CRAFTING AND IMPLEMENTING STRATEGY
Text and Readings

CRAFTING AND IMPLEMENTING STRATEGY
Text and Readings

Arthur A. Thompson, Jr.
A. J. Strickland III

Both of the University of Alabama

Tenth Edition

Boston, Massachusetts   Burr Ridge, Illinois   Dubuque, Iowa
Madison, Wisconsin   New York, New York   San Francisco, California   St. Louis, Missouri

Irwin/McGraw-Hill

*A Division of The **McGraw·Hill** Companies*

ISBN 0-256-24145-7

Vice president and editorial director: *Michael W. Junior*
Publisher: *Craig S. Beytien*
Senior sponsoring editor: *John E. Biernat*
Senior developmental editor: *Laura Hurst Spell*
Marketing manager: *Ellen Cleary*
Senior project manager: *Mary Conzachi*
Production supervisor: *Scott Hamilton*
Designer: *Ellen Pettengell/Michael Warrell*
Compositor: *Shepard Poorman Communications*
Typeface: *10.5/12 Times Roman*
Printer: *R.R. Donnelley & Sons Company*

This book is a tenth edition in honor of the tenth anniversary of *Strategic Management: Concepts and Cases,* from which the chapters are taken. The previous edition of this book was called the sixth edition.

Library of Congress Cataloging-in-Publication Data

Thompson, Arthur A., (date)
   Crafting and implementing strategy : text and readings / Arthur A.
Thompson, Jr. & A.J. Strickland III. — 10th ed.
     p.   c.m.
   Rev. ed. of: Crafting & implementing strategy. 6th ed. c1995.
   Includes bibliographical references and index.
   ISBN 0-256-24145-7
   1. Strategic planning. 2. Business planning. I. Strickland, A.
J. (Alonzo J.) II. Thompson, Arthur A., 1940– Crafting &
implementing strategy. III. Title.
HD30.28.T525 1998
  658.4′012—dc21   97-31063

http://www.mhhe.com

PREFACE

The objective of this tenth edition is to effectively and interestingly cover what every senior-level or MBA student needs to know about crafting, implementing, and executing business strategies. The revisions and enhancements extend from cover to cover. You'll find greatly expanded treatment of the resource-based theory of the firm, much more emphasis on collaborative strategies and strategic partnerships, and a new section on competing in "high velocity" market environments. There's a fresh collection of 18 readings that includes only 2 carryovers from the previous edition. Throughout, the presentation reflects a mainstream conceptual framework, a sharp focus on analytical techniques, and cutting-edge contributions to strategic thinking based on both academic research and practitioner experiences.

CONTENT FEATURES OF THE TENTH EDITION

New concepts, analytical tools, and methods of managing continue to surface at rates that mandate important edition-to-edition changes in content and emphasis. In the interval since the last revision, the conceptual underpinning and articulation of the resource-based view of the firm has blossomed. While SWOT analysis and the attention paid to building and nurturing core competencies have always pointed to the importance of careful internal strength-weakness assessment in formulating strategy, recent contributions to the literature make it clear that there's much more to the resource-based view of the firm than is implied in a simple weighing of company strengths and weaknesses. We have made a concerted attempt throughout this tenth edition to drive home the strategy-making, strategy-implementing relevance of strengthening a company's resource complement and upgrading its competencies and competitive capabilities to match market realities and create competitive advantage. This edition gives balanced treatment to the thesis that a company's strategy must be matched both to its external market circumstances and to its resources and competitive capabilities. Hence, you'll find the resource-based view of the firm prominently integrated into the coverage of crafting business strategy (Chapters 2 and 4) and crafting diversification strategies (Chapters 7 and 8). You'll also find that Chapters 9 and 10 have a strong resource-based perspective in relating to the role of core competencies, competitive capabilities, and organizational resources in implementing and executing strategy.

In addition to the exceptionally thorough resource-based orientation, we've incorporated important new material on cooperative strategies, collaborative alliances, and competing in "high velocity" market environments where the pace of change (from whatever source) places special demands on a company to adapt its strategy and its resource capabilities to rapidly unfolding events. Once again, there's front-to-back coverage of global issues in strategic management, prominent treatment of ethical and social responsibility issues, and margin notes in every chapter that highlight basic concepts, strategic management principles, and kernels of wisdom. Extensive rewriting to sharpen the presentations in every chapter has allowed us to include the new material and still cover everything in less than 365 pages—something that readers and adopters ought to welcome, given the jam-packed content of the course.

Specific Changes in Content and Emphasis

While the overall organizational arrangement of chapters and topics continues to parallel that of the last several editions, we've made a number of noteworthy changes in chapter content and topical emphasis:

- Chapters 1 and 2 contain fresh presentations on the importance of a clear, motivating strategic vision, strategy objectives, and rapid adaptation of strategy to newly unfolding market conditions and customer expectations. We continue to place strong emphasis on how and why a company's strategy emerges from (a) the deliberate and purposeful actions of management and (b) as-needed reactions to unanticipated developments and fresh competitive pressures. The material in Chapter 1 underscores even more strongly that a company's strategic plan is a collection of strategies devised by different managers at different levels in the organizational hierarchy and builds a case for why all managers are on a company's strategy-making, strategy-implementing team. The worldwide organizational shift to empowered employees and managers makes it imperative for company personnel to be "students of the business" and skilled users of the concepts and tools of strategic management.

- Together, the material in Chapters 3 and 4 create the understanding for why managers must carefully match company strategy both to industry and competitive conditions and to company resources and capabilities. The role of Chapter 3 "Industry and Competitive Analysis" is to set forth the now familiar analytical tools and concepts and demonstrate the importance of tailoring strategy to fit the circumstances of a company's industry and competitive environment. The role of Chapter 4 "Evaluating Company Resources and Competitive Capabilities" is to establish the equal importance of doing solid company situation analysis as a basis for matching strategy to organizational resources, competencies, and competitive capabilities.

- Chapter 4 has been thoroughly overhauled and contains a full-blown discussion of all the concepts and analytical tools required to understand why a company's strategy must be well matched to its internal resources and competitive capabilities. The roles of core competencies and organizational resources and capabilities in creating customer value and helping build competitive advantage have been given center stage in the discussions of company strengths and weaknesses. SWOT analysis has been recast as a tool for assessing a company's resource strengths and weaknesses. There are new sections on determining the competitive value of specific company resources and assets and on selecting the competencies and capabilities having the biggest competitive advantage potential. The now standard tools of value-chain analysis, strategic cost analysis, benchmarking, and competitive strength assessments, however, continue to have a prominent role in the methodology of evaluating a company's situation—they are an essential part of understanding a company's relative cost position and competitive standing vis-à-vis rivals.

- Chapter 5 contains a major new section on using cooperative strategies to build competitive advantage. Chapter 6 features a new section on competing in industry situations characterized by rapid-fire technological change, short product life-cycles, frequent moves by competitors, and/or rapidly evolving customer requirements and expectations. It also takes a more extensive look at the use of strategic alliances to enhance a company's competitiveness in both high velocity markets and in global markets.

- We continue to believe that global competition and global strategy issues are best dealt with by integrating the relevant discussions into each chapter rather than partitioning the treatment off in a separate chapter. The globalization of each chapter, a prominent feature of the two previous editions, is carried over and strengthened in this edition, plus we've added more illustration capsules to highlight the strategies of non-U.S. companies.

- We have recast our analytical treatment of corporate diversification strategies in Chapters 7 and 8, eliminating much of the attention formerly given to drawing business portfolio matrixes and, instead, putting the analytical emphasis on (1) assessing industry attractiveness, (2) evaluating the company's competitive strength in each of its lines of business, (3) appraising the degree of strategic fits among a diversified company's different businesses, and (4) appraising the degree of *resource fit* among the different businesses. You'll find a very strong resource-based view of the firm in the recommended methodology for evaluating the pros and cons of a company's diversification strategy. Chapter 8 continues to incorporate analytical use of the industry attractiveness/business strength portfolio matrix because of its conceptual soundness and practical relevance, but we have discarded the coverage of the flawed growth-share matrix and the little-used life-cycle matrix.

- The three-chapter module (Chapters 9–11) on strategy implementation has been retained and continues to be structured around (1) building an organization capable of carrying out the strategy successfully; (2) developing budgets to steer ample resources into those value-chain activities critical to strategic success; (3) establishing strategically appropriate policies and procedures; (4) instituting best practices and mechanisms for continuous improvement; (5) installing information, communication, and operating systems that enable company personnel to carry out their strategic roles successfully day-in and day-out; (6) tying rewards and incentives tightly to the achievement of performance objectives and good strategy execution; (7) creating a strategy-supportive work environment and corporate culture; and (8) exerting the internal leadership needed to drive implementation forward and to keep improving on how the strategy is being executed.

- The eight-task framework for understanding the managerial components of strategy implementation and execution is explained in the first section of Chapter 9. The remainder of Chapter 9 focuses on building an organization with the competencies, capabilities, and resource strengths needed for successful strategy execution. You'll find welcome coverage of what it takes for an organization to build and enhance its competencies and capabilities, develop the dominating depth in competence-related activities needed for competitive advantage, and forge arrangements to achieve the necessary degree of collaboration and cooperation both among internal departments and with outside resource providers. There is much-expanded treatment of the task of building resource strengths through collaborative alliances and partnerships. We've continued the coverage initiated in the last two editions concerning the pros and cons of outsourcing noncritical activities, downsizing and delayering hierarchical structures, employee empowerment, reengineering of core business processes, and the use of cross-functional and self-contained work teams. The result is a powerful treatment of building resource capabilities and structuring organizational activities that ties together and makes strategic sense out of all the revolutionary organizational changes sweeping through today's corporations.

- As before, Chapter 10 surveys the role of strategy-supportive budgets, policies, reward structures, and internal support systems and explains why the benchmarking of best practices, total quality management, reengineering, and continuous improvement programs are important managerial tools for enhancing organizational competencies in executing strategy. Chapter 11 continues to deal with creating a strategy-supportive corporate culture and exercising the internal leadership needed to drive implementation forward. There's coverage of strong versus weak cultures, low performance and unhealthy cultures, adaptive cultures, and the sustained leadership commitment it takes to change a company with a problem culture, plus sections on ethics management and what managers can do to improve the caliber of strategy execution.

- There are 17 new or revised illustration capsules.

As in prior editions, we've kept the spotlight trained squarely on the strategy-related tasks of managers, the concepts and methods of strategic analysis and strategy execution, and sound strategic decision making. Managers at all levels are viewed as being on a company's strategy-making, strategy-implementing team, responsible for thinking strategically, conducting strategic analysis as needed, crafting strategy and leading the process of strategy implementation and execution in their areas of authority. Every key aspect of strategic management is examined—defining the business and developing a strategic vision, setting strategic and financial objectives, conducting industry and competitive analysis, appraising a company's resource strengths and weaknesses, understanding industry and company value chains, doing competitive strength assessments, evaluating a diversified company's strategy and business portfolio, deciding which strategic options make the most sense, probing for sustainable competitive advantage, building and nurturing organizational competencies and capabilities, fitting how the organization performs its work to the requirements for successful strategy execution, shaping the corporate culture, and exerting strategic leadership.

The use of margin notes to highlight basic concepts, major conclusions, and "core" truths was well received in earlier editions and remains a visible feature of this edition. The margin notes serve to distill the subject matter into concise principles, bring the discussion into sharper focus for readers, and point them to what is important.

Diligent attention has been paid to improving content, clarity, and writing style. We've tried to take dead aim on creating a text presentation that is crisply written, clear and convincing, interesting to read, comfortably mainstream, and as close to the frontiers of theory and practice as a basic textbook should be.

THE READINGS SELECTIONS

As in prior editions, we have included a collection of readings to complement the chapter discussions. The readings serve three purposes: to add detailed coverage of important, newly published topics; to provide readers with modest exposure to the strategic management literature; and to respond to the requests of users who, as a regular practice, include articles from current journals in their course syllabus. We have chosen 18 readings for this edition, only 2 of which are carryovers from the last edition.

The first reading, by James C. Collins and Jerry I. Porras, "Building Your Company's Strategic Vision," published in the *Harvard Business Review (HBR)* provides an outstanding discussion of the ins and outs of arriving at a well-conceived strategic vision and long-term direction. The second article, by Ron McTavish at Concordia University in Montreal, covers in some detail why business strategy cannot be set until very basic decisions are made about the definition of business activity to be undertaken and the competitive arena in which strategy will be implemented. The third article, by Gary Hamel, "Strategy as Revolution," was an *HBR* McKinsey award-winner because of its provocative thesis that any strategy that does not challenge the status quo is not a strategy at all; it's one of those landmark articles that every student of strategic management needs to read. We suggest assigning these first three readings following coverage of Chapters 1 and 2.

We've selected four readings to accompany our four-chapter coverage of strategic analysis in single-business enterprises. The leadoff article, "Using Core Capabilities to Create Competitive Advantage," and Jay Barney's article, "Looking Inside for Competitive Advantage," are excellent follow-ons to the resource-based view of the firm presented in Chapter 4. The next article by Michael Porter, "What Is Strategy?," puts the spotlight on four essential elements of strategy: (1) what unique activities to perform, (2) what strategic position to stake out in the marketplace, (3) what trade-offs to make to achieve sustainability, and (4) how to optimize the fit among all the various strategy-related activities. Porter's discussion of these important elements is certain to enrich student understanding of what strategy is all about and why it is important; his article is, we think, best assigned after students have been exposed to the material in Chapter 5. The concluding article by Richard D'Aveni, "Coping with Hypercompetition," discusses the special strategic challenges posed by rapid-fire market change; it is an excellent article for extending coverage of the same topic in Chapter 6.

We've included two articles to complement our discussion of strategic analysis of diversified companies in Chapters 7 and 8. The first article by Michael Goold and Kathleen Lucks, "Why Diversify? Four Decades of Management Thinking," explores all the rationales for diversifying, the causes of diversification success and failure, and the management challenges that diversification poses. It's the finest article we've seen for gaining a good perspective on what sort of diversification strategies make the most business sense. The second article, "Collaborating Across Lines of Business for Competitive Advantage," provides convincing arguments of why related diversification is usually a much superior strategy compared to unrelated diversification.

We chose seven readings to complement the three chapters on strategy implementation. All concern high profile topics that are receiving much attention among both researchers and practitioners. The first article, "The Horizontal Corporation," is the cover story from a recent issue of *Business Week*. It provides an excellent overview of the trend toward flatter organizations, cross-functional and process organization, self-managing teams, and the trend to drive unnecessary work out of the business. The article captures the revolutionary changes in work design and internal organization sweeping through companies and provides a wealth of company examples and experiences. The second article, "Rethinking Organizational Design," endeavors to cut through much of the clutter on organization structure, arguing that the real issues relate to hierarchical control, individual autonomy, and cooperation. Next is an excerpt from Thomas A. Stewart's new book, *Intellectual Capital,* outlining the thesis that brainpower, know-how, and other human capital elements are playing an increasing role in the marketplace and in building sustainable competitive advantage. The fourth article, by James Brian Quinn and Frederick G. Hilmer, looks at the role of strategic outsourcing in building competitively valuable capabilities and in structuring a company's value chain. You'll find Jeffery Pheffer's article, "Producing Sustainable Competitive Advantage through the Effective Management of People," to be a useful complement to the topics in any of the three strategy implementation chapters, but it probably works best when used with Chapters 9 or 10. Steven Kerr's classic, "On the Folly of Rewarding A, While Hoping for B," drives home the critical importance of linking reward systems tightly to the achievement of strategic performance targets; we've found no better article to make this point clear to aspiring managers. The article by Schneider, Gunnarson, and Niles-Jolly, "Creating the Climate and Culture of Success," is intended for use with Chapter 11 and concerns the importance of corporate values, the hows of creating a high performance work climate, and the perceptions employees derive the feelings that pervade the work atmosphere. The next article concerns what managers have to do to be effective strategic leaders; the author, a human resources consultant, gives 10 commandments for CEOs seeking organizational change—all 10 center around core values and a focused strategic vision. The concluding article, by Joe Badaracco and Allen Webb, deals with business ethics; it is based on in-depth interviews with 30 recent MBA graduates about their company's ethical climate, the organizational pressures that existed to do unethical things, and the guidance they got from corporate ethics programs and codes of conduct.

All 18 selections are well-written, quite readable, and help put readers at the cutting edge of strategic thinking. We believe you'll find them well worth assigning and discussing in class.

ADDITIONAL PEDAGOGICAL FEATURES

As in previous editions, all 11 chapters incorporate the liberal use of examples and references to the strategic successes and failures of companies—what has worked, what hasn't, and why. The use of boxed Illustration Capsules to further highlight "strategy in action" was well received in earlier editions and has been continued. Seventeen of the capsules are new to this edition. Together, the examples and the capsules keep the bridge between concept and actual practice always open, giving the reader a stronger feel for how strategic analysis concepts and techniques are utilized in real-world management circumstances.

At the end of the book, we've included "A Guide to Case Analysis" that gives students positive direction in what case method pedagogy is all about and offers suggestions for approaching case analysis. In our experience, many students are unsure about what they are to do in preparing a case, and they are certainly inexperienced in analyzing a company from a "big picture" or strategic point of view. The discussion is intended to provide explicit guidance and to focus student attention on an unusually high level of student motivation and emotional involvement in the course throughout the term.

About the Simulation

We designed *The Business Strategy Game* around athletic footwear because producing and marketing athletic footwear is a business that students can readily understand, and because the athletic footwear market displays the characteristics of globally competitive industries in the fast growth, worldwide use of the product, competition among companies from several continents, production located in low-wage locations, and a market environment where a variety of competitive approaches and business strategies can co-exist. The simulation allows companies to manufacture and sell their brands in North America, Europe, and Asia, plus there's the option to compete for supplying private-label footwear to North American chain retailers. Competition is head-to-head—each team of students must match their strategic wits against the other company teams. Companies can focus their branded marketing efforts on one geographic market or two or all three, or they can deemphasize branded sales and specialize in private-label production (an attractive strategy for low-cost producers). Low-cost leadership, differentiation strategies, best-cost producer strategies, and focus strategies are all viable competitive options. Companies can position their products in the low end of the market, the high end, or stick close to the middle on price, quality, and service; they can have a wide or narrow product line, small or big dealer networks, extensive or limited advertising. Company market shares are based on how each company's competitive effort stacks up against the efforts of rivals. Demand conditions, tariffs, and wage rates vary among geographic areas. Raw materials used in footwear production are purchased in a worldwide commodity market at prices that move up or down in response to supply-demand conditions. If a company's sales volume is unexpectedly low, management has the option to liquidate excess inventories at deep discount prices.

The company that students manage has plants to operate, a workforce to compensate, distribution expenses and inventories to control, capital expenditure decisions to make, marketing and sales campaigns to wage, sales forecasts to consider, and ups and downs in exchange rates, interest rates, and the stock market to take into account. Students must weave functional decisions in production, distribution, marketing, finance, and human resources into a cohesive action plan. They have to react to changing market and competitive conditions, initiate moves to try to build competitive advantage, and decide how to defend against aggressive actions by competitors. And they must endeavor to maximize shareholder wealth via increased dividend payments and stock price appreciation. Each team of students is challenged to use their entrepreneurial and strategic skills to become the next Nike or Reebok and ride the wave of growth to the top of the worldwide athletic footwear industry. The whole exercise is representative of a real world competitive market where companies try to outcompete and outperform rivals—things are every bit as realistic and true to actual business practice as we could make them.

There are built-in planning and analysis features that allow students to (1) craft a five-year strategic plan, (2) gauge the long-range financial impact of current decisions, (3) do the number-crunching to make informed short-run versus long-run tradeoffs, (4) assess the revenue-cost profit consequences of alternative strategic actions, and (5) build different strategy scenarios. Calculations at the bottom of each decision screen provide instantly updated projections of sales revenues, profits, return on equity, cash flow, and other key outcomes as each decision entry is made. The sensitivity of financial and operating outcomes to different decision entries is easily observed on the screen and on detailed printouts of projections. With the speed of today's personal computers, the relevant number-crunching is done in a split-second. The game is designed throughout to lead students to decisions based on "My analysis shows . . ." and away from the quicksand of decisions based on "I think," "It sounds good," "Maybe, it will work out" and other such seat-of-the-pants approaches.

The Business Strategy Game is programmed to work on any PC capable of running Windows 3.1x, Windows95 (or 98), or Windows NT, and it is suitable for both senior-level and MBA courses. The game accommodates a wide variety of disk drives, monitors, and printers and runs quite nicely on a network.

Features of the New Version

In preparing this latest version, we've benefited enormously from the experiences and advice of both adopters and players. We've listened carefully, implemented many suggestions of users, programmed in numerous behind-the-scenes refinements that users have requested, and added a couple of new features. You'll find this latest incarnation of *The Business Strategy Game* to be meaningfully better for players and game administrators in several respects:

- **The New Demand Forecasting Feature.** The biggest change is the addition of a demand forecasting model that allows each company to project the number of branded pairs it is likely to sell in each geographic market, given its contemplated marketing effort and given the overall competitive effort it expects to encounter from rival companies. We think players will be thrilled to have a tool that is capable of projecting the upcoming year's branded sales volumes (usually within 5 percent of what actually happens, *provided that they accurately anticipate the competitive effort of rivals*).

- **The New Inventory Liquidation Option.** A second new feature is that companies are given the option to liquidate any excess inventories at deep discount prices, thereby clearing their warehouses of unwanted stocks of unsold branded or private-label shoes.

- **Assorted Fine-tuning.** We have further tweaked the relationships among decision variables and the interactions among the determinants of company competitiveness to mirror market realities in the athletic footwear business ever more closely. A few minor changes have been made in the Footwear Industry Report and the Administrator's Report. We have executed a number of behind-the-scenes programming changes to make the simulation an easier-to-administer exercise from a technical perspective.

- **The Irwin/McGraw-Hill Website.** We now have the capability to provide users with immediate downloads of software upgrades at the Web site for this text (*www.mhhe.com/thompson*), plus offer some online technical support (including answers to FAQs)—all in addition to the technical support via e-mail and telephone that has been and continues to be in place.

At the same time, we have retained the array of new features and improvements introduced in the previous version: the celebrity endorsements feature, the optional executive compensation feature, the extensive on-screen decision support calculations and what-iffing capability, the much improved five-year strategic plan format, and the added scoring flexibility. As before, instructors have numerous ways to heighten competition and keep things lively as the game progresses. There are options to raise or lower interest rates, alter certain costs up or down, and issue special news flashes announcing new tariff levels, materials cost changes, shipping difficulties, or other new considerations to keep business conditions dynamic and "stir the pot" a bit as needed. And the built-in scoreboard of company performance keeps students constantly informed about where their company stands and how well they are doing. Rapid advances in PC technology continue to cut processing times—it should take no more than 45 minutes for you or a student assistant to process the results on an older PC and well under 30 minutes if you have a PC with a Pentium 120 or faster chip.

A separate instructor's manual for *The Business Strategy Game* describes how to integrate the simulation exercise into your course, provides pointers on how to administer the game, and contains step-by-step processing instructions. Should you encounter technical difficulties or have questions, the College New Media department at Irwin/McGraw-Hill can provide quick assistance via a toll-free number.

THE INSTRUCTOR'S PACKAGE FOR THE TENTH EDITION

A full complement of instructional aids is available to assist adopters in using the tenth edition successfully. The *Instructor's Manual* contains suggestions for using the text materials, various approaches to course design and course organization, a sample syllabus, alternative course outlines, and a set of 940 multiple-choice and essay questions. There is also a computerized test bank for generating examinations, a set of color transparencies depicting the figures and tables in the 11 text chapters, and a PowerPoint presentation package that contains a full set of color visuals for classrooms equipped with computer screen projection capability. The PowerPoint package can also be used to make black-and-white overheads in the event you use an overhead projector to support your lectures. The PowerPoint presentations include over 500 visuals that thoroughly cover the material presented in the 11 chapters, thus providing plenty to select from in creating support for your classroom lectures. We deliberately created enough visuals for each chapter to give you an ample number of choices in putting together a presentation that fits both your preferences and time constraints. There's a special instructor-only section of the publisher-maintained authors' Web site that allows you to download many of the instructional aids (*www.mhhe.com/thompson*).

ACKNOWLEDGMENTS

We have benefited from the help of many people during the evolution of this book. Students, adopters, and reviewers have generously supplied an untold number of insightful comments and helpful suggestions. Our intellectual debt to those academics, writers, and practicing managers who have blazed new trails in the strategy field will be obvious to any reader familiar with the literature of strategic management. We have endeavored to acknowledge their specific contributions in footnote references and in the list of suggested readings at the end of each chapter.

Naturally, as custom properly dictates, we are responsible for whatever errors of fact, deficiencies in coverage or presentation, and oversights that remain. As always we value your recommendations and thoughts about the book. Your comments regarding coverage and contents will be most welcome, as you will your calling our attention to specific errors. Please fax us at (205) 348-6695, e-mail us at athompso@cba.ua.edu, or write us at P.O. Box 870225, Department of Management and Marketing, The University of Alabama, Tuscaloosa, AL 35487-0225.

Arthur A. Thompson, Jr.
A.J. Strickland

CONTENTS

6 MATCHING STRATEGY TO A COMPANY'S SITUATION 174

7 STRATEGY AND COMPETITIVE ADVANTAGE IN DIVERSIFIED COMPANIES 213

11   IMPLEMENTING STRATEGY: CULTURE AND LEADERSHIP   334

PART II: READINGS IN STRATEGIC MANAGEMENT   361

CRAFTING AND IMPLEMENTING STRATEGY
Text and Readings

I

THE CONCEPTS AND TECHNIQUES OF STRATEGIC MANAGEMENT

1

THE STRATEGIC MANAGEMENT PROCESS

An Overview

"Cheshire Puss," she [Alice] began . . . "would you tell me, please, which way I ought to go from here?"

"That depends a good deal on where you want to get to," said the Cat.

Lewis Carroll

Without a strategy the organization is like a ship without a rudder, going around in circles.

Joel Ross and Michael Kami

My job is to make sure the company has a strategy and that everybody follows it.

Kenneth H. Olsen
Former CEO, Digital Equipment Corporation

This book is about the managerial tasks of crafting, implementing, and executing company strategies. *A company's strategy is the "game plan" management has for positioning the company in its chosen market arena, competing successfully, pleasing customers, and achieving good business performance.* Strategy consists of the whole array of competitive moves and business approaches that managers employ in running a company. In crafting a strategic course, management is saying that "among all the paths and actions we could have chosen, we have decided to go in this direction and rely upon these particular ways of doing business." A strategy thus entails managerial choices among alternatives and signals organizational commitment to specific markets, competitive approaches, and ways of operating.

Managers devise company strategies because of two very compelling needs. One is the need to *proactively shape* how a company's business will be conducted. Passively allowing strategy to drift along as the by-product of ongoing business approaches, occasional proposals for improvement, and periodic adjustments to unfolding events is a surefire ticket for inconsistent strategic actions, competitive mediocrity, and lackluster business results. Rather, it is management's responsibility to exert entrepreneurial leadership and commit the enterprise to conducting business in a fashion shrewdly calculated to produce good performance. A strategy provides a roadmap to operate by, a prescription for doing business, a game plan for building customer loyalty and winning a sustainable competitive advantage over rivals. The second need is that of molding the independent decisions and actions initiated by departments, managers, and employees across the company into a *coordinated, companywide* game plan. Absent a strategy, managers have no framework for weaving many different action initiatives into a cohesive whole, no plan for uniting cross-department operations into a team effort.

Crafting, implementing, and executing strategy are thus core management functions. Among all the things managers do, nothing affects a company's ultimate success or failure more fundamentally than how well its management team charts the company's long-term direction, develops competitively effective strategic moves and business approaches, and implements what needs to be done internally to produce good day-in/day-out strategy execution. Indeed, *good strategy and good strategy execution are the most trustworthy signs of good management.* Managers don't deserve a gold star for designing a potentially brilliant strategy, but failing to put the organizational means in place to carry it out in high-caliber fashion—weak implementation and execution—undermines the strategy's potential and paves the way for shortfalls in customer satisfaction and company performance. Competent execution of a mediocre strategy scarcely merits enthusiastic applause for management's efforts either. To truly qualify as excellently managed, a company must exhibit excellent execution of an excellent strategy. Otherwise, any claim of talented management is suspect.

> *Competent execution of a well-conceived strategy is not only a proven recipe for organizational success, but also the best test of managerial excellence.*

Granted, good strategy combined with good strategy execution doesn't *guarantee* that a company will avoid periods of so-so or even subpar performance. Sometimes it takes several years for management's strategy-making/strategy-implementing efforts to show good results. Sometimes blue-chip organizations with showcase practices and reputable managers have performance problems because of surprisingly abrupt shifts in market conditions or internal miscues. But neither the "we need more time" reason nor the bad luck of unforeseeable events excuses mediocre performance year after year. It is the responsibility of a company's management team to adjust to unexpectedly tough conditions by undertaking strategic defenses and business approaches that can overcome adversity. Indeed, the essence of good strategy making is to build a market position strong enough and an organization capable enough to produce successful performance despite unforeseeable events, potent competition, and internal difficulties. The rationale for using the twin standards of good strategy making and good strategy execution to determine whether a company is well managed is therefore compelling: The better conceived a company's strategy and the more competently it is executed, the more likely the company will be a solid performer and a competitive success in the marketplace.

THE FIVE TASKS OF STRATEGIC MANAGEMENT

The strategy-making, strategy-implementing process consists of five interrelated managerial tasks:

1. *Forming a strategic vision of what the company's future business makeup will be and where the organization is headed*—so as to provide long-term direction, delineate what kind of enterprise the company is trying to become, and infuse the organization with a sense of purposeful action.
2. *Setting objectives*—converting the strategic vision into specific performance outcomes for the company to achieve.
3. *Crafting a strategy to achieve the desired outcomes.*
4. *Implementing and executing the chosen strategy efficiently and effectively.*
5. *Evaluating performance and initiating corrective adjustments in vision, long-term direction, objectives, strategy, or implementation in light of actual experience, changing conditions, new ideas, and new opportunities.*

Figure 1.1 displays this process. Together, these five components define what we mean by the term *strategic management.* Let's examine this five-task framework in enough detail to set the stage for all that follows in the forthcoming chapters.

FIGURE 1.1   The Five Tasks of Strategic Management

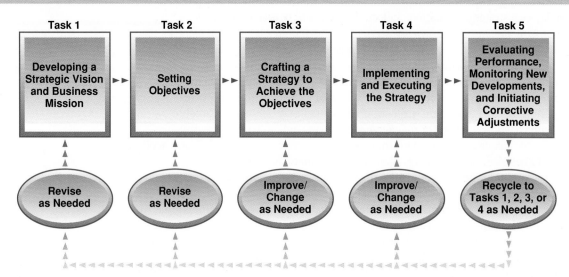

Developing a Strategic Vision and Business Mission

Very early in the strategy-making process, company managers need to pose the issue of "What is our vision for the company—where should the company be headed, what kind of enterprise are we trying to build, what should the company's future business makeup be?" Drawing a carefully reasoned conclusion about what the company's long-term direction should be pushes managers to take a hard look at the company's present business and form a clearer sense of whether and how it needs to change over the next 5 to 10 years. Management's views about "where we plan to go from here—what businesses we want to be in, what customer needs we want to satisfy, what capabilities we're going to develop" charts a course for the organization to pursue and creates organizational purpose and identity.

What a company is currently seeking to do for its customers is often termed the company's *mission*. A mission statement is useful for putting the spotlight on what business a company is presently in and the customer needs it is presently endeavoring to serve. But just clearly setting forth what a company is doing today doesn't speak to the company's future or incorporate a sense of needed change and long-term direction. There is an even greater managerial imperative to consider what the company will have to do to meet its customers' needs tomorrow and whether and how the company's business makeup will have to evolve for the company to grow and prosper. Thus, managers are obligated to look beyond the present business mission and think strategically about the impact of new technologies on the horizon, changing customer needs and expectations, the emergence of new market and competitive conditions, and so on. They have to make some fundamental choices about where they want to take the company and form a vision of the kind of enterprise they believe the company needs to become. In other words, management's concept of the *present* company mission has to be supplemented with a concept of the company's *future* business makeup, product line, and customer base. The faster a company's business environment is changing, the more that coasting along with the status quo is an invitation to disaster and the greater the managerial imperative to consider what the enterprise's future strategic path should be in light of changing conditions and emerging market opportunities.

Management's view of the kind of company it is trying to create and the kind of business position it wants to stake out in the years to come constitutes a *strategic vision* for the company. In the event a company's mission statement not only sets forth a clear definition of the present business but also indicates where the company is headed and what its business will become in the years ahead, then the concepts of company mission (or mission statement) and strategic vision merge into one and the same—in other words, a strategic vision and a future-oriented business mission amount to essentially the same thing. In practice, actual company mission statements tend to exhibit more concern with "what our business is now" than with "what our business will be later," so the conceptual distinction between company mission and strategic vision is relevant. Forming a strategic vision of a company's future is a prerequisite to effective strategic leadership. A manager cannot succeed as an organization leader or a strategy maker without first having drawn some soundly reasoned conclusions about where the enterprise needs to head, the changes in business makeup that are called for, and the organizational capabilities it will take to meet future customer needs and compete successfully. With a clear, well-conceived strategic vision, a manager has a beacon to truly guide managerial decision making, a course for the organization to follow, and a basis for shaping the organization's strategy and operating policies.

A strategic vision is a roadmap of a company's future—the direction it is headed, the business position it intends to stake out, and the capabilities it plans to develop.

Some examples of company mission and vision statements are presented in Illustration Capsule 1.

Setting Objectives

The purpose of setting objectives is to convert managerial statements of strategic vision and business mission into specific performance targets, something the organization's progress can be measured by. Successful managers set company performance targets that require stretch and disciplined effort. The challenge of trying to achieve bold, aggressive performance targets pushes an organization to be more inventive, to exhibit some urgency in improving both its financial performance and its business position, and to be more intentional and focused in its actions. Setting objectives that require real organizational stretch helps build a firewall against complacent coasting and low-grade improvements in organizational performance. As Mitchell Leibovitz, CEO of Pep Boys–Manny, Moe, and Jack, puts it, "If you want to have ho-hum results, have ho-hum objectives."

Objective setting is required of *all* managers. Every unit in a company needs concrete, measurable performance targets that contribute meaningfully toward achieving company objectives. When companywide objectives are broken down into specific targets for each organizational unit and lower-level managers are held accountable for achieving them, a results-oriented climate builds throughout the enterprise. There's little if any internal confusion over what to accomplish. The ideal situation is a team effort where each organizational unit strives to produce results in its area of responsibility that contribute to the achievement of the company's performance targets and strategic vision.

Objectives are yardsticks for tracking an organization's performance and progress.

From a companywide perspective, two very distinct types of performance yardsticks are required: those relating to *financial performance* and those relating to

ILLUSTRATION CAPSULE 1   Examples Of Company Mission and Vision Statements

McDonald's Corporation
McDonald's vision is to dominate the global foodservice industry. Global dominance means setting the performance standard for customer satisfaction while increasing market share and profitability through our Convenience, Value, and Execution Strategies.

Otis Elevator
Our mission is to provide any customer a means of moving people and things up, down, and sideways over short distances with higher reliability than any similar enterprise in the world.

Microsoft Corporation
One vision drives everything we do: A computer on every desk and in every home using great software as an empowering tool.

Avis Rent-a-Car
Our business is renting cars. Our mission is total customer satisfaction.

The Body Shop
We aim to achieve commercial success by meeting our customers' needs through the provision of high quality, good value products with exceptional service and relevant information which enables customers to make informed and responsible choices.

American Red Cross
The mission of the American Red Cross is to improve the quality of human life; to enhance self-reliance and concern for others; and to help people avoid, prepare for, and cope with emergencies.

Eastman Kodak
To be the world's best in chemical and electronic imaging.

Ritz-Carlton Hotels
The Ritz-Carlton Hotel is a place where the genuine care and comfort of our guests is our highest mission.

We pledge to provide the finest personal service and facilities for our guests who will always enjoy a warm, relaxed yet refined ambience.

The Ritz-Carlton experience enlivens the senses, instills well-being, and fulfills even the unexpressed wishes and needs of our guests.

Intel
Intel supplies the computing industry with chips, boards, systems, and software. Intel's products are used as "building blocks" to create advanced computing systems for PC users. Intel's mission is to be the preeminent building block supplier to the new computing industry worldwide.

Compaq Computer
To be the leading supplier of PCs and PC servers in all customer segments.

Long John Silver's
To be America's best quick service restaurant chain. We will provide each guest great tasting, healthful, reasonably priced fish, seafood, and chicken in a fast, friendly manner on every visit.

Bristol-Myers Squibb
The mission of Bristol-Myers Squibb is to extend and enhance human life by providing the highest quality health and personal care products. We intend to be the preeminent global diversified health and personal care company.

---

strategic performance. Achieving acceptable financial results is crucial. Without adequate profitability, a company's pursuit of its vision, as well as its long-term health and ultimate survival, is jeopardized. Neither shareowners nor lenders will continue to sink additional monies into an enterprise that can't deliver satisfactory financial results. Even so, the achievement of satisfactory financial performance, by itself, is not enough. Attention also has to be paid to a company's strategic well-being—its competitiveness and overall long-term business position. Unless a company's performance reflects improving competitive strength and a stronger long-term market position, its progress is less than inspiring and its ability to continue delivering good financial performance is suspect.

The need for both good financial performance and good strategic performance calls for management to set financial objectives and strategic objectives. *Financial objectives* signal commitment to such outcomes as earnings growth, an acceptable return on investment (or economic value added—EVA), dividend growth, stock price appreciation (or market value added—MVA), good cash flow, and creditworthiness.[1] *Strategic objectives*, in contrast, direct efforts toward such outcomes as winning additional market share, overtaking key competitors on product quality or customer service or product innovation, achieving lower overall costs than rivals, boosting the company's reputation with customers, winning a stronger foothold in international markets, exercising technological leadership, gaining a sustainable competitive advantage, and capturing attractive growth opportunities. Strategic objectives serve notice that management not only intends to deliver good financial performance but also intends to improve the organization's competitive strength and long-range business prospects.

Both financial and strategic objectives ought to be time-based—that is, involve both near-term and longer-term performance targets. Short-range objectives focus organizational attention on the need for immediate performance improvements and outcomes. Long-range objectives serve the valuable purpose of prompting managers to consider what to do *now* to put the company in position to perform well over the longer term. As a rule, when trade-offs have to be made between achieving long-run objectives and achieving short-run objectives, long-run objectives should take precedence. Rarely does a company prosper from repeated management actions that put better short-term performance ahead of better long-run performance.

Examples of the kinds of strategic and financial objectives companies set are shown in Illustration Capsule 2.

Crafting a Strategy

A company's strategy represents management's answers to such gut business issues as whether to concentrate on a single business or build a diversified group of businesses, whether to cater to a broad range of customers or focus on a particular market niche, whether to develop a wide or narrow product line, whether to pursue a competitive advantage based on low cost or product superiority or unique organiza-

---

[1]Economic value added (EVA) is profit over and above the company's cost of debt and equity capital. More specifically, it is defined as operating profit less income taxes less the cost of debt less an allowance for the cost of equity capital. For example, if a company has operating profits of $200 million, pays taxes of $75 million, pays interest expenses of $25 million, has shareholders' equity of $400 million with an estimated equity cost of 15 percent (which translates into an equity cost of capital of $60 million), then the company's EVA is $200 million minus $75 million minus $25 million minus $60 million, or $40 million. The EVA of $40 million can be interpreted to mean that the company's management has generated profits well in excess of the benchmark 15 percent equity cost needed to justify or support the shareholder investment of $400 million—all of which represents wealth created for the owners above what they could expect from making investment of comparable risk elsewhere. Such companies as Coca-Cola, AT&T, and Briggs & Stratton use EVA as a measure of their profit performance.

Market value added (MVA) is defined as the amount by which the total value of the company has appreciated above the dollar amount actually invested in the company by shareholders. MVA is equal to a company's current stock price times the number of shares outstanding less shareholders' equity investment; it represents the value that management has added to shareholders' wealth in running the business. For example, if a company's stock price is $50, there are 1,000,000 shares outstanding, and shareholders' equity investment is $40 million, then MVA is $10 million ($50 million in market value of existing shares minus $40 million in equity investment); in other words, management has taken the shareholders' investment of $40 million in the company and leveraged it into a current company value of $50 million, creating an additional $10 million in shareholder value. If shareholder value is to be maximized, management must select a strategy and long-term direction that maximizes the market value of the company's common stock. In recent years, MVA and EVA have gained widespread acceptance as valid measures of a company's financial performance.

ILLUSTRATION CAPSULE 2   Strategic And Financial Objectives Of Well-Known Corporations

Banc One Corporation
To be one of the top three banking companies in terms of market share in all significant markets we serve.

Domino's Pizza
To safely deliver a hot, quality pizza in 30 minutes or less at a fair price and a reasonable profit.

Ford Motor Company
To satisfy our customers by providing quality cars and trucks, developing new products, reducing the time it takes to bring new vehicles to market, improving the efficiency of all our plants and processes, and building on our teamwork with employees, unions, dealers, and suppliers.

Exxon
To provide shareholders a secure investment with a superior return.

Alcan Aluminum
To be the lowest-cost producer of aluminum and to outperform the average return on equity of the Standard and Poor's industrial stock index.

General Electric
To become the most competitive enterprise in the world by being number one or number two in market share in every business the company is in. To achieve an average of 10 inventory turns and a corporate operating profit margin of 16% by 1998.

Bristol-Myers Squibb
To focus globally on those businesses in health and personal care where we can be number one or number two through delivering superior value to the customer.

Atlas Corporation
To become a low-cost, medium-size gold producer, producing in excess of 125,000 ounces of gold a year and building gold reserves of 1,500,000 ounces.

3M
To achieve annual growth in earnings per share of 10% or better, on average; a return on stockholders' equity of 20-25%; a return on capital employed of 27% or better; and have at least 30% of sales come from products introduced in the past four years.

An organization's strategy consists of the actions and business approaches management employs to achieve the targeted organizational performance.

tional capabilities, how to respond to changing buyer preferences, how big a geographic market to try to cover, how to react to new market and competitive conditions, and how to grow the enterprise over the long-term. A strategy thus reflects managerial choices among alternatives and signals organizational commitment to particular products, markets, competitive approaches, and ways of operating the enterprise.

Crafting a winning strategy needs to be a top-priority managerial task in every organization. To begin with, there is a compelling need for managers to be proactive in shaping *how* the company's business will be conducted. It is management's responsibility to exert strategic leadership and commit the enterprise to going about its business in one fashion rather than another. Without a strategy, managers have no prescription for doing business, no roadmap to competitive advantage, no game plan for pleasing customers or achieving objectives. Such a lack is a surefire ticket for organizational drift, competitive mediocrity, and lackluster performance. Moreover, there is an equally compelling need to mold the business decisions and competitive actions taken across various parts of the company into a coordinated, compatible *pattern*. A company's activities necessarily involve the efforts and decisions of many divisions, departments, managers, and employees. All the actions and initiatives being taken in such areas as production, marketing, customer service, human resources, information systems, R&D, and finance need to be mutually supportive if a *companywide* game plan that makes good business sense is to emerge. Absent a company strategy, managers have no framework for weaving many different decisions into a cohesive whole and no overarching business rationale that unites departmental operations into a team effort.

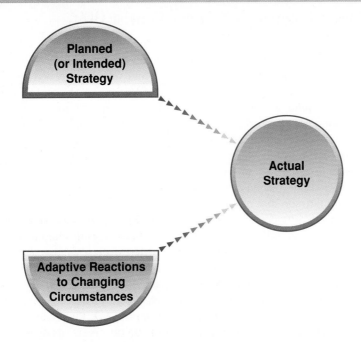

FIGURE 1.2 A Company's Actual Strategy Is Partly Planned and Partly Reactive to Changing Circumstances

Planned (or Intended) Strategy

Actual Strategy

Adaptive Reactions to Changing Circumstances

Strategy making brings into play the critical managerial issue of *how* to achieve the targeted results in light of the organization's situation and prospects. Objectives are the "ends," and strategy is the "means" of achieving them. The hows of a company's strategy are typically a blend of (1) deliberate and purposeful actions and (2) as-needed reactions to unanticipated developments and fresh competitive pressures.[2] As illustrated in Figure 1.2, strategy is more than what managers have carefully plotted out in advance and *intend* to do as part of some grand strategic plan. New circumstances always emerge, whether important technological developments, rivals' successful new product introductions, newly enacted government regulations and policies, widening consumer interest in different kinds of performance features, or whatever. Future business conditions are sufficiently uncertain that managers cannot plan every strategic action in advance and pursue a preplanned or *intended strategy* without any need for alteration. Company strategies end up, therefore, being a composite of planned actions and business approaches (intended strategy) and as-needed reactions to unforeseen conditions ("unplanned" or "adaptive" strategy responses). Consequently, *strategy is best looked upon as being a combination of planned actions and on-the-spot adaptive reactions to freshly developing industry and competitive events.* The strategy-making task involves developing a game plan, or intended strategy, and then adapting it as events unfold. A company's actual strategy is something managers must shape and reshape as events transpire outside and inside the company. It is normal, therefore, for a company's actual strategy to differ from management's

Strategy is both proactive (intended) and reactive (adaptive).

[2]Henry Mintzberg and J. A. Waters, "Of Strategies, Deliberate and Emergent," *Strategic Management Journal*, 6 (1985), pp.257–72.

planned strategy as new strategy features are added and others subtracted to react and adapt to changing conditions.

What Does a Company's Strategy Consist Of?

Company strategies concern *how*: how to grow the business, how to satisfy customers, how to outcompete rivals, how to respond to changing market conditions, how to manage each functional piece of the business and develop needed organizational capabilities, how to achieve strategic and financial objectives. The hows of strategy tend to be company-specific, customized to a company's own situation and performance objectives. In the business world, companies have a wide degree of strategic freedom. They can diversify broadly or narrowly, into related or unrelated industries, via acquisition, joint venture, strategic alliances, or internal start-up. Even when a company elects to concentrate on a single business, prevailing market conditions usually offer enough strategy-making latitude that close competitors can easily avoid carbon-copy strategies—some pursue low-cost leadership, others stress particular attributes of their product or service, and still others concentrate on developing unique capabilities to meet the special needs and preferences of narrow buyer segments. Some compete only locally or regionally, others compete nationally, and others compete globally. Hence, descriptions of the content of company strategy necessarily have to cut broadly across many aspects of the business to be complete.

Company strategies are partly visible and partly hidden to outside view.

Figure 1.3 depicts the kinds of actions and approaches that reflect a company's overall strategy. Because many are visible to outside observers, most of a company's strategy can be deduced from its actions and public pronouncements. Yet, there's an unrevealed portion of strategy outsiders can only speculate about—the actions and moves company managers are considering. Managers often, for good reason, choose not to reveal certain elements of their strategy until the time is right.

To get a better understanding of the content of company strategies, see the overview of McDonald's strategy in Illustration Capsule 3 on page 12.

Strategy and Entrepreneurship.   Crafting strategy is an exercise in entrepreneurship and *outside-in* strategic thinking. The challenge is for company managers to keep their strategies closely matched to such *outside drivers* as changing buyer preferences, the latest actions of rivals, new technological capabilities, the emergence of attractive market opportunities, and newly appearing business conditions. Company strategies can't end up being well matched to the company's present and future environment unless managers exhibit first-rate entrepreneurship in studying market trends, listening to customers, enhancing the company's competitiveness, and steering company activities in whatever new directions are dictated by market conditions and customer preferences. Good strategy making is therefore inseparable from good business entrepreneurship. One cannot exist without the other.

Strategy-making is fundamentally a market-driven and customer-driven entrepreneurial activity—venturesomeness, business creativity, an eye for spotting emerging market opportunities, keen observation of customer needs, and an appetite for risk-taking are inherent to the task of crafting company strategies.

A company encounters two dangers when its managers fail to exercise strategy-making entrepreneurship. One is a stale strategy. The faster a company's business environment is changing, the more critical it becomes for its managers to be good entrepreneurs in diagnosing shifting conditions and instituting whatever strategic adjustments are indicated. Coasting along with a status quo strategy tends to be riskier than making modifications. Managers with weak entrepreneurial skills are usually risk-averse and disinclined to embark on a different strategic course so long as they believe the present strategy can produce acceptable results for a while

FIGURE 1.3   Understanding a Company's Strategy—What to Look For

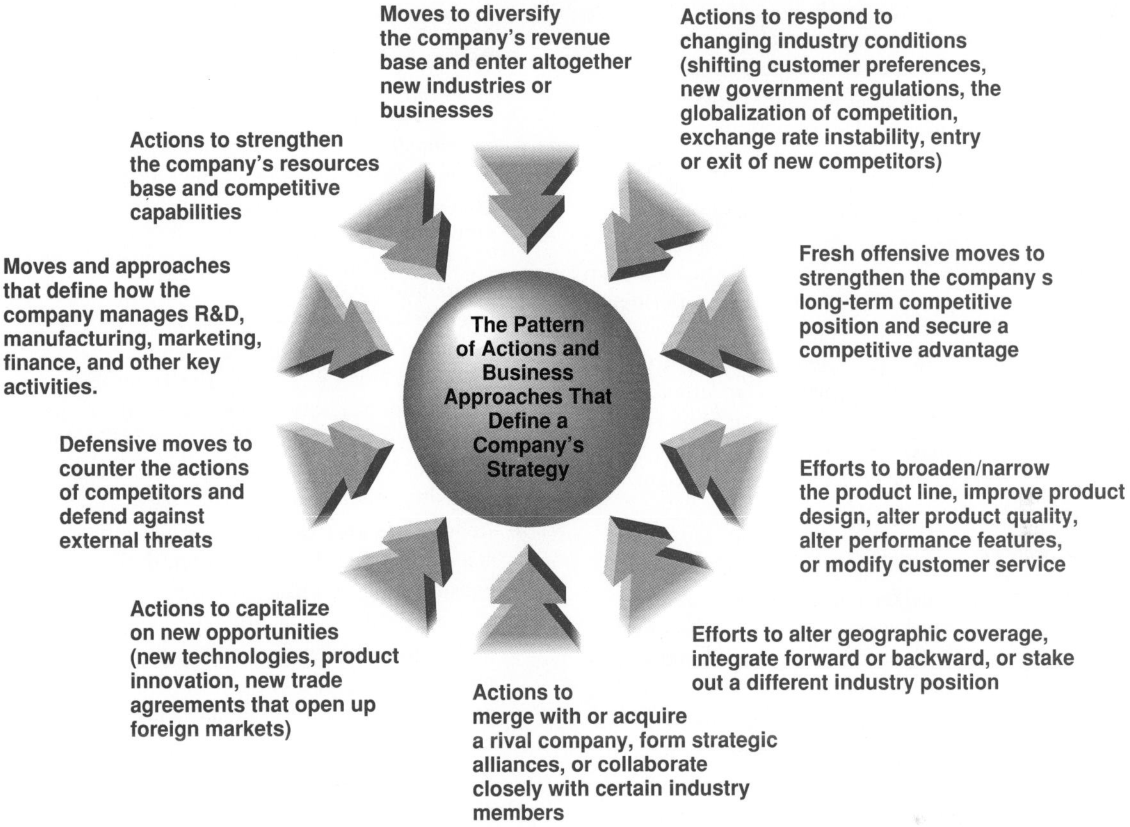

Moves to diversify the company's revenue base and enter altogether new industries or businesses

Actions to respond to changing industry conditions (shifting customer preferences, new government regulations, the globalization of competition, exchange rate instability, entry or exit of new competitors)

Actions to strengthen the company's resources base and competitive capabilities

Moves and approaches that define how the company manages R&D, manufacturing, marketing, finance, and other key activities.

The Pattern of Actions and Business Approaches That Define a Company's Strategy

Fresh offensive moves to strengthen the company s long-term competitive position and secure a competitive advantage

Defensive moves to counter the actions of competitors and defend against external threats

Efforts to broaden/narrow the product line, improve product design, alter product quality, alter performance features, or modify customer service

Actions to capitalize on new opportunities (new technologies, product innovation, new trade agreements that open up foreign markets)

Efforts to alter geographic coverage, integrate forward or backward, or stake out a different industry position

Actions to merge with or acquire a rival company, form strategic alliances, or collaborate closely with certain industry members

longer. They are prone to misread market trends and put too little weight on subtle shifts in customers' needs and behavior. Often, they either dismiss the signs of impending developments as unimportant ("we don't think it will really affect us") or else move so slowly in taking actions that the company is habitually late in responding to market change. There's pervasive resistance to bold strategic change, a wariness of deviating very far from the company's tried-and-true business approaches unless absolutely forced to. Strategies that grow increasingly out of touch with market and customer realities weaken a company's competitiveness and performance.

The second danger of failing to exercise strategy-making entrepreneurship is inside-out strategic thinking. Managers with deficient entrepreneurial skills or an entrepreneurially cautious nature usually focus most of their time and energy inwardly—on solving internal problems, improving organizational processes and procedures, and taking care of daily administrative chores. The strategic actions they do decide to initiate tend to be heavily dictated by inside considerations—what is philosophically comfortable, what is acceptable to various internal political coalitions, and what is safe, both organizationally and career-wise. Often, outside considerations end up being compromised to accommodate internal considerations, resulting in strategies that are as much a reflection of inwardly focused strategic thinking as of the need to respond to changing external market and customer conditions. Inside-out strategies, while not disconnected from external developments, nearly always fall short of being truly market-driven and customer-driven,

Good strategy making is more outside-in than inside-out.

ILLUSTRATION CAPSULE 3   A Strategy Example: McDonald's

In 1997 McDonald's was the leading food service retailer in the global consumer marketplace, with a strong brand name and systemwide restaurant sales approaching $35 billion. Two-thirds of its 22,000-plus restaurants were franchised to nearly 5,000 owner/operators around the world. Sales had grown an average of 6 percent in the United States and 20 percent outside the United States over the past 10 years. McDonald's food quality specifications, equipment technology, marketing and training programs, operating systems, site selection techniques, and supply systems were considered industry standards throughout the world. The company's strategic priorities were continued growth, providing exceptional customer care, remaining an efficient and quality producer, offering high value and good-tasting products, and effectively marketing McDonald's brand on a global scale. McDonald's strategy had eight core elements:

Growth Strategy

- Penetrate the market not currently served by adding 2,500 restaurants annually (an average of 8 per day), some company-owned and some franchised, with about two-thirds outside the United States. Establish a leading market position in foreign countries ahead of competitors.
- Promote more frequent customer visits via the addition of attractive menu items, low-price specials, Extra Value Meals, and children's play areas.

Franchising Strategy

- Grant franchises only to highly motivated, talented entrepreneurs with integrity and business experience and train them to become active, on-premise owners of McDonald's (no franchises were granted to corporations, partnerships, or passive investors).

Store Location and Construction Strategy

- Locate restaurants on sites offering convenience to customers and profitable growth potential. The company's research indicated that 70 percent of all decisions to eat at McDonald's were made on the spur of the moment, so its goal was to pick locations that were as convenient as possible for customers to visit. In the United States, the company supplemented its traditional suburban and urban locations with satellite outlets in food courts, airports, hospitals, universities, large shopping establishments (Wal-Mart, The Home Depot), and service stations; outside the United States, the strategy was to establish an initial presence in center cities, then open freestanding units with drive-thrus outside center cities.
- Reduce site costs and building costs by using standardized, cost-efficient store designs and by consolidating purchases of equipment and materials via a global sourcing system.
- Make sure restaurants are attractive and pleasing inside and out and, where feasible, provide drive-thru service and play areas for children.

Product Line Strategy

- Offer a limited menu.
- Improve the taste appeal of the items offered (especially sandwich selections).
- Expand product offerings into new categories of fast food (chicken, Mexican, pizza, adult-oriented sandwiches, and so on) and include more items for health-conscious customers.
- Do extensive testing to ensure consistent high quality and ample customer appeal before rolling out new menu items systemwide.

---

once again setting the stage for weakened competitiveness, impaired ability to exercise industry leadership, and underperformance.

How boldly managers embrace new strategic opportunities, how much they emphasize outinnovating the competition, and how often they champion actions to improve organizational performance are good barometers of their entrepreneurial spirit. Entrepreneurial strategy-makers are inclined to be first-movers, responding quickly and opportunistically to new developments. They are willing to take prudent risks and initiate trailblazing strategies. In contrast, reluctant entrepreneurs are risk-averse; they tend to be late-movers, hopeful about their chances of soon catching up and alert to how they can avoid whatever "mistakes" they believe first-movers have

ILLUSTRATION CAPSULE 3 (concluded)

Store Operations

- Enforce stringent standards regarding food quality, store and equipment cleanliness, restaurant operating procedures, and friendly, courteous counter service.
- Develop new equipment and production systems that improve the ability to serve hotter, better-tasting food, faster and with greater accuracy.

Sales Promotion, Marketing, and Merchandising

- Enhance the McDonald's image of quality, service, cleanliness, and value globally via heavy media advertising and in-store merchandise promotions funded with fees tied to a percent of sales revenues at each restaurant.
- Use Ronald McDonald to create greater brand awareness among children and the Mc prefix to reinforce the connection of menu items and McDonald's.
- Project an attitude of happiness and interest in children.

Human Resources and Training

- Offer wage rates that are equitable and nondiscriminatory in every location; teach job skills; reward both individual and team performance; create career opportunities; have flexible work hours for student employees.

- Hire restaurant crews with good work habits and courteous attitudes and train them to act in ways that will impress customers; promote promising employees quickly.
- Provide proper training on delivering customer satisfaction and running a fast-food business to franchisees, restaurant managers, and assistant managers. (Instructors at Hamburger University campuses in Illinois, Germany, England, Australia, and Japan annually train over 5,000 students in 22 languages.)

Social Responsibility and Community Citizenship

- Take an active community role—support local charities and community projects; help create a neighborhood spirit; promote educational excellence.
- Sponsor Ronald McDonald Houses (at year-end 1995, there were 168 houses in 12 countries providing a home-away-from-home for families of seriously ill children receiving treatment at nearby hospitals).
- Promote workforce diversity, voluntary affirmative action, and minority-owned franchises (over 25% of McDonald's franchisees were females and minorities).
- Adopt and encourage environmentally friendly practices.
- Provide nutritional information on McDonald's products to customers.

Source: Company annual reports.

made. They prefer incremental strategic change over bold and sweeping strategic moves.

In strategy-making, all managers, not just senior executives, must take prudent risks and exercise entrepreneurship. Entrepreneurship is involved when a district customer service manager, as part of a company's commitment to better customer service, crafts a strategy to speed the response time on service calls by 25 percent and commits $15,000 to equip all service trucks with mobile telephones. Entrepreneurship is involved when a warehousing manager contributes to a company's strategic emphasis on total quality by figuring out how to reduce the error frequency on filling customer orders from one error every 100 orders to one error every 100,000. A sales manager exercises strategic entrepreneurship by deciding to run a special promotion and cut sales prices by 5 percent to wrest market share away from rivals. A manufacturing manager exercises strategic entrepreneurship in deciding, as part of a companywide emphasis on greater cost competitiveness, to source an important component from a lower-priced South Korean supplier instead of making it in-house. Company strategies can't be truly market- and customer-driven unless the strategy-related activities of managers all across the company have an outside-in entrepreneurial character aimed at boosting customer satisfaction and achieving sustainable competitive advantage.

Why Company Strategies Evolve   Frequent fine-tuning and tweaking of a company's strategy, first in one department or functional area and then in another, are quite normal. On occasion, quantum changes in strategy are called for—when a competitor makes a dramatic move, when technological breakthroughs occur, or when crisis strikes and managers are forced to make radical strategy alterations very quickly. Because strategic moves and new action approaches are ongoing across the business, an organization's strategy forms over a period of time and then reforms as the number of changes begin to mount. Current strategy is typically a blend of holdover approaches, fresh actions and reactions, and potential moves in the planning stage. Except for crisis situations (where many strategic moves are often made quickly to produce a substantially new strategy almost overnight) and new company start-ups (where strategy exists mostly in the form of plans and intended actions), it is common for key elements of a company's strategy to emerge piece by piece as events transpire and the enterprise seeks to improve its position and performance.

> *A company's strategy is dynamic, forming in bits and pieces and then reforming as managers see avenues for improvement or a need to adapt business approaches to changing conditions.*

Rarely is a company's strategy so well crafted and durable that it can go unaltered for long. Even the best-laid business plans must be adapted to shifting market conditions, altered customer needs and preferences, the strategic maneuvering of rival firms, the experience of what is working and what isn't, emerging opportunities and threats, unforeseen events, and fresh thinking about how to improve the strategy. This is why strategy-making is an ongoing process and why a manager must reevaluate strategy regularly, refining and recasting it as needed.

However, when managers decide to change strategy so fast and so fundamentally that their business game plan undergoes major overhaul every year, they are almost certainly guilty of poor entrepreneurship, faulty situation analysis, and inept "strategizing." Quantum changes in strategy may well be needed occasionally, especially in crisis situations or during unusually rapid periods of industry change, but they cannot be made on a regular basis without creating a zigzag market wake, generating undue confusion among customers and employees, and undermining performance. Well-crafted strategies normally have a life of at least several years, requiring only minor tweaking to keep them in tune with changing circumstances.

Strategy and Strategic Plans   Developing a strategic vision and mission, establishing objectives, and deciding on a strategy are basic direction-setting tasks. They map out where the organization is headed, its short-range and long-range performance targets, and the competitive moves and internal action approaches to be used in achieving the targeted results. Together, they constitute a *strategic plan*. In some companies, especially those committed to regular strategy reviews and the development of explicit strategic plans, a document describing the company's strategic plan is circulated to managers and employees (although parts of the plan may be omitted or expressed in general terms if they are too sensitive to reveal before they are actually undertaken). In other companies, the strategic plan is not put in writing for widespread distribution but rather exists in the form of oral understandings and commitments among managers about where to head, what to accomplish, and how to proceed.

Organizational objectives are the part of the strategic plan most often spelled out explicitly and communicated to managers and employees. Some companies spell out key elements of their strategic plans in the company's annual report to shareholders or in statements provided to the business media, while others deliberately refrain from candid public discussion of their strategies for reasons of competitive sensitivity.

However, strategic plans seldom anticipate all the strategically relevant events that will transpire in upcoming months and years. Unforeseen events, unexpected opportunities or threats, plus the constant bubbling up of new proposals encourage managers to modify planned actions and forge "unplanned" reactions. Postponing the recrafting of strategy until it's time to work on next year's strategic plan is both foolish and unnecessary. Managers who confine their strategizing to the company's regularly scheduled planning cycle (when they can't avoid turning something in) have a wrongheaded concept of what their strategy-making responsibilities are. Once-a-year strategizing under "have-to" conditions is not a prescription for managerial success.

Implementing and Executing the Strategy

The managerial task of implementing and executing the chosen strategy entails assessing what it will take to make the strategy work and to reach the targeted performance on schedule—the managerial skill here is being good at figuring out what must be done to put the strategy in place, execute it proficiently, and produce good results. Managing the process of implementing and executing strategy is primarily a hands-on, close-to-the-scene administrative task that includes the following principal aspects:

- Building an organization capable of carrying out the strategy successfully.
- Developing budgets that steer resources into those internal activities critical to strategic success.
- Establishing strategy-supportive policies and operating procedures.
- Motivating people in ways that induce them to pursue the target objectives energetically and, if need be, modifying their duties and job behavior to better fit the requirements of successful strategy execution.
- Tying the reward structure to the achievement of targeted results.
- Creating a company culture and work climate conducive to successful strategy implementation and execution.
- Installing information, communication, and operating systems that enable company personnel to carry out their strategic roles effectively day in and day out.
- Instituting best practices and programs for continuous improvement.
- Exerting the internal leadership needed to drive implementation forward and to keep improving on how the strategy is being executed.

The strategy implementer's aim must be to create strong "fits" between the way things are done internally to try to execute the strategy and what it will take for the strategy to succeed. The stronger the methods of implementation fit the strategy's requirements, the better the execution and the better the odds that performance targets will be achieved. The most important fits are between strategy and organizational capabilities, between strategy and the reward structure, between strategy and internal support systems, and between strategy and the organization's culture (the latter emerges from the values and beliefs shared by organizational members, the company's approach to people management, and ingrained behaviors, work practices, and ways of thinking). Fitting the ways the organization does things internally to what is needed for strategic success helps unite the organization behind the accomplishment of strategy.

The strategy-implementing task is easily the most complicated and time-consuming part of strategic management. It cuts across virtually all facets of managing and must be initiated from many points inside the organization. The strategy-implementer's agenda for action emerges from careful assessment of what the organization must do differently and better to carry out the strategic plan proficiently. Each manager has to think through the answer to "What has to be done in my area to carry out my piece of the strategic plan, and how can I best get it done?" How much internal change is needed to put the strategy into place depends on the degree of strategic change, how far internal practices and competencies deviate from what the strategy requires, and how well strategy and organizational culture already match. As needed changes and actions are identified, management must see that all the details of implementation are attended to and apply enough pressure on the organization to convert objectives into results. Depending on the amount of internal change involved, full implementation can take several months to several years.

Strategy implementation is fundamentally an action-oriented, make-it-happen activity—developing competencies and capabilities, budgeting, policy making, motivating, culture building, and leading are all part of the process.

Evaluating Performance, Monitoring New Developments, and Initiating Corrective Adjustments

It is always incumbent on management to evaluate the organization's performance and progress. It is management's duty to stay on top of the company's situation, deciding whether things are going well internally, and monitoring outside developments closely. Subpar performance or too little progress, as well as important new external circumstances, call for corrective actions and adjustments. Long-term direction may need to be altered, the business redefined, and management's vision of the organization's future course narrowed or broadened or radically revised. Performance targets may need raising or lowering in light of past experience and future prospects. Strategy may need to be modified because of shifts in long-term direction, because new objectives have been set, because some elements are not working well, or because of shifting market conditions and customer preferences.

A company's vision, objectives, strategy, and approach to implementation are never final; evaluating performance, monitoring changes in the surrounding environment, and making adjustments are normal and necessary parts of the strategic management process.

Likewise, one or more aspects of implementation and execution may not be going as well as intended. Budget revisions, policy changes, reorganization, personnel changes, revamped activities and work processes, culture-changing efforts, and revised compensation practices are typical managerial actions that may have to be taken to hasten implementation or improve strategy execution. *Proficient strategy execution is always the product of much organizational learning.* It is achieved unevenly—coming quickly in some areas and proving nettlesome in others. Progress reviews, ongoing searches for ways to continuously improve, and corrective adjustments are thus normal.

WHY STRATEGIC MANAGEMENT IS A PROCESS, NOT AN EVENT

The march of external and internal events guarantees that a company's vision, objectives, strategy, and implementation approaches will have to be revisited, reconsidered, and eventually revised. This is why the task of evaluating performance and initiating corrective adjustments is both the end and the beginning of the strategic management *cycle*. Evaluating and adjusting means that prior strategy-related decisions and actions are subject to modification as conditions in the surrounding environment change and ideas for improvement emerge. The choice of whether to continue or change the company's vision, objectives, strategy, and implementation approaches always presents itself. Strategic management is thus an ongoing, never-ending *process*, not a start-stop event that once done can be safely put aside for a while. Managers have everpresent responsibility for detecting when new developments require a strategic response and when they don't. It is their job to track progress, spot problems early, monitor the winds of market and customer change, and initiate adjustments.

Characteristics of the Process

Although forming a strategic vision, setting objectives, crafting a strategy, implementing and executing the strategic plan, and evaluating performance portray what strategic management involves, actually performing these five tasks is not so cleanly divided into separate, neatly sequenced compartments. There is much interplay and recycling among the five tasks, as shown in Figure 1.1. For example, considering what strategic actions to take raises issues about whether and how the strategy can be satisfactorily implemented. Deciding on a company mission and vision shades into setting objectives (both involve directional priorities). Objective setting entails considering current performance, the strategy options available to improve performance, and what the organization can really achieve when pushed and challenged. Deciding on a strategy is entangled with decisions about long-term direction and whether objectives have been set in all the key financial and strategic areas. Clearly, the direction-setting tasks of developing a mission, setting objectives, and crafting strategy need to be integrated and done as a package, not individually.

Strategic management is a process; the boundaries between the five tasks are conceptual, not fences that prevent some or all of them being done together.

Second, the five strategic management tasks are not done in isolation from a manager's other duties and responsibilities—administering day-to-day operations, dealing with crises, going to meetings, reviewing information, handling people problems, and taking on special assignments and civic duties. Thus, while the job of managing strategy is the most important managerial function insofar as organizational success or failure is concerned, it isn't all managers must do or be concerned about.

Third, crafting and implementing strategy make erratic demands on a manager's time. Change does not happen in an orderly or predictable way. Events can build quickly or gradually; they can emerge singly or in rapid-fire succession; and their implications for strategic change can be easy or hard to diagnose. Hence the task of reviewing and adjusting the strategic game plan can take up big chunks of management time in some months and little time in other months. As a practical matter, there is as much skill in knowing *when* to institute strategic changes as there is in knowing what to do.

Last, the big day-in, day-out time-consuming aspect of strategic management involves trying to get the best strategy-supportive performance out of every individual and trying to perfect the current strategy by refining its content and execution. Managers usually spend most of their efforts improving bits and pieces of the current strategy rather than developing and instituting radical changes. Excessive changes in strategy can be disruptive to employees and confusing to customers, and they are usually unnecessary. Most of the time, there's more to be gained from improving execution of the present strategy. Persistence in making a sound strategy work better is often the key to managing the strategy to success.

WHO PERFORMS THE FIVE TASKS OF STRATEGIC MANAGEMENT?

An organization's chief executive officer, as captain of the ship, is the most visible and important strategy manager. The title of CEO carries with it the mantles of chief direction setter, chief objective setter, chief strategy maker, and chief strategy implementer for the total enterprise. Ultimate responsibility for *leading* the tasks of formulating and implementing a strategic plan for the whole organization rests with the CEO, even though other senior managers normally have significant *leadership* roles also. What the CEO views as strategically important usually is reflected in the company's strategy, and the CEO customarily puts a personal stamp of approval on big strategic decisions and actions.

Vice presidents for production, marketing, finance, human resources, and other key departments have important strategy-making and strategy-implementing responsibilities as well. Normally, the production VP has a lead role in developing the company's production strategy; the marketing VP oversees the marketing strategy effort; the financial VP is in charge of devising an appropriate financial strategy; and so on. Usually, senior managers below the CEO are also involved in proposing key elements of the overall company strategy and developing major new strategic initiatives, working closely with the CEO to hammer out a consensus and coordinate various aspects of the strategy more effectively. Only in the smallest, owner-managed companies is the strategy-making, strategy-implementing task small enough for a single manager to handle.

But managerial positions with strategy-making and strategy-implementing responsibility are by no means restricted to CEOs, vice presidents, and owner-entrepreneurs. Every major organizational unit in a company—business unit, division, staff plant, support group, or district office—normally has a leading or supporting role in the company's strategic game plan. And the manager in charge of that organizational unit, with guidance from superiors, usually ends up doing some or most of the strategy making for the unit and deciding how to implement whatever strategic choices are made. While managers farther down in the managerial hierarchy obviously have a narrower, more specific strategy-making/strategy-implementing role than managers closer to the top, *every manager is a strategy maker and strategy implementer for the area he/she supervises.*

Every company manager has a strategy-making, strategy-implementing role—it is flawed thinking to view strategic management as solely a senior executive responsibility.

One of the primary reasons why middle- and lower-echelon managers are part of the strategy-making/strategy-implementing team is that the more geographically scattered and diversified an organization's operations are, the more unwieldy it becomes for senior executives at the company's headquarters to craft and implement all the necessary actions and programs. Managers in the corporate office seldom know enough about the situation in every geographic area and operating unit to direct every move made in the field. It is common practice for top-level managers to grant some strategy-making responsibility to managerial subordinates who head the organizational subunits where specific strategic results must be achieved. Delegating a strategy-making role to on-the-scene managers charged with implementing whatever strategic moves are made in their areas fixes accountability for strategic success or failure. When the managers who implement the strategy are also its architects, it is hard for them to shift blame or make excuses if they don't achieve the target results. And, having participated in developing the strategy they are trying to implement and execute, they are likely to have strong buy-in and support for the strategy, an essential condition for effective strategy execution.

In diversified companies where the strategies of several different businesses have to be managed, there are usually four distinct levels of strategy managers:

- The chief executive officer and other senior corporate-level executives who have primary responsibility and personal authority for big strategic decisions affecting the total enterprise and the collection of individual businesses the enterprise has diversified into.

- Managers who have profit-and-loss responsibility for one specific business unit and who are delegated a major leadership role in formulating and implementing strategy for that unit.

- Functional area heads and department heads within a given business unit who have direct authority over a major piece of the business (manufacturing, marketing and sales, finance, R&D, personnel) and whose role it is to support the business unit's overall strategy with strategic actions in their own areas.

- Managers of major operating units (plants, sales districts, local offices) who have on-the-scene responsibility for developing the details of strategic efforts in their areas and for implementing and executing their piece of the overall strategic plan at the grassroots level.

Single-business enterprises need no more than three of these levels (a business-level strategy manager, functional-area strategy managers, and operating-level strategy managers). In a large single-business company, the team of strategy managers consists of the chief executive, who functions as chief strategist with final authority over both strategy and its implementation; the vice presidents and department heads in charge of key activities (R&D, production, marketing, finance, human resources, and so on); plus as many operating-unit managers of the various plants, sales offices, distribution centers, and staff support departments as it takes to handle the company's scope of operations. Proprietorships, partnerships, and owner-managed enterprises, however, typically have only one or two strategy managers since in small-scale enterprises the whole strategy-making/strategy-implementing function can be handled by just a few key people.

Managerial jobs involving strategy formulation and implementation abound in not-for-profit organizations as well. In federal and state government, heads of local, district, and regional offices function as strategy managers in their efforts to respond to the needs and situations of the areas they serve (a district manager in Portland may need a slightly different strategy than a district manager in Orlando). In municipal government, the heads of various departments (fire, police, water and sewer, parks and recreation, health, and so on) are strategy managers because they have line authority for the operations of their departments and thus can influence departmental objectives, the formation of a strategy to achieve these objectives, and how the strategy is implemented.

Managerial jobs with strategy-making/strategy-implementing roles are thus the norm rather than the exception.[3] The job of crafting and implementing strategy touches virtually every managerial job in one way or another, at one time or another. Strategic management is basic to the task of managing; it is not something just top-level managers deal with.

Is Strategy-Making an Individual Responsibility or a Group Task?

Many companies today are involving teams of managers and key employees in strategy-making exercises, partly because many strategic issues cut across traditional functional and departmental lines, partly to tap into the ideas and problem-solving skills of people with different backgrounds, expertise, and perspectives, and partly to give a greater number of people an ownership stake in the strategy that emerges and win their wholehearted commitment to implementation. Frequently, these teams include line and staff managers from different disciplines and departmental units, a few handpicked junior staffers known for their ability to think creatively, and near-retirement veterans noted for being keen observers, telling it like it is, and giving sage advice. And it is not uncommon for these teams to involve customers and suppliers in assessing the future market situation and deliberating the various strategy options. One of the biggest causes of flawed strategy is insufficient focus on what customers really need and want; another is not seeing the company as part of a wider environment and recognizing the value of reaching out and collaborating closely with key suppliers and customers (and maybe even select competitors) to gain competitive advantage.[4]

Electronic Data Systems recently conducted a yearlong strategy review involving 2,500 of its 55,000 employees that was coordinated by a core of 150 managers and staffers from all over the world.[5] J.M. Smucker, a maker of jams and jellies, formed a team of 140 employees (7 percent of its 2,000-person workforce) who spent 25 percent of their time over a six-month period to seek ways to rejuvenate the company's growth; the team, which solicited input from all employees, came up with 12 initiatives to double the company's revenues over the next five years. Nokia Group, a Finland-based telecommunications company, involved 250 employees in a recent strategy review of how different communications technologies were converging, how this would impact the company's business, and what strategic responses were needed.

Broad participation in a company's strategy-creating exercises is usually a strong plus.

Involving teams of people to dissect complex situations and find market-driven, customer-driven solutions is becoming increasingly necessary in many businesses. Not only are many strategic issues too big or too complex for a single manager to handle but they often are cross-functional and cross-departmental in nature, requiring the contributions of many disciplinary experts and the collaboration of managers from different parts of the organization to decide upon sound strategic actions. The notion that an organization's strategists are at the top and its doers are in the ranks below needs to be cast aside; very often, key pieces of strategy

---

[3]The strategy-making, strategy-implementing roles of middle managers are thoroughly discussed and documented in Steven W. Floyd and Bill Wooldridge, *The Strategic Middle Manager* (San Francisco: Jossey-Bass Publishers, 1996), Chapters 2 and 3.

[4]See James F. Moore, *The Death of Competition* (New York: HarperBusiness, 1996), Chapter 3.

[5]"Strategic Planning," *Business Week*, August 26, 1996, pp. 51–52.

originate in the middle and lower ranks of the organization, with senior managers endorsing what emerges from below and providing the resources necessary for implementation.

Is There a Role for Full-Time Strategic Planners?

If senior and middle managers have the lead roles in strategy making and strategy implementing in their areas of responsibility, supplemented by multidisciplinary strategy teams and broad employee participation in some circumstances, is there any need for full-time strategic planners or staffers with expertise in strategic analysis? The answer is perhaps in a few companies, but even then a planning staff's role and tasks should consist chiefly of helping to gather and organize information that strategy makers decide they need, providing administrative support to line managers in revising their strategic plans, and coordinating the process of higher-level executive review and approval of the strategic plans developed for all the various parts of the company. A strategic planning staff can help line managers and strategy teams crystallize the strategic issues that ought to be addressed; in addition, they can provide data, conduct studies of industry and competitive conditions as requested by the strategy makers, and develop assessments of the company's strategic performance. But strategic planners should not make strategic decisions, prepare strategic plans (for someone else to implement), or make strategic action recommendations that usurp the strategy-making responsibilities of line managers or self-directed work teams in charge of operating units or particular activities.

When strategic planners are asked to go beyond providing staff assistance and actually prepare a strategic plan for management's consideration, any of four adverse consequences may occur. One, weak managers will gladly turn tough strategic problems over to strategic planners to do their strategic thinking for them—a questionable outcome because it deludes managers into thinking they shouldn't be held responsible for crafting a strategy for their own organizational unit or for acting on strategic issues related to their areas of responsibility.

Two, planners, however expert they may be in strategic analysis and writing snappy reports, can't know as much about all the ins and outs of the situation as on-the-scene managers who are responsible for staying on top of things in their assigned area on a daily basis. This puts planning staffers at a severe disadvantage in devising sound action recommendations and taking into account the practical difficulties of implementing what they recommend.

Three, giving planners responsibility for strategy making and line managers responsibility for implementation makes it hard to fix accountability for poor results. Planners can place the blame for poor results on weak implementation; line managers can claim the problem rests with bad strategy.

Four, when line managers see no urgency in or have no ownership stake in the strategic agenda proposed by the planning staff, there's a big risk they will give it lip service, perhaps make a few token implementation efforts, and then let most of the planners' recommendations die through inaction. Handing the strategy-making function off to a strategic planning staff runs the risk that line managers and senior executives will not see the urgency or necessity of following through on what is proposed. Skepticism or disagreement over planners' recommendations breeds inaction. Absent strong concurrence with the actions recommended by planners, their work is likely to fall through the cracks—and strategic planning exercises come to be seen

Strategic Management Principle

Strategy making is a job for line managers, not a staff of planners—the doers should be the strategy makers.

as an unproductive bureaucratic activity. Such outcomes raise the chances that a company will drift along with no strong top-down strategic direction and with fragmented, uncoordinated strategic decisions. The hard truth is that strategy making is not a staff function.

All four consequences are unacceptable. Strategizing efforts get a bum rap as ineffective, line managers don't develop the skills or the discipline to think strategically about the business, and the company encounters much bigger risk of a strategy-making vacuum. On the other hand, when people are expected to be the chief strategy makers and strategy implementers for the areas they head, their own strategy and implementation efforts end up being put to the test. They quickly see the necessity of having a workable strategic plan (their annual performance reviews and perhaps even their future careers with the organization are at risk if their strategies prove unsound and they fail to achieve the target results!). When responsibility for crafting strategy is lodged with the same people charged with implementing strategy, there's no question who is accountable for results. Furthermore, pushing authority for crafting and implementing the strategy down to the people closest to the action puts decision making in the hands of those who *should* know best what to do. Broad participation gives more organizational members experience in thinking strategically about the business and in crafting and implementing strategies. People who consistently prove incapable of crafting and implementing good strategies and achieving target results have to be moved to less responsible positions.

The Strategic Role of the Board of Directors

Since lead responsibility for crafting and implementing strategy falls to key managers, the chief strategic role of an organization's board of directors is to exercise oversight and see that the five tasks of strategic management are done in a manner that benefits shareholders (in the case of investor-owned enterprises) or stakeholders (in the case of not-for-profit organizations). Recent increases in the number of stockholder lawsuits and the escalating costs of liability insurance for directors and officers have underscored that corporate board members do indeed bear ultimate responsibility for the strategic actions taken. Moreover, holders of large blocks of shares (mutual funds and pension funds), regulatory authorities, and the financial press are all calling for board members, especially outside directors, to be more active in their oversight of company strategy.

It is standard procedure for executives to brief board members on important strategic moves and to submit the company's strategic plans to the board for official approval. But directors rarely can or should play a direct, hands-on role in formulating or implementing strategy. Most outside directors lack industry-specific experience; their company-specific knowledge is limited (especially if they are relatively new board members). Boards of directors typically meet once a month (or less) for six to eight hours. Board members can scarcely be expected to have detailed command of all the strategic issues or know the ins and outs of the various strategic options. They can hardly be expected to come up with compelling strategy proposals of their own to debate against those put forward by management. Such a hands-on role is unnecessary for good oversight. The immediate task of directors is to be *supportive critics*, exercising their own independent judgment about whether proposals have been adequately analyzed and whether proposed strategic actions

Strategic Management Principle

A board of directors' role in the strategic management process is to critically appraise and ultimately approve strategic action plans but rarely, if ever, to develop the details.

appear to have greater promise than available alternatives.[6] If executive management is bringing well-supported strategy proposals to the board, there's little reason for board members to aggressively challenge and try to pick apart everything put before them—asking perceptive and incisive questions is usually sufficient to test whether the case for the proposals is compelling and to exercise vigilant oversight. However, if the company is experiencing gradual erosion of profits and market share, and certainly when there is a precipitous collapse in profitability, board members have a duty to be proactive, expressing their concerns about the validity of the strategy, initiating debate about the company's strategic path, having one-on-one discussions with key executives and other board members, and perhaps directly intervening as a group to alter both the strategy and the company's executive leadership.

The real hands-on role of directors is to evaluate the caliber of senior executives' strategy-making and strategy-implementing skills. The board is always responsible for determining whether the current CEO is doing a good job of strategic management (as a basis for awarding salary increases and bonuses and deciding on retention or removal). In recent years, at Apple Computer, General Motors, IBM, American Express, Kmart, W.R. Grace, and Compaq Computer, company directors concluded that top executives were not adapting their company's strategy fast enough and fully enough to the changes sweeping their markets. They pressured the CEOs to resign, and installed new leadership to provide the impetus for strategic renewal. Boards must also exercise due diligence in evaluating the strategic leadership skills of other senior executives in line to succeed the CEO. When the incumbent CEO retires, the board must elect a successor, either going with an insider (frequently nominated by the retiring CEO) or deciding that an outsider is needed to perhaps radically change the company's strategic course.

Hence, the strategic role of the board of directors is twofold: (1) to continuously audit the validity of a company's long-term direction and strategy, typically giving top executives free rein but always monitoring, offering constructive critiques, and standing ready to intervene if circumstances require, and (2) to evaluate the strategic leadership skills of the CEO and other insiders in line to succeed the incumbent CEO, proactively making personnel changes whenever the organization's performance is deemed not to be as good as it should be. Board oversight and vigilance is therefore very much in play in the strategy arena.

THE BENEFITS OF A "STRATEGIC APPROACH" TO MANAGING

The message of this book is that doing a good job of managing inherently requires good strategic thinking and good strategic management. Today's managers have to think strategically about their company's position and about the impact of changing conditions. They have to monitor the external situation closely enough to know when to institute strategy changes. They have to know the business well enough to know what kinds of strategic changes to initiate. Simply said, the fundamentals of strategic

---

[6]For a good discussion of the role of the board of directors in overseeing the strategy-making, strategy-implementing process, see Gordon Donaldson, "A New Tool for Boards: The Strategic Audit," *Harvard Business Review* 73, no.4 (July–August 1995), pp. 99–107.

management need to drive the whole approach to managing organizations. The chief executive officer of one successful company put it well when he said:

> In the main, our competitors are acquainted with the same fundamental concepts and techniques and approaches that we follow, and they are as free to pursue them as we are. More often than not, the difference between their level of success and ours lies in the relative thoroughness and self-discipline with which we and they develop and execute our strategies for the future.

The advantages of first-rate strategic thinking and conscious strategy management (as opposed to freewheeling improvisation, gut feel, and hoping for luck) include (1) providing better guidance to the entire organization on the crucial point of "what it is we are trying to do and to achieve"; (2) making managers more alert to the winds of change, new opportunities, and threatening developments; (3) providing managers with a rationale for evaluating competing budget requests for investment capital and new staff—a rationale that argues strongly for steering resources into strategy-supportive, results-producing areas; (4) helping to unify the numerous strategy-related decisions by managers across the organization; and (5) creating a more proactive management posture and counteracting tendencies for decisions to be reactive and defensive.

The advantage of being proactive is that trailblazing strategies can be the key to better long-term performance. Business history shows that high-performing enterprises often initiate and lead, not just react and defend. They launch strategic offensives to outinnovate and outmaneuver rivals and secure sustainable competitive advantage, then use their market edge to achieve superior financial performance. Aggressive pursuit of a creative, opportunistic strategy can propel a firm into a leadership position, paving the way for its products/services to become the industry standard. High-achieving enterprises are nearly always the product of astute, proactive management, rather than the result of lucky breaks or a long run of good fortune.

TERMS TO REMEMBER

In the chapters to come, we'll be referring to *mission, vision, objectives, strategy, strategic plan*, and other terms common to the language of strategy again and again. In practice, these terms generate a lot of confusion—managers, consultants, and academics often use them imprecisely and sometimes interchangeably. No single, common vocabulary exists. To cut down on the confusion and promote precise meaning, we're going to incorporate the following definitions throughout our presentation.

Strategic vision—a view of an organization's future direction and business makeup; a guiding concept for what the organization is trying to do and to become.

Organization mission—management's customized answer to the question "What is our business and what are we trying to accomplish on behalf of our customers?" A mission statement broadly outlines the organization's activities and present business makeup. Whereas the focus of a strategic vision is on a company's future, the focus of a company's mission *tends* to be on the present. (If the statement of mission speaks as much to the future path the organization intends to follow as to the present organizational purpose, then the mission statement incorporates the strategic vision and there's no *separate* managerial need for a vision.)

Financial objectives—the targets management has established for the organization's financial performance.

Strategic objectives—the targets management has established for strengthening the organization's overall business position and competitive vitality.

Long-range objectives—the results to be achieved either within the next three to five years or else on an ongoing basis year after year.

Short-range objectives—the organization's near-term performance targets; the amount of short-term improvement signals how fast management is trying to achieve the long-range objectives.

Strategy—the pattern of actions and business approaches managers employ to please customers, build an attractive market position, and achieve organizational objectives; a company's actual strategy is partly planned and partly reactive to changing circumstances.

Strategic plan—a statement outlining an organization's mission and future direction, near-term and long-term performance targets, and strategy.

Strategy formulation—the entire direction-setting management function of conceptualizing an organization's mission, setting performance objectives, and crafting a strategy. The end product of strategy formulation is a strategic plan.

Strategy implementation—the full range of managerial activities associated with putting the chosen strategy into place, supervising its pursuit, and achieving the targeted results.

On the following pages, we will probe the strategy-related tasks of managers and the methods of strategic analysis much more intensively. When you get to the end of the book, we think you will see that two factors separate the best-managed organizations from the rest: (1) superior strategy making and entrepreneurship, and (2) competent implementation and execution of the chosen strategy. There's no escaping the fact that the quality of managerial strategy making and strategy implementing has a significant impact on organization performance. A company that lacks clear-cut direction, has vague or undemanding objectives, has a muddled or flawed strategy, or can't seem to execute its strategy competently is a company whose performance is probably suffering, whose business is at long-term risk, and whose management is lacking. In short, the better conceived a company's strategy and the more proficient its execution, the greater the chances the company will be a leading performer in its markets and truly deserve a reputation for talented management.

SUGGESTED READINGS

Andrews, Kenneth R. *The Concept of Corporate Strategy,* 3rd ed. Homewood, Ill.: Richard D. Irwin, 1987, chap. 1.

Collins, James C., and Jerry I. Porras. "Building Your Company's Vision." *Harvard Business Review* 74, no.5 (September–October 1996), pp. 65–77.

Farkas, Charles M., and Suzy Wetlaufer. "The Ways Chief Executive Officers Lead," *Harvard Business Review* 74 no. 3 (May–June 1996), pp. 110–22.

Hamel, Gary. "Strategy as Revolution," *Harvard Business Review* 74 no. 4 (July–August 1996), pp. 69–82.

Lipton, Mark. "Demystifying the Development of an Organizational Vision." *Sloan Management Review* (Summer 1996), pp. 83–92.

Mintzberg, Henry. "Rethinking Strategic Planning: Pitfalls and Fallacies." *Long Range Planning* 27, no. 3 (1994), pp. 12–19.

――――."Rethinking Strategic Planning: New Roles for Planners." *Long Range Planning* 27, no. 3 (1994), pp. 22–29.

――――. "Crafting Strategy." *Harvard Business Review* 65, no. 4 (July–August 1987), pp. 66–75.

Porter, Michael E. "What Is Strategy?" *Harvard Business Review* 74, no. 6 (November–December 1996), pp. 61–78.

Yip, George S. *Total Global Strategy: Managing for Worldwide Competitive Advantage.* Englewood Cliffs, N.J.: Prentice-Hall, 1992, chap. 1.

THE THREE STRATEGY-MAKING TASKS

Developing a Strategic Vision, Setting Objectives, and Crafting a Strategy

2

I n this chapter, we take a more in-depth look at the three strategy-making tasks: developing a strategic vision and business mission, setting performance objectives, and crafting a strategy to produce the desired results. We also examine the kinds of strategic decisions made at each management level, the major determinants of a company's strategy, and four frequently used managerial approaches to forming a strategic plan.

DEVELOPING A STRATEGIC VISION AND MISSION: THE FIRST DIRECTION-SETTING TASK

Early on, a company's senior management has to look to the future and address the issue of "where do we go from here—what customer needs and buyer segments do we need to be concentrating on, what should the company's business makeup be 5 to 10 years down the road?" Management's views and conclusions about the organization's future course, the customer focus it should have, the market position it should try to occupy, and the business activities to be pursued constitute a *strategic vision* for the company. A strategic vision indicates management's aspirations for the organization, providing a panoramic view of "what businesses we want to be in, where we are headed, and the kind of company we are trying to create." It spells out a direction and describes the destination.

The last thing IBM needs right now is a vision. (July 1993) What IBM needs most right now is a vision. (March 1996)

Louis V. Gerstner, Jr
CEO, IBM Corporation

How can you lead if you don't know where you are going?

George Newman
The Conference Board

Management's job is not to see the company as it is . . . but as it can become.

John W. Teets
CEO, Greyhound Corporation

A strategy is a commitment to undertake one set of actions rather than another.

Sharon M. Oster
Professor, Yale University

ILLUSTRATION CAPSULE 4   Delta Airlines' Strategic Vision

In late 1993, Ronald W. Allen, Delta's chief executive officer, described the company's vision and business mission in the following way:

> . . . we want Delta to be the **Worldwide Airline of Choice**.
>
> Worldwide, because we are and intend to remain an innovative, aggressive, ethical, and successful competitor that offers access to the world at the highest standards of customer service. We will continue to look for opportunities to extend our reach through new routes and creative global alliances.
>
> Airline, because we intend to stay in the business we know best—air transportation and related ser-

vices. We won't stray from our roots. We believe in the long-term prospects for profitable growth in the airline industry, and we will continue to focus time, attention, and investment on enhancing our place in that business environment.

> Of Choice, because we value the loyalty of our customers, employees, and investors. For passengers and shippers, we will continue to provide the best service and value. For our personnel, we will continue to offer an ever more challenging, rewarding, and result-oriented workplace that recognizes and appreciates their contributions. For our shareholders, we will earn a consistent, superior financial return.

Source: *Sky Magazine*, December 1993, p. 10.

Why Have a Mission or Strategic Vision?

A clear and entrepreneurially astute strategic vision is a prerequisite to effective strategic leadership. A manager cannot function effectively as either leader or strategy maker without a future-oriented concept of the business—what customer needs to work toward satisfying, what business activities to pursue, and what kind of long-term market position to build vis-à-vis competitors. Forming a strategic vision is thus not a wordsmithing exercise to create a catchy company slogan; rather, it is an exercise in thinking strategically about a company's future, forming a viable concept of the company's future business, and putting the company on a strategic path that management is deeply committed to. It is an exercise in coming up with a coherent and powerful picture of what the company's business can and should be 5 or 10 years hence. When management's strategic vision conveys something substantive about what business position it intends for the company to stake out and what course the company is going to follow, then the vision is truly capable of *guiding* managerial decision making, *shaping* the company's strategy, and *impacting* how the company is run. Such outcomes have *real managerial value*. Illustration Capsule 4 presents Delta Airlines' strategic vision.

Effective strategy making begins with a concept of what the organization should and should not do and a vision of where the organization needs to be headed.

Strategic Visions Chart a Company's Future   The term *strategic vision* is inherently more future oriented than the oft-used terms *business purpose* or *mission statement*. The statements of mission or business purpose that most companies include in their annual reports tend to deal more with the present ("What is our business?") than with the organization's aspirations and long-term direction (where we are headed, what new things we intend to pursue, what we want our business makeup to be in 5 to 10 years, what kind of company we are trying to become, and what sort of long-term market position we aspire to achieve). However, a here-and-now-oriented purpose/mission statement highlighting the boundaries of the company's current business is a logical vantage point from which to look down the road, decide what the enterprise's future business makeup and customer focus need to be, and chart a strategic path for the company to take. As a rule, strategic visions should have a time horizon of a decade or more.

Strategic Visions Are Company-Specific, Not Generic   Strategic visions and company mission statements ought to be highly personalized—unique to the organization for which they were developed. There's nothing unusual about companies in the same industry pursuing significantly, even radically, different strategic paths. For example, the current mission and future direction of a globally active New York bank like Citicorp has little in common with that of a locally owned hometown bank even though both are in the banking industry. IBM, with its mainframe computer business, its line-up of personal computers, and its software and services business, is not on the same long-term strategic course as Compaq Computer (which concentrates on PCs and servers), even though both are leaders in the personal computer industry. *The whole idea behind developing a strategic vision/mission statement is to set an organization apart from others in its industry and give it its own special identity, business emphasis, and path for development.*

Generically worded statements, couched in everything-and-everybody language that could apply just as well to many companies and lines of business, are not managerially useful—they paint no mental picture of where the company is destined and offer no guidance to managers in deciding which business activities to pursue and not to pursue, what strategies make the best sense, or how to operate the company. Nor do they communicate useful information about a company's long-term direction and future business makeup to employees and investors. Ambiguous or vaguely worded mission/vision statements may have some public relations value, but they don't help managers manage. *The best vision statements are worded in a manner that clarifies the direction in which an organization needs to move.*

> *Visionless companies are unsure what business position they are trying to stake out.*

The Mission or Vision Is Not to Make a Profit   Sometimes companies couch their business purpose or mission in terms of making a profit. This is misguided—profit is more correctly an *objective* and a *result* of what the company does. The desire to make a profit says nothing about the business arena in which profits are to be sought. Missions or visions based on making a profit are incapable of distinguishing one type of profit-seeking enterprise from another—the business and long-term direction of Sears are plainly different from the business and long-term direction of Toyota, even though both endeavor to earn a profit. A company that says its mission/business purpose/strategic vision is to make a profit begs the question "What will we do to make a profit?" To understand a company's business and future direction, we must know management's answer to "make a profit doing what and for whom?"

The Elements of a Strategic Vision   There are three distinct pieces to the task of forming a strategic vision of a company's business future:

- Defining what business the company is *presently* in.
- Deciding on a *long-term* strategic course for the company to pursue.
- Communicating the vision in ways that are clear, exciting, and inspiring.

Defining a Company's Present Business

Coming up with a strategically insightful definition of what business an organization is presently in is not as simple as it might seem. Is IBM in the computer business (a product-oriented definition) or the information and data-processing business (a customer service or customer needs type of definition) or the advanced electronics business (a technology-based definition)? Is America Online in the computer services business, the information business, the business of connecting people to the Internet, the on-line content business, or the entertainment business? Is AT&T in the long-distance business or the telephone business or the telecommunications business? Is Coca-Cola in the soft-drink business (in which case management's strategic attention can be concentrated on outselling and outcompeting Pepsi, 7UP, Dr Pepper, Canada Dry, and Schweppes) or is it in the beverage business (in which case management also needs to think strategically about positioning Coca-Cola products to compete against other fruit juices, ready-to-drink teas, bottled water, sports drinks, milk, and coffee)? Whether to take a soft-drink perspective or a beverage perspective is not a trivial question for Coca-Cola management—only partly because Coca-Cola is also the parent of Minute Maid and Hi-C juice products. With a beverage industry vision as opposed to a soft-drink focus, Coca-Cola management can better zero in on how to convince young adults to get their morning caffeine fix by drinking Coca-Cola instead of coffee.

A company's business is defined by what needs it is trying to satisfy, by which customer groups it is targeting, and by the technologies it will use and the functions it will perform in serving the target market.

Incorporating What, Who, and How Into the Business Definition   To arrive at a strategically revealing business definition, three elements need to be incorporated:[1]

1. Customer needs, or *what* is being satisfied.
2. Customer groups, or *who* is being satisfied.
3. The technologies used and functions performed—*how* customers' needs are satisfied.

Defining a business in terms of what to satisfy, who to satisfy, and how the organization will go about producing the satisfaction produces a comprehensive definition of what a company does and what business it is in. Just knowing what products or services a firm provides is never enough. Products or services per se are not important to customers; a product or service becomes a business when it satisfies a need or want. Without the need or want there is no business. Customer groups are relevant because they indicate the market to be served—the geographic domain to be covered and the types of buyers the firm is going after.

Technology and functions performed are important because they indicate *how* the company will satisfy the customers' needs and how much of the industry's production-distribution chain its activities will span. For instance, a firm's business can be *fully integrated*, extending across the entire range of industry activities that must be performed to get a product or service in the hands of end users. Major international oil companies like Exxon, Mobil, BP, Royal Dutch Shell, and Chevron lease drilling sites, drill wells, pump oil, transport crude oil in their own ships and pipelines to their own refineries, and sell gasoline and other refined products through their own networks of branded distributors and service station outlets. Their operations cover all stages of the industry's entire production-distribution chain.

Other firms stake out *partially integrated* positions, participating only in selected stages of the industry. Goodyear, for instance, both manufactures tires and operates a chain of company-owned retail tire stores, but it has not integrated backward into

---

[1]Derek F. Abell, *Defining the Business: The Starting Point of Strategic Planning* (Englewood Cliffs, N.J.: Prentice-Hall, 1980), p. 169.

rubber plantations and other tire-making components. General Motors, the world's most integrated manufacturer of cars and trucks, makes between 60 and 70 percent of the parts and components used in assembling GM vehicles. But GM is moving to outsource a greater fraction of its parts and systems components, and it relies totally on a network of independent, franchised dealers to handle sales and service functions. Still other firms are *specialized*, concentrating on just one stage of an industry's total production-distribution chain. Wal-Mart, Home Depot, Toys-R-Us, Lands' End, and The Limited are essentially one-stage firms. Their operations focus on the retail end of the production-distribution chain; they don't manufacture the items they sell. Delta Airlines is a one-stage enterprise; it doesn't manufacture the airplanes it flies, and it doesn't operate the airports where it lands. Delta has made a conscious decision to limit its business activities to moving travelers from one location to another via commercial jet aircraft.

An example of a company that does a pretty good job of covering the three bases of what, who, and how is Russell Corporation, the largest U. S. manufacturer of athletic uniforms:

> Russell Corporation is a vertically integrated international designer, manufacturer, and marketer of athletic uniforms, activewear, better knit shirts, leisure apparel, licensed sports apparel, sports and casual socks, and a comprehensive line of lightweight, yarn-dyed woven fabrics. The Company's manufacturing operations include the entire process of converting raw fibers into finished apparel and fabrics. Products are marketed to sporting goods dealers, department and specialty stores, mass merchandisers, golf pro shops, college bookstores, screen printers, distributors, mail-order houses, and other apparel manufacturers.

The concepts that McDonald's uses to define its business are a limited menu, good-tasting fast-food products of consistent quality, fast and accurate service, value pricing, exceptional customer care, convenient locations, and global market coverage. McDonald's business mission is built around "serving a limited menu of hot, tasty food quickly in a clean, friendly restaurant for a good value" to a broad base of fast-food customers worldwide (McDonald's serves approximately 30 million customers daily at 20,000-plus restaurants in over 90 countries).

Trying to identify needs served, target market, and functions performed in a single, snappy sentence is a challenge, and many firms' business definitions/mission statements fail to illuminate all three bases explicitly. The business definitions of some companies are thus better than others in terms of how they cut to the chase of what the enterprise is really about and the strategic position it is trying to stake out.[2]

A Broad or Narrow Business Definition?   Merck, one of the world's foremost pharmaceutical companies, has defined its business broadly as "providing society with

---

[2]For a more extensive discussion of the challenges of developing a well-conceived vision, as well as some in-depth examples, see James C. Collins and Jerry I. Porras, "Building Your Company's Vision," *Harvard Business Review* 74, no.5 (September–October 1996), pp. 65–77; Robert A. Burgelman and Andrew S. Grove, "Strategic Dissonance," *California Management Review* 38, no. 2 (Winter 1996), pp. 8–25; and Ron McTavish, "One More Time: What Business Are You In?" *Long Range Planning* 28, no. 2 (April 1995), pp. 49–60. For a discussion of some of the alternative ways a company can position itself in the marketplace, see Michael E. Porter, "What Is Strategy," *Harvard Business Review* 74, no. 6 (November–December 1996), pp. 65–67. Porter argues that the three basic strategic positions are based on (a) the range of customer needs to be served, (b) the variety of products to be offered (anywhere along the spectrum of one to many), and (c) the means by which customers are accessed—the terms Porter uses are needs-based positioning, variety-based positioning, and access-based positioning. For an empirical study of executive success in formulating and implementing a company vision and the difficulties encountered, see Laurie Larwood, Cecilia M. Falbe, Mark Kriger, and Paul Miesing, "Structure and Meaning of Organizational Vision," *Academy of Management Journal*, 38, no. 3 (June 1995), pp. 740–69.

superior products and services—innovations and solutions that satisfy customer needs and improve the quality of life." Such broad language, however, offers no practical strategic guidance. With such a definition Merck could pursue limitless strategic paths—developing innovative computer software, producing and marketing uniquely satisfying snack foods, manufacturing very appealing sports utility vehicles, or providing tax preparation services—businesses well outside its capabilities and actual intent. Trying to go in several business directions at once may be tempting and even fashionable, but it risks lack of business focus and dilution of effort. Few businesses fail because they are clearly focused on one market opportunity; many do badly because they try to pursue too many things at once.

To have managerial value, strategic visions, business definitions, and mission statements must be narrow enough to pin down the company's real arena of business interest. Consider the following definitions based on broad-narrow scope:

Broad Definition	Narrow Definition
• Beverages	• Soft drinks
• Children's products	• Toys
• Furniture	• Wrought-iron lawn furniture
• Global mail delivery	• Overnight package delivery
• Travel and tourism	• Ship cruises in the Caribbean

Broad-narrow definitions are relative to a company's business focus and intent, however. Being in "the furniture business" is probably too broad a concept for a company intent on being the largest manufacturer of wrought-iron lawn furniture in North America. On the other hand, toys has proved too narrow a scope for a growth-oriented company like Toys-R-Us, which, with its desire to capitalize on the potential of providing parents with more of what their children need, has ventured beyond toys and opened Kids-R-Us stores containing a wide selection of children's apparel and Books-R-Us stores specializing in children's books and reading programs. The U.S. Postal Service operates with a broad definition, providing global mail-delivery services to all types of senders. Federal Express, however, operates with a narrow business definition based on handling overnight package delivery for customers who have unplanned emergencies and tight deadlines.

Diversified companies have broader missions and business definitions than single-business enterprises.

Diversified firms, understandably, employ more sweeping business definitions than single-business enterprises. For example, Times Mirror Corp. describes itself broadly as a media and information company (which covers a lot of ground) but then goes on to pin down its business arenas in fairly explicit terms:

> Times Mirror is a media and information company principally engaged in newspaper publishing; book, magazine and other publishing; and cable and broadcast television.

Mission Statements for Functional Departments   There's also a place for mission statements for key functions (R&D, marketing, finance) and support units (human resources, training, information systems). Every department can benefit from a consensus statement spelling out its contribution to the company mission, its principal role and activities, and the direction it needs to be moving. Functional and departmental managers who think through and debate with subordinates and higher-

ILLUSTRATION CAPSULE 5   Intel's Bold Decision to Radically Alter Its Strategic Vision

Sometimes there's an order-of-magnitude change in a company's environment that dramatically alters its future prospects and mandates radical revision of its direction and strategic course—Intel's Chairman Andrew Grove calls such occasions "strategic inflection points." Grove and Intel encountered such an inflection point in the mid-1980s. At the time, memory chips were Intel's principal business, and Japanese manufacturers, intent on dominating the memory chip business, were cutting their prices 10 percent below the prices charged by Intel and other U.S. memory chip manufacturers; each time U.S. companies matched the Japanese price cuts, the Japanese manufacturers responded with another 10 percent price cut. Intel's management explored a number of strategic options to cope with the aggressive pricing of its Japanese rivals—building a giant memory chip factory to overcome the cost advantage of Japanese producers, investing in R&D to come up with a more advanced memory chip, and retreating to niche markets for memory chips that were not of interest to the Japanese. Grove concluded that none of these options offered much promise and that the best long-term solution was

to abandon the memory chip business even though it accounted for 70 percent of Intel's revenue.

Grove then proceeded to commit Intel's full energies to the business of developing ever more powerful microprocessors for personal computers (Intel had invented microprocessors in the early 1970s but had recently been concentrating on memory chips because of strong competition and excess capacity in the market for microprocessors).

Grove's bold decision to withdraw from memory chips, absorb a $173 million write-off in 1986, and go all out in microprocessors produced a new strategic vision for Intel—becoming the preeminent supplier of microprocessors to the personal computing industry, making the PC the central appliance in the workplace and the home, and being the undisputed leader in driving PC technology forward. Grove's vision for Intel and the strategic course he subsequently charted has produced spectacular results. Today, 85 percent of the PCs have "Intel inside," and Intel was one of the five most profitable U.S. companies in 1996, earning after-tax profits of $5.2 billion on revenues of $20.8 billion.

ups what their unit needs to focus on and do have a clearer view of how to lead the unit. Three examples from actual companies indicate how a functional mission statement puts the spotlight on a unit's organizational *role* and *scope*:

- The mission of the human resources department is to contribute to organizational success by developing effective leaders, creating high-performance teams, and maximizing the potential of individuals.
- The mission of the corporate claims department is to minimize the overall cost of liability, workers compensation, and property damage claims through competitive cost containment techniques and loss prevention and control programs.
- The mission of corporate security is to provide services for the protection of corporate personnel and assets through preventive measures and investigations.

Deciding on a Long-Term Strategic Vision for the Company

Coming to grips with what a company's business can and should be 5 or 10 years down the road is something of a daunting task. It requires rational analysis of what the company should be doing to get ready for the changes coming in its present business and to capitalize on newly developing market opportunities. It also requires good entrepreneurial instincts, creativity, and an intuitive sense of what the company is capable of when pushed and challenged. Management's strategic vision ought to be realistic about the market, competitive, technological, economic, regulatory, and societal conditions the company is likely to encounter, and it ought to be realistic about the company's resources and capabilities. A strategic vision is not supposed to be a pipe dream or a fantasy about the company's future. Indeed, it has got to be compelling enough to shape the company's actions and energize its strategy.

The entrepreneurial challenge in developing a strategic vision is to think creatively about how to prepare a company for the future.

Often, the driving consideration is how best to position the enterprise to be successful in light of emerging developments and changes on the horizon. Alertness to the winds of change lessens the chances of the company becoming trapped in a stagnant or declining business or letting attractive new growth opportunities slip away because of inaction. Good entrepreneurs and strategists have a sharp eye for shifting customer wants and needs, new technological developments, openings to enter attractive foreign markets, and other important signs of growing or shrinking business opportunity. They attend quickly to users' problems and complaints with the industry's current products and services. They listen intently when a customer says, "If only . . . " Such clues and information tidbits stimulate them to think creatively and strategically about ways to break new ground. Appraising new customer-market-technology opportunities ultimately leads to entrepreneurial judgments about which fork in the road to take and what kind of strategic position to stake out in the marketplace. It is the strategy maker's job to evaluate the risks and prospects of alternative paths and make direction-setting decisions to position the enterprise for success in the years ahead. *A well-chosen vision and long-term business mission prepare a company for the future.*

> *Many successful organizations need to change direction not to survive but to maintain their success.*

Communicating the Strategic Vision

How to communicate the strategic vision down the line to lower-level managers and employees is almost as important as the strategic soundness of the organization's business concept and long-term direction. One-way communication is seldom adequate, however; conversations with employees that allow for give-and-take discussion work best. People have a need to believe that the company's management knows where it's trying to take the company, where the company's markets are headed, and what changes lie ahead. When management can paint a picture of the company's future path in words that inspire employees and arouse a committed organizational effort, then the strategic vision serves as a powerful motivational tool—the simple, clear, lofty mission of the International Red Cross is a good example: "to serve the most vulnerable." Bland language, platitudes, and dull motherhood-and-apple-pie-style verbiage must be scrupulously avoided—they can be a turn-off rather than a turn-on. Managers need to communicate the vision in words that induce employee buy-in, build pride, and create a strong sense of organizational purpose. People are proud to be associated with a company pursuing a worthwhile strategic course and trying to be the world's best at something competitively significant and beneficial to customers. Hence, expressing the strategic vision in engaging language that reaches out and grabs people, that creates a vivid image in their heads, and that provokes emotion and excitement has enormous motivational value; it lifts thoughts above and beyond the daily routine of the business.

> *A well-articulated strategic vision creates enthusiasm for the future course management has charted and poses a challenge that inspires and engages members of the organization.*

Having an exciting business cause energizes the company's strategy, brings the workforce together, galvanizes people to act, stimulates extra effort, and gets people to live the business instead of just coming to work.[3] In organizations with a just-revised vision and long-term direction, it is particularly important for executives to provide a compelling rationale for the new strategic path and why the company must

---

[3]Tom Peters, *Thriving on Chaos* (New York: Harper & Row, Perennial Library Edition, 1988), pp. 486–87; and Andrall E. Pearson, "Corporate Redemption and The Seven Deadly Sins," *Harvard Business Review* 70, no. 3 (May–June 1992), pp. 66–68.

ILLUSTRATION CAPSULE 6   NovaCare's Business Mission and Vision

NovaCare is a health care company specializing in providing patient rehabilitation services on a contract basis to nursing homes. Rehabilitation therapy is a $12 billion industry, of which 35 percent is provided contractually. In 1996 NovaCare was an $800 million company with 17,000 employees at 2,300 sites in 43 states. The company stated its business mission and vision as follows:

NovaCare is people committed to making a difference . . . enhancing the future of all patients . . . breaking new ground in our professions . . . achieving excellence . . . advancing human capability . . . changing the world in which we live.

We lead the way with our enthusiasm, optimism, patience, drive, and commitment.

We work together to enhance the quality of our patients' lives by reshaping lost abilities and teaching new skills. We heighten expectations for the patient and family. We rebuild hope, confidence, self-respect, and a desire to continue.

We apply our clinical expertise to benefit our patients through creative and progressive techniques. Our ethical and performance standards require us to expend every effort to achieve the best possible results.

Our customers are national and local health care providers who share our goal of enhancing the patients' quality of life. In each community, our customers consider us a partner in providing the best possible care. Our reputation is based on our responsiveness, high standards, and effective systems of quality assurance. Our relationship is open and proactive.

We are advocates of our professions and patients through active participation in the professional, regulatory, educational, and research communities at national, state, and local levels.

Our approach to health care fulfills our responsibility to provide investors with a high rate of return through consistent growth and profitability.

Our people are our most valuable asset. We are committed to the personal, professional, and career development of each individual employee. We are proud of what we do and dedicated to our Company. We foster teamwork and create an environment conducive to productive communication among all disciplines.

NovaCare is a company of people in pursuit of this Vision.

Source: Company annual report and website.

begin to stake out a different future business position. Unless people understand how a company's business environment is changing and why a new course is being charted, a new vision and long-term business mission does little to win employees' commitment and wholehearted cooperation. Employee failure to understand or accept the need for redirecting organizational efforts often produces resistance to change and makes it harder to move the organization down a newly chosen path. Hence, explaining and justifying the new strategic vision in persuasive terms that everyone can understand and agree with is a necessary step in getting the organization redirected and ready to move along the new course.

Well-worded vision statements give employees a larger sense of purpose—so that they see themselves as "building a cathedral" rather than "laying stones."

The best-worded mission statements and visions of a company's future are simple and easy to grasp; they convey unmistakable meaning, generate enthusiasm for the firm's future course, and elicit personal effort and dedication from everyone in the organization. They have to be presented and then repeated over and over as a worthy organizational challenge, one capable of benefiting customers in a valuable and meaningful way—indeed, it is crucial that the mission/vision stress the payoff for customers, not the payoff for stockholders. It goes without saying that the company intends to profit shareholders from its efforts to provide real value to its customers. A crisp, clear, often-repeated, inspiring strategic vision has the power to turn heads in the intended direction and begin a new organizational march. When this occurs, the first step in organizational direction-setting is successfully completed. Illustration Capsule 6 is a good example of an inspiration-oriented company vision and mission.

A well-conceived, well-worded strategic vision/mission statement has real managerial value: (1) it crystallizes senior executives' own views about the firm's long-term direction and future business makeup; (2) it reduces the risk of visionless management and rudderless decision making; (3) it conveys an organizational purpose that arouses employee buy-in and commitment and that motivates employees to go all out and contribute to making the vision a reality; (4) it provides a beacon lower-level managers can use to form departmental missions, set departmental objectives, and craft functional and departmental strategies that are in sync with the company's direction and strategy; and (5) it helps an organization prepare for the future.

ESTABLISHING OBJECTIVES: THE SECOND DIRECTION-SETTING TASK

Setting objectives converts the strategic vision and directional course into specific performance targets. Objectives represent a managerial commitment to achieving specific outcomes and results. They are a call for action and for results. Unless an organization's long-term direction and business mission are translated into specific performance targets and managers are pressured to show progress in reaching these targets, vision and mission statements are likely to end up as nice words, window dressing, and unrealized dreams of accomplishment. The experiences of countless companies and managers teach that *companies whose managers set objectives for each key result area and then press forward with actions aimed directly at achieving these performance outcomes typically outperform companies whose managers exhibit good intentions, try hard, and hope for the best.*

Objectives represent a managerial commitment to achieving specific performance targets within a specific time frame.

For objectives to function as yardsticks of organizational performance and progress, they must be stated in *quantifiable* or measurable terms and they must contain a *deadline for achievement.* They have to spell out *how much* of *what kind* of performance *by when.* This means avoiding generalities like "maximize profits," "reduce costs," "become more efficient," or "increase sales," which specify neither how much or when. As Bill Hewlett, cofounder of Hewlett-Packard, once observed, "You cannot manage what you cannot measure . . . And what gets measured gets done."[4] Spelling out organization objectives in measurable terms and then holding managers accountable for reaching their assigned targets within a specified time frame (1) substitutes purposeful strategic decision making for aimless actions and confusion over what to accomplish and (2) provides a set of benchmarks for judging the organization's performance and progress.

What Kinds of Objectives to Set

Objectives are needed for each *key result* managers deem important to success.[5] Two types of key result areas stand out: those relating to *financial performance*

---

[4]As quoted in Charles H. House and Raymond L. Price, "The Return Map: Tracking Product Teams," *Harvard Business Review* 60, no. 1 (January–February 1991), p. 93.

[5]The literature of management is filled with references to *goals* and *objectives.* These terms are used in a variety of ways, many of them conflicting. Some writers use the term goals to refer to the long-run outcomes an organization seeks to achieve and the term objectives to refer to immediate, short-run performance targets. Some writers reverse the usage, referring to objectives as the desired long-run results and goals as the desired short-run results. Others use the terms interchangeably. And still others use the term goals to refer to broad organizationwide performance targets and the term objectives to designate specific

and those relating to *strategic performance*. Achieving acceptable financial performance is a must; otherwise the organization's financial standing can alarm creditors and shareholders, impair its ability to fund needed initiatives, and perhaps even put its very survival at risk. Achieving acceptable strategic performance is essential to sustaining and improving the company's long-term market position and competitiveness. Representative kinds of financial and strategic performance objectives are listed below:

Strategic Management Principle

Every company needs both strategic objectives and financial objectives.

Financial Objectives	Strategic Objectives
• Growth in revenues	• A bigger market share
• Growth in earnings	• Quicker design-to-market times than rivals
• Higher dividends	
• Wider profit margins	• Higher product quality than rivals
• Higher returns on invested capital	• Lower costs relative to key competitors
• Attractive economic value added (EVA) performance[6]	• Broader or more attractive product line than rivals
• Strong bond and credit ratings	
• Bigger cash flows	• A stronger reputation with customers than rivals
• A rising stock price	
• Attractive and sustainable increases in market value added (MVA)[7]	• Superior customer service
• Recognition as a "blue chip" company	• Recognition as a leader in technology and/or product innovation
• A more diversified revenue base	• Wider geographic coverage than rivals
• Stable earnings during periods of recession	• Higher levels of customer satisfaction than rivals

Illustration Capsule 7 presents the strategic and financial objectives of four well-known enterprises.

---

targets set by operating divisions and functional departments to support achievement of overall company performance targets. In our view, little is gained from semantic distinctions between goals and objectives. The important thing is to recognize that the results an enterprise seeks to attain vary as to both organizational scope and time frame. Nearly always, organizations need to have companywide performance targets and division/department performance targets for both the near-term and long-term. It is inconsequential which targets are called goals and which objectives. To avoid a semantic jungle, we use the single term *objectives* to refer to the performance targets and results an organization seeks to attain. We use the adjectives *long-range* (or long-run) and *short-range* (or short-run) to identify the relevant time frame, and we try to describe objectives in words that indicate their intended scope and level in the organization.

[6]Economic value added (EVA) is profit over and above the company's weighted average after-tax cost of capital; specifically, it is defined as operating profit less income taxes less the weighted average cost of capital. Such companies as Coca-Cola, AT&T, Briggs & Stratton, and Eli Lilly use EVA as a measure of the profit performance. For more details on EVA, consult footnote 1 in Chapter 1.

[7]Market value added (MVA) is defined as the amount by which the total value of the company has appreciated above the dollar amount actually invested in the company by shareholders. MVA is equal to a company's current stock price times the number of shares outstanding less shareholders' equity investment; it represents the value that management has added to shareholders' wealth in running the business. If shareholder value is to be maximized, management must select a strategy and long-term direction that maximizes the market value of the company's common stock.

ILLUSTRATION CAPSULE 7   Examples Of Corporate Objectives: McDonald's, 3M Corp., Anheuser-Busch, and McCormick & Company

McDonald's

- To achieve 100 percent total customer satisfaction . . . everyday . . . in every restaurant . . . for every customer.

Anheuser-Busch

- To make all of our companies leaders in their industries in quality while exceeding customer expectations.
- To achieve a 50% share of the U.S. beer market.
- To establish and maintain a dominant leadership position in the international beer market.
- To provide all our employees with challenging and rewarding work, satisfying working conditions, and opportunities for personal development, advancement, and competitive compensation.
- To provide our shareholders with superior returns by achieving double-digit annual earnings per share growth, increasing dividends consistent with earnings growth, repurchasing shares when the opportunity is right, pursuing profitable international beer expansions, and generating quality earnings and cash flow returns.

3M Corporation

- 30 percent of the company's annual sales must come from products fewer than four years old.

McCormick & Company

- To achieve a 20 percent return on equity.
- To achieve a net sales growth rate of 10 percent per year.
- To maintain an average earnings per share growth rate of 15 percent per year.
- To maintain total debt-to-total capital at 40 percent or less.
- To pay out 25 percent to 35 percent of net income in dividends.
- To make selective acquisitions which complement our current businesses and can enhance our overall returns.
- To dispose of those parts of our business which do not or cannot generate adequate returns or do not fit our business strategy.

Source: Company annual reports.

Strategic Objectives versus Financial Objectives: Which Take Precedence?   Even though an enterprise places high priority on achieving both financial and strategic objectives, what if situations arise where a trade-off has to be made? Should a company under pressure to pay down its debt elect to kill or postpone investments in strategic moves that hold promise for strengthening the enterprise's future business and competitive position? Should a company under pressure to boost near-term profits cut back R&D programs that could help it achieve a competitive advantage over key rivals in the years ahead? The pressures on managers to opt for better near-term financial performance and to sacrifice or cut back on strategic initiatives aimed at building a stronger competitive position become especially pronounced when (1) an enterprise is struggling financially, (2) the resource commitments for strategically beneficial moves will materially detract from the bottom line for several years, and (3) the proposed strategic moves are risky and have an uncertain competitive or bottom-line payoff.

Strategic objectives need to be competitor-focused, often aiming at unseating a rival considered to be the industry's best in a particular category.

Yet, there are dangers in management's succumbing time and again to the lure of immediate gains in profitability when it means paring or forgoing strategic moves that would build a stronger business position. A company that consistently passes up opportunities to strengthen its long-term competitive position in order to realize better near-term financial gains risks diluting its competitiveness, losing momentum in its markets, and impairing its ability to stave off market challenges from ambitious rivals. The business landscape is littered with ex-market leaders who put more emphasis on boosting next quarter's profit than strengthening long-term market position. The danger of trading off long-term gains in market position for near-term gains in bottom-line performance is greatest when a profit-conscious market leader has competitors who invest relentlessly in gaining market share, striving to become big and strong enough to outcompete the leader in a head-to-head market battle. One need look no further than Japanese companies' patient and persistent strategic efforts to gain market ground on their more profit-centered American and European rivals to appreciate the pitfall of letting short-term financial objectives dominate. The surest path to protecting and sustaining a company's profitability quarter after quarter and year after year is for its managers to pursue strategic actions that strengthen the company's competitiveness and business position.

> **Strategic Management Principle**
>
> *Building a stronger long-term competitive position benefits shareholders more lastingly than improving short-term profitability.*

The Concept of Strategic Intent

A company's strategic objectives are important for another reason—they indicate *strategic intent* to stake out a particular business position.[8] The strategic intent of a large company may be industry leadership on a national or global scale. The strategic intent of a small company may be to dominate a market niche. The strategic intent of an up-and-coming enterprise may be to overtake the market leaders. The strategic intent of a technologically innovative company may be to pioneer a promising discovery and create a whole new vista of products that change the way people work and live—as many entrepreneurial companies are now trying to do with the Internet.

> **Basic Concept**
>
> A company exhibits strategic intent *when it relentlessly pursues an ambitious strategic objective and concentrates its competitive actions and energies on achieving that objective.*

The time horizon underlying a company's strategic intent is *long term*. Ambitious companies almost invariably begin with strategic intents that are out of proportion to their immediate capabilities and market positions. But they set aggressive long-term strategic objectives and pursue them relentlessly, sometimes even obsessively, over a 10- to 20-year period. In the 1960s, Komatsu, Japan's leading earthmoving equipment company, was less than one-third the size of Caterpillar, had little market presence outside Japan, and depended on its small bulldozers for most of its revenue. But Komatsu's strategic intent was to eventually "encircle Caterpillar" with a broader product line and then compete globally against Caterpillar. By the late 1980s, Komatsu was the industry's second-ranking company, with a strong sales presence in North America, Europe, and Asia plus a product line that included industrial robots and semiconductors as well as a broad selection of earthmoving equipment.

Often, a company's strategic intent takes on a heroic character, serving as a rallying cry for managers and employees alike to go all out and do their very best. Canon's strategic intent in copying equipment was to "Beat Xerox." Komatsu's motivating battle cry was "Beat Caterpillar." When Yamaha overtook Honda in the motorcycle

---

[8]The concept of strategic intent is described in more detail in Gary Hamel and C. K. Pralahad, "Strategic Intent," *Harvard Business Review* 89, no. 3 (May–June 1989), pp. 63–76; this section draws upon their pioneering discussion. See, also, Michael A. Hitt, Beverly B. Tyler, Camilla Hardee, and Daewoo Park, "Understanding Strategic Intent in the Global Marketplace," *Academy of Management Executive*, 9, no. 2 (May 1995), pp. 12–19. For a discussion of the different ways that companies can position themselves in the marketplace, see Michael E. Porter, "What Is Strategy?" *Harvard Business Review* 74, no. 6 (November–December 1996), pp. 65–67.

market, Honda responded with "Yamaha wo tsubusu" ("We will crush, squash, slaughter Yamaha"). The strategic intent of the U.S. government's Apollo space program was to land a person on the moon ahead of the Soviet Union. Throughout the 1980s, Wal-Mart's strategic intent was to "overtake Sears" as the largest U.S. retailer (a feat accomplished in 1991). Netscape's running battle with Microsoft over whose Internet browser software will reign supreme prompted employees to hang "Beat Microsoft" banners in Netscape's offices. In such instances, strategic intent signals a deep-seated commitment to winning—unseating the industry leader or remaining the industry leader (and becoming more dominant in the process) or otherwise beating long odds to gain a significantly stronger business position. Small, capably managed enterprises determined to achieve ambitious strategic objectives exceeding their present reach and resources often prove to be more formidable competitors than larger, cash-rich companies with modest strategic intents.

The Need for Long-Range and Short-Range Objectives

Objective setting should result in both long-range and short-range performance targets. Absent an impending crisis or pressing reason to bolster a company's long-term position and future performance, managers are prone to focus on the near term and place a higher priority on what has to be done to hit this year's numbers. The trouble with giving too high a priority to short-term objectives, of course, is the potential for managers to neglect actions aimed at enhancing a company's long-term business position and sustaining its capacity to generate good results over the long term. Setting bold, long-range performance targets and then putting pressure on managers to show progress in achieving them helps balance the priorities between better near-term results and actions calculated to ensure the company's competitiveness and financial performance down the road. A strong commitment to achieving long-range objectives forces managers to begin taking actions *now* to reach desired performance levels *later*. (A company that has an objective of doubling its sales within five years can't wait until the third or fourth year of its five-year strategic plan to begin growing its sales and customer base!)

By spelling out the near-term results to be achieved, short-range objectives indicate the *speed* at which management wants the organization to progress as well as the *level of performance* being aimed for over the next two or three periods. Short-range objectives can be identical to long-range objectives anytime an organization is already performing at the targeted long-term level. For instance, if a company has an ongoing objective of 15 percent profit growth every year and is currently achieving this objective, then the company's long-range and short-range profit objectives coincide. The most important situation where short-range objectives differ from long-range objectives occurs when managers are trying to elevate organizational performance and cannot reach the long-range/ongoing target in just one year. Short-range objectives then serve as stairsteps or milestones.

How Much Stretch Should Objectives Entail?

As a starter, objectives should be set high enough to produce outcomes at least incrementally better than current performance. But incremental improvements are not necessarily sufficient, especially if current performance levels are subpar. At a minimum, a company's financial objectives must aim high enough to generate the resources to execute the chosen strategy proficiently. But an "enough-to-get-by" mentality is not the way to approach objective setting. Arriving at an appropriate set of performance targets requires considering what performance is possible in light of external conditions, what performance other comparably situated companies are achieving, what performance it will take to please shareholders, what performance is required for long-term competitive success, and what performance the organization is capable of achieving when pushed. Ideally, objectives ought to serve as a managerial tool for truly *stretching an organization to reach its full potential;* this means setting them high enough to be *challenging*—to energize the organization and its strategy.

Company performance targets should require organizational stretch.

However, there is a school of thought that objectives should be set boldly and aggressively high—above levels that many organizational members would consider "realistic." The idea here is that *more* organizational creativity and energy is unleashed when stretch objectives call for achieving performance levels well beyond the reach of the enterprise's immediate resources and capabilities. One of the most avid practitioners of setting bold, audacious objectives and challenging the organization to go all out to achieve them is General Electric, arguably the world's best-managed corporation. Jack Welch, GE's CEO, believes in setting stretch targets that seem "impossible" and then challenging the organization to go after them. Throughout the 1960s, 1970s, and 1980s, GE's operating margins hovered around 10 percent and its sales-to-inventory ratio averaged about five turns per year. In 1991, Welch set stretch targets for 1995 of at least a 16 percent operating margin and 10 inventory turns. Welch's letter to the shareholders in the company's 1995 annual report said:

> 1995 has come and gone, and despite a heroic effort by our 220,000 employees, we fell short on both measures, achieving a 14.4 percent operating margin and almost seven turns. But in stretching for these "impossible" targets, we learned to do things faster than we would have going after "doable" goals, and we have enough confidence now to set new stretch targets of at least 16 operating margin and more than 10 turns by 1998.

GE's philosophy is that setting very aggressive stretch targets pushes the organization to move beyond being only as good as what is deemed doable to being as good as it possibly can be. GE's management believes challenging the company to achieve the impossible improves the quality of the organization's effort, promotes a can-do spirit, and builds self-confidence. Hence, a case can be made that objectives ought to be set at levels *above* what is doable with a little extra effort; there's merit in setting stretch targets that require something approaching a heroic degree of organizational effort.

Objectives Are Needed at All Organizational Levels

For strategic thinking and strategy-driven decision making to permeate organization behavior, performance targets must be established not only for the organization as a whole but also for each of the organization's separate businesses, product lines, functional areas, and departments. Only when each unit's strategic and financial objectives support achievement of the company's strategic and financial objectives is the objective-setting process sufficiently complete to conclude that each part of the organization knows its strategic role and that the various organizational units are on board in helping the whole organization move down the chosen strategic path.

The Need for Top-Down Objective-Setting   To appreciate why a company's objective-setting process needs to be more top-down than bottom-up, consider the following example. Suppose the senior executives of a diversified corporation establish a corporate profit objective of $5 million for next year. Suppose further, after discussion between corporate management and the general managers of the firm's five different businesses, each business is given a stretch profit objective of $1 million by year-end (i.e., if the five business divisions contribute $1 million each in profit, the corporation can reach its $5 million profit objective). A concrete result has thus been agreed on and translated into measurable action commitments at two levels in the managerial hierarchy. Next, suppose the general manager of business unit X, after some analysis and discussion with functional area managers, concludes that reaching the $1 million profit objective will require selling 100,000 units at an average price of $50 and producing them at an average cost of $40 (a $10 profit margin times 100,000 units equals $1 million profit). Consequently, the general manager and the manufacturing manager settle on a production objective of 100,000 units at a unit cost of $40; and the general manager and the marketing manager agree on a sales objective of 100,000 units and a target selling price of $50. In turn, the marketing manager breaks the

Strategic Management Principle

Objective setting needs to be more of a top-down than a bottom-up process in order to guide lower-level managers and organizational units toward outcomes that support the achievement of overall business and company objectives.

sales objective of 100,000 units into unit sales targets for each sales territory, each item in the product line, and each salesperson. It is logical for organizationwide objectives and strategy to be established first so they can *guide* objective setting and strategy making at lower levels. Top-down objective setting and strategizing steer lower-level units toward objectives and strategies that take their cues from those of the total enterprise.

A top-down process of setting companywide performance targets first and then insisting that the financial and strategic performance targets established for business units, divisions, functional departments, and operating units be directly connected to the achievement of company objectives has two powerful advantages. One, it helps produce *cohesion* among the objectives and strategies of different parts of the organization. Two, it helps *unify internal efforts* to move the company along the chosen strategic course. If top management, in the interest of involving a broad spectrum of organizational members, allows objective setting to start at the bottom levels of an organization without the benefit of companywide performance targets as a guide, then lower-level organizational units have no basis for connecting their performance targets to the company's. Letting organizationwide objectives be the product of whatever priorities and targets bubble up from below simply leaves too much room for the objectives and strategies of lower-level organizational units to be uncoordinated with each other and lacking in what makes good business sense for the company as a whole. Bottom-up objective setting, with little or no guidance from above, nearly always signals an absence of strategic leadership on the part of senior executives.

CRAFTING A STRATEGY: THE THIRD DIRECTION-SETTING TASK

Organizations need strategies to guide *how* to achieve objectives and *how* to pursue the organization's business mission and strategic vision. Strategy making is all about *how*—how to achieve performance targets, how to outcompete rivals, how to achieve sustainable competitive advantage, how to strengthen the enterprise's long-term business position, how to make management's strategic vision for the company a reality. A strategy is needed for the company as a whole, for each business the company is in, and for each functional piece of each business—R&D, purchasing, production, sales and marketing, finance, customer service, information systems, and so on. An organization's overall strategy emerges from the *pattern of actions already initiated and the plans managers have for fresh moves*. In forming a strategy out of the many feasible options, a manager acts as a forger of responses to market change, a seeker of new opportunities, and a synthesizer of the different moves and approaches taken at various times in various parts of the organization.[9]

Basic Concept

An organization's strategy deals with the game plan for moving the company into an attractive business position and building a sustainable competitive advantage.

The strategy-making spotlight, however, needs to be kept trained on the important facets of management's game plan for running the enterprise—those actions that determine what market position the company is trying to stake out and that underpin whether the company will succeed. Low-priority issues (whether to increase the advertising budget, raise the dividend, locate a new plant in country X or country Y) and routine managerial housekeeping (whether to own or lease company vehicles, how to reduce sales force turnover) are not basic to the strategy, even though they must be dealt with. Strategy is inherently action-oriented; it concerns what to do and when to do it. Unless there is action, unless something happens, unless somebody does something, strategic thinking and planning simply go to waste and, in the end, amount to nothing.

An organization's strategy evolves over time. The future is too unknowable for management to plan a company's strategy in advance and encounter no reason for changing one piece or another as time passes. Reacting and responding to unpredictable happenings in the surrounding environment is a normal and necessary part of the strategy-making process. There is always something new to react to and some new strategic window opening up—whether from new competitive developments, budding trends in buyer needs and expectations, unexpected increases or decreases in costs, mergers and acquisitions among major industry players, new regulations, the raising or lowering of trade barriers, or countless other events that make it desirable to alter first one then another aspect of the present strategy.[10] This is why the task of crafting strategy is never ending. And it is why a company's actual strategy turns out to be a blend of managerial plans and intentions and as-needed reactions to fresh developments.

While most of the time a company's strategy evolves incrementally, there are occasions when a company can function as an industry revolutionary by creating a rule-breaking strategy that redefines the industry and how it operates. A strategy can challenge fundamental conventions by reconceiving a product or service (like creating a single-use, disposable camera or a digital camera), redefining the marketplace (the growing potential for electronic commerce on the Internet is allowing companies to market their products anywhere at any time rather than being restricted to making their products available at particular locations during normal shopping times), or redrawing industry boundaries (consumers can now get their credit cards from Shell Oil or General Motors, or have their checking account at Charles Schwab, or get a home mortgage from Merrill Lynch, or get a family-style meal for takeout at the Boston Market or the supermarket).[11]

A company's **actual strategy** *usually turns out to be both more and less than the* **planned** strategy *as new strategy features are added and others are deleted in response to newly emerging conditions.*

[9]Henry Mintzberg, "The Strategy Concept II: Another Look at Why Organizations Need Strategies," *California Management Review* 30, no. 1 (Fall 1987), pp. 25–32.

[10]Henry Mintzberg and J. A. Waters, "Of Strategies, Deliberate and Emergent," *Strategic Management Journal*, 6 (1985), pp.257–72.

[11]For an in-depth discussion of revolutionary strategies, see Gary Hamel, "Strategy as Revolution," *Harvard Business Review* 74, no. 4 (July-August 1996), pp. 69–82.

The Strategy-Making Pyramid

As we emphasized in the opening chapter, strategy making is not just a task for senior executives. In large enterprises, decisions about what business approaches to take and what new moves to initiate involve senior executives in the corporate office, heads of business units and product divisions, the heads of major functional areas within a business or division (manufacturing, marketing and sales, finance, human resources, and the like), plant managers, product managers, district and regional sales managers, and lower-level supervisors. In diversified enterprises, strategies are initiated at four distinct organization levels. There's a strategy for the company and all of its businesses as a whole (*corporate strategy*). There's a strategy for each separate business the company has diversified into (*business strategy*). Then there is a strategy for each specific functional unit within a business (*functional strategy*)—each business usually has a production strategy, a marketing strategy, a finance strategy, and so on. And, finally, there are still narrower strategies for basic operating units—plants, sales districts and regions, and departments within functional areas (*operating strategy*). Figure 2.1 shows the strategy-making pyramids for a diversified company and a single-business company. In single-business enterprises, there are only three levels of strategy (business strategy, functional strategy, and operating strategy) unless diversification into other businesses becomes an active consideration. Table 2.1 highlights the kinds of strategic actions that distinguish each of the four strategy-making levels.

Corporate Strategy

Corporate strategy is the overall managerial game plan for a diversified company. *Corporate strategy extends companywide—an umbrella over all a diversified company's businesses. It consists of the moves made to establish business positions* in different industries and the approaches used to manage the company's group of businesses. Figure 2.2 depicts the core elements that identify a diversified company's corporate strategy. Crafting corporate strategy for a diversified company involves four kinds of initiatives:

Basic Concept

Corporate strategy *concerns how a diversified company intends to establish business positions in different industries and the actions and approaches employed to improve the performance of the group of businesses the company has diversified into.*

1. *Making the moves to establish positions in different businesses and achieve diversification.* In a diversified company, a key piece of corporate strategy is how many and what kinds of businesses the company should be in—specifically, what industries should the company participate in and whether to enter the industries by starting a new business or acquiring another company (an established leader, an up-and-coming company, or a troubled company with turnaround potential). This piece of corporate strategy establishes whether diversification is based narrowly in a few industries or broadly in many industries and whether the different businesses will be related or unrelated.

2. *Initiating actions to boost the combined performance of the businesses the firm has diversified into.* As positions are created in the chosen industries, corporate strategy making concentrates on ways to strengthen the long-term competitive positions and profitabilities of the businesses the firm has invested in. Corporate parents can help their business subsidiaries be more successful by financing additional capacity and efficiency improvements, by supplying missing skills and managerial know-how, by acquiring another company in the same industry and merging the two operations into a stronger business, and/or by acquiring new businesses that strongly complement existing businesses. Management's overall strategy for improving companywide performance usually involves pursuing rapid-growth strategies in the most

FIGURE 2.1   The Strategy-Making Pyramid

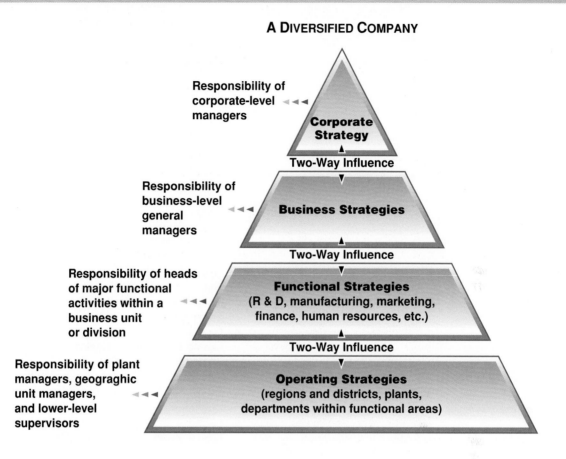

A DIVERSIFIED COMPANY

Responsibility of
corporate-level ◄◄◄
managers

**Corporate
Strategy**

Two-Way Influence

Responsibility of
business-level ◄◄◄
general
managers

Business Strategies

Two-Way Influence

Responsibility of heads
of major functional
activities within a ◄◄◄
business unit
or division

Functional Strategies
(R & D, manufacturing, marketing,
finance, human resources, etc.)

Two-Way Influence

Responsibility of plant
managers, geograghic
unit managers, ◄◄◄
and lower-level
supervisors

Operating Strategies
(regions and districts, plants,
departments within functional areas)

A SINGLE - BUSINESS COMPANY

Responsibility of
executive-level ◄◄◄
managers

**Business
Strategy**

Two-Way Influence

Responsibility of heads
of major functional
activities within a ◄◄◄
business

Functional Strategies
(R & D, manufacturing,
marketing, finance,
human resources, etc.)

Two-Way Influence

Responsibility of plant
managers, geograghic
unit managers, ◄◄◄
and lower-level
supervisors

Operating Strategies
(regions and districts, plants,
departments within functional areas)

TABLE 2.1   How the Strategy-Making Task Tends to Be Shared

Strategy Level	Lead Responsibility	Primary Strategy-Making Concerns at Each Managerial Level
• Corporate strategy	• CEO, other key executives (decisions are typically reviewed/approved by boards of directors)	• Building and managing a high-performing portfolio of business units (making acquisitions, strengthening existing business positions, divesting businesses that no longer fit into management's plans) • Capturing the synergy among related business units and turning it into competitive advantage • Establishing investment priorities and steering corporate resources into businesses with the most attractive opportunities • Reviewing/revising/unifying the major strategic approaches and moves proposed by business-unit managers
• Business strategies	• General manager/head of business unit (decisions are typically reviewed/approved by a senior executive or a board of directors)	• Devising moves and approaches to compete successfully and to secure a competitive advantage • Forming responses to changing external conditions • Uniting the strategic initiatives of key functional departments • Taking action to address company-specific issues and operating problems
• Functional strategies	• Functional managers (decisions are typically reviewed/approved by business-unit head)	• Crafting moves and approaches to support business strategy and to achieve functional/departmental performance objectives • Reviewing/revising/unifying strategy-related moves and approaches proposed by lower-level managers
• Operating strategies	• Field-unit heads/lower-level managers within functional areas (decisions are reviewed/approved by functional area head/department head)	• Crafting still narrower and more specific approaches/moves aimed at supporting functional and business strategies and at achieving operating-unit objectives

promising businesses, keeping the other core businesses healthy, initiating turnaround efforts in weak-performing businesses with potential, and divesting businesses that are no longer attractive or that don't fit into management's long-range plans.

3. *Pursuing ways to capture the synergy among related business units and turn it into competitive advantage.* When a company diversifies into businesses with related technologies, similar operating characteristics, common distribution channels or customers, or some other synergistic relationship, it gains competitive advantage potential not open to a company that diversifies into totally unrelated businesses. Related diversification presents opportunities to transfer skills, share expertise or facilities, and leverage a common brand name, thereby reducing overall costs, strengthening the competitive-

FIGURE 2.2   Identifying the Corporate Strategy of a Diversified Company

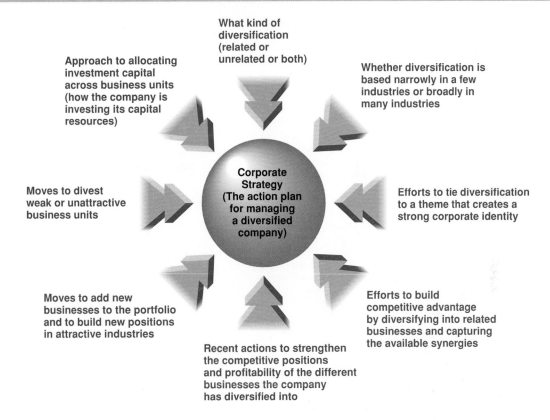

ness of some of the company's products, or enhancing the capabilities of particular business units—any of which can represent a significant source of competitive advantage and provide a basis for greater overall corporate profitability.

4. *Establishing investment priorities and steering corporate resources into the most attractive business units.* A diversified company's different businesses are usually not equally attractive from the standpoint of investing additional funds. This facet of corporate strategy making involves channeling resources into areas where earnings potentials are higher and away from areas where they are lower. Corporate strategy may include divesting business units that are chronically poor performers or those in an increasingly unattractive industry. Divestiture frees up unproductive investments for redeployment to promising business units or for financing attractive new acquisitions.

Corporate strategy is crafted at the highest levels of management. Senior corporate executives normally have lead responsibility for devising corporate strategy and for choosing among whatever recommended actions bubble up from lower-level managers. Key business-unit heads may also be influential, especially in strategic decisions affecting the businesses they head. Major strategic decisions are usually reviewed and approved by the company's board of directors.

Business Strategy

The term *business strategy* (or business-level strategy) refers to the managerial game plan for a single business. It is mirrored in the pattern of approaches and moves crafted by management to produce successful performance in *one specific*

FIGURE 2.3   Identifying Strategy for a Single-Business Company

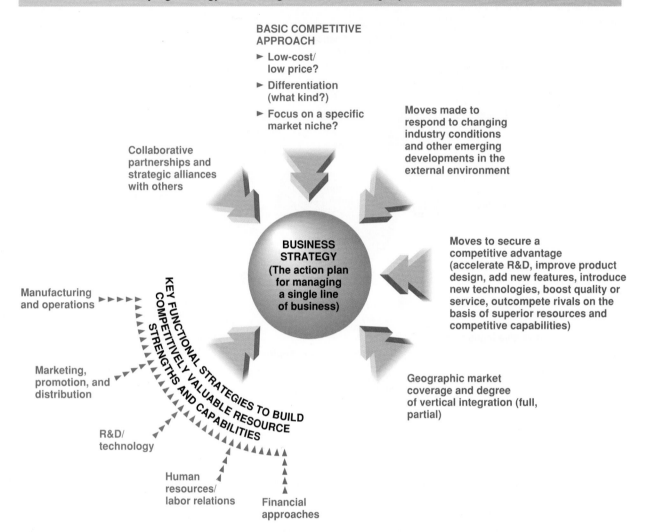

line of business. The core elements of business strategy are illustrated in Figure 2.3. For a stand-alone single-business company, corporate strategy and business strategy are one and the same since there is only one business to form a strategy for. The distinction between corporate strategy and business strategy is relevant only for diversified firms.

The central thrust of business strategy is how to build and strengthen the company's long-term competitive position in the marketplace. Toward this end, business strategy is concerned principally with (1) forming responses to changes under way in the industry, the economy at large, the regulatory and political arena, and other relevant areas, (2) crafting competitive moves and market approaches that can lead to sustainable competitive advantage, (3) building competitively valuable competencies and capabilities, (4) uniting the strategic initiatives of functional departments, and (5) addressing specific strategic issues facing the company's business.

Clearly, business strategy encompasses whatever moves and new approaches managers deem prudent in light of market forces, economic trends and developments, buyer needs and demographics, new legislation and regulatory requirements, and other such broad external factors. *A good strategy is well-matched to the external situation;* as the external environment changes in significant ways, then adjustments in strategy are made on an as-needed basis. Whether a company's response to external change is quick or slow tends to be a function of how long events must unfold before managers can assess their implications and how much longer it then takes to form a strategic response. Some external changes, of course, require little or no response, while others call for significant strategy alterations. On occasion, external factors change in ways that pose a formidable strategic hurdle—for example, cigarette manufacturers face a tough challenge holding their own against mounting efforts to combat smoking.

What separates a powerful business strategy from a weak one is the strategist's ability *to forge a series of moves and approaches capable of producing sustainable competitive advantage.* With a competitive advantage, a company has good prospects for above-average profitability and success in the industry. Without competitive advantage, a company risks being outcompeted by stronger rivals and locked into mediocre performance. Crafting a business strategy that yields sustainable competitive advantage has three facets: (1) deciding what product/service attributes (lower costs and prices, a better product, a wider product line, superior customer service, emphasis on a particular market niche) offer the best chance to win a competitive edge; (2) developing skills, expertise, and competitive capabilities that set the company apart from rivals; and (3) trying to insulate the business as much as possible from the effects of competition.

> *A business strategy is powerful if it produces a sizable and sustainable competitive advantage; it is weak if it results in competitive disadvantage.*

A company's strategy for competing is typically both offensive and defensive— some actions are aggressive and amount to direct challenges to competitors' market positions; others aim at countering competitive pressures and the actions of rivals. Three of the most frequently used competitive approaches are (1) striving to be the industry's low-cost producer (thereby aiming for a cost-based competitive advantage over rivals); (2) pursuing differentiation based on such advantages as quality, performance, service, styling, technological superiority, or unusually good value; and (3) focusing on a narrow market niche and winning a competitive edge by doing a better job than rivals of serving the special needs and tastes of niche members.

Internally, business strategy involves taking actions to develop the capabilities and resource strengths needed to achieve competitive advantage. Successful business strategies usually aim at building strong competencies and competitive capabilities in one or more activities crucial to strategic success and then using them as a basis for winning a competitive edge over rivals. A *distinctive competence* is something a firm does especially well in comparison to rival companies. It thus represents a source of competitive strength. Distinctive competencies can relate to R&D, mastery of a technological process, manufacturing capability, sales and distribution, customer service, or anything else that is a competitively important aspect of creating, producing, or marketing the company's product or service. *A distinctive competence is a basis for competitive advantage because it represents expertise or capability that rivals don't have and cannot readily match.*

> *Having superior internal resource strengths and competitive capabilities is an important way to outcompete rivals.*

On a broader internal front, business strategy must also aim at uniting strategic initiatives in the various functional areas of business (purchasing, production, R&D, finance, human resources, sales and marketing, distribution, and customer service). Strategic actions are needed in each functional area to *support* the company's competitive approach and overall business strategy. Strategic unity and coordination across the various functional areas add power to the business strategy.

Business strategy also extends to action plans for addressing any special strategy-related issues unique to the company's competitive position and internal situation (such as whether to add new capacity, replace an obsolete plant, increase R&D funding for a promising technology, reduce burdensome interest expenses, form strategic alliances and collaborative partnerships, or build competitively valuable competencies and capabilities). Such custom tailoring of strategy to fit a company's specific situation is one of the reasons why companies in the same industry employ different business strategies.

Lead responsibility for business strategy falls in the lap of the manager in charge of the business. Even if the business head does not personally wield a heavy hand in the business strategy-making process, preferring to delegate much of the task to others, he or she is still accountable for the strategy and the results it produces. The business head, as chief strategist for the business, has at least two other responsibilities. The first is seeing that supporting strategies in each of the major functional areas of the business are well conceived and consistent with each other. The second is getting major strategic moves approved by higher authority (the board of directors and/or corporate-level officers) if needed and keeping them informed of important new developments, deviations from plan, and potential strategy revisions. In diversified companies, business-unit heads may have the additional obligation of making sure business-level objectives and strategy conform to corporate-level objectives and strategy themes.

Functional Strategy

The term *functional strategy* refers to the managerial game plan for a particular functional activity, business process, or key department within a business. A company's marketing strategy, for example, represents the managerial game plan for running the marketing part of the business. A company's new product development strategy represents the managerial game plan for keeping the company's product lineup fresh and in tune with what buyers are looking for. A company needs a functional strategy for every competitively relevant business activity and organizational unit—for R&D, production, marketing, customer service, distribution, finance, human resources, information technology, and so on. Functional strategies, while narrower in scope than business strategies, add relevant detail to the overall business game plan by setting forth the actions, approaches, and practices to be employed in managing a particular functional department or business process or key activity. They aim at establishing or strengthening specific competencies and competitive capabilities calculated to enhance the company's market position and standing with its customers. The primary role of a functional strategy is to *support* the company's overall business strategy and competitive approach. Well-executed functional strategies give the enterprise competitively valuable competencies, capabilities, and resource strengths. A related role is to create a managerial roadmap for achieving the functional area's objectives and mission. Thus, functional strategy in the production/manufacturing area represents the game plan for *how* manufacturing activities will be managed to support business strategy and achieve the manufacturing department's objectives and mission. Functional strategy in the finance area consists of *how* financial activities will be managed in supporting business strategy and achieving the finance department's objectives and mission.

Lead responsibility for conceiving strategies for each of the various important business functions and processes is normally delegated to the respective functional

Basic Concept

Functional strategy *concerns the managerial game plan for running a major functional activity or process within a business—R&D, production, marketing, customer service, distribution, finance, human resources, and so on; a business needs as many functional strategies as it has strategy-critical activities.*

department heads and activity managers unless the business-unit head decides to exert a strong influence. In crafting strategy, the manager of a particular business function or activity ideally works closely with key subordinates and touches base with the managers of other functions/processes and the business head often. If functional or activity managers plot strategy independent of each other or the business head, they open the door for uncoordinated or conflicting strategies. Compatible, collaborative, mutually reinforcing functional strategies are essential for the overall business strategy to have maximum impact. Plainly, a business's marketing strategy, production strategy, finance strategy, customer service strategy, new product development strategy, and human resources strategy should be in sync rather than serving their own narrower purposes. Coordination and consistency among the various functional and process/activity strategies are best accomplished during the deliberation stage. If inconsistent functional strategies are sent up the line for final approval, it is up to the business head to spot the conflicts and get them resolved.

Operating Strategy

Operating strategies concern the even narrower strategic initiatives and approaches for managing key operating units (plants, sales districts, distribution centers) and for handling daily operating tasks with strategic significance (advertising campaigns, materials purchasing, inventory control, maintenance, shipping). Operating strategies, while of limited scope, add further detail and completeness to functional strategies and to the overall business plan. Lead responsibility for operating strategies is usually delegated to frontline managers, subject to review and approval by higher-ranking managers.

Basic Concept

Operating strategies concern how to manage frontline organizational units within a business (plants, sales districts, distribution centers) and how to perform strategically significant operating tasks (materials purchasing, inventory control, maintenance, shipping, advertising campaigns).

Even though operating strategy is at the bottom of the strategy-making pyramid, its importance should not be downplayed. For example, a major plant that fails in its strategy to achieve production volume, unit cost, and quality targets can undercut the achievement of company sales and profit objectives and wreak havoc with the whole company's strategic efforts to build a quality image with customers. One cannot reliably judge the strategic importance of a given action by the organizational or managerial level where it is initiated.

Frontline managers are part of an organization's strategy-making team because many operating units have strategy-critical performance targets and need to have strategic action plans in place to achieve them. A regional manager needs a strategy customized to the region's particular situation and objectives. A plant manager needs a strategy for accomplishing the plant's objectives, carrying out the plant's part of the company's overall manufacturing game plan, and dealing with any strategy-related problems that exist at the plant. A company's advertising manager needs a strategy for getting maximum audience exposure and sales impact from the ad budget. The following two examples illustrate how operating strategy supports higher-level strategies:

- A company with a low-price, high-volume business strategy and a need to achieve low manufacturing costs launches a companywide effort to boost worker productivity by 10 percent. To contribute to the productivity-boosting objective: (1) the manager of employee recruiting develops a strategy for interviewing and testing job applicants that is thorough enough to weed out all but the most highly motivated, best-qualified candidates; (2) the manager of information systems devises a way to use office technology to boost the productivity of office workers; (3) the employee compensation manager devises a creative incentive plan to reward increased output by manufacturing employees; and (4) the purchasing manager launches a program to obtain new efficiency-increasing tools and equipment in quicker, less costly fashion.

- A distributor of plumbing equipment emphasizes quick delivery and accurate order-filling as keystones of its customer service approach. To support this strategy, the warehouse manager (1) develops an inventory stocking strategy that allows 99.9 percent of all orders to be completely filled without back-ordering any item and (2) institutes a warehouse staffing strategy that allows any order to be shipped within 24 hours.

Uniting the Strategy-Making Effort

The previous discussion underscores that *a company's strategic plan is a collection of strategies* devised by different managers at different levels in the organizational hierarchy. The larger the enterprise, the more points of strategic initiative it has. Management's direction-setting effort is not complete until the separate layers of strategy are unified into a coherent, supportive pattern. Ideally the pieces and layers of strategy should fit together like the pieces of a picture puzzle. Unified objectives and strategies don't emerge from an undirected process where managers set objectives and craft strategies independently. Indeed, functional and operating-level managers have a duty to work in harmony to set grassroots performance targets and invent frontline strategic actions that will help achieve business objectives and increase the power of business strategy.

Objectives and strategies that are unified from top to bottom of the organizational hierarchy require a team effort.

Harmonizing objectives and strategies piece by piece and level by level can be tedious and frustrating, requiring numerous consultations and meetings, periodic strategy review and approval processes, the experience of trial and error, and months (sometimes years) of consensus building and collaborative effort. The politics of gaining strategic consensus and the battle of trying to keep all managers and departments focused on what's best for the total enterprise (as opposed to what's best for their departments or careers) are often big obstacles in unifying the layers of objectives and strategies and producing the desired degree of cooperation and collaboration.[12] Broad consensus is particularly difficult when there is ample room for opposing views and disagreement. Managerial discussions about an organization's mission and vision, long-term direction, objectives, and strategies often provoke heated debate and strong differences of opinion.

Consistency between business strategy and functional/operating strategies comes from the collaborative efforts of functional and operating-level managers to set performance targets and invent strategic actions in their respective areas of responsibility that contribute directly to achieving business objectives and improving the execution of business strategy.

Figure 2.4 portrays the networking of objectives and strategies through the managerial hierarchy. The two-way arrows indicate that there are simultaneous bottom-up and top-down influences on missions, objectives, and strategies at each level. Furthermore, there are two-way influences across the related businesses of a diversified company and across the related processes, functions, and operating activities within a business. These vertical and horizontal linkages, if man-

---

[12]Functional managers are sometimes more interested in doing what is best for their own areas, building their own empires, and consolidating their personal power and organizational influence than they are in cooperating with other functional managers to unify behind the overall business strategy. As a result, it's easy for functional area support strategies to conflict, thereby forcing the business-level general manager to spend time and energy refereeing functional strategy conflicts and building support for a more unified approach.

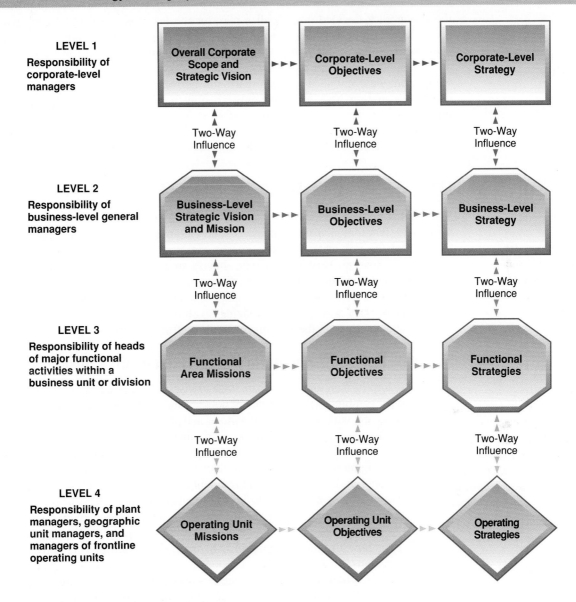

FIGURE 2.4 The Networking of Strategic Visions, Missions, Objectives, and Strategies in the Strategy-Making Pyramid

aged in a way that promotes coordination, can help unify the direction-setting and strategy-making activities of many managers into a mutually reinforcing pattern. The tighter that coordination is enforced, the tighter the linkages in the missions, objectives, and strategies of the various organizational units. Tight linkages safeguard against organizational units straying from the company's charted strategic course.

As a practical matter, however, corporate and business strategic visions, objectives, and strategies need to be clearly outlined and communicated down the line before much progress can be made in direction setting and strategy making at the functional and operating levels. Direction and guidance need to flow from the corporate level to the business level and from the business level to functional and grassroots operating levels. The strategic disarray that occurs in an organization when senior managers don't exercise strong top-down direction setting and strategic leadership is akin to what would happen to a football team's offensive performance if the quarterback decided not to call a play for the team, but instead let each player pick whatever play he thought would work best at his respective position. In business, as in sports, all the strategy makers in a company are on the same team. They are obligated to perform their strategy-making tasks in a manner that benefits the whole company, not in a manner that suits personal or departmental interests. A company's strategy is at full power only when its many pieces are united. This means that the strategizing process has to proceed more from the top down than from the bottom up. Lower-level managers cannot do good strategy making without understanding the company's long-term direction and higher-level strategies.

THE FACTORS THAT SHAPE A COMPANY'S STRATEGY

Many situational considerations enter into crafting strategy. Figure 2.5 depicts the primary factors that shape a company's strategic approaches. The interplay of these factors and the influence that each has on the strategy-making process vary from situation to situation. Very few strategic choices are made in the same context—even in the same industry, situational factors differ enough from company to company that the strategies of rivals turn out to be quite distinguishable from one another rather than imitative. This is why carefully sizing up all the various situational factors, both external and internal, is the starting point in crafting strategy.

Societal, Political, Regulatory, and Citizenship Considerations

What an enterprise can and cannot do strategywise is always constrained by what is legal, by what complies with government policies and regulatory requirements, and by what is in accord with societal expectations and the standards of good community citizenship. Outside pressures also come from other sources—special-interest groups,

Societal, political, regulatory, and citizenship factors limit the strategic actions a company can or should take.

the glare of investigative reporting, a fear of unwanted political action, and the stigma of negative opinion. Societal concerns over health and nutrition, alcohol and drug abuse, environmental pollution, sexual harassment, corporate downsizing, and the impact of plant closings on local communities have caused many companies to temper or revise aspects of their strategies. American concerns over jobs lost to foreign imports and political debate over how to cure the chronic U.S. trade deficit are driving forces in the strategic decisions of Japanese and European companies to locate plants in the United States. Heightened consumer awareness about the hazards of saturated fat and cholesterol have driven most food products companies to phase out high-fat ingredients and substitute low-fat ingredients, despite the extra costs.

Factoring in societal values and priorities, community concerns, and the potential for onerous legislation and regulatory requirements is a regular part of external situation analysis at more and more companies. Intense public pressure and adverse media coverage make such a practice prudent. The task of making an organization's strategy socially responsible means (1) conducting organizational activities within the bounds of what is considered to be in the general public interest; (2) responding positively to emerging societal priorities and expectations; (3) demonstrating a willingness to take action ahead of regulatory confrontation; (4) balancing stockholder interests against the larger interests of society as a whole; and (5) being a good citizen in the community.

FIGURE 2.5 Factors Shaping the Choice of Company Strategy

STRATEGY-SHAPING FACTORS EXTERNAL TO THE COMPANY

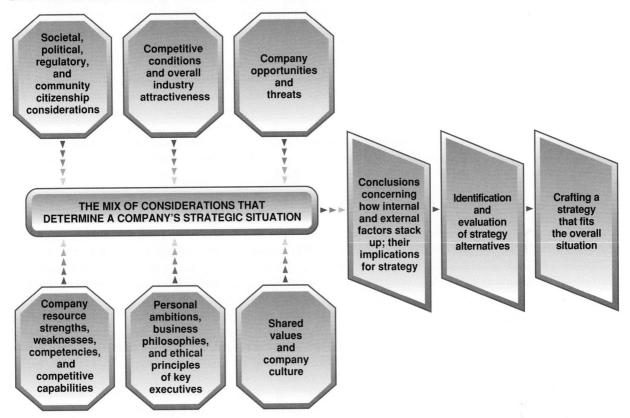

STRATEGY-SHAPING FACTORS INTERNAL TO THE COMPANY

Corporate social responsibility is showing up in company mission statements. John Hancock, for example, concludes its mission statement with the following sentence:

> In pursuit of this mission, we will strive to exemplify the highest standards of business ethics and personal integrity; and shall recognize our corporate obligation to the social and economic well-being of our community.

At Union Electric, a St. Louis-based utility company, the following statement is official corporate policy:

> As a private enterprise entrusted with an essential public service, we recognize our civic responsibility in the communities we serve. We shall strive to advance the growth and welfare of these communities and shall participate in civic activities which fulfill that goal—for we believe this is both good citizenship and good business.

Competitive Conditions and Overall Industry Attractiveness

An industry's competitive conditions and overall attractiveness are big strategy-determining factors. A company's strategy has to be tailored to the nature and mix of competitive factors in play—price, product quality, performance features, service, warranties, and so on. When competitive conditions intensify significantly, a company must respond with strategic actions to protect its position. Competitive weakness on the part of one or more rivals may signal the need for a strategic offensive. Furthermore, fresh moves on the part of rival companies, changes in the industry's price-cost-profit economics, shifting buyer needs and expectations, and new technological developments often alter the requirements for competitive success and mandate reconsideration of strategy. The industry environment, as it exists now and is expected to exist later, thus has a direct bearing on a company's best competitive strategy option and where it should concentrate its efforts. *A company's strategy can't produce real market success unless it is well-matched to the industry and competitive situation.* When a firm concludes its industry environment has grown unattractive and it is better off investing company resources elsewhere, it may begin a strategy of disinvestment and eventual abandonment. A strategist, therefore, has to be a student of industry and competitive conditions.

Strategic Management Principle

A company's strategy should be tailored to fit industry and competitive conditions.

The Company's Market Opportunities and External Threats

The particular business opportunities open to a company and the threatening external developments that it faces are key influences on strategy. Both point to the need for strategic action. A company's strategy needs to be deliberately aimed at capturing its best growth opportunities, especially the ones that hold the most promise for building sustainable competitive advantage and enhancing profitability. Likewise, strategy should be geared to providing a defense against external threats to the company's well-being and future performance. For strategy to be successful, it has to be well matched to market opportunities and threatening external developments; this usually means crafting offensive moves to capitalize on the company's most promising market opportunities and crafting defensive moves to protect the company's competitive position and long-term profitability.

Strategic Management Principle

A well-conceived strategy aims at capturing a company's best growth opportunities and defending against external threats to its well-being and future performance.

Company Resource Strengths, Competencies, and Competitive Capabilities

One of the most pivotal strategy-shaping internal considerations is whether a company has or can acquire the resources, competencies, and capabilities needed to execute a strategy proficiently. An organization's resources, competencies, and competitive capabilities are important strategy-making considerations because of (1) the competitive strengths they provide in capitalizing on a particular opportunity, (2) the competitive edge they may give a firm in the marketplace, and (3) the potential they have for becoming a cornerstone of strategy. The best path to competitive advantage is found where a firm has competitively valuable resources and competencies, where rivals do not have matching or offsetting resources and competencies, and where rivals can't develop comparable capabilities except at high cost and/or over an extended period of time.

Strategic Management Principle

A company's strategy ought to be grounded in its resource strengths and in what it is good at doing (its competencies and competitive capabilities); likewise, it is perilous to craft a strategy whose success is dependent on resources and capabilities that a company lacks.

Even if an organization has no outstanding competencies and capabilities (and many do not), managers still must tailor strategy to fit the enterprise's particular resources and capabilities. It is foolish to develop a strategic plan that cannot be executed with the resources and capabilities a firm is able to assemble. In short, *strategy must be well-matched to a company's resource strengths and weaknesses and to its competitive capabilities.* Experience shows that winning strategies aim squarely at capitalizing on a company's resource strengths and neutralizing its resource deficiencies and skills gaps. An organization's resource strengths make some strategies and market opportunities attractive to pursue; likewise, its resource deficiencies, its gaps in important skills and know-how, and the weaknesses in its present competitive market position make the pursuit of certain strategies or opportunities risky (or even out of the question). Consequently, what resources, competencies, and capabilities a company has and how competitively valuable they are is a very relevant strategy-making consideration.

The Personal Ambitions, Business Philosophies, and Ethical Beliefs of Managers

Managers do not dispassionately assess what strategic course to steer. Their choices are often influenced by their own vision of how to compete and how to position the enterprise and by what image and standing they want the company to have. Both casual observation and formal studies indicate that managers' ambitions, values, business philosophies, attitudes toward risk, and ethical beliefs have important influences on strategy.[13] Sometimes the influence of a manager's personal values, experiences, and emotions is conscious and deliberate; at other times it may be unconscious. As one expert noted in explaining the relevance of personal factors to strategy, "People have to have their hearts in it."[14]

The personal ambitions, business philosophies, and ethical beliefs of managers are usually stamped on the strategies they craft.

Several examples of how business philosophies and personal values enter into strategy making are particularly noteworthy. Ben Cohen and Jerry Greenfield, cofounders and major stockholders in Ben and Jerry's Homemade Ice Cream, have consistently insisted that the company's strategy be supportive of social causes of their choosing and incorporate a strong social mission. Japanese managers are strong proponents of strategies that take a long-term view and that aim at building market share and competitive position. In contrast, some U.S. and European executives have drawn criticism for overemphasizing short-term profits at the expense of long-term competitive positioning because of pressures to meet investors' quarterly and annual earnings expectations. Japanese companies also display a quite different philosophy regarding the role of suppliers. Their preferred supplier strategy is to enter into long-term partnership arrangements with key suppliers because they believe that working closely with the same supplier year after year improves the quality and reliability of component parts, facilitates just-in-time delivery, and reduces inventory carrying costs. In U.S. and European companies, the traditional strategic approach has been to play suppliers off against one another, doing business on a short-term basis with whoever offers the best price and promises acceptable quality.

---

[13]The role of personal values, individual ambitions, and managerial philosophies in strategy making has long been recognized and documented. The classic sources are William D. Guth and Renato Tagiuri, "Personal Values and Corporate Strategy," *Harvard Business Review* 43, no. 5 (September–October 1965), pp. 123–32; Kenneth R. Andrews, *The Concept of Corporate Strategy*, 3rd ed. (Homewood, Ill.: Richard D. Irwin, 1987), chap. 4; and Richard F. Vancil, "Strategy Formulation in Complex Organizations," *Sloan Management Review* 17, no. 2 (Winter 1986), pp. 4–5.

[14]Andrews, *The Concept of Corporate Strategy*, p. 63.

Attitudes toward risk also have a big influence on strategy. Risk-avoiders are inclined toward "conservative" strategies that minimize downside risk, have a quick payback, and produce sure short-term profits. Risk-takers lean more toward opportunistic strategies where visionary moves can produce a big payoff over the long term. Risk-takers prefer innovation to imitation and bold strategic offensives to defensive moves to protect the status quo.

Managerial values also shape the ethical quality of a firm's strategy. Managers with strong ethical convictions take pains to see that their companies observe a strict code of ethics in all aspects of the business. They expressly forbid such practices as accepting or giving kickbacks, badmouthing rivals' products, and buying political influence with political contributions. Instances where a company's strategic actions run afoul of high ethical standards include charging excessive interest rates on credit card balances, employing bait-and-switch sales tactics, continuing to market products suspected of having safety problems, and using ingredients that are known health hazards.

The Influence of Shared Values and Company Culture on Strategy

An organization's policies, practices, traditions, philosophical beliefs, and ways of doing things combine to create a distinctive culture. Typically, the stronger a company's culture the more that culture is likely to shape the strategic actions it decides to employ, sometimes even dominating the choice of strategic moves. This is because

A company's values and culture can dominate the kinds of strategic moves it considers or rejects.

culture-related values and beliefs are so embedded in management's strategic thinking and actions that they condition how the enterprise responds to external events. Such firms have a culture-driven bias about how to handle strategic issues and what kinds of strategic moves it will consider or reject. Strong cultural influences partly account for why companies gain reputations for such strategic traits as leadership in technological advance and product innovation, dedication to superior craftsmanship, a proclivity for financial wheeling and dealing, a desire to grow rapidly by acquiring other companies, having a strong people orientation and being a good company to work for, or unusual emphasis on customer service and total customer satisfaction.

In recent years, more companies have articulated the core beliefs and values underlying their business approaches. One company expressed its core beliefs and values like this:

> We are market-driven. We believe that functional excellence, combined with teamwork across functions and profit centers, is essential to achieving superb execution. We believe that people are central to everything we will accomplish. We believe that honesty, integrity, and fairness should be the cornerstone of our relationships with consumers, customers, suppliers, stockholders, and employees.

Wal-Mart's founder, Sam Walton, was a fervent believer in frugality, hard work, constant improvement, dedication to customers, and genuine care for employees. The company's commitment to these values is deeply ingrained in its strategy of low prices, good values, friendly service, productivity through the intelligent use of technology, and hard-nosed bargaining with suppliers.[15] At Hewlett-Packard, the

---

[15]Sam Walton with John Huey, *Sam Walton: Made in America* (New York: Doubleday, 1992); and John P. Kotter and James L. Heskett, *Corporate Culture and Performance* (New York: Free Press, 1992), pp. 17 and 36.

company's basic values, known internally as "the HP Way," include sharing the company's success with employees, showing trust and respect for employees, providing customers with products and services of the greatest value, being genuinely interested in providing customers with effective solutions to their problems, making profit a high stockholder priority, avoiding the use of long-term debt to finance growth, individual initiative and creativity, teamwork, and being a good corporate citizen.[16] At both Wal-Mart and Hewlett-Packard, the value systems are deeply ingrained and widely shared by managers and employees. Whenever this happens, values and beliefs are more than an expression of nice platitudes; they become a way of life within the company and they mold company strategy.[17]

LINKING STRATEGY WITH ETHICS

Strategy ought to be ethical. It should involve rightful actions, not wrongful ones; otherwise it won't pass the test of moral scrutiny. This means more than conforming to what is legal. Ethical and moral standards go beyond the prohibitions of law and the language of "thou shalt not" to the issues of *duty* and the language of "should do and should not do." Ethics concerns human duty and the principles on which this duty rests.[18]

Every strategic action a company takes should be ethical.

Every business has an ethical duty to each of five constituencies: owners/shareholders, employees, customers, suppliers, and the community at large. Each of these constituencies affects the organization and is affected by it. Each is a stakeholder in the enterprise, with certain expectations as to what the enterprise should do and how it should do it.[19] Owners/shareholders, for instance, rightly expect a return on their investment. Even though investors may individually differ in their preferences for profits now versus profits later, their tolerances for greater risk, and their enthusiasm for exercising social responsibility, business executives have a moral duty to pursue profitable management of the owners' investment.

A company's duty to employees arises out of respect for the worth and dignity of individuals who devote their energies to the business and who depend on the business for their economic well-being. Principled strategy making requires that employee-related decisions be made equitably and compassionately, with concern for due process and for the impact that strategic change has on employees' lives. At best, the chosen strategy should promote employee interests as concerns compensation, career opportunities, job security, and overall working conditions. At worst, the chosen strategy should not disadvantage employees. Even in crisis situations where adverse employee impact cannot be avoided, businesses have an ethical duty to minimize whatever hardships have to be imposed in the form of workforce reductions, plant closings, job transfers, relocations, retraining, and loss of income.

A company has ethical duties to owners, employees, customers, suppliers, the communities where it operates, and the public at large.

The duty to the customer arises out of expectations that attend the purchase of a good or service. Inadequate appreciation of this duty led to product liability laws and a host of regulatory agencies to protect consumers. All kinds of strategy-related

---

[16]Kotter and Heskett, *Corporate Culture and Performance*, pp. 60–61.

[17]For another example of the impact of values and beliefs, see Richard T. Pascale, "Perspectives on Strategy: The Real Story behind Honda's Success," in Glenn Carroll and David Vogel, *Strategy and Organization: A West Coast Perspective* (Marshfield, Mass.: Pitman Publishing, 1984), p. 60.

[18]Harry Downs, "Business Ethics: The Stewardship of Power," working paper provided to the authors.

[19]Ibid.

ethical issues still abound, however. Should a seller voluntarily inform consumers that its product contains ingredients that, though officially approved for use, are suspected of having potentially harmful effects? Is it ethical for the makers of alcoholic beverages to sponsor college events, given that many college students are under 21? Is it ethical for cigarette manufacturers to advertise at all (even though it is legal)? Is it ethical for manufacturers to stonewall efforts to recall products they suspect have faulty parts or defective designs? Is it ethical for supermarkets and department store retailers to lure customers with highly advertised "loss-leader" prices on a few select items, but then put high markups on popular or essential items?

A company's ethical duty to its suppliers arises out of the market relationship that exists between them. They are both partners and adversaries. They are partners in the sense that the quality of suppliers' parts affects the quality of a firm's own product. They are adversaries in the sense that the supplier wants the highest price and profit it can get while the buyer wants a cheaper price, better quality, and speedier service. A company confronts several ethical issues in its supplier relationships. Is it ethical to purchase goods from foreign suppliers who employ child labor and/or pay substandard wages and/or have sweatshop working conditions in their facilities? Is it ethical to threaten to cease doing business with a supplier unless the supplier agrees not to do business with key competitors? Is it ethical to reveal one supplier's price quote to a rival supplier? Is it ethical to accept gifts from suppliers? Is it ethical to pay a supplier in cash? Is it ethical *not* to give present suppliers advance warning of the intent to discontinue using what they have supplied and to switch to components supplied by other enterprises?

A company's ethical duty to the community at large stems from its status as a citizen of the community and as an institution of society. Communities and society are reasonable in expecting businesses to be good citizens—to pay their fair share of taxes for fire and police protection, waste removal, streets and highways, and so on, and to exercise care in the impact their activities have on the environment, on society, and on the communities in which they operate. For example, is it ethical for a liquor firm to advertise its products on TV at times when these ads are likely to be seen by children and people under the age of 21? Is it ethical for liquor firms to even advertise on TV at any time? Some years ago, an oil company was found to have spent $2 million on environmental conservation and $4 million advertising its virtue and good deeds—actions that seem deliberately manipulative and calculated to mislead. A company's community citizenship is ultimately demonstrated by whether it refrains from acting in a manner contrary to the well-being of society and by the degree to which it supports community activities, encourages employees to participate in community activities, handles the health and safety aspects of its operations, accepts responsibility for overcoming environmental pollution, relates to regulatory bodies and employee unions, and exhibits high ethical standards.

Carrying Out Ethical Responsibilities   Management, not constituent groups, is responsible for managing the enterprise. Thus, it is management's perceptions of its ethical duties and of constituents' claims that drive whether and how strategy is linked to ethical behavior. Ideally, managers weigh strategic decisions from each constituent's point of view and, where conflicts arise, strike a rational, objective, and equitable balance among the interests of all five constituencies. If any of the five constituencies conclude that management is not doing its duty, they have their own avenues for recourse. Concerned investors can protest at the annual shareholders' meeting, appeal to the board of directors, or sell their stock. Concerned employees can unionize and

ILLUSTRATION CAPSULE 8   Harris Corporation's Commitments to Its Stakeholders

Harris Corporation is a major supplier of information, communication, and semiconductor products, systems, and services to commercial and governmental customers throughout the world. The company utilizes advanced technologies to provide innovative and cost-effective solutions for processing and communicating data, voice, text, and video information. The company had sales of $3.6 billion in 1996, and it employs nearly 23,000 people. In a recent annual report, the company set forth its commitment to satisfying the expectations of its stakeholders:

Customers—For customers, our objective is to achieve ever-increasing levels of satisfaction by providing quality products and services with distinctive benefits on a timely and continuing basis worldwide. Our relationships with customers will be forthright and ethical, and will be conducted in a manner to build trust and confidence.

Shareholders—For shareholders, the owners of our company, our objective is to achieve sustained growth in earnings-per-share. The resulting stock-price appreciation combined with dividends should provide our shareholders with a total return on investment that is competitive with similar investment opportunities.

Employees—The people of Harris are our company's most valuable asset, and our objective is for every employee to be personally involved in and share the success of the business. The company is committed to providing an environment that encourages all employees to make full use of their creativity and unique talents; to providing equitable compensation, good working conditions, and the opportunity for personal development and growth which is limited only by individual ability and desire.

Suppliers—Suppliers are a vital part of our resources. Our objective is to develop and maintain mutually beneficial partnerships with suppliers who share our commitment to achieving increasing levels of customer satisfaction through continuing improvements in quality, service, timeliness, and cost. Our relationships with suppliers will be sincere, ethical, and will embrace the highest principles of purchasing practice.

Communities—Our objective is to be a responsible corporate citizen. This includes support of appropriate civic, educational, and business activities, respect for the environment, and the encouragement of Harris employees to practice good citizenship and support community programs. Our greatest contribution to our communities is to be successful so that we can maintain stable employment and create new jobs.

Source: 1988 Annual Report.

bargain collectively, or they can seek employment elsewhere. Customers can switch to competitors. Suppliers can find other buyers or pursue other market alternatives. The community and society can do anything from staging protest marches and urging boycotts to stimulating political and governmental action.[20]

A management that truly cares about business ethics and corporate social responsibility is proactive rather than reactive in linking strategic action and ethics. It steers away from ethically or morally questionable business opportunities (for example, in late 1996, Anheuser-Busch announced it would no longer run its beer commercials on MTV). It won't do business with suppliers that engage in activities the company does not condone. It produces products that are safe for its customers to use. It operates a workplace environment that is safe for employees. It recruits and hires employees whose values and behavior match the company's principles and ethical standards. It acts to reduce any environmental pollution it causes. It cares about how it does business and whether its actions reflect integrity and high ethical standards. Illustration Capsule 8 describes Harris Corporation's ethical commitments to its stakeholders.

---

[20]Ibid.

Tests of a Winning Strategy

What are the criteria for weeding out candidate strategies? How can a manager judge which strategic option is best for the company? What are the standards for determining whether a strategy is successful or not? Three tests can be used to evaluate the merits of one strategy over another and to gauge how good a strategy is:

1. *The Goodness of Fit Test*—A good strategy is tailored to fit the company's internal and external situation—without tight situational fit, there's real question whether a strategy appropriately matches the requirements for market success.

2. *The Competitive Advantage Test*—A good strategy leads to sustainable competitive advantage. The bigger the competitive edge that a strategy helps build, the more powerful and effective it is.

3. *The Performance Test*—A good strategy boosts company performance. Two kinds of performance improvements are the most telling of a strategy's caliber: gains in profitability and gains in the company's competitive strength and long-term market position.

Strategic options that clearly come up short on one or more of these tests are candidates to be dropped from further consideration. The strategic option that best

Strategic Management Principle

A winning strategy must fit the enterprise's situation, build sustainable competitive advantage, and improve company performance.

meets all three tests can be regarded as the best or most attractive strategic alternative. Once a strategic commitment is made and enough time elapses to see results, these same tests can be used to determine whether the chosen strategy qualifies as a winning strategy. The more a strategy fits the situation, builds sustainable competitive advantage, and boosts company performance, the more it qualifies as a winner.

There are, of course, some additional criteria for judging the merits of a particular strategy: completeness and coverage of all the bases, internal consistency among all the pieces of strategy, clarity, the degree of risk involved, and flexibility. These criteria are useful supplements and certainly ought to be looked at, but they can in no way replace the three tests posed above.

APPROACHES TO PERFORMING THE STRATEGY-MAKING TASK

Companies and managers go about the task of developing strategic plans differently. In small, owner-managed companies, strategy making usually occurs informally, emerging from the experiences, personal observations and assessments, verbal exchanges and debates, and entrepreneurial judgments of a few key people at the top—with perhaps some data gathering and number-crunching analysis involved. Often, the resulting strategy exists mainly in the entrepreneur's own mind and in oral understandings with key subordinates, but is not reduced to writing and laid out in a formal document called a strategic plan.

Large companies, however, tend to develop their strategic plans more formally (occasionally using prescribed procedures, forms, and timetables) and in deeper detail. There is often considerable data gathering, situational analysis, and intense study of particular issues, involving the broad participation of managers at many organizational levels and numerous meetings to probe, question, sort things out, and hammer out the pieces of the strategy. The larger and more diverse an enterprise, the more managers feel it is better to have a structured process with timetables, studies and debate, and written plans that receive official approval from up the line.

Along with variations in the organizational process of formulating strategy are variations in how managers personally participate in analyzing the company's situation and deliberating what strategy to pursue. The four basic strategy-making styles managers use are:[21]

The Master Strategist Approach   Some managers take on the role of chief strategist and chief entrepreneur, singlehandedly exercising *strong* influence over assessments of the situation, over the strategy alternatives that are explored, and over the details of strategy. This does not mean that the manager personally does all the work; it means that the manager personally becomes the chief architect of strategy and wields a proactive hand in shaping some or all of the major pieces of strategy. Master strategists act as strategy commanders and have a big ownership stake in the chosen strategy.

The Delegate-It-to-Others Approach   Here the manager in charge delegates pieces and maybe all of the strategy-making task to others, perhaps a group of trusted subordinates, a cross-functional task force, or self-directed work teams with authority over a particular process or function. The manager then personally stays in touch with how the strategy deliberations are progressing, offers guidance when appropriate, smiles or frowns as trial balloon recommendations are informally run by him/her for reaction, and reserves final approval until the strategy proposals are formally presented, considered, modified (if needed), and deemed ready for implementation. While strategy delegators may leave little of their own imprint on individual pieces of the strategy proposals presented for approval, they often must still play an integrative role in bringing the separate strategy elements devised by others into harmony and in fleshing out any pieces not delegated. They also must bear ultimate responsibility for the caliber of the strategy-making efforts of subordinates, so their confidence in the business judgments of those to whom strategy-making tasks are delegated must be well placed. This strategy-making style allows for broad participation and input from many managers and areas, plus it gives managers some flexibility in picking and choosing from the smorgasbord of strategic ideas that bubble up from below. The big weakness of delegation is that its success depends heavily on the business judgments and strategy-making skills of those to whom the strategy-making tasks are delegated—for instance, the strategizing efforts of subordinates may prove too short-run oriented and reactive, dealing more with how to address today's problems than with positioning the enterprise and adapting its resources to capture tomorrow's opportunities. Subordinates may not have either the clout or the inclination to tackle changing major components of the present strategy.[22] A second weakness of chartering a group of subordinates to develop strategy is that it sends the wrong signal: Strategy development isn't important enough to warrant a big claim on the boss's personal time and attention. Moreover, a manager can end up too detached from the process to

---

[21]This discussion is based on David R. Brodwin and L. J. Bourgeois, "Five Steps to Strategic Action," in Glenn Carroll and David Vogel, *Strategy and Organization: A West Coast Perspective* (Marshfield, Mass.: Pitman Publishing, 1984), pp. 168–78.

[22]For a case in point of where the needed strategy changes were too big for a chartered group of subordinates to address, see Thomas M. Hout and John C. Carter, "Getting It Done: New Roles for Senior Executives," *Harvard Business Review* 73 no. 6 (November–December 1995), pp. 140–44.

exercise strategic leadership if the group's deliberations bog down in disagreement or go astray, either of which set the stage for rudderless direction setting and/or ill-conceived strategy.

The Collaborative Approach   This is a middle approach whereby the manager enlists the help of key peers and subordinates in hammering out a consensus strategy. The strategy that emerges is the joint product of all concerned, with the collaborative effort usually being personally led by the manager in charge. The collaborative approach is well suited to situations where strategic issues cut across traditional functional and departmental lines, where there's a need to tap into the ideas and problem-solving skills of people with different backgrounds, expertise, and perspectives, and where it makes sense to give as many people as feasible a participative role in shaping the strategy that emerges and help win their wholehearted commitment to implementation. Involving teams of people to dissect complex situations and find market-driven, customer-driven solutions is becoming increasingly necessary in many businesses. Not only are many strategic issues too far-reaching or too involved for a single manager to handle but they often are cross-functional and cross-departmental in nature, thus requiring the contributions of many disciplinary experts and the collaboration of managers from different parts of the organization to decide upon sound strategic actions. A valuable strength of this strategy-making style is that the group of people charged with crafting the strategy can easily include the very people who will also be charged with implementing it. Giving people an influential stake in crafting the strategy they must later help implement is not only motivational but also means they can be held accountable for putting the strategy into place and making it work—the oft-used excuse of "It wasn't my idea to do this" won't fly.

The Champion Approach   In this style, the manager is interested neither in a big personal stake in the details of strategy nor in the time-consuming task of leading others through participative brainstorming or a collaborative "group wisdom" exercise. Rather, the idea is to encourage individuals and teams to develop, champion, and implement sound strategies on their own initiative. Here important pieces of company strategy originate with the "doers" and the "fast-trackers." Executives serve as judges, evaluating the strategy proposals needing their approval. This approach works well in large diversified corporations where the CEO cannot personally orchestrate strategy making in each of many business divisions. For headquarters executives to capitalize on having people in the enterprise who can see strategic opportunities that they cannot, they must delegate the initiative for strategy making to managers at the business-unit level. Corporate executives may well articulate general strategic themes as organizationwide guidelines for strategic thinking, but the key to good strategy making is stimulating and rewarding new strategic initiatives conceived by a champion who believes in the opportunity and badly wants the blessing to go after it. With this approach, the total strategy ends up being the sum of the championed initiatives that get approved.

These four basic managerial approaches to forming a strategy illuminate several aspects about how companies arrive at a planned strategy. When the manager in charge personally functions as the chief architect of strategy, the choice of what strategic course to steer is a product of his/her own vision about how to position the enterprise and of the manager's ambitions, values, business philosophies, and entrepreneurial judgment about what moves to make next. Highly centralized strategy making works fine when the manager in charge has a powerful, insightful vision of where to head and how to get there. The primary weakness of the master strategist approach is that the caliber of the strategy depends so heavily on one person's strategy-making skills and entrepreneurial acumen. It also breaks down in large enterprises where many strategic initiatives are needed and the strategy-making task is too complex for one person to handle alone.

Of the four basic approaches managers can use in crafting strategy, none is inherently superior—each has strengths and weaknesses and each is workable in the "right" situation.

On the other hand, the group approach to strategy making has its risks too. Sometimes, the strategy that emerges from group consensus is a middle-of-the-road compromise, void of bold, creative initiative. Other times, it represents political consensus, with the outcome shaped by influential subordinates, by powerful functional departments, or by majority coalitions that have a common interest in promoting their particular version of what the strategy ought to be. Politics and the exercise of power are most likely to come into play in situations where there is no strong consensus on what strategy to adopt; this opens the door for a political solution to emerge. The collaborative approach is conducive to political strategic choices as well, since powerful departments and individuals have ample opportunity to try to build a consensus for their favored strategic approach. The big weakness of a delegate-it-to-others approach is the potential lack of sufficient top-down direction and strategic leadership.

The strength of the champion approach is also its weakness. The value of championing is that it encourages people at lower organizational levels to be alert for profitable market opportunities, to propose innovative strategies to capture them, and to take on responsibility for new business ventures. Individuals with attractive strategic proposals are given the latitude and resources to try them out, thus helping renew an organization's capacity for innovation and growth. On the other hand, a series of championed actions, because they spring from many places in the organization and can fly off in many directions, are not likely to form a coherent pattern or result in a clear strategic direction for the company as a whole without some strong top-down leadership. With championing, the chief executive has to work at ensuring that what is championed adds power to the overall organization strategy; otherwise, strategic initiatives may be launched in directions that have no integrating links or overarching rationale. Another weakness of the championing approach is that top executives will be more intent on protecting their reputations for prudence than on supporting sometimes revolutionary strategies, in which case innovative ideas can be doused by corporate orthodoxy.[23] It is usually painful and laborious for a lowly employee to champion an out-of-the-ordinary idea up the chain of command.

All four styles of handling the strategy-making task thus have strengths and weaknesses. All four can succeed or fail depending on whether they are used in the right circumstances, on how well the approach is managed, and on the strategy-making skills and judgments of the individuals involved.

Management's direction-setting task involves charting a company's future strategic path, setting objectives, and forming a strategy. Early on in the direction-setting process, managers need to address the question of "What is our business and what will it be?" Management's views and conclusions about the organization's future

KEY POINTS

---

[23]See Hamel, "Strategy as Revolution," pp. 80–81.

course, the market position it should try to occupy, and the business activities to be pursued constitute a *strategic vision* for the company. A strategic vision indicates management's aspirations for the organization, providing a panoramic view of "what businesses we want to be in, where we are headed, and the kind of company we are trying to create." It spells out a direction and describes the destination. Effective visions are clear, challenging, and inspiring; they prepare a firm for the future, and they make sense in the marketplace. A well-conceived, well-said mission/vision statement serves as a beacon of long-term direction, helps channel organizational efforts along the path management has committed to following, builds a strong sense of organizational identity, and creates employee buy-in.

The second direction-setting step is to establish *strategic* and *financial* objectives for the organization to achieve. Objectives convert the business mission and strategic vision into specific performance targets. The agreed-on objectives need to spell out precisely how much by when, and they need to require a significant amount of organizational stretch. Objectives are needed at all organizational levels.

The third direction-setting step entails forming strategies to achieve the objectives set in each area of the organization. A corporate strategy is needed to achieve corporate-level objectives; business strategies are needed to achieve business-unit performance objectives; functional strategies are needed to achieve the performance targets set for each functional department; and operating-level strategies are needed to achieve the objectives set in each operating and geographic unit. In effect, an organization's strategic plan is a collection of unified and interlocking strategies. As shown in Table 2.1, different strategic issues are addressed at each level of managerial strategy making. Typically, the strategy-making task is more top-down than bottom-up. Lower-level strategies should support and complement higher-level strategy and contribute to the achievement of higher-level, companywide objectives.

Strategy is shaped by both outside and inside considerations. The major external considerations are societal, political, regulatory, and community factors; competitive conditions and overall industry attractiveness; and the company's market opportunities and threats. The primary internal considerations are company strengths, weaknesses, and competitive capabilities; managers' personal ambitions, philosophies, and ethics; and the company's culture and shared values. A good strategy must be well matched to all these situational considerations. In addition, a good strategy must lead to sustainable competitive advantage and improved company performance.

There are essentially four basic ways to manage the strategy formation process in an organization: the master strategist approach where the manager in charge personally functions as the chief architect of strategy, the delegate-it-to-others approach, the collaborative approach, and the champion approach. All four have strengths and weaknesses. All four can succeed or fail depending on how well the approach is managed and depending on the strategy-making skills and judgments of the individuals involved.

SUGGESTED READINGS

Campbell, Andrew, and Laura Nash. *A Sense of Mission: Defining Direction for the Large Corporation.* Reading, Mass.: Addison-Wesley, 1993.

Collins, James C. and Jerry I. Porras. " Building Your Company's Vision." *Harvard Business Review* 74, no.5 (September–October 1996), pp. 65–77.

Drucker, Peter. "The Theory of the Business." *Harvard Business Review* 72, no. 5 (September–October 1994), pp. 95–104.

Hamel, Gary, and C. K. Prahalad. "Strategic Intent." *Harvard Business Review* 67, no. 3 (May–June 1989), pp. 63–76.

———. "Strategy as Stretch and Leverage." *Harvard Business Review* 71, no. 2 (March–April 1993), pp. 75–84.

Hamel, Gary. "Strategy as Revolution," *Harvard Business Review* 74 no. 4 (July–August 1996), pp. 69–82.

Hammer, Michael, and James Champy. *Reengineering the Corporation.* New York: HarperBusiness, 1993, chap. 9.

Ireland, R. Duane, and Michael A. Hitt. "Mission Statements: Importance, Challenge, and Recommendations for Development." *Business Horizons* (May–June 1992), pp. 34–42.

Kahaner, Larry. "What You Can Learn from Your Competitors' Mission Statements." *Competitive Intelligence Review* 6 no. 4 (Winter 1995), pp. 35–40.

Lipton, Mark. "Demystifying the Development of an Organizational Vision." *Sloan Management Review* (Summer 1996), pp. 83–92.

McTavish, Ron. "One More Time: What Business Are You In?" *Long Range Planning* 28, no. 2 (April 1995), pp. 49–60.

Mintzberg, Henry. "Crafting Strategy." *Harvard Business Review* 65, no. 4 (July–August 1987), pp. 66–77.

Porter, Michael E. "What Is Strategy?" *Harvard Business Review* 74, no. 6 (November–December 1996), pp. 61–78.

Wilson, Ian. "Realizing the Power of Strategic Vision." *Long Range Planning* 25, no.5 (1992), pp. 18–28.

3

INDUSTRY AND COMPETITIVE ANALYSIS

Crafting strategy is an analysis-driven exercise, not a task where managers can get by with opinions, good instincts, and creative thinking. Judgments about what strategy to pursue need to flow directly from solid analysis of a company's external environment and internal situation. The two biggest considerations are (1) industry and competitive conditions (these are the heart of a single-business company's "external environment") and (2) a company's competitive capabilities, resources, internal strengths and weaknesses, and market position.

Figure 3.1 illustrates what is involved in sizing up a company's situation and deciding on a strategy. The analytical sequence is from strategic appraisal of the company's external and internal situation to identification of issues to evaluation of alternatives to choice of strategy. Accurate diagnosis of the company's situation is necessary managerial preparation for deciding on a sound long-term direction, setting appropriate objectives, and crafting a winning strategy. Without perceptive understanding of the strategic aspects of a company's macro- and microenvironments, the chances are greatly increased that managers will concoct a strategic game plan that doesn't fit the situation well, that holds little prospect for building competitive advantage, and that is unlikely to boost company performance.

This chapter examines the techniques of *industry and competitive analysis*, the term commonly used to refer to assessing the strategically relevant aspects of a company's *macroenvironment* or *business ecosystem*. In the next chapter, we'll cover the methods of *company situation analysis* and see how to appraise the strategy-shaping aspects of a firm's immediate *microenvironment*.

THE METHODS OF INDUSTRY AND COMPETITIVE ANALYSIS

Industries differ widely in their economic characteristics, competitive situations, and future profit prospects. The economic and competitive character of the trucking industry bears little resemblance to that of discount retailing. The economic and competitive traits of the fast-food business have little in common with those of providing Internet-related products or services. The cable-TV business is shaped by industry and competitive conditions radically different from those in the soft-drink business.

FIGURE 3.1 How Strategic Thinking and Strategic Analysis Lead to Good Strategic Choices

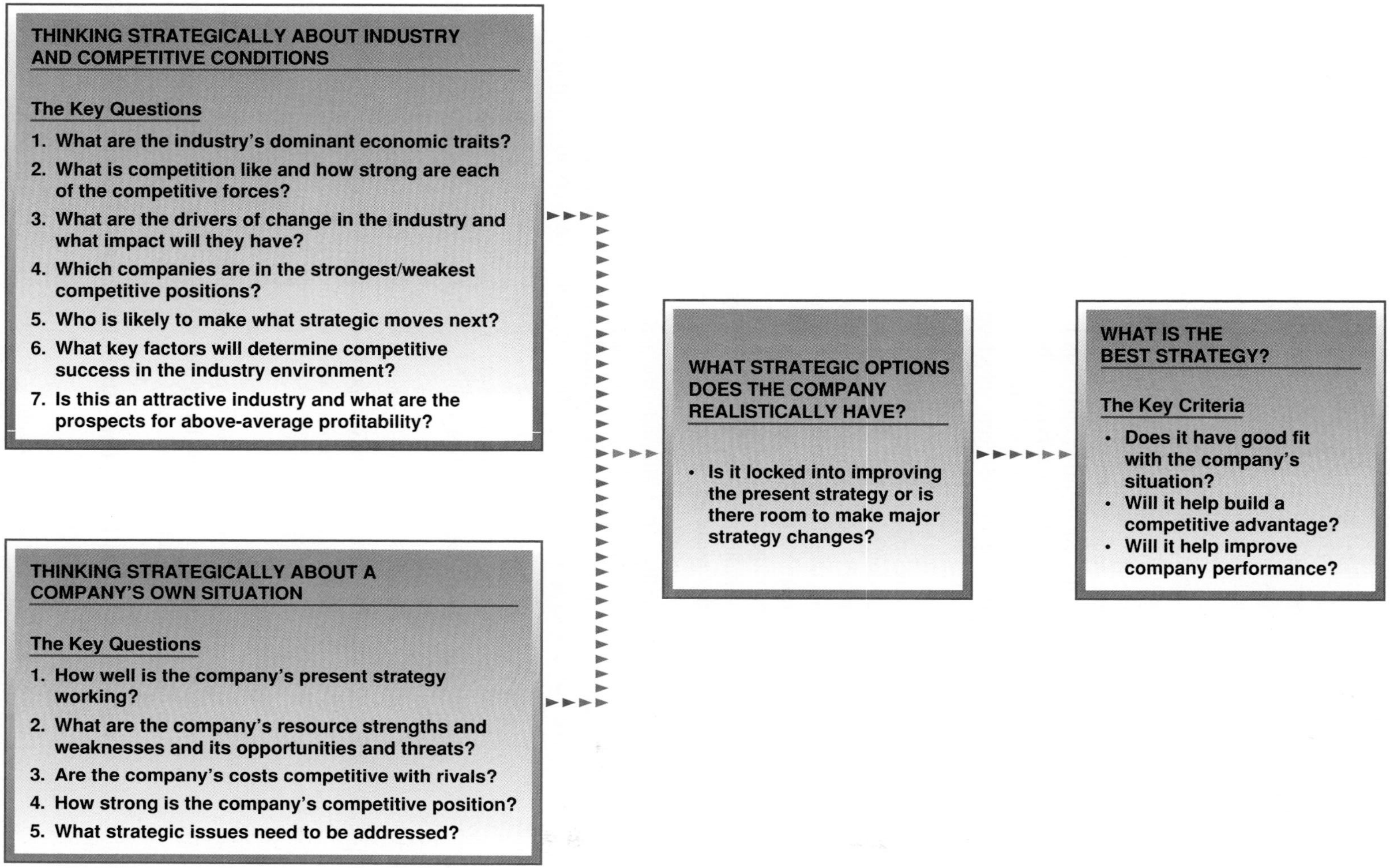

THINKING STRATEGICALLY ABOUT INDUSTRY AND COMPETITIVE CONDITIONS

The Key Questions

1. What are the industry's dominant economic traits?
2. What is competition like and how strong are each of the competitive forces?
3. What are the drivers of change in the industry and what impact will they have?
4. Which companies are in the strongest/weakest competitive positions?
5. Who is likely to make what strategic moves next?
6. What key factors will determine competitive success in the industry environment?
7. Is this an attractive industry and what are the prospects for above-average profitability?

THINKING STRATEGICALLY ABOUT A COMPANY'S OWN SITUATION

The Key Questions

1. How well is the company's present strategy working?
2. What are the company's resource strengths and weaknesses and its opportunities and threats?
3. Are the company's costs competitive with rivals?
4. How strong is the company's competitive position?
5. What strategic issues need to be addressed?

WHAT STRATEGIC OPTIONS DOES THE COMPANY REALISTICALLY HAVE?

• Is it locked into improving the present strategy or is there room to make major strategy changes?

WHAT IS THE BEST STRATEGY?

The Key Criteria

• Does it have good fit with the company's situation?
• Will it help build a competitive advantage?
• Will it help improve company performance?

The economic character of industries varies according to a number of factors: the overall size and market growth rate, the pace of technological change, the geographic

Managers are not prepared to decide on a long-term direction or a strategy until they have a keen understanding of the company's strategic situation— the exact nature of the industry and competitive conditions it faces and how these conditions match up with its resources and capabilities.

boundaries of the market (which can extend from local to worldwide), the number and sizes of buyers and sellers, whether sellers' products are virtually identical or highly differentiated, the extent to which costs are affected by economies of scale, and the types of distribution channels used to access buyers. Competitive forces can be moderate in one industry and fierce, even cutthroat, in another. Moreover, industries differ widely in the degree of competitive emphasis put on price, product quality, performance features, service, advertising and promotion, and new product innovation. In some industries, price competition dominates the marketplace while in others the competitive emphasis is centered on quality or product performance or customer service or brand image/reputation. In other industries, the challenge is for companies to work cooperatively with suppliers, customers, and maybe even select competitors to create the next round of product innovations and open up a whole new vista of market opportunities (as we are witnessing in computer technology and telecommunications).

An industry's economic traits and competitive conditions and how they are expected to change determine whether its future profit prospects will be poor, average, or excellent. Industry and competitive conditions differ so much that leading companies in unattractive industries can find it hard to earn respectable profits, while even weak companies in attractive industries can turn in good performances.

Industry and competitive analysis uses a tool kit of concepts and techniques to get a clear fix on key industry traits, the intensity of competition, the drivers of industry change, the market positions and strategies of rival companies, the keys to competitive success, and the industry's future profit outlook. This tool kit provides a way of thinking strategically about any industry and drawing conclusions about whether the industry represents an attractive investment for company funds. It entails examining a company's business in the context of a much wider environment. Industry and competitive analysis aims at developing probing, insightful answers to seven questions:

1. What are the industry's dominant economic features?
2. What competitive forces are at work in the industry and how strong are they?
3. What are the drivers of change in the industry and what impact will they have?
4. Which companies are in the strongest/weakest competitive positions?
5. Who's likely to make what competitive moves next?
6. What key factors will determine competitive success or failure?
7. How attractive is the industry in terms of its prospects for above-average profitability?

The answers to these questions build understanding of a firm's surrounding environment and, collectively, form the basis for matching its strategy to changing industry conditions and competitive realities.

Question 1: What Are the Industry's Dominant Economic Features?

Because industries differ significantly in their character and structure, industry and competitive analysis begins with an overview of the industry's dominant economic features. As a working definition, we use the word *industry* to mean a group of firms whose products have so many of the same attributes that they compete for the same buyers. The factors to consider in profiling an industry's economic traits are fairly standard:

- Market size.
- Scope of competitive rivalry (local, regional, national, international, or global).
- Market growth rate and where the industry is in the growth cycle (early development, rapid growth and takeoff, early maturity, mature, saturated and stagnant, declining).
- Number of rivals and their relative sizes—is the industry fragmented with many small companies or concentrated and dominated by a few large companies?
- The number of buyers and their relative sizes.
- The prevalence of backward and forward integration.
- The types of distribution channels used to access buyers.
- The pace of technological change in both production process innovation and new product introductions.
- Whether the product(s)/service(s) of rival firms are highly differentiated, weakly differentiated, or essentially identical.
- Whether companies can realize economies of scale in purchasing, manufacturing, transportation, marketing, or advertising.
- Whether certain industry activities are characterized by strong learning and experience effects such that unit costs decline as *cumulative* output (and thus the experience of "learning by doing") grows.
- Whether high rates of capacity utilization are crucial to achieving low-cost production efficiency.
- Resource requirements and the ease of entry and exit.
- Whether industry profitability is above/below par.

Table 3.1 provides a sample profile of the economic character of the sulfuric acid industry.

An industry's economic features are important because of the implications they have for strategy. For example, in capital-intensive industries where investment in a single plant can run several hundred million dollars, a firm can spread the burden of high fixed costs by pursuing a strategy that promotes high utilization of fixed assets and generates more revenue per dollar of fixed-asset investment. Thus commercial airlines try to boost the revenue productivity of their multimillion-dollar jets by cutting ground time at airport gates (to get in more flights per day with the same plane) and by using multi-tiered price discounts to fill up otherwise empty seats. In industries characterized by one product advance after another, companies must spend enough time and money on R&D to keep their technical prowess and innovative capability abreast of competitors—a strategy of continuous product innovation becomes a condition of survival.

An industry's economic features help frame the window of strategic approaches a company can pursue.

In industries like semiconductors, strong *learning/experience* effects in manufacturing cause unit costs to decline about 20 percent each time *cumulative* production volume doubles. With a 20 percent experience curve effect, if the first

TABLE 3.1   A Sample Profile of the Dominant Economic Characteristics of the Sulfuric Acid Industry

Market Size: $400–$500 million annual revenues; 4 million tons total volume.

Scope of Competitive Rivalry: Primarily regional; producers rarely sell outside a 250-mile radius of plant due to high cost of shipping long distances.

Market Growth Rate: 2–3 percent annually.

Stage in Life Cycle: Mature.

Number of Companies in Industry: About 30 companies with 110 plant locations and capacity of 4.5 million tons. Market shares range from a low of 3 percent to a high of 21 percent.

Customers: About 2,000 buyers; most are industrial chemical firms.

Degree of Vertical Integration: Mixed; 5 of the 10 largest companies are integrated backward into mining operations and also forward in that sister industrial chemical divisions buy over 50 percent of the output of their plants; all other companies are engaged solely in the production of sulfuric acid.

Ease of Entry/Exit: Moderate entry barriers exist in the form of capital requirements to construct a new plant of minimum efficient size (cost equals $10 million) and ability to build a customer base inside a 250-mile radius of plant.

Technology/Innovation: Production technology is standard and changes have been slow; biggest changes are occurring in products—1–2 newly formulated specialty chemicals products are being introduced annually, accounting for nearly all of industry growth.

Product Characteristics: Highly standardized; the brands of different producers are essentially identical (buyers perceive little real difference from seller to seller).

Scale Economies: Moderate; all companies have virtually equal manufacturing costs but scale economies exist in shipping in multiple carloads to same customer and in purchasing large quantities of raw materials.

Learning and Experience Effects: Not a factor in this industry.

Capacity Utilization: Manufacturing efficiency is highest between 90–100 percent of rated capacity; below 90 percent utilization, unit costs run significantly higher.

Industry Profitability: Subpar to average; the commodity nature of the industry's product results in intense price-cutting when demand slackens, but prices firm up during periods of strong demand. Profits track the strength of demand for the industry's products.

Basic Concept

When strong economies of learning and experience result in declining unit costs as cumulative production volume builds, a strategy to become the largest-volume manufacturer can yield the competitive advantage of being the industry's lowest-cost producer.

1 million chips cost $100 each, by a production volume of 2 million the unit cost would be $80 (80 percent of $100), by a production volume of 4 million the unit would be $64 (80 percent of $80), and so on. When an industry is characterized by sizable economies of experience in its manufacturing operations, a company that first initiates production of a new-style product and develops a successful strategy to capture the largest market share gains sustainable competitive advantage as the low-cost producer.[1] The bigger the experience-curve effect, the bigger the cost advantage of the company with the largest *cumulative* production volume, as shown in Figure 3.2.

Table 3.2 presents some additional examples of how an industry's economic traits are relevant to managerial strategy making.

---

[1]There are a large number of studies of the size of the cost reductions associated with experience; the median cost reduction associated with a doubling of cumulative production volume is approximately 15 percent, but there is a wide variation from industry to industry. For a good discussion of the economies of experience and learning, see Pankaj Ghemawat, "Building Strategy on the Experience Curve," *Harvard Business Review* 64, no. 2 (March–April 1985), pp. 143–49.

FIGURE 3.2   Comparison of Experience Curve Effects for 10 Percent, 20 Percent, and 30 Percent Cost Reductions for Each Doubling of Cumulative Production Volume

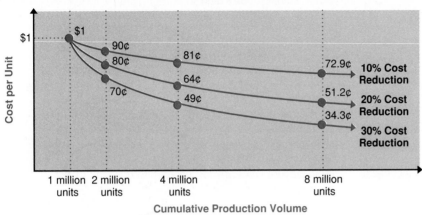

Question 2: What Is Competition Like and How Strong Are Each of the Competitive Forces?

An important part of industry and competitive analysis is to delve into the industry's competitive process to discover the main sources of competitive pressure and how strong each competitive force is. This analytical step is essential because managers cannot devise a successful strategy without understanding the industry's competitive character.

The Five-Forces Model of Competition   Even though competitive pressures in various industries are never precisely the same, the competitive process works similarly enough to use a common analytical framework in gauging the nature and intensity of competitive forces. As Professor Michael Porter of the Harvard Business School has convincingly demonstrated, *the state of competition in an industry is a composite of five competitive forces:*[2]

1. The rivalry among competing sellers in the industry.
2. The market attempts of companies in other industries to win customers over to their own *substitute* products.
3. The potential entry of new competitors.
4. The bargaining power and leverage suppliers of inputs can exercise.
5. The bargaining power and leverage exercisable by buyers of the product.

Porter's *five-forces model*, as depicted in Figure 3.3, is a powerful tool for systematically diagnosing the chief competitive pressures in a market and assessing how

---

[2]For a thoroughgoing treatment of the five-forces model by its originator, see Michael E. Porter, *Competitive Strategy: Techniques for Analyzing Industries and Competitors* (New York: Free Press, 1980), chapter 1.

TABLE 3.2   Examples of the Strategic Importance of an Industry's Key Economic Features

Economic Feature	Strategic Importance
• Market size	• Small markets don't tend to attract big/new competitors; large markets often draw the interest of companies looking to acquire competitors with established positions in attractive industries.
• Market growth rate	• Fast growth breeds new entry; growth slowdowns spawn increased rivalry and a shake-out of weak competitors.
• Capacity surpluses or shortages	• Surpluses push prices and profit margins down; shortages pull them up.
• Industry profitability	• High-profit industries attract new entrants; depressed conditions encourage exit.
• Entry/exit barriers	• High barriers protect positions and profits of existing firms; low barriers make existing firms vulnerable to entry.
• Product is a big-ticket item for buyers	• More buyers will shop for lowest price.
• Standardized products	• Buyers have more power because it is easier to switch from seller to seller.
• Rapid technological change	• Raises risk factor; investments in technology facilities/ equipment may become obsolete before they wear out.
• Capital requirements	• Big requirements make investment decisions critical; timing becomes important; creates a barrier to entry and exit.
• Vertical integration	• Raises capital requirements; often creates competitive differences and cost differences among fully versus partially versus nonintegrated firms.
• Economies of scale	• Increases volume and market share needed to be cost competitive.
• Rapid product innovation	• Shortens product life cycle; increases risk because of opportunities for leapfrogging.

strong and important each one is. Not only is it the most widely used technique of competition analysis, but it is also relatively easy to understand and apply.

The Rivalry among Competing Sellers   The strongest of the five competitive forces is *usually* the jockeying for position and buyer favor that goes on among rival firms. In some industries, rivalry is centered around price competition—sometimes resulting in prices below the level of unit costs and forcing losses on most rivals. In other industries, price competition is minimal and rivalry is focused on such factors as performance features, new product innovation, quality and durability, warranties, after-the-sale service, and brand image.

Competitive jockeying among rivals heats up when one or more competitors sees an opportunity to better meet customer needs or is under pressure to improve its performance. *The intensity of rivalry among competing sellers is a function of how vigorously they employ such tactics as lower prices, snazzier features, expanded customer services, longer warranties, special promotions, and new product introductions.* Rivalry can range from friendly to cutthroat, depending on how frequently and how aggressively companies undertake fresh moves that threaten rivals' profitability. Ordinarily, industry rivals are clever at adding new wrinkles to their product offer-

FIGURE 3.3 The Five-Forces Model of Competition: A Key Analytical Tool

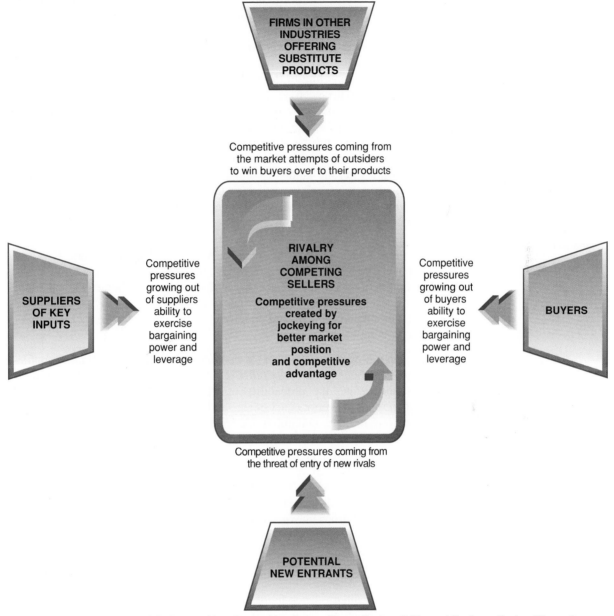

Source: Adapted from Michael E. Porter, "How Competitive Forces Shape Strategy," *Harvard Business Review* 57, no. 2 (March–April 1979), pp. 137–45.

ings that enhance buyer appeal, and they persist in trying to exploit weaknesses in each other's market approaches.

Whether rivalry is lukewarm or heated, every company has to craft a successful strategy for competing—ideally, one that *produces a competitive edge over rivals* and strengthens its position with buyers. The big complication in most industries is that *the success of any one firm's strategy hinges partly on what offensive and defensive maneuvers its rivals employ and the resources rivals are willing and able to put behind their strategic efforts.* The "best" strategy for one firm in its maneuvering for competitive advantage depends, in other words, on the competitive capabilities and strategies of rival companies. Thus, whenever one firm makes a strategic move, its rivals often retaliate with offensive or defensive countermoves. This pattern of action and reaction makes competitive rivalry a "war-games" type of contest conducted according to the rules of fair competition. Indeed, from a strategy-making perspective, *competitive markets are economic battlefields,* with the ebb and flow of the competitive battle varying with the latest strategic moves of the players. In practice, the market outcome is almost always shaped by the strategies of the leading players.

Principle of Competitive Markets

Competitive jockeying among rival firms is a dynamic, ever-changing process as firms initiate new offensive and defensive moves and emphasis swings from one blend of competitive weapons and tactics to another.

Not only do competitive contests among rival sellers assume different intensities but the kinds of competitive pressures that emerge from cross-company rivalry also vary over time. The relative emphasis that rival companies put on price, quality, performance features, customer service, warranties, advertising, dealer networks, new product innovation, and so on shifts as they try different tactics to catch buyers' attention and as competitors launch fresh offensive and defensive maneuvers. Rivalry is thus dynamic; the current competitive scene is ever-changing as companies act and react, sometimes in rapid-fire order and sometimes methodically, and as they swing from one mix of competitive tactics to another.

Regardless of the industry, several common factors seem to influence the tempo of rivalry among competing sellers:[3]

1. *Rivalry intensifies as the number of competitors increases and as competitors become more equal in size and capability.* Up to a point, the greater the number of competitors, the greater the probability of fresh, creative strategic initiatives. In addition, when rivals are more equal in size and capability, they can usually compete on a fairly even footing, making it harder for one or two firms to "win" the competitive battle and dominate the market.

2. *Rivalry is usually stronger when demand for the product is growing slowly.* In a rapidly expanding market, there tends to be enough business for everybody to grow. Indeed, it may take all of a firm's financial and competitive resources just to keep up with buyer demand, much less steal rivals' customers. But when growth slows or when market demand drops unexpectedly, expansion-minded firms and/or firms with excess capacity often cut prices and deploy other sales-increasing tactics, thereby igniting a battle for market share that can result in a shakeout of the weak and less efficient firms. The industry then consolidates into a smaller, but individually stronger, number of sellers.

3. *Rivalry is more intense when industry conditions tempt competitors to use price cuts or other competitive weapons to boost unit volume.* Whenever fixed costs account for a large fraction of total cost, unit costs tend to be lowest at or near full capacity since fixed costs can be spread over more units of production. Unused capacity imposes a significant cost-increasing penalty because there are fewer units

---

[3]These indicators of what to look for in evaluating the intensity of intercompany rivalry are based on Porter, *Competitive Strategy,* pp. 17–21.

carrying the fixed cost burden. In such cases, if market demand weakens and capacity utilization begins to fall off, the pressure of rising unit costs often pushes rival firms into secret price concessions, special discounts, rebates, and other sales-increasing tactics, thus heightening rivalry. Likewise, when a product is perishable, seasonal, or costly to hold in inventory, competitive pressures build when one or more firms decide to dump excess supplies on the market.

4. *Rivalry is stronger when customers' costs to switch brands are low.* The lower the costs of switching, the easier it is for rival sellers to raid one another's customers. High switching costs, however, give sellers a more protected customer base and work against the efforts of rivals to promote brand-switching.

5. *Rivalry is stronger when one or more competitors is dissatisfied with its market position and launches moves to bolster its standing at the expense of rivals.* Firms that are losing ground or in financial trouble often react aggressively by introducing new products, boosting advertising, discounting prices, acquiring smaller rivals to strengthen their capabilities, and so on. Such actions can trigger a new round of maneuvering and a more hotly contested battle for market share.

6. *Rivalry increases in proportion to the size of the payoff from a successful strategic move.* The more rewarding an opportunity, the more likely some firm will aggressively pursue a strategy to capture it. The size of the payoff varies partly with the speed of retaliation. When competitors respond slowly (or not at all), the initiator of a fresh competitive strategy can reap benefits in the intervening period and perhaps gain an advantage that is not easily surmounted. The greater the benefits of moving first, the more likely some competitor will accept the risk and try it.

7. *Rivalry tends to be more vigorous when it costs more to get out of a business than to stay in and compete.* The higher the exit barriers, the stronger the incentive for existing rivals to remain and compete as best they can, even though they may be earning low profits or even incurring losses.

8. *Rivalry becomes more volatile and unpredictable the more diverse competitors are in terms of their visions, strategic intents, objectives, strategies, resources, and countries of origin.* A diverse group of sellers often contains one or more mavericks willing to rock the boat with unconventional moves and market approaches, thus generating a livelier and less predictable environment. Attempts by cross-border rivals to gain stronger footholds in each other's domestic markets boosts the intensity of rivalry, especially when foreign rivals have lower costs or very attractive products.

9. *Rivalry increases when strong companies outside the industry acquire weak firms in the industry and launch aggressive, well-funded moves to transform their newly acquired competitors into major market contenders.* A concerted effort to turn a weak rival into a market leader nearly always entails launching well-financed strategic initiatives to dramatically improve the competitor's product offering, excite buyer interest, and win a much bigger market share. If these actions are successful, they put pressure on rivals to counter with fresh moves of their own.

Two facets of competitive rivalry stand out: (1) the launch of a powerful competitive strategy by one company intensifies the pressures on the remaining companies and (2) the character of rivalry is shaped partly by the strategies of the leading players and partly by the vigor with which industry rivals use competitive weapons to try to outmaneuver one another. In sizing up the competitive pressures created by rivalry among existing competitors, the strategist's job is to identify the current weapons and tactics of competitive rivalry, to stay on top of which tactics are most and least successful, to understand the "rules" that industry rivals play by, and to decide whether and why rivalry is likely to increase or diminish in strength.

Judgments about how much pressure cross-company rivalry is going to put on profitability is the key to concluding whether and why the rivalry among existing sellers is fierce, strong, moderate, or attractively weak. Competitive rivalry is considered intense when the actions of competitors are driving down industry profits, moderate when most companies can earn acceptable profits, and weak when most companies in the industry can earn above-average returns on investment. Chronic outbreaks of cutthroat competition among rival sellers make an industry brutally competitive.

The Competitive Force of Potential Entry   New entrants to a market bring new production capacity, the desire to establish a secure place in the market, and sometimes substantial resources.[4] Just how serious the competitive threat of entry is in a particular market depends on two classes of factors: *barriers to entry* and the *expected reaction of incumbent firms to new entry*. A barrier to entry exists whenever it is hard for a newcomer to break into the market and/or economic factors put a potential entrant at a disadvantage. There are several types of entry barriers:[5]

1. *Economies of scale*—Scale economies deter entry because they force potential competitors either to enter on a large-scale basis (a costly and perhaps risky move) or to accept a cost disadvantage (and lower profitability). Trying to overcome scale economies by entering on a large-scale basis at the outset can result in long-term overcapacity problems for the new entrant (until sales volume builds up), and it can so threaten the market shares of existing firms that they retaliate aggressively (with price cuts, increased advertising and sales promotion, and similar blocking actions). Either way, a potential entrant is discouraged by the prospect of lower profits. Entrants may encounter scale-related barriers not just in production, but in advertising, marketing and distribution, financing, after-sale customer service, raw materials purchasing, and R&D as well.

2. *Inability to gain access to technology and specialized know-how*—Many industries require technological capability and skills not readily available to a newcomer. Key patents can effectively bar entry as can lack of technically skilled personnel and an inability to execute complicated manufacturing techniques. Existing firms often carefully guard know-how that gives them an edge. Unless new entrants can gain access to such proprietary knowledge, they will lack the capability to compete on a level playing field.

3. *The existence of learning and experience curve effects*—When lower unit costs are partly or mostly a result of experience in producing the product and other learning curve benefits, new entrants face a cost disadvantage competing against firms with more know-how.

4. *Brand preferences and customer loyalty*—Buyers are often attached to established brands. Japanese consumers, for example, are fiercely loyal to Japanese brands of motor vehicles, electronics products, cameras, and film. European consumers have traditionally been loyal to European brands of major household appliances. High brand loyalty means that a potential entrant must build a network of distributors and

---

[4]Michael E. Porter, "How Competitive Forces Shape Strategy," *Harvard Business Review* 57, no. 2 (March–April 1979), p. 138.

[5]Porter, *Competitive Strategy*, pp. 7–17.

dealers, then be prepared to spend enough money on advertising and sales promotion to overcome customer loyalties and build its own clientele. Establishing brand recognition and building customer loyalty can be a slow and costly process. In addition, if it is difficult or costly for a customer to switch to a new brand, a new entrant must persuade buyers that its brand is worth the costs. To overcome the switching-cost barrier, new entrants may have to offer buyers a discounted price or an extra margin of quality or service. All this can mean lower profit margins for new entrants—something that increases the risk to start-up companies dependent on sizable, early profits.

5. *Resource requirements*—The larger the total dollar investment and other resource requirements needed to enter the market successfully, the more limited the pool of potential entrants. The most obvious capital requirements are associated with manu-facturing plant and equipment, distribution facilities, working capital to finance inventories and customer credit, introductory advertising and sales promotion to establish a clientele, and cash reserves to cover start-up losses. Other resource barriers include access to technology, specialized expertise and know-how, and R&D requirements, labor force requirements, and customer service requirements.

6. *Cost disadvantages independent of size*—Existing firms may have cost advan-tages not available to potential entrants. These advantages can include access to the best and cheapest raw materials, patents and proprietary technology, the benefits of learning and experience curve effects, existing plants built and equipped years earlier at lower costs, favorable locations, and lower borrowing costs.

7. *Access to distribution channels*—In the case of consumer goods, a potential entrant may face the barrier of gaining access to consumers. Wholesale distributors may be reluctant to take on a product that lacks buyer recognition. A network of retail dealers may have to be set up from scratch. Retailers have to be convinced to give a new brand display space and a trial period. The more existing producers tie up distribution channels, the tougher entry will be. To overcome this barrier, potential entrants may have to "buy" distribution access by offering better margins to dealers and distributors or by giving advertising allowances and other incentives. As a consequence, a potential entrant's profits may be squeezed unless and until its product gains enough acceptance that distributors and retailers want to carry it.

8. *Regulatory policies*—Government agencies can limit or even bar entry by requir-ing licenses and permits. Regulated industries like cable TV, telecommunications, electric and gas utilities, radio and television broadcasting, liquor retailing, and railroads feature government-controlled entry. In international markets, host govern-ments commonly limit foreign entry and must approve all foreign investment appli-cations. Stringent safety regulations and environmental pollution standards are entry barriers because they raise entry costs.

9. *Tariffs and international trade restrictions*—National governments commonly use tariffs and trade restrictions (antidumping rules, local content requirements, and quotas) to raise entry barriers for foreign firms. In 1996, due to tariffs imposed by the South Korean government, a Ford Taurus cost South Korean car buyers over $40,000. The government of India requires that 90 percent of the parts and compo-nents used in Indian truck assembly plants be made in India. And to protect European chipmakers from low-cost Asian competition, European governments instituted a rigid formula for calculating floor prices for computer memory chips.

Whether an industry's entry barriers ought to be considered high or low depends on the resources and competencies possessed by the pool of potential entrants. Entry barriers are usually steeper for new start-up enterprises than for companies in other industries or for current industry participants looking to enter new geographic markets. Indeed, the most likely entrants into a geographic market are often enterprises looking to expand their market reach. A company already well established in one geographic market may have the resources, competencies, and competitive capabilities to hurdle the barriers of entering an attractive new geographic market. In evaluating the potential threat of entry, one must look at (1) how formidable the entry barriers are for each type of potential entrant—new start-up enterprises, candidate companies in other industries, and current industry participants aiming to enter additional geographic markets and (2) how attractive the profit prospects are for new entrants. High profits act as a magnet to potential entrants, motivating them to commit the resources needed to hurdle entry barriers.[6]

Even if a potential entrant has or can acquire the needed competencies and resources to attempt entry, it still faces the issue of how existing firms will react.[7] Will they offer only passive resistance, or will they aggressively defend their market positions using price cuts, increased advertising, new product improvements, and whatever else will give a new entrant (as well as other rivals) a hard time? A potential entrant can have second thoughts when financially strong incumbent firms send clear signals that they will stoutly defend their market positions against newcomers. It may also turn away when incumbent firms can leverage distributors and customers to retain their business.

The best test of whether potential entry is a strong or weak competitive force is to ask if the industry's growth and profit prospects are attractive enough to induce additional entry. When the answer is no, potential entry is a weak competitive force. When the answer is yes and there are entry candidates with enough expertise and resources, then potential entry adds to competitive pressures in the marketplace. The stronger the threat of entry, the more that incumbent firms are driven to fortify their positions against newcomers.

Principle of Competitive Markets

The threat of entry is stronger when entry barriers are low, when there's a sizable pool of entry candidates, when incumbent firms are unable or unwilling to vigorously contest a newcomer's efforts to gain a market foothold, and when a newcomer can expect to earn attractive profits.

One additional point: The threat of entry changes as the industry's prospects grow brighter or dimmer and as entry barriers rise or fall. For example, the expiration of a key patent can greatly increase the threat of entry. A technological discovery can create an economy of scale advantage where none existed before. New actions by incumbent firms to increase advertising, strengthen distributor-dealer relations, step up R&D, or improve product quality can raise the roadblocks to entry. In international markets, entry barriers for foreign-based firms fall as tariffs are lowered, as domestic wholesalers and dealers seek out lower-cost foreign-made goods, and as domestic buyers become more willing to purchase foreign brands.

Competitive Pressures from Substitute Products   Firms in one industry are, quite often, in close competition with firms in another industry because their products are good substitutes. The producers of eyeglasses compete with the makers of contact lenses. The producers of wood stoves compete with such substitutes as kerosene heaters and

---

[6]When profits are sufficiently attractive, entry barriers fail to deter entry; at most, they limit the pool of candidate entrants to enterprises with the requisite competencies and resources and with the creativity to fashion a strategy for competing with incumbent firms. George S. Yip, "Gateways to Entry," *Harvard Business Review* 60, no. 5 (September–October 1982), pp. 85–93.

[7]Porter, "How Competitive Forces Shape Strategy," p. 140, and Porter, *Competitive Strategy*, pp. 14–15.

portable electric heaters. The sugar industry competes with companies that produce artificial sweeteners and high-fructose corn syrup. The producers of glass bottles and jars confront strong competition from manufacturers of plastic containers, paper-board cartons, and metal cans. Aspirin manufacturers compete against the makers of substitute types of pain relievers. Newspapers compete with television in providing news (television has taken over as the preferred source of late-breaking news) and with Internet sources in providing sports results, stock quotes, and job opportunities. Just how strong the competitive pressures are from substitute products depends on three factors: (1) whether attractively priced substitutes are available, (2) how satis-factory the substitutes are in terms of quality, performance, and other relevant attributes, and (3) the ease with which buyers can switch to substitutes.

Readily available and attractively priced substitutes create competitive pressure by placing a ceiling on the prices an industry can charge for its product without giving customers an incentive to switch to substitutes and risking sales erosion.[8] This price ceiling, at the same time, puts a lid on the profits that industry members can earn unless they find ways to cut costs. When substitutes are cheaper than an industry's product, industry members come under heavy competitive pressure to reduce their prices and find ways to absorb the price cuts with cost reductions.

The availability of substitutes inevitably invites customers to compare quality and performance as well as price. For example, ski boat manufacturers are facing strong competition from jet skis because water sports enthusiasts are finding that jet skis have exciting performance features that make them satisfying substitutes. The users of glass bottles and jars constantly weigh the perfor-mance trade-offs with plastic containers, paper cartons, and metal cans. Competition from substitute products pushes industry participants to heighten efforts to convince customers their product has superior attributes.

Another determinant of the strength of competition from substitutes is how difficult or costly it is for the industry's customers to switch to a substitute.[9] Typical switching costs include the extra price premium if any, the costs of additional equipment that may be required, the time and cost in testing the substitute's quality and reliability, the costs of severing old supplier relationships and establishing new ones, payments for technical help in making the changeover, and employee retraining costs. If switching costs are high, sellers of substitutes must offer a major cost or performance benefit in order to entice the industry's customers away. When switching costs are low, it's much easier for sellers of substitutes to convince buyers to change over to their products.

Principle of Competitive Markets

The competitive threat posed by substitute products is strong when substitutes are readily available and attractively priced, buyers believe substitutes have comparable or better features, and buyers' switching costs are low.

As a rule, then, the lower the price of substitutes, the higher their quality and performance, and the lower the user's switching costs, the more intense the competi-tive pressures posed by substitute products. Good indicators of the competitive strength of substitute products are the rate at which their sales and profits are growing, the market inroads they are making, and their plans for expanding produc-tion capacity.

The Power of Suppliers   Whether the suppliers to an industry are a weak or strong competitive force depends on market conditions in the supplier industry and the

---

[8]Porter, "How Competitive Forces Shape Strategy," p. 142, and Porter, *Competitive Strategy*, pp. 23–24.
[9]Porter, *Competitive Strategy*, p. 10.

significance of the item they supply.[10] Supplier-related competitive pressures tend to be minimal whenever the items supplied are standard commodities available on the open market from a large number of suppliers with ample capability. Then it is simple to obtain whatever is needed from a list of capable suppliers, perhaps dividing purchases among several to promote competition for orders. In such cases, suppliers have market power only when supplies become tight and users are so eager to secure what they need that they agree to terms more favorable to suppliers. Suppliers are also relegated to a weak bargaining position whenever there are good substitute inputs and switching is neither costly nor difficult. For example, soft-drink bottlers can check the bargaining power of aluminum can suppliers on price or delivery by using more plastic containers and glass bottles.

Suppliers also tend to have less leverage to bargain over price and other terms of sale when the industry they are supplying is a *major* customer. In such cases, the well-being of suppliers is closely tied to the well-being of their major customers. Suppliers then have a big incentive to protect and enhance their customers' competitiveness via reasonable prices, exceptional quality, and ongoing advances in the technology and performance of the items supplied.

On the other hand, when the item accounts for a sizable fraction of the costs of an industry's product, is crucial to the industry's production process, and/or significantly affects the quality of the industry's product, suppliers have great influence on the competitive process. This is particularly true when a few large companies control most of the available supplies and have pricing leverage. Likewise, a supplier (or group of suppliers) has bargaining leverage the more difficult or costly it is for users to switch to alternate suppliers. Big suppliers with good reputations and growing demand for their output are harder to wring concessions from than struggling suppliers striving to broaden their customer base or more fully utilize their production capacity.

Principle of Competitive Markets

The suppliers to a group of rival firms are a strong competitive force whenever they have sufficient bargaining power to put certain rivals at a competitive disadvantage based on the prices they can command, the quality and performance of the items they supply, or the reliability of their deliveries.

Suppliers are also more powerful when they can supply a component more cheaply than industry members can make it themselves. For instance, most producers of outdoor power equipment (lawnmowers, rotary tillers, snowblowers, and so on) find it cheaper to source small engines from outside manufacturers rather than make their own because the quantity they need is too little to justify the investment, master the process, and capture scale economies. Specialists in small-engine manufacture, by supplying many kinds of engines to the whole power equipment industry, obtain a big enough sales volume to fully realize scale economies, become proficient in all the manufacturing techniques, and keep costs low. Small-engine suppliers, then, are in a position to price the item below what it would cost the user to self-manufacture but far enough above their own costs to generate an attractive profit margin. In such situations, the bargaining position of suppliers is strong *until* the volume of parts a user needs becomes large enough for the user to justify backward integration into self-manufacture of the component. The more credible the threat of backward integration into the suppliers' business becomes, the more leverage users have in negotiating favorable terms with suppliers.

There are a couple of other instances in which the relationship between industry members and suppliers is a competitive force. One is when suppliers, for one reason

---

[10]Ibid., pp. 27–28.

or another, cannot provide items of high or consistent quality. For example, if a manufacturer's suppliers provide components that have a high defect rate or that fail prematurely, they can so increase the warranty and defective goods costs of the manufacturer that its profits, reputation, and competitive position are seriously impaired. A second is when one or more industry members form close working relationships with key suppliers in an attempt to secure lower prices, better quality or more innovative components, just-in-time deliveries, and reduced inventory and logistics costs; such benefits can translate into competitive advantage for industry members who do the best job of managing their relationships with key suppliers.

The Power of Buyers Just as with suppliers, the competitive strength of buyers can range from strong to weak. Buyers have substantial bargaining leverage in a number of situations.[11] The most obvious is when buyers are large and purchase much of the industry's output. Typically, purchasing in large quantities gives a buyer enough leverage to obtain price concessions and other favorable terms. Retailers often have negotiating leverage in purchasing products because of manufacturers' need for broad retail exposure and favorable shelf space. Retailers may stock one or even several brands but rarely all available brands, so competition among sellers for the business of popular or high-volume retailers gives such retailers significant bargaining leverage. In the United States and Britain, supermarket chains have sufficient leverage to require food products manufacturers to make lump-sum payments to gain shelf space for new products. Motor vehicle manufacturers have significant bargaining power in negotiating to buy original-equipment tires not only because they buy in large quantities but also because tire makers believe they gain an advantage in supplying replacement tires to vehicle owners if their tire brand is original equipment on the vehicle. "Prestige" buyers have a degree of clout in negotiating with sellers because a seller's reputation is enhanced by having prestige buyers on its customer list.

> **Principle of Competitive Markets**
>
> *Buyers are a strong competitive force when they are able to exercise bargaining leverage over price, quality, service, or other terms of sale.*

Even if buyers do not purchase in large quantities or offer a seller important market exposure or prestige, they may still have some degree of bargaining leverage in the following circumstances:

- *If buyers' costs of switching to competing brands or substitutes are relatively low*—Anytime buyers have the flexibility to fill their needs by switching brands or sourcing from several sellers, they gain added negotiating room with sellers. When sellers' products are virtually identical, it is relatively easy for buyers to switch from seller to seller at little or no cost. However, if sellers' products are strongly differentiated, buyers may be less able to switch without sizable changeover costs.
- *If the number of buyers is small*—The smaller the number of buyers, the less easy is it for sellers to find alternatives when a customer is lost. The prospect of losing a customer often makes a seller more willing to grant concessions of one kind or another.
- *If buyers are well informed about sellers' products, prices, and costs*—The more information buyers have, the better bargaining position they are in.
- *If buyers pose a credible threat of backward integrating into the business of sellers*—Retailers gain bargaining power by stocking and promoting their

---

[11]Ibid., pp. 24–27.

own private-label brands alongside manufacturers' name brands. Companies like Campbell's soup, Anheuser-Busch, Coors, and Heinz have integrated backward into metal can manufacturing to gain bargaining power in buying cans from otherwise powerful metal can manufacturers.

- *If buyers have discretion in whether they purchase the product*—The buying power of personal computer manufacturers in purchasing from Intel and Microsoft is greatly muted by the critical importance of Intel chips and Microsoft software in making personal computers attractive to PC users. Or, if consumers are unhappy with the sticker prices of new motor vehicles, they can delay purchase or buy a used vehicle instead.

One last point: all buyers of an industry's product are not likely to have equal degrees of bargaining power with sellers, and some may be less sensitive than others to price, quality, or service. For example, apparel manufacturers confront significant customer power when selling to retail chains like Wal-Mart or Sears, but they can command much better prices selling to small owner-managed apparel boutiques. Independent tire retailers have less bargaining power in purchasing replacement tires than do motor vehicle manufacturers in purchasing original-equipment tires and they are also less quality sensitive—motor vehicle manufacturers are very particular about tire quality and tire performance because of the effects on vehicle performance.

Strategic Implications of the Five Competitive Forces   The five-forces model thoroughly exposes what competition is like in a given market—the strength of each of the five competitive forces, the nature of the competitive pressures comprising each force, and the overall structure of competition. As a rule, the stronger the collective impact of competitive forces, the lower the combined profitability of participant firms. The most brutally competitive situation occurs when the five forces create market conditions tough enough to impose prolonged subpar profitability or even losses on most or all firms. The structure of an industry is clearly "unattractive" from a profit-making standpoint if rivalry among sellers is very strong, low entry barriers are allowing new rivals to gain a market foothold, competition from substitutes is strong, and both suppliers and customers are able to exercise considerable bargaining leverage.

A company's competitive strategy is increasingly effective the more it provides good defenses against the five competitive forces, alters competitive pressures in the company's favor, and helps create sustainable competitive advantage.

On the other hand, when competitive forces are not strong, the structure of the industry is "favorable" or "attractive" from the standpoint of earning superior profits. The "ideal" environment from a profit-making perspective is where both suppliers and customers are in weak bargaining positions, there are no good substitutes, entry barriers are relatively high, and rivalry among present sellers is only moderate. However, even when some of the five competitive forces are strong, an industry can be attractive to those firms whose market position and strategy provide a good enough defense against competitive pressures to preserve their ability to earn above-average profits.

To contend successfully against competitive forces, managers must craft strategies that (1) insulate the firm as much as possible from the five competitive forces, (2) influence competitive pressures to change in directions that favor the company, and (3) build a strong, secure position of advantage. Managers cannot expect to develop winning competitive strategies without first identifying what competitive pressures exist, gauging the relative strength of each, and gaining a deep and profound understanding of the industry's whole competitive structure. The five-forces model is a powerful tool for gaining this understanding. Anything less leaves strategy makers short of the competitive insights needed to craft a successful competitive strategy.

Question 3: What Are the Drivers of Change in the Industry and What Impact Will They Have?

An industry's economic features and competitive structure say a lot about the character of industry and competitive conditions but very little about how the industry environment may be changing. All industries are characterized by trends and new developments that gradually or speedily produce changes important enough to require a strategic response from participating firms. The popular hypothesis about industries going through evolutionary phases or life-cycle stages helps explain industry change but is still incomplete.[12] The life-cycle stages are strongly keyed to changes in the overall industry growth rate (which is why such terms as rapid growth, early maturity, saturation, and decline are used to describe the stages). Yet *there are more causes of industry change than an industry's position on the growth curve.*

Industry conditions change because important forces are driving industry participants (competitors, customers, or suppliers) to alter their actions; the driving forces in an industry are the major underlying causes of changing industry and competitive conditions.

The Concept of Driving Forces   While it is important to judge what growth stage an industry is in, there's more value in identifying the factors causing fundamental industry and competitive adjustments. Industry and competitive conditions change *because forces are in motion that create incentives or pressures for change.*[13] The most dominant forces are called driving forces because they have the biggest influence on what kinds of changes will take place in the industry's structure and environment. Driving forces analysis has two steps: identifying what the driving forces are and assessing the impact they will have on the industry.

The Most Common Driving Forces   Many events can affect an industry powerfully enough to qualify as driving forces. Some are one of a kind, but most fall into one of several basic categories.[14]

- *Changes in the long-term industry growth rate*—Shifts in industry growth up or down are a force for industry change because they affect the balance between industry supply and buyer demand, entry and exit, and how hard it will be for a firm to capture additional sales. An upsurge in long-term demand attracts new entrants to the market and encourages established firms to invest in additional capacity. A shrinking market can cause some companies to exit the industry and induce those remaining to close their least efficient plants and retrench.

- *Changes in who buys the product and how they use it*—Shifts in buyer demographics and new ways of using the product can alter the state of competition by forcing adjustments in customer service offerings (credit, technical assistance, maintenance and repair), opening the way to market the industry's product through a different mix of dealers and retail outlets, prompting producers to broaden/narrow their product lines, bringing

---

[12]For more extended discussion of the problems with the life-cycle hypothesis, see Porter, *Competitive Strategy*, pp. 157–62.

[13]Porter, *Competitive Strategy*, p. 162.

[14]What follows draws on the discussion in Porter, *Competitive Strategy*, pp. 164–83.

different sales and promotion approaches into play. Mushrooming popularity of the Internet at home and at work is creating new opportunities for electronic shopping, on-line brokerage services, e-mail services, bulletin board services, data services, and Internet-provider services. The changing demographics generated by longer life expectancies are creating growth markets for residential golf resorts, retirement planning services, mutual funds, and health care.

- *Product innovation*—Product innovation can shake up the structure of competition by broadening an industry's customer base, rejuvenating industry growth, and widening the degree of product differentiation among rival sellers. Successful new product introductions strengthen the market position of the innovating companies, usually at the expense of companies who stick with their old products or are slow to follow with their own versions of the new product. Industries where product innovation has been a key driving force include copying equipment, cameras and photographic equipment, golf clubs, electronic video games, toys, prescription drugs, frozen foods, personal computers, and personal computer software.

- *Technological change*—Advances in technology can dramatically alter an industry's landscape, making it possible to produce new and/or better products at lower cost and opening up whole industry frontiers. Technological developments can also produce significant changes in capital requirements, minimum efficient plant sizes, vertical integration benefits, and learning or experience curve effects. For instance, the pace of technological developments in electronic commerce via the Internet is fast changing the way business is conducted in many industries (stock trading, software sales and distribution, and mail-order retailing, to name a few) and is ushering in "the Information Age."

- *Marketing innovation*—When firms are successful in introducing new ways to market their products, they can spark a burst of buyer interest, widen industry demand, increase product differentiation, and/or lower unit costs— any or all of which can alter the competitive positions of rival firms and force strategy revisions. The Internet is becoming the vehicle for all kinds of marketing innovations.

- *Entry or exit of major firms*—The entry of one or more foreign companies into a market once dominated by domestic firms nearly always shakes up competitive conditions. Likewise, when an established domestic firm from another industry attempts entry either by acquisition or by launching its own start-up venture, it usually applies its skills and resources in some innovative fashion that pushes competition in new directions. Entry by a major firm often produces a "new ball game" with new key players and new rules for competing. Similarly, exit of a major firm changes the competitive structure by reducing the number of market leaders (perhaps increasing the dominance of the leaders who remain) and causing a rush to capture the exiting firm's customers.

- *Diffusion of technical know-how*—As knowledge about how to perform an activity or execute a manufacturing technology spreads, any technically based competitive advantage held by firms originally possessing this know-how erodes. The diffusion of such know-how can occur through scientific journals, trade publications, on-site plant tours, word-of-mouth among suppliers and customers, and the hiring away of knowledgeable employees. It can also occur when the possessors of technological know-how license others to use it for a royalty fee or team up with a company interested in turning the technology into a new business venture. Quite often, technological know-how can be acquired by simply buying a company that has the wanted skills, patents, or manufacturing capabilities. In recent years technology transfer across national boundaries has emerged as one of the most important driving forces in globalizing markets and competition. As companies in more countries gain access to technical know-how, they upgrade their manufacturing capabilities in a long-term effort to compete head-on against established companies. Examples include automobiles, tires, consumer electronics, telecommunications, and computers.

- *Increasing globalization of the industry*—Industries move toward globalization for any of several reasons. One or more nationally prominent firms may launch aggressive long-term strategies to win a globally dominant market position. Demand for the industry's product may pop up in more and more countries. Trade barriers may drop. Technology transfer may open the door for more companies in more countries to enter the industry arena on a major scale. Significant labor cost differences among countries may create a strong reason to locate plants for labor-intensive products in low-wage countries (wages in China, Taiwan, Singapore, Mexico, and Brazil, for example, are about one-fourth those in the United States, Germany, and Japan). Firms with world-scale volumes as opposed to national-scale volumes may gain important cost economies. Multinational companies with the ability to transfer their production, marketing, and management know-how from country to country at very low cost can sometimes gain a significant competitive advantage over domestic-only competitors. As a consequence, global competition usually shifts the pattern of competition among an industry's key players, favoring some and hurting others. Such occurrences make globalization a driving force in industries (1) where scale economies are so large that rival companies need to market their product in many country markets to gain enough volume to drive unit costs down, (2) where low-cost production is a critical consideration (making it imperative to locate plant facilities in countries where the lowest costs can be achieved), (3) where one or more growth-oriented companies are pushing hard to gain a significant competitive position in as many attractive country markets as they can, and (4) based on natural resources (supplies of crude oil, copper, and cotton, for example, are geographically scattered all over the globe).

- *Changes in cost and efficiency*—Widening or shrinking differences in the costs and efficiency among key competitors tends to dramatically alter the state of competition. The low-cost economics of e-mail and faxing has put mounting competitive pressure on the relatively inefficient and high-cost operations of the U.S. Postal Service—sending a one-page fax is cheaper and far quicker than sending a first-class letter. In the electric power industry, sharply lower costs to generate electricity at newly constructed combined-cycle generating plants has put older coal-fired and gas-fired plants under the gun to lower their production costs to remain competitive; moreover, solar power and windpower companies have been forced to aggressively pursue technological breakthroughs to get the costs down far enough to survive against the much-improved cost and efficiency of combined-cycle plants.

- *Emerging buyer preferences for differentiated products instead of a commodity product (or for a more standardized product instead of strongly differentiated products)*—Sometimes growing numbers of buyers decide that a standard "one-size-fits-all" product at a budget price is a better bargain than premium-priced brands with lots of snappy features and personalized services. Such a development tends to shift patronage away from sellers of more expensive differentiated products to sellers of cheaper look-alike products and to create a market characterized by strong price competition. Pronounced shifts toward greater product standardization can so dominate a market that rival producers are limited to driving costs out of the business and remaining price competitive. On the other hand, a shift away from standardized products occurs when sellers are able to win a bigger and more loyal buyer following by introducing new features, making style changes, offering options and accessories, and creating image differences with advertising and packaging. Then the driver of change is the contest among rivals to cleverly outdifferentiate one another. Competition evolves differently depending on whether the market forces are increasing or decreasing the emphasis on product differentiation.

- *Regulatory influences and government policy changes*—Regulatory and governmental actions can often force significant changes in industry practices and strategic approaches. Deregulation has been a potent procompetitive force in the airline, banking, natural gas, telecommunications, and electric utility industries. Governmental efforts to reform Medicare and health insurance have become potent driving forces in the health care industry. In international markets, host governments can drive competitive changes by opening up their domestic markets to foreign participation or closing them off to protect domestic companies.

- *Changing societal concerns, attitudes, and lifestyles*—Emerging social issues and changing attitudes and lifestyles can instigate industry change. Growing antismoking sentiment has emerged as the major driver of change in the tobacco industry. Consumer concerns about salt, sugar, chemical additives, saturated fat, cholesterol, and nutritional value have forced food producers to revamp food-processing techniques, redirect R&D efforts into the use of healthier ingredients, and compete in coming up with healthy, good-tasting products. Safety concerns have transformed products with safety features into a competitive asset in the automobile, toy, and outdoor power equipment industries, to mention a few. Increased interest in physical fitness has spawned whole new industries in exercise equipment, mountain biking, outdoor apparel, sports gyms and recreation centers, vitamin and nutrition supplements, and medically supervised diet programs. Social concerns about air and water pollution have forced industries to add expenses for controlling pollution into their cost structures. Shifting societal concerns, attitudes, and lifestyles usually favor those players that respond quicker and more creatively with products targeted to the new trends and conditions.

- *Reductions in uncertainty and business risk*—A young, emerging industry is typically characterized by an unproven cost structure and uncertainty over potential market size, how much time and money will be needed to surmount technological problems, and what distribution channels to emphasize. Emerging industries tend to attract only risk-taking entrepreneurial companies. Over time, however, if the industry's pioneers succeed and uncertainty about the product's viability fades, more conservative firms are usually enticed to enter the market. Often, these later entrants are larger, financially strong firms looking to invest in attractive growth industries. Lower business risks and less industry uncertainty also affect competition in international markets. In the early stages of a company's entry into foreign markets, conservatism prevails and firms limit their downside exposure by using less risky strategies like exporting, licensing, and joint ventures to accomplish entry. Then, as experience accumulates and perceived risk levels decline, companies move more boldly, constructing plants and making acquisitions to build strong competitive positions in each country market and beginning to link the strategies in each country to create a global strategy.

The many different *potential driving forces* explain why it is too simplistic to view industry change only in terms of the growth stages model and why a full understanding of the *causes* underlying the emergence of new competitive conditions is a fundamental part of industry analysis.

The task of driving forces analysis is to separate the major causes of industry change from the minor ones; usually no more than three or four factors qualify as driving forces.

However, while many forces of change may be at work in a given industry, no more than three or four are likely to qualify as *driving* forces in the sense that they will act as *the major determinants* of why and how the industry is changing. Thus, strategic analysts must resist the temptation to label everything they see changing as driving forces; the analytical task is to evaluate the forces of industry and competitive change carefully enough to separate major factors from minor ones.

The Link between Driving Forces and Strategy Sound analysis of an industry's driving forces is a prerequisite to sound strategy making. Without keen awareness of what external factors will produce the biggest potential changes in the company's business over the next one to three years, managers are ill prepared to craft a strategy tightly matched to emerging conditions. Similarly, if managers are uncertain about the implications of each driving force or if their views are incomplete or off-base, it's difficult for them to craft a strategy that is responsive to the driving forces and their consequences for the industry. So driving forces analysis is not something to take lightly; it has practical strategy-making value and is basic to the task of thinking about where the business is headed and how to prepare for the changes.

Managers can use environmental scanning to spot budding trends and clues of change that could develop into new driving forces.

Environmental Scanning Techniques One way to try to detect future driving forces early on is to systematically monitor the environment for new straws in the wind. *Environmental scanning* involves studying and interpreting the sweep of social, political, economic, ecological, and technological events in an effort to spot budding trends and conditions that could become driving forces. Environmental scanning involves time frames well beyond the next one to three years—for example, it could involve judgments about the demand for energy in the year 2010, what kinds of household appliances and computerized electronic controls will be in the "house of the future," how people will communicate over long distances 10 years from now, or what will happen to the income levels and purchasing habits of retired people in the 21st century if average life expectancies continue to increase. Environmental scanning thus attempts to spot first-of-a-kind happenings and new ideas and approaches that are catching on and to extrapolate their implications 5 to 20 years into the future. *The purpose and value of environmental scanning is to raise the consciousness of managers about potential developments that could have an important impact on industry conditions and pose new opportunities or threats.*

Environmental scanning can be accomplished by monitoring and studying current events, constructing scenarios, and employing the Delphi method (a technique for finding consensus among a group of knowledgeable experts). Environmental scanning methods are highly qualitative and subjective. The appeal of environmental scanning, notwithstanding its speculative nature, is that it helps managers lengthen their planning horizon, translate vague inklings of future opportunities or threats into clearer strategic issues (for which they can begin to develop strategic answers), and think strategically about future developments in the surrounding environment.[15] Companies that undertake formal environmental scanning include General Electric, AT&T, Coca-Cola, Ford, General Motors, Du Pont, and Shell Oil.

Question 4: Which Companies Are in the Strongest/Weakest Positions?

The next step in examining the industry's competitive structure is to study the market positions of rival companies. One technique for revealing the competitive positions of industry participants is *strategic group mapping*.[16] This analytical tool is a bridge between looking at the industry as a whole and considering the standing of each firm separately. It is most useful when an industry has so many competitors that it is not practical to examine each one in depth.

Strategic group mapping is a technique for displaying the competitive positions that rival firms occupy in the industry.

Using Strategic Group Maps to Assess the Competitive Positions of Rival Firms A strategic group consists of those rival firms with similar competitive approaches and positions in the market.[17] Companies in the same strategic group can resemble one another in any of several ways: They may have comparable product line breadth, be vertically integrated to much the same degree, offer buyers similar services and technical assistance, use essentially the same product attributes to appeal to similar types of buyers, emphasize the same distribution channels, depend on identical technological approaches, and/or sell in the same price/quality range. An industry contains only one strategic group when all sellers pursue essentially identical strategies and have comparable market positions. At the other extreme, there are as many strategic groups as there are competitors when each rival pursues a distinct competitive approach and occupies a substantially different competitive position in the marketplace.

Strategic group analysis helps pinpoint a firm's closest competitors.

---

[15]For further discussion of the nature and use of environmental scanning, see Roy Amara and Andrew J. Lipinski, *Business Planning for an Uncertain Future: Scenarios and Strategies* (New York: Pergamon Press, 1983); Harold E. Klein and Robert U. Linneman, "Environmental Assessment: An International Study of Corporate Practice," *Journal of Business Strategy* 5, no. 1 (Summer 1984), pp. 55–75; and Arnoldo C. Hax and Nicolas S. Majluf, *The Strategy Concept and Process* (Englewood Cliffs, N.J.: Prentice-Hall, 1991), chapters 5 and 8.

[16]Porter, *Competitive Strategy,* Chapter 7.

[17]Ibid., pp. 129–30.

The procedure for constructing a strategic group map and deciding which firms belong in which strategic group is straightforward:

- Identify the characteristics that differentiate firms in the industry—typical variables are price/quality range (high, medium, low), geographic coverage (local, regional, national, global), degree of vertical integration (none, partial, full), product line breadth (wide, narrow), use of distribution channels (one, some, all), and degree of service offered (no-frills, limited, full service).
- Plot the firms on a two-variable map using pairs of these differentiating characteristics.
- Assign firms that fall in about the same strategy space to the same strategic group.
- Draw circles around each strategic group, making the circles proportional to the size of the group's respective share of total industry sales revenues.

This produces a two-dimensional *strategic group map* such as the one for the retail jewelry industry portrayed in Illustration Capsule 9.

Several guidelines need to be observed in mapping the positions of strategic groups in the industry's overall strategy space.[18] First, the two variables selected as axes for the map should *not* be highly correlated; if they are, the circles on the map will fall along a diagonal and strategy makers will learn nothing more about the relative positions of competitors than they would by considering just one of the variables. For instance, if companies with broad product lines use multiple distribution channels while companies with narrow lines use a single distribution channel, then looking at broad versus narrow product lines reveals just as much about who is positioned where as looking at single versus multiple distribution channels—one of the variables is redundant. Second, the variables chosen as axes for the map should expose big differences in how rivals position themselves to compete. This, of course, means analysts must identify the characteristics that differentiate rival firms and use these differences as variables for the axes and as the basis for deciding which firm belongs in which strategic group. Third, the variables used as axes don't have to be either quantitative or continuous; rather, they can be discrete variables or defined in terms of distinct classes and combinations. Fourth, drawing the sizes of the circles on the map proportional to the combined sales of the firms in each strategic group allows the map to reflect the relative sizes of each strategic group. Fifth, if more than two good competitive variables can be used as axes for the map, several maps can be drawn to give different exposures to the competitive positioning relationships present in the industry's structure. Because there is not necessarily one best map for portraying how competing firms are positioned in the market, it is advisable to experiment with different pairs of competitive variables.

What Can Be Learned from Strategic Group Maps One thing to look for is whether *industry driving forces and competitive pressures favor some strategic groups and hurt others*.[19] Firms in adversely affected strategic groups may try to shift to a more favorably situated group; how hard such a move is depends on whether entry barriers into the target strategic group are high or low. Attempts by rival firms to enter a new strategic group nearly always increase competition. If certain firms are known to be trying to

---

[18]Ibid., pp. 152–54.
[19]Ibid., pp. 130, 132–38, and 154–55.

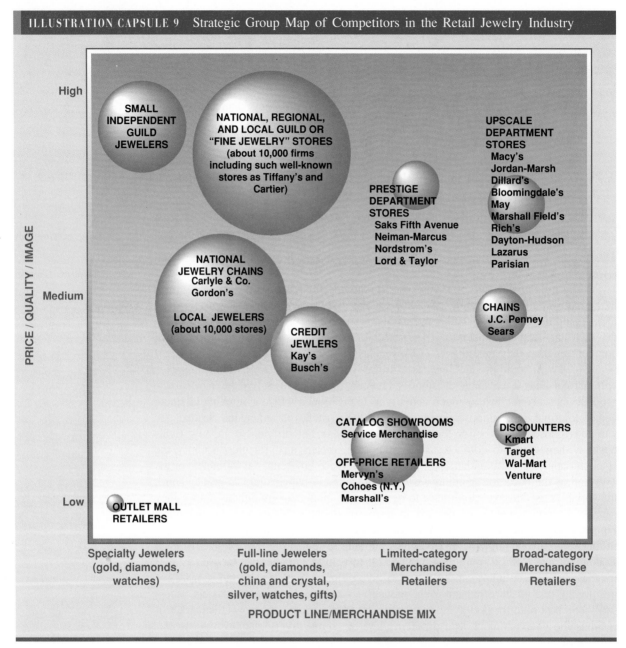

ILLUSTRATION CAPSULE 9   Strategic Group Map of Competitors in the Retail Jewelry Industry

Note: The sizes of the circles are roughly proportional to the market shares of each group of competitors.

change their positions on the map, then attaching arrows to the circles showing the targeted direction helps clarify the picture of competitive jockeying among rivals.

Another consideration is whether *the profit potential of different strategic groups varies due to the competitive strengths and weaknesses in each group's market position*. Differences in profitability can occur because of differing degrees of bargaining leverage with suppliers or customers, differing degrees of exposure to competition from substitute products outside the industry, differing degrees of competitive rivalry within strategic groups, and differing growth rates for the principal buyer segments served by each group. Driving forces and competitive forces do not affect each strategic group evenly.

Generally speaking, *the closer strategic groups are to each other on the map, the* stronger competitive rivalry among member firms tends to be. Although firms in the same strategic group are the closest rivals, the next closest rivals are in the immediately adjacent groups.[20] Often, firms in strategic groups that are far apart on the map hardly compete at all. For instance, Tiffany's and Wal-Mart both sell gold and silver jewelry, but the prices and perceived qualities of their products are much too different to generate any real competition between them. For the same reason, Timex is not a meaningful competitive rival of Rolex, and Subaru is not a close competitor of Lincoln or Mercedes-Benz.

> *Some strategic groups are usually more favorably positioned than other strategic groups.*

Question 5: What Strategic Moves Are Rivals Likely to Make Next?

Unless a company pays attention to what competitors are doing, it ends up flying blind. A company can't expect to outmaneuver its rivals without monitoring their actions, understanding their strategies, and anticipating what moves they are likely to make next. As in sports, scouting the opposition is essential. The strategies rivals are using and the actions they are likely to take next have direct bearing on a company's own best strategic moves— whether it needs to defend against specific actions taken by rivals or whether rivals' moves provide an opening for a new offensive thrust.

> *Successful strategists take great pains in scouting competitors— understanding their strategies, watching their actions, sizing up their strengths and weaknesses, and trying to anticipate what moves they will make next.*

Understanding Competitors' Strategies The best source of information about a competitor's strategy comes from examining what it is doing and what its management is saying about the company's plans (Figure 2.3 indicates what to look for in identifying a company's business strategy). Additional insights can be gotten by considering the rival's geographic market arena, strategic intent, market share objective, competitive position on the industry's strategic group map, willingness to take risks, basic competitive strategy approach, and whether the competitor's recent moves are mostly offensive or defensive.[21] Good sources for such information include the company's annual report and 10-K filings, recent speeches by its managers, the reports of securities analysts, articles in the business media, company press releases, information searches on the Internet, rivals' exhibits at international trade shows, visits to the company's Web site, and talking with a rival's customers, suppliers, and former employees. Many companies have a competitive intelligence unit that gathers information on rivals and makes it available on the company's intranet.

> *It is advantageous to know more about your competitors than they know about you.*

---

[20]Strategic groups act as good reference points for firms' strategies and for predicting future strategies and the evolution of an industry's competitive structure. See Avi Fiegenbaum and Howard Thomas, "Strategic Groups as Reference Groups: Theory, Modeling and Empirical Examination of Industry and Competitive Strategy," *Strategic Management Journal* 16 (1995), pp. 461–76. For a study of how strategic group analysis helps identify the variables that lead to sustainable competitive advantage, see S. Ade Olusoga, Michael P. Mokwa, and Charles H. Noble, "Strategic Groups, Mobility Barriers, and Competitive Advantage," *Journal of Business Research* 33 (1995), pp. 153–64.

[21]For a discussion of legal ways of gathering competitive intelligence on rival companies, see Larry Kahaner, *Competitive Intelligence* (New York: Simon & Schuster, 1996).

Gathering competitive intelligence on rivals can sometimes tread the fine line between honest inquiry and illegal behavior, subterfuge, and unethical conduct, however. For example, calling rivals to get information about prices, the dates of new product introductions, or wage and salary levels is legal, but misrepresenting one's company affiliation is unethical. Pumping rivals' representatives at trade shows is ethical only if one wears an accurate name tag like everyone else. In an effort to learn more about a competitor's strategic plans, Avon in 1991 was able to secure discarded materials about its biggest rival, Mary Kay Cosmetics, by having its personnel search through the garbage dumpsters outside MKC's headquarters.[22] When MKC officials learned of the action and sued, Avon claimed it did nothing illegal (a 1988 Supreme Court case ruled that trash left on public property—in this case, a sidewalk—was anyone's for the taking). Avon even produced a videotape of its removal of the trash at the MKC site. Avon won—but the legality of Avon's action does not mean that what it did was ethical.

Table 3.3 provides an easy-to-apply classification scheme for profiling the objectives and strategies of rival companies. Such profiles, along with a strategic group map, provide a working diagnosis of the strategies and recent moves of rivals and are readily supplemented by whatever additional information is available about each competitor.

Evaluating Who the Industry's Major Players Are Going to Be   It's usually obvious who the *current* major contenders are, but these same firms are not necessarily positioned most strongly for the future. Some may be losing ground or be ill equipped to compete in the future. Smaller companies may be moving into contention and poised for an offensive against larger but vulnerable rivals. Long-standing contenders for market leadership sometimes slide quickly down the industry's ranks; others end up being acquired. Today's industry leaders don't automatically become tomorrow's.

The company that consistently has more and better information about its competitors is better positioned to prevail, other things being equal.

Whether a competitor is favorably or unfavorably positioned to gain market ground depends on why there is potential for it to do better or worse. Usually, how securely a company holds its present market share is a function of its vulnerability to driving forces and competitive pressures, whether it has a competitive advantage or disadvantage, and whether it is the likely target of offensive attack from other industry participants. Pinpointing which rivals are poised to gain market position and which seem destined to lose market share helps a strategist anticipate what kinds of moves they are likely to make next.

Predicting Competitors' Next Moves   This is the hardest yet most useful part of competitor analysis. Good clues about what moves a specific company may make next come from studying its strategic intent, monitoring how well it is faring in the marketplace, and determining how much pressure it is under to improve its financial performance. The likelihood of a company continuing with its present strategy usually depends on how well it is doing and its prospects for continued success with its current strategy. Content rivals are likely to continue their present strategy with only minor fine-tuning. Ailing rivals can be performing so poorly that fresh strategic moves, either offensive or defensive, are virtually certain. Aggressive rivals with ambitious strategic intent are strong candidates for pursuing emerging market opportunities and exploiting weaker rivals.

Since managers generally operate from assumptions about the industry's future and beliefs about their own firm's situation, insights into the strategic thinking of

---

[22]Kahaner, *Competitive Intelligence*, pp. 84–85.

TABLE 3.3   Categorizing the Objectives and Strategies of Competitors

Competitive Scope	Strategic Intent	Market Share Objective	Competitive Position/Situation	Strategic Posture	Competitive Strategy
• Local • Regional • National • Multicountry • Global	• Be the dominant leader • Overtake the present industry leader • Be among the industry leaders (top 5) • Move into the top 10 • Move up a notch or two in the industry rankings • Overtake a particular rival (not necessarily the leader) • Maintain position • Just survive	• Aggressive expansion via both acquisition and internal growth • Expansion via internal growth (boost market share at the expense of rival firms) • Expansion via acquisition • Hold on to present share (by growing at a rate equal to the industry average) • Give up share if necessary to achieve short-term profit objectives (stress profitability, not volume)	• Getting stronger; on the move • Well-entrenched; able to maintain its present position • Stuck in the middle of the pack • Going after a different market position (trying to move from a weaker to a stronger position) • Struggling; losing ground • Retrenching to a position that can be defended	• Mostly offensive • Mostly defensive • A combination of offense and defense • Aggressive risk-taker • Conservative follower	• Striving for low cost leadership • Mostly focusing on a market niche —High end —Low end —Geographic —Buyers with special needs —Other • Pursuing differentiation based on —Quality —Service —Technological superiority —Breadth of product line —Image and reputation —More value for the money —Other attributes

Note: Since a focus strategy can be aimed at any of several market niches and a differentiation strategy can be keyed to any of several attributes, it is best to be explicit about what kind of focus strategy or differentiation strategy a given firm is pursuing. All focusers do not pursue the same market niche, and all differentiators do not pursue the same differentiating attributes.

rival company managers can be gleaned from their public pronouncements about where the industry is headed and what it will take to be successful, what they are saying about their firm's situation, information from the grapevine about what they are doing, and their past actions and leadership styles. Another thing to consider is whether a rival has the flexibility to make major strategic changes or whether it is locked into pursuing its same basic strategy with minor adjustments.

Managers who fail to study competitors closely risk being blindsided by "surprise" actions on the part of rivals.

To succeed in predicting a competitor's next moves, one has to have a good feel for the rival's situation, how its managers think, and what its options are. Doing the necessary detective work can be tedious and time-consuming since the information comes in bits and pieces from many sources. But scouting competitors well enough to anticipate their next moves allows managers to prepare effective countermoves (perhaps even beat a rival to the punch!).

Question 6: What Are the Key Factors for Competitive Success?

An industry's *key success factors* (KSFs) are those things that most affect the ability of industry members to prosper in the marketplace—the particular strategy elements, product attributes, resources, competencies, competitive capabilities, and business outcomes that spell the difference between profit and loss. *Key success factors concern what every industry member must be competent at doing or concentrate on achieving in order to be competitively and financially successful.* KSFs are so important that all firms in the industry must pay them close attention—they are the *prerequisites* for industry success. The answers to three questions help identify an industry's key success factors:

An industry's key success factors concern the product attributes, competencies, competitive capabilities, and market achievements with the greatest direct bearing on company profitability.

- On what basis do customers choose between the competing brands of sellers?
- What must a seller do to be competitively successful—what resources and competitive capabilities does it need?
- What does it take for sellers to achieve a sustainable competitive advantage?

In the beer industry, the KSFs are full utilization of brewing capacity (to keep manufacturing costs low), a strong network of wholesale distributors (to gain access to as many retail outlets as possible), and clever advertising (to induce beer drinkers to buy a particular brand). In apparel manufacturing, the KSFs are appealing designs and color combinations (to create buyer interest) and low-cost manufacturing efficiency (to permit attractive retail pricing and ample profit margins). In tin and aluminum cans, because the cost of shipping empty cans is substantial, one of the keys is having plants located close to end-use customers so that the plant's output can be marketed within economical shipping distances (regional market share is far more crucial than national share). Table 3.4 provides a shopping list of the most common types of key success factors.

Determining the industry's key success factors is a top priority. At the very least, managers need to understand the industry situation well enough to know what is more important to competitive success and what is less important. They need to know what kinds of resources are valuable. Misdiagnosing the industry factors critical to long-term competitive success greatly raises the risk of a misdirected strategy—one that overemphasizes less important competitive targets and under-emphasizes more important competitive capabilities. On the other hand, a company with perceptive understanding of industry KSFs can gain sustainable competitive advantage by training its strategy on industry KSFs and devoting its energies to being better than rivals on one or more of these factors. Indeed, *key success factors represent golden opportunities for competitive advantage*—companies that stand out on a particular KSF enjoy a stronger market position for their efforts. Hence using one or more of the industry's KSFs as *cornerstones* for the company's strategy and trying to gain sustainable competitive advantage by excelling at one particular KSF is a fruitful approach.[23]

Strategic Management Principle

A sound strategy incorporates efforts to be competent on all industry key success factors and to excel on at least one factor.

Key success factors vary from industry to industry and even from time to time within the same industry as driving forces and competitive conditions change. Only rarely does an industry have more than three or four key success factors at any one time. And even among these three or four, one or two usually outrank the others in importance. Managers, therefore, have to resist the temptation to include factors that

---

[23]Some experts dispute the strategy-making value of key success factors. Professor Ghemawat claims that the "whole idea of identifying a success factor and then chasing it seems to have something in common with the ill-considered medieval hunt for the *philosopher's stone*, a substance which would transmute everything it touched into gold." Pankaj Ghemawat, *Commitment: The Dynamic of Strategy* (New York: Free Press, 1991), p.11.

TABLE 3.4 Common Types of Key Success Factors

Technology-Related KSFs

Scientific research expertise (important in such fields as pharmaceuticals, medicine, space exploration, other "high-tech" industries)
Technical capability to make innovative improvements in production processes
Product innovation capability
Expertise in a given technology
Capability to use the Internet to disseminate information, take orders, deliver products or services

Manufacturing-Related KSFs

Low-cost production efficiency (achieve scale economies, capture experience curve effects)
Quality of manufacture (fewer defects, less need for repairs)
High utilization of fixed assets (important in capital intensive/high fixed-cost industries)
Low-cost plant locations
Access to adequate supplies of skilled labor
High labor productivity (important for items with high labor content)
Low-cost product design and engineering (reduces manufacturing costs)
Flexibility to manufacture a range of models and sizes/take care of custom orders

Distribution-Related KSFs

A strong network of wholesale distributors/dealers (or electronic distribution capability via the Internet)
Gaining ample space on retailer shelves
Having company-owned retail outlets
Low distribution costs
Fast delivery

Marketing-Related KSFs

Fast, accurate technical assistance
Courteous customer service
Accurate filling of buyer orders (few back orders or mistakes)
Breadth of product line and product selection
Merchandising skills
Attractive styling/packaging
Customer guarantees and warranties (important in mail-order retailing, big-ticket purchases, new product introductions)
Clever advertising

Skills-Related KSFs

Superior workforce talent (important in professional services like accounting and investment banking)
Quality control know-how
Design expertise (important in fashion and apparel industries and often one of the keys to low-cost manufacture)
Expertise in a particular technology
An ability to develop innovative products and product improvements
An ability to get newly conceived products past the R&D phase and out into the market very quickly

Organizational Capability

Superior information systems (important in airline travel, car rental, credit card, and lodging industries)
Ability to respond quickly to shifting market conditions (streamlined decision making, short lead times to bring new products to market)
Superior ability to employ the Internet and other aspects of electronic commerce to conduct business
More experience and managerial know-how

Other Types of KSFs

Favorable image/reputation with buyers
Overall low cost (not just in manufacturing)
Convenient locations (important in many retailing businesses)
Pleasant, courteous employees in all customer contact positions
Access to financial capital (important in newly emerging industries with high degrees of business risk and in capital-intensive industries)
Patent protection

have only minor importance on their list of key success factors—the purpose of identifying KSFs is to make judgments about what things are more important and what things are less important. To compile a list of every factor that matters even a little bit defeats the purpose of concentrating management attention on the truly critical factors.

Question 7: Is the Industry Attractive and What Are Its Prospects for Above-Average Profitability?

The final step of industry and competitive analysis is to use the answers to the previous six questions to draw conclusions about the relative attractiveness or unattractiveness of the industry, both near term and long term. Important factors for company managers to consider include:

- The industry's growth potential.
- Whether competition currently permits adequate profitability and whether competitive forces will become stronger or weaker.
- Whether industry profitability will be favorably or unfavorably impacted by the prevailing driving forces.
- The company's competitive position in the industry and whether its position is likely to grow stronger or weaker (being a well-entrenched leader or strongly positioned contender in an otherwise lackluster industry can still produce good profitability; on the other hand, having to fight an uphill battle against much stronger rivals can make an otherwise attractive industry unattractive).
- The company's potential to capitalize on the vulnerabilities of weaker rivals (perhaps converting an unattractive *industry* situation into a potentially rewarding *company* opportunity).
- Whether the company is insulated from, or able to defend against, the factors that make the industry unattractive.
- How well the company's competitive capabilities match the industry's key success factors.
- The degrees of risk and uncertainty in the industry's future.
- The severity of problems/issues confronting the industry as a whole.
- Whether continued participation in this industry adds to the firm's ability to be successful in other industries in which it may have interests.

As a general proposition, *if an industry's overall profit prospects are above average, the industry can be considered attractive.* If its profit prospects are below average, it is unattractive. However, it is a mistake to think of industries as being

A company that is uniquely well situated in an otherwise unattractive industry can, under certain circumstances, still earn unusually good profits.

attractive or unattractive *to all industry participants and all potential entrants.* Attractiveness is relative, not absolute, and conclusions one way or the other are in the eye of the beholder—industry attractiveness *always* has to be appraised from the standpoint of a particular company. Industries unattractive to outsiders may be attractive to insiders. Industry environments unattractive to weak competitors may be attractive to strong competitors. Companies on the outside may look at an industry's environment and conclude that it is an unattractive business for them to get into; they may see more profitable opportunities elsewhere, given their particular resources and competencies. But a favorably positioned company already in the industry may survey the very same business environment and conclude that the industry is attractive because it has the resources and competitive capabilities to take sales and market share away from weaker rivals, build a strong leadership position, and earn good profits.

An assessment that the industry is fundamentally attractive suggests that current industry participants employ strategies that strengthen their long-term competitive positions in the business, expanding sales efforts and investing in additional facilities and capabilities as needed. If the industry and competitive situation is relatively unattractive, more successful industry participants may choose to invest cautiously, look for ways to protect their long-term competitiveness and profitability, and perhaps acquire smaller firms if the price is right; over the longer term, strong companies may consider diversification into more attractive businesses. Weak companies in unattractive industries may consider merging with a rival to bolster market share and profitability or, alternatively, begin looking outside the industry for attractive diversification opportunities.

ACTUALLY DOING AN INDUSTRY AND COMPETITIVE ANALYSIS

Table 3.5 provides a *format* for presenting the pertinent findings and conclusions of industry and competitive analysis. It embraces all seven questions discussed above and leads would-be analysts to do the strategic thinking and evaluation needed to draw conclusions about the state of the industry and competitive environment.

Two things should be kept in mind in doing industry and competitive analysis. One, the task of analyzing a company's external situation is not a mechanical, formula-like exercise in which facts and data are plugged in and definitive conclusions come pouring out. Strategic analysis always leaves room for differences of opinion about how all the factors add up and what future industry and competitive conditions will be like. There can be several appealing scenarios about how an industry will evolve, how attractive it will be, and how good the profit outlook is. However, while no methodology can guarantee a conclusive diagnosis, it doesn't make sense to shortcut strategic analysis and rely on opinion and casual observation. Managers become better strategists when they know what analytical questions to pose, have the skills to read clues about which way the winds of industry and competitive change are blowing, and can use situation analysis techniques to find answers and identify strategic issues. This is why we concentrated on suggesting the right questions to ask, explaining concepts and analytical approaches, and indicating the kinds of things to look for.

Two, sweeping industry and competitive analyses need to be done every one to three years; in the interim, managers are obliged to continually update and reexamine their thinking as events unfold. There's no substitute for being a good student of industry and competitive conditions and staying on the cutting edge of what's happening in the industry. Anything else leaves a manager unprepared to initiate shrewd and timely strategic adjustments.

Thinking strategically about a company's external situation involves probing for answers to the following seven questions:

KEY POINTS

1. *What are the industry's dominant economic traits?* Industries differ significantly on such factors as market size and growth rate, the geographic scope of competitive

TABLE 3.5   Sample Form for an Industry and Competitive Analysis Summary

1. **Dominant Economic Characteristics of the Industry Environment** (market size and growth rate, geographic scope, number and sizes of buyers and sellers, pace of technological change and innovation, scale economies, experience curve effects, capital requirements, and so on)

2. **Competition Analysis**
   - Rivalry among competing sellers (a strong, moderate, or weak force/weapons of competition)

   - Threat of potential entry (a strong, moderate, or weak force/assessment of entry barriers)

   - Competition from substitutes (a strong, moderate, or weak force/why)

   - Power of suppliers (a strong, moderate, or weak force/why)

   - Power of customers (a strong, moderate, or weak force/why)

3. **Driving Forces**

4. **Competitive Position of Major Companies/Strategic Groups**
   - Favorably positioned/why

   - Unfavorably positioned/why

5. **Competitor Analysis**
   - Strategic approaches/predicted moves of key competitors

   - Whom to watch and why

6. **Key Success Factors**

7. **Industry Prospects and Overall Attractiveness**
   - Factors making the industry attractive

   - Factors making the industry unattractive

   - Special industry issues/problems

   - Profit outlook (favorable/unfavorable)

rivalry, the number and relative sizes of both buyers and sellers, ease of entry and exit, whether sellers are vertically integrated, how fast basic technology is changing, the extent of scale economies and experience curve effects, whether the products of rival sellers are standardized or differentiated, and overall profitability. An industry's economic characteristics are important because of the implications they have for crafting strategy.

2. *What is competition like and how strong are each of the five competitive forces?* The strength of competition is a composite of five forces: the rivalry among competing sellers, the presence of attractive substitutes, the potential for new entry, the leverage major suppliers have, and the bargaining power of customers. The task of competition analysis is to understand the competitive pressures associated with each force, determine whether these pressures add up to a strong or weak competitive force in the marketplace, and then think strategically about what sort of competitive strategy, given the "rules" of competition in the industry, the company will need to employ to (a) insulate the firm as much as possible from the five competitive forces, (b) influence the industry's competitive rules in the company's favor, and (c) gain a competitive edge.

3. *What are the drivers of change in the industry and what impact will they have?* Industry and competitive conditions change because forces are in motion that create incentives or pressures for change. The most common driving forces are changes in the long-term industry growth rate, changes in buyer composition, product innovation, entry or exit of major firms, globalization, changes in cost and efficiency, changing buyer preferences for standardized versus differentiated products or services, regulatory influences and government policy changes, changing societal and lifestyle factors, and reductions in uncertainty and business risk. Sound analysis of driving forces and their implications for the industry is a prerequisite to sound strategy making.

4. *Which companies are in the strongest/weakest competitive positions?* Strategic group mapping is a valuable, if not necessary, tool for understanding the similarities, differences, strengths, and weaknesses inherent in the market positions of rival companies. Rivals in the same or nearby strategic group(s) are close competitors whereas companies in distant strategic groups usually pose little or no immediate threat.

5. *What strategic moves are rivals likely to make next?* This analytical step involves identifying competitors' strategies, deciding which rivals are likely to be strong contenders and which weak contenders, evaluating their competitive options, and predicting what moves they are likely to make next. Scouting competitors well enough to anticipate their actions helps prepare effective countermoves (perhaps even beat a rival to the punch) and allows managers to take rivals' probable actions into account in designing their own company's best course of action. Managers who fail to study competitors closely risk being blindsided by "surprise" actions on the part of rivals. A company can't expect to outmaneuver its rivals without monitoring their actions and anticipating what moves they may make next.

6. *What key factors will determine competitive success or failure?* Key success factors are the particular strategy elements, product attributes, competitive capabilities, and business outcomes that spell the difference between profit and loss and, ultimately, between competitive success or failure. KSFs point to the things all firms in an industry must be competent at doing or must concentrate on achieving in order to be competitively and financially successful—they are the *prerequisites* for good performance in the industry. Frequently, a company can gain sustainable competitive

advantage by training its strategy on industry KSFs and devoting its energies to being distinctively better than rivals at succeeding on these factors. Companies that only dimly perceive what factors are truly crucial to long-term competitive success are less likely to have winning strategies.

7. *Is the industry attractive and what are its prospects for above-average profitability?* The answer to this question is a major driver of company strategy. An assessment that the industry and competitive environment is fundamentally attractive typically suggests employing a strategy calculated to build a stronger competitive position in the business, expanding sales efforts, and investing in additional facilities and capabilities as needed. If the industry is relatively unattractive, outsiders considering entry may decide against it and look elsewhere for opportunities, weak companies in the industry may merge with or be acquired by a rival, and strong companies may restrict further investments and employ cost-reduction strategies and/or product innovation strategies to boost long-term competitiveness and protect their profitability. On occasion, an industry that is unattractive overall is still very attractive to a favorably situated company with the skills and resources to take business away from weaker rivals.

Good industry and competitive analysis is a prerequisite to good strategy making. A competently done industry and competitive analysis provides the understanding of a company's macroenvironment needed for shrewdly matching strategy to the company's external situation.

SUGGESTED READINGS

D'Aveni, Richard A. *Hypercompetition*. New York: Free Press, 1994, chaps. 5 and 6.

Ghemawat, Pankaj. "Building Strategy on the Experience Curve." *Harvard Business Review* 64, no. 2 (March–April 1985), pp. 143–49.

Kahaner, Larry. "What You Can Learn from Your Competitors' Mission Statements." *Competitive Intelligence Review* 6 no. 4 (Winter 1995), pp. 35–40.

Langley, Ann. "Between 'Paralysis by Analysis' and 'Extinction by Instinct.'" *Sloan Management Review* (Spring 1995), pp. 63–75.

Linneman, Robert E., and Harold E. Klein. "Using Scenarios in Strategic Decision Making." *Business Horizons* 28, no. 1 (January–February 1985), pp. 64–74.

Porter, Michael E. "How Competitive Forces Shape Strategy." *Harvard Business Review* 57, no. 2 (March–April 1979), pp. 137–45.

_____. *Competitive Strategy: Techniques for Analyzing Industries and Competitors*. New York: Free Press, 1980, chap. 1.

_____. *Competitive Advantage*. New York: Free Press, 1985, chap. 2.

Yip, George S. *Total Global Strategy: Managing for Worldwide Competitive Advantage*. Englewood Cliffs, N.J.: Prentice-Hall, 1992, chap. 10.

Zahra, Shaker A., and Sherry S. Chaples. "Blind Spots in Competitive Analysis." *Academy of Management Executive* 7, no. 2 (May 1993), pp. 7–28.

EVALUATING COMPANY RESOURCES AND COMPETITIVE CAPABILITIES

4

I n the previous chapter we described how to use the tools of industry and competitive analysis to assess a company's external situation. In this chapter we discuss the techniques of evaluating a company's resource capabilities, relative cost position, and competitive strength versus rivals. Company situation analysis prepares the groundwork for matching the company's strategy *both* to its external market circumstances and to its internal resources and competitive capabilities. The spotlight of company situation analysis is trained on five questions:

1. How well is the company's present strategy working?
2. What are the company's resource strengths and weaknesses and its external opportunities and threats?
3. Are the company's prices and costs competitive?
4. How strong is the company's competitive position relative to its rivals?
5. What strategic issues does the company face?

To explore these questions, four new analytical techniques will be introduced: SWOT analysis, value chain analysis, strategic cost analysis, and competitive strength assessment. These techniques are basic strategic management tools because they expose the company's resource strengths and deficiencies, its best market opportunities, the outside threats to its future profitability, and its competitive standing relative to rivals. Insightful company situation analysis is a precondition for identifying the strategic issues that management needs to address and for tailoring strategy to company resources and competitive capabilities as well as to industry and competitive conditions.

Organizations succeed in a competitive marketplace over the long run because they can do certain things their customers value better than can their competitors.

Robert Hayes, Gary Pisano, and David Upton

The greatest mistake managers make when evaluating their resources is failing to assess them relative to competitors'.

David J. Collis and Cynthia A. Montgomery

Only firms who are able to continually build new strategic assets faster and cheaper than their competitors will earn superior returns over the long term.

C. C. Markides and P. J. Williamson

QUESTION 1: HOW WELL IS THE PRESENT STRATEGY WORKING?

In evaluating how well a company's present strategy is working, a manager has to start with what the strategy is (see Figure 2.3 in Chapter 2 to refresh your recollection of the key components of business strategy). The first thing to pin down is the company's competitive approach—whether it is (1) striving to be a low-cost leader or stressing ways to differentiate its product offering and (2) concentrating its efforts on serving a broad spectrum of customers or a narrow market niche. Another strategy-defining consideration is the firm's competitive scope within the industry—how many stages of the industry's production-distribution chain it operates in (one, several, or all), what its geographic market coverage is, and the size and makeup of its customer base. The company's functional strategies in production, marketing, finance, human resources, information technology, new product innovation, and so on further characterize company strategy. In addition, the company may have initiated some recent strategic moves (for instance, a price cut, newly designed styles and models, stepped-up advertising, entry into a new geographic area, or merger with a competitor) that are integral to its strategy and that aim at securing an improved competitive position and, optimally, a competitive advantage. The strategy being pursued can be further nailed down by probing the logic behind each competitive move and functional approach.

While there's merit in evaluating the strategy from a qualitative standpoint (its completeness, internal consistency, rationale, and suitability to the situation), the best quantitative evidence of how well a company's strategy is working comes from studying the company's recent strategic and financial performance and seeing what story the numbers tell about the results the strategy is producing. The two best empirical indicators of whether a company's strategy is working well are (1) whether the company is achieving its stated financial and strategic objectives and (2) whether it is an above-average industry performer. Persistent shortfalls in meeting company performance targets and weak performance relative to rivals are reliable warning signs that the company suffers from either a malfunctioning strategy or less-than-competent strategy execution (or both). Sometimes company objectives are not explicit enough (especially to company outsiders) to benchmark actual performance against, but it is nearly always feasible to evaluate the performance of a company's strategy by looking at:

The stronger a company's financial performance and market position, the more likely it has a well-conceived, well-executed strategy.

- Whether the firm's market share ranking in the industry is rising, stable, or declining.
- Whether the firm's profit margins are increasing or decreasing and how large they are relative to rival firms' margins.
- Trends in the firm's net profits, return on investment, and economic value added and how these compare to the same trends in profitability for other companies in the industry.
- Whether the company's overall financial strength and credit rating is improving or on the decline.
- Trends in the company's stock price and whether the company's strategy is resulting in satisfactory gains in shareholder value (relative to the MVA gains of other companies in the industry).
- Whether the firm's sales are growing faster or slower than the market as a whole.

- The firm's image and reputation with its customers.
- Whether the company is regarded as a leader in technology, product innovation, product quality, customer service, or other relevant factor on which buyers base their choice of brands.

The stronger a company's current overall performance, the less likely the need for radical changes in strategy. The weaker a company's financial performance and market standing, the more its current strategy must be questioned. Weak performance is almost always a sign of weak strategy or weak execution or both.

QUESTION 2: WHAT ARE THE COMPANY'S RESOURCE STRENGTHS AND WEAKNESSES AND ITS EXTERNAL OPPORTUNITIES AND THREATS?

Sizing up a firm's resource strengths and weaknesses and its external opportunities and threats, commonly known as *SWOT analysis*, provides a good overview of whether a firm's business position is fundamentally healthy or unhealthy. SWOT analysis is grounded in the basic principle that *strategy-making efforts must aim at producing a good fit between a company's resource capability and its external situation*. A clear view of a company's resource capabilities and deficiencies, its market opportunities, and the external threats to the company's future well-being is essential. Otherwise, the task of conceiving a strategy becomes a chancy proposition indeed.

Identifying Company Strengths and Resource Capabilities

A *strength* is something a company is good at doing or a characteristic that gives it enhanced competitiveness. A strength can take any of several forms:

- *A skill or important expertise*—low-cost manufacturing know-how, technological know-how, a proven track record in defect-free manufacture, expertise in providing consistently good customer service, skills in developing innovative products, excellent mass merchandising skills, or unique advertising and promotional know-how.
- *Valuable physical assets*—state-of-the-art plants and equipment, attractive real estate locations, worldwide distribution facilities, natural resource deposits, or cash on hand.
- *Valuable human assets*—an experienced and capable workforce, talented employees in key areas, motivated employees, managerial know-how, or the collective learning and know-how embedded in the organization and built up over time.
- *Valuable organizational assets*—proven quality control systems, proprietary technology, key patents, mineral rights, a base of loyal customers, a strong balance sheet and credit rating, a company intranet for accessing and exchanging information both internally and with suppliers and key customers, computer-assisted design and manufacturing systems, systems for conducting business on the World Wide Web, or e-mail addresses for many or most of the company's customers.
- *Valuable intangible assets*—brand-name image, company reputation, buyer goodwill, a high degree of employee loyalty, or a positive work climate and organization culture.

- *Competitive capabilities*—short development times in bringing new products to market, build-to-order manufacturing capability, a strong dealer network, strong partnerships with key suppliers, an R&D organization with the ability to keep the company's pipeline full of innovative new products, organizational agility in responding to shifting market conditions and emerging opportunities, or state-of-the-art systems for doing business via the Internet.

- *An achievement or attribute that puts the company in a position of market advantage*—low overall costs, market share leadership, having a better product, wider product selection, stronger name recognition, or better customer service.

- *Alliances or cooperative ventures*—partnerships with others having expertise or capabilities that enhance the company's own competitiveness.

Company strengths thus have diverse origins. Sometimes they relate to fairly specific skills and expertise (like know-how in researching consumer tastes and buying habits or training customer contact employees to be cordial and helpful) and sometimes they flow from different resources teaming together to create a competitive capability (like continuous product innovation—which tends to result from a combination of knowledge of consumer needs, technological know-how, R&D, product design and engineering, cost-effective manufacturing, and market testing). The regularity with

Basic Concept

A company is positioned to succeed if it has a good complement of resources at its command.

which employees from different parts of the organization pool their knowledge and expertise, their skills in exploiting and building upon the organization's physical and intangible assets, and the effectiveness with which they collaborate can create competitive capabilities not otherwise achievable by a single department or organizational unit.

Taken together, a company's strengths—its skills and expertise, its collection of assets, its competitive capabilities, and its market achievements—determine the complement of *resources* with which it competes. These resources, in conjunction with industry and competitive conditions, are big drivers in how well the company will be able to perform in a dynamic competitive marketplace.[1]

Identifying Company Weaknesses and Resource Deficiencies

A *weakness* is something a company lacks or does poorly (in comparison to others) or a condition that puts it at a disadvantage. A company's internal weaknesses can relate to (a) deficiencies in competitively important skills or expertise, (b) a lack of competitively important physical, human, organizational, or intangible assets, or (c) missing or weak competitive capabilities in key areas. *Internal weaknesses are thus shortcomings in a company's complement of resources.* A weakness may or may not make a company competitively vulnerable, depending on how much the weakness matters in the market-

---

[1] In the past decade, there's been considerable research into the role a company's resources and competitive capabilities play in crafting strategy and in determining company profitability. The findings and conclusions have coalesced into what is called the resource-based view of the firm. Among the most insightful articles are Birger Wernerfelt, "A Resource-Based View of the Firm," *Strategic Management Journal*, September–October 1984, pp. 171–80; Jay Barney, "Firm Resources and Sustained Competitive Advantage," *Journal of Management*, 17, no. 1, 1991, pp. 99–120; Margaret A. Peteraf, "The Cornerstones of Competitive Advantage: A Resource-Based View," *Strategic Management Journal*, March 1993, pp. 179–91; Birger Wernerfelt, "The Resource-Based View of the Firm: Ten Years After," *Strategic Management Journal*, 16 (1995), pp. 171–74 and Jay B. Barney, "Looking Inside for Competitive Advantage," *Academy of Management Executive* 9, no. 4 (November 1995), pp. 49–61.

TABLE 4.1   SWOT Analysis—What to Look for in Sizing Up a Company's Strengths, Weaknesses, Opportunities, and Threats

Potential Resource Strengths and Competitive Capabilities

- A powerful strategy supported by good skills and expertise in key areas
- A strong financial condition; ample financial resources to grow the business
- Strong brand-name image/company reputation
- A widely recognized market leader and an attractive customer base
- Ability to take advantage of economies of scale and/or learning and experience curve effects
- Proprietary technology/superior technological skills/important patents
- Cost advantages
- Strong advertising and promotion
- Product innovation skills
- Proven skills in improving production processes
- A reputation for good customer service
- Better product quality relative to rivals
- Wide geographic coverage and distribution capability
- Alliances/joint ventures with other firms

Potential Resource Weaknesses and Competitive Deficiencies

- No clear strategic direction
- Obsolete facilities
- A weak balance sheet; burdened with too much debt
- Higher overall unit costs relative to key competitors
- Missing some key skills or competencies/lack of management depth
- Subpar profitability because . . .
- Plagued with internal operating problems
- Falling behind in R&D
- Too narrow a product line relative to rivals
- Weak brand image or reputation
- Weaker dealer or distribution network than key rivals
- Subpar marketing skills relative to rivals
- Short on financial resources to fund promising strategic initiatives
- Lots of underutilized plant capacity
- Behind on product quality

Potential Company Opportunities

- Serving additional customer groups or expanding into new geographic markets or product segments
- Expanding the company's product line to meet a broader range of customer needs
- Transferring company skills or technological know-how to new products or businesses
- Integrating forward or backward
- Falling trade barriers in attractive foreign markets
- Openings to take market share away from rival firms
- Ability to grow rapidly because of strong increases in market demand
- Acquisition of rival firms
- Alliances or joint ventures that expand the firm's market coverage and competitive capability
- Openings to exploit emerging new technologies
- Market openings to extend the company's brand name or reputation to new geographic areas

Potential External Threats to a Company's Well-Being

- Likely entry of potent new competitors
- Loss of sales to substitute products
- Slowdowns in market growth
- Adverse shifts in foreign exchange rates and trade policies of foreign governments
- Costly new regulatory requirements
- Vulnerability to recession and business cycle
- Growing bargaining power of customers or suppliers
- A shift in buyer needs and tastes away from the industry's product
- Adverse demographic changes
- Vulnerability to industry driving forces

place and whether it can be overcome by the resources and strengths in the company's possession.

Table 4.1 indicates the kinds of factors to be considered in determining a company's resource strengths and weaknesses. Sizing up a company's resource capabilities and deficiencies is akin to constructing *a strategic balance sheet* where resource strengths represent *competitive assets* and resource weaknesses represent *competitive liabilities*. Obviously, the ideal condition is for the company's strengths/competitive assets to outweigh its weaknesses/competitive liabilities by an ample margin—50-50 balance is definitely not the desired condition!

Basic Concept

A company's resource strengths represent competitive assets; its resource weaknesses represent competitive liabilities.

Once managers identify a company's resource strengths and weaknesses, the two compilations need to be carefully evaluated for their competitive and strategy-making implications. Some strengths are more *competitively important* than others because they matter more in forming a powerful strategy, in contributing to a strong market position, and in determining profitability. Likewise, some weaknesses can prove fatal if not remedied, while others are inconsequential, easily corrected, or offset by company strengths. A company's resource weaknesses suggest a need to review its resource base: What existing resource deficiencies need to be remedied? Does the company have important resource gaps that need to be filled? What needs to be done to augment the company's future resource base?

Identifying Company Competencies and Capabilities

Core Competencies: A Valuable Company Resource   One of the most valuable resources a company has is the ability to perform a competitively relevant activity very well. A competitively important internal activity that a company performs better than other competitively important internal activities is termed a *core competence.* What distinguishes a *core* competence from a competence is that a *core* competence is *central* to a company's competitiveness and profitability rather than peripheral. A core competence can relate to demonstrated expertise in performing an activity, to a company's scope and depth of technological know-how, or to a *combination* of specific skills that result in a competitively valuable capability. Frequently, a core competence is the product of effective collaboration among different parts of the organization, of individual resources teaming together. Typically, *core competencies reside in a company's people, not in its assets on the balance sheet.* They tend to be grounded in skills, knowledge, and capabilities.

Basic Concept

A core competence is something a company does well relative to other internal activities; a distinctive competence is something a company does well relative to competitors.

In practice, companies exhibit many different types of core competencies: skills in manufacturing a high-quality product, know-how in creating and operating a system for filling customer orders accurately and swiftly, fast development of new products, the capability to provide good after-sale service, skills in selecting good retail locations, innovativeness in developing popular product features, skills in merchandising and product display, expertise in an important technology, a well-conceived methodology for researching customer needs and tastes and spotting new market trends, skills in working with customers on new applications and uses of the product, and expertise in integrating multiple technologies to create whole families of new products.

Plainly, *a core competence gives a company competitive capability* and thus qualifies as a genuine company strength and resource. A company may have more than one core competence, but rare is the company that can legitimately claim more than several.

Strategic Management Principle

A distinctive competence empowers a company to build competitive advantage.

Distinctive Competencies: A Competitively Superior Company Resource
Whether a company's core competence represents a *distinctive* competence depends on how good the competence is relative to what competitors are capable of—is it a competitively superior competence or just an internal company competence? *A distinctive competence is a competitively important activity that a company performs well in comparison to its competitors.*[2] Most every com-

---

[2]For a fuller discussion of the core competence concept, see C. K. Prahalad and Gary Hamel, "The Core Competence of the Corporation," *Harvard Business Review* 68, no. 3 (May–June 1990), pp. 79–93.

pany does one competitively important activity *enough better than other activities* that it can claim its best-performed activity as a core competence. But an internal assessment of what a company does best doesn't translate into a distinctive competence unless the company performs that activity in a *competitively superior* fashion. For instance, most all retailers believe they have core competencies in product selection and in-store merchandising, but many retailers who build strategies on these competencies run into trouble because they encounter rivals whose competencies in these areas are better. Consequently, *a core competence becomes a basis for competitive advantage only when it is a distinctive competence.*

Sharp Corporation's distinctive competence in flat-panel display technology has enabled it to dominate the worldwide market for liquid-crystal-displays (LCDs). The distinctive competencies of Toyota, Honda, and Nissan in low-cost, high-quality manufacturing and in short design-to-market cycles for new models have proven to be considerable competitive advantages in the global market for motor vehicles. Intel's distinctive competence in rapidly developing new generations of ever more powerful semiconductor chips for personal computers has given the company a dominating position in the personal computer industry. Motorola's distinctive competence in virtually defect-free manufacture (six-sigma quality—an error rate of about one per million) has contributed significantly to the company's world leadership in cellular telephone equipment. Rubbermaid's distinctive competence in developing innovative rubber and plastics products for household and commercial use has made it the clear leader in its industry.

The importance of a distinctive competence to strategy making rests with (1) the competitively valuable capability it gives a company, (2) its potential for being a cornerstone of strategy, and (3) the competitive edge it can potentially produce in the marketplace. It is always easier to build competitive advantage when a firm has a distinctive competence in performing activities important to market success, when rival companies do not have offsetting competencies, and when it is costly and time-consuming for rivals to imitate the competence. A distinctive competence is thus an especially valuable competitive asset, with potential to be the mainspring of a company's success—unless it is trumped by more powerful resources of rivals.

Determining the Competitive Value of a Company Resource No two companies are alike in their resources. They don't have the same skill sets, assets (physical, human, organizational, and intangible), competitive capabilities, and market achievements—a condition that results in different companies having different resource strengths and weaknesses. *Differences in company resources are an important reason why some companies are more profitable and more competitively successful than others.* A company's success is more certain when it has appropriate and ample resources with which to compete, and especially when it has a valuable strength, asset, capability, or achievement with the potential to produce competitive advantage.

For a particular company resource—whether it be a distinctive competence, an asset (physical, human, organizational, or intangible), an achievement, or a competitive capability—to qualify as the basis for sustainable competitive advantage, it must pass four tests of competitive value:[3]

---

[3]See David J. Collis and Cynthia A. Montgomery, "Competing on Resources: Strategy in the 1990s," *Harvard Business Review* 73, no. 4 (July–August 1995), pp. 120–23.

1. *Is the resource hard to copy?* The more difficult and more expensive it is to imitate a resource, the greater its potential competitive value. Hard-to-copy resources limit competition, making any profit stream they are able to generate more sustainable. Resources can be difficult to copy because of their uniqueness (a fantastic real estate location, patent protection), because they must be built over time in ways that are difficult to accelerate (a brand name, mastery of a technology), and because they carry big capital requirements (a new cost-effective plant to manufacture semiconductor chips can cost $1 to $2 billion).

2. *How long does the resource last?* The longer a resource lasts, the greater its value. Some resources lose their value quickly because of the rapid speeds with which technologies or industry conditions are moving. The value of FedEx's resources to provide overnight package delivery is rapidly being undercut by fax machines and electronic mail. The value of the programming know-how underlying Netscape's software for browsing the Internet is a rapidly depreciating asset because of the lightning speed with which Internet technology is advancing.

3. *Is the resource really competitively superior?* Companies have to guard against pridefully believing that their core competences are distinctive competences or that their brand name is more powerful than those of rivals. Who can really say whether Coca-Cola's consumer marketing skills are better than Pepsi-Cola's or whether Mercedes-Benz's brand name is more powerful than BMW's or Lexus's?

4. *Can the resource be trumped by the different resources/capabilities of rivals?* Many commercial airlines (American Airlines, Delta Airlines, United Airlines, Singapore Airlines) have succeeded because of their resources and capabilities in offering safe, convenient, reliable air transportation services and in providing an array of amenities to passengers. However, Southwest Airlines has been more consistently profitable by building the capabilities to provide safe, reliable, fewer frills services at radically lower fares. Intel's and Microsoft's resources have trumped those of IBM in personal computers—IBM's long-standing industry experience and prestigious brand name has faded as a dominating factor in choosing what PC to buy; whether a PC has the "Intel inside" sticker and the ability to run the latest Windows programs have become bigger buying considerations than the brand name on the PC.

The vast majority of companies are not well endowed with competitively valuable resources, much less with competitively superior resources capable of passing the above four tests with flying colors. Most businesses have a mixed bag of strengths/assets/competencies/capabilities—one or two quite valuable, some good, many satisfactory to mediocre. Only a few companies, usually industry leaders or future leaders, possess a superior resource of great competitive value. Furthermore, nearly all companies have competitive liabilities: internal weaknesses, a lack of assets, missing expertise or capabilities, or resource deficiencies.

Strategic Management Principle

Successful strategists seek to capitalize on what a company does best—its expertise, resource strengths, and strongest competitive capabilities.

Even if a company doesn't possess a competitively superior resource, the potential for competitive advantage is not lost. *Sometimes a company derives significant competitive vitality, even competitive advantage, from a collection of good to adequate resources that, in combination, have competitive power.* Toshiba's laptop computers are the market share leader—an indicator that Toshiba is good at something. Yet, Toshiba's laptops are not demonstrably faster than rivals' laptops, nor do they have superior performance features than rival brands (bigger screens, more memory, longer battery power, a better pointing device, and so on), nor does Toshiba provide clearly superior technical support services. And Toshiba laptops are definitely not cheaper, model for model, than comparable brands. But while Toshiba laptops do not consistently rank first in performance ratings or have low-price appeal, Toshiba's competitive superiority springs from a *combination* of "good" resource strengths and capabilities—its strategic partnerships with suppliers of laptop components, its efficient assembly capability, its design expertise, its skills in choosing quality components, its creation of a wide selection of models, the attractive mix of built-in performance features found in each model when balanced against price, the much-better-than-average reliability of its laptops (based on buyer ratings), and its very good technical support services (based on buyer ratings). The verdict from the marketplace is that Toshiba laptops are better, *all things considered*, than rival brands.

From a strategy-making perspective, a company's resource strengths are significant because they can form the cornerstones of strategy and the basis for creating competitive advantage. If a company doesn't have ample resources and competitive capabilities around which to craft an attractive strategy, managers need to take decisive remedial action to upgrade existing organizational resources and capabilities and add others. At the same time, managers have to look toward correcting competitive weaknesses that make the company vulnerable, hold down profitability, or disqualify it from pursuing an attractive opportunity. The strategy-making principle here is simple: *A company's strategy should be tailored to fit its resource capabilities—taking both strengths and weaknesses into account.* It is foolhardy to pursue a strategic plan that can be undermined by company weaknesses or that cannot be competently executed. As a rule, managers should build their strategies around exploiting and leveraging company capabilities—*its most valuable resources*—and avoid strategies that place heavy demands on areas where the company is weakest or has unproven ability. Companies fortunate enough to have a distinctive competence or other competitively superior resource must be wise in realizing that its value will be eroded by time and competition.[4] So attention to building a strong resource base for the future and to maintaining the competitive superiority of an existing distinctive competence are ever-present requirements.

Selecting the Competencies and Capabilities to Concentrate On   Enterprises succeed over time because they can do certain things that their customers value better than their rivals. The essence of astute strategy making is selecting the competencies and capabilities to concentrate on and to underpin the strategy. Sometimes the company already has competitively valuable competencies and capabilities in place and sometimes it has to be proactive in developing and building new competencies and capabilities to complement and strengthen its existing resource base. Sometimes the desired competencies and capabilities need to be developed internally, and sometimes it is best to outsource them by working with key suppliers and forming strategic alliances.

Identifying a Company's Market Opportunities

Market opportunity is a big factor in shaping a company's strategy. Indeed, managers can't properly tailor strategy to the company's situation without first identifying each company opportunity, appraising the growth and profit potential each one holds, and

---

[4]Collis and Montgomery, "Competing on Resources: Strategy in the 1990s," p. 124.

ILLUSTRATION CAPSULE 10   TCI's Retreat to a Vision and Strategy in Line with Its Resources and Market Opportunities

In early 1997, Tele-Communications Inc., the biggest cable TV provider in the United States with 14 million subscribers, announced that its much heralded vision of transforming itself into an information superhighway and multimedia powerhouse providing cable television, telephone, Internet access, and an array of futuristic data and telecommunications services to all customers in its cable franchise territories was too sweeping, overhyped, and infeasible for the company to pursue profitably within the announced time frame. John Malone, the company's CEO and widely regarded as one of the most astute and influential visionaries of how new information superhighway technologies could transform the world of media and communications, said:

> We were just chasing too many rabbits at the same time. The company got overly ambitious about the things it could do simultaneously.
>
> If you read our annual report last year, you'd think we're one-third data, one-third telephone and one-third video entertainment, instead of 100 percent video entertainment and two experiments. Right now, we've got zero revenue from residential telephone service, diminishing revenue from high-speed Internet, and $6 billion in revenue from video entertainment.
>
> My job is to prick the bubble. Let's get real.

For years, Malone and TCI had been touting the potential of deploying newly discovered telecommunications technologies over the company's existing cable connections to deliver a dazzling array of information and telecommunications products and services in head-on competition against the telephone companies. The first generation of expanded services was to be rolled out in 1996 and 1997 via a new digital-cable box installed on residential TVs that would access 500 channels, provide on-screen viewer guides, and deliver better sound and picture quality. However, the manufacturer of the boxes encountered problems and was able to produce only

small quantities. Meanwhile, aggressive investment in new technological infrastructure ($1.6 billion in 1996) to deliver the expanded array of products/services put a strain on TCI's cash flow and prompted bond-rating agencies to put the company on their watch lists for possible credit rating downgrade. TCI's stock price went nowhere in a strong stock market. Plus the new Telecommunications Act enacted into law in 1996 created a swirl of strategic maneuvers by local and long-distance telephone companies to position themselves to compete nationwide in both the telephone business and in information superhighway products and services, a development that meant cable operators suddenly confronted a whole new set of larger, resource-rich competitors.

TCI's new, narrower vision was to focus more on the cable TV business (under attack from alternative providers utilizing satellite dish technology as well as from the fiber optic wire capability being installed by telephone companies) and to push the vision of information superhighway and multimedia provider farther out into the future, conditional upon clearer technological opportunities to profit from investments to modify the existing cable system and provide a wider array of products and services. The retrenched strategy involved slower rollout of the new digital cable box (to give the supplier time to ramp up production and work out quality bugs), continued market testing of telephone service, curtailed investment in two-way communications capabilities until the company's debt levels were reduced and cash flows were stronger, and until it was clear that the new technologies would be both cost-effective and competitive against the fiberoptic and wireless technologies being installed by rivals. TCI also decided to spin off some of the company's businesses into independent companies (Liberty Media's programming assets, a satellite operation, international operations, and telephone operations) and put some life back into the company's languishing stock price.

Source: Based on information in "Malone Says TCI Push Into Phones, Internet Isn't Working for Now," *The Wall Street Journal*, January 2, 1997, pp. A1 and A3.

crafting strategic initiatives to capture the most promising of the company's market opportunities. Depending on industry conditions, a company's opportunities can be plentiful or scarce and can range from wildly attractive (an absolute "must" to pursue) to marginally interesting (low on the company's list of strategic priorities). Table 4.1 presents a checklist of things to be alert for in identifying a company's market opportunities.

In appraising a company's market opportunities and ranking their attractiveness, managers have to guard against viewing every *industry* opportunity as a *company* opportunity. Not every company in an industry is equipped with the resources to pursue each opportunity that exists—some companies have more capabilities to go after particular opportunities than others, and a few companies may be hopelessly outclassed in trying to contend for a piece of the action. Wise strategists are alert to when a company's resource strengths and weaknesses make it better suited to pursuing some market opportunities than others. Wise strategists are also alert to opportunities that don't match especially well with existing resources, but still offer attractive growth potential if the company aggressively moves to develop or acquire the missing resource capabilities. *The market opportunities most relevant to a company are those that offer important avenues for profitable growth, those where a company has the most potential for competitive advantage, and those that match up well with the financial and organizational resource capabilities which the company already possesses or can acquire.*

Strategic Management Principle

A company is well-advised to pass on a particular market opportunity unless it has or can build the resource capabilities to capture it.

Identifying the Threats to a Company's Future Profitability

Often, certain factors in a company's external environment pose *threats* to its profitability and market standing: the emergence of cheaper technologies, rivals' introduction of new or better products, the entry of lower-cost foreign competitors into a company's market stronghold, new regulations that are more burdensome to a company than to its competitors, vulnerability to a rise in interest rates, the potential of a hostile takeover, unfavorable demographic shifts, adverse changes in foreign exchange rates, political upheaval in a foreign country where the company has facilities, and the like. External threats may pose no more than a moderate degree of adversity (all companies confront some threatening elements in the course of doing business) or they may be so imposing as to make a company's situation and outlook quite tenuous. Management's job is to identify the threats to the company's future well-being and evaluate what strategic actions can be taken to neutralize or lessen their impact.

Table 4.1 presents a list of potential threats to a company's future profitability and market position. Opportunities and threats point to the need for strategic action. Tailoring strategy to a company's situation entails (1) pursuing market opportunities well suited to the company's resource capabilities and (2) building a resource base that helps defend against external threats to the company's business.

Strategic Management Principle

Successful strategists aim at capturing a company's best growth opportunities and creating defenses against external threats to its competitive position and future performance.

SWOT analysis is therefore more than an exercise in making four lists. The important part of SWOT analysis involves *evaluating* a company's strengths, weaknesses, opportunities, and threats and *drawing conclusions* about (1) how best to deploy the company's resources in light of the company's internal and external situation and (2) how to build the company's future resource base. SWOT analysis isn't complete until several questions about the company's resource base are answered: What adjustments in the company's resource base are needed to respond to emerging industry and competitive conditions? Are there resource gaps that need to be filled? In what ways does the company need to strengthen its resource base? What actions are needed to build the company's future resource base? Which opportunities should be given top priority in allocating resources?

QUESTION 3: ARE THE COMPANY'S PRICES AND COSTS COMPETITIVE?

Company managers are often stunned when a competitor cuts price to "unbelievably low" levels or when a new market entrant comes on strong with a very low price. The competitor may not, however, be "dumping," buying market share, or waging a desperate move to gain sales; it may simply have substantially lower costs. *One of the most telling signs of whether a company's business position is strong or precarious is whether its prices and costs are competitive with industry rivals.* Price-cost comparisons are especially critical in a commodity-product industry where the value provided to buyers is the same from seller to seller, price competition is typically the ruling market force, and lower-cost companies have the upper hand. But even in industries where products are differentiated and competition centers around the different attributes of competing brands as much as around price, rival companies have to keep their costs *in line* and make sure that any added costs they incur create added buyer value and don't result in prices that customers consider "out-of-line."

Assessing whether a company's costs are competitive with those of its close rivals is a necessary and crucial part of company situation analysis.

Competitors usually don't incur the same costs in supplying their products to end users. The cost disparities can range from tiny to competitively significant and can stem from any of several factors:

- Differences in the prices paid for raw materials, components parts, energy, and other items purchased from suppliers.
- Differences in basic technology and the age of plants and equipment. (Because rival companies usually invest in plants and key pieces of equipment at different times, their facilities have somewhat different technological efficiencies and different fixed costs (depreciation, maintenance, property taxes, and insurance. Older facilities are typically less efficient, but if they were less expensive to construct or were acquired at bargain prices, they *may* still be reasonably cost competitive with modern facilities.)
- Differences in production costs from rival to rival due to different plant efficiencies, different learning and experience curve effects, different wage rates, different productivity levels, and the like.
- Differences in marketing costs, sales and promotion expenditures, advertising expenses, warehouse distribution costs, and administrative costs.
- Differences in inbound transportation costs and outbound shipping costs.
- Differences in forward channel distribution costs (the costs and markups of distributors, wholesalers, and retailers associated with getting the product from the point of manufacture into the hands of end users).

Principle of Competitive Markets

The higher a company's costs are above those of close rivals, the more competitively vulnerable it becomes.

- Differences in rival firms' exposure to the effects of inflation, changes in foreign exchange rates, and tax rates (a frequent occurrence in global industries where competitors have operations in different nations with different economic conditions and governmental taxation policies).

For a company to be competitively successful, its costs must be in line with those of close rivals. While some cost disparity is justified so long as the products or services of closely competing companies are sufficiently differentiated, a high-cost firm's market position becomes increasingly vulnerable the more its costs exceed those of close rivals.

Strategic Cost Analysis and Value Chains

Competitors must be ever alert to how their costs compare with rivals'. While every firm engages in *internal* cost analysis to stay on top of what its own costs are and how they might be changing, *strategic* cost analysis goes a step further to explore how costs compare against rivals. *Strategic cost analysis focuses on a firm's cost position relative to its rivals'.*

Every company's business consists of a *collection of activities* undertaken in the course of designing, producing, marketing, delivering, and supporting its product or service. Each of these activities give rise to costs. The combined costs of all these various activities define the company's internal cost structure. Further, the cost of each activity contributes to whether the company's overall cost position relative to rivals is favorable or unfavorable. The task of strategic cost analysis is to compare a company's costs *activity by activity* against the costs of key rivals and to learn which internal activities are a source of cost advantage or disadvantage. A company's relative cost position is a function of how the overall costs of the activities it performs in conducting its business compare to the overall costs of the activities performed by rivals.

> **Basic Concept**
>
> *Strategic cost analysis involves comparing how a company's unit costs stack up against the unit costs of key competitors activity by activity, thereby pinpointing which internal activities are a source of cost advantage or disadvantage.*

The Concept of a Company Value Chain   The primary analytical tool of strategic cost analysis is a *value chain* identifying the separate activities, functions, and business processes performed in designing, producing, marketing, delivering, and supporting a product or service.[5] The chain starts with raw materials supply and continues on through parts and components production, manufacturing and assembly, wholesale distribution, and retailing to the ultimate end user of the product or service.

A *company's value chain* shows the linked set of activities and functions it performs internally (see Figure 4.1). The value chain includes a profit margin because a markup over the cost of performing the firm's value-creating activities is customarily part of the price (or total cost) borne by buyers—creating value that exceeds the cost of doing so is a fundamental objective of business. Disaggregating a company's operations into strategically relevant activities and business processes exposes the major elements of the company's cost structure. Each activity in the value chain incurs costs and ties up assets; assigning the company's operating costs and assets to each individual activity in the chain provides cost estimates for each activity. Quite often, there are linkages between activities such that the way one activity is performed can spill over to affect the costs of performing other activities (for instance, Japanese VCR producers were able to reduce prices from $1,300 in 1977 to under $300 in 1984 by spotting the impact of an early step in the value chain, product design, on a later step, production, and deciding to drastically reduce the number of parts).[6]

> **Basic Concept**
>
> *A company's value chain identifies the primary activities that create value for customers and the related support activities.*

Why the Value Chains of Rival Companies Often Differ   A company's value chain and the manner in which it performs each activity reflect the evolution of its own

---

[5]Value chains and strategic cost analysis are described at greater length in Michael E. Porter, *Competitive Advantage* (New York: Free Press, 1985), chapters 2 and 3; Robin Cooper and Robert S. Kaplan, "Measure Costs Right: Make the Right Decisions," *Harvard Business Review* 66, no. 5 (September–October, 1988), pp. 96–103; and John K. Shank and Vijay Govindarajan, *Strategic Cost Management* (New York: Free Press, 1993), especially chapters 2–6 and 10.

[6]M. Hegert and D. Morris, "Accounting Data for Value Chain Analysis," *Strategic Management Journal* 10 (1989), p. 183.

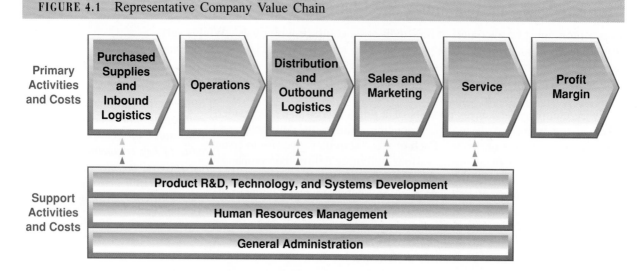

FIGURE 4.1   Representative Company Value Chain

Primary Activities

- **Purchased Supplies and Inbound Logistics**—Activities, costs, and assets associated with purchasing fuel, energy, raw materials, parts components, merchandise, and consumable items from vendors; receiving, storing, and disseminating inputs from suppliers; inspection; and inventory management.
- **Operations**—Activities, costs, and assets associated with converting inputs into final product form (production, assembly, packaging, equipment maintenance, facilities, operations, quality assurance, environmental protection).
- **Distribution and Outbound Logistics**—Activities, costs, and assets dealing with physically distributing the product to buyers (finished goods warehousing, order processing, order picking and packing, shipping, delivery vehicle operations, establishing and maintaining a network of dealers and distributors).
- **Sales and Marketing**—Activities, costs, and assets related to sales force efforts, advertising and promotion, market research and planning, and dealer/distributor support.
- **Service**—Activities, costs, and assets associated with providing assistance to buyers, such as installation, spare parts delivery, maintenance and repair, technical assistance, buyer inquiries, and complaints.

Support Activities

- **Research, Technology, and Systems Development**—Activities, costs, and assets relating to product R&D, process R&D, process design improvement, equipment design, computer software development, telecommunications systems, computer-assisted design and engineering, new database capabilities, and development of computerized support systems.
- **Human Resources Management**—Activities, costs, and assets associated with the recruitment, hiring, training, development, and compensation of all types of personnel; labor relations activities; development of knowledge-based skills and core competencies.
- **General Administration**—Activities, costs, and assets relating to general management, accounting and finance, legal and regulatory affairs, safety and security, management information systems, forming strategic alliances and collaborating with strategic partners, and other "overhead" functions.

Source: Adapted from Michael E. Porter, *Competitive Advantage* (New York: The Free Press, 1985), pp. 37–43.

business and internal operations, its strategy, the approaches it is using to execute its strategy, and the underlying economics of the activities themselves.[7] Consequently, it is normal for the value chains of rival companies to differ, perhaps substantially—a

_____

[7]Porter, *Competitive Advantage*, p. 36.

condition that complicates the task of assessing rivals' relative cost positions. For instance, competing companies may differ in their degrees of vertical integration. Comparing the value chain for a fully integrated rival against a partially integrated rival requires adjusting for differences in scope of activities performed—clearly the *internal* costs for a manufacturer that makes all of its own parts and components will be greater than the *internal* costs of a producer that buys the needed parts and components from outside suppliers and only performs assembly operations.

Likewise, there is legitimate reason to expect value chain and cost differences between a company that is pursuing a low-cost/low-price strategy and a rival positioned at the high-end of the market with a prestige quality product that possesses a wealth of features. In the case of the low-cost firm, the costs of certain activities along the company's value chain should indeed be relatively low whereas the high-end firm may understandably be spending relatively more to perform those activities that create the added quality and extra features.

Moreover, cost and price differences among rival companies can have their origins in activities performed by suppliers or by forward channel allies involved in getting the product to end users. Suppliers or forward channel allies may have excessively high cost structures or profit margins that jeopardize a company's cost competitiveness even though its costs for internally performed activities are competitive. For example, when determining Michelin's cost competitiveness vis-à-vis Goodyear and Bridgestone in supplying replacement tires to vehicle owners, one has to look at more than whether Michelin's tire manufacturing costs are above or below Goodyear's and Bridgestone's. If a buyer has to pay $400 for a set of Michelin tires and only $350 for comparable sets of Goodyear or Bridgestone tires, Michelin's $50 price disadvantage in the replacement tire marketplace can stem not only from higher manufacturing costs (reflecting, *perhaps*, the added costs of Michelin's strategic efforts to build a better quality tire with more performance features) but also from (1) differences in what the three tire makers pay their suppliers for materials and tire-making components and (2) differences in the operating efficiencies, costs, and markups of Michelin's wholesale distributors and retail dealers versus those of Goodyear and Bridgestone. Thus, determining whether a company's prices and costs are competitive from an end user's standpoint requires looking at the activities and costs of competitively relevant suppliers and forward allies, as well as the costs of internally performed activities.

A company's cost competitiveness depends not only on the costs of internally performed activities (its own value chain) but also on costs in the value chains of its suppliers and forward channel allies.

The Value Chain System for an Entire Industry   As the tire industry example makes clear, a company's value chain is embedded in a larger system of activities that includes the value chains of its upstream suppliers and downstream customers or allies engaged in getting its product/service to end users.[8] Accurately assessing a company's competitiveness in end-use markets requires that company managers understand the entire value chain system for delivering a product or service to end-users, not just the company's own value chain. At the very least, this means considering the value chains of suppliers and forward channel allies (if any)—as shown in Figure 4.2. Suppliers' value chains are relevant because suppliers perform activities and incur costs in creating and delivering the purchased inputs used in a company's own value chain; the cost and quality of these inputs influence a company's own cost and/or differentiation capabilities. Anything a company can do to reduce its suppliers' costs or improve suppliers'

[8]Porter, *Competitive Advantage*, p. 34.

FIGURE 4.2   The Value Chain System

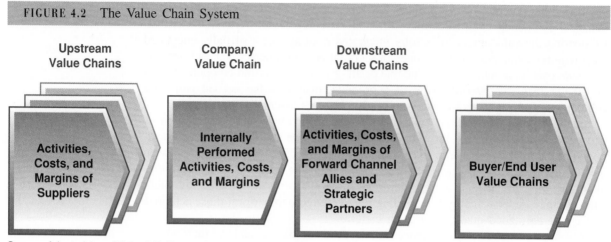

Source: Adapted from Michael E. Porter, *Competitive Advantage* (New York: The Free Press, 1985), p. 35.

effectiveness can enhance its own competitiveness—a powerful reason for working collaboratively or partnering with suppliers. Forward channel value chains are relevant because (1) the costs and margins of downstream companies are part of the price the ultimate end user pays and (2) the activities performed by forward channel allies affect the end user's satisfaction. There are powerful reasons for a company to work closely with forward channel allies to revise or reinvent their value chains in ways that enhance their mutual competitiveness. Furthermore, a company may be able to improve its competitiveness by undertaking activities that beneficially impact *both* its own value chain and its customers' value chains. For instance, some aluminum can producers constructed plants next to beer breweries and delivered cans on overhead conveyors directly to brewers' can-filling lines. This resulted in significant savings in production scheduling, shipping, and inventory costs for both container producers and breweries.[9] The lesson here is that a company's relative cost position and overall competitiveness is linked to the entire industry value chain system and to customers' value chains as well.

Although the value chains in Figures 4.1 and 4.2 are representative, the activity makeup of the chains and the relative importance of the activities within them vary by industry and by company position. Value chains for products differ from value chains for services. The major value chain elements for the pulp and paper industry (timber farming, logging, pulp mills, papermaking, printing, and publishing) differ from the major chain elements for the home appliance industry (parts and components manufacture, assembly, wholesale distribution, retail sales). The value chain for the soft-drink industry (processing of basic ingredients, syrup manufacture, bottling and can filling, wholesale distribution, retailing) differs from the makeup of the chain for the computer software industry (programming, disk loading, marketing, distribution). A producer of bathroom and kitchen faucets depends heavily on the activities of wholesale distributors and building supply retailers in winning sales to homebuilders and do-it-yourselfers. A wholesaler's most important activities and costs deal with purchased goods, inbound logistics, and outbound logistics. A hotel's most important activities and costs are in operations—check-in and check-out, maintenance and housekeeping, dining and room service, conventions and meetings, and

[9]Hegert and Morris, "Accounting Data for Value Chain Analysis," p. 180.

accounting. A global public accounting firm's most important activities and costs revolve around customer service and human resources management (recruiting and training a highly competent professional staff). Outbound logistics is a crucial activity at Domino's Pizza but comparatively insignificant at Blockbuster. Sales and marketing are dominant activities at Nike but only minor activities at electric and gas utilities. Consequently, generic value chains like those in Figures 4.1 and 4.2 are illustrative, not absolute, and may have to be adapted to fit a particular company's circumstances.

Developing the Data for Strategic Cost Analysis   Once the major value chain elements are identified, the next step in strategic cost analysis involves breaking down a firm's departmental cost accounting data into the costs of performing specific activities.[10] The appropriate degree of disaggregation depends on the economics of the activities and how valuable it is to develop cross-company cost comparisons for narrowly defined activities as opposed to broadly defined activities. A good guideline is to develop separate cost estimates for activities having different economics and for activities representing a significant or growing proportion of cost.[11]

Traditional accounting identifies costs according to broad categories of expenses—wages and salaries, employee benefits, supplies, travel, depreciation, R&D, and other fixed charges. *Activity-based costing* entails defining expense categories based on the specific activities being performed and then assigning costs to the appropriate activity responsible for creating the cost. An example is shown in Table 4.2.[12] Perhaps 10 percent of the companies that have explored the feasibility of activity-based costing have adopted this accounting approach. To fully understand the costs of activities all along the industry value chain, cost estimates for activities performed in suppliers' and customers' value chains also have to be developed.

To benchmark the firm's cost position against rivals, costs for the same activities for each rival must be estimated—an advanced art in competitive intelligence. But despite the tediousness of developing cost estimates activity by activity and the imprecision of some of the estimates for rivals, the payoff in exposing the costs of particular internal tasks and functions and the company's cost competitiveness makes activity-based costing a valuable strategic analysis tool.[13] Illustration Capsule 11 shows a simplified value chain comparison for two prominent brewers of beer—Anheuser-Busch (the U.S. industry leader) and Adolph Coors (the third-ranking U.S. brewer).

The most important application of value chain analysis is to expose how a particular firm's cost position compares with its rivals'. What is needed is competitor versus competitor cost estimates for supplying a product or service to a well-defined customer group or market segment. The size of a company's cost advantage/disadvantage can vary from item to item in the product line, from customer group to customer group (if different distribution channels are used), and from geographic market to geographic market (if cost factors vary across geographic regions).

---

[10]For discussions of the accounting challenges in calculating the costs of value chain activities, see Shank and Govindarajan, *Strategic Cost Management*, pp. 62–72 and chapter 5, and Hegert and Morris, "Accounting Data for Value Chain Analysis," pp. 175–88.

[11]Porter, *Competitive Advantage*, p. 45.

[12]For a discussion of activity-based cost accounting, see Cooper and Kaplan, "Measure Costs Right: Make the Right Decisions," pp. 96–103; Shank and Govindarajan, *Strategic Cost Management*, Chapter 11; and Joseph A. Ness and Thomas G. Cucuzza, "Tapping the Full Potential of ABC," *Harvard Business Review* 73 no. 4 (July–August 1995), pp. 130–38.

[13]Shank and Govindarajan, *Strategic Cost Management*, p. 62.

TABLE 4.2   The Difference between Traditional Cost Accounting and Activity-Based
Cost Accounting

Traditional Cost Accounting Categories in Departmental Budget		Cost of Performing Specific Departmental Activities Using Activity-Based Cost Accounting	
Wages and salaries	$350,000	Evaluate supplier capabilities	$135,750
Employee benefits	115,000	Process purchase orders	82,100
Supplies	6,500	Expedite supplier deliveries	23,500
Travel	2,400	Expedite internal processing	15,840
Depreciation	17,000	Check quality of items purchased	94,300
Other fixed charges	124,000	Check incoming deliveries against purchase orders	48,450
Miscellaneous operating expenses	25,250	Resolve problems	110,000
		Internal administration	130,210
	$640,150		$640,150

Source: Adapted from information in Terence P. Paré, "A New Tool for Managing Costs," *Fortune*, June 14, 1993, pp. 124–29.

Benchmarking the Costs of Key Activities

Many companies today are benchmarking the costs of performing a given activity against competitors' costs (and/or against the costs of a noncompetitor in another industry that efficiently and effectively performs much the same activity or business process). Benchmarking focuses on cross-company comparisons of how well basic functions and processes in the value chain are performed—how materials are purchased, how suppliers are paid, how inventories are managed, how employees are trained, how payrolls are processed, how fast the company can get new products to market, how the quality control function is performed, how customer orders are filled and shipped, and how maintenance is performed.[14] *The objectives of benchmarking are to understand the best practices in performing an activity, to learn how lower costs are actually achieved, and to take action to improve a company's cost competitiveness whenever benchmarking reveals that the costs of performing an activity are out of line with those of other companies.*

Benchmarking the performance of company activities against rivals and other best-practice companies provides hard evidence of a company's cost competitiveness.

In 1979, Xerox became an early pioneer in the use of benchmarking when Japanese manufacturers began selling midsize copiers in the United States for $9,600 each—less than Xerox's production costs.[15] Although Xerox management suspected its Japanese competitors were dumping, it sent a team of line managers to Japan, including the head of manufacturing, to study competitors' business processes and costs. Fortunately, Xerox's joint venture partner in Japan, Fuji-Xerox, knew the competitors well. The team found that Xerox's costs were excessive due to gross

[14]For more details, see Gregory H. Watson, *Strategic Benchmarking: How to Rate Your Company's Performance Against the World's Best* (New York: John Wiley, 1993) and Robert C. Camp, *Benchmarking: The Search for Industry Best Practices That Lead to Superior Performance* (Milwaukee: ASQC Quality Press, 1989). See also Alexandra Biesada, "Strategic Benchmarking," *Financial World*, September 29, 1992, pp. 30–38.

[15]Jeremy Main, "How to Steal the Best Ideas Around," *Fortune*, October 19, 1992, pp. 102–3.

ILLUSTRATION CAPSULE 11 Value Chains for Anheuser-Busch and Adolph Coors Beers

In the table below are average cost estimates for the combined brands of beer produced by Anheuser-Busch and Coors. The example shows raw material costs, other manufacturing costs, and forward channel distribution costs. The data are for 1982.

	Estimated Average Cost Breakdown for Combined Anheuser-Busch Brands		Estimated Average Cost Breakdown for Combined Adolph Coors Brands	
Value Chain Activities and Costs	Per 6-Pack of 12-oz. Cans	Per Barrel Equivalent	Per 6-Pack of 12-oz Cans	Per Barrel Equivalent
1. Manufacturing costs:				
Direct production costs:				
Raw material ingredients	$0.1384	$ 7.63	$0.1082	$ 5.96
Direct labor	0.1557	8.58	0.1257	6.93
Salaries for nonunionized personnel	0.0800	4.41	0.0568	3.13
Packaging	0.5055	27.86	0.4663	25.70
Depreciation on plant and equipment	0.0410	2.26	0.0826	4.55
Subtotal	0.9206	50.74	0.8396	46.27
Other expenses:				
Advertising	0.0477	2.63	0.0338	1.86
Other marketing costs and general administrative expenses	0.1096	6.04	0.1989	10.96
Interest	0.0147	0.81	0.0033	0.18
Research and development	0.0277	1.53	0.0195	1.07
Total manufacturing costs	$1.1203	$ 61.75	$1.0951	$ 60.34
2. Manufacturer's operating profit	0.1424	7.85	0.0709	3.91
3. Net selling price	1.2627	69.60	1.1660	64.25
4. Plus federal and state excise taxes paid by brewer	0.1873	10.32	0.1782	9.82
5. Gross manufacturer's selling price to distributor/wholesaler	1.4500	79.92	1.3442	74.07
6. Average margin over manufacturer's cost	0.5500	30.31	0.5158	28.43
7. Average wholesale price charged to retailer (inclusive of taxes in item 4 above but exclusive of other taxes)	$ 2.00	$110.23	$ 1.86	$102.50
8. Plus other assorted state and local taxes levied on wholesale and retail sales (this varies from locality to locality)	0.60		0.60	
9. Average 20% retail markup over wholesale cost	0.40		0.38	
10. Average price to consumer at retail	$ 3.00		$ 2.84	

Note: The difference in the average cost structures for Anheuser-Busch and Adolph Coors is, to a substantial extent, due to A-B's higher proportion of super-premium beer sales. A-B's super-premium brand, Michelob, was the best-seller in its category and somewhat more costly to brew than premium and popular-priced beers.

Source: Compiled by Tom McLean, Elsa Wischkaemper, and Arthur A. Thompson, Jr., from a wide variety of documents and field interviews.

ILLUSTRATION CAPSULE 12   Ford Motor Company's Benchmarking of Its Accounts Payable Activity

In the 1980s Ford's North American accounts payable department employed more than 500 people. Clerks spent the majority of their time straightening out the relatively few situations where three documents—the purchase order issued by the purchasing department, the receiving document prepared by clerks at the receiving dock, and the invoice sent by the vendor/supplier to accounts payable—did not match. Sometimes resolving the discrepancies took weeks of time and the efforts of many people. Ford managers believed that by using computers to automate some functions performed manually, head count could be reduced to 400. Before proceeding, Ford managers decided to visit Mazda—a company in which Ford had recently acquired a 25 percent ownership interest. To their astonishment, Mazda handled its accounts payable function with only five people. Following Mazda's lead, Ford benchmarkers created an invoiceless system where payments to suppliers were triggered automatically when the goods were received. The reengineered system allowed Ford to reduce its accounts payable staff to under 200, a lot more than Mazda but much better than would have resulted without benchmarking the accounts payable activity.

Sources: Michael Hammer and James Champy, *Reengineering the Corporation* (New York: HarperBusiness, 1993), pp. 39–43, and Jeremy Main, "How to Steal the Best Ideas Around," *Fortune*, October 19, 1992, p. 106.

inefficiencies in its manufacturing processes and business practices; the study proved instrumental in Xerox's efforts to become cost competitive and prompted Xerox to embark on a long-term program to benchmark 67 of its key work processes against companies identified as having the "best practices" in performing these processes. Xerox quickly decided not to restrict its benchmarking efforts to its office equipment rivals but to extend them to any company regarded as "world class" in performing an activity relevant to Xerox's business. Illustration Capsule 12 describes one of Ford Motor's benchmarking experiences.

Sometimes cost benchmarking can be accomplished by collecting information from published reports, trade groups, and industry research firms and by talking to knowledgeable industry analysts, customers, and suppliers (customers, suppliers, and joint-venture partners often make willing benchmarking allies). Usually, though, benchmarking requires field trips to the facilities of competing or noncompeting companies to observe how things are done, ask questions, compare practices and processes, and perhaps exchange data on productivity, staffing levels, time requirements, and other cost components. However, benchmarking involves competitively sensitive information about how lower costs are achieved, and close rivals can't be expected to be completely open, even if they agree to host facilities tours and answer questions. But the explosive interest of companies in benchmarking costs and identifying best practices has prompted consulting organizations (for example, Andersen Consulting, A. T. Kearney, Best Practices Benchmarking & Consulting, and Towers Perrin) and several newly formed councils and associations (the International Benchmarking Clearinghouse and the Strategic Planning Institute's Council on Benchmarking) to gather benchmarking data, do benchmarking studies, and distribute information about best practices and the costs of performing activities to clients/members without identifying the sources. The ethical dimension of benchmarking is discussed in Illustration Capsule 13. Over 80 percent of *Fortune* 500 companies now engage in some form of benchmarking.

Benchmarking is a manager's best tool for determining whether the company is performing particular functions and activities efficiently, whether its costs are in line with competitors, and which activities and processes need to be improved. It is a way

---

ILLUSTRATION CAPSULE 13   Benchmarking and Ethical Conduct

Because actions between benchmarking partners can involve competitively sensitive data and discussions, conceivably raising questions about possible restraint of trade or improper business conduct, the SPI Council on Benchmarking and The International Benchmarking Clearinghouse urge all individuals and organizations involved in benchmarking to abide by a code of conduct grounded in ethical business behavior. The code is based on the following principles and guidelines:

- In benchmarking with competitors, establish specific ground rules up front, e.g., "We don't want to talk about those things that will give either of us a competitive advantage; rather, we want to see where we both can mutually improve or gain benefit." Do not discuss costs with competitors if costs are an element of pricing.

- Do not ask competitors for sensitive data or cause the benchmarking partner to feel that sensitive data must be provided to keep the process going. Be prepared to provide the same level of information that you request. Do not share proprietary information without prior approval from the proper authorities of both parties.

- Use an ethical third party to assemble and blind competitive data, with inputs from legal counsel, for direct competitor comparisons.

- Consult with legal counsel if any information gathering procedure is in doubt, e.g., before contacting a direct competitor.

- Any information obtained from a benchmarking partner should be treated as internal, privileged information. Any external use must have the partner's permission.

- Do not:

  - Disparage a competitor's business or operations to a third party.

  - Attempt to limit competition or gain business through the benchmarking relationship.

  - Misrepresent oneself as working for another employer.

- Demonstrate commitment to the efficiency and effectiveness of the process by being adequately prepared at each step, particularly at initial contact. Be professional, honest, and courteous. Adhere to the agenda—maintain focus on benchmarking issues.

Sources: The SPI Council on Benchmarking, The International Benchmarking Clearinghouse, and conference presentation of AT&T Benchmarking Group, Des Moines, Iowa, October 1993.

---

of learning which companies are best at performing certain activities and functions and then imitating—or, better still, improving on—their techniques. Toyota managers got their idea for just-in-time inventory deliveries by studying how U.S. supermarkets replenished their shelves. Southwest Airlines reduced the turnaround time of its aircraft at each scheduled stop by studying pit crews on the auto racing circuit.

Strategic Options for Achieving Cost Competitiveness

Value chain analysis and benchmarking can reveal a great deal about a firm's cost competitiveness. One of the fundamental insights of strategic cost analysis is that a company's competitiveness depends on how well it manages its value chain relative to how well competitors manage theirs.[16] Examining the makeup of a company's own value chain and comparing it to rivals' indicates who has how much of a cost advantage/disadvantage and which cost components are responsible. Such information is vital in crafting strategies to eliminate a cost disadvantage or create a cost advantage.

---

[16]Shank and Govindarajan, *Strategic Cost Management*, p. 50.

Looking again at Figure 4.2, observe that important differences in the costs of competing firms can occur in three main areas: in the suppliers' part of the industry value chain, in a company's own activity segments, or in the forward channel portion of the industry chain. If a firm's lack of cost competitiveness lies either in the backward (upstream) or forward (downstream) sections of the value chain, then reestablishing cost competitiveness may have to extend beyond the firm's own in-house operations. When a firm's cost disadvantage stems from the costs of items purchased from suppliers (the upstream end of the industry chain), company managers can take any of several strategic steps:[17]

Strategic actions to eliminate a cost disadvantage need to be linked to the location in the value chain where the cost differences originate.

- Negotiate more favorable prices with suppliers.
- Work with suppliers to help them achieve lower costs.
- Integrate backward to gain control over the costs of purchased items.
- Try to use lower-priced substitute inputs.
- Do a better job of managing the linkages between suppliers' value chains and the company's own chain; for example, close coordination between a company and its suppliers can permit just-in-time deliveries that lower a company's inventory and internal logistics costs and that may also allow its suppliers to economize on their warehousing, shipping, and production scheduling costs—a win-win outcome for both (instead of a zero-sum game where a company's gains match supplier concessions).[18]
- Try to make up the difference by cutting costs elsewhere in the chain.

A company's strategic options for eliminating cost disadvantages in the forward end of the value chain system include:[19]

- Pushing distributors and other forward channel allies to reduce their markups.
- Working closely with forward channel allies/customers to identify win-win opportunities to reduce costs. A chocolate manufacturer learned that by shipping its bulk chocolate in liquid form in tank cars instead of 10-pound molded bars, it saved its candy bar manufacturing customers the cost of unpacking and melting, and it eliminated its own costs of molding bars and packing them.
- Changing to a more economical distribution strategy, including forward integration.
- Trying to make up the difference by cutting costs earlier in the cost chain.

When the source of a firm's cost disadvantage is internal, managers can use any of nine strategic approaches to restore cost parity:[20]

---

[17]Porter, *Competitive Advantage*, chapter 3.

[18]In recent years, most companies have moved aggressively to collaborate with and partner with key suppliers to implement better supply chain management, often achieving cost savings of 5 to 25 percent. For a discussion of how to develop a cost-saving supply chain strategy, see Shashank Kulkarni, "Purchasing: A Supply-side Strategy," *Journal of Business Strategy* 17, no. 5 (September–October 1996), pp. 17–20.

[19]Porter, *Competitive Advantage*, Chapter 3.

[20]Ibid.

1. Streamline the operation of high-cost activities.

2. Reengineer business processes and work practices (to boost employee productivity, improve the efficiency of key activities, increase the utilization of company assets, and otherwise do a better job of managing the cost drivers).

3. Eliminate some cost-producing activities altogether by revamping the value chain system (for example, shifting to a radically different technological approach or maybe bypassing the value chains of forward channel allies and marketing directly to end users).

4. Relocate high-cost activities to geographic areas where they can be performed more cheaply.

5. See if certain activities can be outsourced from vendors or performed by contractors more cheaply than they can be done internally.

6. Invest in cost-saving technological improvements (automation, robotics, flexible manufacturing techniques, computerized controls).

7. Innovate around the troublesome cost components as new investments are made in plant and equipment.

8. Simplify the product design so that it can be manufactured more economically.

9. Make up the internal cost disadvantage through savings in the backward and forward portions of the value chain system.

From Value Chain Activities to Competitive Capabilities to Competitive Advantage

How well a company manages its value chain activities is a key to building valuable competencies and capabilities and leveraging them into sustainable competitive advantage. With rare exceptions, a firm's products or services are not a basis for sustainable competitive advantage—it is too easy for a resourceful company to clone, improve on, or find a substitute for them.[21] Rather, a company's competitive edge is usually grounded in its skills, know-how, and capabilities relative to those of its rivals and, more specifically, in the scope and depth of its ability to perform competitively crucial activities along the value chain better than rivals.

Developing the capability to perform competitively crucial value chain activities better than rivals is a dependable source of competitive advantage.

Competitively valuable competencies and capabilities emerge from a company's experience, learned skills, organizational routines and operating practices, and focused efforts in performing one or more related value chain components—they are not simply a consequence of the company's collection of resources. FedEx has purposefully built and integrated its resources to create the internal capabilities for providing customers with guaranteed overnight delivery services. McDonald's ability to turn out virtually identical-quality hamburgers at some 20,000-plus outlets around the world reflects impressive capability to replicate its operating systems at many locations through detailed rules and procedures and intensive training of franchise operators and outlet managers. Merck and Glaxo, two of the world's most competitively capable pharmaceutical companies, built their strategic

---

[21]James Brian Quinn, *Intelligent Enterprise* (New York: Free Press, 1993), p. 54.

positions around expert performance of a few key activities: extensive R&D to achieve first discovery of new drugs, a carefully constructed approach to patenting, skill in gaining rapid and thorough clinical clearance from regulatory bodies, and unusually strong distribution and sales force capabilities.[22]

Creating valuable competitive capabilities typically involves integrating the knowledge and skills of individual employees, leveraging the economies of learning and experience, effectively coordinating related value chain activities, making trade-offs between efficiency and flexibility, and exerting efforts to gain dominating expertise over rivals in one or more value chain activities critical to customer satisfaction and market success. Valuable capabilities enhance a company's competitiveness. The strategy-making lesson here is that sustainable competitive advantage can flow from concentrating company resources and talent on one or more competitively sensitive value chain activities; competitive advantage results from developing distinctive capabilities to serve customers—capabilities that buyers value highly and that company rivals don't have and are unable or unwilling to match.

QUESTION 4: HOW STRONG IS THE COMPANY'S COMPETITIVE POSITION?

Using the tools of value chains, strategic cost analysis, and benchmarking to determine a company's cost competitiveness is necessary but not sufficient. A broader assessment needs to be made of a company's competitive position and competitive strength. Particular issues that merit examination include (1) whether the firm's market position can be expected to improve or deteriorate if the present strategy is continued (allowing for fine-tuning), (2) how the firm ranks *relative to key rivals* on each industry key success factor and each relevant measure of competitive strength and resource capability, (3) whether the firm enjoys a competitive advantage over key rivals or is currently at a disadvantage, and (4) the firm's ability to defend its market position in light of industry driving forces, competitive pressures, and the anticipated moves of rivals.

Systematic assessment of whether a company's overall competitive position is strong or weak relative to close rivals is an essential step in company situation analysis.

Table 4.3 lists some indicators of whether a firm's competitive position is improving or slipping. But company managers need to do more than just identify the areas of competitive improvement or slippage. They have to judge whether the company has a net competitive advantage or disadvantage vis-á-vis key competitors and whether the company's market position and performance can be expected to improve or deteriorate under the current strategy.

Managers can begin the task of evaluating the company's competitive strength by using benchmarking techniques to compare the company against industry rivals not just on cost but also on such important measures as product quality, customer service, customer satisfaction, financial strength, technological skills, product cycle time (how quickly new products can be taken from idea to design to market), and the possession of competitively important resources and capabilities. It is not enough to benchmark the costs of activities and identify best practices; a company should benchmark itself against competitors on all strategically and competitively important aspects of its business.

---

[22]Quinn, *Intelligent Enterprise*, p. 34.

TABLE 4.3   The Signs of Strength and Weakness in a Company's Competitive Position

Signs of Competitive Strength	Signs of Competitive Weakness
• Important resource strengths, core competencies, and competitive capabilities • A distinctive competence in a competitively important value chain activity • Strong market share (or a leading market share) • A pace-setting or distinctive strategy • Growing customer base and customer loyalty • Above-average market visibility • In a favorably situated strategic group • Well positioned in attractive market segments • Strongly differentiated products • Cost advantages • Above-average profit margins • Above-average technological and innovational capability • A creative, entrepreneurially alert management • In position to capitalize on emerging market opportunities	• Confronted with competitive disadvantages • Losing ground to rival firms • Below-average growth in revenues • Short on financial resources • A slipping reputation with customers • Trailing in product development and product innovation capability • In a strategic group destined to lose ground • Weak in areas where there is the most market potential • A higher-cost producer • Too small to be a major factor in the marketplace • Not in good position to deal with emerging threats • Weak product quality • Lacking skills, resources, and competitive capabilities in key area • Weaker distribution capability than rivals

Competitive Strength Assessments

The most telling way to determine how strongly a company holds its competitive position is to quantitatively assess whether the company is stronger or weaker than close rivals on each of the industry's key success factors and on each pertinent indicator of competitive capability and potential competitive advantage. Much of the information for competitive strength assessment comes from prior analytical steps. Industry and competitive analysis reveals the key success factors and competitive determinants that separate industry winners from losers. Competitor analysis and benchmarking data provide information for judging the strengths and capabilities of key rivals.

Step one is to make a list of the industry's key success factors and most telling determinants of competitive advantage or disadvantage (6 to 10 measures usually suffice). Step two is to rate the firm and its key rivals on each strength indicator. Rating scales from 1 to 10 are best to use, although ratings of stronger (+), weaker (−), and about equal (=) may be appropriate when information is scanty and assigning numerical scores conveys false precision. Step three is to sum the individual strength overall ratings to get an measure of competitive strength for each competitor. Step four is to draw conclusions about the size and extent of the company's net competitive advantage or disadvantage and to take specific note of those strength measures where the company is strongest and weakest.

High competitive strength ratings signal a strong competitive position and possession of competitive advantage; low ratings signal a weak position and competitive disadvantage.

Table 4.4 provides two examples of competitive strength assessment. The first one employs an *unweighted rating scale*. With unweighted ratings each key success factor/competitive strength measure is assumed to be *equally important* (a rather dubious assumption). Whichever company has the highest strength rating on a given measure has an implied edge on that factor; the size of its edge is mirrored in the margin of difference between its rating and the ratings assigned to rivals. Summing a company's strength ratings on all the

TABLE 4.4   Illustrations of Unweighted and Weighted Competitive Strength Assessments

A. Sample of an Unweighted Competitive Strength Assessment

Rating scale: 1 = Very weak; 10 = Very strong

Key Success Factor/Strength Measure	ABC Co.	Rival 1	Rival 2	Rival 3	Rival 4
Quality/product performance	8	5	10	1	6
Reputation/image	8	7	10	1	6
Manufacturing capability	2	10	4	5	1
Technological skills	10	1	7	3	8
Dealer network/distribution capability	9	4	10	5	1
New product innovation capability	9	4	10	5	1
Financial resources	5	10	7	3	1
Relative cost position	5	10	3	1	4
Customer service capabilities	5	7	10	1	4
Unweighted overall strength rating	61	58	71	25	32

B. Sample of a Weighted Competitive Strength Assessment

Rating scale: 1 = Very weak; 10 = Very strong

Key Success Factor/Strength Measure	Weight	ABC Co.	Rival 1	Rival 2	Rival 3	Rival 4
Quality/product performance	0.10	8/0.80	5/0.50	10/1.00	1/0.10	6/0.60
Reputation/image	0.10	8/0.80	7/0.70	10/1.00	1/0.10	6/0.60
Manufacturing capability	0.10	2/0.20	10/1.00	4/0.40	5/0.50	1/0.10
Technological skills	0.05	10/0.50	1/0.05	7/0.35	3/0.15	8/0.40
Dealer network/distribution capability	0.05	9/0.45	4/0.20	10/0.50	5/0.25	1/0.05
New product innovation capability	0.05	9/0.45	4/0.20	10/0.50	5/0.25	1/0.05
Financial resources	0.10	5/0.50	10/1.00	7/0.70	3/0.30	1/0.10
Relative cost position	0.35	5/1.75	10/3.50	3/1.05	1/0.35	4/1.40
Customer service capabilities	0.15	5/0.75	7/1.05	10/1.50	1/0.15	4/1.60
Sum of weights	1.00					
Weighted overall strength rating		6.20	8.20	7.00	2.15	4.90

measures produces an overall strength rating. The higher a company's overall strength rating, the stronger its competitive position. The bigger the margin of difference between a company's overall rating and the scores of lower-rated rivals, the greater its implied net competitive advantage. Thus, ABC's total score of 61 (see the top half of Table 4.4) signals a greater net competitive advantage over Rival 4 (with a score of 32) than over Rival 1 (with a score of 58).

A weighted competitive strength analysis is conceptually stronger than an unweighted analysis because of the inherent weakness in assuming that all the strength measures are equally important.

However, it is better methodology to use a weighted rating system because the different measures of competitive strength are unlikely to be equally important. In a commodity-product industry, for instance, having low unit costs relative to rivals is nearly always the most important determinant of competitive strength. But in an industry with strong product differentiation the most significant measures of competitive strength may be brand awareness, amount of advertising, reputation for quality, and distribution capability. In a *weighted rating system* each measure of competitive strength is assigned a weight based on its perceived importance in shaping competitive success. The largest weight could be as high as .75 (maybe even higher) when one particular competitive variable is overwhelmingly decisive or as low as .20 when two or three strength measures are more important than the rest. Lesser competitive strength indicators can carry weights of .05 or .10. No matter whether the differences between the weights are big or little, *the sum of the weights must add up to 1.0.*

Weighted strength ratings are calculated by deciding how a company stacks up on each strength measure (using the 1 to 10 rating scale) and multiplying the assigned rating by the assigned weight (a rating score of 4 times a weight of .20 gives a weighted rating of .80). Again, the company with the highest rating on a given measure has an implied competitive edge on that measure, with the size of its edge reflected in the difference between its rating and rivals' ratings. The weight attached to the measure indicates how important the edge is. Summing a company's weighted strength ratings for all the measures yields an overall strength rating. Comparisons of the weighted overall strength scores indicate which competitors are in the strongest and weakest competitive positions and who has how big a net competitive advantage over whom.

The bottom half of Table 4.4 shows a sample competitive strength assessment for ABC Company using a weighted rating system. Note that the unweighted and weighted rating schemes produce a different ordering of the companies. In the weighted system, ABC Company dropped from second to third in strength, and Rival 1 jumped from third into first because of its high strength ratings on the two most important factors. Weighting the importance of the strength measures can thus make a significant difference in the outcome of the assessment.

Competitive strength assessments provide useful conclusions about a company's competitive situation. The ratings show how a company compares against rivals, factor by factor or capability by capability. Moreover, the overall competitive strength scores indicate whether the company is at a net competitive advantage or disadvantage against each rival. The firm with the largest overall competitive strength rating can be said to have a net competitive advantage over each rival.

Knowing where a company is competitively strong and where it is weak is essential in crafting a strategy to strengthen its long-term competitive position. As a general rule, a company should try to convert its competitive strengths into sustainable competitive advantage and take strategic actions to protect against its competitive weaknesses. At the same time, competitive strength ratings point to which rival companies may be vulnerable to competitive attack and the areas where they are weakest. When a company has important competitive strengths in areas where one or more rivals are weak, it makes sense to consider offensive moves to exploit their competitive weaknesses.

Competitive strengths and competitive advantages enable a company to improve its long-term market position.

QUESTION 5: WHAT STRATEGIC ISSUES DOES THE COMPANY FACE?

The final analytical task is to zero in on the issues management needs to address in forming an effective strategic action plan. Here, managers need to draw upon all the prior analysis, put the company's overall situation into perspective, and get a lock on exactly where they need to focus their strategic attention. This step should not be taken lightly. Without a precise fix on what the issues are, managers are not prepared to start crafting a strategy—a good strategy must offer a plan for dealing with all the strategic issues that need to be addressed.

To pinpoint issues for the company's strategic action agenda, managers ought to consider the following:

- Does the present strategy offer attractive defenses against the five competitive forces—particularly those that are expected to intensify in strength?
- Should the present strategy be adjusted to better respond to the driving forces at work in the industry?
- Is the present strategy closely matched to the industry's *future* key success factors?
- Does the present strategy adequately capitalize on the company's resource strengths?
- Which of the company's opportunities merit top priority? Which should be given lowest priority? Which are best suited to the company's resource strengths and capabilities?
- What does the company need to do to correct its resource weaknesses and to protect against external threats?
- To what extent is the company vulnerable to the competitive efforts of one or more rivals and what can be done to reduce this vulnerability?
- Does the company possess competitive advantage or must it work to offset competitive disadvantage?
- Where are the strong spots and weak spots in the present strategy?
- Are additional actions needed to improve the company's cost position, capitalize on emerging opportunities, and strengthen the company's competitive position?

The answers to these questions point to whether the company can continue the same basic strategy with minor adjustments or whether major overhaul is called for.

The better matched a company's strategy is to its external environment and to its resource strengths and capabilities, the less need there is to contemplate big shifts in strategy. On the other hand, when the present strategy is not well-suited for the road ahead, managers need to give top priority to the task of crafting a better strategy.

Table 4.5 provides a format for doing company situation analysis. It incorporates the concepts and analytical techniques discussed in this chapter and provides a way of reporting the results of company situation analysis in a systematic, concise manner.

KEY POINTS

There are five key questions to consider in performing company situation analysis:

1. *How well is the present strategy working?* This involves evaluating the strategy from both a qualitative standpoint (completeness, internal consistency, rationale, and suitability to the situation) and a quantitative standpoint (the strategic and financial

TABLE 4.5   Company Situation Analysis

1. Strategic Performance Indicators

Performance Indicator	19__	19__	20__	20__	20__
Market share	___	___	___	___	___
Sales growth	___	___	___	___	___
Net profit margin	___	___	___	___	___
Return on equity investment	___	___	___	___	___
Other?	___	___	___	___	___

2. Internal Resource Strengths and Competitive Capabilities

Internal Weaknesses and Resource Deficiencies

External Opportunities

External Threats to the Company's Well-Being

3. Competitive Strength Assessment

Rating scale: 1 = Very weak; 10 = Very strong

Key Success Factor/ Competitive Strength Measure	Weight	Firm A	Firm B	Firm C	Firm D	Firm E
Quality/product performance	___	___	___	___	___	___
Reputation/image	___	___	___	___	___	___
Manufacturing capability	___	___	___	___	___	___
Technological skills and know-how	___	___	___	___	___	___
Dealer network/distribution capability	___	___	___	___	___	___
New product innovation capability	___	___	___	___	___	___
Financial resources	___	___	___	___	___	___
Relative cost position	___	___	___	___	___	___
Customer service capability	___	___	___	___	___	___
Other?	___	___	___	___	___	___
Overall strength rating	___	___	___	___	___	___

4. Conclusions Concerning Competitive Position

(Improving/slipping? Competitive advantages/disadvantages?)

5. Major Strategic Issues the Company Must Address

results the strategy is producing). The stronger a company's current overall performance, the less likely the need for radical strategy changes. The weaker a company's performance and/or the faster the changes in its external situation (which can be gleaned from industry and competitive analysis), the more its current strategy must be questioned.

2. *What are the company's resource strengths and weaknesses and its external opportunities and threats?* A SWOT analysis provides an overview of a firm's situation and is an essential component of crafting a strategy tightly matched to the company's situation. A company's resource strengths, competencies, and competitive capabilities are important because they are the most logical and appealing building blocks for strategy; resource weaknesses are important because they may represent vulnerabilities that need correction. External opportunities and threats come into play because a good strategy necessarily aims at capturing a company's most attractive opportunities and at defending against threats to its well-being.

3. *Are the company's prices and costs competitive?* One telling sign of whether a company's situation is strong or precarious is whether its prices and costs are competitive with industry rivals. Strategic cost analysis and value chain analysis are essential tools in benchmarking a company's prices and costs against rivals, determining whether the company is performing particular functions and activities cost effectively, learning whether its costs are in line with competitors, and deciding which internal activities and business processes need to be scrutinized for improvement. Value chain analysis teaches that how competently a company manages its value chain activities relative to rivals is a key to building valuable competencies and competitive capabilities and then leveraging them into sustainable competitive advantage.

4. *How strong is the company's competitive position?* The key appraisals here involve whether the company's position is likely to improve or deteriorate if the present strategy is continued, how the company matches up against key rivals on industry KSFs and other chief determinants of competitive success, and whether and why the company has a competitive advantage or disadvantage. Quantitative competitive strength assessments, using the methodology presented in Table 4.4, indicate where a company is competitively strong and weak and provide insight into the company's ability to defend or enhance its market position. As a rule a company's competitive strategy should be built around its competitive strengths and should aim at shoring up areas where it is competitively vulnerable. Also, the areas where company strengths match up against competitor weaknesses represent the best potential for new offensive initiatives.

5. *What strategic issues does the company face?* The purpose of this analytical step is to develop a complete strategy-making agenda using the results of both company situation analysis and industry and competitive analysis. The emphasis here is on drawing conclusions about the strengths and weaknesses of a company's strategy and framing the issues that strategy makers need to consider.

Good company situation analysis, like good industry and competitive analysis, is crucial to good strategy making. A competently done evaluation of a company's resources and competencies exposes strong and weak elements in the present strategy, points to important company capabilities and vulnerabilities, and indicates the company's ability to protect or improve its competitive position in light of driving forces, competitive pressures, and the competitive strength of rivals. Managers need such understanding to craft a strategy that fits the company's situation well.

Collis, David J., and Cynthia A. Montgomery. "Competing on Resources: Strategy in the 1990s." *Harvard Business Review* 73 no. 4 (July–August 1995), pp. 118–28.

Fahey, Liam, and H. Kurt Christensen. "Building Distinctive Competencies into Competitive Advantages." Reprinted in Liam Fahey, *The Strategic Planning Management Reader*. Englewood Cliffs, N.J.: Prentice-Hall, 1989, pp. 113–18.

Prahalad, C. K., and Gary Hamel. "The Core Competence of the Corporation." *Harvard Business Review* 90, no. 3 (May–June 1990), pp. 79–93.

Shank, John K., and Vijay Govindarajan. *Strategic Cost Management: The New Tool for Competitive Advantage*. New York: Free Press, 1993.

Stalk, George, Philip Evans, and Lawrence E. Shulman. "Competing on Capabilities: The New Rules of Corporate Strategy." *Harvard Business Review* 70, no. 2 (March–April 1992), pp. 57–69.

Watson, Gregory H. *Strategic Benchmarking: How to Rate Your Company's Performance Against the World's Best*. New York: John Wiley & Sons, 1993.

SUGGESTED READINGS

5 | STRATEGY AND COMPETITIVE ADVANTAGE

Successful business strategy is about actively shaping the game you play, not just playing the game you find.

**Adam M. Brandenburger and
Barry J. Nalebuff**

The essence of strategy lies in creating tomorrow's competitive advantages faster than competitors mimic the ones you possess today.

Gary Hamel and C. K. Prahalad

Competitive strategy is about being different. It means deliberately choosing to perform activities differently or to perform different activities than rivals to deliver a unique mix of value.

Michael E. Porter

Strategies for taking the hill won't necessarily hold it.

Amar Bhide

Winning business strategies are grounded in sustainable competitive advantage. A company has *competitive advantage* whenever it has an edge over rivals in attracting customers and defending against competitive forces. There are many routes to competitive advantage: developing a product that becomes the industry standard, manufacturing the best-made product on the market, delivering superior customer service, achieving lower costs than rivals, having a more convenient geographic location, developing proprietary technology, incorporating features and styling with more buyer appeal, having the capability to bring new products to market faster than rivals, having greater technological expertise than rivals, developing unique competencies in customized mass production techniques, doing a better job of supply chain management than rivals, building a better-known brand name and reputation, and providing buyers more value for the money (a combination of good quality, good service, and acceptable price). *Investing aggressively in creating sustainable competitive advantage is a company's single most dependable contributer to above-average profitability.*

To succeed in building a competitive advantage, a company's strategy must aim at providing buyers with what they perceive as superior value—a good product at a lower price or a better product that is worth paying more for. This translates into performing value chain activities differently than rivals and building competencies and resource capabilities that are not readily matched.

This chapter focuses on how a company can achieve or defend a competitive advantage.[1] We begin by describing the basic types of competitive strategies in some depth. Next are sections examining the pros and cons of a vertical integration strategy and the merits of cooperative strategies. There are also major sections surveying the use of offensive moves to build competitive advantage and the use of defensive moves to protect it. In the concluding section we look at the competitive importance of timing strategic moves—when it is advantageous to be a first-mover and when it is better to be a fast-follower or late-mover.

---

[1]The definitive work on this subject is Michael E. Porter, *Competitive Advantage* (New York: Free Press, 1985). The treatment in this chapter draws heavily on Porter's pioneering contribution.

THE FIVE GENERIC COMPETITIVE STRATEGIES

A company's competitive strategy consists of its business approaches and initiatives to attract customers and fulfill their expectations, to withstand competitive pressures, and to strengthen its market position.[2] The competitive aim, quite simply, is to do a significantly better job of providing what buyers are looking for, enabling the company to earn a competitive advantage and outcompete rivals. The core of a company's competitive strategy consists of its internal initiatives to deliver superior value to customers. But it also includes offensive and defensive moves to counter the maneuvering of key rivals, actions to shift resources around to improve the firm's long-term competitive capabilities and market position, and tactical efforts to respond to whatever market conditions prevail at the moment.

The objective of competitive strategy is to knock the socks off rival companies by doing a significantly better job of providing what buyers are looking for.

Companies the world over are imaginative in conceiving strategies to win customer favor, outcompete rivals, and secure a market edge. Because a company's strategic initiatives and market maneuvers are usually tailor-made to fit its specific situation and industry environment, there are countless variations in the strategies that companies employ—strictly speaking, there are as many competitive strategies as there are competitors. However, when one strips away the details to get at the real substance the biggest and most important differences among competitive strategies boil down to (1) whether a company's market target is broad or narrow and (2) whether it is pursuing a competitive advantage linked to low costs or product differentiation. Five distinct approaches stand out:[3]

1. *A low-cost leadership strategy*—Appealing to a broad spectrum of customers based on being the overall low-cost provider of a product or service.

2. *A broad differentiation strategy*—Seeking to differentiate the company's product offering from rivals' in ways that will appeal to a broad spectrum of buyers.

3. *A best-cost provider strategy*—Giving customers more value for the money by combining an emphasis on low cost with an emphasis on upscale differentiation; the target is to have the best (lowest) costs and prices relative to producers of products with comparable quality and features.

4. *A focused or market niche strategy based on lower cost*—Concentrating on a narrow buyer segment and outcompeting rivals by serving niche members at a lower cost than rivals.

5. *A focused or market niche strategy based on differentiation*—Concentrating on a narrow buyer segment and outcompeting rivals by offering niche members a customized product or service that meets their tastes and requirements better than rivals' offerings.

Each of these five generic competitive approaches stakes out a different market position—as shown in Figure 5–1. Each involves distinctively different approaches to competing and operating the business. The listing in Table 5–1 highlights the

---

[2]Competitive strategy has a narrower scope than business strategy. Competitive strategy deals exclusively with management's action plan for competing successfully and providing superior value to customers. Business strategy not only concerns how to compete but also how management intends to address the full range of strategic issues confronting the business.

[3]The classification scheme is an adaptation of one presented in Michael E. Porter, *Competitive Strategy: Techniques for Analyzing Industries and Competitors* (New York: Free Press, 1980), chapter 2 and especially pp. 35–39 and 44–46.

FIGURE 5-1   The Five Generic Competitive Strategies

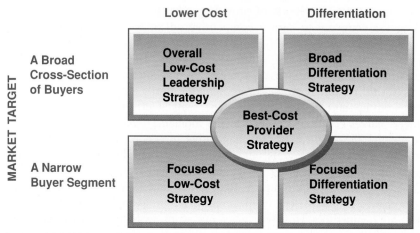

Source: Adapted from Michael E. Porter, *Competitive Strategy* (New York: Free Press, 1980), pp. 35–40.

contrasting features of these generic competitive strategies (for simplicity, the two strains of focused strategies are combined under one heading since they differ fundamentally on only one feature—the basis of competitive advantage).

Low-Cost Provider Strategies

Striving to be the industry's overall low-cost provider is a powerful competitive approach in markets where many buyers are price sensitive. The aim is to operate the business in a highly cost-effective manner and open up a sustainable cost advantage over rivals. A low-cost provider's strategic target is *low cost relative to competitors*, not the absolutely lowest possible cost. In pursuing low-cost leadership, managers must take care to include features and services that buyers consider essential—a product that is too spartan and frills-free weakens rather than strengthens competitiveness. Furthermore, it matters greatly whether the company achieves its cost advantage in ways difficult for rivals to copy or match. The value of a cost advantage depends on its sustainability. If rivals find it relatively easy and/or inexpensive to imitate the leader's low-cost methods, then the low-cost leader's advantage is too short-lived to yield a valuable edge.

A low-cost leader's basis for competitive advantage is lower overall costs than competitors. Successful low-cost leaders are exceptionally good at finding ways to drive costs out of their businesses.

A low-cost leader has two options for achieving superior profit performance. Option one is to use the lower-cost edge to underprice competitors and attract price-sensitive buyers in great enough numbers to increase total profits.[4] Option two is to

---

[4]The trick to profitably underpricing rivals is either to keep the size of the price cut smaller than the size of the firm's cost advantage (thus reaping the benefits of both a bigger profit margin per unit sold and the added profits on incremental sales) or to generate enough added volume to increase total profits despite thinner profit margins (larger volume can make up for smaller margins provided the price reductions bring in enough extra sales).

TABLE 5-1 Distinctive Features of the Generic Competitive Strategies

Type of Feature	Low-Cost Leadership	Broad Differentiation	Best-Cost Provider	Focused Low-Cost and Focused Differentiation
Strategic target	• A broad cross-section of the market.	• A broad cross-section of the market.	• Value-conscious buyers.	• A narrow market niche where buyer needs and preferences are distinctively different from the rest of the market.
Basis of competitive advantage	• Lower costs than competitors	• An ability to offer buyers something different from competitors.	• Give customers more value for the money	• Lower cost in serving the niche (focused low cost) *or* an ability to offer niche buyers something customized to their requirements and tastes (focused differentiation).
Product line	• A good basic product with few frills (acceptable quality and limited selection).	• Many product variations, wide selection, strong emphasis on the chosen differentiating features.	• Good-to-excellent attributes, several-to-many upscale features.	• Customized to fit the specialized needs of the target segment
Production emphasis	• A continuous search for cost reduction without sacrificing acceptable quality and essential features.	• Invent ways to create value for buyers; strive for product superiority.	• Incorporate upscale features and attributes at low cost.	• Tailor-made for the niche.
Marketing emphasis	• Try to make a virtue out of product features that lead to low cost.	• Build in whatever features buyers are willing to pay for. • Charge a premium price to cover the extra costs of differentiating features.	• Underprice rival brands with comparable features	• Communicate the focuser's unique ability to satisfy the buyer's specialized requirements
Sustaining the strategy	• Economical prices/ good value. • All elements of strategy aim at contributing to a sustainable cost advantage—the key is to manage costs down, year after year, in every area of the business.	• Communicate the points of difference in credible ways. • Stress constant improvement and innovation to stay ahead of imitative competitors. • Concentrate on a few key differentiating features; tout them to create a reputation and brand image.	• Unique expertise in managing costs down and product/ service caliber up simultaneously.	• Remain totally dedicated to serving the niche better than other competitors; don't blunt the firm's image and efforts by entering segments with substantially different buyer requirements or adding other product categories to widen market appeal.

refrain from price-cutting altogether, be content with the present market share, and use the lower-cost edge to earn a higher profit margin on each unit sold, thereby raising the firm's total profits and overall return on investment.

Illustration Capsule 14 describes ACX Technologies' strategy for gaining low-cost leadership in aluminum cans.

Opening Up a Cost Advantage   To achieve a cost advantage, a firm's cumulative costs across its value chain must be lower than competitors' cumulative costs. There are two ways to accomplish this:[5]

- Do a better job than rivals of performing internal value chain activities efficiently and of managing the factors that drive the costs of value chain activities.
- Revamp the firm's value chain to permit some cost-producing activities to be bypassed altogether.

Let's look at each of the two avenues.

Controlling the Cost Drivers   A firm's cost position is the result of the behavior of costs in each activity in its total value chain. Any of nine different cost drivers can come into play in determining a company's costs in a particular value chain activity:[6]

1. *Economies or diseconomies of scale.* The costs of a particular value chain activity are often subject to economies or diseconomies of scale. Economies of scale arise whenever activities can be performed more cheaply at larger volumes than smaller volumes and from the ability to spread out certain costs like R & D and advertising over a greater sales volume. Astute management of those activities subject to scale economies or diseconomies can be a major source of cost savings. For example, manufacturing economies can usually be achieved by simplifying the product line, by scheduling longer production runs for fewer models, and by using common parts and components in different models. In global industries, making separate products for each country market instead of selling a standard product worldwide tends to boost unit costs because of lost time in model changeover, shorter production runs, and inability to reach the most economic scale of production for each country model. Scale economies or diseconomies also arise in how a company manages its sales and marketing activities. A geographically organized sales force can realize economies as regional sales volume grows because a salesperson can write larger orders at each sales call and/or because of reduced travel time between calls; on the other hand, a sales force organized by product line can encounter travel-related diseconomies if salespersons have to spend travel time calling on distantly spaced customers. Boosting local or regional market share can lower sales and marketing costs per unit, whereas opting for a bigger national share by entering new regions can create scale diseconomies unless and until market penetration reaches efficient proportions.

2. *Learning and experience curve effects.* The cost of performing an activity can decline over time due to economies of experience and learning. Experience-based cost savings can come from much more than just personnel learning how to perform their tasks more efficiently and the debugging of new technologies. Other valuable

---

[5]Michael E. Porter, *Competitive Advantage* (New York: Free Press, 1985), p. 97.

[6]The list and explanations are condensed from Porter, *Competitive Advantage*, pp. 70–107.

ILLUSTRATION CAPSULE 14 ACX Technologies' Strategy to Become a Low-Cost Producer of Aluminum Cans

ACX Technologies began as an idea of William Coors, CEO of Adolph Coors beer company, to recycle more used aluminum cans back into new cans. Typical aluminum can-making operations involved producing thick aluminum slabs from a smelter using bauxite ore combined with as much as 50 percent scrap aluminum, including used aluminum beverage cans; the slabs of aluminum ingot were fed into a rolling mill to achieve the required thickness. Cans were then formed by stamping pieces of thin aluminum sheet into a seamless can with the top open for filling.

Coors's idea was to produce aluminum-can sheet from 95 percent recycled cans. He began by purchasing rights to technology that his company had helped develop in Europe; the technology used lower-cost electric arc furnaces to melt aluminum scrap directly, short-cutting the smelter process, which required heavy capital investment and big production volumes to be competitive. Coors then built a plant in Colorado that could grind and melt used cans and pour hot aluminum through a continuous caster to make aluminum sheet suitable for the tops and tabs of beverage cans. It took seven years to develop alloys with the desired attributes and to fine-tune the process—Coors originally believed it could be done in less than two years.

In mid-1991 Coors announced it would build a new $200 million mill in Texas to make sheet aluminum for the body of the can—the product with the most exacting specifications but also the number one end use for aluminum in the United States. Production was expected to begin by mid-1992, but problems and delays soon pushed the start-up date into fall 1993. The new plant's low-cost advantages stemmed from several factors:

- Lower capital investment.
- Use of 95 percent recycled aluminum cans as feedstock—reducing raw material costs in producing aluminum sheet by 10 to 15.
- Lower electricity requirements—electric arc technology used only about one-fifth of the electricity of bauxite-smelter technology.
- Comparatively low electric rates at the Texas location.

- Reduced labor costs as compared to bauxite-smelter technology.

Overall, production costs were expected to be anywhere from 20 to 35 percent below the costs of aluminum can producers using traditionally produced aluminum sheet, depending on the prevailing market prices for aluminum ingot and scrap aluminum. In addition, the mill had greater flexibility than traditional producers to vary its alloy mixes to meet different customer specifications.

Meanwhile, in December 1992 during construction of the Texas plant, Coors decided to spin off all aluminum can operations (along with a paper-packaging operation making patented polyethylene cartons with high-quality metallic graphics—packaging for Cascade boxes and Lever 2000 soapbars are examples; a ceramics unit making materials for high-tech applications; and several developmental businesses) into a new publicly owned company called ACX Technologies. The new company had 1992 revenues of $570 million, about 28 percent of which were sales to Coors. The breakdown of revenues in 1992 was aluminum for cans 17 percent, graphics packaging 37 percent, ceramics materials 32 percent, and developmental businesses 14 percent (including corn wet milling, biotechnology, defense electronics, and biodegradable polymers).

In summer 1993, the Texas plant was in start-up and can makers began testing the quality of its aluminum sheet. Coors was the first to qualify ACX's output for use; at year-end 1993 four other can users were testing the suitability of the plant's output for their products. ACX expected the plant to ship close to 50 million pounds of aluminum by year-end 1993 and 100 million pounds or more in 1994 as new customers placed orders. Analysts believed that ACX, given its cost advantage, could grow its annual volume to 1.0 to 1.5 billion pounds in 10 years as it perfected the process and gained acceptance for the quality of its output.

The company's new shares were issued at $10.75 in December 1992 when it went public. In the first 20 days of trading the price climbed to $21.75. Later in 1993, shares traded as high as $46. In May 1994 they were trading in the mid-$30s.

Sources: Based on information published by The Robinson-Humphrey Company and on Marc Charlier, "ACX Strives to Become Aluminum's Low-Cost Producer," *The Wall Street Journal*, September 29, 1993, p. B2.

sources of learning/experience economies include seeing ways to improve plant layout and work flows, to modify product designs to enhance manufacturing efficiency, to redesign machinery and equipment to gain increased operating speed, and to tailor parts and components in ways that streamline assembly. Learning can also reduce the cost of constructing and operating new retail outlets, new plants, or new distribution facilities. Plus there are learning benefits from getting samples of a rival's products and having design engineers study how they are made, benchmarking company activities against the performance of similar activities in other companies, and interviewing suppliers, consultants, and ex-employees of rival firms to tap into their wisdom. Learning tends to vary with the amount of management attention devoted to capturing the benefits of experience of both the firm and outsiders. Astute managers make a conscious effort not only to capture learning benefits but also to keep the benefits proprietary by building or modifying production equipment in-house, endeavoring to retain knowledgeable employees (to reduce the risk of them going to work for rivals firms), limiting the dissemination of cost-saving information through employee publications that can fall into rivals' hands, and enforcing strict nondisclosure provisions in employment contracts.

3. *The cost of key resource inputs.* The cost of performing value chain activities depends in part on what a firm has to pay for key resource inputs. All competitors do not incur the same costs for items purchased from suppliers or for resources used in performing value chain activities. How well a company manages the costs of acquiring inputs is often a big driver of costs. Input costs are a function of three factors:

- *Union versus nonunion labor*—Avoiding the use of union labor is often a key to low-cost manufacturing, not just to escape paying high wages (because such prominent low-cost manufacturers as Nucor and Cooper Tire are noted for their incentive compensation systems that allow their nonunion workforces to earn more than their unionized counterparts at rival companies) but rather to escape union work rules that stifle productivity.
- *Bargaining power vis-à-vis suppliers*—Many large enterprises (Wal-Mart, Home Depot, the world's major motor vehicle producers) have used their bargaining clout in purchasing large volumes to wrangle good prices on their purchases from suppliers. Differences in buying power among industry rivals can be an important source of cost advantage or disadvantage.
- *Locational variables*—Locations differ in their prevailing wage levels, tax rates, energy costs, inbound and outbound shipping and freight costs, and so on. Opportunities may exist for reducing costs by relocating plants, field offices, warehousing, or headquarters operations.

4. *Linkages with other activities in the company or industry value chain.* When the cost of one activity is affected by how other activities are performed, costs can be reduced by making sure that linked activities are performed in cooperative and coordinated fashion. For example, when a company's quality control costs or materials inventory costs are linked to the activities of suppliers, costs can be saved by working cooperatively with key suppliers on the design of parts and components, quality-assurance procedures, just-in-time delivery, and integrated materials supply. The costs of new product development can often be reduced by having cross-functional task forces (perhaps including representatives of suppliers and key customers) jointly work on R&D, product design, manufacturing plans, and market launch. Linkages with forward channels tend to center on location of warehouses,

materials handling, outbound shipping, and packaging (nail manufacturers, for example, learned that nails delivered in prepackaged 1-pound, 5-pound, and 10-pound assortments instead of 100-pound bulk cartons could reduce a hardware dealer's labor costs in filling individual customer orders). The lesson here is that effective coordination of linked activities holds potential for cost reduction.

5. *Sharing opportunities with other organizational or business units within the enterprise.* Different product lines or business units within an enterprise can often share the same order processing and customer billing systems, use a common sales force to call on customers, share the same warehouse and distribution facilities, or rely upon a common customer service and technical support team. Such combining of like activities and the sharing of resources across sister units can create significant cost savings. Cost sharing can help achieve scale economies, shorten the learning curve in mastering a new technology, and/or promote fuller capacity utilization. Furthermore, the know-how gained in one division or geographic unit can be used to help lower costs in another; sharing know-how across organizational lines has significant cost-saving potential when the activities are similar and know-how is readily transferred from one unit to another.

6. *The benefits of vertical integration versus outsourcing.* Partially or fully integrating into the activities of either suppliers or forward channel allies can allow an enterprise to detour suppliers or buyers with bargaining power. Vertical integration forward or backward also has potential if merging or tightly coordinating adjacent activities in the industry value chain offers significant cost savings. On the other hand, it is sometimes cheaper to outsource certain functions and activities to outside specialists who by virtue of their expertise and volume, can perform the activity/function more cheaply.

7. *Timing considerations associated with first-mover advantages and disadvantages.* Sometimes the first major brand in the market is able to establish and maintain its brand name at a lower cost than later brand arrivals—being a first-mover turns out to be cheaper than being a late-mover. On other occasions, such as when technology is developing fast, late purchasers can benefit from waiting to install second- or third-generation equipment that is both cheaper and more efficient; first-generation users often incur added costs associated with debugging and learning how to use an immature and unperfected technology. Likewise, companies that follow rather than lead new product development efforts sometimes avoid many of the costs that pioneers incur in performing pathbreaking R&D and opening up new markets.

8. *The percentage of capacity utilization.* Capacity utilization is a big cost driver for value chain activities that have substantial fixed costs associated with them. Higher rates of capacity utilization allow depreciation and other fixed costs to be spread over a larger unit volume, thereby lowering fixed costs per unit. The more capital-intensive the business and/or the higher the percentage of fixed costs as a percentage of total costs, the more important this cost driver becomes because there's such a stiff unit-cost penalty for underutilizing existing capacity. In such cases, finding ways to operate close to full capacity on a year-round basis can be an important source of cost advantage.[7]

---

[7]A firm can improve its capacity utilization by *(a)* serving a mix of accounts with peak volumes spread throughout the year, *(b)* finding off-season uses for its products, *(c)* serving private-label customers that can intermittently use the excess capacity, *(d)* selecting buyers with stable demands or demands that are counter to the normal peak/valley cycle, *(e)* letting competitors serve the buyer segments whose demands fluctuate the most, and *(f)* sharing capacity with sister units having a different seasonal production pattern (producing snowmobiles for the winter season and jet skis for summer water sports).

9. *Strategic choices and operating decisions.* A company's costs can be driven up or down by a fairly wide assortment of managerial decisions:

- Increasing/decreasing the number of products or varieties offered.
- Adding/cutting the services provided to buyers.
- Incorporating more/fewer performance and quality features into the product.
- Paying higher/lower wages and fringes to employees relative to rivals and firms in other industries.
- Increasing/decreasing the number of different forward channels used in distributing the firm's product.
- Lengthening/shortening delivery times to customers.
- Putting more/less emphasis than rivals on the use of incentive compensation to motivate employees and boost worker productivity.
- Raising/lowering the specifications for purchased materials.

Managers intent on achieving low-cost leader status have to develop sophisticated understanding of how the above nine factors drive the costs of each activity in the value chain. Then they not only have to use their knowledge to reduce costs for every activity where cost savings can be identified but they have to do so with enough ingenuity and commitment that the company ends up with a sustainable cost advantage over rivals.

Outperforming rivals in controlling the factors that drive costs is a very demanding managerial exercise.

Revamping the Makeup of the Value Chain   Dramatic cost advantages can emerge from finding innovative ways to restructure processes and tasks, cut out frills, and provide the basics more economically. The primary ways companies can achieve a cost advantage by reconfiguring their value chains include:

- Simplifying product design (utilizing computer-assisted design techniques, reducing the number of parts, standardizing parts and components across models and styles, shifting to an easy-to-manufacture product design).
- Stripping away the extras and offering only a basic, no-frills product or service, thereby cutting out activities and costs of multiple features and options.
- Shifting to a simpler, less capital-intensive, or more streamlined or flexible technological process (computer-assisted design and manufacture, flexible manufacturing systems that accommodate both low-cost efficiency and product customization).
- Finding ways to bypass the use of high-cost raw materials or component parts.
- Using direct-to-end-user sales and marketing approaches that cut out the often large costs and margins of wholesalers and retailers (costs and margins in the wholesale-retail portions of the value chain often represent 50 percent of the price paid by final consumers).
- Relocating facilities closer to suppliers, customers, or both to curtail inbound and outbound costs.
- Dropping the "something-for-everyone" approach and focusing on a limited product/service to meet a special, but important, need of the target buyer, thereby eliminating activities and costs of numerous product versions.

- Reengineering core business processes to consolidate work steps and cut out low-value-added activities (many low-cost providers are adept at learning how to operate with exceptionally small corporate staffs and corporate overheads).

- Using electronic communications technologies to eliminate paperwork (paperless invoice systems and electronic funds transfer), reduce printing and copying costs, speed communications via e-mail, curtail travel costs via teleconferencing, distribute information via company intranets, and establish relationships with customers using Websites and Web pages—companies the world over are using such technologies to restructure how they do business. Ford Motor has aggressively adopted videoconferencing and computer-assisted design and manufacturing technologies—its new "global car" (marketed as the Contour in North America) was developed by a team of designers at Ford locations around the world who used an on-line computer network to share ideas, create the actual designs, integrate the designs for the various parts and components (the chassis, engine, transmission, body. and instrumentation), and build and test prototypes via computer simulations. The Internet is fast becoming an attractive channel for retailing new software products (downloading new software directly from the Internet eliminates the costs of producing and packaging disks, then shipping and distributing them through wholesale and retail channels).

Companies can sometimes achieve dramatic cost advantages from creating altogether new value chain systems or from restructuring existing value chains and slicing out cost-producing activities that produce little customer value. For example, both Hallmark and American Greetings are marketing CD-ROM software that allows customers to select or design a card electronically, type in the recipient's name and address, and click on an "order" icon; computer technicians at the company take over from there—printing and mailing the card to arrive via regular mail or e-mail on the appropriate date. Card senders can pick out all the cards they want to send for an entire year at a single time if they wish and get a confirmation from the company that the appropriate card has been sent on its way. Such electronic value chains can radically alter how greeting cards are designed, produced, distributed, sold, and delivered.

Dell Computer has proved a pioneer in revamping the value chain in manufacturing and marketing PCs. Whereas most PC makers produce their models in volume and sell them through independent dealers and distributors, Dell markets directly to consumers, building its PCs as customers order them and shipping them to customers within a few days of receiving the order. Dell's value chain approach has proved cost effective in coping with the PC industry's blink-of-an-eye product life cycle (new models equipped with faster chips and new features appear every few months). Dell's build-to-order strategy enables it to avoid misjudging buyer demand for its various models and being saddled with fast-obsoleting components and finished goods inventories; its sell-direct strategy slices dealer/distributor costs and margins out of the value chain (although some of these savings are offset by the cost of Dell's direct marketing and customer support activities—functions that would otherwise be performed by dealers and distributors). In 1996, Dell's shipments of PCs grew 58 percent compared to growth of 30 percent for industry leader Compaq Computer and of 15 percent for the industry as a whole. In a number of industries, efforts are under way to restructure the value chain to remove the inefficiencies and costs of getting goods and services from the producer to the end users. Illustration Capsule 15 provides additional examples of the cost advantages of value chain restructuring.

ILLUSTRATION CAPSULE 15   Winning A Cost Advantage via Value Chain Restructuring: Iowa Beef Packers, FedEx, Southwest Airlines, and the Internet Entrepreneurs

Iowa Beef Packers, FedEx, and Southwest Airlines have been able to win strong competitive positions by restructuring the traditional value chains in their industries.

In beef packing, the traditional cost chain involved raising cattle on scattered farms and ranches, shipping them live to labor-intensive, unionized slaughtering plants, and then transporting whole sides of beef to grocery retailers whose butcher departments cut them into smaller pieces and packaged them for sale to grocery shoppers. Iowa Beef Packers revamped the traditional chain with a radically different strategy—large automated plants employing nonunion labor were built near economically transportable supplies of cattle, and the meat was partially butchered at the processing plant into smaller high-yield cuts (sometimes sealed in plastic casing ready for purchase), boxed, and shipped to retailers. IBP's inbound cattle transportation expenses, traditionally a major cost item, were cut significantly by avoiding the weight losses that occurred when live animals were shipped long distances; major outbound shipping cost savings were achieved by not having to ship whole sides of beef with their high waste factor. Iowa Beef's strategy was so successful that it became the largest U.S. meatpacker, surpassing the former industry leaders, Swift, Wilson, and Armour.

FedEx innovatively redefined the value chain for rapid delivery of small parcels. Traditional firms like Emery and Airborne Express operated by collecting freight packages of varying sizes, shipping them to their destination points via air freight and commercial airlines, and then delivering them to the addressee. Federal Express opted to focus only on the market for overnight delivery of small packages and documents. These were collected at local drop points during the late afternoon hours and flown on company-owned planes during early evening hours to a central hub in Memphis where from 11 P.M. to 3 A.M. each night all parcels were sorted, then reloaded on company planes, and flown during the early morning hours to their destination points, where they were delivered the next morning by company personnel using company trucks. The cost structure achieved by FedEx is low enough to permit it to guarantee overnight delivery of a small parcel anywhere in the United States for a price as low as $13.

Southwest Airlines has tailored its value chain to deliver low-cost, convenient service to passengers. It has mastered fast turnarounds at the gates (about 15 minutes versus 45 minutes for rivals); because the short turnarounds allow the planes to fly more hours per day, Southwest can schedule more flights per day with fewer aircraft. Southwest does not offer inflight meals, assigned seating, baggage transfer to connecting airlines, or first-class seating and service, thereby eliminating all the cost-producing activities associated with these features. Automated ticketing at its airport ticket counters and gates encourages customers to bypass travel agents (allowing Southwest to avoid paying commissions and to avoid the costs of maintaining an elaborate on-line computerized reservation system readily available to every travel agent) and also reduces the need for so many agents. Southwest's full-service rivals have higher costs because they must perform all the activities associated with providing meal service, assigned seating, premium classes of service, interline baggage checking, and computerized reservation systems.

Internet entrepreneurs are currently leading a revolution to revamp the value chains for providing traditional mail services, for providing all sorts of information to businesses and households, for conducting meetings via cameras and computers while the attendees sit at their desks in their offices, for providing long-distance telephone services via the Internet, for shopping for goods and services, for trading stocks, and on and on. They are employing "virtual value chains" and exploiting the new economics of doing business in the market*space* of the World Wide Web and commercial on-line services. Web pages are fast becoming retail showrooms and a new retail channel where business can sometimes be transacted faster, better, and less expensively than in the physical world of the marketplace. The shift to E-mail, faxing, and electronic funds transfer (which utilize digital or virtual value chains) is undermining the business of the U.S. Postal Service (which estimates that 25 percent of its revenues are at risk).

Source: Based in part on information in Michael E. Porter, *Competitive Advantage* (New York: Free Press, 1985), p. 109 and Jeffrey F. Rayport and John J. Sviokla, "Exploiting the Virtual Value Chain," *Harvard Business Review* 73, no. 6 (November–December 1995), pp. 75–85.

The Keys to Success in Achieving Low-Cost Leadership Managers intent on pursuing a low-cost-provider strategy have to scrutinize each cost-creating activity and determine what drives its cost. Then they have to use their knowledge about the cost drivers to manage the costs of each activity downward. They have to be proactive in restructuring the value chain, reengineering business processes, and eliminating nonessential work steps—some companies have been able to reduce the costs of reengineered activities by 30 to 70 percent, compared to the 5 to 10 percent possible with creative tinkering and adjusting.

Successful low-cost providers usually achieve their cost advantages by exhaustively pursuing cost savings throughout the value chain. All avenues for reducing costs are explored and no area of potential is overlooked—the success of Japanese manufacturers is largely due to their persistent search for continuous cost reductions across all aspects of their operations. Normally, low-cost producers have cost-conscious corporate cultures featuring broad employee participation in cost-control efforts, ongoing efforts to benchmark costs against best-in-class performers of an activity, intensive scrutiny of operating expenses and budget requests, programs to promote continuous cost improvement, limited perks and frills for executives, and adequate, but not lavish, facilities.

But while low-cost providers are champions of frugality, they are usually aggressive in investing in resources and capabilities that promise to drive costs out of the business. Wal-Mart, for example, employs state-of-the-art technology throughout its operations—its distribution facilities are an automated showcase, it uses on-line computer systems to order goods from suppliers and manage inventories, its stores are equipped with cutting-edge sales-tracking and check-out systems, and it operates a private satellite-communications system that daily sends point-of-sale data to 4,000 vendors.

Companies that employ low-cost leadership strategies include Lincoln Electric in arc-welding equipment, Briggs and Stratton in small gasoline engines, BIC in ball-point pens, Black & Decker in power tools, Stride Rite in footwear, Beaird-Poulan in chain saws, Ford in heavy-duty trucks, General Electric in major home appliances, Toys-R-Us in discount retailing, and Southwest Airlines in commercial airline travel.

The Competitive Defenses of Low-Cost Leadership Being the low-cost provider in an industry provides some attractive defenses against the five competitive forces.

- In meeting the challenges of *rival competitors*, the low-cost company is in the best position to compete on the basis of price, to use the appeal of lower price to grab sales (and market share) from rivals, to remain profitable in the face of strong price competition, and to survive price wars and earn above-average profits (based on bigger profit margins or greater sales volume). Low cost is a powerful defense in markets where many buyers are price sensitive and price competition thrives.

- In defending against the power of *buyers*, low costs provide a company with partial profit-margin protection, since powerful customers are rarely able to bargain price down past the survival level of the next most cost-efficient seller.

- In countering the bargaining leverage of *suppliers*, the low-cost producer is more insulated than competitors from powerful suppliers if the primary source of its cost advantage is greater internal efficiency. (A low-cost provider whose cost advantage stems from being able to buy components at favorable prices from outside suppliers could be vulnerable to the actions of powerful suppliers.)

- As concerns *potential entrants*, the low-cost leader can use price-cutting to make it harder for a new rival to win customers; the pricing power of the low-cost provider acts as a barrier for new entrants.
- In competing against *substitutes*, a low-cost leader is better positioned to use low price as a defense against companies trying to gain market inroads with a substitute product or service.

A low-cost leader is in the strongest position to win the business of price-sensitive buyers, set the floor on market price, and still earn a profit.

A low-cost company's ability to set the industry's price floor and still earn a profit erects protective barriers around its market position. Anytime price competition becomes a major market force, less efficient rivals get squeezed the most. Firms in a low-cost position relative to rivals have a competitive edge in profitably selling to price-sensitive buyers.

When a Low-Cost Provider Strategy Works Best   A competitive strategy predicated on low-cost leadership is particularly powerful when

1. Price competition among rival sellers is especially vigorous.
2. The industry's product is essentially standardized or a commodity readily available from a host of sellers (a condition that allows buyers to shop for the best price).
3. There are few ways to achieve product differentiation that have value to buyers (put another way, the differences between brands do not matter much to buyers), thereby making buyers very sensitive to price differences.

In markets where rivals compete mainly on price, low cost relative to competitors is the only competitive advantage that matters.

4. Most buyers use the product in the same ways—with common user requirements, a standardized product can satisfy the needs of buyers. In this case low selling price, not features or quality, becomes the dominant factor in causing buyers to choose one seller's product over another's.
5. Buyers incur low switching costs in changing from one seller to another, thus giving them the flexibility to switch readily to lower-priced sellers having equally good products.
6. Buyers are large and have significant power to bargain down prices.

As a rule, the more price sensitive buyers are and the more inclined they are to base their purchasing decisions on which seller offers the best price, the more appealing a low-cost strategy becomes.

The Pitfalls of a Low-Cost Provider Strategy   Perhaps the biggest pitfall of a low-cost provider strategy, however, is getting carried away with overly aggressively price-cutting and ending up with lower, rather than higher, profitability. A low-cost/low-price advantage results in superior profitability only if (1) prices are cut by less than the size of the cost advantage or (2) the added gains in unit sales are large enough to bring in a bigger total profit despite lower margins per unit sold—a company with a 5 percent cost advantage cannot cut prices 20 percent, end up with a volume gain of only 10 percent, and still expect to earn higher profits!

A second big pitfall is not emphasizing avenues of cost advantage that can be kept proprietary or that relegate rivals to playing catch-up. The value of a cost advantage depends on its sustainability. Sustainability, in turn, hinges on whether the company achieves its cost advantage in ways difficult for rivals to copy or match.

A third pitfall is becoming too fixated on cost reduction. Low cost cannot be pursued so zealously that a firm's offering ends up being too spartan and frills-free to generate buyer appeal. Furthermore, a company driving zealously to push its costs down has to guard against misreading or ignoring subtle but significant market swings—like growing buyer interest in added features or service, declining buyer sensitivity to price, or new developments that start to alter how buyers use the product. A low-cost zealot risks getting left behind if buyers begin to opt for enhanced quality, innovative performance features, faster service, and other differentiating features.

A low-cost provider's product offering must always contain enough attributes to be attractive to prospective buyers.

Even if these mistakes are avoided, a low-cost competitive approach still carries risk. Technological breakthroughs can open up cost reductions for rivals that nullify a low-cost leader's past investments and hard-won gains in efficiency. Heavy investments in cost reduction can lock a firm into both its present technology and present strategy, leaving it vulnerable to new technologies and to growing customer interest in something other than a cheaper price.

Differentiation Strategies

Differentiation strategies are an attractive competitive approach when buyer preferences are too diverse to be fully satisfied by a standardized product or when buyer requirements are too diverse to be fully satisfied by sellers with identical capabilities. To be successful with a differentiation strategy, a company has to study buyers' needs and behavior carefully to learn what they consider important, what they think has value, and what they are willing to pay for. Then the company has to either incorporate selected buyer-desired attributes that set its offering visibly and distinctively apart from rivals or else develop *unique* capabilities to serve buyer requirements. Competitive advantage results once a sufficient number of buyers become strongly attached to the differentiated attributes, features, or capabilities. The stronger the buyer appeal of the differentiated offering, the more that customers *bond* with the company and the stronger the resulting competitive advantage.

The essence of a differentiation strategy is to be unique in ways that are valuable to customers and that can be sustained.

Successful differentiation allows a firm to

- Command a premium price for its product, and/or
- Increase unit sales (because additional buyers are won over by the differentiating features), and/or
- Gain buyer loyalty to its brand (because some buyers are strongly attracted to the differentiating features and bond with the company and its products).

Differentiation enhances profitability whenever the extra price the product commands outweighs the added costs of achieving the differentiation. Company differentiation strategies fail when buyers don't value the brand's uniqueness enough to buy it instead of rivals' brands and/or when a company's approach to differentiation is easily copied or matched by its rivals.

Types of Differentiation Themes   Companies can pursue differentiation from many angles: a unique taste (Dr Pepper and Listerine), a host of features (America Online), reliable service (FedEx in overnight package delivery), spare parts availability (Caterpillar guarantees 48-hour spare parts delivery to any customer anywhere in the world or else the part is furnished free), more for the money (McDonald's and Wal-Mart), engineering design and performance (Mercedes in automobiles), prestige and distinctiveness (Rolex in watches), product reliability (Johnson & Johnson in baby products), quality manufacture (Karastan in carpets and Honda in automobiles), technological leadership (3M Corporation in bonding and coating products), a full range of services (Merrill Lynch), a complete line of products (Campbell's soups), and top-of-the-line image and reputation (Gucci, Ralph Lauren, and Chanel in fashions and accessories, Ritz-Carlton in hotels, and Mont Blanc and Cross in writing instruments).

Easy-to-copy differentiating features cannot produce sustainable competitive advantage.

The most appealing approaches to differentiation are those that are hard or expensive for rivals to duplicate. Indeed, resourceful competitors can, in time, clone almost any product or feature or attribute—if American Airlines creates a program for frequent fliers, so can Delta; if Ford offers a 30,000-mile bumper-to-bumper warranty on its new cars, so can Chrysler and Nissan. This is why *sustainable* differentiation usually has to be linked to unique internal skills, core competencies, and capabilities. When a company has competencies and capabilities that competitors cannot readily match and when its expertise can be used to perform activities in the value chain where differentiation potential exists, then it has a strong basis for sustainable differentiation. As a rule, differentiation yields a longer-lasting and more profitable competitive edge when it is based on new product innovation, technical superiority, product quality and reliability, and comprehensive customer service. Such attributes are widely perceived by buyers as having value; moreover, the competencies and competitive capabilities required to produce them tend to be tougher for rivals to copy or overcome profitably.

Where Along the Value Chain to Create the Differentiating Attributes   Differentiation is not something hatched in marketing and advertising departments, nor is it limited to the catchalls of quality and service. Differentiation is about understanding what the customer values, about where along the value chain to create the differentiating attributes, and about what resources and capabilities are needed to produce brand uniqueness. Differentiation possibilities exist in virtually every activity along an industry's value chain, most commonly in:

1. *Purchasing and procurement activities* that ultimately spill over to affect the performance or quality of the company's end product. (McDonald's gets high ratings on its french fries partly because it has very strict specifications on the potatoes purchased from suppliers.)

2. *Product R&D activities* that aim at improved product designs and performance features, expanded end uses and applications, shorter lead times in developing new models, more frequent first-on-the-market victories, wider product variety, added user safety, greater recycling capability, or enhanced environmental protection.

3. *Production R&D and technology-related activities* that permit custom-order manufacture at an efficient cost, make production methods more environmentally safe, or improve product quality, reliability, and appearance. (Vehicle manufacturers have developed flexible manufacturing systems that allow different models to be made on the same assembly line and to equip models with different options as they come down the assembly line.)

4. *Manufacturing activities* that reduce product defects, prevent premature product failure, extend product life, allow better warranty coverages, improve

economy of use, result in more end-user convenience, or enhance product appearance. (The quality edge enjoyed by Japanese automakers stems partly from their distinctive competence in performing assembly-line activities.)

5. *Outbound logistics and distribution activities* that allow for faster delivery, more accurate order filling, and fewer warehouse and on-the-shelf stockouts.

6. *Marketing, sales, and customer service activities* that can result in superior technical assistance to buyers, faster maintenance and repair services, more and better product information, more and better training materials for end users, better credit terms, quicker order processing, more frequent sales calls, or greater customer convenience.

Managers need to fully understand the value-creating differentiation options and the activities that drive uniqueness to devise a sound differentiation strategy and evaluate various differentiation approaches.[8]

Achieving a Differentiation-Based Competitive Advantage   The cornerstone of a successful differentiation strategy is creating buyer value in ways unmatched by rivals. There are four differentiation-based approaches to creating buyer value. One is to incorporate product attributes and user features that lower the buyer's overall costs of using the company's product—Illustration Capsule 16 lists options for making a company's product more economical. A second approach is to incorporate features that raise the performance a buyer gets out of the product—Illustration Capsule 17 contains differentiation avenues that enhance product performance and buyer value.

> *A differentiator's basis for competitive advantage is either a product/service offering whose attributes differ significantly from the offerings of rivals or a set of capabilities for delivering customer value that are unmatched by rivals.*

A third approach is to incorporate features that enhance buyer satisfaction in noneconomic or intangible ways. Goodyear's new Aquatread tire design appeals to safety-conscious motorists wary of slick roads in rainy weather. Wal-Mart's campaign to feature products "Made in America" appeals to customers concerned about the loss of American jobs to foreign manufacturers. Rolls-Royce, Tiffany's, and Gucci have competitive advantages linked to buyer desires for status, image, prestige, upscale fashion, superior craftsmanship, and the finer things in life. L. L. Bean makes its mail-order customers feel secure in their purchases by providing an unconditional guarantee with no time limit: "All of our products are guaranteed to give 100 percent satisfaction in every way. Return anything purchased from us at anytime if it proves otherwise. We will replace it, refund your purchase price, or credit your credit card, as you wish."

A fourth approach is to compete on the basis of capabilities—to deliver value to customers via competitive capabilities that rivals don't have or can't afford to match.[9] *The strategy-making challenge is selecting which differentiating capabilities to develop.* Successful capabilities-driven differentiation begins with a deep understanding of what customers need and ends with building organizational capabilities to satisfy these needs better than rivals. The Japanese auto manufacturers have the capability to bring new models to market faster than American and European automakers, thereby allowing them to satisfy changing consumer preferences for one

---

[8]Porter, *Competitive Advantage*, p. 124.

[9]For a more detailed discussion, see George Stalk, Philip Evans, and Lawrence E. Schulman, "Competing on Capabilities: The New Rules of Corporate Strategy," *Harvard Business Review* 70, no.2 (March–April 1992), pp. 57–69.

ILLUSTRATION CAPSULE 16   Differentiating Features That Lower Buyer Costs

A company doesn't have to resort to price cuts to make it cheaper for a buyer to use its product. An alternative is to incorporate features and attributes into the company's product/service package that

- Reduce the buyer's scrap and raw materials waste. Example of differentiating feature: cut-to-size components.
- Lower the buyer's labor costs (less time, less training, lower skill requirements). Examples of differentiating features: snap-on assembly features, modular replacement of worn-out components.
- Cut the buyer's downtime or idle time. Examples of differentiating features: greater product reliability, ready spare parts availability, or less frequent maintenance requirements.
- Reduce the buyer's inventory costs. Example of differentiating feature: just-in-time delivery.
- Reduce the buyer's pollution control costs or waste disposal costs. Example of differentiating feature: scrap pickup for use in recycling.
- Reduce the buyer's procurement and order-processing costs. Example of differentiating feature: computerized on-line ordering and billing procedures.

- Lower the buyer's maintenance and repair costs. Example of differentiating feature: superior product reliability.
- Lower the buyer's installation, delivery, or financing costs. Example of differentiating feature: 90-day payment same as cash.
- Reduce the buyer's need for other inputs (energy, safety equipment, security personnel, inspection personnel, other tools and machinery). Example of differentiating feature: fuel-efficient power equipment.
- Raise the trade-in value of used models.
- Lower the buyer's replacement or repair costs if the product unexpectedly fails later. Example of differentiating feature: longer warranty coverage.
- Lower the buyer's need for technical personnel. Example of differentiating feature: free technical support and assistance.
- Boost the efficiency of the buyer's production process. Examples of differentiating features: faster processing speeds, better interface with ancillary equipment.

Source: Adapted from Michael E. Porter, *Competitive Advantage* (New York: Free Press, 1985), pp. 135–37.

vehicle style versus another. CNN has the capability to cover breaking news stories faster and more completely than the major networks. Microsoft, with its three PC operating systems (DOS, Windows 95, and Windows NT), its large project teams of highly talented and antibureaucratic programmers who thrive on developing complex products and systems, and its marketing savvy and know-how, has greater capabilities to design, create, distribute, advertise, and sell an array of software products for PC applications than any of its rivals. Microsoft's capabilities are especially suited to fast-paced markets with short product life cycles and competition centered around evolving product features.

Real Value, Perceived Value, and Signals of Value   Buyers seldom pay for value they don't perceive, no matter how real the unique extras may be.[10] Thus the price premium that a differentiation strategy commands reflects *the value actually delivered* to the buyer and *the value perceived* by the buyer (even if not actually delivered). Actual and perceived value can differ whenever buyers have trouble assessing what their experience with the product will be. Incomplete knowledge on the part of buyers often causes them to judge value based on such *signals* as price (where price

---

[10]This discussion draws from Porter, *Competitive Advantage*, pp. 138–42. Porter's insights here are particularly important to formulating differentiating strategies because they highlight the relevance of "intangibles" and "signals."

ILLUSTRATION CAPSULE 17   Differentiating Features That Raise the Performance a User Gets

To enhance the performance a buyer gets from using its product/service, a company can incorporate features and attributes that

- Provide buyers greater reliability, durability, convenience, or ease of use.
- Make the company's product/service cleaner, safer, quieter, or more maintenance-free than rival brands.
- Exceed environmental or regulatory standards.

- Meet the buyer's needs and requirements more completely, compared to competitors' offerings.
- Give buyers the option to add on or to upgrade later as new product versions come on the market.
- Give buyers more flexibility to tailor their own products to the needs of their customers.
- Do a better job of meeting the buyer's future growth and expansion requirements.

Source: Adapted from Michael E. Porter, *Competitive Advantage* (New York: Free Press, 1985), pp. 135–38.

---

connotes quality), attractive packaging, extensive ad campaigns (i.e., how well known the product is), ad content and image, the quality of brochures and sales presentations, the seller's facilities, the seller's list of customers, the firm's market share, length of time the firm has been in business, and the professionalism, appearance, and personality of the seller's employees. Such signals of value may be as important as actual value (1) when the nature of differentiation is subjective or hard to quantify, (2) when buyers are making a first-time purchase, (3) when repurchase is infrequent, and (4) when buyers are unsophisticated.

> *A firm whose differentiation strategy delivers only modest extra value but clearly signals that extra value may command a higher price than a firm that actually delivers higher value but signals it poorly.*

Keeping the Cost of Differentiation in Line   Once a company's managers identify what approach to creating buyer value and establishing a differentiation-based competitive advantage makes the most sense, given the company's situation and what rivals are doing, they must develop the capabilities and build in the value-creating attributes at an acceptable cost. Differentiation usually raises costs. The trick to profitable differentiation is either to keep the costs of achieving differentiation below the price premium the differentiating attributes can command in the marketplace (thus increasing the profit margin per unit sold) or to offset thinner profit margins with enough added volume to increase total profits (larger volume can make up for smaller margins provided differentiation adds enough extra sales). It usually makes sense to incorporate extra differentiating features that are not costly but add to buyer satisfaction—FedEx installed systems that allowed customers to track packages in transit by connecting to FedEx's World Wide Web site and entering the airbill number; some hotels and motels provide in-room coffeemaking amenities for the convenience of guests or early-morning complimentary coffee-to-go in their lobbies; many McDonald's outlets have play areas for small children.

What Makes a Differentiation Strategy Attractive   Differentiation offers a buffer against the strategies of rivals when it results in enhanced buyer loyalty to a company's brand or model and greater willingness to pay a little (perhaps a lot!) more for it. In addition, successful differentiation (1) erects entry barriers in the form of customer loyalty and uniqueness that newcomers find hard to hurdle, (2) lessens buyers' bargaining power since the products of alternative sellers are less attractive to them, and (3) helps a firm fend off threats from substitutes not having comparable features or attributes. If differentiation allows a company to charge a higher price and have bigger profit margins, it is in a stronger position to withstand the efforts of powerful vendors to get a higher price for the items they supply. Thus, as with cost leadership, successful differentiation creates lines of defense for dealing with the five competitive forces.

For the most part, differentiation strategies work best in markets where (1) there are many ways to differentiate the company's offering from that of rivals and many buyers perceive these differences as having value, (2) buyer needs and uses of the item or service are diverse, (3) few rival firms are following a similar differentiation approach, and (4) technological change is fast-paced and competition revolves around evolving product features.

The Pitfalls of a Differentiation Strategy There are, of course, no guarantees that differentiation will produce a meaningful competitive advantage. If buyers see little value in the unique attributes or capabilities a company stresses, then its differentiation strategy will get a "ho-hum" reception in the marketplace. In addition, attempts at differentiation are doomed to fail if competitors can quickly copy most or all of the appealing product attributes a company comes up with. Rapid imitation means that a firm never achieves real differentiation, since competing brands keep changing in like ways each time a company makes a new move to set its offering apart from rivals'. Thus, to build competitive advantage through differentiation a firm must search out lasting sources of uniqueness that are burdensome for rivals to overcome. Other common pitfalls and mistakes in pursuing differentiation include:[11]

Any differentiating element that works well tends to draw imitators.

- Trying to differentiate on the basis of something that does not lower a buyer's cost or enhance a buyer's well-being, as perceived by the buyer.
- Overdifferentiating so that price is too high relative to competitors or that the array of differentiating attributes exceeds buyers' needs.
- Trying to charge too high a price premium (the bigger the price differential the harder it is to keep buyers from switching to lower-priced competitors).
- Ignoring the need to signal value and depending only on intrinsic product attributes to achieve differentiation.
- Not understanding or identifying what buyers consider as value.

A low-cost producer strategy can defeat a differentiation strategy when buyers are satisfied with a basic product and don't think "extra" attributes are worth a higher price.

The Strategy of Being a Best-Cost Provider

This strategy aims at giving customers *more value for the money*. It combines a strategic emphasis on low cost with a strategic emphasis on *more than minimally acceptable* quality, service, features, and performance. The idea is to create superior value by meeting or exceeding buyers' expectations on key quality-service-features-performance attributes and by beating their expectations on price. The aim is to become the low-cost provider of a product or service with *good-to-excellent* attributes, then use the cost advantage to underprice brands with comparable attributes. Such a competitive approach is termed a *best-cost provider strategy* because the producer has the best (lowest) cost relative to producers whose brands have comparable quality-service-features-performance attributes.

---

[11]Porter, *Competitive Advantage*, pp. 160–62.

ILLUSTRATION CAPSULE 18   Toyota's Best-Cost Producer Strategy for Its Lexus Line

Toyota Motor Co. is widely regarded as a low-cost producer among the world's motor vehicle manufacturers. Despite its emphasis on product quality, Toyota has achieved absolute low-cost leadership because of its considerable skills in efficient manufacturing techniques and because its models are positioned in the low-to-medium end of the price spectrum where high production volumes are conducive to low unit costs. But when Toyota decided to introduce its new Lexus models to compete in the luxury-car market, it employed a classic best-cost producer strategy. Toyota's Lexus strategy had three features:

- Transferring its expertise in making high-quality Toyota models at low cost to making premium quality luxury cars at costs below other luxury-car makers, especially Mercedes and BMW. Toyota executives reasoned that Toyota's manufacturing skills should allow it to incorporate high-tech performance features and upscale quality into Lexus models at less cost than other luxury-car manufacturers.

- Using its relatively lower manufacturing costs to underprice Mercedes and BMW, both of which had models selling in the $40,000 to $75,000 range (and some even higher). Toyota believed that with its cost advantage it could price

attractively equipped Lexus models in the $38,000 to $42,000 range, drawing price-conscious buyers away from Mercedes and BMW and perhaps inducing quality-conscious Lincoln and Cadillac owners to trade up to a Lexus.

- Establishing a new network of Lexus dealers, separate from Toyota dealers, dedicated to providing a level of personalized, attentive customer service unmatched in the industry.

The Lexus 400 series models were priced in the $48,000 to $55,000 range and competed against Mercedes's 300/400E series, BMW's 535i/740 series, Nissan's Infiniti Q45, Cadillac Seville, Jaguar, and Lincoln Continental. The lower-priced Lexus 300 series, priced in the $30,000 to $38,000 range, competed against Cadillac Eldorado, Acura Legend, Infiniti J30, Buick Park Avenue, Mercedes's C-Class series, BMW's 315 series, and Oldsmobile's Aurora line.

Lexus's best-cost producer strategy was so successful that Mercedes introduced a new C-Class series, priced in the $30,000 to $35,000 range, to become more competitive. The Lexus LS 400 models and the Lexus SC 300/400 models ranked first and second, respectively, in the widely watched J. D. Power & Associates quality survey for 1993 cars; the entry-level Lexus ES 300 model ranked eighth.

The competitive advantage of a best-cost provider comes from matching close rivals on quality-service-features-performance and beating them on cost. To become a best-cost provider, a company must match quality at a lower cost than rivals, match features at a lower cost than rivals, match product performance at a lower cost than rivals, and so on. What distinguishes a successful best-cost provider is having the resources, know-how, and capabilities to incorporate upscale product or service attributes at a low cost. The most successful best-cost producers have competencies and capabilities to simultaneously drive unit costs down and product caliber up—see Illustration Capsule 18.

A best-cost provider strategy has great appeal from the standpoint of competitive positioning. It produces superior customer value by balancing a strategic emphasis on low cost against a strategic emphasis on differentiation. In effect, it is a *hybrid* strategy that allows a company to combine the competitive advantage of both low cost and differentiation to deliver superior buyer value. In markets where buyer diversity makes product differentiation the norm and many buyers are price and value sensitive, a best-cost producer strategy can be more advantageous than either a pure low-cost producer strategy or a pure differentiation strategy keyed to product superiority. This is because a best-cost provider can position itself near the middle of the market with either a medium-quality product at a below-average price or a very good product at a medium price. Often the

> *The most powerful competitive approach a company can pursue is to strive relentlessly to become a lower-and-lower-cost producer of a higher-and-higher-caliber product, aiming at eventually becoming the industry's absolute lowest-cost producer and, simultaneously, the producer of the industry's overall best product.*

majority of buyers prefer a midrange product rather than the cheap, basic product of a low-cost producer or the expensive product of a top-of-the-line differentiator.

Focused or Market Niche Strategies

What sets focused strategies apart from low-cost or differentiation strategies is concentrated attention on a narrow piece of the total market. The target segment or niche can be defined by geographic uniqueness, by specialized requirements in using the product, or by special product attributes that appeal only to niche members. The aim of a focus strategy is to do a better job of serving buyers in the target market niche than rival competitors. *A focuser's basis for competitive advantage is either (1) lower costs than competitors in serving the market niche or (2) an ability to offer niche members something they perceive is better.* A focused strategy based on low cost depends on there being a buyer segment whose requirements are less costly to satisfy compared to the rest of the market. A focused strategy based on differentiation depends on there being a buyer segment that wants or needs special product attributes or company capabilities.

Examples of firms employing some version of a focused strategy include Netscape (a specialist in software for browsing the World Wide Web), Porsche (in sports cars), Cannondale (in top-of-the-line mountain bikes), commuter airlines like Horizon, Comair, and Atlantic Southeast (specializing in low-traffic, short-haul flights linking major airports with smaller cities 100 to 250 miles away), Jiffy Lube International (a specialist in quick oil changes, lubrication, and simple maintenance for motor vehicles), and Bandag (a specialist in truck tire recapping that promotes its recaps aggressively at over 1,000 truck stops). Microbreweries, local bakeries, bed-and-breakfast inns, and local owner-managed retail boutiques are all good examples of enterprises that have scaled their operations to serve narrow or local customer segments. Illustration Capsule 19 describes Motel 6's focused low-cost strategy and Ritz-Carlton's focused differentiation strategy.

Focused low-cost strategies are fairly common. Producers of private-label goods are able to lower product development, marketing, distribution, and advertising costs by concentrating on making generic items imitative of name-brand merchandise and selling directly to retail chains wanting a basic house brand to sell at a discount to price-sensitive shoppers. Discount stock brokerage houses have lowered costs by focusing on customers who are willing to forgo the investment research, advice, and financial services offered by full-service firms like Merrill Lynch in return for 30 percent or more commission savings on their buy-sell transactions. Pursuing a cost advantage via focusing works well when a firm can lower costs significantly by concentrating its energies and resources on a well-defined market segment.

At the other end of the market spectrum, focusers like Godiva Chocolates, Chanel, Rolls-Royce, Häagen-Dazs, and W. L. Gore (the maker of Gore-Tex) employ successful differentiation strategies targeted at upscale buyers. Indeed, most markets contain a buyer segment willing to pay a big price premium for the very finest items available, thus opening the window for some competitors to pursue differentiation-based focus strategies aimed at the very top of the market. Another successful focused differentiator is a "fashion food retailer" called Trader Joe's, a 74-store chain that is a combination gourmet deli and food warehouse.[12] Customers shop Trader Joe's as much for entertainment as for conventional grocery items—the store stocks all kinds of out-of-the-ordinary culinary treats like raspberry salsa, salmon burgers, and jasmine fried rice, as well as the standard goods normally found in

---

[12]Gary Hamel, "Strategy as Revolution," *Harvard Business Review* 74, no. 4 (July–August 1996), p. 72.

ILLUSTRATION CAPSULE 19   Focused Strategies in the Lodging Industry: Motel 6 and Ritz-Carlton

Motel 6 and Ritz-Carlton compete at opposite ends of the lodging industry. Motel 6 employs a focused strategy keyed to low cost; Ritz-Carlton employs a focused strategy based on differentiation.

Motel 6 caters to price-conscious travelers who want a clean, no-frills place to spend the night. To be a low-cost provider of overnight lodging, Motel 6 (1) selects relatively inexpensive sites on which to construct its units—usually near interstate exits and high traffic locations but far enough away to avoid paying prime site prices; (2) builds only basic facilities—no restaurant or bar and only rarely a swimming pool; (3) relies on standard architectural designs that incorporate inexpensive materials and low-cost construction techniques; and (4) has simple room furnishings and decorations. These approaches lower both investment costs and operating costs. Without restaurants, bars, and all kinds of guest services, a Motel 6 unit can be operated with just front desk personnel, room cleanup crews, and skeleton building-and-grounds maintenance. To promote the Motel 6 concept with travelers who have simple overnight requirements, the chain uses unique, recognizable radio ads done by nationally syndicated radio personality Tom Bodett; the ads describe Motel 6's clean rooms, no-frills facilities, friendly atmosphere, and dependably low rates (usually under $30 per night).

In contrast, the Ritz-Carlton caters to discriminating travelers and vacationers willing and able to pay for top-of-the-line accommodations and world-class personal service. Ritz-Carlton hotels feature (1) prime locations and scenic views from many rooms, (2) custom architectural designs, (3) fine dining restaurants with gourmet menus prepared by accomplished chefs, (4) elegantly appointed lobbies and bar lounges, (5) swimming pools, exercise facilities, and leisure-time options, (6) upscale room accommodations, (7) an array of guest services and recreation opportunities appropriate to the location, and (8) large, well-trained professional staffs who do their utmost to make each guest's stay an enjoyable experience.

Both companies concentrate their attention on a narrow piece of the total market. Motel 6's basis for competitive advantage is lower costs than competitors in providing basic, economical overnight accommodations to price-constrained travelers. Ritz-Carlton's advantage is its capability to provide superior accommodations and unmatched personal service for a well-to-do clientele. Each is able to succeed, despite polar opposite strategies, because the market for lodging consists of diverse buyer segments with diverse preferences and abilities to pay.

supermarkets. What sets Trader Joe's apart is not just its unique combination of food novelties and competitively priced grocery items but the opportunity it provides to turn an otherwise mundane shopping trip into a whimsical treasure hunt.

When Focusing Is Attractive   A focused strategy based either on low cost or differentiation becomes increasingly attractive as more of the following conditions are met:

- The target market niche is big enough to be profitable.
- The niche has good growth potential.
- The niche is not crucial to the success of major competitors.
- The focusing firm has the capabilities and resources to serve the targeted niche effectively.
- The focuser can defend itself against challengers based on the customer goodwill it has built up and its superior ability to serve buyers comprising the niche.

A focuser's specialized competencies and capabilities in serving the target market niche provide a basis for defending against the five competitive forces. Multisegment rivals may not have the capability to truly meet the expectations of the focused firm's target clientele. Entry into a focuser's target segment is made harder by the focused firm's unique capabilities in serving the market niche—the barrier of trying to match the focuser's capabilities deters potential newcomers. A focuser's capabilities in serving the niche also present a hurdle that makers of substitute products must overcome. The bargaining leverage of powerful customers is blunted somewhat by their own unwillingness to shift their business to rival companies less capable of meeting their expectations.

Focusing works best (1) when it is costly or difficult for multisegment competitors to meet the specialized needs of the target market niche, (2) when no other rival is attempting to specialize in the same target segment, (3) when a firm doesn't have the resources or capabilities to go after a bigger piece of the total market, and (4) when the industry has many different niches and segments, allowing a focuser to pick an attractive niche suited to its resource strengths and capabilities.

The Risks of a Focused Strategy   Focusing carries several risks. One is the chance that competitors will find effective ways to match the focused firm in serving the target niche. A second is that the niche buyer's preferences and needs might shift toward the product attributes desired by the majority of buyers. An erosion of the differences across buyer segments lowers entry barriers into a focuser's market niche and provides an open invitation for rivals to compete for the focuser's customers. A third risk is that the segment becomes so attractive it is soon inundated with competitors, splintering segment profits.

VERTICAL INTEGRATION STRATEGIES AND COMPETITIVE ADVANTAGE

Vertical integration extends a firm's competitive scope within the same industry. It involves expanding the firm's range of activities backward into sources of supply and/or forward toward end users of the final product. Thus, if a manufacturer invests in facilities to produce certain component parts rather than purchase them from outside suppliers, it remains in essentially the same industry as before. The only change is that it has business units in two production stages in the industry's value chain system. Similarly, if a paint manufacturer elects to integrate forward by opening 100 retail stores to market its products directly to consumers, it remains in the paint business even though its competitive scope extends further forward in the industry chain.

Vertical integration strategies can aim at *full integration* (participating in all stages of the industry value chain) or *partial integration* (building positions in just some stages of the industry's total value chain). A firm can accomplish vertical integration by starting its own operations in other stages in the industry's activity chain or by acquiring a company already performing the activities it wants to bring in-house.

The Strategic Advantages of Vertical Integration

The only good reason for investing company resources in vertical integration is to strengthen the firm's competitive position.[13] Unless vertical integration produces sufficient cost savings to justify the extra investment or yields a differentiation-based competitive advantage, it has no real payoff profitwise or strategywise.

---

[13]See Kathryn R. Harrigan, "Matching Vertical Integration Strategies to Competitive Conditions," *Strategic Management Journal* 7, no. 6 (November–December 1986), pp. 535–56; for a discussion of the advan-

Backward Integration   Integrating backward generates cost savings only when the volume needed is big enough to capture the same scale economies suppliers have and when suppliers' production efficiency can be matched or exceeded with no drop-off in quality. The best potential for being able to reduce costs via backward integration exists when suppliers have sizable profit margins, when the item being supplied is a major cost component, and when the needed technological skills are easily mastered. Backward vertical integration can produce a differentiation-based competitive advantage when a company, by performing activities in-house that were previously outsourced, ends up with a better-quality product/service offering, improves the caliber of its customer service, or in other ways enhances the performance of its final product. On occasion, integrating into more stages along the value chain can add to a company's differentiation capabilities by allowing it to build or strengthen its core competencies, better master key skills or strategy-critical technologies, or add features that deliver greater customer value.

A vertical integration strategy has appeal only if it significantly strengthens a firm's competitive position.

Backward integration can also spare a company the uncertainty of depending on suppliers of crucial components or support services, and it can lessen a company's vulnerability to powerful suppliers that raise prices at every opportunity. Stockpiling, fixed-price contracts, multiple-sourcing, long-term cooperative partnerships, or the use of substitute inputs are not always attractive ways for dealing with uncertain supply conditions or with economically powerful suppliers. Companies that are low on a key supplier's priority list can find themselves waiting on shipments every time supplies get tight. If this occurs often and wreaks havoc in a company's own production and customer relations activities, backward integration may be an advantageous strategic solution.

Forward Integration   The strategic impetus for forward integration has much the same roots. In many industries, independent sales agents, wholesalers, and retailers handle competing brands of the same product; they have no allegiance to any one company's brand and tend to push "what sells" or earns them the biggest profits. Undependable sales and distribution channels can give rise to costly inventory pile-ups and frequent underutilization of capacity, undermining the economies of a steady, near-capacity production operation. In such cases, a manufacturer may find it competitively advantageous to integrate forward into wholesaling and/or retailing in order to have outlets fully committed to representing its products. A manufacturer can sometimes profit from investing in company-owned distributorships, franchised dealer networks, and/or a chain of retail stores if it is able to realize higher rates of capacity utilization or build a stronger brand image. There are also occasions when integrating forward into the activity of selling directly to end users can produce important cost savings and permit lower selling prices by eliminating many of the costs of using wholesale-retail channels.

For a raw materials producer, integrating forward into manufacturing may permit greater product differentiation and provide an avenue of escape from the price-oriented competition of a commodity business. Often, in the early phases of an industry's value chain, intermediate goods are commodities in the sense that they have essentially identical technical specifications irrespective of producer (as is the case with crude oil, poultry, sheet steel, cement, and textile fibers). Competition in

---

tages and disadvantages of vertical integration, see John Stuckey and David White, "When and When *Not* to Vertically Integrate," *Sloan Management Review* (Spring 1993), pp. 71–83.

the markets for commodity products is usually fiercely price competitive, with the shifting balance between supply and demand giving rise to volatile profits. However, the closer the activities in the chain get to the ultimate consumer, the greater the opportunities for a firm to break out of a commodity-like competitive environment and differentiate its end product through design, service, quality features, packaging, promotion, and so on. Product differentiation often reduces the importance of price compared to other value-creating activities and improves profit margins.

The Strategic Disadvantages of Vertical Integration

Vertical integration has some substantial drawbacks, however. It boosts a firm's capital investment in the industry, increasing business risk (what if the industry goes sour?) and perhaps denying financial resources to more worthwhile pursuits. A vertically integrated firm has vested interests in protecting its present investments in technology and production facilities. Because of the high costs of abandoning such investments before they are worn out, fully integrated firms tend to adopt new technologies slower than partially integrated or nonintegrated firms. Second, integrating forward or backward locks a firm into relying on its own in-house activities and sources of supply (that later may prove more costly than outsourcing) and may result in less flexibility in accommodating buyer demand for greater product variety.

The big disadvantage of vertical integration is that it locks a firm deeper into the industry; unless operating across more stages in the industry's value chain builds competitive advantage, it is a questionable strategic move.

Third, vertical integration can pose problems of balancing capacity at each stage in the value chain. The most efficient scale of operation at each activity link in the value chain can vary substantially. Exact self-sufficiency at each interface is the exception not the rule. Where internal capacity is insufficient to supply the next stage, the difference has to be bought externally. Where internal capacity is excessive, customers need to be found for the surplus. And if by-products are generated, they have to be disposed of.

Fourth, integration forward or backward often calls for radically different skills and business capabilities. Parts and components manufacturing, assembly operations, wholesale distribution, and retailing are different businesses with different key success factors. Managers of a manufacturing company should consider carefully whether it makes good business sense to invest time and money in developing the expertise and merchandising skills to integrate forward into wholesaling or retailing. Many manufacturers learn the hard way that owning and operating wholesale-retail networks present many headaches, fit poorly with what they do best, and don't always add the kind of value to their core business they thought they would. Integrating backward into parts and components manufacture isn't as simple or profitable as it sometimes sounds either. Personal computer makers, for example, frequently have trouble getting timely deliveries of the latest semiconductor chips at favorable prices. Most, though, don't come close to having the resources or capabilities to integrate backward into chip manufacture; the semiconductor business is technologically sophisticated and entails heavy capital requirements and ongoing R&D effort, and mastering the manufacturing process takes a long time.

Fifth, backward vertical integration into the production of parts and components can reduce a company's manufacturing flexibility, lengthening the time it takes to make design and model changes and to bring new products to market. Companies that alter designs and models frequently in response to shifting buyer preferences often find vertical integration into parts and components burdensome because of constant retooling and redesign costs and the time it takes to implement coordinated changes. Outsourcing parts and components is often cheaper and less complicated than making them in-house, allowing a company to be more nimble in adapting its product offering to buyer preferences. Most of the world's automakers, despite their expertise in automotive technology and manufacturing, have concluded that they are better off from the standpoints of quality, cost, and design flexibility purchasing many of their parts and components from manufacturing specialists rather than trying to supply their own needs.

Unbundling and Outsourcing Strategies   In recent years, some vertically integrated companies have found operating in many stages of the industry value chain to be so competitively burdensome that they have adopted *vertical deintegration* (or unbundling) strategies. Deintegration involves withdrawing from certain stages/activities in the value chain system and relying on outside vendors to supply the needed products, support services, or functional activities. Outsourcing pieces of the value chain formerly performed in-house makes strategic sense whenever:

- An activity can be performed better or more cheaply by outside specialists.
- The activity is not crucial to the firm's ability to achieve sustainable competitive advantage and won't hollow out its core competencies, capabilities, or technical know-how. (Outsourcing of maintenance services, data processing, accounting, and other administrative support activities to companies specializing in these services has become commonplace.)
- It reduces the company's risk exposure to changing technology and/or changing buyer preferences.
- It streamlines company operations in ways that improve organizational flexibility, cut cycle time, speed decision making, and reduce coordination costs.
- It allows a company to concentrate on its core business.

Often, many of the advantages of vertical integration can be captured and many of the disadvantages avoided by forging close, long-term cooperative partnerships with key suppliers and tapping into the capabilities that able suppliers have developed. In years past, many companies' relationships with suppliers were of an arms-length nature where the nature of the items supplied were specified in detailed, short-term contracts.[14] Although a company might engage the same supplier repeatedly, there was no expectation that this would be the case; price was usually the determining factor for awarding contracts to suppliers, and companies maneuvered for leverage over suppliers to get the lowest possible prices. The threat of switching suppliers was the primary weapon. To make this threat credible, short-term contracts with multiple suppliers were preferred to long-term ones with single suppliers in order to promote lively competition among suppliers. Today, such approaches are being abandoned in favor of dealing with fewer, highly capable suppliers that are treated as long-term *strategic partners*. Cooperative relationships and alliances with key suppliers are replacing contractual, purely price-oriented relationships. There's more of a concerted effort to coordinate related value chain activities and to build important capabilities by working closely with suppliers.

---

[14]Robert H. Hayes, Gary P. Pisano, and David M. Upton, *Strategic Operations: Competing Through Capabilities* (New York: Free Press, 1996), pp. 419–22.

Weighing the Pros and Cons of Vertical Integration

All in all, then, a strategy of vertical integration can have both important strengths and weaknesses. Which direction the scales tip on vertical integration depends on (1) whether it can enhance the performance of strategy-critical activities in ways that lower cost or increase differentiation, (2) its impact on investment costs, flexibility and response times, and administrative overheads associated with coordinating operations across more stages, and (3) whether it creates competitive advantage. The issue of vertical integration hinges on which capabilities and value-chain activities need to be performed in-house in order for a company to be successful and which can be safely delegated to outside suppliers. Absent solid benefits, vertical integration is not likely to be an attractive competitive strategy option.

COOPERATIVE STRATEGIES AND COMPETITIVE ADVANTAGE

Many companies have begun forming strategic alliances and cooperative relationships with other companies to complement their own strategic initiatives and strengthen their competitiveness in domestic and international markets. Strategic alliances are cooperative agreements between firms that go beyond normal company-to-company dealings but that fall short of merger or full partnership and ownership ties.[15] Alliances and/or cooperative agreements can involve joint research efforts, technology sharing, joint use of production facilities, marketing one another's products, or joining forces to manufacture components or assemble finished products.

Companies enter into alliances or establish cooperative agreements for several strategically beneficial reasons.[16] The five most important are to collaborate on technology or the development of promising new products, to improve supply chain efficiency, to gain economies of scale in production and/or marketing, to fill gaps in their technical and manufacturing expertise, and to acquire or improve market access. Allies learn much from one another in performing joint research, sharing technological know-how, and collaborating on complementary new technologies and products. Manufacturers pursue alliances with parts and components suppliers to gain the efficiencies of better supply chain management and to speed new products to market. By joining forces in producing components, assembling models, or marketing their products, companies can realize cost savings not achievable with their own small volumes; they can also learn how to improve their quality control and production procedures by studying one another's manufacturing methods. Often alliances are formed to share distribution facilities and dealer networks or to jointly promote complementary products, thereby mutually strengthening their access to buyers.

While a few firms can pursue their strategies alone, it is becoming increasingly common for companies to pursue their strategies in collaboration with suppliers, distributors, makers of complementary products, and sometimes even select competitors.

Not only can alliances offset competitive disadvantages but they also can result in the allied companies' directing their competitive energies more toward mutual rivals and less toward one another. Who partners with whom affects the pattern of industry rivalry. Many runner-up companies, wanting to preserve their independence, resort to

---

[15]A number of strategic alliances do involve minority ownership by one, occasionally both, alliance members however. See C. A. Bartlett and S. Ghoshal, *Managing Across Borders: The Transnational Solution* (Boston: Harvard Business School Press, 1989), p. 65 and Kenichi Ohmae, "The Global Logic of Strategic Alliances," *Harvard Business Review* 89, no. 2 (March–April 1989), pp. 143–54.

[16]Porter, *The Competitive Advantage of Nations*, p. 66; see also Jeremy Main, "Making Global Alliances Work," *Fortune*, December 17, 1990, pp. 121–26.

alliances rather than merger to try to close the competitive gap on leading companies—*they rely on collaboration with others to enhance their own capabilities,
develop valuable new strategic resources, and compete effectively.* Industry leaders
pursue cooperative alliances in order to better fend off ambitious rivals and to open
up new opportunities.

Strategic cooperation is a much-favored, indeed necessary, approach in industries
like electronics, semiconductors, computer hardware and software, and telecommunications where technological developments are occurring at a furious pace along
many different paths and advances in one technology spill over to affect others (often
blurring industry boundaries). Whenever industries are experiencing high-
velocity technological change in many areas simultaneously, firms find it
essential to have cooperative relationships with other enterprises to stay on
the leading edge of technology and product performance even in their own
area of specialization. They cooperate in technology development, in sharing R&D information of mutual interest, in developing new products that
complement each other, and in building networks of dealers and distributors to handle their products. Competitive advantage emerges when a
company acquires valuable resources and capabilities through alliances and cooperative agreements that it could not otherwise obtain on its own—this requires real in-
the-trenches collaboration between the partners to create new value together, not
merely an arm's-length exchange of ideas and information. Unless partners value the
skills, resources, and contributions each brings to the alliance and the cooperative
arrangement results in win-win outcomes, it is doomed.

Alliances and cooperative agreements between companies can lead to competitive advantage in ways that otherwise are beyond a company's reach.

Cooperative strategies and alliances to penetrate international markets are also
common between domestic and foreign firms. Such partnerships are useful in putting
together the resources and capabilities to do business over more country markets. For
example, U.S., European, and Japanese companies wanting to build market footholds
in the fast-growing China market have all pursued partnership arrangements with
Chinese companies to help in dealing with governmental regulations, to supply
knowledge of local markets, to provide guidance on adapting their products to
Chinese consumers, to set up local manufacturing capabilities, and to assist in
distribution, marketing, and promotional activities.

General Electric has formed over 100 cooperative partnerships in a wide range of
areas; IBM has joined in over 400 strategic alliances.[17] Alliances are so central to
Corning's strategy that the company describes itself as a "network of
organizations." Microsoft and Netscape have both been aggressive users of
cooperative strategies, forming scores of alliances with the providers of
complementary technologies and products to build and strengthen their
competitive positions. In the PC industry cooperative alliances are pervasive because the different components of PCs and the software to run them
is supplied by so many different companies—one set of companies provide
the microprocessors, another group makes the motherboards, another the
monitors, another the keyboards, another the printers, and so on. Moreover,
their facilities are scattered across the United States, Japan, Taiwan, Singapore, and Malaysia. Close collaboration on product development, logistics, production, and the timing of new product releases works to the advantage of nearly all PC
industry members.

Alliances and cooperative arrangements, whether they bring together companies from different parts of the industry value chain or different parts of the world, are a fact of life in business today.

---

[17]Michael A. Hitt, Beverly B. Tyler, Camilla Hardee, and Daewoo Park, "Understanding Strategic Intent in
the Global Marketplace," *Academy of Management Executive*, 9, no. 2 (May 1995), p. 13.

The Achilles' heel of alliances and cooperative strategies is the danger of becoming dependent on other companies for *essential* expertise and capabilities over the long term. To be a market leader (and perhaps even a serious market contender), a company must develop its own capabilities in areas where internal strategic control is pivotal to protecting its competitiveness and building competitive advantage. Moreover, acquiring essential know-how and capabilities from one's allies sometimes holds only limited potential (because one's partners guard their most valuable skills and expertise); in such instances, acquiring or merging with a company possessing the desired know-how and resources is a better solution.

USING OFFENSIVE STRATEGIES TO SECURE COMPETITIVE ADVANTAGE

Competitive advantage is nearly always achieved by successful offensive strategic moves—moves calculated to yield a cost advantage, a differentiation advantage, or a resource or capabilities advantage. Defensive strategies can protect competitive advantage but rarely are the basis for creating the advantage. How long it takes for a successful offensive to create an edge varies with the competitive circumstances.[18] The

Competitive advantage is usually acquired by employing a creative offensive strategy that isn't easily thwarted by rivals.

buildup period, shown in Figure 5–2, can be short, if the requisite resources and capabilities are already in place or if the offensive produces immediate buyer response (as can occur with a dramatic price cut, an imaginative ad campaign, or a new product that proves to be a smash hit). Or the buildup can take much longer, if winning consumer acceptance of an innovative product will take some time or if the firm may need several years to debug a new technology and bring new capacity on-line. Ideally, an offensive move builds competitive advantage quickly; the longer it takes, the more likely rivals will spot the move, see its potential, and begin a counterresponse. The size of the advantage (indicated on the vertical scale in Figure 5–2) can be large (as in pharmaceuticals where patents on an important new drug produce a substantial advantage) or small (as in apparel where popular new designs can be imitated quickly).

Following a successful competitive offensive is a *benefit period* during which the fruits of competitive advantage can be enjoyed. The length of the benefit period depends on how much time it takes rivals to launch counteroffensives and begin closing the gap. A lengthy benefit period gives a firm valuable time to earn above-average profits and recoup the investment made in creating the advantage. The best strategic offensives produce big competitive advantages and long benefit periods.

As rivals respond with counteroffensives to close the competitive gap, the *erosion period* begins. Competent, resourceful competitors can be counted on to counterattack with initiatives to overcome any market disadvantage they face—they are not going to stand idly by and passively accept being outcompeted without a fight.[19] Thus, to sustain an initially won competitive advantage, a firm must come up with follow-on offensive and defensive moves. Preparations for the next round of strategic moves ought to be made during the benefit period so that the needed resources are in place when competitors mount efforts to cut into the leader's advantage. Unless the firm stays a step ahead of rivals by initiating one series of offensive and defensive

---

[18]Ian C. MacMillan, "How Long Can You Sustain a Competitive Advantage?" reprinted in Liam Fahey, *The Strategic Planning Management Reader* (Englewood Cliffs, N.J.: Prentice-Hall, 1989), pp. 23–24.

[19]Ian C. MacMillan, "Controlling Competitive Dynamics by Taking Strategic Initiative," *The Academy of Management Executive* 2, no. 2 (May 1988), p. 111.

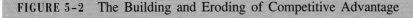

FIGURE 5-2   The Building and Eroding of Competitive Advantage

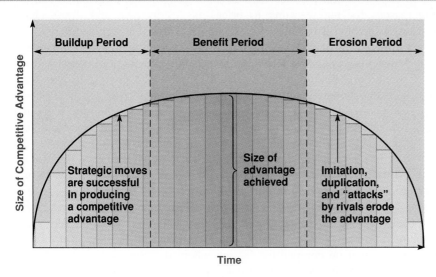

moves after another to protect its market position and retain customer favor, its market advantage will erode.

There are six basic types of strategic offensives:[20]

- Initiatives to match or exceed competitor strengths.
- Initiatives to capitalize on competitor weaknesses.
- Simultaneous initiatives on many fronts.
- End-run offensives.
- Guerrilla offensives.
- Preemptive strikes.

Initiatives to Match or Exceed Competitor Strengths

There are two instances in which it makes sense to mount offensives aimed at neutralizing or overcoming the strengths and capabilities of rival companies. The first is when a company has no choice but to try to whittle away at a strong rival's competitive advantage. The second is when it is possible to gain profitable market share at the expense of rivals despite whatever resource strengths and capabilities they have. Attacking the strengths of rivals is most likely to meet with success when a firm has either a *superior* product offering or *superior* organizational resources and capabilities. The merit of challenging a rival's strengths head-on depends on the trade-off between the costs of the offensive and its competitive benefits. Absent good prospects for added profitability and a more solidified competitive position, such an offensive is ill advised.

One of the most powerful offensive strategies is to challenge rivals with an equally good or better product at a lower price.

[20]Philip Kotler and Ravi Singh, "Marketing Warfare in the 1980s," *The Journal of Business Strategy* 1, no. 3 (Winter 1981), pp. 30–41; Philip Kotler, *Marketing Management*, 5th ed. (Englewood Cliffs, N.J.: Prentice-Hall, 1984), pp. 401–6; and Ian MacMillan, "Preemptive Strategies," *Journal of Business Strategy* 14, no. 2 (Fall 1983), pp. 16–26.

The classic avenue for attacking a strong rival is with an equally good offering at a lower price.[21] This can produce market share gains if the targeted competitor has strong reasons for not resorting to price cuts of its own and if the challenger convinces buyers that its product is just as good. However, such a strategy increases total profits only if the gains in unit sales are enough to offset the impact of lower prices and thinner margins per unit sold. A more potent and sustainable basis for mounting a price-aggressive challenge is to *first* achieve a cost advantage and then hit competitors with a lower price.[22] Price-cutting supported by a cost advantage can be continued indefinitely. Without a cost advantage, price-cutting works only if the aggressor has more financial resources and can outlast its rivals in a war of attrition.

Challenging larger, entrenched competitors with aggressive price-cutting is foolhardy unless the aggressor has either a cost advantage or greater financial strength.

Other strategic options for attacking a competitor's strengths include leapfrogging into next-generation technologies to make the rival's products and/or production processes obsolete, adding new features that appeal to the rival's customers, running comparison ads, constructing major new plant capacity in the rival's backyard, expanding the product line to match the rival model for model, and developing customer service capabilities that the rival doesn't have. As a rule, challenging a rival on competitive factors where it is strong is an uphill struggle. Success can be long in coming and usually hinges on developing a cost advantage, a service advantage, a product with attractive differentiating features, or unique competitive capabilities (fast design-to-market times, greater technical know-how, or agility in responding to shifting customer requirements).

Initiatives to Capitalize on Competitor Weaknesses

In this offensive approach, a company tries to gain market inroads by directing its competitive attention to the weaknesses of rivals. There are a number of ways to achieve competitive gains at the expense of rivals' weaknesses:

- Concentrate on geographic regions where a rival has a weak market share or is exerting less competitive effort.
- Pay special attention to buyer segments that a rival is neglecting or is weakly equipped to serve.
- Go after the customers of rivals whose products lag on quality, features, or product performance; in such cases, a challenger with a better product can often convince the most performance-conscious customers to switch to its brand.
- Make special sales pitches to the customers of rivals who provide subpar customer service—it may be relatively easy for a service-oriented challenger to win a rival's disenchanted customers.
- Try to move in on rivals that have weak advertising and weak brand recognition—a challenger with strong marketing skills and a recognized brand name can often win customers away from lesser-known rivals.
- Introduce new models or product versions that exploit gaps in the product lines of key rivals; sometimes "gap fillers" turn out to be a market hit and develop into new growth segments—witness Chrysler's success in minivans. This initiative works well when new product versions satisfy neglected buyer needs.

---

[21]Kotler, *Marketing Management*, p. 402.
[22]Ibid., p. 403.

As a rule, initiatives that exploit competitor weaknesses stand a better chance of succeeding than do those that challenge competitor strengths, especially if the weaknesses represent important vulnerabilities and the rival is caught by surprise with no ready defense.[23]

Simultaneous Initiatives on Many Fronts

On occasion a company may see merit in launching a grand competitive offensive involving multiple initiatives (price cuts, increased advertising, new product introductions, free samples, coupons, in-store promotions, rebates) across a wide geographic front. Such all-out campaigns can throw a rival off-balance, diverting its attention in many directions and forcing it to protect many pieces of its customer base simultaneously. Microsoft is employing a grand offensive to outmaneuver rivals in securing a prominent role on the Internet for its software products.[24] It allocated $160 million and 500 of its most talented programmers to the task of rapidly introducing upgraded versions of Internet Explorer (to overtake Netscape's Navigator Web browser), incorporated Explorer in the Windows 95 package and allowed Internet users to download Explorer free, negotiated deals with America Online and CompuServe to utilize Internet Explorer, put several thousand programmers to work on a variety of Internet-related projects (with R&D budgets of over $500 million), assigned another large group of programmers the task of retrofitting Microsoft's product line to better mesh with the Internet, entered into a joint venture with NBC to form a new cable channel called MSNBC, invested $1 billion in the common stock of Comcast (the second largest U.S. cable provider) to give it leverage in pushing for faster advances in Internet-related cable technologies to speed data transfer, and formed alliances with NBC, ESPN, Disney, Dreamworks, and others to provide content for Microsoft Network and MSNBC. Multifaceted offensives have their best chance of success when a challenger not only comes up with an especially attractive product or service but also has a brand name and reputation to secure broad distribution and retail exposure. Then it can blitz the market with advertising and promotional offers and perhaps entice significant numbers of buyers to switch their brand allegiance.

End-Run Offensives

End-run offensives seek to avoid head-on challenges tied to aggressive price-cutting, escalated advertising, or costly efforts to outdifferentiate rivals. Instead the idea is to maneuver *around* competitors, capture unoccupied or less contested market territory, and change the rules of the competitive game in the aggressor's favor. Examples of end-run offensives include launching initiatives to build strong positions in geographic areas where close rivals have little or no market presence, trying to create new segments by introducing products with different attributes and performance features to better meet the needs of selected buyers, and leapfrogging into next-generation technologies. A successful end-run offensive allows a company to gain a significant first-mover advantage in a new arena and force competitors to play catch-up.

---

[23]For a discussion of the use of surprise, see William E. Rothschild, "Surprise and the Competitive Advantage," *Journal of Business Strategy* 4, no. 3 (Winter 1984), pp. 10–18.

[24]A more detailed account of Microsoft's grand offensive is presented in Brent Schendler, "Software Hardball," *Fortune*, September 30, 1996, pp.106–16.

Guerrilla Offensives

Guerrilla offensives are particularly well-suited to small challengers who have neither the resources nor the market visibility to mount a full-fledged attack on industry leaders.[25] A guerrilla offensive uses the hit-and-run principle, selectively trying to grab sales and market share wherever and whenever an underdog catches rivals napping or spots an opening to lure their customers away. There are several ways to wage a guerrilla offensive:[26]

1. Go after buyer groups that are not important to major rivals.

2. Go after buyers whose loyalty to rival brands is weakest.

3. Focus on areas where rivals are overextended and have spread their resources most thinly (possibilities include going after selected customers located in isolated geographic areas, enhancing delivery schedules at times when competitors' deliveries are running behind, adding to quality when rivals have quality control problems, and boosting technical services when buyers are confused by competitors' proliferation of models and optional features).

4. Make small, scattered, random raids on the leaders' customers with such tactics as occasional lowballing on price (to win a big order or steal a key account).

5. Surprise key rivals with sporadic but intense bursts of promotional activity to pick off buyers who might otherwise have selected rival brands.

6. If rivals employ unfair or unethical competitive tactics and the situation merits it, file legal actions charging antitrust violations, patent infringement, or unfair advertising.

Preemptive Strikes

Preemptive strategies involve moving first to secure an advantageous position that rivals are foreclosed or discouraged from duplicating. What makes a move "preemptive" is its one-of-a-kind nature—whoever strikes first stands to acquire competitive assets that rivals can't readily match. A firm can bolster its competitive capabilities with several preemptive moves:[27]

- Expand production capacity well ahead of market demand in hopes of discouraging rivals from following with expansions of their own. When rivals are "bluffed" out of adding capacity for fear of creating long-term excess supply and having to struggle with the bad economics of underutilized plants, the preemptor stands to win a bigger market share as market demand grows and it has the production capacity to take on new orders.

---

[25]For an interesting study of how small firms can successfully employ guerrilla-style tactics, see Ming-Jer Chen and Donald C. Hambrick, "Speed, Stealth, and Selective Attack: How Small Firms Differ from Large Firms in Competitive Behavior," *Academy of Management Journal* 38, no. 2 (April 1995), pp. 453–82.

[26]For more details, see Ian MacMillan "How Business Strategists Can Use Guerrilla Warfare Tactics," *Journal of Business Strategy* 1, no. 2 (Fall 1980), pp. 63–65; Kathryn R. Harrigan, *Strategic Flexibility* (Lexington, Mass.: Lexington Books, 1985), pp. 30–45; and Liam Fahey, "Guerrilla Strategy: The Hit-and-Run Attack," in Fahey, *The Strategic Management Planning Reader,* pp. 194–97.

[27]The use of preemptive moves is treated comprehensively in Ian MacMillan, "Preemptive Strategies," *Journal of Business Strategy* 14, no. 2 (Fall 1983), pp. 16–26. What follows in this section is based on MacMillan's article.

- Tie up the best (or the most) raw material sources and/or the most reliable, high-quality suppliers with long-term contracts or backward vertical integration. This move can relegate rivals to struggling for second-best supply positions.

- Secure the best geographic locations. An attractive first-mover advantage can often be locked up by moving to obtain the most favorable site along a heavily traveled thoroughfare, at a new interchange or intersection, in a new shopping mall, in a natural beauty spot, close to cheap transportation or raw material supplies or market outlets, and so on.

- Obtain the business of prestigious customers.

- Build a "psychological" image in the minds of consumers that is unique and hard to copy and that establishes a compelling appeal and rallying cry. Examples include Nike's "Just do it" tag line, Avis's well-known "We try harder" theme; Frito-Lay's guarantee to retailers of "99.5% service"; and Prudential's "piece of the rock" image of safety and permanence.

- Secure exclusive or dominant access to the best distributors in an area.

To be successful, a preemptive move doesn't have to totally block rivals from following or copying; it merely needs to give a firm a "prime" position that is not easily circumvented. Fox's stunning four-year, $6.2 billion contract to televise NFL football (a preemptive strike that ousted CBS) represented a bold strategic move to transform Fox into a major TV network alongside ABC, CBS, and NBC. DeBeers became the dominant world distributor of diamonds by buying up the production of most of the important diamond mines. Du Pont's aggressive capacity expansions in titanium dioxide, while not blocking all competitors from expanding, did discourage enough to give it a leadership position in the industry.

Choosing Whom to Attack

Aggressor firms need to analyze which of their rivals to challenge as well as how to outcompete them. Any of four types of firms can make good targets:[28]

1. *Market leaders.* Offensive attacks on a market leader make the best sense when the leader in terms of size and market share is not a "true leader" in serving the market well. Signs of leader vulnerability include unhappy buyers, a product line that is inferior to what several rivals have, a competitive strategy that lacks real strength based on low-cost leadership or differentiation, strong emotional commitment to an aging technology the leader has pioneered, outdated plants and equipment, a preoccupation with diversification into other industries, and mediocre or declining profitability. Offensives to erode the positions of market leaders have real promise when the challenger is able to revamp its value chain or innovate to gain a fresh cost-based or differentiation-based advantage.[29] Attacks on leaders don't have to result in making the aggressor the new leader to be judged successful; a challenger may "win" by simply wresting enough sales from the leader to become a stronger runner-up. Caution is well advised in challenging strong market leaders—there's a significant risk of squandering valuable resources in

[28]Kotler, *Marketing Management*, p. 400.
[29]Porter, *Competitive Advantage*, p. 518.

a futile effort or starting a fierce and profitless industrywide battle for market share.

2. *Runner-up firms.* Runner-up firms are an especially attractive target when a challenger's resource strengths and competitive capabilities are well suited to exploiting their weaknesses.

3. *Struggling enterprises that are on the verge of going under.* Challenging a hard-pressed rival in ways that further sap its financial strength and competitive position can weaken its resolve and hasten its exit from the market.

4. *Small local and regional firms.* Because these firms typically have limited expertise and resources, a challenger with broader capabilities is well positioned to raid their biggest and best customers—particularly those who are growing rapidly, have increasingly sophisticated requirements, and may already be thinking about switching to a full-service supplier.

Choosing the Basis for Attack   A firm's strategic offensive should, at a minimum, be tied to its most potent competitive assets—its core competencies, resource strengths, and competitive capabilities. Otherwise the prospects for success are indeed dim. The centerpiece of the offensive can be a new-generation technology, a newly developed competitive capability, an innovative new product, introduction of attractive new performance features, a cost advantage in manufacturing or distribution, or some kind of differentiation advantage. If the challenger's resources and competitive strengths amount to a competitive advantage over the targeted rivals, so much the better.

At the very least, an offensive must be tied to a firm's resource strengths; more optimally, it is grounded in competitive advantage.

USING DEFENSIVE STRATEGIES TO PROTECT COMPETITIVE ADVANTAGE

In a competitive market, all firms are subject to challenges from rivals. Market offensives can come both from new entrants in the industry and from established firms seeking to improve their market positions. The purpose of defensive strategy is to lower the risk of being attacked, weaken the impact of any attack that occurs, and influence challengers to aim their efforts at other rivals. While defensive strategy usually doesn't enhance a firm's competitive advantage, it helps fortify a firm's competitive position, protect its most valuable resources and capabilities from imitation, and sustain whatever competitive advantage it does have.

The foremost purpose of defensive strategy is to protect competitive advantage and fortify the firm's competitive position.

A company can protect its competitive position in several ways. One is trying to block the avenues challengers can take in mounting an offensive. The options include:[30]

- Hiring additional employees to broaden or deepen the company's core competencies or capabilities in key areas (so as to be able to overpower rivals who attempt to imitate its skills and resources).

- Enhancing the flexibility of resource assets and competencies (so that they can be quickly redeployed or adapted to meet changing market conditions),

---

[30]Porter, *Competitive Advantage*, pp. 489–94.

thereby being in a greater state of readiness for new developments than rivals.

- Broadening the firm's product line to close off vacant niches and gaps to would-be challengers.
- Introducing models or brands that match the characteristics challengers' models already have or might have.
- Keeping prices low on models that most closely match competitors' offerings.
- Signing exclusive agreements with dealers and distributors to keep competitors from using the same ones.
- Granting dealers and distributors volume discounts to discourage them from experimenting with other suppliers.
- Offering free or low-cost training to product users.
- Endeavoring to discourage buyers from trying competitors' brands by (1) providing coupons and sample giveaways to buyers most prone to experiment and (2) making early announcements about impending new products or price changes to induce potential buyers to postpone switching.
- Raising the amount of financing provided to dealers and buyers.
- Reducing delivery times for spare parts.
- Lengthening warranty coverages.
- Participating in alternative technologies.
- Protecting proprietary know-how in product design, production technologies, and other value chain activities.
- Contracting for all or most of the output of the best suppliers to make it harder for rivals to obtain parts and components of equal quality.
- Avoiding suppliers that also serve competitors.
- Purchasing natural resource reserves ahead of present needs to keep them from competitors.
- Challenging rivals' products or practices in regulatory proceedings.

Moves such as these not only buttress a firm's present position, they also present competitors with a moving target. Protecting the status quo isn't enough. A good defense entails adjusting quickly to changing industry conditions and, on occasion, being a first-mover to block or preempt moves by would-be aggressors. A mobile defense is preferable to a stationary defense.

A second approach to defensive strategy entails signaling challengers that there is a real threat of strong retaliation if a challenger attacks. The goal is to dissuade challengers from attacking at all or at least divert them to options that are less threatening to the defender. Would-be challengers can be signaled by:[31]

- Publicly announcing management's commitment to maintain the firm's present market share.
- Publicly announcing plans to construct adequate production capacity to meet and possibly surpass the forecasted growth in industry volume.

---

[31]Ibid., pp. 495–97. The listing here is selective; Porter offers a greater number of options.

- Giving out advance information about a new product, technology breakthrough, or the planned introduction of important new brands or models in hopes that challengers will delay moves of their own until they see if the announced actions actually happen.
- Publicly committing the company to a policy of matching competitors' terms or prices.
- Maintaining a war chest of cash and marketable securities.
- Making an occasional strong counterresponse to the moves of weak competitors to enhance the firm's image as a tough defender.

Another way to dissuade rivals is to try to lower the profit inducement for challengers to launch an offensive. When a firm's or industry's profitability is enticingly high, challengers are more willing to tackle high defensive barriers and combat strong retaliation. A defender can deflect attacks, especially from new entrants, by deliberately forgoing some short-run profits and using accounting methods that obscure profitability.

FIRST-MOVER ADVANTAGES AND DISADVANTAGES

When to make a strategic move is often as crucial as *what* move to make. Timing is especially important when *first-mover advantages* or *disadvantages* exist.[32] Being first to initiate a strategic move can have a high payoff when (1) pioneering helps build a firm's image and reputation with buyers, (2) early commitments to supplies of raw materials, new technologies, distribution channels, and so on can produce an absolute cost advantage over rivals, (3) first-time customers remain strongly loyal to pioneering firms in making repeat purchases, and (4) moving first constitutes a preemptive strike, making imitation extra hard or unlikely. The bigger the first-mover advantages, the more attractive that making the first move becomes.

Because of first-mover advantages and disadvantages, competitive advantage is often attached to when *a move is made as well as to* what *move is made.*

However, a wait-and-see approach doesn't always carry a competitive penalty. Being a first-mover may entail greater risks than being a late-mover. First-mover disadvantages (or late-mover advantages) arise when (1) pioneering leadership is much more costly than followership and the leader gains negligible experience curve effects, (2) technological change is so rapid that early investments are soon obsolete (thus allowing following firms to gain the advantages of next-generation products and more efficient processes), (3) it is easy for latecomers to crack the market because customer loyalty to pioneering firms is weak, and (4) the hard-earned skills and know-how developed by the market leaders during the early competitive phase are easily copied or even surpassed by late-movers. Good timing, therefore, is important in deciding whether to be a first-mover, a fast-follower, or a cautious late-mover.

KEY POINTS

The challenge of competitive strategy—whether it be overall low-cost, broad differentiation, best-cost, focused low-cost, or focused differentiation—is to create a competitive advantage for the firm. Competitive advantage comes from positioning a

---

[32]Porter, *Competitive Strategy*, pp. 232–33.

firm in the marketplace so it has an edge in coping with competitive forces and in attracting buyers.

A strategy of trying to be the low-cost provider works well in situations where:

- The industry's product is essentially the same from seller to seller (brand differences are minor).

- Many buyers are price-sensitive and shop for the lowest price.

- There are only a few ways to achieve product differentiation that have much value to buyers.

- Most buyers use the product in the same ways and thus have common user requirements.

- Buyers' costs in switching from one seller or brand to another are low (or even zero).

- Buyers are large and have significant power to negotiate pricing terms.

To achieve a low-cost advantage, a company must become more skilled than rivals in managing the cost drivers and/or it must find innovative cost-saving ways to revamp its value chain. Successful low-cost providers usually achieve their cost advantages by imaginatively and persistently ferreting out cost savings throughout the value chain. They are good at finding ways to drive costs out of their businesses.

Differentiation strategies seek to produce a competitive edge by incorporating attributes and features into a company's product/service offering that rivals don't have or by developing competencies and capabilities that buyers value and that rivals don't have. Anything a firm can do to create buyer value represents a potential basis for differentiation. Successful differentiation is usually keyed to lowering the buyer's cost of using the item, raising the performance the buyer gets, or boosting a buyer's psychological satisfaction. To be sustainable, differentiation usually has to be linked to unique internal expertise, core competencies, and resources that give a company capabilities its rivals can't easily match. Differentiation tied just to unique physical features seldom is lasting because resourceful competitors are adept at cloning, improving on, or finding substitutes for almost any feature or trait that appeals to buyers.

Best-cost provider strategies combine a strategic emphasis on low cost with a strategic emphasis on more than minimal quality, service, features, or performance. The aim is to create competitive advantage by giving buyers more value for the money; this is done by matching close rivals on key quality-service-features-performance attributes and beating them on the costs of incorporating such attributes into the product or service. To be successful with a best-cost provider strategy, a company must have unique expertise in incorporating upscale product or service attributes at a lower cost than rivals; it must have the capability to manage unit costs down and product/service caliber up simultaneously.

The competitive advantage of focusing is earned either by achieving lower costs in serving the target market niche or by developing an ability to offer niche buyers something appealingly different from rival competitors—in other words, it is either *cost-based* or *differentiation-based*. Focusing works best when:

- Buyer needs or uses of the item are diverse.

- No other rival is attempting to specialize in the same target segment.

- A firm lacks the capability to go after a wider part of the total market.

- Buyer segments differ widely in size, growth rate, profitability, and intensity in the five competitive forces, making some segments more attractive than others.

Vertically integrating forward or backward makes strategic sense only if it strengthens a company's position via either cost reduction or creation of a differentiation-based advantage. Otherwise, the drawbacks of vertical integration (increased investment, greater business risk, increased vulnerability to technological changes, and less flexibility in making product changes) outweigh the advantages (better coordination of production flows and technological know-how from stage to stage, more specialized use of technology, greater internal control over operations, greater scale economies, and matching production with sales and marketing). There are ways to achieve the advantages of vertical integration without encountering the drawbacks.

A variety of offensive strategic moves can be used to secure a competitive advantage. Strategic offensives can be aimed either at competitors' strengths or at their weaknesses; they can involve end-runs or simultaneously launched initiatives on many fronts; they can be designed as guerrilla actions or as preemptive strikes; and the target of the offensive can be a market leader, a runner-up firm, or the smallest and/or weakest firms in the industry.

The strategic approaches to defending a company's position usually include (1) making moves that fortify the company's present position, (2) presenting competitors with a moving target to avoid "out of date" vulnerability, and (3) dissuading rivals from even trying to attack.

The timing of strategic moves is important. First-movers sometimes gain strategic advantage; at other times, such as when technology is developing fast, it is cheaper and easier to be a follower than a leader.

SUGGESTED READINGS

Aaker, David A. "Managing Assets and Skills: The Key to a Sustainable Competitive Advantage." *California Management Review* 31, no. 2 (Winter 1989), pp. 91–106.

Barney, Jay B. *Gaining and Sustaining Competitive Advantage.* Reading, Mass.: Addison-Wesley, 1997, especially chapters 6, 7, 9, 10, and 14.

Cohen, William A. "War in the Marketplace." *Business Horizons* 29, no. 2 (March–April 1986), pp. 10–20.

Coyne, Kevin P. "Sustainable Competitive Advantage—What It Is, What It Isn't." *Business Horizons* 29, no. 1 (January–February 1986), pp. 54–61.

D'Aveni, Richard A. *Hypercompetition: The Dynamics of Strategic Maneuvering* (New York: Free Press, 1994), chaps. 1, 2, 3, and 4.

Hamel, Gary, "Strategy as Revolution." *Harvard Business Review* 74, no. 4 (July–August 1996), pp. 69–82.

Harrigan, Kathryn R. "Guerrilla Strategies of Underdog Competitors." *Planning Review* 14, no. 16 (November 1986), pp. 4–11.

———. "Formulating Vertical Integration Strategies." *Academy of Management Review* 9, no. 4 (October 1984), pp. 638–52.

———. "Matching Vertical Integration Strategies to Competitive Conditions." *Strategic Management Journal* 7, no. 6 (November–December 1986), pp. 535–56.

Hout, Thomas, Michael E. Porter, and Eileen Rudden. "How Global Companies Win Out." *Harvard Business Review* 60, no. 5 (September–October 1982), pp. 98–108.

MacMillan, Ian C. "Preemptive Strategies." *Journal of Business Strategy* 14, no. 2 (Fall 1983), pp. 16–26.

———. "Controlling Competitive Dynamics by Taking Strategic Initiative." *The Academy of Management Executive* 2, no. 2 (May 1988), pp. 111–18.

Porter, Michael E. *Competitive Advantage* (New York: Free Press, 1985), chaps. 3, 4, 5, 7, 14, and 15.

———. "What Is Strategy." *Harvard Business Review* 74, no. 6 (November–December 1996), pp. 61–78.

Rothschild, William E. "Surprise and the Competitive Advantage." *Journal of Business Strategy* 4, no. 3 (Winter 1984), pp. 10–18.

Schnarrs, Steven P. *Managing Imitation Strategies: How Later Entrants Seize Markets from Pioneers*. New York: Free Press, 1994.

Stuckey, John and David White, "When and When *Not* to Vertically Integrate." *Sloan Management Review* (Spring 1993), pp. 71–83.

Venkatesan, Ravi. "Strategic Outsourcing: To Make or Not to Make." *Harvard Business Review* 70, no. 6 (November–December 1992), pp. 98–107.

6 MATCHING STRATEGY TO A COMPANY'S SITUATION

The task of matching strategy to a company's situation is complicated because of the many external and internal factors managers have to weigh. However, while the number and variety of considerations is necessarily lengthy, the most important drivers shaping a company's best strategic options fall into two broad categories:

- The nature of industry and competitive conditions.
- The firm's own resources and competitive capabilities, market position, and best opportunities.

The dominant *strategy-shaping industry and competitive conditions* revolve around what stage in the life cycle the industry is in (emerging, rapid growth, mature, declining), the industry's structure (fragmented versus concentrated), the relative strength of the five competitive forces, the impact of industry driving forces, and the scope of competitive rivalry (particularly whether the company's market is globally competitive). The pivotal *company-specific considerations* are (1) whether the company is an industry leader, an up-and-coming challenger, a content runner-up, or an also-ran struggling to survive, and (2) the company's set of resource strengths and weaknesses, competitive capabilities, and market opportunities and threats. But even these few categories occur in too many combinations to cover here. However, we can demonstrate what the task of matching strategy to the situation involves by considering the strategy-making challenges that exist in six classic types of industry environments:

1. Competing in emerging and rapidly growing industries.
2. Competing in high-velocity markets.
3. Competing in maturing industries.
4. Competing in stagnant or declining industries.
5. Competing in fragmented industries.
6. Competing in international markets.

and in three classic types of company situations:

1. Firms in industry leadership positions.
2. Firms in runner-up positions.
3. Firms that are competitively weak or crisis-ridden.

STRATEGIES FOR COMPETING IN EMERGING INDUSTRIES

An emerging industry is one in the early, formative stage. Most companies in an emerging industry are in a start-up mode, adding people, acquiring or constructing facilities, gearing up production, trying to broaden distribution and gain buyer acceptance. Often, there are important product design and technological problems to be worked out as well. Emerging industries present managers with some unique strategy-making challenges:[1]

- Because the market is new and unproven, there are many uncertainties about how it will function, how fast it will grow, and how big it will get. Firms have to scramble to get hard information about competitors, how fast products are gaining buyer acceptance, and users' experiences with the product; because of the industry's newness, there are no organizations or trade associations gathering and distributing information to industry members. The little historical data available is virtually useless in making sales and profit projections because the past is an unreliable guide to the future.

- Much of the technological know-how tends to be proprietary and closely guarded, having been developed in-house by pioneering firms; some firms may file patents to secure competitive advantage.

- Often, there are conflicting judgments about which of several competing technologies will win out or which product attributes will gain the most buyer favor. Until market forces sort these things out, wide differences in product quality and performance are typical and rivalry centers around each firm's efforts to get the market to ratify its own strategic approach to technology, product design, marketing, and distribution.

- Entry barriers tend to be relatively low, even for entrepreneurial start-up companies; well-financed, opportunity-seeking outsiders are likely to enter if the industry has promise for explosive growth.

- Strong experience curve effects often result in significant cost reductions as volume builds.

- Since all buyers are first-time users, the marketing task is to induce initial purchase and to overcome customer concerns about product features, performance reliability, and conflicting claims of rival firms.

- Many potential buyers expect first-generation products to be rapidly improved, so they delay purchase until technology and product design mature.

- Sometimes, firms have trouble securing ample supplies of raw materials and components (until suppliers gear up to meet the industry's needs).

- Many companies, finding themselves short of funds to support needed R&D and get through several lean years until the product catches on, end up merging with competitors or being acquired by financially strong outsiders looking to invest in a growth market.

The two critical strategic issues confronting firms in an emerging industry are (1) how to finance start-up and initial operations until sales take off and (2) what

---

[1]Michael E. Porter, *Competitive Strategy* (New York: Free Press, 1980), pp. 216–23.

market segments and competitive advantages to go after in trying to secure a leading position.[2] Competitive strategies keyed either to low cost or differentiation are usually viable. Focusing should be considered when financial resources are limited and the industry has too many technological frontiers to pursue at once. Because an emerging industry has no established "rules of the game" and industry participants employ widely varying strategic approaches, a well-financed firm with a powerful strategy can shape the rules and become the recognized industry leader.

Strategic success in an emerging industry calls for bold entrepreneurship, a willingness to pioneer and take risks, an intuitive feel for what buyers will like, quick response to new developments, and opportunistic strategy making.

Dealing with all the risks and opportunities of an emerging industry is one of the most challenging business strategy problems. To be successful, companies usually have to pursue one or more of the following avenues:[3]

1. Try to win the early race for industry leadership with bold entrepreneurship and a creative strategy. Broad or focused differentiation strategies keyed to product superiority typically offer the best chance for early competitive advantage.

2. Push to perfect the technology, to improve product quality, and to develop attractive performance features.

3. As technological uncertainty clears and a dominant technology emerges, adopt it quickly. (However, while there's merit in trying to be the industry standard bearer on technology and to pioneer the "dominant product design," firms have to beware of betting too heavily on their own preferred technological approach or product design—especially when there are many competing technologies, R&D is costly, and technological developments can quickly move in surprising new directions.)

4. Form strategic alliances with key suppliers to gain access to specialized skills, technological capabilities, and critical materials or components.

5. Try to capture any first-mover advantages by commiting early to promising technologies, allying with the most capable suppliers, expanding product selection, improving styling, capturing experience curve effects, and getting well-positioned in new distribution channels.

6. Pursue new customer groups, new user applications, and entry into new geographical areas (perhaps utilizing joint ventures if financial resources are constrained).

7. Make it easier and cheaper for first-time buyers to try the industry's first-generation product. Then as the product becomes familiar to a wide portion of the market, begin to shift the advertising emphasis from creating product awareness to increasing frequency of use and building brand loyalty.

8. Use price cuts to attract the next layer of price-sensitive buyers.

9. Expect well-financed outsiders to move in with aggressive strategies as industry sales start to take off and the perceived risk of investing in the industry lessens. Try to prepare for the entry of powerful competitors by forecasting *(a)* who the probable entrants will be (based on present and future entry barriers) and *(b)* the types of strategies they are likely to employ.

---

[2]Charles W. Hofer and Dan Schendel, *Strategy Formulation: Analytical Concepts* (St. Paul, Minn.: West Publishing, 1978), pp. 164–65.

[3]Phillip Kotler, *Marketing Management*, 5th ed. (Englewood Cliffs, N.J.: Prentice-Hall, 1984), p. 366, and Porter, *Competitive Strategy*, chapter 10.

The short-term value of winning the early race for growth and market share leadership has to be balanced against the longer-range need to build a durable competitive edge and a defendable market position.[4] New entrants, attracted by the growth and profit potential, may crowd the market. Aggressive newcomers, aspiring to industry leadership, can quickly become major players by acquiring and merging the operations of weaker competitors. Young companies in fast-growing markets face three strategic hurdles: (1) managing their own rapid expansion, (2) defending against competitors trying to horn in on their success, and (3) building a competitive position extending beyond their initial product or market. Up-and-coming companies can help their cause by selecting knowledgeable members for their boards of directors, by hiring entrepreneurial managers with experience in guiding young businesses through the start-up and takeoff stages, by concentrating on outinnovating the competition, and perhaps by merging with or acquiring another firm to gain added expertise and a stronger resource base.

STRATEGIES FOR COMPETING IN HIGH VELOCITY MARKETS

Some companies find themselves in markets characterized by rapid-fire technological change, short product life cycles (because of the pace with which next-generation products are being introduced) entry of important new rivals, frequent launches of new competitive moves by rivals (including mergers and acquisitions to build a stronger, if not dominant, market position), and rapidly evolving customer requirements and expectations—all occurring at once. High-velocity change is the prevailing condition in microelectronics, in personal computer hardware and software, in telecommunications, in the whole cyberspace arena of the Internet and company intranets, and in health care.

High-velocity market environments pose a big strategy-making challenge.[5] Since news of this or that important competitive development is a daily happening, it is an imposing task just to monitor, assess, and react to unfolding events. Competitive success in fast-changing markets tends to hinge on building the following elements into company strategies:

1. *Invest aggressively in R&D to stay on the leading edge of technological know-how.* Having the expertise and capability to advance the state of technological know-how and translate the advances into innovative new products (and to remain close on the heels of whatever advances and features are pioneered by rivals) is a necessity in high-tech markets. But it is often important to focus the R&D effort in a few critical areas not only to avoid stretching the company's resources too thinly but also to deepen the firm's expertise, master the technology, fully capture experience curve effects, and become the dominant leader in a particular technology or product category.[6]

---

[4]Hofer and Schendel, *Strategy Formulation*, pp. 164–65.

[5]The strategic issues companies must address in fast-changing market environments are thoroughly explored in Richard A. D'Aveni, *Hyper-Competition: Managing the Dynamics of Strategic Manuevering* (New York: Free Press, 1994). See, also, Richard A. D'Aveni, "Coping with Hypercompetition: Utilizing the New 7S's Framework," *Academy of Management Executive,* 9, no. 3 (August 1995), pp. 45–56 and Bala Chakravarthy, "A New Strategy Framework for Coping with Turbulence," *Sloan Management Review* (Winter 1997), pp. 69–82.

[6]For insight into building competitive advantage through R&D and technological innovation, see Shaker A. Zahra, Sarah Nash, and Deborah J. Bickford, "Transforming Technological Pioneering into Competitive Advantage," *Academy of Management Executive,* 9, no. 1 (February 1995), pp. 32–41.

2. Develop the organizational capability to respond quickly to important new events. Quick reaction times are essential because it is impossible to predict or foresee all of the changes that will occur. Moreover, a competitor has to alertly and swiftly shift resources to respond to the actions of rivals or new technological developments or evolving customer needs or opportunities to move against slower competitiors. Resource flexibility tends to be a key success factor, as does the ability to *adapt* existing competencies and capabilities, to *create new competencies and capabilities*, and to *match rivals* on whatever technological approaches and product features they are able to pioneer successfully. Absent such organizational capabilities as speed, agility, flexibility, and innovativeness in finding new and better ways to please customers, a company soon loses its competitiveness. Being a fast follower, if not the first mover, is critical.

3. Rely on strategic partnerships with outside suppliers and with companies making tie-in products to perform those activities in the total industry value chain where they have specialized expertise and capabilities. In many high-velocity industries, technology is branching off to create so many new paths and product categories that no company has the resources and competencies to pursue them all. Specialization (to promote the necessary technical depth) and focus strategies (to preserve organizational agility and leverage the firm's expertise) are essential. Companies build their competitive position not just by strengthening their own resource base but also by partnering with suppliers making state-of-the-art parts and components and by collaborating with the leading makers of tie-in products. For example, the makers of personal computers rely heavily on the makers of faster chips, the makers of monitors and screens, the makers of hard disks and disk drives, and software developers to be the source of most of the innovative advances in PCs. The makers of PCs concentrate on *assembly*— none have integrated backward into parts and components, because the most effective way to provide a state-of-the-art product is to outsource the latest, most advanced components from technologically sophisticated suppliers. An outsourcing strategy also allows a company the flexibility to replace suppliers that fall behind on technology or product features or that cease to be competitive on price. Moreover, computer software developers collaborate with the various hardware manufacturers to have cutting-edge software products ready for the market when next-generation hardware products are introduced.

In fast-paced markets, in-depth expertise, speed, agility, innovativeness, opportunism, and resource flexibility are critical organizational capabilities.

When a fast-evolving market environment entails many technological areas and product categories, competitors have little choice but to employ some type of focus strategy and concentrate on being the leader in a particular category. Cutting-edge know-how and first-to-market capabilities are very valuable competitive assets. Moreover, the pace of competition demands that a company have quick reaction times and flexible, adaptable resources—organizational agility is a huge asset. So is the ability to collaborate with suppliers, effectively combining and meshing their resources with the firm's own resources. The challenge is to strike a good balance between building a rich internal resource base that, on the one hand, keeps the firm from being at the mercy of its suppliers and allies and, on the other hand, maintains organizational agility by relying on the resources and expertise of outsiders.

STRATEGIES FOR COMPETING IN MATURING INDUSTRIES

Rapid growth or fast-paced market change doesn't go on forever. However, the transition to a slower-growth, maturing industry environment does not begin on an easily predicted schedule, and the transition can be forestalled by further technological advances, product innovations, or other driving forces that keep rejuvenating market demand. Nonetheless, when growth rates do slacken, the transition to market maturity usually produces fundamental changes in the industry's competitive environment:[7]

1. *Slowing growth in buyer demand generates more head-to-head competition for market share.* Firms that want to continue on a rapid-growth track start looking for ways to take customers away from competitors. Outbreaks of price-cutting, increased advertising, and other aggressive tactics to gain market share are common.

2. *Buyers become more sophisticated, often driving a harder bargain on repeat purchases.* Since buyers have experience with the product and are familiar with competing brands, they are better able to evaluate different brands and can use their knowledge to negotiate a better deal with sellers.

3. *Competition often produces a greater emphasis on cost and service.* As sellers all begin to offer the product attributes buyers prefer, buyer choices increasingly depend on which seller offers the best combination of price and service.

4. *Firms have a "topping out" problem in adding production capacity.* Slower rates of industry growth mean slowdowns in capacity expansion. Each firm has to monitor rivals' expansion plans and time its own capacity additions to minimize industry oversupply. With slower industry growth, the mistake of adding too much capacity too soon can adversely affect company profits well into the future.

5. *Product innovation and new end-use applications are harder to come by.* Producers find it increasingly difficult to create appealing new performance features, find further uses for the product, and sustain buyer excitement.

6. *International competition increases.* Growth-minded domestic firms start to seek out sales opportunities in foreign markets. Some companies, looking for ways to cut costs, relocate plants to countries with lower wage rates. Greater product standardization and diffusion of technology reduce entry barriers and make it possible for enterprising foreign companies to become serious market contenders in more countries. Industry leadership passes to companies that build strong competitive positions in most of the world's major geographic markets and win the biggest global market shares.

7. *Industry profitability falls temporarily or permanently.* Slower growth, increased competition, more sophisticated buyers, and occasional periods of overcapacity put pressure on industry profit margins. Weaker, less-efficient firms are usually the hardest hit.

8. *Stiffening competition leads to mergers and acquisitions among former competitors, drives the weakest firms out of the industry, and, in general, produces industry consolidation.* Inefficient firms and firms with weak competitive strategies can achieve respectable results in a fast-growing industry with booming sales. But the intensifying competition that accompanies industry maturity exposes competitive weakness and throws second- and third-tier competitors into a survival-of-the-fittest contest.

---

[7]Porter, *Competitive Strategy*, pp. 238–40.

As the new competitive character of industry maturity begins to hit full force, there are several strategic moves that firms can initiate to strengthen their positions.[8]

Pruning the Product Line   A wide selection of models, features, and product options has competitive value during the growth stage when buyers' needs are still evolving. But such variety can become too costly as price competition stiffens and profit margins are squeezed. Maintaining too many product versions prevents firms from achieving the economies of long production runs. In addition, the prices of slow-selling versions may not cover their true costs. Pruning marginal products from the line lowers costs and permits more concentration on items whose margins are highest and/or where the firm has a competitive advantage.

In a maturing industry, strategic emphasis needs to be on efficiency-increasing, profit-preserving measures: pruning the product line, improving production methods, reducing costs, accelerating sales promotion efforts, expanding internationally, and acquiring distressed competitors.

More Emphasis on Process Innovations   Efforts to "reinvent" the manufacturing process can have a fourfold payoff: lower costs, better production quality, greater capability to turn out multiple or customized product versions, and shorter design-to-market cycles. Process innovation can involve mechanizing high-cost activities, revamping production lines to improve labor efficiency, building flexibility into the assembly process so that customized product versions can be easily produced, creating self-directed work teams, reengineering the manufacturing portion of the value chain, and increasing use of advanced technology (robotics, computerized controls, and automatic guided vehicles). Japanese firms have become remarkably adept at using manufacturing process innovation to become lower-cost producers of higher-quality products.

A Stronger Focus on Cost Reduction   Stiffening price competition gives firms extra incentive to reduce unit costs. Such efforts can cover a broad front: Companies can push suppliers for better prices, switch to lower-priced components, develop more economical product designs, cut low-value activities out of the value chain, streamline distribution channels, and reengineer internal processes.

Increasing Sales to Present Customers   In a mature market, growing by taking customers away from rivals may not be as appealing as expanding sales to existing customers. Strategies to increase purchases by existing customers can involve providing complementary items and ancillary services, and finding more ways for customers to use the product. Convenience food stores, for example, have boosted average sales per customer by adding video rentals, automatic bank tellers, and deli counters.

Purchasing Rival Firms at Bargain Prices   Sometimes the facilities and assets of distressed rivals can be acquired cheaply. Bargain-priced acquisitions can help create a low-cost position if they also present opportunities for greater operating efficiency. In addition, an acquired firm's customer base can provide expanded market coverage. The most desirable acquisitions are those that enhance the acquiring firm's competitive strength.

Expanding Internationally   As its domestic market matures, a firm may seek to enter foreign markets where attractive growth potential exists and where competitive

---

[8]The following discussion draws on Porter, *Competitive Strategy* pp. 241–46.

pressures are not especially strong. Several manufacturers in highly industrialized nations found international expansion attractive because equipment no longer suitable for domestic operations could be used in plants in less-developed foreign markets (a condition that lowered entry costs). Such possibilities arise when (1) foreign buyers have less sophisticated needs and have simpler, old-fashioned, end-use applications, and (2) foreign competitors are smaller, less formidable, and do not employ the latest production technology. Strategies to expand internationally also make sense when a domestic firm's skills, reputation, and product are readily transferable to foreign markets. Even though the U.S. market for soft drinks is mature, Coca-Cola has remained a growth company by upping its efforts to penetrate foreign markets where soft-drink sales are expanding rapidly.

Building New or More Flexible Capabilities   The stiffening pressures of competition in a maturing or already mature market can often be combatted by strengthening the company's resource base and competitive capabilities. This can mean adding new competencies or capabilities, deepening existing competencies to make them harder to imitate, or striving to make core competencies more flexible and adaptable to changing customer requirements and expectations. Microsoft has responded to competitors' challenges by expanding its already large cadre of talented programmers. Chevron has developed a best-practices discovery team and a best-practices resource map to enhance its speed and effectiveness in transferring efficiency improvements in one oil refinery to its other refineries.

Strategic Pitfalls

Perhaps the greatest strategic mistake a company can make as an industry matures is steering a middle course between low cost, differentiation, and focusing— blending efforts to achieve low cost with efforts to incorporate differentiating features and efforts to focus on a limited target market. Such strategic compromises typically result in a firm ending up "stuck in the middle" with a fuzzy strategy, too little commitment to winning a competitive advantage based on either low cost or differentiation, an average image with buyers, and little chance of springing into the ranks of the industry leaders. Other strategic pitfalls include being slow to adapt existing competencies and capabilities to changing customer expectations, concentrating more on short-term profitability than on building or maintaining long-term competitive position, waiting too long to respond to price-cutting, getting caught with too much capacity as growth slows, overspending on marketing efforts to boost sales growth, and failing to pursue cost reduction soon enough and aggressively enough.

One of the biggest mistakes a firm can make in a maturing industry is pursuing a compromise between low-cost, differentiation, and focusing such that it ends up with a fuzzy strategy, an ill-defined market identity, no competitive advantage, and little prospect of becoming an industry leader.

STRATEGIES FOR FIRMS IN STAGNANT OR DECLINING INDUSTRIES

Many firms operate in industries where demand is barely growing, flat, or even declining. Although harvesting the business to obtain the greatest cash flow, selling out, or preparing for close-down are obvious end-game strategies for uncommitted competitors with dim long-term prospects, strong competitors may be able to achieve good performance in a stagnant market environment.[9] Stagnant demand by itself is not enough to make an industry unattractive. Selling out may or may not be practical, and closing operations is always a last resort. Businesses competing in slow-growth/declining industries have to accept the difficult realities of a stagnating market environment and resign themselves to performance targets consistent with available market opportunities. Cash flow and return-on-investment criteria are more appropriate than growth-oriented performance measures, but sales and market share growth are by no means ruled out. Strong competitors may be able to take sales from weaker rivals, and the acquisition or exit of weaker firms creates opportunities for the remaining companies to capture greater market share.

Achieving competitive advantage in stagnant or declining industries usually requires pursuing one of three competitive approaches: focusing on growing market segments within the industry, differentiating on the basis of better quality and frequent product innovation, or becoming a lower cost producer.

In general, companies that succeed in stagnant industries employ one of three strategic themes:[10]

1. *Pursue a focused strategy by identifying, creating, and exploiting the growth segments within the industry.* Stagnant or declining markets, like other markets, are composed of numerous segments or niches. Frequently, one or more of these segments is growing rapidly, despite stagnation in the industry as a whole. An astute competitor who is first to concentrate on the attractive growth segments can escape stagnating sales and profits and possibly achieve competitive advantage in the target segments.

2. *Stress differentiation based on quality improvement and product innovation.* Either enhanced quality or innovation can rejuvenate demand by creating important new growth segments or inducing buyers to trade up. Successful product innovation opens up an avenue for competing besides meeting or beating rivals' prices. Such differentiation can have the additional advantage of being difficult and expensive for rival firms to imitate.

3. *Work diligently and persistently to drive costs down.* When increases in sales cannot be counted on to increase earnings, companies can improve profit margins and return on investment by stressing continuous productivity improvement and cost reduction year after year. Potential cost-saving actions include (a) outsourcing functions and activities that can be performed more cheaply by outsiders, (b) completely redesigning internal business processes, (c) consolidating underutilized production facilities, (d) adding more distribution channels to ensure the unit volume needed for low-cost production, (e) closing low-volume, high-cost distribution outlets, and (f) cutting marginally beneficial activities out of the value chain.

These three strategic themes are not mutually exclusive.[11] Introducing new, innovative versions of a product can *create* a fast-growing market segment. Similarly, relentless pursuit of greater operating efficiencies permits price reductions that can bring price-conscious buyers back into the market. Note that all three themes are spin-offs of the generic competitive strategies, adjusted to fit the circumstances of a tough industry environment.

The most attractive declining industries are those in which sales are eroding only slowly, there is large built-in demand, and some profitable niches remain. The most

---

[9]R. G. Hamermesh and S. B. Silk, "How to Compete in Stagnant Industries," *Harvard Business Review* 57, no. 5 (September–October 1979), p. 161.

[10]Ibid., p. 162.

[11]Ibid., p. 165.

ILLUSTRATION CAPSULE 20   Yamaha's Strategy in the Piano Industry

For some years now, worldwide demand for pianos has been declining—in the mid-1980s the decline was 10 percent annually. Modern-day parents have not put the same stress on music lessons for their children as prior generations of parents did. In an effort to see if it could revitalize its piano business, Yamaha conducted a market research survey to learn what use was being made of pianos in households that owned one. The survey revealed that the overwhelming majority of the 40 million pianos in American, European, and Japanese households were seldom used. In most cases, the reasons the piano had been purchased no longer applied. Children had either stopped taking piano lessons or were grown and had left the household; adult household members played their pianos sparingly, if at all—only a small percentage were accomplished piano players. Most pianos were serving as a piece of fine furniture and were in good condition despite not being tuned regularly. The survey

also confirmed that the income levels of piano owners were well above average.

Yamaha's piano strategists saw the idle pianos in these upscale households as a potential market opportunity. The strategy that emerged entailed marketing an attachment that would convert the piano into an old-fashioned automatic player piano capable of playing a wide number of selections recorded on 3.5-inch floppy disks (the same kind used to store computer data). The player piano conversion attachment carried a $2,500 price tag. Concurrently, Yamaha introduced Disklavier, an upright acoustic player piano model that could play *and record* performances up to 90 minutes long; the Disklavier retailed for $8,000. At year-end 1988 Yamaha offered 30 prerecorded disks for $29.95 each and since then has released a continuing stream of new selections. Yamaha believed that these new high-tech products held potential to reverse the downtrend in piano sales.

---

common strategic mistakes companies make in stagnating or declining markets are (1) getting trapped in a profitless war of attrition, (2) diverting too much cash out of the business too quickly (thus further eroding performance), and (3) being overly optimistic about the industry's future and spending too much on improvements in anticipation that things will get better.

Illustration Capsule 20 describes the creative approach taken by Yamaha to reverse declining market demand for pianos.

STRATEGIES FOR COMPETING IN FRAGMENTED INDUSTRIES

A number of industries are populated by hundreds, even thousands, of small and medium-sized companies, many privately held and none with a substantial share of total industry sales.[12] The standout competitive feature of a fragmented industry is the absence of market leaders with king-sized market shares or widespread buyer recognition. Examples of fragmented industries include book publishing, landscaping and plant nurseries, real estate development, banking, mail-order catalog sales, computer software development, custom printing, kitchen cabinets, trucking, auto repair, restaurants and fast food, public accounting, apparel manufacture and apparel retailing, paperboard boxes, log homes, hotels and motels, and furniture.

Any of several reasons can account for why the supply side of an industry is fragmented:

- Low entry barriers allow small firms to enter quickly and cheaply.
- The technologies embodied in the industry's value chain are exploding into so many new areas and along so many different paths that specialization is essential just to keep abreast in any one area of expertise.

---

[12]This section is summarized from Porter, *Competitive Strategy*, chapter 9.

- An absence of large-scale production economies permits small companies to compete on an equal cost footing with larger firms.
- Buyers require relatively small quantities of customized products (as in business forms, interior design, and advertising); because demand for any particular product version is small, sales volumes are not adequate to support producing, distributing, or marketing on a scale that yields advantages to a large firm.
- The market for the industry's product/service is becoming more global, allowing competitors in more and more countries to be drawn into the same competitive market arena (as in apparel manufacture).
- Market demand is so large and so diverse that it takes very large numbers of firms to accommodate buyer requirements (restaurants, energy, apparel, computer products and computer software).
- The industry is so new that no firms have yet developed their resource base and competitive capabilities to command a significant market share.

Some fragmented industries consolidate naturally as they mature. The stiffer competition that accompanies slower growth shakes out weak, inefficient firms leading to a greater concentration of larger, more visible sellers. Others remain atomistically competitive because it is inherent in the nature of their businesses. And still others remain stuck in a fragmented state because existing firms lack the resources or ingenuity to employ a strategy powerful enough to drive industry consolidation.

Competitive rivalry in fragmented industries can vary from moderately strong to fierce. Low barriers make entry of new competitors an ongoing threat. Competition from substitutes may or may not be a major factor. The relatively small size of companies in fragmented industries puts them in a weak position to bargain with powerful suppliers and buyers, although sometimes they can become members of a cooperative, using their combined leverage to negotiate better sales and purchase terms. In such an environment, the best a firm can expect is to cultivate a loyal customer base and grow a bit faster than the industry average. Competitive strategies based either on low cost or product differentiation are viable unless the industry's product is highly standardized or a commodity (like sand, concrete blocks, paperboard boxes). Focusing on a well-defined market niche or buyer segment usually offers more competitive advantage potential than striving for broad market appeal. Suitable options in a fragmented industry include

- *Constructing and operating "formula" facilities*—This strategic approach is frequently employed in restaurant and retailing businesses operating at multiple locations. It involves constructing standardized outlets in favorable locations at minimum cost and then polishing to a science how to operate all outlets in a superefficient manner. McDonald's, Home Depot, and 7-Eleven have pursued this strategy to perfection, earning excellent profits in their respective industries.
- *Becoming a low-cost operator*—When price competition is intense and profit margins are under constant pressure, companies can stress no-frills operations featuring low overhead, high-productivity/low-cost labor, lean capital budgets, and dedicated pursuit of total operating efficiency. Successful low-cost producers in a fragmented industry can play the price-cutting game and still earn profits above the industry average.
- *Increasing customer value through integration*—Backward or forward integration into additional value chain activities may contain opportunities

to lower costs or enhance the value provided to customers. One example is a supplier taking on the manufacture of several related parts, assembling them into a modular component system, and providing the ultimate manufacturer with something that is readily inserted or attached to the final product. Another example is a manufacturer opening a series of regional distribution centers to provide overnight delivery to area retailers.

- *Specializing by product type*—When a fragmented industry's products include a range of styles or services, a strategy to focus on one product/service category can be very effective. Some firms in the furniture industry specialize in only one furniture type such as brass beds, rattan and wicker, lawn and garden, or early American. In auto repair, companies specialize in transmission repair, body work, or speedy oil changes.

In fragmented industries competitors usually have wide enough strategic latitude to (1) compete broadly or focus and (2) pursue either a low-cost or a differentiation-based competitive advantage.

- *Specialization by customer type*—A firm can stake out a market niche in a fragmented industry by catering to those customers (1) who are interested in unique product attributes, customized features, carefree service, or other "extras," (2) who are the least price sensitive, or (3) who have the least bargaining leverage (because they are small in size or purchase small amounts).

- *Focusing on a limited geographic area*—Even though a firm in a fragmented industry can't win a big share of total industrywide sales, it can still try to dominate a local/regional area. Concentrating company efforts on a limited territory can produce greater operating efficiency, speed delivery and customer services, promote strong brand awareness, and permit saturation advertising, while avoiding the diseconomies of stretching operations out over a much wider area. Supermarkets, banks, and sporting goods retailers successfully operate multiple locations within a limited geographic area.

In fragmented industries, firms generally have the strategic freedom to pursue broad or narrow market targets and low-cost or differentiation-based competitive advantages. Many different strategic approaches can exist side by side.

STRATEGIES FOR COMPETING IN INTERNATIONAL MARKETS

Companies are motivated to expand into international markets for any of several reasons:

- *To seek new customers for their products or services*—Selling in additional country markets can propel higher revenues and profits and provide an avenue for sustaining attractively high rates of growth over the long-term.

- *A competitive need to achieve lower costs*—Many companies are driven to sell in more than one country because the sales volume in their own domestic markets is not large enough to fully capture manufacturing economies of scale; moreover, locating plants or other operations in countries where labor, materials, or technology costs are lower can often substantially improve a firm's cost competitiveness.

- *To capitalize on its competencies and resource strengths*—A company with valuable competencies and capabilities may be able to leverage them into a position of advantage in foreign markets as well as in its own domestic market.

- *To obtain valuable natural resource deposits in other countries*—In natural resource-based industries (like oil and gas, minerals, rubber, and lumber), companies often find it necessary to pursue access to attractive raw material supplies in foreign countries.

- *To spread its business risk across a wider market base*—A company spreads business risk by operating in a number of different foreign countries rather than depending entirely on operations in its own domestic market.

Whatever the motivation for foreign country operations, strategies for competing internationally have to be situation-driven. Special attention has to be paid to how national markets differ in buyer needs and habits, distribution channels, long-run growth potential, driving forces, and competitive pressures. Aside from the basic market differences from country to country, four other situational considerations are unique to international operations: cost variations among countries, fluctuating exchange rates, host government trade policies, and the pattern of international competition.

Competing in international markets poses a bigger strategy-making challenge than competing in only the company's home market.

Country-to-Country Cost Variations   Differences in wage rates, worker productivity, inflation rates, energy costs, tax rates, government regulations, and the like create sizable variations in manufacturing costs from country to country. Plants in some countries have major manufacturing cost advantages because of lower input costs (especially labor), relaxed government regulations, or unique natural resources. In such cases, the low-cost countries become principal production sites, with most of the output being exported to markets in other parts of the world. Companies with facilities in these locations (or that source their products from contract manufacturers in these countries) have a competitive advantage. The competitive role of low manufacturing costs is most evident in low-wage countries like Taiwan, South Korea, China, Singapore, Malaysia, Vietnam, Mexico, and Brazil, which have become production havens for goods with high labor content.

Another important manufacturing cost consideration in international competition is the concept of *manufacturing share* as distinct from brand share or market share. For example, although less than 40 percent of all the video recorders sold in the United States carry a Japanese brand, Japanese companies do 100 percent of the manufacturing—all sellers source their video recorders from Japanese manufacturers.[13] In microwave ovens, Japanese brands have less than a 50 percent share of the U.S. market, but the manufacturing share of Japanese companies is over 85 percent. *Manufacturing share is significant because it is a better indicator than market share of the industry's low-cost producer.* In a globally competitive industry where some competitors are intent on global dominance, being the worldwide low-cost producer is a powerful competitive advantage. Achieving low-cost producer status often requires a company to have the largest worldwide manufacturing share, with production centralized in one or a few superefficient plants. However, important marketing and distribution economies associated with multinational operations can also yield low-cost leadership.

---

[13]C. K. Prahalad and Yves L. Doz, *The Multinational Mission* (New York: Free Press, 1987), p. 60.

Fluctuating Exchange Rates   The volatility of exchange rates greatly complicates the issue of geographic cost advantages. Currency exchange rates often fluctuate as much as 20 to 40 percent annually. Changes of this magnitude can totally wipe out a country's low-cost advantage or transform a former high-cost location into a competitive-cost location. A strong U.S. dollar makes it more attractive for U.S. companies to manufacture in foreign countries. A falling dollar can eliminate much of the cost advantage that foreign manufacturers have over U.S. manufacturers and can even prompt foreign companies to establish production plants in the United States.

Host Government Trade Policies   National governments enact all kinds of measures affecting international trade and the operation of foreign companies in their markets. Host governments may impose import tariffs and quotas, set local content requirements on goods made inside their borders by foreign-based companies, and regulate the prices of imported goods. In addition, outsiders may face a web of regulations regarding technical standards, product certification, prior approval of capital spending projects, withdrawal of funds from the country, and minority (sometimes majority) ownership by local citizens. Some governments also provide subsidies and low-interest loans to domestic companies to help them compete against foreign-based companies. Other governments, anxious to obtain new plants and jobs, offer foreign companies a helping hand in the form of subsidies, privileged market access, and technical assistance.

Multicountry Competition versus Global Competition

There are important differences in the patterns of international competition from industry to industry.[14] At one extreme is *multicountry* or *multidomestic competition* where each country market is self-contained—buyers in different countries have different expectations and like different styling and features, competition in each national market is independent of competition in other national markets, and the set of rivals competing in each country differ from place to place. For example, there is a banking industry in France, one in Brazil, and one in Japan, but market conditions and buyer expectations in banking differ markedly among the three countries, the lead banking competitors in France differ from those in Brazil or in Japan, and the competitive battle going on among the leading banks in France is unrelated to the rivalry taking place in Brazil or Japan. Because each country market is self-contained in multicountry competition, a company's reputation, customer base, and competitive position in one nation have little or no bearing on its ability to compete successfully in another. As a consequence, the power of a company's strategy in any one nation and any competitive advantage it yields are largely confined to that nation and do not spill over to other countries where it operates. *With multicountry competition there is no "international market," just a collection of self-contained country markets.* Industries characterized by multicountry competition include beer, life insurance, apparel, metals fabrication, many types of food products (coffee, cereals, canned goods, frozen foods), and many types of retailing.

Multicountry (or multidomestic) competition exists when competition in one national market is independent of competition in another national market—there is no "international market," just a collection of self-contained country markets.

At the other extreme is *global competition* where prices and competitive conditions across country markets are strongly linked together and the term international

---

[14]Michael E. Porter, *The Competitive Advantage of Nations* (New York: Free Press, 1990), pp. 53–54.

or global market has true meaning. In a global industry, a company's competitive position in one country both affects and is affected by its position in other countries. Rival companies compete against each other in many different countries, but especially so in countries where sales volumes are large and where having a competitive presence is strategically important to building a strong global position in the industry. In global competition, a firm's overall advantage grows out of its entire worldwide operations; the competitive advantage it enjoys at its home base are linked to advantages growing out of its operations in other countries (having plants in low-wage countries, a capability to serve corporate customers with multinational operations of their own, and a brand reputation that is transferable from country to country). *A global competitor's market strength is directly proportional to its portfolio of country-based competitive advantages.* Global competition exists in automobiles, television sets, tires, telecommunications equipment, copiers, watches, and commercial aircraft.

Global competition *exists when competitive conditions across national markets are linked strongly enough to form a true international market and when leading competitors compete head-to-head in many different countries.*

In multicountry competition, rival firms vie for national market leadership. In globally competitive industries, rival firms vie for worldwide leadership.

An industry can have segments that are globally competitive and segments where competition is country by country.[15] In the hotel-motel industry, for example, the low- and medium-priced segments are characterized by multicountry competition because competitors mainly serve travelers within the same country. In the business and luxury segments, however, competition is more globalized. Companies like Nikki, Marriott, Sheraton, and Hilton have hotels at many international locations and use worldwide reservation systems and common quality and service standards to gain marketing advantages with frequent travelers.

In lubricants, the marine engine segment is globally competitive because ships move from port to port and require the same oil everywhere they stop. Brand reputations have a global scope, and successful marine engine lubricant producers (Exxon, British Petroleum, and Shell) operate globally. In automotive motor oil, however, multicountry competition dominates. Countries have different weather conditions and driving patterns, production is subject to limited scale economies, shipping costs are high, and retail distribution channels differ markedly from country to country. Thus domestic firms, like Quaker State and Pennzoil in the United States and Castrol in Great Britain, can be leaders in their home markets without competing globally.

All these considerations, along with the obvious cultural and political differences between countries, shape a company's strategic approach in international markets.

Types of International Strategies

A company participating in international markets has seven strategic options:

1. *License foreign firms to use the company's technology or produce and distribute the company's products* (in which case international revenues will equal the royalty income from the licensing agreement).

2. *Maintain a national (one-country) production base and export goods to foreign markets* using either company-owned or foreign-controlled forward distribution channels.

[15]Ibid., p. 61.

3. *Follow a multicountry strategy,* varying the company's strategic approach (perhaps a little, perhaps a lot) from country to country in accordance with differing buyer needs and competitive conditions. While the company may use the same basic competitive theme (low cost, differentiation, best cost) in most or all country markets, product attributes are customized to fit local buyers' preferences and expectations and the target customer base may vary from broad in some countries to narrowly focused in others. Furthermore, strategic moves in one country are made independent of those in another country; cross-country strategy coordination is a lower priority than matching company strategy to host-country market and competitive conditions.

4. *Follow a global low-cost strategy* and strive to be a low-cost supplier to buyers in most or all strategically important markets of the world. The company's strategic efforts are coordinated worldwide to achieve a low-cost position relative to all competitors.

5. *Follow a global differentiation strategy* whereby the company's product is differentiated on the same attributes in all countries to create a globally consistent image and a consistent competitive theme. The firm's strategic moves are coordinated across countries to achieve consistent differentiation worldwide.

6. *Follow a global focus strategy,* serving the same identifiable niche in each of many strategically important country markets. Strategic actions are coordinated globally to achieve a consistent low-cost or differentiation-based competitive approach in the target niche worldwide.

7. *Follow a global best-cost provider strategy* and strive to match rivals on the same product attributes and beat them on cost and price *worldwide*. The firm's strategic moves in each country market are coordinated to achieve a consistent best-cost position worldwide.

Licensing makes sense when a firm with valuable technical know-how or a unique patented product has neither the internal capability nor the resources to compete effectively in foreign markets. By licensing the technology or the production rights to foreign-based firms, the firm at least realizes income from royalties.

Using domestic plants as a production base for exporting goods to foreign markets is an excellent initial strategy for pursuing international sales. It minimizes both risk and capital requirements, and it is a conservative way to test the international waters. With an export strategy, a manufacturer can limit its involvement in foreign markets by contracting with foreign wholesalers experienced in importing to handle the entire distribution and marketing function in their countries or regions. If it is better to maintain control over these functions, a manufacturer can establish its own distribution and sales organizations in some or all of the target foreign markets. Either way, a firm minimizes its direct investments in foreign countries because of its home-based production and export strategy. Such strategies are commonly favored by Korean and Italian companies—products are designed and manufactured at home and only marketing activities are performed abroad. Whether such a strategy can be pursued successfully over the long run hinges on the relative cost competitiveness of a home-country production base. In some industries, firms gain additional scale economies and experience curve benefits from centralizing production in one or several giant plants whose output capability exceeds demand in any one country market; obviously, to capture such economies a company must export to markets in other countries. However, this strategy is vulnerable when manufacturing costs in the home country are much higher than in foreign countries where rivals have plants. The pros and cons of a multicountry strategy versus a global strategy are a bit more complex.

A Multicountry Strategy or a Global Strategy?

The need for a multicountry strategy derives from the sometimes vast differences in cultural, economic, political, and competitive conditions in different countries. The more diverse national market conditions are, the stronger the case for a *multicountry strategy* where the company tailors its strategic approach to fit each host country's market situation. Usually, but not always, companies employing a multicountry strategy use the same basic competitive theme (low-cost, differentiation, or best-cost) in each country, making whatever country-specific variations are needed to best satisfy customers and to position itself against local rivals. They may aim at broad market targets in some countries and focus more narrowly on a particular niche in others. The bigger the country-to-country variations, the more that a company's overall international strategy becomes a collection of its individual country strategies.[16]

A multicountry strategy is appropriate for industries where multicountry competition dominates, but a global strategy works best in markets that are globally competitive or beginning to globalize.

While multicountry strategies are best suited for industries where multicountry competition dominates, global strategies are best suited for globally competitive industries. A *global strategy* is one where a company's approach to competing is mostly the same in all countries. Although *minor* country-to-country differences in strategy do exist to accommodate specific conditions in host countries, the company's fundamental approach (low-cost, differentiation, best-cost or focused) remains the same worldwide. Moreover, a global strategy involves (1) integrating and coordinating the company's strategic moves worldwide and (2) selling in many if not all nations where there is significant buyer demand. Table 6–1 provides a point-by-point comparison of multicountry versus global strategies. The question of which of these two strategies to pursue is the foremost strategic issue firms face when they compete in international markets.

The strength of a multicountry strategy is that it matches the company's competitive approach to host country circumstances. A multicountry strategy is essential when there are significant country-to-country differences in customers' needs and buying habits (see Illustration Capsule 21), when buyers in a country insist on special-order or highly customized products, when regulations require that products sold locally meet strict manufacturing specifications or performance standards, and when trade restrictions are so diverse and complicated they preclude a uniform, coordinated worldwide market approach. However, a multicountry strategy has two big drawbacks: It is very difficult to transfer and exploit a company's competencies and resources across country boundaries, and it does not promote building a single, unified competitive advantage. The primary orientation of a multicountry strategy is responsiveness to local country conditions, not building well-defined competencies and competitive capabilities that can ultimately produce a competitive advantage over other international competitors and the domestic companies of host countries.

A global strategy, because it is more uniform from country to country, can concentrate on building the resource strengths to secure a sustainable low-cost or

---

[16]It is, however, possible to connect the strategies in different countries by making an effort to transfer ideas, technologies, competencies, and capabilities that work successfully in one country market to another country market whenever such transfers appear advantageous. Operations in each country can be thought of as "experiments" that result in learning and in capabilities that merit transfer to other country markets. For more details on the usefulness of such a "transnational" strategy, see C. A. Bartlett and S. Ghoshal, *Managing Across Borders: The Transnational Solution* (Boston: Harvard Business School Press, 1989).

TABLE 6-1 Differences between Multicountry and Global Stategies

	Multicountry Strategy	Global Strategy
Strategic Arena	• Selected target countries and trading areas.	• Most countries which constitute critical markets for the product, at least North America, the European Community, and the Pacific Rim (Australia, Japan, South Korea, and Southeast Asia).
Business Strategy	• Custom strategies to fit the circumstances of each host country situation; little or no strategy coordination across countries.	• Same basic strategy worldwide; minor country-by-country variations where essential.
Product-line Strategy	• Adapted to local needs.	• Mostly the same attributes and variety of models/styles worldwide.
Production Strategy	• Plants scattered across many host countries.	• Plants located on the basis of maximum competitive advantage (in low-cost countries, close to major markets, geographically scattered to minimize shipping costs, or use of a few world-scale plants to maximize economies of scale—as most appropriate).
Source of Supply for Raw Materials and Components	• Suppliers in host country preferred (local facilities meeting local buyer needs; some local sourcing may be required by host government).	• Attractive suppliers located anywhere in the world.
Marketing and Distribution	• Adapted to practices and culture of each host country.	• Much more worldwide coordination; minor adaptation to host country situations if required.
Company Organization	• Form subsidiary companies to handle operations in each host country; each subsidiary operates more or less autonomously to fit host country conditions.	• All major strategic decisions are closely coordinated at global headquarters; a global organizational structure is used to unify the operations in each country.

differentiation-based advantage over both international and domestic rivals. Whenever country-to-country differences are small enough to be accommodated within the framework of a global strategy, a global strategy is preferable to a multicountry strategy because of the value of uniting a company's efforts worldwide to create strong, competitively valuable competencies and capabilities not readily matched by rivals.

Global Strategy and Competitive Advantage

A firm can gain competitive advantage (or offset domestic disadvantages) with a global strategy in two ways.[17] One way exploits a global competitor's ability to deploy R&D, parts manufacture, assembly, distribution centers, sales and marketing, customer service centers and other activities among nations in a manner that

[17]Ibid., p. 54.

ILLUSTRATION CAPSULE 21   Multicountry Strategies: Microsoft in PC Software and Nestlé in Instant Coffee

In order to best serve the needs of users in foreign countries, Microsoft localizes many of its software products to reflect local languages. In France, for example, all user messages and documentation are in French and all monetary references are in French francs. In the United Kingdom, monetary references are in British pounds and user messages and documentation reflect certain British conventions. Various Microsoft products have been localized into more than 30 languages.

Nestlé is the world's largest food company with over $50 billion in revenues, market penetration on all major continents, and plants in over 70 countries. A star performer in Nestlé's food products lineup is coffee, accounting for sales of over $5 billion and operating profits of $600 million. Nestlé is the world's largest producer of coffee. Nestlé produces 200 types of instant coffee, from lighter blends for the U.S. market to dark espressos for Latin America. To keep its instant coffees matched to consumer tastes in different countries (and

areas within some countries), Nestlé operates four coffee research labs to experiment with new blends in aroma, flavor, and color. The strategy is to match the blends marketed in each country to the tastes and preferences of coffee drinkers in that country, introducing new blends to develop new segments when opportunities appear, and altering blends as needed to respond to changing tastes and buyer habits.

In Britain, Nescafé was promoted extensively to build a wider base of instant coffee drinkers. In Japan, where Nescafé was considered a luxury item, the company made its Japanese blends available in fancy containers suitable for gift-giving. In 1993 Nestlé began introducing Nescafé instant coffee and Coffee-Mate creamer in several large cities in China. As of 1992 the company's Nescafé brand was the leader in the instant coffee segment in virtually every national market but the U.S., where it ranked number two behind Maxwell House.

Sources: Company annual reports and Shawn Tully, "Nestlé Shows How to Gobble Markets," *Fortune*, January 16, 1989, pp. 74–78 and "Nestlé: A Giant in a Hurry," *Business Week*, March 22, 1993, pp. 50–54.

lowers costs or achieves greater product differentiation. A second way draws on a global competitor's ability to deepen or broaden its resource strengths and capabilities and to coordinate its dispersed activities in ways that a domestic-only competitor cannot.

Locating Activities   To use location to build competitive advantage, a global firm must consider two issues: (1) whether to concentrate each activity it performs in one or two countries or to spread it across many nations and (2) in which countries to locate particular activities. Activities tend to be concentrated in one or two locations when there are significant economies of scale in performing them, when there are advantages in locating related activities in the same area to better coordinate them, and when a steep learning or experience curve is associated with performing an activity in a single location. Thus in some industries scale economies in parts manufacture or assembly are so great that a company establishes one large plant from which it serves the world market. Where just-in-time inventory practices yield big cost savings and/or where the assembly firm has long-term partnering arrangements with its key suppliers, parts manufacturing plants may be clustered around final assembly plants.

A global strategy enables a firm to pursue sustainable competitive advantage by locating activities in the most advantageous nations and coordinating its strategic actions worldwide; a domestic-only competitor forfeits such opportunities.

On the other hand, dispersing activities is more advantageous than concentrating them in several instances. Buyer-related activities—such as distribution to dealers, sales and advertising, and after-sale service—usually must take place close to buyers. This means physically locating the ability to perform such activities in every country market where a global firm has major customers (unless buyers in several adjoining countries can be served quickly from a nearby central location). For example, firms that make mining and oil-drilling equipment maintain operations in many international locations to support customers' needs for speedy equipment repair and technical assistance. Large public accounting firms have numerous international offices to service the foreign operations of their multinational corporate clients. A global competitor that effectively disperses its buyer-related activities can gain a service-based competitive edge in world markets over rivals whose buyer-related activities are more concentrated—this is one reason the Big Six public accounting firms have been so successful relative to second-tier firms. Dispersing activities to many locations is also advantageous when high transportation costs, diseconomies of large size, and trade barriers make it too expensive to operate from a central location. Many companies distribute their products from multiple locations to shorten delivery times to customers. In addition, dispersing activities to hedge against the risks of fluctuating exchange rates, supply interruptions (due to strikes, mechanical failures, and transportation delays), and adverse political developments has advantages. Such risks are greater when activities are concentrated in a single location.

The classic reason for locating an activity in a particular country is lower costs.[18] Even though a global firm has strong reason to disperse buyer-related activities to many locations, such activities as materials procurement, parts manufacture, finished goods assembly, technology research, and new-product development can frequently be performed wherever advantage lies. Components can be made in Mexico, technology research done in Frankfurt, new products developed and tested in Phoenix, and assembly plants located in Spain, Brazil, Taiwan, and South Carolina. Capital can be raised in whatever country it is available on the best terms.

Low cost is not the only locational consideration, however. A research unit may be situated in a particular nation because of its pool of technically trained personnel. A customer service center or sales office may be opened in a particular country to help develop strong relationships with pivotal customers. An assembly plant may be located in a country in return for the host government's allowing freer import of components from large-scale, centralized parts plants located elsewhere.

Strengthening the Resource Base and Coordinating Cross Border Activities   A global strategy allows a firm to leverage its core competencies and resource strengths to compete successfully in additional country markets. Relying upon use of the same types of competencies, capabilities, and resource strengths in country after country contributes to the development of broader/deeper competencies and capabilities—ideally helping a company achieve *dominating depth* in some valuable area (whether it be competent performance of certain value chain activities, superior technical expertise, marketing know-how, or some other competitive asset). Dominating depth in a valuable capability or resource or value chain activity is a strong basis for sustainable competitive advantage. A company may not be able to achieve dominating depth with a domestic-only strategy because a one-country customer base may simply be too small to support such a resource buildup.

Aligning and coordinating company activities located in different countries contributes to sustainable competitive advantage in several different ways. If a firm learns how to assemble its product more efficiently at its Brazilian plant, the accumulated knowledge and expertise can be transferred to its assembly plant in Spain. Knowledge gained in marketing a company's product in Great Britain can be used to

---

[18]Ibid., p. 57.

introduce the product in New Zealand and Australia. A company can shift production from one country to another to take advantage of exchange rate fluctuations, to enhance its leverage with host country governments, and to respond to changing wage rates, energy costs, or trade restrictions. A company can enhance its brand reputation by consistently incorporating the same differentiating attributes in its products in all worldwide markets where it competes. The reputation for quality that Honda established worldwide first in motorcycles and then in automobiles gave it competitive advantage in positioning its lawnmowers at the upper end of the market—the Honda name gave the company instant credibility with buyers.

A global competitor can choose where and how to challenge rivals. It may decide to retaliate against aggressive rivals in the country market where the rival has its biggest sales volume or its best profit margins in order to reduce the rival's financial resources for competing in other country markets. It may decide to wage a price-cutting offensive against weak rivals in their home markets, capturing greater market share and subsidizing any short-term losses with profits earned in other country markets.

A company operating only in its home country can't pursue the competitive advantage opportunities of locating activites in the lowest-cost countries, using the added sales in foreign markets to broaden/deepen company competencies and capabilities, and coordinating cross-border activities. When a domestic company finds itself at a competitive disadvantage against global companies, one option is shifting from a domestic strategy to a global strategy.

The Use of Strategic Alliances to Enhance Global Competitiveness

Strategic alliances and cooperative agreements are a potentially fruitful means for firms in the same industry to compete on a more global scale while still preserving their independence. Typically such arrangements involve joint research efforts, technology sharing, joint use of production facilities, marketing one another's products, or joining forces to manufacture components or assemble finished products. Historically, export-minded firms in industrialized nations sought alliances with firms in less-developed

Strategic alliances can help companies in globally competitive industries strengthen their competitive positions while still preserving their independence.

countries to import and market their products locally—such arrangements were often necessary to win local government approval to enter a less-developed country's market or to comply with governmental requirements for local ownership. More recently, companies from different parts of the world have formed strategic alliances and partnership arrangements to strengthen their mutual ability to serve whole continents and move toward more global market participation. Both Japanese and American companies are actively forming alliances with European companies to strengthen their ability to compete in the 12-nation European Community and to capitalize on the opening up of Eastern European markets. Many U.S. and European companies are allying with Asian companies in their efforts to enter markets in China, India, and other Asian countries. Illustration Capsule 22 describes Toshiba's successful use of strategic alliances and joint ventures to pursue related technologies and product markets.

Cooperative arrangements between domestic and foreign companies have strategic appeal for reasons besides market access.[19] One is to capture economies of scale in production and/or marketing—the cost reductions can be the difference that allows a

---

[19]Porter, *The Competitive Advantage of Nations*, p. 66; see also Jeremy Main, "Making Global Alliances Work," *Fortune*, December 17, 1990, pp. 121–26.

ILLUSTRATION CAPSULE 22   Toshiba's Use of Strategic Alliances and Joint Ventures

Toshiba, Japan's oldest and third largest electronics company (after Hitachi and Matsushita), over the years has made technology licensing agreements, joint ventures, and strategic alliances cornerstones of its corporate strategy. Using such partnerships to complement its own manufacturing and product innovation capabilities, it has become a $37 billion maker of electrical and electronics products—from home appliances to computer memory chips to telecommunications equipment to electric power generation equipment.

Fumio Sato, Toshiba's CEO, contends that joint ventures and strategic alliances are a necessary component of strategy for a high-tech electronics company with global ambitions:

It is no longer an era in which a single company can dominate any technology or business by itself. The technology has become so advanced, and the markets so complex, that you simply can't expect to be the best at the whole process any longer.

Among Toshiba's two dozen major joint ventures and strategic alliances are

- A five-year-old joint venture with Motorola to design and make dynamic random access memory chips (DRAMs) for Toshiba and microprocessors for Motorola. Initially the two partners invested $125 million apiece in the venture and have since invested another $480 million each.

- A joint venture with IBM to make flat-panel liquid crystal displays in color for portable computers.

- Two other joint ventures with IBM to develop computer memory chips (one a "flash" memory chip that remembers data even after the power is turned off).

- An alliance with Sweden-based Ericsson, one of the world's biggest telecommunications manufacturers, to develop new mobile telecommunications equipment.

- A partnership with Sun Microsystems, the leading maker of microprocessor-based

workstations, to provide portable versions of the workstations to Sun and to incorporate Sun's equipment in Toshiba products to control power plants, route highway traffic, and monitor automated manufacturing processes.

- A $1 billion strategic alliance with IBM and Siemens to develop and produce the next-generation DRAM—a single chip capable of holding 256 million bits of information (approximately 8,000 typewritten pages).

- An alliance with Apple Computer to develop CD-ROM-based multimedia players that plug into a TV set.

- A joint project with the entertainment division of Time Warner to design advanced interactive cable television technology.

Other alliances and joint ventures with General Electric, United Technologies, National Semiconductor, Samsung (Korea), LSI Logic (Canada), and European companies like Olivetti, SCS-Thomson, Rhone-Poulenc, Thomson Consumer Electronics, and GEC Alstholm are turning out such products as fax machines, copiers, medical equipment, computers, rechargeable batteries, home appliances, and nuclear and steam power generating equipment.

So far, none of Toshiba's relationships with partners have gone sour despite potential conflicts among related projects with competitors (Toshiba has partnerships with nine other chip makers to develop or produce semiconductors). Toshiba attributes this to its approach to alliances: choosing partners carefully, being open about Toshiba's connections with other companies, carefully defining the role and rights of each partner in the original pact (including who gets what if the alliance doesn't work out), and cultivating easy relations and good friendships with each partner. Toshiba's management believes that strategic alliances and joint ventures are an effective way for the company to move into new businesses quickly, share the design and development costs of ambitious new products with competent partners, and achieve greater access to important geographic markets outside Japan.

Source: Based on Brenton R. Schlender, "How Toshiba Makes Alliances Work," *Fortune*, October 4, 1993, pp. 116–20.

company to be cost competitive. By joining forces in producing components, assembling models, and marketing their products, companies can realize cost savings not achievable with their own small volumes. A second reason is to fill gaps in technical expertise and/or knowledge of local markets (buying habits and product preferences of consumers, local customs, and so on). Allies learn much from one another in performing joint research, sharing technological know-how, and studying one another's manufacturing methods. A third reason is to share distribution facilities and dealer networks, thus mutually strengthening their access to buyers. And finally, allied companies can direct their competitive energies more toward mutual rivals and less toward one another; by teaming up, both may end up stronger and better able to close the gap on leading companies.

Alliances between domestic and foreign companies have their pitfalls, however. Collaboration between independent companies, each with different motives and perhaps conflicting objectives, is not easy.[20] It requires many meetings of many people working in good faith over a period of time to iron out what is to be shared, what is to remain proprietary, and how the cooperative arrangements will work. Cross-border allies typically have to overcome language and cultural barriers; the communication, trust-building, and coordination costs are high in terms of management time. Often, once the bloom is off the rose, partners discover they have deep differences of opinion about how to proceed and conflicting objectives and strategies. Tensions build up, working relationships cool, and the hoped-for benefits never materialize.[21] Many times, allies find it difficult to collaborate effectively in competitively sensitive areas, thus raising questions about mutual trust and forthright exchanges of information and expertise. There can also be clashes of egos and company cultures. The key people on whom success or failure depends may have little personal chemistry, be unable to work closely together or form a partnership, or be unable to come to consensus. For example, the alliance between Northwest Airlines and KLM Royal Dutch Airlines linking their hubs in Detroit and Amsterdam resulted in a bitter feud among the top officials of both companies (who, according to some reports, refuse to speak to each other) and precipitated a battle for control of Northwest Airlines engineered by KLM; the dispute was rooted in a clash of philosophies about how to run an airline business (the American way versus the European way), basic cultural differences between the two companies, and an executive power struggle over who should call the shots.[22]

Strategic alliances are more effective in combating competitive disadvantage than in gaining competitive advantage.

Most important, though, is the danger of depending on another company for essential expertise and capabilities over the long term. To be a serious market contender, a company must ultimately develop internal capabilities in most all areas instrumental in strengthening its competitive position and building a competitive advantage. When learning essential know-how and capabilities from one's allies holds only limited potential (because one's partners guard their most valuable skills and expertise), acquiring or merging with a company possessing the desired know-how and resources is a better solution. Strategic alliances are best used as a transitional way to combat competitive disadvantage in international markets; rarely can they be relied on as ways to create competitive

---

[20]For an excellent discussion of company experiences with alliances and partnerships, see Rosabeth Moss Kanter, "Collaborative Advantage: The Art of the Alliance," *Harvard Business Review* 72, no. 4 (July–August 1994), pp. 96–108.

[21]Jeremy Main, "Making Global Alliances Work," p. 125.

[22]Details of the disagreements are reported in Shawn Tully, "The Alliance from Hell," *Fortune*, June 24, 1996, pp. 64–72.

ILLUSTRATION CAPSULE 23   Company Experiences With Cross-Border Strategic Alliances

As the chairman of British Aerospace recently observed, a strategic alliance with a foreign company is "one of the quickest and cheapest ways to develop a global strategy." AT&T formed joint ventures with many of the world's largest telephone and electronics companies. Boeing, the world's premier manufacturer of commercial aircraft, partnered with Kawasaki, Mitsubishi, and Fuji to produce a long-range, wide-body jet for delivery in 1995. General Electric and Snecma, a French maker of jet engines, have a 50-50 partnership to make jet engines to power aircraft made by Boeing, McDonnell-Douglas, and Airbus Industrie (Airbus, the leading European maker of commercial aircraft, was formed by an alliance of aerospace companies from Britain, Spain, Germany, and France). The GE/Snecma alliance is regarded as a model because it existed for 17 years and it produced orders for 10,300 engines, totaling $38 billion.

Since the early 1980s, hundreds of strategic alliances have been formed in the motor vehicle industry as car and truck manufacturers and automotive parts suppliers moved aggressively to get in stronger position to compete globally. Not only have there been alliances between automakers strong in one region of the world and automakers strong in another region but there have also been strategic alliances between vehicle makers and key parts suppliers (especially those with high-quality parts and strong technological capabilities). General Motors and Toyota in 1984 formed a 50-50 partnership called New United Motor Manufacturing Inc. (NUMMI) to produce cars for both companies at an old GM plant in Fremont, California. The strategic value of the GM-Toyota alliance was that Toyota would learn how to deal with suppliers and workers in the United States (as a prelude to building its own plants in the United States) while GM would learn about Toyota's approaches to

manufacturing and management. Each company sent managers to the NUMMI plant to work for two or three years to learn and absorb all they could, then transferred their NUMMI "graduates" to jobs where they could be instrumental in helping their companies apply what they learned. Toyota moved quickly to capitalize on its experiences at NUMMI. By 1991 Toyota had opened two plants on its own in North America, was constructing a third plant, and was producing 50 percent of the vehicles it sold in North America in its North American plants. While General Motors incorporated much of its NUMMI learning into the management practices and manufacturing methods it was using at its newly opened Saturn plant in Tennessee, it proceeded more slowly than Toyota. American and European companies are generally regarded as less skilled than the Japanese in transferring the learning from strategic alliances into their own operations.

Many alliances fail or are terminated when one partner ends up acquiring the other. A 1990 survey of 150 companies involved in terminated alliances found that three-fourths of the alliances had been taken over by Japanese partners. A nine-year alliance between Fujitsu and International Computers, Ltd., a British manufacturer, ended when Fujitsu acquired 80 percent of ICL. According to one observer, Fujitsu deliberately maneuvered ICL into a position of having no better choice than to sell out to its partner. Fujitsu began as a supplier of components for ICL's mainframe computers, then expanded its role over the next nine years to the point where it was ICL's only source of new technology. When ICL's parent, a large British electronics firm, saw the mainframe computer business starting to decline and decided to sell, Fujitsu was the only buyer it could find.

Source: Jeremy Main, "Making Global Alliances Work," *Fortune*, December 17, 1990, pp. 121–26.

advantage. Illustration Capsule 23 relates the experiences of companies with cross-border strategic alliances.

Companies can realize the most from a strategic alliance by observing five guidelines:[23]

1. Pick a compatible partner; take the time to build strong bridges of communication and trust, and don't expect immediate payoffs.

2. Choose an ally whose products and market strongholds *complement* rather than compete directly with the company's own products and customer base.

---

[23]Ibid.

3. Learn thoroughly and rapidly about a partner's technology and management; transfer valuable ideas and practices into one's own operations promptly.

4. Don't share competitively sensitive information with a partner.

5. View the alliance as temporary (5 to 10 years); continue longer if it's beneficial but don't hesitate to terminate the alliance and go it alone when the payoffs run out.

Strategic Intent, Profit Sanctuaries, and Cross-Subsidization

Competitors in international markets can be distinguished not only by their strategies but also by their long-term strategic objectives and strategic intent. Four types of competitors stand out:[24]

- Firms whose strategic intent is *global dominance* or, at least, a high ranking among the global market leaders (such firms typically have operations in most or all of the world's biggest and most important country markets and are pursuing global low-cost, best-cost or differentiation strategies).

- Firms whose primary strategic objective is *achieving or maintaining domestic dominance* in their home market, but who pursue international sales in several or many foreign markets as a "sideline" to bolster corporate growth; the international sales of such firms is usually under 20 percent of total corporate sales.

- *Multinational firms employing multicountry strategies* to build their international sales revenues; the strategic intent of such firms is usually to expand sales in foreign markets at a fast enough pace to produce respectable revenue and profit growth.

- *Domestic-only firms* whose strategic intent does not extend beyond building a strong competitive position in their home country market; such firms base their competitive strategies on domestic market conditions and watch events in the international market only for their impact on the domestic situation.

When all four types of firms find themseves competing head-on in the same market arena, the playing field is not necessarily level for all the players. Consider the case of a purely domestic U.S. company in competition with a Japanese company operating in many country markets and aspiring to global dominance. Because of its multicountry sales and profit base, the Japanese company has the option of lowballing its prices in the U.S. market to gain market share at the expense of the U.S. company, subsidizing any losses with profits earned in Japan and its other foreign markets. If the U.S. company, with all of its business being in the U.S. market, retaliates with matching price cuts, it exposes its entire revenue and profit base to erosion. Its profits can be squeezed and its competitive strength gradually sapped even if it is the U.S. market leader. However, if the U.S. company is a multinational competitor and operates in Japan as well as elsewhere, it can counter Japanese pricing in the United States with retaliatory price cuts in Japan (its competitor's main profit sanctuary) and in other countries where it competes against the same Japanese company.

The point here is that a domestic-only company can have a hard time competing on an equal footing with either multinational or global rivals that can rely on profits earned in other country markets to support a price-cutting offensive. When aggressive

---

[24]Prahalad and Doz, *The Multinational Mission*, p. 52.

global or multinational competitors enter a domestic-only company's market, one of the domestic-only competitor's best defenses is to switch to a multinational or global strategy to give it the same cross-subsidizing capabilities the aggressors have.

Profit Sanctuaries and Critical Markets   *Profit sanctuaries* are country markets where a company derives substantial profits because of its strong or protected market position. Japan, for example, is a profit sanctuary for most Japanese companies because trade barriers erected around Japanese industries by the Japanese government effectively block foreign companies from competing for a large share of Japanese sales. Protected from the threat of foreign competition in their home market, Japanese companies can safely charge higher prices to their Japanese customers and thus earn attractively large profits on sales made in Japan. In most cases, a company's biggest and most strategically crucial profit sanctuary is its home market, but multinational companies also have profit sanctuaries in those country markets where they enjoy strong competitive positions, big sales volumes, and attractive profit margins.

Profit sanctuaries are valuable competitive assets in global industries. Companies with large, protected profit sanctuaries have competitive advantage over companies that don't have a dependable sanctuary. Companies with multiple profit sanctuaries have a competitive advantage over companies with a single sanctuary—not only do they have a broader and more diverse market base, but their multiple profit sanctuaries give them multiple financial pockets and the flexibility to redeploy profits and cash flows generated in their market strongholds to support new strategic offensives to gain market share in additional country markets. The resource advantage of multiple profit sanctuaries gives a global or multinational competitor the ability to wage a market offensive against a domestic competitor whose only profit sanctuary is its home market.

> *A particular nation is a* company's **profit sanctuary** *when the company, either because of its strong competitive position or protective governmental trade policies, derives a substantial part of its total profits from sales in that nation.*

To defend against competitive strength of global competitors with multiple profit sanctuaries, companies don't have to compete in all or even most foreign markets, but they do have to compete in all critical markets. *Critical markets* are markets in countries

- That are the profit sanctuaries of key competitors.
- That have big sales volumes.
- That contain prestigious customers whose business it is strategically important to have.
- That offer exceptionally good profit margins due to weak competitive pressures.[25]

The more critical markets a company participates in, the greater its ability to draw upon its resources and competitive strength in these markets to cross-subsidize its efforts to defend against offensives waged by competitors intent on global dominance.

The Competitive Power of Cross-Subsidization   Cross-subsidization—supporting competitive efforts in one market with resources and profits diverted from operations in other markets—is a powerful competitive weapon. Take the case of an aggressive

---

[25]Ibid., p. 61.

A competent global competitor with multiple profit sanctuaries can wage and generally win a competitive offensive against a domestic competitor whose only profit sanctuary is its home market.

To defend against aggressive international competitors intent on global dominance, a domestic-only competitor usually has to abandon its domestic focus, become a multinational competitor, and craft a multinational competitive strategy.

global firm with multiple profit sanctuaries that is intent on achieving global market dominance over the long-term and that seeks to improve its market share at the expense of a domestic-only competitor and a multicountry competitor. The global competitor can charge a low enough price to draw customers away from a domestic-only competitor, all the while gaining market share, building name recognition, and *covering any losses with profits earned in its other critical markets.* It can adjust the depth of its price-cutting to move in and capture market share quickly, or it can shave prices slightly to make gradual market inroads over a decade or more so as not to threaten domestic firms precipitously and perhaps trigger protectionist government actions. When attacked in this manner, a domestic company's best short-term hope is to pursue immediate and perhaps dramatic cost reduction and, if the situation warrants, to seek government protection in the form of tariff barriers, import quotas, and antidumping penalties. In the long term, the domestic company has to find ways to compete on a more equal footing—a difficult task when it must charge a price to cover full unit costs plus a margin for profit while the global competitor can charge a price only high enough to cover the incremental costs of selling in the domestic company's profit sanctuary. The best long-term defenses for a domestic company are to enter into strategic alliances with foreign firms or to compete on an international scale, although sometimes it is possible to drive enough costs out of the business over the long term to survive with a domestic-only strategy. As a rule, however, competing only domestically is a perilous strategy in an industry populated with global competitors who engage in cross-subsidization tactics.

While a company with a multicountry strategy has some cross-subsidy defense against a company with a global strategy, its vulnerability comes from a probable cost disadvantage and more limited competitive advantage opportunities. A global competitor with a big manufacturing share and world-scale state-of-the-art plants is almost certain to be a lower-cost producer than a multicountry strategist with many small plants and short production runs turning out specialized products country by country. Companies pursuing a multicountry strategy thus need differentiation and focus-based advantages keyed to local responsiveness in order to defend against a global competitor. Such a defense is adequate in industries with significant enough national differences to impede use of a global strategy. But if an international rival can accommodate necessary local needs within a global strategy and still retain a cost edge, then a global strategy can defeat a multicountry strategy.[26]

STRATEGIES FOR INDUSTRY LEADERS

The competitive positions of industry leaders normally range from stronger-than-average to powerful. Leaders typically are well-known, and strongly entrenched leaders have proven strategies (keyed either to low-cost leadership or to differentiation). Some of the best-known industry leaders are Anheuser-Busch (beer), Intel (microprocessors), McDonald's (fast food), Gillette (razor blades), Campbell Soup

---

[26]One way a global competitor can attack a multicountry competitor is by developing the capability to manufacture products customized for each country market at its world-scale plants; many manufacturers have become expert at designing assembly lines with the flexibility to turn out customized versions of a mass-produced product—so-called flexible mass production techniques. The advantage of flexible mass production is that it permits product customization and low-cost mass production *at the same time.*

(canned soups), Gerber (baby food), AT&T (long-distance telephone service), Eastman Kodak (camera film), and Levi Strauss (jeans). The main strategic concern for a leader revolves around how to sustain a leadership position, perhaps becoming the *dominant* leader as opposed to *a* leader. However, the pursuit of industry leadership and large market share per se is primarily important because of the competitive advantage and profitability that accrue to being the industry's biggest company.

Three contrasting strategic postures are open to industry leaders and dominant firms:[27]

1. **Stay-on-the-offensive strategy**—This strategy rests on the principle that the best defense is a good offense. Offensive-minded leaders stress being first-movers to sustain their competitive advantage (lower cost or differentiation) and to reinforce their reputation as *the* leader. A low-cost provider aggressively pursues cost reduction, and a differentiator constantly tries new ways to set its product apart from rivals' brands and become the standard against which rivals' products are judged. The theme of a stay-on-the-offensive strategy is relentless pursuit of continuous improvement and innovation. Striving to be first with new products, better performance features, quality enhancements, improved customer services, or ways to cut production costs not only helps a leader avoid complacency but it also keeps rivals on the defensive scrambling to keep up. Offensive options can also include initiatives to expand overall industry demand—discovering new uses for the product, attracting new users of the product, and promoting more frequent use. In addition, a clever offensive leader stays alert for ways to make it easier and less costly for potential customers to switch their purchases from runner-up firms to its own products. Unless a leader's market share is already so dominant that it presents a threat of antitrust action (a market share under 60 percent is usually "safe"), a stay-on-the-offensive strategy means trying to grow *faster* than the industry as a whole and wrest market share from rivals. A leader whose growth does not equal or outpace the industry average is losing ground to competitors.

> *Industry leaders can strengthen their long-term competitive positions with strategies keyed to aggressive offense, aggressive defense, or muscling smaller rivals into a follow-the-leader role.*

2. **Fortify-and-defend strategy**—The essence of "fortify and defend" is to make it harder for new firms to enter and for challengers to gain ground. The goals of a strong defense are to hold on to the present market share, strengthen current market position, and protect whatever competitive advantage the firm has. Specific defensive actions can include:

- Attempting to raise the competitive ante for challengers and new entrants by increased spending for advertising, higher levels of customer service, and bigger R&D outlays.

- Introducing more product versions or brands to match the product attributes of challengers' brands or to fill vacant niches that competitors could slip into.

- Adding personalized services and other "extras" that boost customer loyalty and make it harder or more costly for customers to switch to rival products.

- Keeping prices reasonable and quality attractive.

- Building new capacity ahead of market demand to discourage smaller competitors from adding capacity of their own.

---

[27]Kotler, *Marketing Management*, chapter 23; Michael E. Porter, *Competitive Advantage* (New York: Free Press, 1985), chapter 14; and Ian C. MacMillan, "Seizing Competitive Initiative," *The Journal of Business Strategy* 2, no. 4 (Spring 1982), pp. 43–57.

- Investing enough to remain cost competitive and technologically progressive.
- Patenting the feasible alternative technologies.
- Signing exclusive contracts with the best suppliers, distributors, and dealers.

A fortify-and-defend strategy best suits firms that have already achieved industry dominance and don't wish to risk antitrust action. It also works when a firm wishes to milk its present position for profits and cash flow because the industry's prospects for growth are low or because further gains in market share do not appear profitable enough to go after. But a fortify-and-defend strategy always entails trying to grow as fast as the market as a whole (to stave off market share slippage) and requires reinvesting enough capital in the business to protect the leader's ability to compete.

3. Follow-the-leader strategy—With this strategy the leader uses its competitive muscle (ethically and fairly!) to encourage runner-up firms to be content followers rather than aggressive challengers. The leader plays competitive hardball when smaller rivals rock the boat with price cuts or mount new market offensives that threaten its position. Specific responses can include quickly matching and perhaps exceeding challengers' price cuts, using large promotional campaigns to counter challengers' moves to gain market share, and offering better deals to the major customers of maverick firms. Leaders can also court distributors to dissuade them from carrying rivals' products, provide salespersons with documented information about the weaknesses of an aggressor's products, or try to fill any vacant positions in their own firms by making attractive offers to the better executives of rivals that "get out of line." When a leader consistently meets any moves to cut into its business with strong retaliatory tactics, it sends clear signals that offensive attacks on the leader's position will be met head-on and probably won't pay off. However, leaders pursuing this strategic approach should choose their battles. For instance, it makes sense to assume a hands-off posture and not respond in hardball fashion when smaller rivals attack each other's customer base in ways that don't affect the leader.

STRATEGIES FOR RUNNER-UP FIRMS

Runner-up firms have smaller market shares than the industry leader(s). Some runner-up firms are up-and-coming *market challengers*, using offensive strategies to gain market share and build a stronger market position. Others behave as *content followers*, willing to coast along in their current positions because profits are adequate. Follower firms have no urgent strategic issue to confront beyond "What kinds of strategic changes are the leaders initiating and what do we need to do to follow along?"

Rarely can a runner-up firm successfully challenge an industry leader with a copycat strategy.

A challenger firm interested in improving its market standing needs a strategy aimed at building a competitive advantage of its own. *Rarely can a runner-up firm improve its competitive position by imitating the strategies of leading firms. A cardinal rule in offensive strategy is to avoid attacking a leader head-on with an imitative strategy, regardless of the resources and staying power an underdog may have.*[28] Moreover, if a challenger has a 5 percent market share and needs a 20 percent share to earn attractive returns, it needs a more creative approach to competing than just "try harder."

---

[28]Porter, *Competitive Advantage*, p. 514.

In industries where large size yields *significantly* lower unit costs and gives large-share competitors an *important* cost advantage, small-share firms have only two viable strategic options: initiate offensive moves to gain sales and market share (so as to build the production volumes needed to approach the scale economies enjoyed by larger rivals) or withdraw from the business (gradually or quickly). The competitive strategies most underdogs use to build market share are based on (1) a combination of actions to drive down costs and to lower prices to win customers from weak, higher-cost rivals and (2) using differentiation strategies based on quality, technological superiority, better customer service, best cost, or innovation. Achieving low-cost leadership is usually open to an underdog only when one of the market leaders is not already solidly positioned as the industry's low-cost producer. But a small-share firm may still be able to narrow any cost disadvantage by eliminating marginal activities from the value chain, finding ways to better manage cost drivers and improve operating efficiency, or merging with or acquiring rival firms (the combined production volumes may provide the scale needed to achieve size-related economies).

When scale economies or experience curve effects are small and a large market share produces no cost advantage, runner-up companies have more strategic flexibility and can consider any of the following six approaches:[29]

1. **Vacant-niche strategy**—This version of a focused strategy involves concentrating on customer or end-use applications that market leaders have bypassed or neglected. An ideal vacant niche is of sufficient size and scope to be profitable, has some growth potential, is well-suited to a firm's own capabilities and resources, and is not interesting to leading firms. Two examples where vacant-niche strategies worked successfully are regional commuter airlines serving cities with too few passengers to attract the interest of major airlines and health foods producers (like Health Valley, Hain, and Tree of Life) that cater to local health food stores—a market segment traditionally ignored by Pillsbury, Kraft General Foods, Heinz, Nabisco, Campbell Soup, and other leading food products firms.

2. **Specialist strategy**—A specialist firm trains its competitive effort on one market segment: a single product, a particular end use, or buyers with special needs. The aim is to build competitive advantage through product uniqueness, expertise in special-purpose products, or specialized customer services. Smaller companies that successfully use a specialist focused strategy include Formby's (a specialist in stains and finishes for wood furniture, especially refinishing), Liquid Paper Co. (a leader in correction fluid for writers and typists), Canada Dry (known for its ginger ale, tonic water, and carbonated soda water), and American Tobacco (a leader in chewing tobacco and snuff).

3. **Ours-is-better-than-theirs strategy**—The approach here is to use a differentiation-based focus strategy keyed to superior product quality or unique attributes. Sales and marketing efforts are aimed directly at quality-conscious and performance-oriented buyers. Fine craftsmanship, prestige quality, frequent product innovations, and/or close contact with customers to solicit their input in developing a better product usually undergird this "superior product" approach. Some examples include Beefeater and Tanqueray in gin, Tiffany in diamonds and jewelry, Chicago

---

[29]For more details, see Kotler, *Marketing Management*, pp. 397–412; R. G. Hamermesh, M. J. Anderson, Jr., and J. E. Harris, "Strategies for Low Market Share Businesses," *Harvard Business Review* 56, no. 3 (May–June 1978), pp. 95–102; and Porter, *Competitive Advantage*, chapter 15.

Cutlery in premium-quality kitchen knives, Baccarat in fine crystal, Cannondale in mountain bikes, Bally in shoes, and Patagonia in apparel for outdoor recreation enthusiasts.

4. Content-follower strategy—Follower firms deliberately refrain from initiating trendsetting strategic moves and from aggressive attempts to steal customers away from the leaders. Followers prefer approaches that will not provoke competitive retaliation, often opting for focus and differentiation strategies that keep them out of the leaders' paths. They react and respond rather than initiate and challenge. They prefer defense to offense. And they rarely get out of line with the leaders on price. Union Camp (in paper products) has been a successful market follower by consciously concentrating on selected product uses and applications for specific customer groups, focused R&D, profits rather than market share, and cautious but efficient management.

5. Growth-via-acquisition strategy—One way to strengthen a company's position is to merge with or acquire weaker rivals to form an enterprise that has more competitive strength and a larger share of the market. Commercial airline companies such as Northwest, US Airways, and Delta owe their market share growth during the past decade to acquisition of smaller, regional airlines. Likewise, the Big Six public accounting firms extended their national and international coverage by merging or forming alliances with smaller CPA firms at home and abroad.

6. Distinctive-image strategy—Some runner-up companies build their strategies around ways to make themselves stand out from competitors. A variety of strategic approaches can be used: creating a reputation for charging the lowest prices, providing prestige quality at a good price, going all-out to give superior customer service, designing unique product attributes, being a leader in new product introduction, or devising unusually creative advertising. Examples include Dr Pepper's strategy in calling attention to its distinctive taste and Mary Kay Cosmetics' distinctive use of the color pink.

In industries where big size is definitely a key success factor, firms with low market shares have some obstacles to overcome: (1) less access to economies of scale in manufacturing, distribution, or sales promotion; (2) difficulty in gaining customer recognition; (3) an inability to afford mass media advertising on a grand scale; and (4) difficulty in funding capital requirements.[30] But *it is erroneous to view runner-up firms as inherently less profitable or unable to hold their own against the biggest firms.* Many firms with small market shares earn healthy profits and enjoy good reputations with customers. Often, the handicaps of smaller size can be surmounted and a profitable competitive position established by (1) focusing on a few market segments where the company's resource strengths and capabilities can yield a competitive edge; (2) developing technical expertise that will be highly valued by customers; (3) getting new or better products into the market ahead of rivals and building a reputation for product leadership; and (4) being more agile and innovative in adapting to evolving market conditions and customer expectations than stodgy, slow-to-change market leaders. Runner-up companies have a golden opportunity to make big market share gains if they pioneer a leapfrog technological breakthrough, if they are first to market with a new or dramatically improved product, or if the leaders stumble or become complacent.

---

[30]Hamermesh, Anderson, and Harris, "Strategies for Low Market Share Businesses," p. 102.

Otherwise, runner-up companies have to patiently nibble away at the leaders and build sales at a more moderate pace over time.

STRATEGIES FOR WEAK BUSINESSES

A firm in an also-ran or declining competitive position has four basic strategic options. If it can come up with the financial resources, it can launch an *offensive* turnaround strategy keyed either to low-cost or "new" differentiation themes, pouring enough money and talent into the effort to move up a notch or two in the industry rankings and become a respectable market contender within five years or so. It can employ a *fortify-and-defend* strategy, using variations of its present strategy and fighting hard to keep sales, market share, profitability, and competitive position at current levels. It can opt for an *immediate abandonment strategy* and get out of the business, either by selling out to another firm or by closing down operations if a buyer cannot be found. Or it can employ a *harvest strategy*, keeping reinvestment to a bare-bones minimum and taking actions to maximize short-term cash flows in preparation for an orderly market exit. The gist of the first three options is self-explanatory. The fourth merits more discussion.

The strategic options for a competitively weak company include waging a modest offensive to improve its position, defending its present position, being acquired by another company, or employing a harvest strategy.

A *harvest strategy* steers a middle course between preserving the status quo and exiting as soon as possible. Harvesting is a phasing down or endgame strategy that involves sacrificing market position in return for bigger near-term cash flows or profits. The overriding financial objective is to reap the greatest possible harvest of cash to use in other business endeavors. The operating budget is chopped to a rock-bottom level; reinvestment in the business is held to a bare minimum. Capital expenditures for new equipment are put on hold or given low priority (unless replacement needs are unusually urgent); instead, efforts are made to stretch the life of existing equipment and make do with present facilities as long as possible. Price may be raised gradually, promotional expenses slowly cut, quality reduced in not-so-visible ways, nonessential customer services curtailed, and the like. Although such actions may result in shrinking sales and market share, if cash expenses can be cut even faster, then after-tax profits and cash flows are bigger (at least temporarily). The business gradually declines, but not before a sizable cash harvest is realized.

Harvesting is a reasonable strategic option for a weak business in the following circumstances:[31]

1. When the industry's long-term prospects are unattractive.
2. When rejuvenating the business would be too costly or at best marginally profitable.
3. When the firm's market share is becoming more costly to maintain or defend.
4. When reduced competitive effort will not trigger an immediate or rapid fall-off in sales.
5. When the enterprise can redeploy the freed resources in higher opportunity areas.

---

[31]Phillip Kotler, "Harvesting Strategies for Weak Products," *Business Horizons* 21, no. 5 (August 1978), pp. 17–18.

6. When the business is *not* a crucial or core component of a diversified company's overall lineup of businesses (harvesting a sideline business is strategically preferable to harvesting a mainline or core business).

7. When the business does not contribute other desired features (sales stability, prestige, a product that complements others in the company's lineup of offerings) to a diversified company's overall business portfolio.

The more of these seven conditions present, the more ideal the business is for harvesting.

Turnaround Strategies for Businesses in Crisis

Turnaround strategies are needed when a business worth rescuing goes into crisis; the objective is to arrest and reverse the sources of competitive and financial weakness as quickly as possible. Management's first task is to diagnose what lies at the root of poor performance. Is it an unexpected downturn in sales brought on by a weak economy? An ill-chosen competitive strategy? Poor execution of an otherwise workable strategy? High operating costs? Important resource deficiencies? An overload of debt? Can the business be saved, or is the situation hopeless? Understanding what is wrong with the business and how serious its problems are is essential because different diagnoses lead to different turnaround strategies.

Some of the most common causes of business trouble include: taking on too much debt, overestimating the potential for sales growth, ignoring the profit-depressing effects of an overly aggressive effort to "buy" market share with deep price cuts, being burdened with heavy fixed costs because of an inability to utilize plant capacity, betting on R&D efforts to boost competitive position and profitability and failing to come up with effective innovations, betting on technological long shots, being too optimistic about the ability to penetrate new markets, making frequent changes in strategy (because the previous strategy didn't work out), and being overpowered by the competitive advantages enjoyed by more successful rivals. Curing these kinds of problems and turning the firm around can involve any of the following actions:

- Selling off assets to raise cash to save the remaining part of the business.
- Revising the existing strategy.
- Launching efforts to boost revenues.
- Pursuing cost reduction.
- Using a combination of these efforts.

Selling Off Assets   Assets reduction/retrenchment strategies are essential when cash flow is critical and when the most practical ways to generate cash are (1) through sale of some of the firm's assets and (2) through retrenchment (pruning of marginal products from the product line, closing or selling older plants, reducing the workforce, withdrawing from outlying markets, cutting back customer service, and the like). Sometimes crisis-ridden companies sell off assets not so much to unload losing operations and to stem cash drains as to raise funds to save and strengthen the remaining business activities.

Strategy Revision   When weak performance is caused by bad strategy, the task of strategy overhaul can proceed along any of several paths: (1) shifting to a new competitive approach to rebuild the firm's market position; (2) overhauling internal operations, resource capabilities, and functional strategies to better support the same overall business strategy; (3) merging with another firm in the industry and forging a new strategy keyed to the newly merged firm's strengths; and (4) retrenching into a reduced core of products and customers more closely matched to the firm's resource capabilities. The most appealing path depends on prevailing industry conditions, the firm's resource strengths and weaknesses, its competitive capabilities, and the severity of the crisis. Situation analysis of the industry, major competitors, and the firm's own competitive position and its competencies and resources are prerequisites for action. As a rule, successful strategy revision must be tied to the ailing firm's strengths and near-term competitive capabilities and directed at its best market opportunities.

Boosting Revenues   Revenue-increasing turnaround efforts aim at generating increased sales volume. There are a number of options: price cuts, increased promotion, a bigger sales force, added customer services, and quickly achieved product improvements. Attempts to increase revenues and sales volumes are necessary (1) when there is little or no room in the operating budget to cut expenses and still break even and (2) when the key to restoring profitability is increased use of existing capacity. If buyer demand is not especially price sensitive because of differentiating features, the quickest way to boost short-term revenues may be to raise prices rather than opt for volume-building price cuts.

Cutting Costs   Cost-reducing turnaround strategies work best when an ailing firm's value chain and cost structure are flexible enough to permit radical surgery, when it can identify and correct operating inefficiencies, when the firm's costs are obviously bloated and there are many places where savings can be quickly achieved, and when the firm is relatively close to its break-even point. Accompanying a general belt-tightening can be an increased emphasis on paring administrative overheads, elimination of nonessential and low-value-added activities, modernization of existing plant and equipment to gain greater productivity, delay of nonessential capital expenditures, and debt restructuring to reduce interest costs and stretch out repayments.

Combination Efforts   Combination turnaround strategies are usually essential in grim situations that require fast action on a broad front. Likewise, combination actions frequently come into play when new managers are brought in and given a free hand to make whatever changes they see fit. The tougher the problems, the more likely the solutions will involve multiple strategic initiatives.

Turnaround efforts tend to be high-risk undertakings, and they often fail. A landmark study of 64 companies found no successful turnarounds among the most troubled companies in eight basic industries.[32] Many of the troubled businesses waited too long to begin a turnaround. Others found themselves short of both the cash and entrepreneurial talent needed to compete in a slow-growth industry. Better-positioned rivals simply proved too strong to defeat in a long, head-to-head contest. Even when successful, many troubled companies go through a series of turnaround

[32]William K. Hall, "Survival Strategies in a Hostile Environment," *Harvard Business Review* 58, no. 5 (September–October 1980), pp. 75–85. See also Frederick M. Zimmerman, *The Turnaround Experience: Real-World Lessons in Revitalizing Corporations* (New York: McGraw-Hill, 1991), and Gary J. Castrogiovanni, B. R. Baliga, and Roland E. Kidwell, "Curing Sick Businesses: Changing CEOs in Turnaround Efforts," *Academy of Management Executive* 6, no. 3 (August 1992), pp. 26–41.

attempts and management changes before long-term competitive viability and profitability are finally restored.

THIRTEEN COMMANDMENTS FOR CRAFTING SUCCESSFUL BUSINESS STRATEGIES

Business experiences over the years prove again and again that disastrous courses of action can be avoided by adhering to good strategy-making principles. The wisdom gained from these past experiences can be distilled into 13 commandments that, if faithfully observed, can help strategists craft better strategic action plans.

1. *Place top priority on crafting and executing strategic moves that enhance the company's competitive position for the long term.* An ever-stronger competitive position pays off year after year, but the glory of meeting one quarter's and one year's financial performance targets quickly fades. Shareholders are never well served by managers who let short-term financial performance rule out strategic initiatives that will bolster the company's long-term position and strength. The best way to protect a company's long-term profitability is to strengthen the company's long-term competitiveness.

2. *Understand that a clear, consistent competitive strategy, when well crafted and well executed, builds reputation and recognizable industry position; a frequently changed strategy aimed at capturing momentary market opportunities yields fleeting benefits.* Short-run financial opportunism, absent any long-term strategic consistency, tends to produce the worst kind of profits: one-shot rewards that are unrepeatable. Over the long haul, a company that has a well-conceived, consistent competitive strategy aimed at securing an ever-stronger market position will outperform and defeat a rival whose strategic decisions are driven by a desire to meet Wall Street's short-term expectations. In an ongoing enterprise, the game of competition ought to be played for the long term, not the short term.

3. *Avoid "stuck in the middle" strategies that represent compromises between lower costs and greater differentiation and between broad and narrow market appeal.* Middle-of-the-road strategies rarely produce sustainable competitive advantage or a distinctive competitive position—well-executed best-cost producer strategies are the only exception where a compromise between low cost and differentiation succeeds. Usually, companies with compromise or middle-of-the-road strategies end up with average costs, average features, average quality, average appeal, an average image and reputation, a middle-of-the-pack industry ranking, and little prospect of climbing into the ranks of the industry leaders.

4. *Invest in creating a sustainable competitive advantage.* It is the single most dependable contributor to above-average profitability.

5. *Play aggressive offense to build competitive advantage and aggressive defense to protect it.*

6. *Avoid strategies capable of succeeding only in the most optimistic circumstances.* Expect competitors to employ countermeasures and expect times of unfavorable market conditions.

7. *Be cautious in pursuing a rigid or inflexible strategy that locks the company in for the long term with little room to maneuver—inflexible strategies can*

be made obsolete by changing market conditions. While long-term strategic consistency is usually a virtue, some adapting of the strategy to changing circumstances is normal and necessary. Moreover, strategies to achieve top quality or lowest cost should be interpreted as *relative to competitors'* and/ or *in line with customers' needs and expectations* rather than based on single-mindedly striving to make the absolute highest quality or lowest cost product possible no matter what.

8. *Don't underestimate the reactions and the commitment of rival firms.* Rivals are most dangerous when they are pushed into a corner and their well-being is threatened.

9. *Avoid attacking capable, resourceful rivals without solid competitive advantage and ample financial strength.*

10. *Consider that attacking competitive weakness is usually more profitable and less risky than attacking competitive strength.*

11. *Be judicious in cutting prices without an established cost advantage.* Only a low-cost producer can win at price-cutting over the long term.

12. *Be aware that aggressive moves to wrest market share away from rivals often provoke retaliation in the form of a marketing "arms race" and/or price wars*—to the detriment of everyone's profits. Aggressive moves to capture a bigger market share invite cutthroat competition, particularly in markets with high inventories and excess production capacity.

13. *Strive to open up very meaningful gaps in quality or service or performance features when pursuing a differentiation strategy.* Tiny differences between rivals' product offerings may not be visible or important to buyers.

KEY POINTS

It is not enough to understand that a company's basic competitive strategy options are overall low-cost leadership, broad differentiation, best cost, focused low cost, and focused differentiation and that there are a variety of offensive, defensive, first-mover, and late-mover initiatives and actions to choose from. Managers must also understand that the array of strategic options is narrowed and shaped by (1) the nature of industry and competitive conditions and (2) a firm's own competitive capabilities, market position, and best opportunities. Some strategic options are better suited to certain specific industry and competitive environments than others. Some strategic options are better suited to certain specific company situations than others. This chapter describes the multifaceted task of matching strategy to a firm's external and internal situations by considering six classic types of industry environments and three classic types of company situations.

Rather than try to summarize the main points we made about choosing strategies for these eight sets of circumstances (the relevant principles can't really be encapsulated in three or four sentences each), we think it more useful to conclude by outlining a broader framework for matching strategy to *any* industry and company situation. Table 6–2 provides a summary checklist of the most important situational considerations and strategic options. Matching strategy to the situation starts with an overview of the industry environment and the firm's competitive standing in the industry (columns 1 and 2 in Table 6–2):

1. What basic type of industry environment does the company operate in (emerging, rapid growth, high velocity, mature, fragmented, global,

TABLE 6–2   Matching Strategy to the Situation (A Checklist of Optional Strategies and Generic Situations)

Industry Environments	Company Positions/ Situations	Situational Considerations	Market Share and Investment Options	Strategy Options

• Young, emerging industry
• Rapid growth
• High velocity/rapid change
• Consolidating to a smaller group of competitors
• Mature/slow growth
• Aging/declining
• Fragmented
• International/global
• Commodity product orientation
	• Dominant leader
	  –Global/ multinational
	  –National
	  –Regional
	  –Local
	• Leader
	• Aggressive challenger
	• Content follower
	• Weak/distressed candidate for turnaround or exit
	• "Stuck in the middle"/no clear strategy or market image
		• External
		  –Driving forces
		  –Competitive pressures
		  –Anticipated moves of key rivals
		  –Key success factors
		  –Industry attractiveness
		• Internal
		  –Current company performance
		  –Strengths and weaknesses
		  –Opportunities and threats
		  –Cost position
		  –Competitive strength
		  –Strategic issues and problems
			• Grow and build
			  –Capture a bigger market share by growing faster than industry as a whole
			  –Invest heavily to capture growth potential
			• Fortify and defend
			  –Protect market share; grow at least as fast as whole industry
			  –Invest enough resources to maintain competitive strength and market position
			• Retrench and retreat
			  –Surrender weakly held positions when forced to, but fight hard to defend core markets/customer base
			  –Maximize short-term cash flow
			  –Minimize reinvestment of capital in the business
			• Overhaul and reposition
			  –Pursue a turnaround
			• Abandon/liquidate
			  –Sell out
			  –Close down
				• Competitive approach
				  –Overall low-cost
				  –Differentiation
				  –Best-cost
				  –Focused low-cost
				  –Focused differentiation
				• Offensive initiatives
				  –Competitor strengths
				  –Competitor weaknesses
				  –End run
				  –Guerrilla warfare
				  –Preemptive strikes
				• Defensive initiatives
				  –Fortify/protect
				  –Retaliatory
				  –Harvest
				• International initiatives
				  –Licensing
				  –Export
				  –Multicountry
				  –Global
				• Vertical integration initiatives
				  –Forward
				  –Backward

commodity-product)? What strategic options and strategic postures are usually best suited to this generic type of environment?

2. What position does the firm have in the industry (strong vs. weak vs. crisis-ridden; leader vs. runner-up vs. also-ran)? How does the firm's standing influence its strategic options given the stage of the industry's development—in particular, which courses of action have to be ruled out?

Next, strategists need to factor in the primary external and internal situational considerations (column 3) and decide how all the factors add up. This should narrow the firm's basic market share and investment options (column 4) and strategic options (column 5).

The final step is to custom-tailor the chosen generic strategic approaches (columns 4 and 5) to fit *both* the industry environment and the firm's standing vis-à-vis competitors. Here, it is important to be sure that (1) the customized aspects of the proposed strategy are well-matched to the firm's competencies and competitive capabilities and (2) the strategy addresses all strategic issues the firm confronts.

In weeding out weak strategies and weighing the pros and cons of the most attractive ones, the answers to the following questions often point to the "best" course of action, all things considered:

- What kind of competitive edge can the company *realistically* achieve and whether the company can execute the strategic moves/approaches to secure this edge?
- Does the company have the capabilities and resources to succeed in these moves and approaches? If not, can they be acquired?
- Once built, how can the competitive advantage be protected? What defensive strategies need to be employed? Will rivals counterattack? What will it take to blunt their efforts?
- Are any rivals particularly vulnerable? Should the firm mount an offensive to capitalize on these vulnerabilities? What offensive moves need to be employed?
- What additional strategic moves are needed to deal with driving forces in the industry, specific threats and weaknesses, and any other issues/problems unique to the firm?

As the choice of strategic initiatives is developed, there are several pitfalls to avoid:

- Designing an overly ambitious strategic plan—one that overtaxes the company's resources and capabilities.
- Selecting a strategy that represents a radical departure from or abandonment of the cornerstones of the company's prior success—a radical strategy change need not be rejected automatically, but it should be pursued only after careful risk assessment.
- Choosing a strategy that goes against the grain of the organization's culture or that conflicts with the values and philosophies of the most senior executives.
- Being unwilling to *commit wholeheartedly* to one of the five competitive strategies—picking and choosing features of the different strategies usually produces so many compromises between low cost, best cost, differentiation, and focusing that the company fails to achieve any kind of advantage and ends up stuck in the middle.

Table 6–3 provides a generic format for outlining a strategic action plan for a single-business enterprise.

Bleeke, Joel A. "Strategic Choices for Newly Opened Markets." *Harvard Business Review* 68, no. 5 (September–October 1990), pp. 158–65.

Bolt, James F. "Global Competitors: Some Criteria for Success." *Business Horizons* 31, no. 1 (January–February 1988), pp. 34–41.

SUGGESTED READINGS

TABLE 6-3   Sample Format for a Strategic Action Plan

1. Strategic Vision and Mission

2. Strategic Objectives
• Short term
• Long term

3. Financial Objectives
• Short term
• Long term

4. Overall Business Strategy

5. Supporting Functional Strategies
• Production
• Marketing/sales
• Finance
• Personnel/human resources
• Other

6. Recommended Actions
• Immediate
• Longer-range

Cooper, Arnold C., and Clayton G. Smith. "How Established Firms Respond to Threatening Technologies." *Academy of Management Executive* 6, no. 2 (May 1992), pp. 55–57.

D'Aveni, Richard A. *Hypercompetition: Managing the Dynamics of Strategic Maneuvering.* New York: Free Press, 1994, chaps. 3 and 4.

Gordon, Geoffrey L., Roger J. Calantrone, and C. Anthony di Benedetto. "Mature Markets and Revitalization Strategies: An American Fable." *Business Horizons* (May–June 1991), pp. 39–50.

Lei, David. "Strategies for Global Competition." *Long Range Planning* 22, no. 1 (February 1989), pp. 102–9.

Mayer, Robert J. "Winning Strategies for Manufacturers in Mature Industries." *Journal of Business Strategy* 8, no. 2 (Fall 1987), pp. 23–31.

Ohmae, Kenichi. "The Global Logic of Strategic Alliances." *Harvard Business Review* 67, no. 2 (March–April 1989), pp. 143–54.

Porter, Michael E. *Competitive Strategy: Techniques for Analyzing Industries and Competitors.* New York: Free Press, 1980, chaps. 9–13.

Porter, Michael E. *The Competitive Advantage of Nations.* New York: Free Press, 1990, chap. 2.

Rackham, Neil, Lawrence Friedman, and Richard Ruff. *Getting Partnering Right: How Market Leaders Are Creating Long-Term Competitive Advantage.* New York: McGraw-Hill, 1996.

Sugiura, Hideo, "How Honda Localizes Its Global Strategy." *Sloan Management Review* 33 (Fall 1990), pp. 77–82.

Yip, George S. *Total Global Strategy.* Englewood Cliffs, N.J.: Prentice-Hall, 1992, chaps. 1, 2, 3, 5, and 7.

Zimmerman, Frederick M. *The Turnaround Experience: Real-World Lessons in Revitalizing Corporations.* New York: McGraw-Hill, 1991.

STRATEGY AND COMPETITIVE ADVANTAGE IN DIVERSIFIED COMPANIES

7

In this chapter and the next, we move up one level in the strategy-making hierarchy, from strategic analysis of a single-business enterprise to strategic analysis of a diversified enterprise. Because a diversified company is a collection of individual businesses, corporate strategy making is a bigger-picture exercise than crafting line-of-business strategy. In a single-business enterprise, management has to contend with how to compete success-fully in only one industry environment. But in a diversified company managers must come up with a strategic action plan for several different business divisions competing in diverse industry environments—their challenge is to craft a multi-industry, multibusiness strategy.

Crafting corporate strategy for a diversified company has four elements:

1. *Making the moves to enter new businesses*. The first concern in diversifying is what new industries to get into and whether to enter by starting a new business from the ground up or acquiring a company already in the target industry. Picking what industries to diversify into establishes whether the company's diversification effort is based narrowly in a few industries or broadly in many industries. The choice of how to enter each target industry (by launching a new start-up operation or by acquisition of an established leader, an up-and-coming company, or a troubled company with turn-around potential) shapes what position the company will initially stake out for itself going into each of the chosen industries.

2. *Initiating actions to boost the combined performance of the businesses the firm has diversified into*. As positions are created in the chosen industries, corporate strategy making concentrates on ways to strengthen the long-term competitive positions and profits of the businesses the firm has invested in. Corporate parents can help their business subsidiaries be more successful by providing financial resources, by supplying missing skills or technological know-how or managerial expertise to better perform key value chain activities, by providing new avenues

> . . . to acquire or not to acquire: that is the question.
>
> **Robert J. Terry**
>
> Strategy is a deliberate search for a plan of action that will develop a business's competitive advantage and compound it.
>
> **Bruce D. Henderson**
>
> Fit between a parent and its businesses is a two-edged sword: a good fit can create value: a bad one can destroy it.
>
> **Andrew Campbell, Michael Goold, and Marcus Alexander**

for cost reduction, by acquiring another company in the same industry and merging the two operations into a stronger business, and/or by acquiring new businesses that complement existing businesses. Typically, rapid-growth strategies are pursued in a diversified company's most promising businesses, turnaround efforts are initiated in weak-performing businesses with potential, and businesses that are no longer attractive or that don't fit into management's strategic vision long-range plans for the company are divested.

3. *Finding ways to capture the synergy among related business units and turn it into competitive advantage.* When a company diversifies into businesses with related technologies, similar value chain activities, the same distribution channels, common customers, or some other synergistic relationship, it gains competitive advantage potential not open to a company that diversifies into unrelated businesses. Related diversification presents opportunities to transfer skills, share expertise, or share facilities, thereby reducing overall costs, strengthening the competitiveness of some of the company's products, or enhancing the capabilities of business units—any of which can represent a source of competitive advantage.

4. *Establishing investment priorities and steering corporate resources into the most attractive business units.* A diversified company's different businesses are usually not equally attractive from the standpoint of investing additional funds. Management has to (1) decide on the priorities for investing capital in the company's different businesses, (2) channel resources into areas where earnings potentials are higher and away from areas where they are lower, and (3) divest business units that are chronically poor performers or are in increasingly unattractive industries. Divesting poor performers and businesses in unattractive industries frees up unproductive investments for redeployment to promising business units or for financing attractive new acquisitions.

These four tasks are so demanding and time-consuming that corporate-level decision makers generally do not become immersed in the details of crafting and implementing business-level strategies, preferring instead to delegate responsibility for business strategy to the heads of each business unit.

In this chapter we describe the various approaches a company can take in becoming diversified, explain how a company can use diversification to create or compound competitive advantage for its business units, and survey the strategic options an already-diversified company has to improve the overall performance of its business units. In Chapter 8 we will examine the techniques and procedures for assessing the attractiveness of a diversified company's business portfolio.

WHEN TO DIVERSIFY

Most companies begin as small single-business enterprises serving a local or regional market. During a company's early years, its product line tends to be limited, its resource base thin, and its competitive position vulnerable. Usually, a young company's strategic emphasis is on growing the business—increasing sales, boosting market share, and cultivating a loyal clientele. Profits are reinvested and new debt is taken on to expand facilities, add resources, and build competitive capabilities as fast as conditions permit. Price, quality, service, and promotion are tailored more precisely to customer needs. As soon as practical, the product line is broadened to meet variations in customer wants and to capture sales opportunities in related end-use applications.

Opportunities for geographic expansion are normally pursued next. The natural sequence of expansion proceeds from local to regional to national to international markets, though the degree of penetration may be uneven from area to area because of varying profit potentials. Geographic expansion may, of course, stop well short of global or even national proportions because of intense competition, lack of resources, or the unattractiveness of further extending a firm's market coverage.

Somewhere along the way, the potential of vertical integration, either backward to sources of supply or forward to the ultimate consumer, may become a strategic consideration. Generally, integrating forward or backward into more activities along the industry value chain makes strategic sense only if it significantly enhances a company's profitability and competitive strength.

The Conditions That Make Diversification Attractive

Companies with diminishing growth prospects in their present business, with competencies and capabilities that are readily transferable to other businesses, and with the resources and managerial depth to expand into other industry arenas are prime candidates for diversifying. So long as a company has its hands full trying to capitalize on profitable growth opportunities in its present industry, there is no urgency to diversify. But when growth opportunities in the company's mainstay business begin to peter out, diversification is the most viable option for reviving the firm's prospects. Diversification also has to be considered when a firm possesses core competencies, competitive capabilities, and resource strengths that are well suited for competing successfully in other industries.

When to diversify depends partly on a company's growth opportunities in its present industry and partly on the available opportunities to utilize its resources, expertise, and capabilities in other market arenas.

A decision to diversify into new businesses raises the question "What kind and how much diversification?" The strategic possibilities are wide open. A company can diversify into closely related businesses or into totally unrelated businesses. It can expand into businesses where existing competencies and capabilities are key success factors and valuable competitive assets. It can pursue opportunities to get into other product markets where its present technological know-how can be applied and possibly yield competitive advantage. It can diversify to a small extent (less than 10 percent of total revenues and profits) or to a large extent (up to 50 percent). It can move into one or two large new businesses or a greater number of small ones. Joint ventures with other organizations into new fields of endeavor are another possibility.

Why Rushing to Diversify Isn't Necessarily a Good Strategy   Companies that continue to concentrate on a single business can achieve success over many decades without relying upon diversification. McDonald's, Delta Airlines, Coca-Cola, Domino's Pizza, Apple Computer, Wal-Mart, Federal Express, Timex, Campbell Soup, Anheuser-Busch, Xerox, Gerber, and Polaroid all won their reputations in a single business. In the nonprofit sector, continued emphasis on a single activity has proved successful for the Red Cross, Salvation Army, Christian Children's Fund, Girl Scouts, Phi Beta Kappa, and American Civil Liberties Union. Coca-Cola, wanting to escape market maturity for soft drinks in the United States, abandoned most of its early efforts to diversify (into wine and into entertainment) when it realized that the opportunities to sell Coca-Cola products in foreign markets (especially in China, India, and other parts of Asia) would allow it to grow its sales and profits at rates of 15–20 percent for decades to come.

Diversification doesn't need to become a strategic priority until a company begins to run out of attractive growth opportunities in its main business.

There are important organizational, managerial, and strategic advantages to concentrating on just one business.

Concentrating on a single line of business (totally or with a small dose of diversification) has important advantages. It makes clearer "who we are and what we do." The energies of the *total* organization are directed down *one* business path, creating less chance that senior management's time will be diluted or resources will be stretched thinly by the demands of several different businesses. The company can devote the full force of its resources to expanding into geographic markets it doesn't serve and to becoming better at what it does. Important competencies and competitive skills are more likely to emerge. Entrepreneurial efforts can be trained exclusively on keeping the firm's business strategy and competitive approach responsive to industry change and fine-tuned to customer needs.

With management's attention focused exclusively on one business, the probability is higher that good ideas will emerge on how to improve production technology, better meet customer needs with new product features, and enhance efficiencies or differentiation capabilities along the value chain. All the firm's managers, especially top executives, can have hands-on contact with the core business and in-depth knowledge of operations. Most senior officers will usually have risen through the ranks and have firsthand experience in field operations. (In broadly diversified enterprises, corporate managers seldom have had the opportunity to work in more than one or two of the company's businesses.) The more successful a single-business enterprise is, the more able it is to parlay its accumulated experience, distinctive competence, and brand-name reputation into a sustainable competitive advantage and an industry leadership position.

The Risks of Concentrating on a Single Business   The big risk of single-business concentration, of course, is putting all of a firm's eggs in one industry basket. If the market becomes saturated or becomes competitively unattractive or can be made obsolete bynew technologies or new products or fast-shifting buyer preferences, then a company's prospects can quickly dim. It is not unusual for changing customer needs, technological innovation, or new substitute products to undermine or wipe out a single-business firm—consider, for example, what the word-processing capabilities of personal computers have done to the electric typewriter business, what compact disk technology is doing to the market for cassette tapes and 3.5-inch disks, and what companies coming out with good-tasting low-fat and nonfat food products are doing to the sales of companies dependent on items with high fat content.

Factors That Signal When It's Time to Diversify   Judgments about when to diversify have to be made case-by-case on the basis of a company's own situation—the growth potential remaining in its present business, the attractiveness of opportunities to tranfer its competencies and capabilities to new business arenas, any cost-saving opportunites that can be exploited by being in closely related businesses, whether it has the resources to support a diversification effort, and whether it has the managerial breadth and depth to operate a multibusiness enterprise. Indeed, because companies in the same industry occupy different market positions and have different resource strengths and weaknesses, it is entirely rational for them to choose different diversification approaches and launch them at different times.

BUILDING SHAREHOLDER VALUE: THE ULTIMATE JUSTIFICATION FOR DIVERSIFYING

Diversifying into new businesses is justifiable only if it builds shareholder value. To enhance shareholder value, more must be accomplished than simply spreading the company's business risk across more than one industry. Shareholders can easily diversify risk on their own by purchasing stock in companies in different industries. Strictly speaking, *diversification does not create shareholder value unless a diversified group of businesses perform better under a single corporate umbrella than they would operating as independent, standalone businesses.* For example, if company A diversifies by purchasing company B and if A and B's consolidated profits in the years to come prove no greater than what each would have earned on its own, then A's diversification into business B won't provide its shareholders with added value. Company A's shareholders could have achieved the same 2 + 2 = 4 result by merely purchasing stock in company B. Shareholder value is not *created* by diversification unless it produces a 2 + 2 = 5 effect where sister businesses perform better together as part of the same firm than they could have performed as independent companies.

To create shareholder value, a diversifying company must get into businesses that can perform better under common management than they could perform as standalone enterprises.

Three Tests for Judging a Diversification Move

The problem with such a strict benchmark of whether diversification has enhanced shareholder value is that it requires speculation about how well a diversified company's businesses would have performed on their own. Comparisons of actual performance against the hypothetical of what performance might have been under other circumstances are never very satisfactory and, besides, they represent after-the-fact assessments. Strategists have to base diversification decisions on *future* expectations. Attempts to gauge the impact of particular diversification moves on shareholder value do not have to be abandoned, however. Corporate strategists can make before-the-fact assessments of whether a particular diversification move can increase shareholder value by using three tests:[1]

1. **The attractiveness test:** The industry chosen for diversification must be attractive enough to yield consistently good returns on investment. Whether an industry is attractive depends chiefly on the presence of favorable competitive conditions and a market environment conducive to long-term profitability. Such indicators as rapid growth or a sexy product are unreliable proxies of attractiveness.

2. **The cost-of-entry test:** The cost to enter the target industry must not be so high as to erode the potential for good profitability. A catch-22 can prevail here, however. The more attractive the industry, the more expensive it can be to get into. Entry barriers for start-up companies are nearly always high—were barriers low, a rush of new entrants would soon erode the potential for high profits. And buying a company already in the business often entails a high acquisition cost because of the industry's strong appeal.

3. **The better-off test:** The diversifying company must bring some potential for competitive advantage to the new business it enters, or the new business

---

[1]Michael E. Porter, "From Competitive Advantage to Corporate Strategy," *Harvard Business Review* 45, no. 3 (May–June 1987), pp. 46–49.

must offer added competitive advantage potential to the company's present businesses. The opportunity to create sustainable competitive advantage where none existed before means there is also opportunity for added profitability and shareholder value. The better-off test entails examining potential new businesses to determine if they have competitively valuable value chain matchups with the company's existing businesses—matchups that offer opportunities to reduce costs, to transfer skills or technology from one business to another, to create valuable new capabilities, or to leverage existing resources. Without such matchups, one has to be skeptical about the potential for the businesses to perform better together than apart.

Diversification moves that satisfy all three tests have the greatest potential to build shareholder value over the long term. Diversification moves that can pass only one or two tests are suspect.

DIVERSIFICATION STRATEGIES

Once the decision is made to diversify, a choice must be made whether to diversify into *related* businesses or *unrelated* businesses or some mix of both. Businesses are related when there are competitively valuable relationships among their value chains activities. Businesses are unrelated when there are no common similarities or match-ups in their respective value chains. Figure 7–1 shows the paths a company can take in moving from a single-business enterprise to a diversified enterprise. Vertical integration strategies may or may not enter the picture depending on whether forward or backward integration strengthens a firm's competitive position. Once diversification is accomplished, management's task is to figure out how to manage the collection of businesses the company has invested in—the six fundamental strategic options are shown in the last box of Figure 7–1.

We can better understand the strategic issues corporate managers face in creating and managing a diversified group of businesses by looking at six diversification-related strategies:

1. Strategies for entering new industries—acquisition, start-up, and joint ventures.
2. Related diversification strategies.
3. Unrelated diversification strategies.
4. Divestiture and liquidation strategies.
5. Corporate turnaround, retrenchment, and restructuring strategies.
6. Multinational diversification strategies.

The first three are ways to diversify; the last three are strategies to strengthen the positions and performance of companies that have already diversified.

Strategies for Entering New Businesses

Entry into new businesses can take any of three forms: acquisition, internal start-up, and joint ventures.

Acquisition of an Existing Business   Acquisition is the most popular way to diversify into another industry. Not only is it a quicker way to enter the target market than trying to launch a brand-new operation from the ground up but it offers an effective way to hurdle such entry barriers as acquiring technological experience, establishing

FIGURE 7-1   Corporate Strategy Alternatives

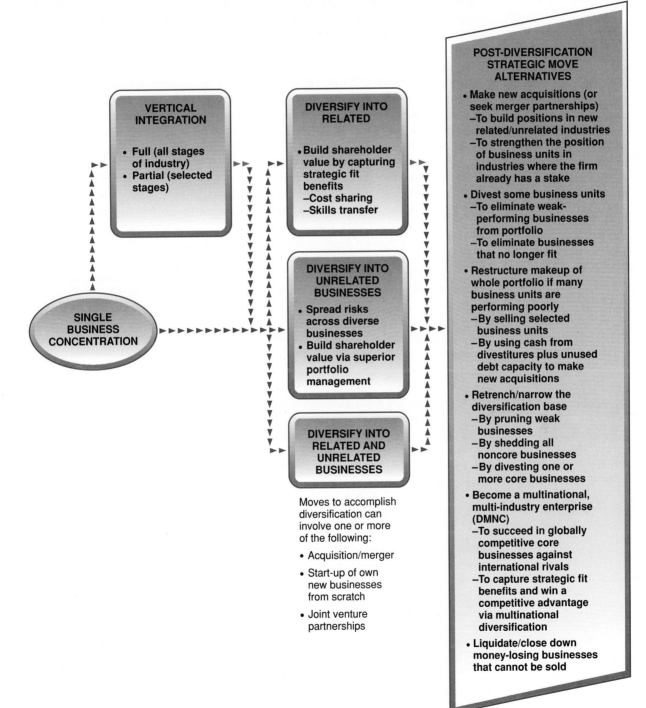

supplier relationships, becoming big enough to match rivals' efficiency and unit costs, having to spend large sums on introductory advertising and promotions to gain market visibility and brand recognition, and securing adequate distribution.[2] In many industries, going the internal start-up route and trying to develop the knowledge, resources, scale of operation, and market reputation necessary to become an effective competitor can take years. Acquiring an already established concern allows the entrant to move directly to the task of building a strong market position in the target industry.

However, finding the right kind of company to acquire sometimes presents a challenge.[3] The big dilemma an acquisition-minded firm faces is whether to pay a premium price for a successful company or to buy a struggling company at a bargain price. If the buying firm has little knowledge of the industry but ample capital, it is often better off purchasing a capable, strongly posi- tioned firm—unless the price of such an acquisition is prohibitive and flunks the cost-of-entry test. On the other hand, when the acquirer sees promising ways to transform a weak firm into a strong one and has the resources, the know-how, and the patience to do it, a struggling company can be the better long-term investment.

One of the big stumbling blocks to entering attractive industries by acquisition is the difficulty of finding a suitable company at a price that satisfies the cost-of- entry test.

The cost-of-entry test requires that the expected profit stream of an acquired business provide an attractive return on the total acquisition cost and on any new capital investment needed to sustain or expand its operations. A high acquisition price can make meeting that test improbable or difficult. For instance, suppose that the price to purchase a company is $3 million and that the business is earning after- tax profits of $200,000 on an equity investment of $1 million (a 20 percent annual return). Simple arithmetic requires that the acquired business's profits be tripled for the purchaser to earn the same 20 percent return on the $3 million acquisition price that the previous owners were getting on their $1 million equity investment. Building the acquired firm's earnings from $200,000 to $600,000 annually could take several years—and require additional investment on which the purchaser would also have to earn a 20 percent return. Since the owners of a successful and growing company usually demand a price that reflects their business's future profit prospects, it's easy for such an acquisition to fail the cost-of-entry test. A would-be diversifier can't count on being able to acquire a desirable company in an appealing industry at a price that still permits attractive returns on investment.

Internal Start-Up   Achieving diversification through *internal start-up* involves creating a new company under the corporate umbrella to compete in the desired industry. A newly formed organization not only has to overcome entry barriers, it also has to invest in new production capacity, develop sources of supply, hire and train employees, build channels of distribution, grow a customer base, and so on. Generally, forming a start-up company to enter a new industry is more attractive when (1) there is ample time to launch the business from the ground up, (2) incumbent firms are likely to be slow or ineffective in responding to a new entrant's efforts to crack the market, (3) internal entry has lower costs than entry via acquisition, (4) the company already has in-house most or

---

[2]In recent years, hostile takeovers have become a hotly debated and sometimes abused approach to acqui- sition. The term *takeover* refers to the attempt (often sprung as a surprise) of one firm to acquire owner- ship or control over another firm against the wishes of the latter's management (and perhaps some of its stockholders).

[3]Michael E. Porter, *Competitive Strategy: Techniques for Analyzing Industries and Competitors* (New York: Free Press, 1980), p. 354–55.

all of the skills it needs to compete effectively, (5) adding new production capacity will not adversely impact the supply-demand balance in the industry, and (6) the targeted industry is populated with many relatively small firms so the new start-up does not have to compete head-to-head against larger, more powerful rivals.[4]

Joint Ventures   Joint ventures are a useful way to gain access to a new business in at least three types of situations.[5] First, a joint venture is a good way to do something that is uneconomical or risky for an organization to do alone. Second, joint ventures make sense when pooling the resources and competencies of two or more organizations produces an organization with more resources and competitive assets to be a strong market contender. In such cases, each partner brings special talents or resources that the other doesn't have and that are important for success. Third, joint ventures with foreign partners are sometimes the only or best way to surmount import quotas, tariffs, nationalistic political interests, and cultural roadblocks. The economic, competitive, and political realities of nationalism often require a foreign company to team up with a domestic partner to gain access to the national market in which the domestic partner is located. Domestic partners offer outside companies the benefits of local knowledge, managerial and marketing personnel, and access to distribution channels. However, such joint ventures often pose complicated questions about how to divide efforts among the partners and about who has effective control.[6] Conflicts between foreign and domestic partners can arise over whether to use local sourcing of components, how much production to export, whether operating procedures should conform to the foreign company's standards or to local preferences, who has control of cash flows, and how to distribute profits.

> *The biggest drawbacks to entering an industry by forming a start-up company internally are the costs of overcoming entry barriers and the extra time it takes to build a strong and profitable competitive position.*

RELATED DIVERSIFICATION STRATEGIES

A related diversification strategy involves diversifying into businesses whose value chains possess competitively valuable "strategic fits" with those of the company's present business(es). *Strategic fit* exists between different businesses whenever their value chains are similiar enough to present opportunities for technology sharing, for exercising more bargaining leverage with common suppliers, for joint manufacture of parts and components, for sharing a common sales force, for using the same distribution facilities, for using the same wholesale distributors or retail dealers, for combining after-sale service activities, for exploiting common use of a well-known brand name, for transferring competitively valuable know-how or capabilities from one business to another, or for combining similar value chain activites to achieve lower costs. Strategic fits can exist anywhere along the businesses' respective value chains—in the relationships with suppliers, in R&D and technology activiities, in manufacturing, in sales and marketing, or in distribution activities.

> *Related diversification involves diversifying into businesses with competitively valuable strategic fits and matchups in their value chains.*

What makes related diversification an attractive strategy is the opportunity to convert the strategic fit relationships between the value chains of different businesses

---

[4]Ibid., pp. 344–45.

[5]Peter Drucker, *Management: Tasks, Responsibilities, Practices* (New York: Harper & Row, 1974), pp. 720–24. Strategic alliances offer much the same benefits as joint ventures, but represent a weaker commitment to entering a new business.

[6]Porter, *Competitive Strategy*, p. 340.

ILLUSTRATION CAPSULE 24   Koch Industries' Efforts to Link Its Diversification Strategy to Core Competencies and Capabilities

At Koch Industries, one of the five largest privately held companies in America, development of a company vision and strategy involved an analysis of the company's competencies and capabilities and deciding how to match these competencies and capabilities with perceived market opportunities. One executive observed, "We thought we were in the oil business, but we found out our real expertise is in the gathering, transportation, processing, and trading business." While the company developed these competencies in gathering, refining, transporting, and trading crude oil, management realiza-

tion of what the company's capabilities were led to expansion into gas liquids, and then into gas gathering, transportation, processing, and trading. Involvement in gas operations led Koch into ammonia transportation and trading, operations more closely related to Koch's oil business than service station operations. More recent acquisitions have involved transferring Koch's core capabilities to grain gathering and cattle feedlots, business activities which draw on the company's expertise in gathering, transportation, processing, and trading.

Source: Tyler Cowen and Jerry Ellig, "Market-Based Management at Koch Industries: Discovery, Dissemination, and Integration of Knowledge," *Competitive Intelligence Review* 6, no. 4 (Winter 1995), p. 7.

What makes related diversification attractive is the opportunity to turn strategic fits into competitive advantage.

into competitive advantage. When a company diversifies into businesses that present opportunities to (1) transfer expertise or capabilities or technology from one business to another, (2) combine the related activities of separate businesses into a single operation and reduce costs, (3) leverage a company's brand-name reputation in new businesses, and/or (4) conduct the related value chain activities in such collaborative fashion as to create valuable competitive capabilities, it gains competitive advantage over rivals that have not diversified or that have diversified in ways that don't give them access to such strategic-fit benefits.[7] The greater the relatedness among the businesses of a diversified company, the greater the opportunities for skills transfer and/or combining value chain activities to lower costs and/or collaborating to create new resource strengths and capabilities and/or using a common brand name and the bigger the window for creating competitive advantage.[8]

Moreover, *a diversified firm that exploits these value-chain matchups and captures the benefits of strategic fit can achieve a consolidated performance greater than the sum of what the businesses can earn pursuing independent strategies.* Competitively valuable strategic fits (assuming corporate management is able to effectively capture the benefits of the value chain matchups) make related diversification a $2 + 2 = 5$ phenomenon. The competitive edge flowing from strategic fits along the value chains of related businesses provides a basis for them performing better together than as stand-alone enterprises. The bigger the strategic-fit benefits, the more that related diversification is capable of $2 + 2 = 5$ performance—thereby satisfying the better-off test for building shareholder value.

---

[7]Michael E. Porter, *Competitive Advantage* (New York: Free Press, 1985), pp. 318–19 and pp. 337–53; Kenichi Ohmae, *The Mind of the Strategist* (New York: Penguin Books, 1983), pp. 121–24; and Porter, "From Competitive Advantage to Corporate Strategy," pp. 53–57. For an empirical study confirming that strategic fits are capable of enhancing performance (provided the resulting resource strengths are competitively valuable and difficult to duplicate by rivals), see Constantinos C. Markides and Peter J. Williamson, "Corporate Diversification and Organization Structure: A Resource-Based View," *Academy of Management Journal*, 39, no. 2 (April 1996), pp. 340–67.

[8]For a discussion of the strategic significance of cross-business coordination and insight into how it works, see Jeanne M. Liedtka, "Collaboration across Lines of Business for Competitive Advantage," *Academy of Management Executive* 10, no. 2 (May 1996), pp. 20–34.

Related Diversification in Actual Practice   Some of the most commonly used approaches to related diversification are

- Entering businesses where sales force, advertising, brand name, and distribution facilities can be shared (a maker of cookies and crackers diversifying into salty snack foods).

- Exploiting closely related technologies and technical expertise (a creator of software for mainframe computers diversifying into software for networking of PCs, for company intranets, and for stand-alone PCs).

- Transferring know-how and expertise from one business to another (a successful operator of Italian restaurants acquiring a chain specializing in Mexican food).

- Transferring the organization's brand name and reputation with consumers to a new product/service (a tire manufacturer acquiring a chain of car care centers specializing in brake repair and muffler and shock-absorber replacement).

- Acquiring new businesses that will uniquely help the firm's position in its existing businesses (a cable TV broadcaster purchasing a sports team or a movie production company to provide original programming).

Examples of related diversification abound. BIC Pen, which pioneered inexpensive disposable ballpoint pens, used its core competencies in low-cost manufacturing and mass merchandising as its basis for diversifying into disposable cigarette lighters and disposable razors—both of which required low-cost production know-how and skilled consumer marketing for success. Sony, a leading consumer electronics company, employed a technology-related and marketing-related diversification strategy when it decided to enter the videogame industry and to transfer its competencies and capabilities in electronics technology, its marketing know-how, and its brand name credibility to the manufacture and sale of videogame players and the marketing of videogames. Procter & Gamble's lineup of products includes Jif peanut butter, Duncan Hines cake mixes, Folger's coffee, Tide laundry detergent, Crisco vegetable oil, Crest toothpaste, Ivory soap, Charmin toilet tissue, and Head and Shoulders shampoo—all different businesses with different competitors and different production requirements. But P&G's products still represent related diversification because they all move through the same wholesale distribution systems, are sold in common retail settings to the same shoppers, are advertised and promoted in the same ways, and use the same marketing and merchandising skills. Illustration Capsule 25 shows the business portfolios of several companies that have pursued a strategy of related diversification.

Strategic Fit, Economies of Scope, and Competitive Advantage

A related diversification strategy is appealing from several angles. It allows a firm to preserve a degree of unity in its business activities, reap the benefits of skills transfer and/or lower costs and/or common brand-name usage and/or stronger competitive capabilities, and still spread investor risks over a broader business base.

Diversifying into businesses where technology, facilities, functional activities, or distribution channels can be shared can lead to lower costs because of economies of scope. *Economies of scope* exist whenever it is less costly for two or more businesses to be operated under centralized management than to function as independent businesses. These economies can arise from

Strategic fits among related businesses offer the competitive advantage potential of (a) lower costs, (b) efficient transfer of key skills, technological expertise, or managerial know-how from one business to another, (c) ability to share a common brand name, and/or (d) enhanced resource strengths and competitive capabilities.

ILLUSTRATION CAPSULE 25   Examples of Companies with Related Business Portfolios

Presented below are the business portfolios of three companies that have pursued some form of related diversification. Can you identify the strategic fits and value chain relationships that exist among their businesses?

Gillette

- Blades and razors
- Toiletries (Right Guard, Foamy, Dry Idea, Soft & Dry, White Rain)
- Jafra skin care products
- Oral-B toothbrushes and dental care products
- Writing instruments and stationery products (Paper Mate pens, Parker pens, Waterman pens, Liquid Paper correction fluids)
- Braun shavers, coffeemakers, alarm clocks, mixers, hair dryers, and electric toothbrushes

Philip Morris Companies

- Cigarettes (Marlboro, Virginia Slims, Benson & Hedges, Merit, and numerous other brands)

- Miller Brewing Company (Miller Genuine Draft, Miller Lite, Icehouse, Red Dog)
- Kraft General Foods (Maxwell House, Sanka, Oscar Mayer, Kool-Aid, Jell-O, Post cereals, Birds-Eye frozen foods, Kraft cheeses, Crystal Light, Tombstone pizza)
- Mission Viejo Realty

Johnson & Johnson

- Baby products (powder, shampoo, oil, lotion)
- Band-Aids and wound care products
- Stayfree, Carefree, and Sure & Natural, feminine hygiene products
- Nonprescription drugs (Tylenol, Pepcid AC, Mylanta, Motrin, Monistat-7)
- Prescription drugs
- Surgical and hospital products
- Reach dental products
- Accuvue contact lenses
- Skin care products

Source: Company annual reports

Economies of scope arise from the ability to eliminate costs by operating two or more businesses under the same corporate umbrella; the cost-saving opportunities can stem from interrelationships anywhere along the businesses' value chains.

cost-saving opportunities to share resources or combine activities anywhere along the respective value chains of the businesses and from shared use of an established brand name. The greater the economies of scope, the greater the potential for creating a competitive advantage based on lower costs.

Both skills transfer and combining the performance of closely related value chain activies enable the diversifier to earn greater profits from joint operation of different businesses than the businesses could earn as independent, stand-alone enterprises. The key to skills transfer opportunities and to cost saving economies of scope is diversification into businesses with strategic fit. While strategic-fit relationships can occur throughout the value chain, most fall into one of four categories.

Technology Fits   Different businesses have *technology fit* when there is potential for sharing common technology, exploiting the full range of business opportunities associated with a particular technology, or transferring technological know-how from one business to another. Businesses with technology-sharing benefits can perform better together than apart because of potential cost-savings in technology development and new product R&D, because of shorter times in getting new products to market, important complementarity or interdependence between the resulting products that leads to increased sales of both, and/or the technology transfer potential between businesses allows more effective or efficient performance of technology-related activities.

Operating Fits   Different businesses have *operating fit* when there are opportunities to combine activities or transfer skills/capabilities in procuring materials, conducting

R&D, improving production processes, manufacturing components, assembling finished goods, or performing administrative support functions. Sharing-related operating fits usually present cost-saving opportunities; some derive from the economies of combining activities into a larger-scale operation *(economies of scale)*, and some derive from the ability to eliminate costs by performing activities together rather than independently *(economies of scope)*. The bigger the proportion of cost that a shared activity represents, the more significant the shared cost savings become and the bigger the cost advantage that can result. With operating fit, the most important skills transfer opportunities usually relate to situations where supply chain management or manufacturing expertise in one business has beneficial applications in another.

Distribution and Customer-Related Fits   When the value chains of different businesses overlap such that the products are used by the same customers, distributed through common dealers and retailers, or marketed and promoted in similar ways, then the businesses enjoy *market-related strategic fit.* A variety of cost-saving opportunities (or economies of scope) spring from market-related strategic fit: using a single sales force for all related products rather than having separate sales forces for each business, advertising the related products in the same ads and brochures, using a common brand name, coordinating delivery and shipping, combining after-sale service and repair organizations, coordinating order processing and billing, using common promotional tie-ins (cents-off couponing, free samples and trial offers, seasonal specials, and the like), and combining dealer networks. Such value-chain matchups usually allow a firm to economize on its marketing, selling, and distribution costs.

In addition to economies of scope, market-related fit can involve opportunities to transfer selling skills, promotional skills, advertising skills, or product differentiation skills from one business to another. Moreover, a company's brand name and reputation in one product can often be transferred to other products. Honda's name in motorcycles and automobiles gave it instant credibility and recognition in entering the lawnmower business without spending large sums on advertising. Canon's reputation in photographic equipment was a competitive asset that aided the company's diversification into copying equipment. Panasonic's name in consumer electronics (radios, TVs) was readily transferred to microwave ovens, making it easier and cheaper for Panasonic to diversify into the microwave oven market.

Managerial Fits   This type of fit emerges when different business units have comparable types of entrepreneurial, administrative, or operating problems, thereby allowing managerial know-how in one line of business to be transferred to another. Transfers of managerial expertise can occur anywhere in the value chain. Ford transferred its automobile financing and credit management know-how to the savings and loan industry when it acquired some failing savings and loan associations during the 1989 bailout of the crisis-ridden S&L industry. Wal-Mart transferred its managerial know-how in discount merchandising to its newly created Sam's Wholesale Club division and thereby successfully entered the wholesale discounting business.

Capturing Strategic-Fit Benefits

It is one thing to diversify into industries with strategic fit and another to actually realize the benefits of doing so. To capture economies of scope, related activities must be merged into a single operating unit and coordinated; then the cost savings must be squeezed out. Merged functions and coordination can entail reorganization costs, and management must determine that the benefit of *some* centralized strategic control is great enough to warrant sacrifice of business-unit autonomy. Likewise, where skills or technology transfer is the cornerstone of strategic fit, managers must find a way to make the transfer effective without stripping too many skilled personnel from the business with the expertise. The more a company's diversification strategy is tied to skills or technology transfer, the more it has to develop a big enough and talented enough pool of specialized personnel not only to supply new businesses with the skill or technology but also to master the skill/technology enough to create competitive advantage.

A company with the know-how to expand its stock of strategic assets faster and at lower cost than rivals obtains sustainable competitive advantage.

One additional benefit flows from companies becoming adept at capturing strategic fits across businesses: the potential for the firm to expand its pool of resources and strategic assets and to create new ones *faster and more cheaply* than rivals who are not diversified across related businesses.[9] One reason some firms pursuing related diversification perform better over the long-term than others is that they are better at exploiting the linkages between their related businesses; such know-how over the long term translates into an ability to *accelerate* the creation of valuable new core competencies and competitive capabilities. In a competitively dynamic world, the ability to accumulate strategic assets faster than rivals is a potent and dependable way for a diversified company to earn superior returns over the long term.

UNRELATED DIVERSIFICATION STRATEGIES

Despite the strategic-fit benefits associated with related diversification, a number of companies opt for unrelated diversification strategies—diversifying into *any industry* with a good profit opportunity. *In unrelated diversification there is no deliberate effort to seek out businesses having strategic fit with the firm's other businesses.* While companies pursuing unrelated diversification may try to make certain their diversification targets meet the industry-attractiveness and cost-of-entry tests, the conditions needed for the better-off test are either disregarded or relegated to secondary status. Decisions to diversify into one industry versus another are the product of a search for "good" companies to acquire—*the basic premise of unrelated diversification is that any company that can be acquired on good financial terms and that has satisfactory profit prospects represents a good business to diversify into.* Much time and effort goes into finding and screening acquisition candidates using such criteria as:

A strategy of unrelated diversification involves diversifying into whatever industries and businesses hold promise for attractive financial gain; exploiting strategic-fit relationships is secondary.

- Whether the business can meet corporate targets for profitability and return on investment.
- Whether the new business will require infusions of capital to replace fixed assets, fund expansion, and provide working capital.
- Whether the business is in an industry with significant growth potential.
- Whether the business is big enough to contribute significantly to the parent firm's bottom line.

[9]Constantinos C. Markides and Peter J. Williamson, "Related Diversification, Core Competences and Corporate Performance," *Strategic Management Journal* 15 (Summer 1994), pp. 149–65.

- Whether there is a potential for union difficulties or adverse government regulations concerning product safety or the environment.

- Whether the industry is unusually vulnerable to recession, inflation, high interest rates, or shifts in government policy.

Sometimes, companies with unrelated diversification strategies concentrate on identifying acquisition candidates that offer quick opportunities for financial gain because of their "special situation." Three types of businesses may hold such attraction:

- *Companies whose assets are undervalued*—opportunities may exist to acquire such companies for less than full market value and make substantial capital gains by reselling their assets and businesses for more than the purchase price.

- *Companies that are financially distressed*—such businesses can often be purchased at a bargain price, their operations turned around with the aid of the parent companies' financial resources and managerial know-how, and then either held as long-term investments (because of their strong earnings or cash flow potential) or sold at a profit, whichever is more attractive.

- *Companies that have bright growth prospects but are short on investment capital*—capital poor, opportunity-rich companies are usually coveted diversification candidates for a financially strong, opportunity-seeking firm.

Companies that pursue unrelated diversification nearly always enter new businesses by acquiring an established company rather than by forming a start-up subsidiary within their own corporate structures. Their premise is that growth by acquisition translates into enhanced shareholder value. Suspending application of the better-off test is seen as justifiable so long as unrelated diversification results in sustained growth in corporate revenues and earnings and so long as none of the acquired businesses end up performing badly.

Illustration Capsule 26 shows the business portfolios of several companies that have pursued unrelated diversification. Such companies are frequently labeled *conglomerates* because there is no strategic theme in their diversification makeup and because their business interests range broadly across diverse industries.

The Pros and Cons of Unrelated Diversification

Unrelated or conglomerate diversification has appeal from several financial angles:

1. Business risk is scattered over a set of *diverse* industries—a superior way to diversify financial risk as compared to related diversification because the company's investments can be spread over businesses with totally different technologies, competitive forces, market features, and customer bases.[10]

2. The company's financial resources can be employed to maximum advantage by investing in *whatever industries* offer the best profit prospects (as opposed

---

[10]While such arguments have logical appeal, there is research showing that related diversification is less risky from a financial perspective than is unrelated diversification; see, Michael Lubatkin and Sayan Chatterjee, "Extending Modern Portfolio Theory into the Domain of Corporate Diversification: Does It Apply?" *Academy of Management Journal* 37, no. 1 (February 1994), pp. 109–36.

ILLUSTRATION CAPSULE 26   Diversified Companies with Unrelated Business Portfolios

Union Pacific Corporation
- Railroad operations (Union Pacific Railroad Company)
- Oil and gas exploration
- Mining
- Microwave and fiber optic transportation information and control systems
- Hazardous waste management disposal
- Trucking (Overnite Transportation Company)
- Oil refining
- Real estate

Rockwell International
- Industrial automation products (Reliance electric, Allen-Bradley, Sprecher & Schuh, Datamyte, Rockwell, Dodge, Electro Craft)
- Commercial aviation electronics systems
- Semiconductors
- PC modems
- Defense electronics systems
- Aerospace (Rocketdyne reusable Space Shuttle Main Engines, codeveloper of the X-33 and X-34 reusable launcher for satellites and heavy payloads)
- Heavy-duty automotive systems (axles, brakes, clutches, transmissions)
- Light automobile systems (sunroofs, doors, access controls, seat adjustment controls, suspension systems, electric motors, wheels)
- Newspaper printing press systems

Cooper Industries
- Crescent wrenches and Nicholson files
- Champion spark plugs
- Gardner-Denver mining equipment

United Technologies, Inc.
- Pratt & Whitney aircraft engines
- Carrier heating and air-conditioning equipment
- Otis elevators
- Norden defense systems
- Hamilton Standard controls
- Automotive components

Textron, Inc.
- Bell helicopters
- Paul Revere Insurance
- Cessna Aircraft
- E-Z-Go golf carts
- Missile reentry systems
- Textron automotive interior and exterior parts
- Specialty fasteners
- Avco Financial Services
- Jacobsen turf care equipment
- Tanks and armored vehicles,

The Walt Disney Company
- Theme parks
- Movie production (for both children and adults)
- Videos
- Children's apparel
- Toys and stuffed animals
- Television broadcasting (ABC network and The Disney Channel)

American Standard
- Air-conditioning products (Trane, American Standard)
- Plumbing products (American Standard, Ideal Standard, Standard, Porcher)
- Automotive Products (commercial and utility vehicle braking and control systems)

Source: Company annual reports.

to considering only opportunities in related industries). Specifically, cash flows from company businesses with lower growth and profit prospects can be diverted to acquiring and expanding businesses with higher growth and profit potentials.

3. Company profitability may prove somewhat more stable because hard times in one industry may be partially offset by good times in another—ideally, cyclical downswings in some of the company's businesses are counterbalanced by cyclical upswings in other businesses the company has diversified into.

4. To the extent that corporate-level managers are exceptionally astute at spotting bargain-priced companies with big upside profit potential, shareholder wealth can be enhanced.

While entry into an unrelated business can often pass the attractiveness and the cost-of-entry tests (and sometimes even the better-off test), a strategy of unrelated diversification has drawbacks. One Achilles' heel of conglomerate diversification is the big demand it places on corporate-level management to make sound decisions regarding fundamentally different businesses operating in fundamentally different industry and competitive environments. The greater the number of businesses a company is in and the more diverse they are, the harder it is for corporate-level executives to oversee each subsidiary and spot problems early, to have real expertise in evaluating the attractiveness of each business's industry and competitive environment, and to judge the caliber of strategic actions and plans proposed by business-level managers. As one president of a diversified firm expressed it:

> *The two biggest drawbacks to unrelated diversification are the difficulties of competently managing many different businesses and being without the added source of competitive advantage that strategic fit provides.*

> . . . we've got to make sure that our core businesses are properly managed for solid, long-term earnings. We can't just sit back and watch the numbers. We've got to know what the real issues are out there in the profit centers. Otherwise, we're not even in a position to check out our managers on the big decisions.[11]

With broad diversification, corporate managers have to be shrewd and talented enough to (1) tell a good acquisition from a bad acquisition, (2) select capable managers to run each of many different businesses, (3) discern when the major strategic proposals of business-unit managers are sound, and (4) know what to do if a business unit stumbles.[12] Because every business tends to encounter rough sledding, a good way to gauge the risk of diversifying into new unrelated areas is to ask, "If the new business got into trouble, would we know how to bail it out?" When the answer is no, unrelated diversification can pose significant financial risk and the business's profit prospects are more chancy.[13] As the former chairman of a *Fortune* 500 company advised, "Never acquire a business you don't know how to run." It takes only one or two big strategic mistakes (misjudging industry attractiveness, encountering unexpected problems in a newly acquired business, or being too optimistic about how hard it will be to turn a struggling subsidiary around) to cause corporate earnings to plunge and crash the parent company's stock price.

Second, without the competitive advantage potential of strategic fit, consolidated performance of an unrelated multibusiness portfolio tends to be no better than the sum of what the individual business units could achieve if they were independent, and it may be worse to the extent that corporate managers meddle unwisely in business-unit operations or hamstring them with corporate policies. Except, perhaps, for the added financial backing that a cash-rich corporate parent can provide, a strategy of unrelated diversification does nothing for the competitive strength of the individual business units. Each business is on its own in trying to build a competitive edge—the unrelated nature of sister businesses offers no common ground for cost reduction, skills transfer, or technology sharing. In a widely diversified firm, the value added by corporate managers depends primarily on how good they are at deciding what new businesses to add, which ones to get rid of, how best to deploy available financial resources to build

---

[11]Carter F. Bales, "Strategic Control: The President's Paradox," *Business Horizons* 20, no. 4 (August 1977), p. 17.

[12]For a review of the experiences of companies that have pursued unrelated diversification successfully, see Patricia L. Anslinger and Thomas E. Copeland, "Growth through Acquisitions: A Fresh Look," *Harvard Business Review* 74, no. 1 (January–February 1996), pp. 126–35.

[13]Of course, management may be willing to assume the risk that trouble will not strike before it has had time to learn the business well enough to bail it out of almost any difficulty. But there is research that shows this is very risky from a financial perspective; see, for example, Lubatkin and Chatterjee, "Extending Modern Portfolio Theory into the Domain of Corporate Diversification: Does It Apply?" pp. 132–33.

a higher-performing collection of businesses, and the quality of the guidance they give to the managers of their business subsidiaries.

Third, although in theory unrelated diversification offers the potential for greater sales-profit stability over the course of the business cycle, in practice attempts at countercyclical diversification fall short of the mark. Few attractive businesses have opposite up-and-down cycles; the great majority of businesses are similarly affected by economic good times and hard times. There's no convincing evidence that the consolidated profits of broadly diversified firms are more stable or less subject to reversal in periods of recession and economic stress than the profits of less diversified firms.

Despite these drawbacks, unrelated diversification can sometimes be a desirable corporate strategy. It certainly merits consideration when a firm needs to diversify away from an endangered or unattractive industry and has no distinctive competencies or capabilities it can transfer to an adjacent industry. There's also a rationale for pure diversification to the extent owners have a strong preference for investing in several unrelated businesses instead of a family of related ones. Otherwise, the argument for unrelated diversification hinges on the case-by-case prospects for financial gain.

A key issue in unrelated diversification is how wide a net to cast in building the business portfolio. In other words, should a company invest in few or many unrelated businesses? How much business diversity can corporate executives successfully manage? A reasonable way to resolve the issue of how much diversification is to ask "What is the least diversification it will take to achieve acceptable growth and profitability?" and "What is the most diversification that can be managed given the complexity it adds?"[14] The optimal amount of diversification usually lies between these two extremes.

Unrelated Diversification and Shareholder Value

Unrelated diversification is fundamentally a finance-driven approach to creating shareholder value whereas related diversification is fundamentally strategy-driven.

Unrelated diversification is a financial approach to creating shareholder value; related diversification, in contrast, represents a strategic approach.

Related diversification represents a strategic approach to building shareholder value because it is predicated on exploiting the linkages between the value chains of different businesses to lower costs, transfer skills and technological expertise across businesses, and gain other strategic-fit benefits. The objective is to convert the strategic fits among the firm's businesses into an extra measure of competitive advantage that goes beyond what business subsidiaries are able to achieve on their own. The added competitive advantage a firm achieves through related diversification is the driver for building greater shareholder value.

In contrast, *unrelated diversification is principally a financial approach to creating shareholder value* because it is predicated on astute deployment of corporate financial resources and executive skill in spotting financially attractive business opportunities. Since unrelated diversification produces no strategic-fit opportunities of consequence, corporate strategists can't build shareholder value by acquiring companies that create or compound competitive advantage for its business subsidiaries—in a conglomerate, competitive advantage doesn't go beyond what each business subsidiary can achieve independently through its own competitive strategy. Consequently, for unrelated diversification to result in enhanced shareholder

---

[14]Drucker, *Management: Tasks, Responsibilities, Practices,* pp. 692–93.

value (above the 2 + 2 = 4 effect that the subsidiary businesses could produce operating independently), corporate strategists must exhibit *superior skills* in creating and managing a portfolio of diversified business interests. This specifically means:

For corporate strategists to build shareholder value in some way other than through strategic fits and competitive advantage, they must be smart enough to produce financial results from a group of businesses that exceed what business-level managers can produce.

- Doing a superior job of diversifying into new businesses that can produce consistently good returns on investment (satisfying the attractiveness test).
- Doing a superior job of negotiating favorable acquisition prices (satisfying the cost-of-entry test).
- Being shrewd enough to sell previously acquired business subsidiaries at their peak and getting premium prices (this requires skills in discerning when a business subsidiary is on the verge of confronting adverse industry and competitive conditions and probable declines in long-term profitability).
- Wisely and aggressively shifting corporate financial resources out of businesses where profit opportunities are dim and into businesses where rapid earnings growth and high returns on investment are occurring.
- Doing such a good job overseeing the firm's business subsidiaries and contributing to how they are managed (by providing expert problem-solving skills, creative strategy suggestions, and decision-making guidance to business-level managers) that the businesses perform at a higher level than they would otherwise be able to do (a possible way to satisfy the better-off test).

To the extent that corporate executives are able to craft and execute a strategy of unrelated diversification that produces enough of the above outcomes for an enterprise to consistently outperform other firms in generating dividends and capital gains for stockholders, then a case can be made that shareholder value has truly been enhanced. Achieving such results consistently requires supertalented corporate executives, however. Without them, unrelated diversification is a very dubious and unreliable way to try to build shareholder value—there are far more who have tried and failed than who have tried and succeeded.

DIVESTITURE AND LIQUIDATION STRATEGIES

Even a shrewd corporate diversification strategy can result in the acquisition of business units that, down the road, just do not work out. Misfits cannot be completely avoided because it is difficult to foresee how getting into a new line of business will actually work out. In addition, long-term industry attractiveness changes with the times; what was once a good diversification move into an attractive industry may later turn sour. Subpar performance by some business units is bound to occur, thereby raising questions of whether to keep them or divest them. Other business units, despite adequate financial performance, may not mesh as well with the rest of the firm as was originally thought.

A business needs to be considered for divestiture when corporate strategists conclude it no longer fits or is an attractive investment.

Sometimes, a diversification move that seems sensible from a strategic-fit standpoint turns out to lack *cultural fit*.[15] Several pharmaceutical companies had just this experience. When they diversified into cosmetics and perfume, they discov-

---

[15]Ibid., p. 709.

ered their personnel had little respect for the "frivolous" nature of such products compared to the far nobler task of developing miracle drugs to cure the ill. The absence of shared values and cultural compatibility between the medical research and chemical-compounding expertise of the pharmaceutical companies and the fashion-marketing orientation of the cosmetics business was the undoing of what otherwise was diversification into businesses with technology-sharing potential, product-development fit, and some overlap in distribution channels.

When a particular line of business loses its appeal, the most attractive solution usually is to sell it. Normally such businesses should be divested as fast as is practical. To drag things out serves no purpose unless time is needed to get it into better shape to sell. The more business units in a diversified firm's portfolio, the more likely that it will have occasion to divest poor performers, "dogs," and misfits. A useful guide to determine if and when to divest a business subsidiary is to ask the question, "If we were not in this business today, would we want to get into it now?"[16] When the answer is no or probably not, divestiture should be considered.

Divestiture can take either of two forms. The parent can spin off a business as a financially and managerially independent company in which the parent company may or may not retain partial ownership. Or the parent may sell the unit outright, in which case a buyer needs to be found. As a rule, divestiture should not be approached from the angle of "Who can we pawn this business off on and what is the most we can get for it?"[17] Instead, it is wiser to ask "For what sort of organization would this business be a good fit, and under what conditions would it be viewed as a good deal?" Organizations for which the business is a good fit are likely to pay the highest price.

Of all the strategic alternatives, liquidation is the most unpleasant and painful, especially for a single-business enterprise where it means the organization ceases to exist. For a multi-industry, multibusiness firm to liquidate one of its lines of business is less traumatic. The hardships of job eliminations, plant closings, and so on, while not to be minimized, still leave an ongoing organization, perhaps one that is healthier after its pruning. In hopeless situations, an early liquidation effort usually serves owner-stockholder interests better than an inevitable bankruptcy. Prolonging the pursuit of a lost cause exhausts an organization's resources and leaves less to liquidate; it can also mar reputations and ruin management careers. The problem, of course, is differentiating between when a turnaround is achievable and when it isn't. It is easy for managers to let their emotions and pride overcome sound judgment when a business gets in such deep trouble that a successful turnaround is remote.

CORPORATE TURNAROUND, RETRENCHMENT, AND PORTFOLIO RESTRUCTURING STRATEGIES

Turnaround, retrenchment, and portfolio restructuring strategies come into play when a diversified company's management has to restore an ailing business portfolio to good health. Poor performance can be caused by large losses in one or more business units that pull the corporation's overall financial performance down, a disproportion-

---

[16]Ibid., p. 94.
[17]Ibid., p. 719.

ate number of businesses in unattractive industries, a bad economy adversely impacting many of the firm's business units, an excessive debt burden, or ill-chosen acquisitions that haven't lived up to expectations.

Corporate turnaround strategies focus on efforts to restore a diversified company's money-losing businesses to profitability instead of divesting them. The intent is to get the whole company back in the black by curing the problems of those businesses that are most responsible for pulling overall performance down. Turnaround strategies are most appropriate when the reasons for poor performance are short-term, the ailing businesses are in attractive industries, and divesting the money losers does not make long-term strategic sense.

Corporate retrenchment strategies involve reducing the scope of diversification to a smaller number of businesses. Retrenchment is usually undertaken when corporate management concludes that the company is in too many businesses and needs to narrow its business base. Sometimes diversified firms retrench because they can't make certain businesses profitable after several frustrating years of trying or because they lack funds to support the investment needs of all of their business subsidiaries. More commonly, however, corporate executives conclude that the firm's diversification efforts have ranged too far afield and that the key to improved long-term performance lies in concentrating on building strong positions in a smaller number of businesses. Retrenchment is usually accomplished by divesting businesses that are too small to make a sizable contribution to earnings or that have little or no strategic fit with the businesses that management wants to concentrate on. Divesting such businesses frees resources that can be used to reduce debt, to support expansion of the remaining businesses, or to make acquisitions that strengthen the company's competitive position in one or more of the remaining businesses.

Portfolio restructuring strategies involve radical surgery on the mix and percentage makeup of the types of businesses in the portfolio. For instance, one company over a two-year period divested 4 business units, closed down the operations of 4 others, and added 25 new lines of business to its portfolio, 16 through acquisition and 9 through internal start-up. Other companies have elected to demerge their businesses and split into two or more independent companies—AT&T, for instance, has divided into three companies (one for long distance and other telecommunications services that will retain the AT&T name, one for manufacturing telephone equipment callent Lucent Technologies, and one for computer systems, called NCR, that essentially represents the divestiture of AT&T's earlier acquisition of NCR). Restructuring can be prompted by any of several conditions:

1. When a strategy review reveals that the firm's long-term performance prospects have become unattractive because the portfolio contains too many slow-growth, declining, or competitively weak business units.

2. When one or more of the firm's principal businesses fall prey to hard times.

3. When a new CEO takes over and decides to redirect where the company is headed.

4. When "wave of the future" technologies or products emerge and a major shakeup of the portfolio is needed to build a position in a potentially big new industry.

5. When the firm has a unique opportunity to make an acquisition so big that it has to sell several existing business units to finance the new acquisition.

6. When major businesses in the portfolio have become more and more unattractive, forcing a shakeup in the portfolio in order to produce satisfactory long-term corporate performance.

7. When changes in markets and technologies of certain businesses proceed in such different directions that it is better to split the company into separate pieces rather than remain together under the same corporate umbrella.

Portfolio restructuring involves revamping a diversified company's business makeup through a series of divestitures and new acquisitions.

Candidates for divestiture typically include not only weak or up-and-down performers or those in unattractive industries, but also those that no longer fit (even though they may be profitable and in attractive-enough industries). Many broadly diversified companies, disenchanted with the performance of some acquisitions and having only mixed success in overseeing so many unrelated business units, restructure to enable concentration on a smaller core of at least partially related businesses. Business units incompatible with newly established related diversification criteria are divested, the remaining units regrouped and aligned to capture more strategic fit benefits, and new acquisitions made to strengthen the parent company's position in the industries it has chosen to emphasize.[18]

Most recently, portfolio restructuring has centered on demerging—splitting a broadly diversified company into several independent companies. Notable examples of companies pursuing demerger include ITT, Westinghouse, and Britian's Imperial Chemical and Hanson, plc. Before beginning to divest and demerge in 1995, Hanson owned companies with more than $20 billion in revenues in businesses as diverse as beer, exercise equipment, tools, construction cranes, tobacco, cement, chemicals, coal mining, electricity, hot tubs and whirlpools, cookware, rock and gravel, bricks, and asphalt; understandably, investors and analysts had a hard time understanding the company and its strategies. By early 1997, Hanson had demerged into a $3.8 billion enterprise focused more narrowly on gravel, crushed rock, cement, asphalt, bricks, and construction cranes; the remaining businesses were divided into four groups and divested. Another example of portfolio restructuring is presented in Illustration Capsule 26 (see p. 226).

The strategies of broadly diversified companies to demerge and deconglomerate have been driven by a growing preference among company executives and investors for building diversification around the creation of strong competitive positions in a few, well-selected industries. Indeed, investor disenchantment with the conglomerate approach to diversification has been so pronounced (evident in the fact that conglomerates often have *lower* price-earnings ratios than companies with related diversification strategies) that some broadly diversified companies have restructured their portfolios and retrenched to escape being regarded as a conglomerate.

MULTINATIONAL DIVERSIFICATION STRATEGIES

The distinguishing characteristics of a multinational diversification strategy are a *diversity of businesses* and a *diversity of national markets*.[19] Not only do the managers of a diversified multinational corporation (DMNC) have to conceive and execute

---

[18]Evidence that corporate restructuring and pruning down to a narrower business base produces improved corporate performance is contained in Constantinos C. Markides, "Diversification, Restructuring and Economic Performance," *Strategic Management Journal* 16 (February 1995), pp. 101–18.

[19]C. K. Prahalad and Yves L. Doz, *The Multinational Mission* (New York: Free Press, 1987), p. 2.

a substantial number of strategies—at least one for each industry, with as many multinational variations as conditions in each country market dictate—but they also have the added challenge of conceiving good ways to coordinate the firm's strategic actions across industries and countries. This effort can do more than just bring the full force of corporate resources and capabilities to the task of building a strong competitive position in each business and national market. *Capitalizing on opportunities for strategic coordination across businesses and countries provides an avenue for sustainable competitive advantage not open to a company that competes in only one country or one business.*[20]

The Emergence of Multinational Diversification

Until the 1960s, multinational companies (MNCs) operated fairly autonomous subsidiaries in each host country, each catering to the special requirements of its own national market.[21] Management tasks at company headquarters primarily involved finance functions, technology transfer, and export coordination. Even though their products and competitive strategies were tailored to market conditions in each country, a multinational company could still realize competitive advantage by learning to transfer technology, manufacturing know-how, brand-name identification, and marketing and management skills from country to country quite efficiently, giving them an edge over smaller host country competitors. Standardized administrative procedures helped minimize overhead costs, and once an initial organization for managing foreign subsidiaries was put in place, entry into additional national markets could be accomplished at low incremental costs.

During the 1970s, however, buyer preferences for some products converged enough that it became feasible to market common product versions across different country markets. No longer was it essential or even desirable to have strategies and products custom-tailored to customer preferences and competitive conditions prevailing in specific country markets. Moreover, as Japanese, European, and U.S. companies pursued international expansion in the wake of trade liberalization and the opening up of market opportunities in both industrialized and less-developed countries, they found themselves in head-to-head competition in country after country.[22] *Global competition*—where the leading companies in an industry competed head to head in most of the world's major country markets—began to emerge.

As the relevant market arena in more and more industries shifted from national to international to global, traditional MNCs were driven to integrate their operations across national borders in a quest for better efficiencies and lower manufacturing costs. Instead of separately manufacturing a complete product range in each country, plants became more specialized in their production operations to gain the economies of longer production runs, to permit use of faster automated equipment, and to capture experience curve effects. Country subsidiaries obtained the rest of the product range they needed from sister plants in other countries. Gains in manufacturing efficiencies from converting to state-of-the-art, world-scale manufacturing plants more than offset increased international shipping costs, especially in light of the other advantages globalized strategies offered. With a global strategy, an MNC could

---

[20]Ibid., p. 15.

[21]Yves L. Doz, *Strategic Management in Multinational Companies* (New York: Pergamon Press, 1985), p. 1.

[22]Ibid., pp. 2–3.

locate plants in countries with low labor costs—a key consideration in industries whose products have high labor content. With a global strategy, an MNC could also exploit differences in tax rates, setting transfer prices in its integrated operations to produce higher profits in low-tax countries and lower profits in high-tax countries. Global strategic coordination also increased MNC's ability to take advantage of country-to-country differences in interest rates, exchange rates, credit terms, government subsidies, and export guarantees. These advantages made it increasingly difficult for a company that produced and sold its product in only one country to succeed in an industry populated with multinational competitors intent on achieving global dominance.

During the 1980s another source of competitive advantage began to emerge: using the strategic fit advantages of related diversification to build stronger competitive positions in several related global industries simultaneously. Being a diversified MNC (DMNC) became competitively superior to being a single-business MNC in cases where strategic fits existed across globally competitive industries. Related diversification proved most capable of producing competitive advantage when a multinational company's expertise in a core technology could be applied in different industries (at least one of which was global) and where there were important economies of scope and brand name advantages to being in a family of related businesses.[23] Illustration Capsule 27 describes how Honda has exploited gasoline engine technology and its well-known name by diversifying into a variety of products powered by gasoline engines.

> *A multinational corporation can gain competitive advantage by diversifying into global industries having related technologies or possessing value chain relationships that yield economies of scope.*

Sources of Competitive Advantage for a DMNC

A strategy of related diversification into industries where global competition prevails opens several avenues of competitive advantage not available to a domestic-only competitor or a single-business competitor:

1. A diversified multinational company can realize competitive advantage by transferring its expertise in a core technology to other lines of business able to benefit from its technical know-how and capabilities.

2. A diversified multinational company with expertise in a core technology and a family of businesses using this technology can capture competitive advantage through a collaborative and strategically coordinated R&D effort on behalf of all the related businesses as a group.

3. A diversified multinational company with businesses that use the same distributors and retail dealers worldwide can (a) diversify into new businesses using the same worldwide distribution capabilities at relatively little expense and use the distribution-related economies of scope as a source of cost advantage over less diversified rivals, (b) can exploit its worldwide distribution capability by diversifying into businesses having attractive sales growth opportunites in the very country markets where its distribution capability is already established, and (c) can gain added bargaining leverage with retailers in securing attractive shelf space for any new products and businesses as its family of businesses grows in number and sales importance to the retailer. Sony, for example, has attractive competitive advantage potential in diversifying into the videogame industry to take on giants like

---

[23]Pralahad and Doz, *The Multinational Mission*, pp. 62–63.

ILLUSTRATION CAPSULE 27   Honda's Competitive Advantage

Expertise in the Technology of Gasoline Engines

At first blush anyone looking at Honda's lineup of products—cars, motorcycles, lawn mowers, power generators, outboard motors, snowmobiles, snowblowers, and garden tillers—might conclude that Honda has pursued unrelated diversification. But underlying the obvious product diversity is a common core: the technology of gasoline engines.

Honda's strategy involves transferring the company's expertise in gasoline engine technology to additional products, exploiting its capabilities in low-cost/high-quality manufacturing, using the widely known and respected Honda brand name on all the products, and promoting several products in the same ad (one Honda ad teased consumers with the question, "How do you put six Hondas in a two-car garage?" and then showed a garage containing a Honda car, a Honda motorcycle, a Honda snowmobile, a Honda lawnmower, a Honda power generator, and a Honda outboard motor). The relatedness in the value chains for the products in Honda's business lineup produces competitive advantage for Honda in the form of economies of scope, beneficial opportunities to transfer technology and capabilities from one business to another, and economical use of a common brand name.

Honda's Competitive Advantage

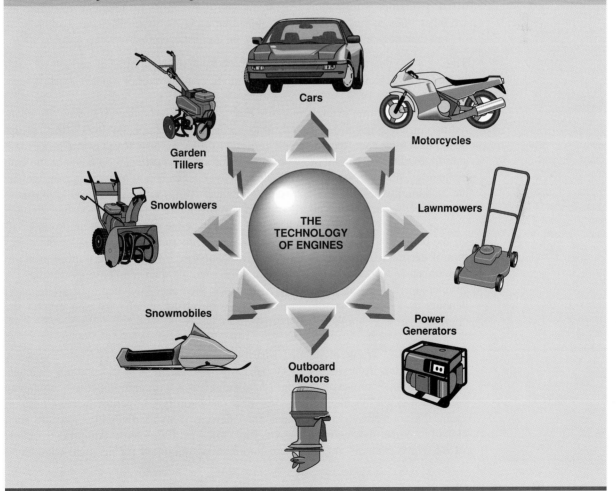

Source: Adapted from C. K. Prahalad and Yves L. Doz, *The Multinational Mission* (New York: Free Press, 1987), p. 62.

Nintendo and SEGA because (a) it has well-established distribution capabilities in consumer electronics worldwide that can be used for videogame game products, (b) it has the capability to go after videogame sales in all country markets where it presently does business, and (c) it has the marketing clout to persuade retailers to give Sony videogame products good visibility in retail stores.

4. A diversified multinational company can leverage its brand name by diversifying into additional businesses able to use its already established brand, thereby capturing economies of scope and marketing benefits. Sony, for example, doesn't have to spend nearly as much advertising and promoting its new videogame products against the offerings of Nintendo and Sega because the Sony brand name already has a strong reputation in consumer electronics worldwide.

5. A diversified multinational company can use the financial and organizational resources it has from operations in other countries to cross-subsidize a competitive assault on the market position of a one-country competitor.

6. A diversified multinational company can draw upon the financial resources in other lines of business to cross-subsidize a competitive offensive against a one-business multinational company or domestic company.

There's a growing evidence that all these advantages are significant enough to result in DMNCs' achieving high returns and having lower overall business risk.[24]

The Competitive Power of a Collaborative R&D Effort and Technology Transfer   By channeling corporate resources directly into a *combined* R&D/technology effort, as opposed to letting each business unit fund and direct its own R&D effort however it sees fit, the DMNC can merge its expertise and efforts *worldwide* to advance the core technology, pursue promising technological avenues to create new businesses, generate technology-based manufacturing economies within and across product/business lines, expedite across-the-board product improvements in existing businesses, and develop new products that complement and enhance the sales of existing products. If, on the other hand, R&D activities are decentralized and put totally under the direction of each existing business unit, R&D/technology investments are more prone to end up narrowly aimed at each business's own product-market opportunities. A splintered R&D effort is unlikely to produce the range and depth of strategic fit benefits as a broad, coordinated companywide effort to advance and exploit the company's full technological expertise.[25]

The Competitive Power of Related Distribution and Common Brand Name Usage   A DMNC that has diversified into global industries with related distribution channels and opportunities to use a common brand name has important competitive advantage potential a single-business competitor or a one-country competitor lacks. Consider, again, the competitive strength that Sony derives from its diversification into such globally competitive consumer goods industries as TVs, stereo equipment, radios, VCRs, video cameras, monitors and multimedia equipment for personal computers,

---

[24]See, for example, W. Chan Kim, Peter Hwang, and Willem P. Burgers, "Multinational's Diversification and the Risk-Return Tradeoff," *Strategic Management Journal* 14 (May 1993) pp. 275–86.
[25]Ibid.

CDs, and videogames—all distributed and marketed through the same types of distributors and retail dealers worldwide and all able to capitalize on use of the Sony brand name. Sony's approach to diversification has allowed it to build worldwide distribution capabilities in consumer electronics products, capture logistical and distribution-related economies of scope, and establish high levels of brand awareness for its products in countries all across the world.[26] A single-business competitor is disadvantaged in competing against Sony because it lacks access to distribution-related economies of scope, it doesn't have Sony's ability to transfer its brand reputation in one line of business to another and achieve advertising economies, and it can't match Sony's clout in bargaining for favorable shelf space in retail stores. A domestic-only competitor is at a disadvantage on costs if its national sales volume is too small to achieve the scale economies afforded by Sony's global-sized sales volume.

A multinational corporation can also gain competitive advantage by diversifying into global industries with related distribution channels and opportunities for common use of a well-known brand.

Moreover, Sony's already-established *global* distribution capabilities and *global* brand-name recognition give it an important cost advantage over a one-country competitor looking at the costs of trying to expand into foreign country markets for the first time and better position itself as a global competitor against Sony. Similarly, Sony's economies of scope (both distribution-related and brand name-related) give it a cost advantage over a one-business competitor (with no existing economies of scope) that might be looking to diversify into a business that Sony is already in.

The Competitive Power of Using Cross-Subsidization to Outcompete a One-Business Company Both a one-business domestic company and a one-business multinational company are weakly positioned to defend their market positions against a DMNC determined to establish a solid long-term competitive position in their market and willing to accept lower short-term profits in order to do so. A one-business domestic company has only one profit sanctuary—its home market. A one-business multinational company may have profit sanctuaries in several country markets but all are in the same business. Each is vulnerable to a DMNC that launches a major strategic offensive in their profit sanctuaries and lowballs its prices and/or spends extravagantly on advertising to win market share at their expense. A DMNC's ability to keep hammering away at competitors with lowball prices year after year may reflect either a cost advantage growing out of its related diversification strategy or a willingness to cross-subsidize low profits or even losses with earnings from its profit sanctuaries in other country markets and/or its earnings from other businesses. Sony, for example, by pursuing related diversification keyed to product-distribution-technology strategic fit and managing its product families on a global scale, has the ability to put strong competitive pressure on domestic companies like Zenith (which manufactures TVs and small computer systems) and Magnavox (which manufactures TVs, VCRs, stereo equipment, and monitors for personal computers). Sony can lowball its prices on TVs or fund special promotions for its TVs, using earnings from its other country markets and lines of business to help support its assault. If Sony chooses, it can keep its prices low or spend lavishly on advertising for several years, persistently pecking away at Zenith's and Magnavox's market shares in TVs over time. At the same time, it can draw upon its considerable resources in R&D, its ability to transfer technology from one product

A well-diversified family of businesses and a multinational market base give a DMNC the power and resource strength to subsidize a long-term market offensive against one-market or one-business competitors with earnings from one or more of its country market profit sanctuaries and/or earnings in other businesses.

---

[26]Ibid., p. 64.

ILLUSTRATION CAPSULE 28   Mitsubishi: The Competitive Power of a Japanese Keiretsu

Mitsubishi is Japan's largest *keiretsu*—a family of affiliated companies. With combined 1995 sales of $184 billion, the Mitsubishi keiretsu consists of 28 core companies: Mitsubishi Corp. (the trading company), Mitsubishi Heavy Industries (the group's biggest manufacturer—shipbuilding, air conditioners, forklifts, robots, gas turbines), Mitsubishi Motors, Mitsubishi Steel, Mitsubishi Aluminum, Mitsubishi Oil, Mitsubishi Petrochemical, Mitsubishi Gas Chemical, Mitsubishi Plastics, Mitsubishi Cable, Mitsubishi Electric, Mitsubishi Construction, Mitsubishi Paper Mills, Mitsubishi Mining and Cement, Mitsubishi Rayon, Nikon, Asahi Glass, Kirin Brewery, Mitsubishi Bank (the world's fifth largest bank and the lead bank for family companies), Tokio Marine and Fire Insurance (one of the world's largest insurance companies), and eight others. Beyond this core group are hundreds of other Mitsubishi-related subsidiaries and affiliates.

The 28 core companies of the Mitsubishi *keiretsu* are bound together by cross-ownership of each other's stock (the percentage of shares of each core company owned by other members ranges from 17 percent to 100 percent, with an average of 27 percent), by interlocking directorships (it is standard for officers of one company to sit on the boards of other *keiretsu* members), joint ventures, and long-term business relationships. They use each other's products and services in many instances—among the suppliers to Mitsubishi Motor's Diamond

Star plant in Bloomington, Illinois, are 25 Mitsubishi and Mitsubishi-related suppliers. It is common for them to join forces to make acquisitions—five Mitsubishi companies teamed to buy a cement plant in California; Mitsubishi Corp. bought an $880 million chemical company in Pittsburgh with financial assistance from Mitsubishi Bank and Mitsubishi Trust, then sold pieces to Mitsubishi Gas Chemical, Mitsubishi Rayon, Mitsubishi Petrochemical, and Mitsubishi Kasei. Mitsubishi Bank and occasionally other Mitsubishi financial enterprises serve as a primary financing source for new ventures and as a financial safety net if *keiretsu* members encounter tough market conditions or have financial problems.

Despite these links, there's no grand Mitsubishi strategy. Each company operates independently, pursuing its own strategy and markets. On occasion, group members find themselves going after the same markets competing with each other. Nor do member companies usually get sweetheart deals from other members; for example, Mitsubishi Heavy Industries lost out to Siemens in competing to supply gas turbines to a new power plant that Mitsubishi Corp.'s wholly owned Diamond Energy subsidiary constructed in Virginia. But operating independence does not prevent them from recognizing their mutual interests, cooperating voluntarily without formal controls, or turning inward to *keiretsu* members for business partnerships on ventures perceived as strategically important.

---

family to another, and its expertise in product innovation to introduce appealing new features and better picture quality. Such competitive actions not only enhance Sony's own brand image but they make it very tough for Zenith and Magnavox to match its prices, advertising, and product development efforts and still earn acceptable profits. Sony can turn its attention to becoming attractively profitable once the battle for market share and competitive position is won.[27] Some additional aspects of the competitive power of broadly diversified enterprises is described in Illustration Capsule 28.

Although cross-subsidization is a potent competitive weapon, it can only be used sparingly because of its adverse impact on overall corporate profitability.

The Combined Effects of These Advantages Is Potent   Companies with a strategy of (1) diversifying into *related* industries and (2) competing *globally* in each of these industries thus can draw upon any of several competitive advantage opportunities to overcome a domestic-only rival or a single business rival. A DMNC's biggest competitive advantage potential comes from concentrating its diversification efforts in industries where there are technology-sharing and technology-transfer opportunities and where there are important economies of scope and brand-name benefits. The more a company's diversification

---

[27]Ibid.

A President's Council, consisting of 49 chairmen and presidents, meets monthly, usually the second Friday of the month. While the formal agenda typically includes a discussion of joint philanthropical and public relations projects and a lecture by an expert on some current topic, participants report instances where strategic problems or opportunities affecting several group members are discussed and major decisions made. It is common for a Mitsubishi company involved in a major undertaking (initiating its first foray into the U.S. or European markets or developing a new technology) to ask for support from other members. In such cases, group members who can take business actions that contribute to solutions are expected to do so. The President's Council meetings also serve to cement personal ties, exchange information, identify mutual interests, and set up follow-on actions by subordinates. Other ways that Mitsubishi uses to foster an active informal network of contacts, information sharing, cooperation, and business relationships among member companies include regular get-togethers of Mitsubishi-America and Mitsubishi-Europe executives and even a matchmaking club where member company employees can meet prospective spouses.

In recent years, Mitsubishi companies introduced a number of consumer products in the United States and elsewhere, all branded with a three-diamond logo derived from the crest of the founding samurai family—cars and trucks made by Mitsubishi Motors, big-screen TVs and mobile phones made by Mitsubishi Electric, and air conditioners produced by Mitsubishi Heavy Industries. Mitsubishi executives believe common logo usage has produced added brand awareness; for example, in the United States Mitsubishi Motors' efforts to advertise and market its cars and trucks helped boost brand awareness of Mitsubishi TVs. In several product categories one or more Mitsubishi companies operate in stages all along the industry value chain—from components production to assembly to shipping, warehousing, and distribution.

Similar practices exist in the other five of the six largest Japanese *keiretsu*: Dai-Ichi Kangin with 47 core companies, Mitsui Group with 24 core companies (including Toyota and Toshiba), Sanwa with 44 core companies, Sumitomo with 20 core companies (including NEC, a maker of telecommunications equipment and personal computers), and Fuyo with 29 core companies (including Nissan and Canon). Most observers agree that Japan's keiretsu model gives Japanese companies major competitive advantages in international markets. According to a Japanese economics professor at Osaka University, "Using group power, they can engage in cutthroat competition."

Source: Based on information in "Mighty Mitsubishi Is on the Move" and "Hands across America: The Rise of Mitsubishi," *Business Week*, September 24, 1990, pp. 98–107.

strategy yields these kinds of strategic fit benefits, the more powerful a competitor it becomes and the better its profit and growth performance is likely to be. Relying on strategic fit advantages to outcompete rivals is inherently more attractive than resorting to cross-subsidization.

While a DMNC can employ cross-subsidization tactics to muscle its way into attractive new markets or outcompete a particular rival, its ability to use cross-subsidization is limited by the need to maintain respectable levels of overall profitability. It is one thing to *occasionally* use a *portion* of the profits and cash flows from existing businesses to cover *reasonable* short-term losses to gain entry to a new business or a new country market or wage a competitive offensive against certain rivals. It is quite another thing to *regularly* use cross-subsidization tactics to fund competitive inroads in new areas and *weaken overall company performance* on an *ongoing* basis. A DMNC is under the same pressures as any other company to earn consistently acceptable profits across its whole business portfolio. At some juncture, every business and every market entered needs to make a profit contribution or become a candidate for abandonment. As a general rule, *cross-subsidization is justified only if there is a good prospect that the short-term impairment to corporate profitability will be offset by stronger competitiveness and better overall profitability over the long term.*

COMBINATION RELATED-UNRELATED DIVERSIFICATION STRATEGIES

Nothing prevents a company from diversifying into both related and unrelated businesses. Indeed, in actual practice the business makeup of diversified companies varies considerably. Some diversified companies are really *dominant-business enterprises*—one major "core" business accounts for 50 to 80 percent of total revenues and a collection of small related or unrelated businesses account for the remainder. Some diversified companies are *narrowly diversified* around a few (two to five) *related* or *unrelated* businesses. Some diversified companies are *broadly diversified* and have a wide ranging collection of either *related* businesses or *unrelated* businesses. And a few multibusiness enterprises have diversified into unrelated areas but have a collection of related businesses within each area—thus giving them a business portfolio consisting of *several unrelated groups of related businesses*. Companies have ample room to customize their diversification strategies to suit their own risk preferences and to fit most any strategic vision.

Moreover, the geographic markets of individual businesses within a diversified company can range from local to regional to national to multinational to global. Thus, a diversified company can be competing locally in some businesses, nationally in others, and globally in still others.

KEY POINTS

Most companies have their business roots in a single industry. Even though they may have since diversified into other industries, a substantial part of their revenues and profits still usually comes from the original or "core" business. Diversification becomes an attractive strategy when a company runs out of profitable growth opportunities in its core business (including any opportunities to integrate backward or forward to strengthen its competitive position). The purpose of diversification is to build shareholder value. Diversification builds shareholder value when a diversified group of businesses can perform better under the auspices of a single corporate parent than they would as independent, stand-alone businesses. Whether a particular diversification move is capable of increasing shareholder value hinges on the attractiveness test, the cost-of-entry test, and the better-off test.

There are two fundamental approaches to diversification—into related businesses and into unrelated businesses. The rationale for related diversification is *strategic:* diversify into businesses with strategic fit, capitalize on strategic-fit relationships to gain competitive advantage, then use competitive advantage to achieve the desired 2 + 2 = 5 impact on shareholder value. Businesses have strategic fit when their value chains offer potential (1) for realizing economies of scope or cost-saving efficiencies associated with sharing technology, facilities, distribution outlets, or combining related value chain activities; (2) for efficient transfer of key skills, technological expertise, or managerial know-how, (3) for using a common brand name, and/or (4) for strengthening a firm's resources and competitive capabilities.

The basic premise of unrelated diversification is that any business that has good profit prospects and can be acquired on good financial terms is a good business to diversify into. Unrelated diversification is basically a *financial* approach to diversification; strategic fit is a secondary consideration compared to the expectation of financial gain. Unrelated diversification surrenders the competitive advantage potential of strategic fit in return for such advantages as (1) spreading business risk over a variety of industries and (2) gaining opportunities for quick financial gain (if candidate acquisitions have undervalued assets, are bargain-priced and have good upside potential given the right management, or need the backing of a financially strong parent to capitalize on attractive opportunities). In theory, unrelated diversification also offers greater earnings stability over the business cycle, a third advantage. However, achieving these three outcomes consistently requires corporate executives who are smart enough to avoid the considerable disadvantages of unrelated diversification. The greater the number of businesses a conglomerate company is in and the more diverse these businesses are, the more that corporate executives are stretched to know enough about each business to distinguish a good acquisition from a risky one, select capable managers to run each business, know when the major strategic proposals of business units are sound, or wisely decide what to do when a business unit stumbles. Unless corporate managers are exceptionally shrewd and talented, unrelated diversification is a dubious and unreliable approach to building shareholder value when compared to related diversification.

Once diversification is accomplished, corporate management's task is to manage the firm's business portfolio for maximum long-term performance. Six options for improving a diversified company's performance include: (1) make new acquisitions, (2) divest weak-performing business units or those that no longer fit, (3) restructure the makeup of the portfolio when overall performance is poor and future prospects are bleak, (4) retrench to a narrower diversification base, (5) pursue multinational diversification, and (6) liquidate money-losing businesses with poor turnaround potential.

The most popular option for getting out of a business that is unattractive or doesn't fit is to sell it—ideally to a buyer for whom the business has attractive fit. Sometimes a business can be divested by spinning it off as a financially and managerially independent enterprise in which the parent company may or may not retain an ownership interest.

Corporate turnaround, retrenchment, and restructuring strategies are used when corporate management has to restore an ailing business portfolio to good health. Poor performance can be caused by large losses in one or more businesses that pull overall corporate performance down, by too many business units in unattractive industries, by an excessive debt burden, or by ill-chosen acquisitions that haven't lived up to expectations. Corporate turnaround strategies aim at restoring money-losing businesses to profitability instead of divesting them. Retrenchment involves reducing the scope of diversification to a smaller number of businesses by divesting those that are too small to make a sizable contribution to corporate earnings or those that don't fit with the narrower business base on which corporate management wants to concentrate company resources and energies. Restructuring strategies involve radical portfolio shakeups, divestiture of some businesses and acquisition of others to create a group of businesses with much improved performance potential.

Multinational diversification strategies feature a diversity of businesses and a diversity of national markets. Despite the complexity of having to devise and manage so many strategies (at least one for each industry, with as many variations for country markets as may be needed), multinational diversification can be a competitively advantageous strategy. DMNCs can use the strategic-fit advantages of related diversification (economies of scope, technology and skills transfer, and shared brand names) to build competitively strong positions in several related global industries simultaneously. Such advantages, if competently exploited, can allow a DMNC to outcompete a one-business domestic rival or a one-business multinational rival over time. A one-business domestic company has only one profit sanctuary—its home market. A single-business multinational company may have profit sanctuaries in several countries, but all are in the same business. Both are vulnerable to a DMNC that launches offensive campaigns in their profit sanctuaries. A DMNC can use a lower-cost advantage growing out of its economies of scope to underprice rivals and gain market share at their expense. Even without a cost advantage, the DMNC can decide to underprice such rivals and subsidize its lower profit margins (or even losses) with the profits earned in its other businesses. A well-financed and competently managed DMNC can sap the financial and competitive strength of one-business domestic-only and multinational rivals. A DMNC gains the biggest competitive advantage potential by diversifying into *related* industries where it can capture significant economies of scope, share technology and expertise, and leverage use of a well-known brand name.

SUGGESTED READINGS

Barney, Jay B. *Gaining and Sustaining Competitive Advantage*. Reading, Mass.: Addison-Wesley, 1997, chaps. 11 and 13.

Campbell, Andrew, Michael Goold, and Marcus Alexander. "Corporate Strategy: The Quest for Parenting Advantage." *Harvard Business Review* 73, no. 2 (March–April 1995), pp. 120–32.

————. "The Value of the Parent Company." *California Management Review* 38, no. 1 (Fall 1995), pp. 79–97.

Goold, Michael, and Kathleen Luchs. "Why Diversify? Four Decades of Management Thinking." *Academy of Management Executive* 7, no. 3 (August 1993), pp. 7–25.

Hoffman, Richard C. "Strategies for Corporate Turnarounds: What Do We Know about Them?" *Journal of General Management* 14, no. 3 (Spring 1989), pp. 46–66.

Liedtka, Jeanne M. "Collaboration across Lines of Business for Competitive Advantage." *Academy of Management Executive* 10, no.2 (May 1996), pp. 20–34.

Prahalad, C. K., and Yves L. Doz. *The Multinational Mission*. New York: Free Press, 1987, chaps. 1 and 2.

EVALUATING THE STRATEGIES OF DIVERSIFIED COMPANIES

8

Once a company diversifies and has operations in a number of different industries, three issues dominate the agenda of the company's top strategy makers:

- How attractive is the group of businesses the company is in?
- Assuming the company sticks with its present lineup of businesses, how good is its performance outlook in the years ahead?
- If the previous two answers are not satisfactory: (a) should the company divest itself of low-performing or unattractive businesses, (b) what actions should the company take to strengthen the growth and profit potential of the businesses it intends to remain in, and (c) should the company move into additional businesses to boost its long-term performance prospects?

Crafting and implementing action plans to improve the overall attractiveness and competitive strength of a company's business lineup is the central strategic task of corporate-level managers.

Strategic analysis of diversified companies builds on the concepts and methods used for single-business companies. But there are also new aspects to consider and additional analytical approaches to master. The procedure for critiquing a diversified company's strategy, evaluating the attractiveness of the industries it diversified into, assessing the competitive strength and performance potential of its businesses, and deciding on what strategic actions to take next involves the following steps:

> If we can know where we are and something about how we got there, we might see where we are trending—and if the outcomes which lie naturally in our course are unacceptable, to make timely change.
>
> **Abraham Lincoln**
>
> The corporate strategies of most companies have dissipated instead of created shareholder value.
>
> **Michael Porter**
>
> Achieving superior performance through diversification is largely based on relatedness.
>
> **Philippe Very**

1. *Identifying the present corporate strategy*—whether the company is pursuing related or unrelated diversification (or a mixture of both), the nature and purpose of any recent acquisitions and divestitures, and the kind of diversified company that corporate management is trying to create.

2. *Applying the industry attractiveness test*—evaluating the long-term attractiveness of each industry the company is in.

3. *Applying the competitive strength test*—evaluating the competitive strength of the company's business units to see which ones are strong contenders in their respective industries.

4. *Applying the strategic fit test*—determining the competitive advantage potential of any value chain relationships and strategic fits among existing business units.

5. *Applying the resource fit test*—determining whether the firm's resource strengths match the resource requirements of its present business lineup.

6. *Ranking the businesses from highest to lowest on the basis of both historical performance and future prospects.*

7. *Ranking the business units in terms of priority for resource allocation* and deciding whether the strategic posture for each business unit should be aggressive expansion, fortify and defend, overhaul and reposition, or harvest/divest. (The task of initiating *specific* business-unit strategies to improve the business unit's competitive position is usually delegated to business-level managers, with corporate-level managers offering suggestions and having authority for final approval.)

8. *Crafting new strategic moves to improve overall corporate performance*—changing the makeup of the portfolio via acquisitions and divestitures, improving coordination among the activities of related business units to achieve greater cost-sharing and skills-transfer benefits, and steering corporate resources into the areas of greatest opportunity.

The rest of this chapter describes this eight-step process and introduces analytical techniques needed to arrive at sound corporate strategy appraisals.

IDENTIFYING THE PRESENT CORPORATE STRATEGY

Analysis of a diversified company's situation and prospects needs to begin with an understanding of its present strategy and business makeup. Recall from Figure 2–2 in Chapter 2 that one can get a good handle on a diversified company's corporate strategy by looking at:

Evaluating a diversified firm's business portfolio needs to begin with a clear identification of the firm's diversification strategy.

- The extent to which the firm is diversified (as measured by the proportion of total sales and operating profits contributed by each business unit and by whether the diversification base is broad or narrow).

- Whether the firm is pursuing related or unrelated diversification, or a mixture of both.

- Whether the scope of company operations is mostly domestic, increasingly multinational, or global.

- Any moves to add new businesses to the portfolio and build positions in new industries.

- Any moves to divest weak or unattractive business units.

- Recent moves to boost performance of key business units and/or strengthen existing business positions.

- Management efforts to capture strategic-fit benefits and use value-chain relationships among its businesses to create competitive advantage.

- The percentage of total capital expenditures allocated to each business unit in prior years (a strong indicator of the company's resource allocation priorities).

Getting a clear fix on the current corporate strategy and its rationale sets the stage for probing the strengths and weaknesses in its business portfolio and drawing conclusions about whatever refinements or major alterations in strategy are appropriate.

EVALUATING INDUSTRY ATTRACTIVENESS: THREE TESTS

A principal consideration in evaluating a diversified company's business makeup and the caliber of its strategy is the attractiveness of the industries it has diversified into. The more attractive these industries, the better the company's long-term profit prospects. Industry attractiveness needs to be evaluated from three angles:

The more attractive the industries that a company has diversified into, the better its performance prospects.

1. *The attractiveness of each industry represented in the business portfolio.* Management must examine each industry the firm has diversified into to determine whether it represents a good business for the company to be in. What are the industry's prospects for long-term growth? Do competitive conditions and emerging market opportunities offer good prospects for long-term profitability? Are the industry's capital, technology, and other resource requirements well-matched to company capabilities?

2. *Each industry's attractiveness relative to the others.* The issue here is "Which industries in the portfolio are the most attractive and which are the least attractive?" Comparing the attractiveness of the industries and ranking them from most attractive to least attractive is a prerequisite for deciding how best to allocate corporate resources.

3. *The attractiveness of all the industries as a group.* The question here is "How appealing is the mix of industries?" A company whose revenues and profits come chiefly from businesses in unattractive industries probably needs to consider restructuring its portfolio.

Evaluating the Attractiveness of Each Industry the Company Has Diversified Into

All the industry attractiveness considerations discussed in Chapter 3 come into play in assessing the long-term appeal of the industries a company has diversified into:

- *Market size and projected growth rate*—big industries are more attractive than small industries, and fast-growing industries tend to be more attractive than slow-growing industries, other things being equal.

- *The intensity of competition*—industries where competitive pressures are relatively weak are more attractive than industries where competitive pressures are strong.

- *Emerging opportunities and threats*—industries with promising opportunities and minimal threats on the near horizon are more attractive than industries with modest opportunities and imposing threats.

- *Seasonal and cyclical factors*—industries where demand is relatively steady year-round and not unduly vulnerable to economic ups and downs are more attractive than industries where there are wide swings in buyer demand within or across years.

- *Capital requirements and other special resource requirements*—industries with low capital requirements (or amounts within the company's reach) are relatively more attractive than industries where investment requirements could strain corporate financial resources. Likewise, industries which do *not* require specialized technology, hard-to-develop competencies, or unique capabilities (unless such requirements match well with a diversifier's own capabilities) are more attractive than industries where the resource requirements outstrip a firm's resources and capabilities.
- *Strategic fits and resource fits with the firm's present businesses*—an industry is more attractive to a particular firm if its value chain and resource requirements match up well with the value chain activities of other industries the company has diversified into and with the company's resource capabilities.
- *Industry profitability*—industries with healthy profit margins and high rates of return on investment are generally more attractive than industries where profits have historically been low or where the business risks are high.
- *Social, political, regulatory, and environmental factors*—industries with significant problems in such areas as consumer health, safety, or environmental pollution or that are subject to intense regulation are less attractive than industries where such problems are no worse than most businesses encounter.
- *Degree of risk and uncertainty*—industries with less uncertainty and business risk are more attractive than industries where the future is uncertain and business failure is common.

How well each industry stacks up on these factors determines how many are able to satisfy the *attractiveness test*. The ideal situation is for all of the industries represented in the company's portfolio to be attractive.

Measuring Each Industry's Attractiveness Relative to the Others

It is not enough, however, that an industry be attractive. Corporate resources need to be allocated to those industries of *greatest* long-term opportunity. Shrewd resource allocation is aided by ranking the industries in the company's business portfolio from most attractive to least attractive—a process that calls for quantitative measures of industry attractiveness.

The first step in developing a quantitative measure of long-term industry attractiveness is to select a set of industry attractiveness measures (such as those listed above). Next, weights are assigned to each attractiveness measure—it is weak methodology to assume that the various measures are equally important. While judgment is obviously involved in deciding how much weight to put on each attractiveness measure, it makes sense to place the highest weights on those important to achieving the company's vision or objective and that match up well with the company's needs and capabilities. The sum of the weights must add up to 1.0. Each industry is then rated on each of the chosen industry attractivenesss measures, using a 1 to 5 or 1 to 10 rating scale (where *a high rating signifies high attractiveness and a low rating signifies low attractiveness or unattractiveness*). Weighted attractiveness ratings are calculated by multiplying the industry's rating on each factor by the factor's weight. For example, a rating score of 8 times a weight of .30 gives a weighted rating of 2.40. The sum of weighted ratings for all the attractiveness factors provides a quantitative measure of the industry's long-term attractiveness. The procedure is shown below:

Industry Attractiveness Factor	Weight	Rating	Weighted Industry Attractiveness Rating
Market size and projected growth	.15	5	0.75
Intensity of competition	.30	8	2.40
Emerging industry opportunities and threats	.05	2	0.10
Resource requirements	.10	6	0.60
Strategic fit with other company businesses	.15	4	0.60
Social, political, regulatory, and environmental factors	.05	7	0.35
Industry profitability	.10	4	0.40
Degree of risk	.10	5	0.50
Sum of the assigned weights	1.00		
Industry Attractiveness Rating			5.70

Once industry attractiveness ratings are calculated for each industry in the corporate portfolio, it is a simple task to rank the industries from most to least attractive.

Calculating industry attractiveness scores presents two difficulties. One is deciding on appropriate weights for the industry attractiveness measures. The other is getting reliable data on which to assign accurate and objective ratings. Without good information, the ratings necessarily become subjective, and their validity hinges on whether management has probed industry conditions sufficiently to make dependable judgments. Generally, a company can come up with the statistical data needed to compare its industries on such factors as market size, growth rate, seasonal and cyclical influences, and industry profitability. The attractiveness measure where judgment weighs most heavily is in comparing the industries on intensity of competition, resource requirements, strategic fits, degree of risk, and social, regulatory, and environmental considerations. It is not always easy to conclude whether competition in one industry is stronger or weaker than in another industry because of the different types of competitive influences and the differences in their relative importance. Nonetheless, industry attractiveness ratings are a reasonably reliable method for ranking a diversified company's industries from most attractive to least attractive—they tell a valuable story about just how and why some of the industries a company has diversified into are more attractive than others.

The Attractiveness of the Mix of Industries as a Whole

For a diversified company to be a strong performer, a substantial portion of its revenues and profits must come from business units judged to be in attractive industries—those with relatively high attractiveness scores. It is particularly important that the company's principal businesses be in industries with a good outlook for growth and above-average profitability. Having a big fraction of the company's revenues and profits come from industries that are growing slowly or have low returns on investment tends to drag overall company performance down. Business units in the least attractive industries are potential candidates for divestiture, unless they are positioned strongly enough to overcome the unattractive aspects of their industry environments or they are a strategically important component of the portfolio.

EVALUATING THE COMPETITIVE STRENGTH OF EACH OF THE COMPANY'S BUSINESS UNITS

The task here is to evaluate whether each business unit in the corporate portfolio is well-positioned in its industry and whether it already is or can become a strong market contender. Appraising each business unit's strength and competitive position in its industry not only reveals its chances for success but also provides a basis for comparing the relative competitive strength of the different business units to determine which ones are strongest and which are weakest. Quantitative measures of each business unit's competitive strength and market position can be calculated using a procedure similar to that for measuring industry attractiveness.[1] Assessing the competitive strength of a diversified company's business subsidiaries should be based on such factors as;

- *Relative market share*—business units with higher *relative* market shares normally have greater competitive strength than those with lower shares. A business unit's *relative market share* is defined as the ratio of its market share to the market share of the largest rival firm in the industry, with market share measured in unit volume, not dollars. For instance, if business A has a 15 percent share of its industry's total volume and A's largest rival has 30 percent, A's relative market share is 0.5. If business B has a market-leading share of 40 percent and its largest rival has 30 percent, B's relative market share is 1.33.[2] Using *relative* market share instead of *actual* or *absolute* market share to measure competitive strength is analytically superior because a 10 percent market share is much stronger if the leader's share is 12 percent than if it is 50 percent; the use of relative market share captures this difference.[3]

- *Ability to compete on cost*—business units that are very cost competitive tend to be more strongly positioned in their industries than business units struggling to achieve cost parity with major rivals.

- *Ability to match industry rivals on quality and/or service*—a company's competitiveness depends in part on being able to satisfy buyer expectations with regard to features, product performance, reliability, service, and other important attributes.

- *Ability to exercise bargaining leverage with key suppliers or customers*—having bargaining leverage is a source of competitive advantage.

---

[1] The procedure also parallels the methodology for doing competitive strength assessments presented in Chapter 4 (see Table 4-4).

[2] Given this definition, only business units that are market share leaders in their respective industries will have relative market shares greater than 1.0. Business units that trail rivals in market share will have ratios below 1.0. The further below 1.0 a business unit's relative market share, the weaker is its competitive strengh and market position relative to the industry's market share leader.

[3] Equally important, relative market share is likely to reflect relative cost based on experience in producing the product and economies of large-scale production. Businesses with large reative market shares may be able to operate at lower unit costs than low-share firms because of technological and efficiency gains that attach to larger production and sales volume. As was discussed in Chapter 3, the phenomenon of lower unit costs can go beyond just the effects of scale economies; as the cumulative volume of production increases, the knowledge gained from the firm's growing production experience can lead to the discovery of additional efficiencies and ways to reduce costs even further. For more details on how the relationship between experience and cumulative production volume results in lower unit costs, see Figure 3–1 in Chapter 3. A sizable experience curve effect in an industry's value chain places a strategic premium on market share: the competitor that gains the largest market share tends to realize important cost advantages which, in turn, can be used to lower prices and gain still additional customers, sales, market share, and profit. Such conditions are an important contributor to the competitive strength that a company has in that business.

- *Technology and innovation capabilities*—business units recognized for their technological leadership and track record in innovation are usually strong competitors in their industry.
- *How well the business unit's competitive assets and competencies match industry key success factors*—the more a business unit's strengths match the industry's key success factors, the stronger its competitive position tends to be.
- *Brand-name recognition and reputation*—a strong brand name is nearly always a valuable competitive asset.
- *Profitability relative to competitors*—business units that consistently earn above-average returns on investment and have bigger profit margins than their rivals usually have stronger competitive positions than those with below-average profitability for their industry.

Other competitive strength indicators include knowledge of customers and markets, production capabilities, skills in supply chain management, marketing skills, ample financial resources, and proven know-how in managing the business. Analysts have a choice between rating each business unit on the same generic factors or rating each business unit's strength on those strength measures most pertinent to its industry. Either approach can be defended, although using strength measures specific to each industry is conceptually stronger because the relevant measures of competitive strength, along with their relative importance, vary from industry to industry.

As was done in evaluating industry attractiveness, weights need to be assigned to each of the strength measures to indicate their relative importance (using different weights for different business units is conceptually stronger when the importance of the strength measures differs significantly from business to business). As before, the sum of the weights must add up to 1.0. Each business unit is then rated on each of the chosen strength measures, using a 1 to 5 or 1 to 10 rating scale (where *a high rating signifies high competitive strength and a low rating signifies low strength*). Weighted strength ratings are calculated by multiplying the business unit's rating on each strength measure by the assigned weight. For example, a strength score of 6 times a weight of .25 gives a weighted strength rating of 1.50. The sum of weighted ratings across all the strength measures provides a quantitative measure of a business unit's overall competitive strength. The procedure is shown below:

Competitive Strength Measure	Weight	Strength Rating	Weighted Strength Rating
Relative market share	.20	5	1.00
Costs relative to competitors	.25	8	2.00
Ability to match or beat rivals on key product attributes	.10	2	0.20
Bargaining leverage with buyers/suppliers	.10	6	0.60
Technology and innovation capabilities	.05	4	0.20
How well resources are matched to industry key success factors	.15	7	1.05
Brand name reputation/image	.05	4	0.20
Profitability relative to competitors	.10	5	0.50
Sum of the assigned weights	1.00		
Competitive Strength Rating			5.75

Business units with relatively high overall competitive strength ratings (above 6.7 on a rating scale of 1 to 10) are strong market contenders in their industries. Businesses with relatively low overall ratings (below 3.3 on a 1 to 10 rating scale) are in competitively weak market positions.[4] Managerial evaluations of which businesses in the portfolio are strong and weak market contenders are a valuable consideration in deciding where to steer resources. *Shareholder interests are generally best served by concentrating corporate resources on businesses that can contend for market leadership in their industries.*

Using a Nine-Cell Matrix to Simultaneously Portray Industry Attractiveness and Competitive Strength

In the attractiveness-strength matrix, each business's location is plotted using quantitative measures of long-term industry attractiveness and business strength/competitive position.

The industry attractiveness and business strength scores can be used to graphically portray the strategic positions of each business a diversified company is in. Long-term industry attractiveness is plotted on the vertical axis and competititive strength on the horizontal axis. A nine-cell grid emerges from dividing the vertical axis into three regions (high, medium, and low attractiveness) and the horizontal axis into three regions (strong, average, and weak competitive strength). High attractiveness is associated with scores of 6.7 or greater on a rating scale of 1 to 10, medium attractiveness is assigned to scores of 3.3 to 6.7, and so on; likewise, strong competitive strength is defined as a strength score greater than 6.7, average strength entails scores of 3.3 to 6.7, and so on—as shown in Figure 8-1. Each business unit in the corporate portfolio is plotted on the resulting nine-cell grid based on its overall attractiveness score and strength score and then shown as a "bubble," with the size of each bubble or circle scaled to what percent of revenues it generates relative to total corporate revenues.

The attractiveness-strength matrix helps assign investment priorities to each of the company's business units. Businesses in the three cells at the upper left, where long-term industry attractiveness and business strength/competitive position are favorable, have top investment priority. The strategic prescription for businesses falling in these three cells is "grow and build," with businesses in the high-strong cell having the highest claim on investment funds. Next in priority come businesses positioned in the three diagonal cells stretching from the lower left to the upper right. These businesses are usually given medium priority. They merit steady reinvestment to maintain and protect their industry positions; however, if such a business has an unusually attractive opportunity, it can win a higher investment priority and be given the go-ahead to employ a more aggressive strategic approach. The strategy prescription for businesses in the three cells in the lower right corner of the matrix is typically harvest or divest (in exceptional cases where good turnaround potential exists, it can be "overhaul and reposition" using some type of turnaround approach).[5]

---

[4]If analysts lack sufficient data to do detailed strength ratings, they can rely on their knowledge of each business unit's competitive situation to classify it as being in a "strong," "average," or "weak" competitive position. If trustworthy, such subjective assessments of business-unit strength can substitute for quantitative measures.

[5]At General Electric, each business actually ended up in one of five types of categories: (1) *high-growth potential* businesses deserving top investment priority, (2) *stable base* businesses deserving steady reinvestment to maintain position, (3) *support* businesses deserving periodic investment funding, (4) *selective pruning or rejuvenation* businesses deserving reduced investment funding, and (5) *venture* businesses deserving heavy R&D investment.

FIGURE 8-1 A Representative Nine-Cell Industry Attractiveness-Competitive Strength Matrix

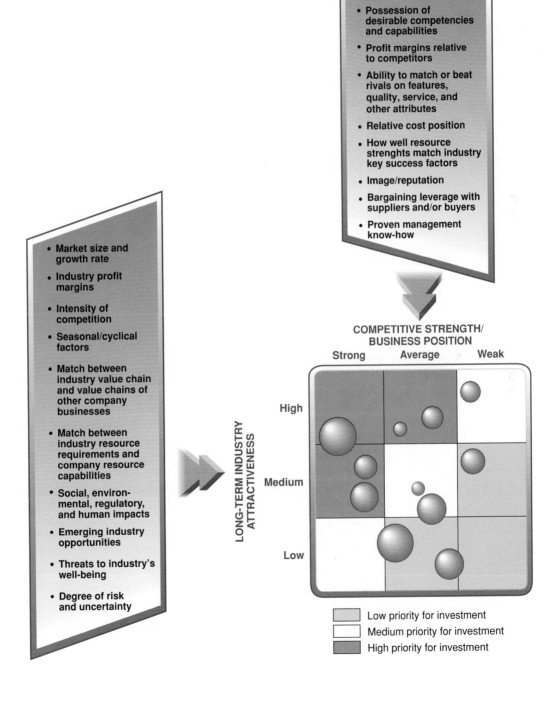

The nine-cell attractiveness-strength grid provides strong logic for concentrating resources in those businesses that enjoy a higher degree of attractiveness and competitive strength, being very selective in making investments in businesses with intermediate positions, and with drawing resources from businesses that are lower in attractiveness and strength unless they offer exceptional turnaround potential. This is why a diversified company needs to consider *both* industry attractiveness and business strength in allocating resources and investment capital to its different businesses.

> *A company may earn larger profits over the long term by investing in a business with a competitively strong position in a moderately attractive industry than by investing in a weak business in a glamour industry.*

More and more diversified companies are concentrating their resources on industries where they can be strong market contenders and divesting businesses that are not good candidates for becoming market leaders. At General Electric, the whole thrust of corporate strategy and corporate resource allocation is to put GE's businesses into a number one or two position in both the United States and globally—see Illustration Capsule 29.

STRATEGIC-FIT ANALYSIS: CHECKING FOR COMPETITIVE ADVANTAGE POTENTIAL

The next analytical step is to determine the competitive advantage potential of any value chain relationships and strategic fits among the company's existing businesses. Fit needs to be looked at from two angles: (1) whether one or more business units have valuable strategic fit with other businesses the firm has diversified into and (2) whether each business unit meshes well with the firm's long-term strategic direction.

When a company's business portfolio includes subsidiaries with related technologies, similar value chain activities, overlapping distribution channels, common customers, or some other competitively valuable relationship, it gains competitive advantage potential not open to a company that diversifies into totally unrelated businesses. The more businesses it has with competitively valuable strategic fits, the greater a diversified company's potential for realizing economies of scope, enhancing the competitive capabilities of particular business units, strengthening the competitiveness of its product and business lineup, and leveraging its resources into a combined performance greater than the units could achieve operating independently.

Consequently, one essential part of evaluating a diversified company's strategy is to check its business portfolio for competitively valuable value chain matchups among the company's existing businesses:

- Which business units have value chain matchups that offer opportunities to combine the performance of related activities and thereby reduce costs?

- Which business units have value chain matchups that offer opportunities to transfer skills or technology from one business to another?

- Which business units offer opportunities to use a common brand name? to gain greater leverage with distributors/dealers in winning more favorable shelf space for the company's products?

- Which business units have value chain matchups that offer opportunities to create valuable new competitive capabilities or to leverage existing resources?

ILLUSTRATION CAPSULE 29   General Electric's Approach to Managing Diversification

When Jack Welch became CEO of General Electric in 1981, he launched a corporate strategy effort to reshape the company's diversified business portfolio. Early on he issued a challenge to GE's business-unit managers to become number one or number two in their industry; failing that, the business units either had to capture a decided technological advantage translatable into a competitive edge or face possible divestiture.

By 1990, GE was a different company. Under Welch's prodding, GE divested operations worth $9 billion—TV operations, small appliances, a mining business, and computer chips. It spent a total of $24 billion acquiring new businesses, most notably RCA, Roper (a maker of major appliances whose biggest customer was Sears), and Kidder Peabody (a Wall Street investment banking firm). Internally, many of the company's smaller business operations were put under the direction

of larger "strategic business units." But, most significantly, in 1989, 12 of GE's 14 strategic business units were market leaders in the United States and globally (the company's financial services and communications units served markets too fragmented to rank).

During the 1990s, having divested most of the weak businesses and having built existing businesses into leading contenders, Welch launched initiatives to dramatically boost productivity and reduce the size of GE's bureaucracy. Welch argued that for GE to continue to be successful in a global marketplace, the company had to press hard for continuous cost reduction in each of its businesses, cut through bureaucratic procedures to shorten response times to changing market conditions, and dramatically improve its profit margins. In 1997, GE had the highest market capitalization of any company in the world.

GE Strategic Business Units	Market Standing in the United States	Market Standing in the World
Aircraft engines	First	First
Broadcasting (NBC)	First	Not applicable
Circuit breakers	Tied for first with two others	Tied for first with three others
Defense electronics	Second	Second
Electric motors	First	First
Engineering plastics	First	First
Factory automation	Second	Third
Industrial and power systems	First	First
Lighting	First	Second
Locomotives	First	Tied for first
Major home apliances	First	Tied for second
Medical diagnostic imaging	First	First

Source: Developed from information in Stratford P. Sherman, "Inside the Mind of Jack Welch," *Fortune,* March 27, 1989, pp. 39–50.

Figure 8-2 illustrates the process of identifying the value chains of each of the businesses, then searching for competitively valuable value chain matchups. Without a number of such matchups, one has to be skeptical about the potential for the company's businesses to perform better together than apart and whether its diversification approach is truly capable of enhancing shareholder value.

A second aspect of strategic fit that bears checking out is whether any businesses in the portfolio do not fit in well with the company's overall long-term direction and strategic vision. Sometimes a business, despite having certain value chain matchups, doesn't mesh well with the strategic markets or customer groups or product categories that corporate mangement is concentrating on—in other words, it doesn't fit strategically into the company's overall business picture. In such instances, the business probably needs to be considered for divestiture even though it may be making a positive contribution to company profits and cash flows. Businesses with no real

FIGURE 8-2 Comparing Value Chains to Identify Strategic Fits Among a Diversified Company's Business Units

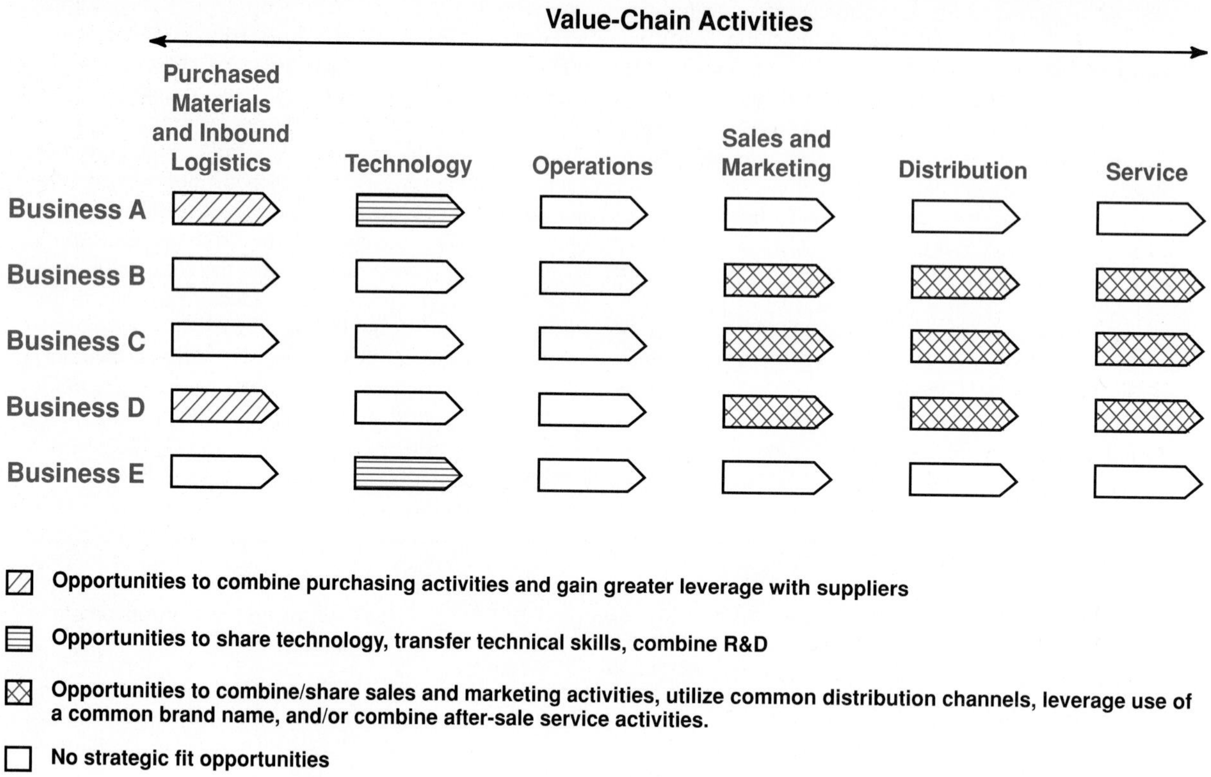
Value-Chain Activities
Purchased Materials and Inbound Logistics
Technology
Operations
Sales and Marketing
Distribution
Service
Business A
Business B
Business C
Business D
Business E
Opportunities to combine purchasing activities and gain greater leverage with suppliers
Opportunities to share technology, transfer technical skills, combine R&D
Opportunities to combine/share sales and marketing activities, utilize common distribution channels, leverage use of a common brand name, and/or combine after-sale service activities.
No strategic fit opportunities

strategic value often end up being treated like an unwanted stepchild and are a distraction to top management. The only reasons to retain such businesses are if they are unusually good financial performers or offer superior growth opportunities—that is to say, if they are valuable *financially* even though they are not valuable strategically.

RESOURCE FIT ANALYSIS: DETERMINING HOW WELL THE FIRM'S RESOURCES MATCH BUSINESS UNIT REQUIREMENTS

The businesses in a diversified company's lineup need to exhibit good *resource fit* as well as good strategic fit. Resource fit exists when (1) businesses add to a company's resource strengths, either financially or strategically and (2) a company has the resources to adequately support the resource requirements of its businesses as a group without spreading itself too thinly. One important dimension of resource fit concerns whether the company's business lineup is well-matched to its financial resources.

Checking Financial Resource Fit: Cash Hog and Cash Cow Businesses

Different businesses have different cash flow and investment characteristics. For example, business units in rapidly growing industries are often "cash hogs"—so labeled because their annual cash flows aren't big enough to cover their annual capital requirements. To keep pace with rising demand, rapid-growth businesses frequently are looking at sizable annual capital investments for some years to come—for new facilities and equipment, for new product development or technology improvements, and for additional working capital to support inventory expansion and a larger base of operations. A business in a fast-growing industry becomes an even bigger cash hog when it has a relatively low market share and is pursuing a strategy to outgrow the market and gain enough market share to become an industry leader. When a rapid-growth business cannot generate a big enough cash flow from operations to finance its capital requirements internally, the needed financial resources must be provided by the corporate parent. Corporate management has to decide whether it is strategically and financially worthwhile to fund the perhaps considerable investment requirements of a cash hog business.

A "cash hog" business is one whose internal cash flows are inadequate to fully fund its needs for working capital and new capital investment.

Business units with leadership positions in slow-growing industries with modest capital requirements may, however, be "cash cows," in the sense that they generate substantial cash surpluses over what is needed for capital reinvestment and other initiatives to sustain their leadership position. It is not unusual for businesses that are market leaders in industries where capital requirements are modest to generate sizable positive cash flows *over and above what is needed for reinvestment in operations.* Cash cow businesses, though often less attractive from a growth standpoint, are valuable businesses from a financial resources perspectives. The surplus cash flows they generate can be used to pay corporate dividends, finance acquisitions, and provide funds for investing in the company's promising cash hog businesses. It makes good financial and strategic sense for diversified companies to keep cash cow businesses in healthy condition, fortifying and defending their market position to preserve their cash-generating capability over the long term and thereby maintain an ongoing source of positive cash flows to redeploy elsewhere.

A "cash cow" business is a valuable part of a diversified company's business portfolio because it generates cash for financing new acquisitions, funding the capital requirements of cash hog businesses, and paying dividends.

Viewing a diversified group of businesses as a collection of cash flows and cash requirements (present and future) is a major step forward in understanding the financial aspects of corporate strategy. Assessing the cash requirements of different businesses in a company's portfolio and determining which are cash hogs and which are cash cows highlights opportunities for shifting corporate financial resources between business subsidiaries to optimize the performance of the whole corporate portfolio, explains why priorities for corporate resource allocation can differ from business to business, and provides good rationalizations for both invest-and-expand strategies and divestiture. For instance, a diversified company can use the excess cash generated by cash cow business units to fund the investment requirements of *promising* cash hog businesses, eventually growing the hogs into self-supporting "stars" having strong competitive positions in attractive, high-growth markets.[6] Star businesses are the cash cows of the future—when the markets of star businesses begin to mature and their growth slows, their competitive strength should produce self-

---

[6]A star business, as the name implies, is one with a leading market share, a widely respected reputation, a solid track record of profitability, and excellent future growth and profit opportunities. Star businesses vary as to their cash hog status. Some can cover their investment needs with self-generated cash flows; others require capital infusions from their corporate parents to stay abreast of rapid industry growth. Normally, strongly positioned star businesses in industries where growth is beginning to slow tend to be self-sustaining in terms of cash flow and make little claim on the corporate parent's treasury. Young stars, however, may require substantial investment capital *beyond what they can generate on their own* and still be cash hogs.

generated cash flows more than sufficient to cover their investment needs. The "success sequence" is thus cash hog to young star (but perhaps still a cash hog) to self-supporting star to cash cow.

On the other hand, if a cash hog business has questionable promise (either because of low industry attractiveness or a weak competitive position), then it becomes a logical candidate for divestiture. Pursuing an aggressive invest-and-expand strategy for a competitively weak cash hog business seldom makes sense if the company has other attractive opportunities and if it will strain the corporate parent's financial resources to keep pumping more capital into the business to keep abreast of fast-paced market growth *and* to build an attractively strong competitive position. Such businesses are a financial drain and lack good financial resource fit. Divesting a less attractive cash hog business is usually the best alternative *unless* (1) it has valuable strategic fits with other business units or (2) the capital infusions needed from the corporate parent are modest relative to the funds available and there's a decent chance of growing the business into a solid bottom-line contributor.

Aside from cash flow considerations, a business has good financial fit when it contributes to the achievement of corporate performance objectives (profit growth, above-average return on investment, recognition as an industry leader, and so on) and when it enhances shareholder value. A business exhibits poor financial fit if it soaks up a disproportionate share of the company's financial resources, if it is a subpar or inconsistent bottom-line contributor, if it is unduly risky and failure would jeopardize the entire enterprise, or if it is too small to make a material earnings contribution even though it performs well. In addition, a diversified company's business portfolio lacks financial fit if its financial resources are stretched thinly across too many businesses. Severe financial strain can occur if a company borrows so heavily to finance new acquisitions that it has to trim way back on new capital expenditures for existing businesses and use the big majority of its financial resources to meet interest obligations and to pay down debt. Some diversified companies have found themselves in such an overextended or overleveraged financial situation that they have had to sell off some businesses to raise the money to meet existing debt obligations and fund essential capital expenditures for the remaining businesses.

Business subsidiaries that don't exhibit good strategic fit and good resource fit should be considered for divestiture unless their financial performance is outstanding.

Checking Competitive and Managerial Resource Fits

A diversified company's strategy must aim at producing a good fit between its resource capability and the competitive and managerial requirements of its businesses.[7] Diversification is most likely to result in added shareholder value when the company has or can develop the competitive and managerial capabilities to be successful in each of the businesses/industries it has diversified into. The absence of good resource fit with one or more business units is serious enough to make such businesses prime divestiture candidates. Likewise, when a company's resources and capabilities are well suited to competing in new industries, it makes sense to take a hard look at acquiring companies in these industries and expanding the company's business lineup.

---

[7]For an excellent discussion of how to assess these fits, see Andrew Campbell, Michael Goold, and Marcus Alexander, "Corporate Strategy: The Quest for Parenting Advantage," *Harvard Business Review* 73, no. 2 (March–April 1995), pp. 120–32.

Checking a diversified company's business portfolio for competitive and managerial resource fits involves the following:

- Determining whether the company's resource strengths (skills, technological expertise, competitive capabilities) are well matched to the key success factors of the businesses it has diversified into.

- Determining whether the company has adequate managerial depth and expertise to cope with the assortment of managerial and operating problems posed by its present lineup of businesses (plus those it may be contemplating getting into).

- Determining whether competitive capabilities in one or more businesses can be transferred them to other businesses (capabilities that are often good candidates for transfer include short development times in bringing new products to market, strong partnerships with key suppliers, an R&D organization capable of generating technological and product opportunites in several different industry arenas simultaneously, a high degree of organizational agility in responding to shifting market conditions and emerging opportunities, or state-of-the-art systems for doing business via the Internet).

- Determining whether the company needs to invest in upgrading its resources or capabilities to stay ahead of (or at least abreast of) the efforts of rivals to upgrade their resource base. In a world of fast-paced change and competition, managers have to be alert to the need to continually invest in and upgrade the company's resources, however potent its current resources are. All resources depreciate in value as competitors mimic them or retaliate with a different (and perhaps more attractive) resource combination.[8] Upgrading resources and competencies often means going beyond just strengthening what the company already is capable of doing— it may involve adding new resource capabilities (like the ability to manage a group of diverse international manufacturing plants or developing technological expertise in related or complementary disciplines or a state-of-the-art-company intranet or an innovative Web page that draws many visits and gives all of its business units greater market exposure), building competencies that allow the company to enter another attractive industry, or widening the company's range of capabilities to match certain competitively valuable capabilities of rivals.

The complement of resources and capabilities at a firm's command determine its competitive strengths. The more a company's diversification strategy is tied to leveraging its resources and capabilities in new businesses, the more it has to develop a big enough and deep enough resource pool to supply these businesses with enough capability to create competitive advantage. Otherwise its strengths end up being stretched too thinly across too many businesses and the opportunity for competitive advantage lost.

Some Notes of Caution   Many diversification strategies built around transferring resource capabilities to new businesses never live up to their promise because the transfer process is not as easy as it might seem. Developing a resource capability in

---

[8]David J. Collis and Cynthia A. Montgomery, "Competing on Resources: Strategy in the 90s," *Harvard Business Review* 73, no. 4 (July–August 1995), p. 124.

one business nearly always involves much trial and error and much organizational learning, and is usually the product of close collaboration of many people working together over a period of time. The first step in transferring a resource capability developed in this manner to another business involves moving people with much of the know-how to the new business. Then these people not only have to learn the ins and outs of the new business well enough to see how best to integrate the capability into the operation of the receiving business but they also have to be adept in implanting all the needed organizational learning from the donor business. As a practical matter, transferring a resource capability in one business to another business can't be done without the receiving business undergoing significant organizational learning and team-building on its own to get up to speed in executing the transferred capability. It takes time, money, and patience for the transferred capability to be implanted and made fully operational. Sometimes unforeseen problems occur, resulting in debilitating delays or prohibitive expenses or inability on the part of the receiving business to execute the capability proficiently. As a consequence, the new business never performs up to expectations.

A second reason for the failure of a diversification move into a new business with seemingly good resource fit is that the causes of a firm's success in one business are sometimes quite entangled and the means of re-creating them hard to replicate.[9] It is easy to be overly optimistic about the ease with which a company that has hit a home run in one business can enter a new business with similar resource requirements and hit a second home run. Noted British retailer Marks & Spencer, despite its impressive resource capabilities (ability to choose excellent store locations, having a supplier chain that gives it both low costs and high merchandise quality, loyal employees, an excellent reputation with consumers, and strong management expertise) that have made it one of Britain's premier retailers for 100 years, has failed repeatedly in its efforts to diversify into department store retailing in the United States.

Diversifying into businesses with seemingly good resource fit is, by itself, not sufficient to produce success.

A third reason for diversification failure, despite apparent resource fit, is misjudging the difficulty of overcoming the resource strengths and capabilities of the rivals it will have to face in a new business. For example, Philip Morris, even though it had built powerful consumer marketing capabilities in its cigarette and beer businesses, floundered in soft drinks and ended up divesting its acquisition of 7UP after several frustrating years because of difficulties in competing against strongly entrenched and resource-capable rivals like Coca-Cola and PepsiCo.

RANKING THE BUSINESS UNITS ON THE BASIS OF PAST PERFORMANCE AND FUTURE PROSPECTS

Once a diversified company's businesses have been rated on the basis of industry attractiveness, competitive strength, strategic fit, and resource fit, the next step is to evaluate which businesses have the best performance prospects and which the worst. The most important considerations are sales growth, profit growth, contribution to company earnings, and the return on capital invested in the business (more and more companies are evaluating business performance on the basis of economic value added—the return on invested capital over and above the firm's cost of capital). Sometimes, cash flow generation is a big consideration, especially for cash cow businesses and businesses with potential for harvesting.

---

[9]Collis and Montgomery, "Competing on Resources: Strategy in the 90s," pp.121–22.

Information on each business's past performance can be gleaned from financial records.[10] While past performance is not necessarily a good predictor of future performance, it does signal which businesses have been strong performers and which have been weak performers. The industry attractiveness–competitive strength evaluations should provide a solid basis for judging future prospects. Normally, strong business units in attractive industries have better prospects than weak businesses in unattractive industries.

The growth and profit outlooks for a diversified company's principal or core businesses generally determine whether its portfolio as a whole is capable of strong, mediocre, or weak performance. Noncore businesses with subpar track records and long-term prospects are logical candidates for divestiture. Business subsidiaries with the brightest profit and growth prospects generally should head the list for corporate resource support.

DECIDING ON RESOURCE ALLOCATION PRIORITIES AND A GENERAL STRATEGIC DIRECTION FOR EACH BUSINESS UNIT

Using the information and results of the preceding evaluation steps, corporate strategists can decide what the priorities should be for allocating resources to the various business units and settle on a general strategic direction for each business unit. The task here is to draw some conclusions about which business units should have top priority for corporate resource support and new capital investment and which should carry the lowest priority. In doing the ranking, special attention needs to be given to whether and how *corporate* resources and capabilities can be used to enhance the competitiveness of particular business units.[11] Opportunities for capabilities/technology transfer or for combining activities to reduce costs or for infusions of new financial capital become especially important when a diversified firm has business units in less than desirable competitive positions, when improvement in some key success area could make a big difference to a particular business unit's performance, and when a cash hog business needs financial support to grow into a star performer.

Improving a diversified company's long-term financial performance entails concentrating company resources on businesses with good to excellent prospects and allocating only minimal resources to businesses with subpar prospects.

Ranking the businesses from highest to lowest priority process should also clarify management thinking about what the basic strategic approach for each business unit should be—*invest-and-grow* (aggressive expansion), *fortify-and-defend* (protect current position by strengthening and adding resource capabilities in needed areas), *overhaul-and-reposition* (make major competitive strategy changes to move the business into a different and ultimately stronger industry position), or *harvest-divest*. In deciding whether to divest a business unit, corporate managers should rely on a number of evaluating criteria: industry attractiveness, competitive strength, strategic fit with other businesses, resource fit, performance potential (profit, return on capital employed, economic value added, contribution to cash flow), compatibility with the

---

[10]Financial performance by line of business is typically contained in a company's annual report, usually in the notes to corporate financial statements. Line of business performance can also be found in a publicly owned firm's 10-K report filed annually with the Securities and Exchange Commission.

[11]Collis and Montgomery, "Competing on Resources: Strategy in the 90s," pp.126–28; Hofer and Schendel, *Strategy Formulation: Analytical Concepts*, p. 80; and Michael E. Porter, *Competitive Advantage* (New York: Free Press, 1985), chapter 9.

companies strategic vision and long-term direction, and ability to contribute to enhanced shareholder value.

To get ever-higher levels of performance out of a diversified company's business portfolio, corporate managers have to do an effective job of steering resources out of low-opportunity areas into high-opportunity areas. Divesting marginal businesses is one of the best ways of freeing unproductive assets for redeployment. Surplus funds from cash cow businesses and businesses being harvested also add to the corporate treasury. Options for allocating a diversified company's financial resources include (1) investing in ways to strengthen or expand existing businesses, (2) making acquisitions to establish positions in new industries, (3) funding long-range R&D ventures, (4) paying off existing long-term debt, (5) increasing dividends, and (6) repurchasing the company's stock. The first three are *strategic* actions to add shareholder value; the last three are *financial* moves to enhance shareholder value. Ideally, a company will have enough funds to do what is needed, both strategically and financially. If not, strategic uses of corporate resources should usually take precedence unless there is a compelling reason to strengthen the firm's balance sheet or divert financial resources to pacify shareholders.

CRAFTING A CORPORATE STRATEGY

The preceding analytical steps set the stage for crafting strategic moves to improve a diversified company's overall performance. The basic issue of "what to do" hinges on the conclusions drawn about the strategic and financial attractiveness of the group of businesses the company has diversified into.[12] Key considerations here are:

- Does the company have enough businesses in very attractive industries?
- Is the proportion of mature or declining businesses so great that corporate growth will be sluggish?
- Are the company's businesses overly vulnerable to seasonal or recessionary influences?
- Is the firm burdened with too many businesses in average to weak competitive positions?
- Is there ample strategic fit among the company's different businesses?
- Does the portfolio contain businesses that the company really doesn't need to be in?
- Is there ample resource fit among the company's business units?
- Does the firm have enough cash cows to finance the cash hog businesses with potential to be star performers?
- Can the company's principal or core businesses be counted on to generate dependable profits and/or cash flow?
- Does the makeup of the business portfolio put the company in good position for the future?

Answers to these questions indicate whether corporate strategists should consider divesting certain businesses, making new acquisitions, restructuring the makeup of the portfolio, altering the pattern of corporate resource allocation, or sticking with the existing business lineup and pursuing the opportunities they present.

---

[12]Barry Hedley, "Strategy and the Business Portfolio," *Long Range Planning* 10, no. 1 (February 1977), p. 13; and Hofer and Schendel, *Strategy Formulation*, pp. 82–86.

The Performance Test

A good test of the strategic and financial attractiveness of a diversified firm's business portfolio is whether the company can attain its performance objectives with its current lineup of businesses and resource capabilities. If so, no major corporate strategy changes are indicated. However, if a performance shortfall is probable, corporate strategists can take any of several actions to close the gap:[13]

1. *Alter the strategic plans for some (or all) of the businesses in the portfolio.* This option involves renewed corporate efforts to get better performance out of its present business units. Corporate managers can push business-level managers for strategy changes that yield better business-unit performance and, perhaps, provide higher-than-planned corporate resource support for these efforts. However, pursuing better short-term performance by zealously trimming resource initiatives aimed at bolstering a business's long-term competitive position has dubious value—it merely trades off better long-term performance for better short-term financial performance. In any case there are limits on how much extra near-term performance can be squeezed out.

2. *Add new business units to the corporate portfolio.* Boosting overall performance by making new acquisitions and/or starting new businesses internally raises some new strategy issues. Expanding the corporate portfolio means taking a close look at (*a*) whether to acquire related or unrelated businesses, (*b*) what size acquisition(s) to make, (*c*) how the new unit(s) will fit into the present corporate structure, (*d*) what specific features to look for in an acquisition candidate, and (*e*) whether acquisitions can be financed without shortchanging present business units on their new investment requirements. Nonetheless, adding new businesses is a major strategic option, one frequently used by diversified companies to escape sluggish earnings performance.

3. *Divest weak-performing or money-losing businesses.* The most likely candidates for divestiture are businesses in a weak competitive position, in a relatively unattractive industry, or in an industry that does not "fit." Funds from divestitures can, of course, be used to finance new acquisitions, pay down corporate debt, or fund new strategic thrusts in the remaining businesses.

4. *Form strategic alliances and collaborative partnerships to try to alter conditions responsible for subpar performance potentials.* In some situations, cooperative alliances with domestic or foreign firms, suppliers, customers, or special interest groups may help ameliorate adverse performance prospects.[14] Instituting resource sharing agreements with suppliers, select competitors, or firms with complementary products and collaborating closely on mutually advantageous initiatives are becoming increasingly used avenues for improving the competitiveness and performance potential of a company's businesses. Forming or supporting a political action group may be an

---

[13]Hofer and Schendel, *Strategy Formulation: Analytical Concepts,* pp. 93–100.

[14]For an excellent discussion of the benefits of alliances among competitors in global industries, see Kenichi Ohmae, "The Global Logic of Strategic Alliances," *Harvard Business Review* 67, no. 2 (March–April 1989), pp. 143–54.

effective way of lobbying for solutions to import-export problems, tax disincentives, and onerous regulatory requirements.

5. *Upgrade the company's resource base.* Achieving better performance may well hinge on corporate efforts to develop new resource strengths that will help select business units match the competitively valuable capabilities of their rivals or, better still, allow them to secure competitive advantage. One of the biggest ways that corporate-level managers of diversified companies can contribute to added shareholder value is to lead the development of cutting-edge capabilities and to marshal new kinds of corporate resources for deployment in a number of the company's businesses.

6. *Lower corporate performance objectives.* Adverse market circumstances or declining fortunes in one or more core business units can render companywide performance targets unreachable. So can overly ambitious objective setting. Closing the gap between actual and desired performance may then require downward revision of corporate objectives to bring them more in line with reality. Lowering performance objectives is usually a "last resort" option.

Identifying Additional Diversification Opportunities

One of the major corporate strategy-making concerns in a diversified company is whether to diversify further and, if so, how to identify the "right" kinds of industries and businesses to get into. For firms pursuing unrelated diversification, the issue of where to diversify next is based more on spotting a good financial opportunity and having the financial resources to pursue it than on industry or strategic criteria. Decisions to diversify into additional unrelated businesses are usually based on such considerations as whether the firm has the financial ability to make another acquisition, whether new acquisitions are badly needed to boost overall corporate performance, whether one or more acquisition opportunities have to be acted on before they are purchased by other firms, whether the timing is right for another acquisition (corporate management may have its hands full dealing with the current portfolio of businesses), and whether corporate management believes it possesses the range and depth of expertise to supervise an additional business.

Firms with unrelated diversification strategies hunt for businesses that offer attractive financial returns—regardless of what industry they're in.

Further diversification in firms with related diversification strategies involves identifying attractive industries having good strategic or resource fit with one or more existing businesses.

With a related diversification strategy, however, the search for new industries to diversify into is aimed at identifying other businesses (1) whose value chains have fits with the value chains of one or more businesses in the company's business portfolio and (2) whose resource requirements are well-matched to the firm's corporate resource capabilities.[15] Once strategic-fit and resource-fit opportunities in *attractive* new industries are identified, corporate strategists have to distinguish between opportunities where important competitive advantage potential exists (through cost savings, technology or capabilities transfer, leveraging a well-known brand name, and so on) and those where the strategic-fit and resource-fit benefits are marginally valuable. The size of the competitive advantage potential depends on whether the fits are competitively significant and on the costs and difficulties of merging or coordinating the business unit interrelationships to capture the fits.[16] Often, careful analysis reveals

[15]Porter, *Competitive Advantage*, pp. 370–71.
[16]Ibid., pp. 371–72.

that while there are many actual and potential business unit interrelationships and linkages, only a few have enough strategic importance to generate meaningful competitive advantage.

GUIDELINES FOR MANAGING THE PROCESS OF CRAFTING CORPORATE STRATEGY

Although formal analysis and entrepreneurial brainstorming normally undergird the corporate strategy-making process, there is more to where corporate strategy comes from and how it evolves. Rarely is there an all-inclusive grand formulation of the total corporate strategy. Instead, corporate strategy in major enterprises emerges incrementally from the unfolding of many different internal and external events, the result of probing the future, experimenting, gathering more information, sensing problems, building awareness of the various options, spotting new opportunities, developing responses to unexpected crises, communicating consensus as it emerges, and acquiring a feel for all the strategically relevant factors, their importance, and their interrelationships.[17]

Strategic analysis is not something that the executives of diversified companies do all at once. Such big reviews are sometimes scheduled, but research indicates that major strategic decisions emerge gradually rather than from periodic, full-scale analysis followed by prompt decision. Typically, top executives approach major strategic decisions a step at a time, often starting from broad, intuitive conceptions and then embellishing, fine-tuning, and modifying their original thinking as more information is gathered, as formal analysis confirms or modifies their judgments about the situation, and as confidence and consensus build for what strategic moves need to be made. Often attention and resources are concentrated on a few critical strategic thrusts that illuminate and integrate corporate direction, objectives, and strategies.

Strategic analysis in diversified companies is an eight-step process:

KEY POINTS

Step 1: *Get a clear fix on the present strategy.* Determine whether the company's strategic emphasis is on related or unrelated diversification; whether the scope of company operations is mostly domestic or increasingly multinational, what moves have been made recently to add new businesses and build positions in new industries, the rationale underlying recent divestitures, the nature of any efforts to capture strategic fits and create competitive advantage based on economies of scope and/or resource transfer, and the pattern of resource allocation to the various business units. This step sets the stage for thorough evaluation of the need for strategy changes.

Step 2: *Evaluate the long-term attractiveness of each industry the company is in.* Industry attractiveness needs to be evaluated from three angles: the attractiveness of each industry on its own, the attractiveness of each industry relative to the others, and the attractiveness of all the industries as a group. Quantitative measures of industry attractiveness, using the methodology presented, are a reasonably reliable method for ranking a diversified company's industries from most attractive to least attractive—they tell a

---

[17]Ibid., pp. 58 and 196.

valuable story about just how and why some of the industries a company has diversified into are more attractive than others. The two hardest parts of calculating industry attractiveness scores are deciding on appropriate weights for the industry attractiveness measures and knowing enough about each industry to assign accurate and objective ratings.

Step 3: *Evaluate the relative competitive positions and business strength of each of the company's business units.* Again, quantitative ratings of competitive strength are preferable to subjective judgments. The purpose of rating the competitive strength of each business is to gain clear understanding of which businesses are strong contenders in their industries, which are weak contenders, and the underlying reasons for their strength or weakness. One of the most effective ways to join the conclusions about industry attractiveness with the conclusions about competitive strength is to draw an industry attractiveness/competitive strength matrix displaying the positions of each business on a nine-cell grid.

Step 4: *Determine the competitive advantage potential of any value chain relationships and strategic fits among existing business units.* A business is more attractive *strategically* when it has value chain relationships with other business units that present opportunities to transfer skills or technology, reduce overall costs, share facilities, or share a common brand name—any of which can represent a significant avenue for producing competitive advantage beyond what any one business can achieve on its own. The more businesses with competitively valuable strategic fits, the greater a diversified company's potential for achieving economies of scope, enhancing the competitive capabilities of particular business units, and/or strengthening the competitiveness of its product and business lineup, thereby leveraging its resources into a combined performance greater than the units could achieve operating independently.

Step 5: *Determine whether the firm's resource strengths match the resource requirements of its present business lineup.* The businesses in a diversified company's lineup need to exhibit good *resource fit* as well as good strategic fit. Resource fit exists when (1) businesses add to a company's resource strengths, either financially or strategically and (2) a company has the resources to adequately support the resource requirements of its businesses as a group without spreading itself too thinly. One important dimension of resource fit concerns whether the company's business lineup is well-matched to its financial resources. Assessing the cash requirements of different businesses in a diversified company's portfolio and determining which are cash hogs and which are cash cows highlights opportunities for shifting corporate financial resources between business subsidiaries to optimize the performance of the whole corporate portfolio, explains why priorities for corporate resource allocation can differ from business to business, and provides good rationalizations for both invest-and-expand strategies and divestiture.

Step 6: *Rank the past performance of different business units from best to worst and rank their future performance prospects from best to worst.* The most important considerations in judging business-unit performance are sales growth, profit growth, contribution to company earnings, and the return on capital invested in the business. Sometimes, cash flow generation is a big consideration. Normally, strong business units in attractive industries have significantly better performance prospects than weak businesses or businesses in unattractive industries.

Step 7: *Rank the business units in terms of priority for resource allocation and decide whether the strategic posture for each business unit should be aggressive expansion, fortify and defend, overhaul and reposition, or harvest/ divest.* In doing the ranking, special attention needs to be given to whether and how *corporate* resources and capabilities can be used to enhance the competitiveness of particular business units. Options for allocating a diversified company's financial resources include (1) investing in ways to strengthen or expand existing businesses, (2) making acquisitions to establish positions in new industries, (3) funding long-range R&D ventures, (4) paying off existing long-term debt, (5) increasing dividends, and (6) repurchasing the company's stock. Ideally, a company will have the financial strength to accomplish what is needed strategically and financially; if not, strategic uses of corporate resources should usually take precedence.

Step 8: *Use the preceding analysis to craft a series of moves to improve overall corporate performance.* Typical actions include (1) making acquisitions, starting new businesses from within, and divesting marginal businesses or businesses that no longer match the company's long-term direction and strategy, (2) devising moves to strengthen the long-term competitive positions of the company's businesses, (3) capitalizing on strategic-fit and resource-fit opportunities and turning them into long-term competitive advantage, and (4) steering corporate resources out of low-opportunity areas into high-opportunity areas.

Campbell, Andrew, Michael Goold, and Marcus Alexander. "Corporate Strategy: The Quest for Parenting Advantage." *Harvard Business Review* 73, no. 2 (March–April 1995), pp. 120–32.

Haspeslagh, Phillippe C., and David B. Jamison. *Managing Acquisitions: Creating Value through Corporate Renewal.* New York: Free Press, 1991.

Naugle, David G., and Garret A. Davies. "Strategic-Skill Pools and Competitive Advantage." *Business Horizons* 30, no. 6 (November–December 1987), pp. 35–42.

Porter, Michael E. "From Competitive Advantage to Corporate Strategy." *Harvard Business Review* 65, no. 3 (May–June 1987), pp. 43–59.

SUGGESTED READINGS

9

IMPLEMENTING STRATEGY: BUILDING RESOURCE CAPABILITIES AND STRUCTURING THE ORGANIZATION

We strategize beautifully, we implement pathetically.

An auto-parts firm executive

Strategies are intellectually simple; their execution is not.

Lawrence A. Bossidy
CEO, Allied-Signal

Just being able to conceive bold new strategies is not enough. The general manager must also be able to translate his or her strategic vision into concrete steps that "get things done."

Richard G. Hamermesh

O nce managers have decided on a strategy, the emphasis turns to converting it into actions and good results. Putting a strategy into place and getting the organization to execute it well call for a different set of managerial tasks and skills. While crafting strategy is largely a market-driven entrepreneurial activity, implementing strategy is primarily an operations-driven activity revolving around the management of people and business processes. While successful strategy making depends on business vision, shrewd industry and competitive analysis, and good resource fit, successful strategy implementation depends on doing a good job of leading, working with and through others, allocating resources, building and strengthening competitive capabilities, installing strategy-supportive policies, and matching how the organization performs its core business activities to the requirements for good strategy execution. Implementing strategy is an action-oriented, make-things-happen task that tests a manager's ability to direct organizational change, motivate people, develop core competencies, build valuable organizational capabilities, achieve continuous improvement in business processes, create a strategy-supportive corporate culture, and meet or beat performance targets.

Experienced managers are emphatic in declaring that it is a whole lot easier to develop a sound strategic plan than it is to make it happen. According to one executive, "It's been rather easy for us to decide where we wanted to go. The hard part is to get the organization to act on the new priorities."[1] What makes strategy

---

[1]As quoted in Steven W. Floyd and Bill Wooldridge, "Managing Strategic Consensus: The Foundation of Effective Implementation," *Academy of Management Executive* 6, no. 4 (November 1992), p. 27.

implementation a tougher, more time-consuming management challenge than crafting strategy is the wide array of managerial activities that have to be attended to, the many ways managers can proceed, the demanding people-management skills required, the perseverance it takes to get a variety of initiatives launched and moving, the number of bedeviling issues that must be worked out, the resistance to change that must be overcome, and the difficulties of integrating the efforts of many different work groups into a smoothly functioning whole. *Just because managers announce a new strategy doesn't mean that subordinates will agree with it or cooperate in implementing it.* Some may be skeptical about the merits of the strategy, seeing it as contrary to the organization's best interests, unlikely to succeed, or threatening to their own careers. Moreover, company personnel may interpret the new strategy differently, be uncertain about how their departments will fare, and have different ideas about what internal changes are needed to execute the new strategy. Long-standing attitudes, vested interests, inertia, and ingrained organizational practices don't melt away when managers decide on a new strategy and start to implement it—especially when only a handful of people have been involved in crafting the strategy and the rationale for strategic change has to be sold to enough organization members to root out the status quo. It takes adept managerial leadership to overcome pockets of doubt and disagreement, build consensus for how to proceed, secure commitment and cooperation, and get all the implementation pieces into place and integrated. Depending on how much consensus building and organizational change is involved, the implementation process can take several months to several years.

> *The strategy-implementer's task is to convert the strategic plan into action and get on with what needs to be done to achieve the vision and targeted objectives.*

> *Companies don't implement strategies, people do.*

A FRAMEWORK FOR IMPLEMENTING STRATEGY

Implementing strategy entails converting the organization's strategic plan into action and then into results. Like crafting strategy, it's a job for the whole management team, not a few senior managers. While an organization's chief executive officer and the heads of business divisions, departments, and key operating units are ultimately responsible for seeing that strategy is implemented successfully, the implementation process typically impacts every part of the organizational structure, from the biggest organizational unit to the smallest frontline work group. Every manager has to think through the answer to "What has to be done in my area to implement our part of the strategic plan, and what should I do to get these things accomplished?" In this sense, *all managers become strategy implementers in their areas of authority and responsibility, and all employees are participants.*

> *Every manager has an active role in the process of implementing and executing the firm's strategic plan.*

One of the keys to successful implementation is for management to communicate the case for organizational change so clearly and persuasively that there is determined commitment throughout the ranks to carry out the strategy and meet performance targets. The ideal condition is for managers to arouse enough enthusiasm for the strategy to turn the implementation process into a companywide crusade. Management's handling of strategy implementation is successful when the company achieves the targeted strategic and financial performance and shows good progress in realizing its long-range strategic vision.

Unfortunately, there are no 10-step checklists, no proven paths, and few concrete guidelines for tackling the job—strategy implementation is the least charted, most open-ended part of strategic management. The best evidence on dos and don'ts comes from the reported experiences and "lessons learned" of managers and companies—and the wisdom they yield is inconsistent. What's worked well for some managers has been tried by others and found lacking. The reasons are understandable. Not only are some managers more effective than others in employing this or that recommended approach to organizational change, but each instance of strategy implementation takes place in a different organizational context. Different business practices and competitive circumstances, work environments and cultures, policies, compensation incentives, and mixes of personalities and organizational histories require a customized approach to strategy implementation—one based on individual company situations and circumstances and on the strategy implementer's best judgment and ability to use particular change techniques adeptly.

Implementing strategy is more art than science.

THE PRINCIPAL STRATEGY-IMPLEMENTING TASKS

While managers' approaches should be tailor-made for the situation, certain bases have to be covered no matter what the organization's circumstances; these include

- Building an organization with the competencies, capabilities, and resource strengths to carry out the strategy successfully.
- Developing budgets to steer ample resources into those value chain activities critical to strategic success.
- Establishing strategy-supportive policies and procedures.
- Instituting best practices and pushing for continuous improvement in how value chain activities are performed.
- Installing information, communication, and operating systems that enable company personnel to carry out their strategic roles successfully day in and day out.
- Tying rewards and incentives to the achievement of performance objectives and good strategy execution.
- Creating a strategy-supportive work environment and corporate culture.
- Exerting the internal leadership needed to drive implementation forward and to keep improving on how the strategy is being executed.

These managerial tasks, depicted in Figure 9–1, crop up repeatedly in the strategy implementation process, no matter what the specifics of the situation. One or two of these tasks usually end up being more crucial or time-consuming than others, depending on how radically different the strategy changes are that have to be implemented, the organization's financial condition and competitive capabilities, whether there are important resource weaknesses to correct or new competencies to develop, the extent to which the company is already able to meet the resource requirements for creating sustainable competitive advantage, the strength of ingrained behavior patterns that have to be changed, the personal and organizational relationships in the firm's history, any pressures for quick results and near-term financial improvements, and perhaps other important factors.

In devising an action agenda, *strategy implementers should begin with a probing assessment of what the organization must do differently and better to carry out the strategy successfully*, then consider how to make the necessary internal changes as rapidly as practical. The strategy implementer's actions should center on fitting how the organization performs its value chain activities and conducts its internal business to what it takes for first-rate strategy execution. A series of "fits" are needed. Organiza-

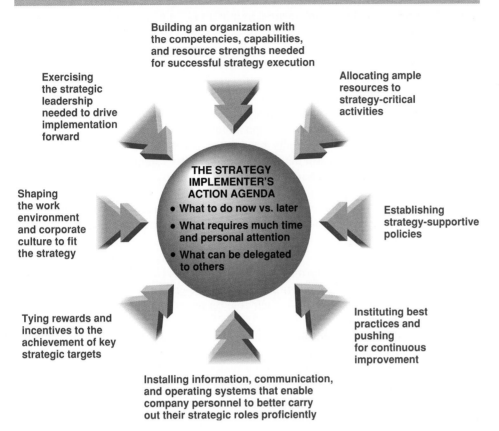

FIGURE 9-1 The Eight Big Managerial Components of Implementing Strategy

Building an organization with the competencies, capabilities, and resource strengths needed for successful strategy execution

Allocating ample resources to strategy-critical activities

Exercising the strategic leadership needed to drive implementation forward

THE STRATEGY IMPLEMENTER'S ACTION AGENDA
- What to do now vs. later
- What requires much time and personal attention
- What can be delegated to others

Establishing strategy-supportive policies

Shaping the work environment and corporate culture to fit the strategy

Instituting best practices and pushing for continuous improvement

Tying rewards and incentives to the achievement of key strategic targets

Installing information, communication, and operating systems that enable company personnel to better carry out their strategic roles proficiently

tional capabilities and resources must be carefully matched to the requirements of strategy—especially if the chosen strategy is based on a competence-based or resource-based competitive advantage. Financial resources must be allocated to provide departments with the people and operating budgets needed to execute their strategic roles effectively. The company's reward structure, policies, information systems, and operating practices need to push for strategy execution, rather than playing a merely passive role or, even worse, acting as obstacles. Equally important is the need for managers to do things in a manner and style that create and nurture a strategy-supportive work environment and corporate culture. The stronger such fits, the better the chances for successful strategy implementation. Systematic management efforts to match how the organization goes about its business with the needs of good strategy execution help unite the organization and produce a team effort to meet or beat performance targets. Successful strategy implementers have a knack for diagnosing what their organizations need to do to execute the chosen strategy well, and they are creative in finding ways to perform key value chain activities effectively.

LEADING THE IMPLEMENTATION PROCESS

One make-or-break determinant of successful strategy implementation is how well management leads the process. Managers can employ any of several leadership styles in pushing the implementation process along. They can play an active, visible, take-charge role or a quiet, low-key, behind-the-scenes one. They can make decisions authoritatively or on the basis of consensus; delegate much or little; be personally involved in the details of implementation or stand on the sidelines and coach others; proceed swiftly (launching implementation initiatives on many fronts) or deliberately (remaining content with gradual progress over a long time frame). How managers lead the implementation task tends to be a function of (1) their experience and knowledge about the business; (2) whether they are new to the job or veterans; (3) their network of personal relationships with others in the organization; (4) their own diagnostic, administrative, interpersonal, and problem-solving skills; (5) the authority they've been given; (6) the leadership style they're comfortable with; and (7) their view of the role they need to play to get things done.

Although major initiatives usually have to be led by the CEO and other senior officers, top-level managers still have to rely on the active support and cooperation of middle and lower managers to push strategy changes and see that key activities are performed well on a daily basis. Middle- and lower-level managers not only are responsible for initiating and supervising the implementation process in their areas of authority but they also are instrumental in getting subordinates to continuously improve on how strategy-critical value chain activities are performed and produce the frontline results that allow company performance targets to be met. How successful middle and lower managers are determines how proficiently the company executes its strategy on a daily basis—their role on the company's strategy implementation team is by no means minimal.

It is the job of middle and lower-level managers to push needed implementation actions on the front lines and to see that the strategy is well-executed on a daily basis.

The action agenda of senior-level strategy implementers, especially in big organizations with geographically scattered operating units, mostly involves communicating the case for change to others, building consensus for how to proceed, installing strong allies in positions where they can push implementation along in key organizational units, urging and empowering subordinates to get the process moving, establishing measures of progress and deadlines, recognizing and rewarding those who reach implementation milestones, reallocating resources, and personally presiding over the strategic change process. Thus, the bigger the organization, the more the success of the chief strategy implementer depends on the cooperation and implementing skills of operating managers who can push needed changes at the lowest organizational levels. In small organizations, the chief strategy implementer doesn't have to work through middle managers and can deal directly with frontline managers and employees. They can personally orchestrate the action steps and implementation sequence, observe firsthand how implementation is progressing, and decide how hard and how fast to push the process along. Either way, *the most important leadership trait is a strong, confident sense of "what to do" to achieve the desired results.* Knowing "what to do" comes from a savvy understanding of the business and the organization's circumstances.

The real strategy-implementing skill is being good at figuring out what it will take to execute the strategy proficiently.

In the remainder of this chapter and the next two chapters, we survey the ins and outs of the manager's role as chief strategy implementer. The discussion is framed around the eight managerial components of the strategy-implementation process. This chapter explores the management tasks of building a capable organization. Chapter 10 looks at budget allocations, policies, best practices, internal support systems, and strategically appropriate reward structures. Chapter 11 deals with creating a strategy-supportive corporate culture and exercising strategic leadership.

BUILDING A CAPABLE ORGANIZATION

Proficient strategy execution depends heavily on competent personnel, better-than-adequate competencies and competitive capabilities, and effective organization. Building a capable organization is thus always a top strategy-implementing priority. Three types of organization-building actions are paramount:

- Selecting able people for key positions.
- Making certain that the organization has the skills, core competencies, managerial talents, technical know-how, competitive capabilities, and resource strengths it needs.
- Organizing business processes, value chain activities, and decision making in a manner that is conducive to successful strategy execution.

Selecting People for Key Positions

Assembling a capable management team is one of the first cornerstones of the organization-building task. Strategy implementers must determine the kind of core management team they need to execute the strategy and then find the right people to fill each slot. Sometimes the existing management team is suitable; sometimes it needs to be strengthened or expanded by promoting qualified people from within or by bringing in outsiders whose experience, skills, and leadership styles suit the situation. In turnaround and rapid-growth situations, and in instances when a company doesn't have insiders with the needed experience and management know-how, filling key management slots from the outside is a fairly standard approach.

Putting together a strong management team with the right personal chemistry and mix of skills is one of the first strategy-implementing steps.

Putting together a core executive group starts with deciding what mix of backgrounds, experiences, know-how, values, beliefs, management styles, and personalities are needed to reinforce and contribute to successful strategy execution. As with any kind of team-building exercise, it is important to put together a compatible group of managers who possess the full set of skills to get things done. The personal chemistry needs to be right, and the talent base needs to be appropriate for the chosen strategy. Picking a solid management team is an essential organization-building function—often the first strategy implementation step to take.[2] Until key slots are filled with able people, it is hard for strategy implementation to proceed at full speed.

But a good management team is not enough. The task of staffing the organization with talented people must go much deeper into the organizational ranks. Companies like Electronic Data Systems (EDS), Microsoft, and McKinsey & Co. (one of the world's premier management consulting companies) make a concerted effort to recruit and retain the best and brightest talent they can find—having a cadre of people with strong technical skills is essential to their business. EDS requires college graduates to have at least a 3.5 grade-point average (on a 4.0 scale) just to qualify for an interview; Microsoft seeks out the world's most talented programmers to write code for its programs; McKinsey recruits MBAs only at the top ten business schools. The Big Six accounting firms screen candidates not only on the basis of their accounting expertise but also on whether they possess the people skills to relate well

---

[2]For an analytical framework in top-management team analysis, see Donald C. Hambrick, "The Top Management Team: Key to Strategic Success," *California Management Review* 30, no. 1 (Fall 1987), pp. 88–108.

with clients and colleagues. Southwest Airlines goes to considerable lengths to hire people who can have fun and be fun on the job; Southwest uses specially developed methods, including interviews with customers, to determine whether applicants for customer-contact jobs have outgoing personality traits that match its strategy of creating a high-spirited, fun-loving, in-flight atmosphere for passengers and going all-out to make flying Southwest a pleasant experience. The company is so selective that only about 3 percent of the candidates interviewed are offered jobs.

Building Core Competencies and Competitive Capabilities

Strategic Management Principle

Building core competencies, resource strengths, and organizational capabilities that rivals can't match is a sound foundation for sustainable competitive advantage.

Two of the most important organization-building concerns are that of (1) staffing operating units with the specialized talents, skills, and technical expertise needed to give the firm a competitive edge over rivals in performing one or more critical value chain activities and (2) building competitively valuable organizational capabilities. When ease of imitation makes it difficult or impossible to beat rivals on the basis of a superior strategy, the other main avenue to industry leadership is to outexecute them (beat them with superior strategy implementation—more resources, superior talent, stronger or better capabilities, more attention to detail). Superior strategy execution is essential in situations where rival firms have very similar strategies and can readily duplicate one another's strategic maneuvers. Building core competencies, resource strengths, and organizational capabilities that rivals can't match is one of the best ways to outexecute them. This is why one of management's most important strategy-implementing tasks is to build competitively advantageous competencies and organizational capabilities.

Developing and Strengthening Core Competencies   Core competencies can relate to any strategically relevant factor. Honda's core competence is its depth of expertise in gasoline engine technology and small engine design. Intel's is in the design of complex chips for personal computers. Procter & Gamble's core competencies reside in its superb marketing-distribution skills and its R&D capabilities in five core technologies—fats, oils, skin chemistry, surfactants, and emulsifiers.[3] Sony's core competencies are its expertise in electronic technology and its ability to translate that expertise into innovative products (miniaturized radios and video cameras, TVs and VCRs with unique features, attractively designed PCs). Most often, a company's core competencies emerge incrementally as it moves either to bolster skills that contributed to earlier successes or to respond to customer problems, new technological and market opportunities, and the moves of rivals.[4] Wise company managers try to foresee coming changes in customer-market requirements and proactively build new competencies and capabilities that offer a competitive edge.

Four traits concerning core competencies and competitive capabilities are important to a strategy implementer's organization-building task:[5]

- Core competencies rarely consist of narrow skills or the work efforts of a single department. Rather, they are composites of skills and activities

---

[3]James Brian Quinn, *Intelligent Enterprise* (New York: Free Press, 1992), p. 76.
[4]Ibid.
[5]Quinn, *Intelligent Enterprise*, pp. 52–53, 55, 73, and 76.

performed at different locations in the firm's value chain that, when linked, create unique organizational capability.

- Because core competencies typically reside in the combined efforts of different work groups and departments, individual supervisors and department heads can't be expected to see building the overall corporation's core competencies as their responsibility.

- The key to leveraging a company's core competencies into long-term competitive advantage is concentrating more effort and more talent than rivals on deepening and strengthening these competencies.

- Because customers' needs change in often unpredictable ways and the know-how and capabilities needed for competitive success cannot always be accurately forecasted, a company's selected bases of competence need to be broad enough and flexible enough to respond to an unknown future.

The multiskill, multiactivity character of core competencies makes building and strengthening them an exercise in (1) managing human skills, knowledge bases, and intellect and (2) coordinating and networking the efforts of different work groups and departments at every related place in the value chain. It's an exercise best orchestrated by senior managers who appreciate the strategy-implementing signifi- cance of creating valuable competencies/capabilities and who have the clout to enforce the necessary cooperation among individuals, groups, departments, and ex- ternal allies. Moreover, organization builders have to concentrate enough resources and management attention on core competence-related activities to achieve the *domi- nating depth* needed for competitive advantage.[6] This does not necessarily mean spending more money on competence-related activities than present or potential competitors. It does mean consciously focusing more talent on them and making appropriate internal and external benchmarking comparisons to move toward best-in- industry, if not best-in-world, status. To achieve dominance on lean financial re- sources, companies like Cray in large computers, Lotus in software, and Honda in small engines leveraged the expertise of their talent pool by frequently re-forming high-intensity teams and reusing key people on special projects.[7] In leveraging internal knowledge and skills rather than physical assets or market position, it is superior selection, training, powerful cultural influences, cooperative networking, motivation, empowerment, attractive incentives, organizational flexibility, short deadlines, and good databases—not big operating budgets—that are the usual keys to success.[8] One of Microsoft's keys to success in computer software is hiring the very brightest and most talented programmers it can find and motivating them with both good monetary incentives and the challenge of working on cutting-edge software design projects (although Microsoft also assigns small armies of these programmers to work on projects with high-priority or short deadlines).

> *Core competencies don't come into being or reach strategic fruition without conscious management attention.*

Strategy implementers can't afford to become complacent once core competencies are in place and functioning. It's a constant organization- building challenge to broaden, deepen, or modify them in response to ongoing customer-market changes. But it's a task worth pursuing. Core competencies that are

---

[6]Ibid., p. 73.
[7]Ibid.
[8]Ibid., pp. 73–74.

finely honed and kept current with shifting circumstances can provide a big executional advantage. Distinctive core competencies and organizational capabilities are not easily duplicated by rival firms; thus any competitive advantage that results from them is likely to be durable. Dedicated management attention to the task of building strategically relevant internal skills and capabilities is always one of the keys to effective strategy implementation.

Developing and Strengthening Organizational Capabilities   Whereas the essence of astute strategy-making is *selecting* the competencies and capabilities to underpin the strategy, the essence of good strategy implementation is *building and strengthening* the competencies and capabilities to execute the chosen strategy proficiently. Sometimes a company already has the needed competencies and capabilities in place, in which case the strategy implementation task only involves efforts to strengthen and nurture them so as to promote better execution. Sometimes, however, management has be be proactive in developing *new* competencies and capabilities to complement the company's existing resource base and promote more proficient strategy execution. It is useful here to think of companies as a bundle of evolving competencies and capabilities, with the challenge being one of developing new capabilities and strengthening existing ones to achieve competitive advantage through superior strategy execution.

Organization-building that succeeds in developing valuable new competitive capabilities and strengthening existing ones can enable an enterprise to outcompete rivals on the basis of superior resources.

One issue is whether to develop the desired competencies and capabilities internally or whether it makes more sense to outsource them by partnering with key suppliers or forming strategic alliances. Decisions about whether to outsource or develop in-house capability often turn on the issue of what can be safely delegated to outside suppliers versus what internal capabilities are key to the company's long-term success. Either way, though, implementation actions are called for. Outsourcing involves identifying the most attractive providers and establishing collaborative relationships. Developing the capabilities in-house means hiring new personnel with skills and experience relevant to the desired capability, linking the individual skills/know-how to form organizational capability (a group's capabilities are partly a function of the working relationships among its members), building the desired levels of proficiency through repetition ("practice makes perfect"), and linking all the capability-related value chain activities.[9] Strong linkages with related activities are important. The capability to do something really complex (like design and manufacture a sports utility vehicle or create software that allows secure credit card transactions over the Internet) usually involves a number of skills, technological disciplines, competencies, and capabilities—some performed in-house and some provided by suppliers/allies. An important part of organization building is to think about which skills and activities need to be linked and made mutually reinforcing and then to forge the necessary collaboration and cooperation both internally and with outside resource providers.

Managers create organizational capabilities by integrating the skills and know-how of different people and groups in competitively valuable ways, and continuously tuning and recalibrating the components to match new strategic requirements over time.

All this should reemphasize that capability building is a time-consuming, hard-to-replicate exercise. Capabilities are difficult to purchase (except through outsiders who already have them and will agree to supply them) and difficult to imitate just by

---

[9] Robert H. Hayes, Gary P. Pisano, and David M. Upton, *Strategic Operations: Competing through Capabilities* (New York: Free Press, 1996), pp. 503–07.

watching others (just as one cannot become a good golfer by watching Tiger Woods play golf, a company cannot put a new capability in place by creating a new department and assigning it the task of emulating a capability rivals have). Capability building requires a series of organizational steps:

- First, the organization must develop the *ability* to do something, however imperfectly or inefficiently. This means selecting people with the needed skills and experience, upgrading or expanding individual abilities as needed, and then molding the efforts and work products of individuals into a cooperative group effort to create organizational *ability*.
- Then as experience builds, such that the organization can accomplish the activity consistently well and at an acceptable cost, the ability begins to translate into a *competence* and/or a *capability*.
- Should the organization get so good (by continuing to polish and refine and deepen its skills and know-how) that it is better than rivals at the activity, the capability becomes a *distinctive competence* with potential for competitive advantage.

Building capabilities either internally or in collaboration with others takes time and considerable organizing skill.

Sometimes these steps can be short-circuited by acquiring the desired capability through collaborative efforts with external allies or by buying a company that has the needed capability. Indeed, a pressing need to acquire certain capabilities quickly is one reason to acquire another company—an acquisition aimed at building greater capability can be every bit as competitively valuable as an acquisition aimed at adding the acquired company's products/services to the acquirer's business lineup. Capabilities-motivated acquisitions are essential (1) when an opportunity can disappear faster than a needed capability can be created internally and (2) when industry conditions, technology, or competitors are moving at such a rapid clip that time is of the essence.

Organizational competencies and capabilities emerge from establishing and nurturing collaborative working relationships between individuals and groups in different departments and between a company and its external allies.

The Strategic Role of Employee Training   Training and retraining are important parts of the strategy implementation process when a company shifts to a strategy requiring different skills, managerial approaches, and operating methods. Training is also strategically important in organizational efforts to build skills-based competencies. And it is a key activity in businesses where technical know-how is changing so rapidly that a company loses its ability to compete unless its skilled people have cutting-edge knowledge and expertise. Successful strategy implementers see that the training function is adequately funded and that effective training programs are in place. If the chosen strategy calls for new skills, deeper technological capability, or building and using new capabilities, training should be placed near the top of the action agenda because it needs to be done early in the strategy implementation process.

Matching Organization Structure to Strategy

There are few hard-and-fast rules for organizing the work effort in a strategy-supportive fashion. Every firm's organization chart is idiosyncratic, reflecting prior organizational patterns, executive judgments about how best to arrange reporting relationships, the politics of who to give which assignments, and varying internal circumstances. Moreover, every strategy is grounded in its own set of key success factors and value chain activities. So a customized organization structure is appropriate. The following are helpful guidelines in fitting structure to strategy:

- Pinpoint the primary value chain activities, competencies, and competitive capabilities that are important in successfully executing the strategy.
- Determine whether some value chain activities (especially noncritical support activities, but perhaps selected primary activities) can be outsourced more efficiently or effectively than they can be performed internally.
- Determine which of the strategy-critical activities/capabilities require close collaboration with suppliers, forward channel allies (distributors or dealers or franchisees), makers of complementary products, or even competitors.
- Make those primary value chain activities and capabilities to be performed/ developed internally and strategy-critical organizational units the main building blocks in the organization structure.
- Determine the degrees of authority needed to manage each organizational unit, striking a balance between centralizing decision making under the coordinating authority of a single manager and pushing decision making down to the lowest organizational level capable of making timely, informed, competent decisions.
- If all facets of an internal strategy-critical activity/capability cannot be placed under the authority of a single manager, establish ways to bridge departmental lines and achieve the necessary coordination.
- Determine how the relationships with outsiders are to be managed and assign responsibility for building the necessary organizational bridges.

Pinpointing Strategy-Critical Activities and Competitive Capabilities   In any business, some activities in the value chain are always more critical to success than others. From a strategy perspective, a certain portion of an organization's work involves routine administrative housekeeping (doing the payroll, administering employee benefit programs, handling grievances, providing corporate security, maintaining fleet vehicles). Others are support functions (data processing, accounting, training, public relations, market research, purchasing). Among the primary value chain activities are certain crucial business processes that have to be performed either exceedingly well or in closely coordinated fashion for the organization to develop the capabilities needed for strategic success. For instance, hotel/motel enterprises have to be good at fast check-in/check-out, room maintenance, food service, and creating a pleasant ambiance. A manufacturer of chocolate bars must be skilled in purchasing quality cocoa beans at low prices, efficient production (a fraction of a cent in cost savings per bar can mean seven-figure improvement in the bottom line), merchandising, and promotional activities. In discount stock brokerage, the strategy-critical activities are fast access to information, accurate order execution, efficient record-keeping and transactions processing, and good customer service. In specialty chemicals, the critical activities are R&D, product innovation, getting new products onto the market quickly, effective marketing, and expertise in assisting customers. In the electronics industry, where technology is racing along, a company's cycle time in getting new, cutting-edge products to market is the critical organizational capability. Strategy-critical activities and capabilities vary according to the particulars of a firm's strategy, value chain makeup, and competitive requirements.

Two questions help identify what an organization's strategy-critical activities are: "What functions have to be performed extra well or in timely fashion to achieve sustainable competitive advantage?" and "In what value chain activities would malperformance seriously endanger strategic success?"[10] The answers generally point to the crucial activities and organizational capabilities where organization-building efforts must be concentrated.

Reasons to Consider Outsourcing Certain Value Chain Activities   Managers too often spend inordinate amounts of time, psychic energy, and resources wrestling with functional support groups and other internal bureaucracies, diverting attention from the company's strategy-critical activities. One way to detour such distractions is to cut the number of internal staff support activities and, instead, source more of what is needed from outside vendors.

Each supporting activity in a firm's value chain and within its traditional staff groups can be considered a "service."[11] Indeed, most overheads are just services the company chooses to produce internally. However, many such services can typically be purchased from outside vendors. What makes outsourcing attractive is that an outsider, by concentrating specialists and technology in its area of expertise, can frequently perform these services *as well or better and usually more cheaply* than a company that performs the activities only for itself. But there are other reasons to consider outsourcing. From a strategic point of view, outsourcing non-crucial support activities (and maybe selected primary activities in the value chain) can decrease internal bureaucracies, flatten the organization structure, heighten the company's strategic focus, and increase competitive responsiveness.[12] The experiences of companies that obtain many support services from outside vendors indicate that *outsourcing activities not crucial to building those organizational capabilities needed for long-term competitive success allows a company to concentrate its own energies and resources on those value chain activities where it can create unique value, where it can be best in the industry (or, better still, best in the world), and where it needs strategic control to build core competencies, achieve competitive advantage, and manage key customer-supplier-distributor relationships.*

> *Outsourcing noncritical value chain activities and even select primary activities has many advantages.*

Critics contend that extensive outsourcing can hollow out a company, leaving it at the mercy of outside suppliers and barren of the competencies and organizational capabilities needed to be master of its own destiny.[13] However, a number of companies have successfully relied on outside components suppliers, product designers, distribution channels, advertising agencies, and financial services firms to perform significant value chain activities. For years Polaroid Corporation bought its film medium from Eastman Kodak, its electronics from Texas Instruments, and its cameras from Timex and others, while it concentrated on producing its unique self-developing film packets and designing its next generation of cameras and films. Nike concentrates on design, marketing, and distribution to retailers, while outsourcing virtually all production of its shoes and sporting apparel. Many mining companies outsource geological work, assaying, and drilling. Ernest and Julio Gallo Winery outsources 95 percent of its grape production, letting farmers take on the weather and

---

[10]Peter F. Drucker, *Management: Tasks, Responsibilities, Practices* (New York: Harper & Row, 1974), pp. 530, 535.

[11]Quinn, *Intelligent Enterprise*, p. 32.

[12]Ibid., pp. 33 and 89. See, also, James Brian Quinn and Frederick G. Hilmer, "Strategic Outsourcing," *Sloan Management Review* (Summer 1994), pp. 43–55.

[13]Ibid., pp. 39–40.

other grape-growing risks while it concentrates on wine production and the marketing-sales function.[14] The major airlines outsource their in-flight meals even though food quality is important to travelers' perception of overall service quality. Eastman Kodak, Ford, Exxon, Merrill Lynch, and Chevron have outsourced their data-processing activities to computer service firms, believing that outside specialists can perform the needed services at lower costs and equal or better quality. Chrysler has transformed itself from a high-cost producer into a low-cost producer by abandoning internal production of many parts and components and instead outsourcing them from more efficient suppliers; greater reliance on outsourcing has also enabled Chrysler to shorten the time it takes to bring new models to market. *Outsourcing certain value chain activities makes strategic sense whenever outsiders can perform them at lower cost and/or with higher value-added than the buyer company can perform them internally.*[15]

Reasons to Consider Partnering with Others to Gain Competitively Valuable Capabilities But there is another equally important reason to look outside for help. *Strategic partnerships, alliances, and close collaboration with select suppliers, distributors, the makers of complementary products and services, and even competitors can add to a company's arsenal of capabilities and contribute to better strategy execution.* Partnering with outsiders can result in bringing new technology on-line quicker, in quicker delivery and/or lower inventories of parts and components, in providing better or faster technical assistance to customers, in geographically wider distribution capability, in the development of multiple distribution outlets, in deeper technological know-how, in economical custom manufacture, in more extensive after-sale support services, and so on. By building, continually improving, and then leveraging these kinds of organizational capabilities, a company develops the resource strengths needed for competitive success—it puts in place enhanced ability to do things for its customers that deliver value to customers and that rivals can't quite match.

Microsoft's Bill Gates and Intel's Andrew Grove meet periodically to explore how their organizations can share information, work in parallel, and team together to sustain the "Wintel" standard that pervades the PC industry. The automobile manufacturers work closely with their suppliers to advance the design and functioning of parts and components, to incorporate new technology, to better integrate individual parts and components to form engine cooling systems, transmission systems, electrical systems, and so on—all of which helps shorten the cycle time for new models, improve the quality and performance of their vehicles, and boost overall production efficiency. The soft-drink producers (Coca-Cola and PepsiCo) and the beer producers (Anheuser-Busch and Miller Brewing) all cultivate their relationships with their bottlers/distributors to strengthen access to local markets and build the loyalty, support, and commitment for corporate marketing programs, without which their own sales and growth are weakened. Similarly, the fast-food enterprises like McDonald's and Taco Bell find it essential to work hand-in-hand with franchisees on outlet cleanliness, consistency of product quality, in-store ambience, courtesy and friendliness of store personnel, and other aspects of store operations—unless franchisees

---

[14]Ibid., p. 43.

[15]Ibid., p. 47. The growing tendency of companies to outsource important activities and the many reasons for building cooperative, collaborative alliances and partnerships with other companies is detailed in James F. Moore, *The Death of Competition* (New York: HarperBusiness, 1996), especially Chapter 3.

deliver sufficient customer satisfaction to attract repeat business on an ongoing basis, a fast-food chain's sales and competitive standing suffer quickly. *Strategic partnerships, alliances, and close collaboration with suppliers, distributors, the makers of complementary products/services and competitors make good strategic sense whenever the result is to enhance organizational resources and capabilities.*

Making Strategy-Critical Activities/Capabilities the Main Building Blocks of the Internal Organization   The rationale for making strategy-critical activities and capabilities the main building blocks in structuring a business is compelling: If activities/capabilities crucial to strategic success are to have the resources, decision-making influence, and organizational impact needed, they have to be centerpieces in the organizational scheme. Plainly, a new or changed strategy is likely to lead to new or different key activities, competencies, or capabilities and, therefore, require new or different organizational arrangements; without them, the resulting mismatch between strategy and structure can open the door to implementation and performance problems.[16]

Strategic Management Principle

Attempting to carry out a new strategy with an old organizational structure is usually unwise.

Senior executives seldom send a stronger signal about what is strategically important than by making key business units and critical activities prominent organizational building blocks and, further, giving the managers of these units a visible, influential position in the organizational pecking order. When key business units are put down on a level with or, worse, superseded by less important divisions or departments, they usually end up with fewer resources and less clout than they deserve in the organization's power structure. When top management fails to devote attention to organizing in a way that produces effective performance of strategy-critical activities and processes and develops needed capabilities, the whole strategy implementation effort is weakened. It is thus essential that the primary value-creating, success-causing activities and business processes be prominent in the company's organization structure and deeply ingrained in how the organization does its work. Anything else risks a serious mismatch between structure and strategy.

Strategic Management Principle

Matching structure to strategy requires making strategy-critical activities and strategy-critical organizational units the main building blocks in the organization structure.

---

[16]The importance of matching organization design and structure to the particular needs of strategy was first brought to the forefront in a landmark study of 70 large corporations conducted by Professor Alfred Chandler of Harvard University. Chandler's research revealed that changes in an organization's strategy bring about new administrative problems which, in turn, require a new or refashioned structure for the new strategy to be successfully implemented. He found that structure tends to follow the growth strategy of the firm—but often not until inefficiency and internal operating problems provoke a structural adjustment. The experiences of these firms followed a consistent sequential pattern: new strategy creation, emergence of new administrative problems, a decline in profitability and performance, a shift to a more appropriate organizational structure, and then recovery to more profitable levels and improved strategy execution. That managers should reassess their company's internal organization whenever strategy changes is pretty much common sense. A new or different strategy is likely to entail new or different key activities, competencies, or capabilities and, therefore, require new or different internal organizational arrangements; if workable organizational adjustments are not forthcoming, the resulting mismatch between strategy and structure can open the door to implementation and performance problems. For more details, see Alfred Chandler, *Strategy and Structure* (Cambridge, Mass.: MIT Press, 1962).

Although the stress here is on designing the organization structure around the needs of effective strategy execution, it is worth noting that structure can and does influence the choice of strategy. A good strategy must be doable. When an organization's present structure is so far out of line with the requirements of a particular strategy that the organization would have to be turned upside down to implement it, the strategy may not be doable and should not be given further consideration. In such cases, structure shapes the choice of strategy. The point here, however, is that once strategy is chosen, structure must be modified to fit the strategy if, in fact, an approximate fit does not already exist. Any influences of structure on strategy should, logically, come before the point of strategy selection rather than after it.

In grafting routine and staff support activities onto the basic structure, company managers should be guided by the strategic relationships among the primary and support functions comprising the value chain. Activities can be related by the flow of work along the value chain, the type of customer served, the distribution channels used, the technical skills and know-how needed to perform them, their contribution to building a core competence or competitive capability, their role in a work process that spans traditional departmental lines, their role in how customer value is created, their sequence in the value chain, the skills or technology transfer opportunities they present, and the potential for combining or coordinating them in a manner that will reduce total costs, to mention some of the most obvious. If the needs of successful strategy execution are to drive organization design, then the relationships to look for are those that (1) link one work unit's performance to another and (2) can be melded into a competitively valuable competence or capability.

Managers need to be particularly alert to the fact that *in traditional functionally organized structures, pieces of strategically relevant activities and capabilities often end up scattered across many departments.* The process of filling customer orders accurately and promptly is a case in point. The order fulfillment process begins when a customer places an order, ends when the goods are delivered, and typically includes a dozen or so steps performed by different people in different departments.[17] Someone in customer service receives the order, logs it in, and checks it for accuracy and completeness. It may then go to the finance department, where someone runs a credit check on the customer. Another person may be needed to approve credit terms or

Functional specialization can result in the pieces of strategically relevant activities and capabilities being scattered across many different departments.

special financing. Someone in sales calculates or verifies the correct pricing. When the order gets to inventory control, someone has to determine if the goods are in stock. If not, a back order may be issued or the order routed to production planning so that it can be factored into the production schedule. When the goods are ready, warehouse operations prepares a shipment schedule. Personnel in the traffic department determine the shipment method (rail, truck, air, water) and choose the route and carrier. Product handling picks the product from the warehouse, verifies the picking against the order, and packages the goods for shipment. Traffic releases the goods to the carrier, which takes responsibility for delivery to the customer. Each handoff from one department to the next entails queues and wait times. Although such organization incorporates Adam Smith's division of labor principle (every person involved has specific responsibility for performing one simple task) and allows for tight management control (everyone in the process is accountable to a manager for efficiency and adherence to procedures), *no one oversees the whole process and its result.*[18] Accurate, timely order fulfillment, despite its relevance to effective strategy execution, ends up being neither a single person's job nor the job of any one functional department—it is a capability that grows out of the combined pieces of many people's jobs in different units.[19] Other strategy-critical activities that are often fragmented include obtaining feedback from customers and making product modifications to meet their needs, speeding new products to market (a task that is often fragmented among R&D, engineering, purchasing, manufacturing, and market-

---

[17]Michael Hammer and James Champy, *Reengineering the Corporation* (New York: HarperBusiness, 1993), pp. 26–27.
[18]Ibid.
[19]Ibid., pp. 27–28.

ILLUSTRATION CAPSULE 30   Process Organization at Lee Memorial Hospital and St. Vincent's Hospital

At acute care hospitals such as Lee Memorial in Fort Myers, Florida, and St. Vincent's in Melbourne, Australia, medical care is delivered by interdisciplinary teams of doctors, nurses, laboratory technicians, and so on that are organized around the needs of the patients and their families rather than around functional departments within the hospital; these hospitals have created focused care or treatment-specific wards within the hospital to treat most of a patient's needs, from admission to discharge. Patients are no longer wheeled from department to department for procedures and tests; instead, teams have the equipment and resources within each focused care unit to provide total care for the patient. While the hospitals had some concern about functional inefficiency in the use of some facilities, process organization has resulted in substantially lower operating cost, faster patient recovery, and greater satisfaction on the part of patients and caregivers.

Source: Iain Somerville and John Edward Mroz, "New Competencies for a New World," in *The Organization of the Future*, edited by Frances Hesselbein, Marshall Goldsmith, and Richard Beckard, (San Francisco: Jossey-Bass, 1997), p.71.

ing), improving product quality, managing relationships with key suppliers, and building the capability to conduct business via the Internet.

Managers have to guard against organization designs that unduly fragment strategically relevant activities. Parceling strategy-critical work efforts across many specialized departments contributes to an obsession with activity (performing the assigned tasks in the prescribed manner) rather than result (lower costs, short product development times, higher product quality, customer satisfaction, competitive advantage). So many handoffs lengthen completion time and frequently drive up overhead costs since coordinating the fragmented pieces can soak up hours of effort on the parts of many people. *One obvious solution is to pull the pieces of strategy-critical processes out of the functional silos and create process-complete departments able to perform all the cross-functional steps needed to produce a strategy-critical result*—see Illustration Capsule 30 for an example of process organization. In recent years, many companies have reengineered their work flows, moving from functional structures to process structures pursued this solution where it was feasible to do so.[20] Nonetheless, some fragmentation is necessary, even desirable. Traditional functional centralization works to good advantage in support activities like finance and accounting, human resource management, and engineering, and in such primary activities as R&D, manufacturing, and marketing.

Thus the primary organizational building blocks within a business are usually a combination of traditional functional departments and process-complete departments. In enterprises with operations in various countries around the world, the basic building blocks may also include geographic organizational units, each of which has profit-loss responsibility for its area. In vertically integrated firms, the major building blocks are divisional units, each of which performs one (or more) of the major processing steps along the value chain (raw materials production, components manufacture, assembly, wholesale distribution, retail store operations); each division in the value chain sequence may operate as a profit center for performance measurement purposes. The typical building blocks of a diversified company are its individual

---

[20]For a detailed review of one company's experiences with reengineering, see Donna B. Stoddard, Sirkka L. Jarvenpaa, and Michael Littlejohn, "The Reality of Business Reengineering: Pacific Bell's Centrex Provisioning Process," *California Management Review* 38, no. 3 (Spring 1996), pp. 57–76.

businesses, with each business unit usually operating as an independent profit center and with corporate headquarters performing support functions for all the businesses.

Determining the Degree of Authority and Independence to Give Each Unit and Each Employee

Companies must decide how much authority to give managers of each organization unit (especially the heads of business subsidiaries, functional departments, and process departments) and how much decision-making latitude to give individual employees in performing their jobs. In a highly centralized organization, top executives retain authority for most strategic and operating decisions and keep a tight rein on business-unit heads and department heads; comparatively little discretionary authority is granted to subordinate managers and individual employees. One weakness of centralized organization is that its vertical, hierarchical character tends to stall decision making until the review-approval process runs its course through the layers of the management bureaucracy. Furthermore, to work well, centralized decision making requires top-level managers to gather and process whatever knowledge is relevant to the decision. When the relevant knowledge resides at lower organizational levels or is technical or detailed or hard to express in words, it is difficult and time-consuming to get all of the facts and nuances in front of the decision maker—knowledge cannot be "copied" from one mind to another. In many cases, it is better to put decision-making authority in the hands of the people most familiar with the situation and train them to exercise good judgment, rather than trying to convey the knowledge and information up the line to the person with the decision-making authority.

There are serious disadvantages to having a small number of all-knowing, top-level managers micromanage the business.

In a highly decentralized organization, managers (and, increasingly, many nonmanagerial employees) are empowered to act on their own in their areas of responsibility—plant managers are empowered to order new equipment as needed and make arrangements with suppliers for parts and components; process managers (or teams) are empowered to manage and improve their assigned process; and employees with customer contact are empowered to do what it takes to please customers. At Starbucks, for example, employees are empowered to exercise initiative in promoting customer satisfaction—there's the story of a store employee, who when the computerized cash register system went off-line, enthusiastically told waiting customers "free coffee."[21] In a diversified company operating on the principle of decentralized decision making, business unit heads have broad authority to run the subsidiary with comparatively little interference from corporate headquarters; moreover, the business head gives functional and process department heads considerable decision-making latitude.

The purpose of decentralization is not to push decisions down to lower levels but to lodge decision-making authority in those persons or teams closest to and most knowledgeable about the situation.

Delegating greater authority to subordinate managers and employees creates a more horizontal organization structure with fewer layers. Whereas in a centralized vertical structure managers and workers have to go up the ladder of authority for an answer, in a decentralized horizontal structure they develop their own answers and action plans—making decisions and being accountable for results is part of their job. Decentralized decision making usually shortens organizational response times, plus it spurs new ideas, creative thinking, innovation, and greater involvement on the part of subordinate managers and employees.

---

[21]Iain Somerville and John Edward Mroz, "New Competencies for a New World," in *The Organization of the Future*, ed. Frances Hesselbein, Marshall Goldsmith, and Richard Beckard, (San Francisco: Jossey-Bass, 1997), p.70.

In recent years, there's been a decided shift from authoritarian, hierarchical structures to flatter, more decentralized structures that stress employee empowerment. The new preference for leaner management structures and empowered employees is grounded in three tenets.

1. *With the world economy moving swiftly from the Industrial Age to the Knowledge/Information/Systems Age, traditional hierarchical structures built around functional specialization have to undergo radical surgery to accommodate greater emphasis on building competitively valuable cross-functional capabilities*; the best companies have to be able to act and react quickly and to create, package, and rapidly move information to the point of need—in short, companies have to reinvent their organizational arrangements.

2. *Decision-making authority should be pushed down to the lowest organizational level capable of making timely, informed, competent decisions*—to those people (managers or nonmanagers) nearest the scene who are knowledgeable about the issues and trained to weigh all the factors. Insofar as strategic management is concerned, decentralization means that the managers of each organizational unit should not only lead the crafting of their unit's strategy but also lead the decision making on how to implement it. Decentralization thus requires selecting strong managers to head each organizational unit and holding them accountable for crafting and executing appropriate strategies for their units. Managers who consistently produce unsatisfactory results and have poor track records in strategy making and strategy implementing have to be weeded out.

3. *Employees below the management ranks should be empowered to exercise judgment on matters pertaining to their jobs*. The case for empowering employees to make decisions and be accountable for their performance is based on the belief that a company that draws on the combined brainpower of all its employees can outperform a company where people management means transferring executives' decisions about what to do and how to do it into the actions of workers-doers. To ensure that the decisions of empowered people are as well-informed as possible, great pains have to be taken to put accurate, timely data into everyone's hands and make sure they understand the links between their performance and company performance. Delayered corporate hierarchies coupled with today's electronic communication systems make greater empowerment feasible. It's possible now to create "a wired company" where people at all organizational levels have direct electronic access to data, other employees, managers, suppliers, and customers; they can access information quickly (via the Internet or company intranet), check with superiors or whoever else as needed, and take responsible action. Typically, there are genuine morale gains when people are well-informed and allowed to operate in a self-directed way. But there is an organizing challenge as well: how to exercise adequate control over the actions of empowered employes so that the business is not put at risk at the same time that the benefits of empowerment are realized.[22]

> *Successful strategy inplementation involves empowering others to act on doing all the things needed to put the strategy into place and execute it proficiently.*

---

[22]Exercising adequate control in businesses that demand short response times, innovation, and creativity is a serious requirement. For example, Kidder, Peabody & Co. lost $350 million when a trader allegedly booked fictitious profits; Sears took a $60 million write-off after admitting that employees in its automobile service departments recommended unnecessary repairs to customers. For a discussion of the problems

One of the biggest exceptions to decentralizing strategy-related decisions and giving lower-level managers more operating rein arises in diversified companies with related businesses. In such cases, strategic-fit benefits are often best captured by either centralizing decision-making authority or enforcing close cooperation and shared decision making.[23] For example, if businesses with overlapping process and product technologies have their own independent R&D departments, each pursuing their own priorities, projects, and strategic agendas, it's hard for the corporate parent to prevent duplication of effort, capture either economies of scale or economies of scope, or broaden the vision of the company's R&D efforts to embrace new technological paths, product families, end-use applications, and customer groups. Likewise, centralizing control over the related activities of separate businesses makes sense when there are opportunities to share a common sales force, use common distribution channels, rely upon a common field service organization to handle customer requests for technical assistance or provide maintenance and repair services, and so on. And for reasons previously discussed, limits also have to be placed on the independence of functional managers when pieces of strategy-critical processes are located in different organizational units and require close coordination for maximum effectiveness.

Centralizing strategy-implementing authority at the corporate level has merit when the related activities of related businesses need to be tightly coordinated.

Reporting Relationships and Cross-Unit Coordination   The classic way to coordinate the activities of organizational units is to position them so that those most closely related report to a single person (a functional department head, a process manager, a geographic area head). Managers higher up in the pecking order generally have authority over more organizational units and thus the clout to coordinate and unify the activities of units under their supervision. In such structures, the chief executive officer, chief operating officer, and business-level managers end up as central points of coordination. When a firm is pursuing a related diversification strategy, coordinating the related activities of independent business units often requires the centralizing authority of a single corporate-level officer. Also, companies with either related or unrelated diversification strategies commonly centralize such staff support functions as public relations, finance and accounting, employee benefits, and information systems at the corporate level.

But, as the customer order fulfillment example illustrates, it isn't always feasible to position all the pieces of a strategy-critical process and/or all interrelated organizational units vertically under the coordinating authority of a single executive. Formal reporting relationships have to be supplemented. Options for unifying the strategic efforts of interrelated organizational units include the use of coordinating teams, cross-functional task forces, dual reporting relationships, informal organizational networking, voluntary cooperation, incentive compensation tied to group performance measures, and strong executive-level insistence on teamwork and interdepartmental cooperation (including removal of recalcitrant managers who stonewall collaborative efforts).[24] See Illustration

---

and possible solutions, see Robert Simons, "Control in an Age of Empowerment," *Harvard Business Review* 73 (March–April 1995), pp. 80–88.

[23] For a discussion of the importance of cross-business coordination, see Jeanne M. Liedtka, "Collaboration across Lines of Business for Competitive Advantage," *Academy of Management Executive* 10, no. 2 (May 1996), pp. 20–34.

[24] At ABB, a $30 billion European-based company that makes power generation and electrical equipment and offers a wide range of engineering services, a top executive promptly replaced the managers of several plants who were not fully committed to collaborating closely on eliminating duplication in product development and production efforts among plants in several different countries. Earlier, the executive, noting that negotiations among the managers had stalled on which labs and plants to close, had met with all

ILLUSTRATION CAPSULE 31   Cross-Unit Coordination on Technology at 3M Corp.

At 3M, technology experts in more than 100 3M labs around the world have come to work openly and cooperatively without resorting to turf protection tactics or not-invented-here mind-sets. 3M management has been successful in creating a collegial working environment that results in the scientists calling upon one another for assistance and advice and in rapid technology transfer.

Mangement formed a Technical Council, composed of the heads of the major labs; the Council meets monthly and has a three-day annual retreat to discuss ways to improve cross-unit transfer of technology and other issues of common interest. In addition, management created a broader-based Technical Forum, composed of scientists and technical experts chosen as

representatives, to facilitate grassroots communication among employees in all the labs. One of the Forum's responsibilities is to organize employees with similar technical interests from all the labs into chapters; chapter members attend regular seminars with experts from outside the company. There's also an annual three-day technology fair at which 3M scientists showcase their latest findings for colleagues and expand their network of acquaintances.

As a result of these collaborative efforts, 3M has developed a portfolio of more than 100 technologies and it has created the capability to routinely utilize these technologies in product applications in three different divisions that each serve multiple markets.

Source: Adapted from Sumantra Ghoshal and Christopher A. Bartlett, "Changing the Role of Top Management: Beyond Structure to Process," *Harvard Business Review* 73, no. 1 (January–February 1995), pp. 93–94.

Capsule 31 for a more detailed example of putting the necessary organizational arrangements into place and creating the desired results.

The key in weaving support activities into the organization design is to establish reporting and coordinating arrangements that:

- Maximize how support activities contribute to enhanced performance of the primary activities in the firm's value chain.
- Contain the costs of support activities and minimize the time and energy internal units have to spend doing business with each other.

Without such arrangements, the cost of transacting business internally becomes excessive, and the managers of individual organizational units, forever diligent in guarding their turf, can weaken the strategy execution effort and become part of the strategy-implementing problem rather than part of the solution.

Assigning Responsibility for Collaboration with Outsiders   Someone or some group must be given authority and responsibility for collaborating with each major outside constituency involved in strategy execution. This means having managers with responsibility for making particular strategic partnerships or alliances generate the intended benefits. If close working relationships with suppliers are crucial, then authority and responsibility for supply chain management must be given formal status on the company's organization chart and a significant position in the pecking order. If distributor/dealer/franchisee relationships are important, someone must be assigned the task of building the bridges of cooperation and nurturing the relationships. If working in parallel with providers of complementary products and services contributes to enhanced organizational capability, then cooperative organizational arrangements of some kind have to be put in place and managed to good effect. Just appointing and empowering relationship managers is not enough; there have to be

the managers, asked them to cooperate to find a solution, discussed with them which options were unacceptable, and given them a deadline to find a solution. When the asked-for teamwork wasn't forthcoming from several managers attending the meeting, they were replaced.

multiple ties at multiple levels to ensure proper communication, coordination, and control.[25]

The key to cooperative alliances and partnerships is effectively managing the relationship and capturing the potential gain in resource capability, not in doing the deal.

The organizing challenge is to find ways to span the boundaries of independent organizations and produce the collaborative efforts needed to enhance a company's own competitive capabilites and resource strengths.[26] *Forming alliances and cooperative relationships presents immediate opportunities and opens the door to future possibilities, but nothing valuable is realized until the relationship grows, develops, and blossoms.* Unless top management sees that such bridge building occurs and that ample effort goes into creating productive working relationships, the company's power to execute its strategy is weakened.

The Strategic Advantages And Disadvantages Of Different Organizational Structures

There are five basic building block schemes for matching structure to strategy: (1) functional and/or process specialization, (2) geographic organization, (3) decentralized business divisions, (4) strategic business units, and (5) matrix structures featuring dual lines of authority and strategic priority. Each has strategic advantages and disadvantages, and each has to be supplemented with formal and informal organizational arrangements to fully coordinate the work effort, develop core competencies, and build competitive capabilities.

Functional and Process Organization Structures Organizational structures anchored around functionally specialized departments and strategy-critical processes are far and away the most popular way to match structure to strategy in single-business enterprises. However, just what form the functional and process specialization takes varies according to the nature of the value chain. For instance, a technical instruments manufacturer may be organized around research and development, engineering, production, technical services, quality control, marketing, personnel, and finance and accounting. A hotel may have an organization based on front-desk operations, housekeeping, building maintenance, food service, convention services and special events, guest services, personnel and training, and accounting. A discount retailer may divide its organizational units into purchasing, warehousing and distribution, store operations, advertising, merchandising and promotion, customer service, and corporate administrative services. Functional and process organizational approaches are diagrammed in Figure 9–2.

Making specialized functions or processes the main organizational building blocks works well so long as strategy-critical activities closely match functional specialties and/or business processes, there's minimal need for interdepartmental coordination, and top-level management is able to short-circuit departmental rivalries and create a spirit of teamwork, trust, and internal cooperation. Departmental units having expertise in performing every facet of the activity is an attractive way (1) to exploit any learning/experience curve benefits or economy-of-scale opportunities of division of

---

[25]Rosabeth Moss Kanter, "Collaborative Advantage: The Art of the Alliance," *Harvard Business Review* 72, no. 4 (July–August 1994), pp. 105–06.

[26]For an excellent review of ways to effectively manage the relationship between alliance partners, see Kanter, *op. cit.*, pp. 96–108.

FIGURE 9-2 Functional and Process Organizational Structures

A. The Building Blocks of a "Typical" Functional Organizational Structure

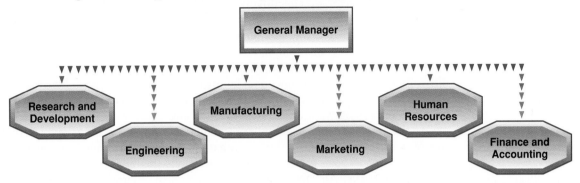

B. The Building Blocks of a Process-Oriented Structure

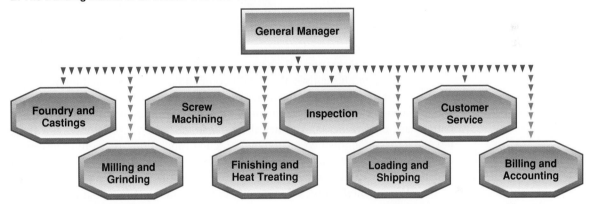

STRATEGIC ADVANTAGES	STRATEGIC DISADVANTAGES
• Centralized control of strategic results.	• Functional specialization is conducive to fragmentation of strategy-critical processes.
• Best suited for structuring a single business.	
• Well-suited to businesses where the strategy-critical value chain components consist of discipline-specific or process-oriented activities.	• Emphasis on functional specialization poses organizational barriers to creating cross-functional core competencies and to close collaboration across departmental lines.
• Promotes in-depth functional expertise.	• Can lead to interfunctional rivalry and conflict, rather than team-play and cooperation.
• Well suited to developing functional and/or process related skills and competencies.	
• Conducive to exploiting learning/experience curve effects associated with functional specialization or process specialization.	• Multilayered management bureaucracies and centralized decision-making slow response times.
	• Organizing around functional departments development of managers with cross-functional experience because the ladder of advancement is up the ranks within the same functional area.
• Enhances operating efficiency where tasks are routine and repetitive.	
• Can be a basis for competitive advantage when dominating depth in a function or process is a key success factor.	• Forces profit responsibility to the top.
	• Functional specialists often attach more importance to what's best for the functional area than to what's best for the whole business.
• Process organization provides a way to avoid fragmentation of strategy-critical activities across functional departments.	• Functional myopia often works against creative entrepreneurship and rapid adaptation to changing market circumstances.
	• Functional specialization poses barriers to creating cross-functional competencies and close departmental collaboration.

labor and the use of specialized technology and equipment and (2) to develop deep expertise in an important business function or process. When dominating depth in one or more functional specialties or business processes enhances operating efficiency and/or creates a competitively valuable competence, it becomes a basis for competitive advantage (lower cost or greater organizational capability).

The traditional functional structures that used to dominate single-business enterprises have three big shortcomings: excessive functional myopia, the potential for fragmentation of strategy-critical business processes across functional lines, and the difficulty of building cross-functional competencies and capabilities. Functional specialists are prone to focus inward on departmental matters and upward at their boss's priorities but not outward on the business, the customer, or the industry.[27] Members of functional departments usually have strong departmental loyalties and are protective of departmental interests. There's a natural tendency for each functional department to push for solutions and decisions that advance its well-being and influence. All this creates an organizational environment where functional departments operate as vertical silos or stovepipes and become a breeding ground for bureaucracies, empire building, authoritarian decision making, and narrow perspectives. In addition, the preoccupation of functional departments with developing deeper expertise and improving functional performance works against devising creative responses to major customer-market-technological changes; functional heads are often quick to oppose ideas or alternatives that aren't compatible with functional interests. Classical functional structures also worsen the problems of process fragmentation whenever a firm's value chain includes strategy-critical activities that, by their very nature, are cross-functional rather than discipline specific. Likewise, it's tough to develop cross-functional core competencies and capabilities in an environment dominated by strongly entrenched functional empires that don't "talk the same language" and that prefer to do their own thing without outside interference.

A big weakness of functional departments is that they are prone to develop strong functional mind-sets and approach strategic issues more from a functional than a business perspective.

Interdepartmental politics, functional empire building, functional myopia, process fragmentation, and a need to build cross-functional competencies and capabilities can impose a time-consuming administrative burden on the general manager, who is the only person on a functionally dominated organization chart with authority to contain rivalries and to enforce interdepartmental cooperation. In a functionally dominated structure, much of a GM's time and energy is spent keeping lines of communication open across departments, tempering departmental rivalries, convincing stovepipe thinkers of the merits of broader solutions, devising ways to secure cooperation, and working to mold desirable cross-functional core competencies and capabilities. To achieve the cross-functional coordination necessary for strategic success, a GM either has to (1) supplement the functional organization structure by creating process-complete departments to handle strategy-critical activities that cross functional lines or (2) be tough and uncompromising in insisting that functional department heads be team players and that functional specialists collaborate and cooperate.

Increasingly during the last decade, companies have found that rather than continuing to scatter related pieces of a business process across several functional departments and scrambling to integrate their efforts, it is better to reengineer the work effort and create process departments by pulling the people who performed the pieces in functional departments into a group that works together to perform the whole

---

[27]Hammer and Champy, *Reengineering the Corporation*, p. 28.

process.[28] This is what Bell Atlantic did in cutting through its bureaucratic procedures for connecting a telephone customer to its long-distance carrier.[29] In Bell
Atlantic's functional structure, when a business customer requested a connection
between its telephone system and a long-distance carrier for data services, the request
traveled from department to department, taking two to four weeks to complete all the
internal processing steps. In reengineering that process, Bell Atlantic pulled workers
doing the pieces of the process from the many functional departments and put them
on teams that, working together, could handle most customer requests in a matter of
days and sometimes hours. Because the work was recurring—similar customer
requests had to be processed daily—the teams were permanently grouped into a
process department. In the electronics industry where product life cycles are often
less than a year, companies have formed process departments charged with cutting
the time it takes to develop new technologies and get new products to market. Some
companies, however, have stopped short of creating process departments and, instead, either appointed process managers or interdisciplinary teams to oversee coordination of fragmented processes and strategy-critical activities. While the means of
unifying the performance of strategy-critical processes and activities has varied,
many companies have now incorporated some form of process organization to
counteract the weaknesses of a purely functional structure. The methods of reengineering fragmented processes and creating more process-complete work flows, as well
as the results that reengineering can produce, are presented in Illustration Capsule 32.

Geographic Forms of Organization   Organizing on the basis of geographic areas or
territories is a common structural form for enterprises operating in diverse geographic markets or serving an expansive geographic area. As Figure 9–3 indicates,
geographic organization has advantages and disadvantages, but the chief reason for
its popularity is that it promotes improved performance.

In the private sector, a territorial structure is typically used by discount retailers,
power companies, cement firms, restaurant chains, and dairy products enterprises. In
the public sector, such organizations as the Internal Revenue Service, the
Social Security Administration, the federal courts, the U.S. Postal Service,   *A geographic organization*
state troopers, and the Red Cross have adopted territorial structures in order   *structure is well-suited to firms*
to be directly accessible to geographically dispersed clienteles. Multina-   *pursuing different strategies in*
tional enterprises use geographic structures to manage the diversity they   *different geographic regions.*
encounter operating across national boundaries, often dividing into a do-
mestic division and an international division or, when international operations are quite large, dividing into divisions for each continent or major country.

Raymond Corey and Steven Star cite Pfizer International as a good example of a
company whose strategic requirements made geographic decentralization advantageous:

> Pfizer International operated plants in 27 countries and marketed in more than 100 coun-
> tries. Its product lines included pharmaceuticals (antibiotics and other ethical prescription
> drugs), agricultural and veterinary products (such as animal feed supplements and vaccines
> and pesticides), chemicals (fine chemicals, bulk pharmaceuticals, petrochemicals, and
> plastics), and consumer products (cosmetics and toiletries).

---

[28]Ibid., p. 66.
[29]Ibid., pp. 66–67.

ILLUSTRATION CAPSULE 32   Reengineering: How Companies Do It and the Results They Have Gotten

Reengineering strategy-critical business processes to reduce fragmentation across traditional departmental lines and cut bureaucratic overheads has proven to be a legitimate organization design tool. It's not a passing fad or another management program of the month. Process organization is every bit as valid an organizing principle as functional specialization. Strategy execution is improved when the pieces of strategy-critical activities and core business processes performed by different departments are properly integrated and coordinated.

Companies that have reengineered some of their business processes have ended up compressing formerly separate steps and tasks into jobs performed by a single person and integrating jobs into team activities. Reorganization then follows, a natural consequence of task synthesis and job redesign. The experiences of companies that have successfully reengineered and restructured their operations in strategy-supportive ways suggest attacking process fragmentation and overhead reduction in the following fashion:

- Develop a flow chart of the total business process, including its interfaces with other value-chain activities.

- Try to simplify the process first, eliminating tasks and steps where possible and analyzing how to streamline the performance of what remains.

- Determine which parts of the process can be automated (usually those that are repetitive, time-consuming, and require little thought or decision); consider introducing advanced technologies that can be upgraded to achieve next-generation capability and provide a basis for further productivity gains down the road.

- Reengineer, then reorganize.

- Evaluate each activity in the process to determine whether it is strategy-critical or not. Strategy-critical activities are candidates for benchmarking to achieve best-in-industry or best-in-world performance status.

- Weigh the pros and cons of outsourcing activities that are noncritical or that contribute little to organizational capabilities and core competencies.

- Design a structure for performing the activities that remain; reorganize the personnel and groups who perform these activities into the new structure.

Reengineering can produce dramatic gains in productivity and organizational capability when done properly. In the order-processing section of General Electric's circuit breaker division, elapsed time from order receipt to delivery was cut from three weeks to three days by consolidating six production units into one, reducing a variety of former inventory and handling steps, automating the design system to replace a human custom-design process, and cutting the organizational layers between managers and workers from three to one. Productivity rose 20 percent in one year, and unit manufacturing costs dropped 30 percent.

Northwest Water, a British utility, used reengineering to eliminate 45 work depots that served as home base to crews who installed and repaired water and sewage lines and equipment. Now crews work directly from their vehicles, receiving assignments and reporting work completion from computer terminals in their trucks. Crew members are no longer employees but contractors to Northwest Water. These reengineering efforts not only eliminated the need for the work depots but also allowed Northwest Water to eliminate a big percentage of the bureaucratic personnel and supervisory organization that managed the crews.

There's no escaping the conclusion that reengineering, in concert with electronic communication systems, empowerment, and the use of self-directed work teams, provides company managers with important new organization design options. Organizational hierarchies can be flattened and middle-management layers removed. Responsibility and decision-making authority can be pushed downward and outward to those places in the organization where customer contacts are made. Strategy-critical processes can be unified, performed more quickly and at lower cost, and made more responsive to changing customer preferences and expectations. Used properly, these new design approaches can trigger big gains in organizational creativity and employee productivity.

Sources: Based on information in James Brian Quinn, *Intelligent Enterprise* (New York: Free Press, 1992), p. 162; T. Stuart, "GE Keeps Those Ideas Coming," *Fortune*, August 12, 1991; Gene Hall, Jim Rosenthal, and Judy Wade, "How to Make Reengineering Really Work," *Harvard Business Review* 71, no. 6 (November–December 1993), pp. 119–31; and Ann Majchrzak and Qianwei Wang, "Breaking the Functional Mind-Set in Process Organizations," *Harvard Business Review* 74, no. 5 (September–October 1996), pp. 93–99.

FIGURE 9-3   A Representative Geographic Organizational Structure

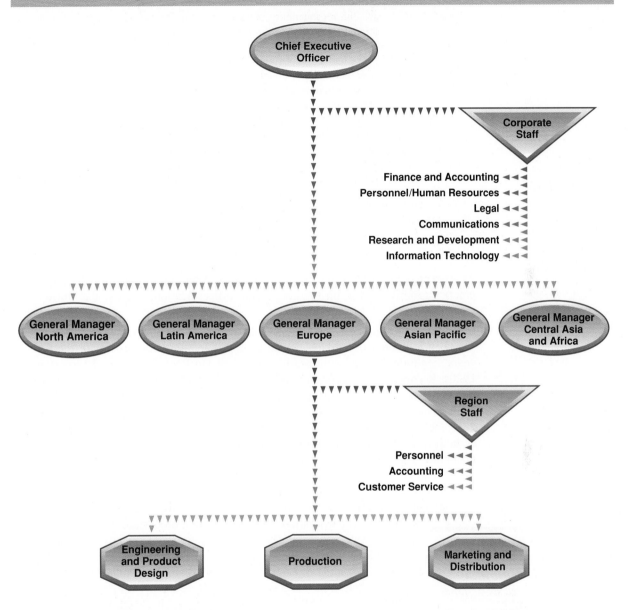

STRATEGIC ADVANTAGES

- Allows tailoring of strategy to needs of each geographical market.
- Delegates profit/loss responsibility to lowest strategic level.
- Improves functional coordination within the target market.
- Takes advantage of economies of local operations.
- Regional units make an excellent training ground for higher-level general managers.

STRATEGIC DISADVANTAGES

- Poses a problem of how much geographic uniformity headquarters should impose versus how much geographic diversity should be allowed.
- Greater difficulty in maintaining consistent company image/reputation from area to area when geographic managers exercise much strategic freedom.
- Adds another layer of management to run the geographic units.
- Can result in duplication of staff services at headquarters and geographic levels, creating a cost disadvantage.

Ten geographic Area Managers reported directly to the President of Pfizer International and exercised line supervision over Country Managers. According to a company position description, it was "the responsibility of each Area Manager to plan, develop, and carry out Pfizer International's business in the assigned foreign area in keeping with company policies and goals."

Country Managers had profit responsibility. In most cases a single Country Manager managed all Pfizer activities in his country. In some of the larger, well-developed countries of Europe there were separate Country Managers for pharmaceutical and agricultural products and for consumer lines.

Except for the fact that New York headquarters exercised control over the to-the-market prices of certain products, especially prices of widely used pharmaceuticals, Area and Country Managers had considerable autonomy in planning and managing the Pfizer International business in their respective geographic areas. This was appropriate because each area, and some countries within areas, provided unique market and regulatory environments. In the case of pharmaceuticals and agricultural and veterinary products (Pfizer International's most important lines), national laws affected formulations, dosages, labeling, distribution, and often price. Trade restrictions affected the flow of bulk pharmaceuticals and chemicals and packaged products, and might in effect require the establishment of manufacturing plants to supply local markets. Competition, too, varied significantly from area to area.[30]

At Andersen Consulting, the basic organizational building blocks are the individual practice groups making up the geographic offices scattered across the world.

Decentralized Business Units   Grouping activities along business and product lines has been a favored organizing device among diversified enterprises for the past 75 years, beginning with the pioneering efforts of Du Pont and General Motors in the 1920s. Separate business/product divisions emerged because diversification made a functionally specialized manager's job incredibly complex. Imagine the problems a manufacturing executive and his/her staff would have if put in charge of, say, 50 different plants using 20 different technologies to produce 30 different products in eight different businesses/industries. In a multibusiness enterprise, the practical organizational sequence is corporate to business to functional area within a business rather than corporate to functional area (aggregated for all businesses).

Thus while functional departments, process departments, and geographic divisions are the standard organizational building blocks in a single-business enterprise, in a multibusiness corporation the basic building blocks are the individual businesses.[31] Authority over each business unit is typically delegated to a business-level manager. The approach is to put entrepreneurial general managers in charge of each business unit, give them authority to formulate and implement a business strategy, motivate them with performance-based incentives, and hold them accountable for results. Each business unit then operates as a stand-alone profit center and is organized around whatever functional/process departments and geographic units suit the business's strategy, key activities, and operating requirements.

In a diversified firm, the basic organizational building blocks are its business units; each business is operated as a stand-alone profit center.

Fully independent business units, however, pose an obstacle to companies pursuing related diversification: *There is no mechanism for coordinating related activities across business units or for sharing/tranferring/developing mutually beneficial resource*

---

[30]Raymond Corey and Steven H. Star, *Organization Strategy: A Marketing Approach* (Boston: Harvard Business School, 1971), pp. 23–24.

[31]Over 90 percent of the *Fortune* 500 firms employ a business unit or divisional organizational structure.

strengths. As the label implies, divisions divide, creating potentially insulated units with barriers that inhibit sharing or building mutually beneficial resource strengths. It can be tough to get independent business units and autonomy-conscious business-unit managers to coordinate related activities and collaborate in ways that leverage resource strengths and enhance organizational capabilities. They are prone to argue about turf and resist being held accountable for activities outside their control.

To capture strategic-fit and resource-fit benefits in a diversified company, corporate headquarters must superimpose some internal organizational means of cutting across boundaries and coordinating related business-unit activities. One option is to centralize related functions at the corporate level—for example, set up a corporate R&D department (if there are technology and product development fits), create a special corporate sales force to call on customers who purchase from several of the company's business units, combine the dealer networks and sales force organizations of closely related businesses, merge the order processing and shipping functions of businesses with common customers, or consolidate the production of related components and products into fewer, more efficient plants. In addition, corporate officers can develop bonus arrangements that give business-unit managers strong incentives to work together. If the strategic-fit relationships involve skills or technology transfers across businesses, corporate headquarters can mandate the transfer of people with the requisite experience and know-how from one business to another or form interbusiness teams to open the flow of proprietary technology, managerial know-how, and related skills between businesses.

Strategic Management Principle

A decentralized business-unit structure can block success of a related diversification strategy unless specific organizational arrangements are devised to coordinate the related activities of related businesses.

A typical line-of-business organization structure is shown in Figure 9–4, along with the strategy-related pros and cons of this organizational form.

Strategic Business Units   In broadly diversified companies, the number of decentralized business units can be so great that the span of control is too much for a single chief executive. Then it may be useful to group related businesses and to delegate authority over them to a senior executive who reports directly to the chief executive officer. While this imposes a layer of management between business-level managers and the chief executive, it may nonetheless improve strategic planning and top-management coordination of diverse business interests. This explains both the popularity of the group vice president concept among multibusiness companies and the creation of strategic business units.

Basic Concept

A strategic business unit (SBU) is a grouping of related businesses under the supervision of a senior executive.

A *strategic business unit* (SBU) is a grouping of business subsidiaries based on important strategic elements common to all. The elements can be an overlapping set of competitors, closely related value chain activities, a common need to compete globally, emphasis on the same kind of competitive advantage (low cost or differentiation), common key success factors, or technologically related growth opportunities. At General Electric, a pioneer in the concept of SBUs, 190 businesses were grouped into 43 SBUs and then aggregated further into six "sectors."[32] At Union Carbide, 15 groups and divisions were decomposed into 150 "strategic planning units" and then regrouped and combined into 9 new "aggregate planning units." At General Foods, SBUs were

[32]William K. Hall, "SBUs: Hot, New Topic in the Management of Diversification," *Business Horizons* 21, no. 1 (February 1978), p. 19. For an excellent discussion of the problems of implementing the SBU concept at 13 companies, see Richard A. Bettis and William K. Hall, "The Business Portfolio Approach— Where It Falls Down in Practice," *Long Range Planning* 16, no. 2 (April 1983), pp. 95–104.

FIGURE 9-4   A Decentralized Line-of-Business Organization Structure

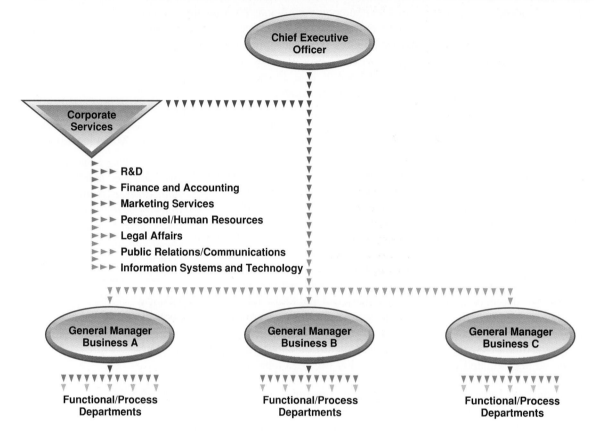

STRATEGIC ADVANTAGES

- Offers a logical and workable means of decentralizing responsibility and delegating authority in diversified organizations.

- Puts responsibility for crafting and implementing business strategy in closer proximity to each business's unique environment.

- Allows each business unit to organize around its own key value chain activities, business processes, and functional requirements.

- Frees CEO to handle corporate strategy issues.

- Puts clear profit/loss accountability on shoulders of business-unit managers.

STRATEGIC DISADVANTAGES

- May lead to costly duplication of staff functions at corporate and business-unit levels, thus raising administrative overhead costs.

- Poses a problem of what decisions to centralize and what decisions to decentralize (business managers need enough authority to get the job done, but not so much that corporate management loses control of key business-level decisions).

- May lead to excessive division rivalry for corporate resources and attention.

- Business/division autonomy works against achieving coordination of related activities in different business units, thus blocking to some extent the capture of strategic-fit and resource-fit benefits.

- Corporate management becomes heavily dependent on business-unit managers.

- Corporate managers can lose touch with business-unit situations, end up surprised when problems arise, and not know much about how to fix such problems.

originally defined on a product-line basis but were later redefined according to menu segments (breakfast foods, beverages, main meal products, desserts, and pet foods). SBUs make headquarters' reviews of the strategies of lower-level units less imposing (there is no practical way for a CEO to conduct in-depth reviews of a hundred or more different businesses). A CEO can, however, effectively review the strategic plans of a lesser number of SBUs, leaving detailed business strategy reviews and direct supervision of individual businesses to the SBU heads. Figure 9–5 illustrates the SBU form of organization, along with its strategy-related pros and cons.

The SBU concept provides broadly diversified companies with a way to rationalize the organization of many different businesses and a management arrangement for capturing strategic-fit benefits and streamlining strategic planning and budgeting processes. The strategic function of the group vice president is to provide the SBU with some cohesive direction, enforce coordination across related businesses, and keep an eye out for trouble at the business-unit level, providing counsel and support as needed. The group vice president, as coordinator for all businesses in the SBU, can promote resource sharing and skills/technology transfers where appropriate and unify the decisions and actions of businesses in the SBU. The SBU, in effect, becomes a strategy-making, strategy-implementing unit with a wider field of vision and operations than a single business unit. It serves as a broadly diversified company's mechanism for capturing strategic-fit benefits across businesses and adding to the competitive advantage that each business in the SBU is able to build on its own. Moreover, it affords opportunity to "cross-pollinate" the activities of separate businesses, ideally creating enough new capability to stretch a company's strategic reach into adjacent products, technologies, and markets.

> *SBU structures are a means for managing broad diversification and enforcing strategic coordination across related businesses.*

Matrix Forms of Organization

A matrix organization is a structure with two (or more) channels of command, two lines of budget authority, and two sources of performance and reward. The key feature of the matrix is that authority for a business/product/project/venture and authority for a function or business process are overlaid (to form a matrix or grid), and decision-making responsibility in each unit/cell of the matrix is shared between the business/project/venture team manager and the functional/process manager—as shown in Figure 9–6. In a matrix structure, subordinates have a *continuing dual assignment*: to the product line/project/business/venture and to their home-base function/process. The resulting structure is a compromise between organizing solely around functional/process specialization or around product line, project, line-of-business, or special venture divisions.

> *Matrix structures, although complex to manage and sometimes unwieldy, allow a firm to be organized in two different strategy-supportive ways at the same time.*

A matrix-type organization is a genuinely different structural form and represents a "new way of life." It breaks the unity-of-command principle; two reporting channels, two bosses, and shared authority create a new kind of climate. In essence, the matrix is a conflict-resolution system through which strategic and operating priorities are negotiated, power is shared, and resources are allocated on the basis of "strongest case" for what is best overall for the unit.[33]

---

[33]For two excellent critiques of matrix organizations, see Stanley M. Davis and Paul R. Lawrence, "Problems of Matrix Organizations," *Harvard Business Review* 56, no. 3 (May–June 1978), pp. 131–42, and Erik W. Larson and David H. Gobeli, "Matrix Management: Contradictions and Insights," *California Management Review* 29, no. 4 (Summer 1987), pp. 126–38.

FIGURE 9-5   An SBU Organization Structure

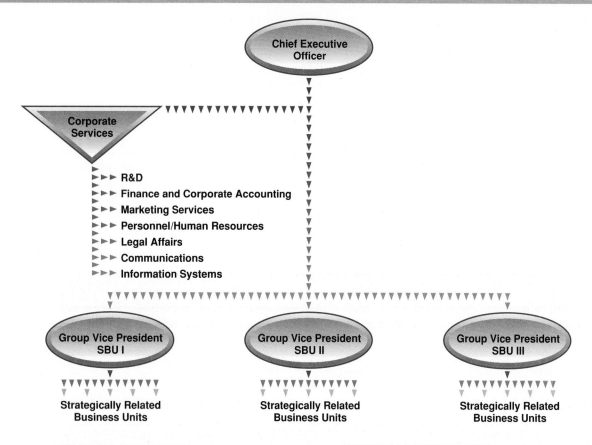

STRATEGIC ADVANTAGES

- Provides a strategically relevant way to organize the business-unit portfolio of a broadly diversified company.
- Facilitates the coordination of related activities within an SBU, thus helping to capture the benefits of strategic fits and resource fits among related businesses.
- Promotes more cohesiveness and collaboration among separate but related businesses.
- Allows strategic planning to be done at the most relevant level within the total enterprise.
- Makes the task of strategic review by top executives more objective and more effective.
- Helps allocate corporate resources to areas with greatest growth and profit opportunities.
- Group VP position is a good training ground for future CEOs.

STRATEGIC DISADVANTAGES

- It is easy for the definition and grouping of businesses into SBUs to be so arbitrary that the SBU serves no other purpose than administrative convenience. If the criteria for defining SBUs are rationalizations and have little to do with the nitty-gritty of strategy coordination, then the groupings lose real strategic significance.
- The SBUs can still be myopic in charting their future direction.
- Adds another layer to top management.
- The roles and authority of the CEO, the group vice president, and the business-unit manager have to be carefully worked out or the group vice president gets trapped in the middle with ill-defined authority.
- Unless the SBU head is strong willed, very little strategy coordination or collaboration is likely to occur across business units in the SBU.
- Performance recognition gets blurred; credit for successful business units tends to go to corporate CEO, then to business-unit head, last to group vice president.

FIGURE 9-6   A Matrix Organization Structure

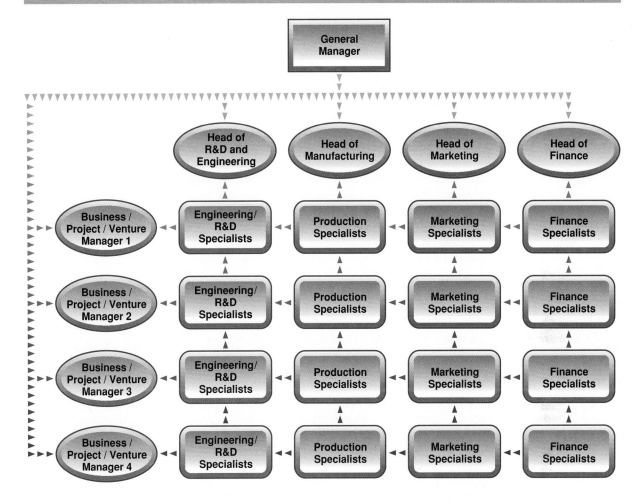

STRATEGIC ADVANTAGES

- Gives formal attention to each dimension of strategic priority.
- Creates checks and balances among competing viewpoints.
- Facilitates capture of functionally based strategic fits in diversified companies.
- Promotes making trade-off decisions on the basis of "what's best for the organization as a whole."
- Encourages cooperation, consensus-building, conflict resolution, and coordination of related activities.

STRATEGIC DISADVANTAGES

- Very complex to manage.
- Hard to maintain "balance" between the two lines of authority.
- So much shared authority can result in a transactions logjam and disproportionate amounts of time being spent on communications, consensus building, and collaboration.
- It is hard to move quickly and decisively without checking with or getting clearance from many other people.
- Promotes organizational bureaucracy and hamstrings creative entrepreneurship and initiative.
- Works at cross purposes with efforts to empower down-the-line managers and employees.

The impetus for matrix organizations stems from growing use of strategies that create a simultaneous need for process teams, special project managers, product managers, functional managers, geographic area managers, new-venture managers, and business-level managers—all of whom have important responsibilities. When at least two of several variables (product, customer, technology, geography, functional area, business process, and market segment) have roughly equal priorities, a matrix organization can be an effective structural form. A matrix structure promotes internal checks and balances among competing viewpoints and perspectives, with separate managers for different dimensions of strategic initiative. A matrix arrangement thus allows each of several strategic considerations to be managed directly and to be formally represented in the organization structure. In this sense, it helps middle managers make trade-off decisions from an organizationwide perspective.[34] The other big advantage of matrix organization is that it can help capture strategic fit. When the strategic fits in a diversified company are related to a specific functional area (R&D, technology, marketing), or cross traditional functional lines, matrix organization can be a reasonable structural arrangement for coordinating activity sharing and skills transfer. Companies using matrix structures include General Electric, Texas Instruments, Citibank, Shell Oil, TRW, Bechtel, Boeing, and Dow Chemical. Illustration Capsule 33 describes how one broadly diversified company with global strategies in each of its businesses developed a matrix structure to manage its operations worldwide. However, in most companies, use of matrix organization is confined to a *portion* of what the firm does rather than its whole organizing scheme.

Many companies and managers shun matrix organization because of its chief weaknesses.[35] It is a complex structure to manage; people end up confused or frustrated over who to report to for what. Working relationships among different organizational units become more complicated. Moreover, because the matrix signals a need for communication and consensus, a "transactions logjam" can result. People in one area are pushed into transacting business with people in another area and networking their way through bureaucracies. Action turns into paralysis since, with shared authority, it is hard to move decisively without first checking with other people and getting clearance. Much time and psychic energy get eaten up in meetings and communicating back and forth. Sizable transactions costs and longer decision times can result with little value-added work accomplished. Even so, in some situations the benefits of conflict resolution, consensus building, and coordination outweigh these weaknesses, as the ABB example in Illustration Capsule 33 indicates.

Supplementing the Basic Organization Structure   None of the basic structural designs is wholly adequate for organizing the total work effort in strategy-supportive ways. Some weaknesses can be corrected by using two or more of the structural designs simultaneously—many companies are large enough and diverse enough to have SBUs, business units with functional and/or process departments, geographic organizational structures in one or more businesses, and units employing matrix principles. But in many companies strategy-supportive organization requires supplementing the formal structure with special coordinating mechanisms and efforts to build

[34]Davis and Lawrence, "Problems of Matrix Organizations," p. 132.
[35]Thomas J. Peters and Robert H. Waterman, Jr., *In Search of Excellence* (New York: Harper & Row, 1982), pp. 306–7.

ILLUSTRATION CAPSULE 33   Matrix Organization in a Diversified Global Company: The Case of Asea Brown Boveri

Asea Brown Boveri (ABB) is a diversified multinational corporation headquartered in Zurich, Switzerland. ABB was formed in 1987 through the merger of Asea, one of Sweden's largest industrial enterprises, and Brown Boveri, a major Swiss company. Both companies manufactured electrical products and equipment. Following the merger, ABB acquired or took minority positions in 60 companies, mostly outside Europe. In 1996 ABB had annual revenues of $34 billion and employed 210,000 people around the world, including 130,000 in Western Europe, 30,000 in North America, 10,000 in South America, and 10,000 in India. The company was a world leader in the global markets for electrical products, electrical installations and service, and power-generation equipment and was the dominant European producer. European sales accounted for 60 percent of revenues, while North America accounted for 30 percent and Asia 15 percent.

To manage its global operations, ABB had devised a matrix organization that leveraged its core competencies in electrical-power technologies and its ability to achieve global economies of scale while, at the same time, maximizing its national market visibility and responsiveness. At the top of ABB's corporate organization structure was an executive committee composed of the CEO and 12 colleagues; the committee consisted of Swedes, Swiss, Germans, and Americans, several of whom were based outside Switzerland. The group, which met every three weeks at various locations around the world, was responsible for ABB's corporate strategy and performance.

Along one dimension of ABB's global matrix were 50 or so business areas (BAs), each representing a closely related set of products and services. The BAs were grouped into eight "business segments"; each segment was supervised by a different member of the executive committee. Each BA had a leader charged with responsibility for (1) devising and championing a global strategy, (2) setting quality and cost standards for the BA's factories worldwide, (3) deciding which factories would export to which country markets, (4) rotating people across borders to share technical expertise, create mixed-nationality teams to solve BA problems, and build a culture of trust and communication, and (5) pooling expertise and research funds for the benefit of the BA worldwide. BA leaders worked out of whatever world location made the most sense for their BA.

Along the other dimension of the matrix was a group of national enterprises with presidents, boards of directors, financial statements, and career ladders. The presidents of ABB's national enterprises had responsibility for maximizing the performance and effectiveness of all ABB activities within their country's borders. Country presidents worked closely with the BA leaders to evaluate and improve what was happening in ABB's business areas in their countries.

Inside the matrix were 1,300 "local" ABB companies with an average of 200 employees, each headed by a president. The local company president reported both to the national president in whose country the local company operated and to the leader of the BA to which its products/services were assigned. Each local company was a subsidiary of the ABB national enterprise where it was located. Thus, all of ABB's local companies in Norway were subsidiaries of ABB Norway, the national company for Norway; all ABB operations in Portugal were subsidiaries of ABB Portugal, and so on. The 1,300 presidents of ABB's local companies were expected to be excellent profit center managers, able to answer to two bosses effectively. The local president's global boss was the BA manager who established the local company's role in ABB's global strategy and, also, the rules a local company had to observe in supporting this strategy. The local president's country boss was the national CEO, with whom it was necessary to cooperate on local issues.

ABB believed that its matrix structure allowed it to optimize its pursuit of global business strategies and, at the same time, maximize its performance in every country market where it operated. The matrix was a way of being global and big strategically, yet small and local operationally. Decision making was decentralized (to BA leaders, country presidents, and local company presidents), but reporting and control was centralized (through the BA leaders, the country presidents, and the executive committee). ABB saw itself as a federation of national companies with a global coordination center.

Only about 100 professionals were located in ABB's corporate headquarters in Zurich. A management information system collected data on all profit centers monthly, comparing actual performance against budgets and forecasts. Data was collected in local currencies but translated into U.S. dollars to allow for cross-border analysis. ABB's corporate financial statements were reported in U.S. dollars, and English was ABB's official language. All high-level meetings were conducted in English.

Source: Compiled from information in William Taylor, "The Logic of Global Business: An Interview with ABB's Percy Barnevik," *Harvard Business Review* 69, no. 2 (March–April 1991), pp. 90–105 and company annual reports.

organizational capabilities. Seven of the most frequently used devices for supplementing the basic building block structure are:

- *Special project teams*—creating a separate, largely self-sufficient work group to oversee the completion of a special activity (setting up a new technological process, bringing out a new product, starting up a new venture, merging with another company, seeing through the completion of a government contract, supervising the construction and opening of a new plant). Project teams are especially suitable for short-term, one-of-a-kind situations when the normal organization is not equipped to achieve the same results in addition to regular duties. (At 3M Corp. project teams are the basic organizational building blocks for the company's 3,900 profit centers.)

- *Cross-functional task forces*—bringing a number of top-level executives and/or specialists together to solve problems requiring specialized expertise from several parts of the organization, coordinating strategy-related activities that span departmental boundaries, or exploring ways to leverage the skills of different functional specialists into broader core competencies. Task forces seem to be most effective when they have fewer than 10 members, membership is voluntary, the seniority of the members is proportional to the importance of the problem, the task force moves swiftly to deal with its assignment, they are used sparingly, no staff is assigned, and documentation is scant.[36] Companies that have used task forces successfully form them to solve pressing problems, produce some solutions efficiently, and then disband them.

- *Venture teams*—forming a group of individuals to manage the launch of a new product, entry into a new geographic market, or creation of a specific new business. Dow, General Mills, Westinghouse, General Electric, and Monsanto used the venture-team approach to renew an entrepreneurial spirit. The difficulties with venture teams include deciding who the venture manager should report to; whether funding for ventures should come from corporate, business, or departmental budgets; how to keep the venture clear of bureaucratic and vested interests; and how to coordinate large numbers of different ventures.

- *Self-contained work teams*—forming a group of people drawn from different disciplines who work together on a semipermanent basis to continuously improve organizational performance in such strategy-related areas as shortening the lab-to-market cycle time, boosting product quality, improving customer service, cutting delivery times, eliminating stockouts, reducing the costs of purchased materials and components, increasing assembly-line productivity, trimming equipment downtime and maintenance expenses, or designing new models. American Express cut out three layers of hierarchy when it developed self-managed teams to handle all types of customer inquiries in a single-call, quick-resolution manner.[37]

- *Process teams*—putting functional specialists who perform pieces of a business process together on a team instead of assigning them to their home-base functional department. Such teams can be empowered to reengineer the process, held accountable for results, and rewarded on the

---

[36]Ibid., pp. 127–32.

[37]Quinn, *Intelligent Enterprise*, p. 163.

basis of how well the process is performed. Much of Chrysler's revitalization is due to dramatically revamping its new-model development process using "platform teams."[38] Each platform team consists of members from engineering, design, finance, purchasing, and marketing. The team is responsible for the car's design from beginning to end, has broad decision-making power, and is held accountable for the success or failure of their design. Teams coordinate their designs with manufacturing so that the models will be easier to build and consult regularly with purchasing agents about parts quality. In one case Chrysler purchasing agents elected to pay 30 percent more for a better part because the engineer on the platform team believed the added cost would be offset by the time saved during assembly.

- *Contact managers*—appointing someone to serve as a single point of contact for customers when customer-related activities are so multi-faceted that integrating them for a single person or team to perform is impractical.[39] Acting as a buffer between internal processes and the customer, the contact person answers customer questions and coordinates the solutions to customer problems as if he or she were responsible for performing the called-for activities. To perform this role, contact persons need access to all the information that the persons actually performing the activities use and the ability to contact those people with questions and requests for further assistance when necessary. The best results are achieved when contact persons are empowered to use their own judgment to get things done in a manner that will please customers. Duke Power, a Charlotte-based electric utility, uses empowered customer service representatives to resolve the problems of residential customers while shielding them from whatever goes on "behind the scenes" to produce solutions.

- *Relationship managers*—appointing people who have responsibility for orchestrating and integrating company efforts to build strong working relationships with allies and strategic partners. Relationship managers have many roles and functions: getting the right people together, promoting good rapport, seeing that plans for specific activities are developed and carried out, helping adjust procedures to link the partners better and iron out operating dissimilarities, and nurturing interpersonal ties. Lines of communication have to be established and kept open, with enough information sharing to make the relationship work and frank discussion of conflicts, trouble spots, and changing situations.

Organizational capabilities emerge from effectively coordinating and networking the efforts of different work groups, departments, and external allies, not from how the boxes on the organization chart are arranged.

The ways of developing stronger core competencies and organizational capabilities (or creating altogether new ones) are much more idiosyncratic. Not only do different companies and executives tackle the challenge in different ways but different capabilities require different organizing techniques. Thus generalizing about *how* to build capabilities is misleading. Suffice it to say here that it entails *a process of consciously knitting the efforts of individuals and groups together* and that it is a task senior management must lead and be deeply involved in. Effectively managing both internal processes and external bridge-building with partners to create and develop valuable

---

[38]"Can Jack Smith Fix GM?" *Business Week*, November 1, 1993, pp. 130–31.

[39]Hammer and Champy, *Reengineering the Corporation*, pp. 62–63.

competencies and capabilities ranks very high on the "things to do" list of senior executives in today's companies.

Perspectives on Organizing the Work Effort and Building Capabilities   All the basic building block designs have their strengths and weaknesses. To do a good job of matching structure to strategy, strategy implementers have to pick a basic design, modify it as needed to fit the company's business makeup, and then supplement it with coordinating mechanisms and communication arrangements to support execution of the firm's strategy. Building core competencies and competitive capabilities is a *process* that nearly always involves close collaboration between individuals and groups in different departments and between a company and its external allies—they emerge from establishing and nurturing cooperative working relationships among people and groups to perform activities in a more customer-satisfying fashion, not from rearranging boxes on an organization chart. While companies may not set up "ideal" organizational arrangements in order to avoid disturbing certain existing reporting relationships or to accommodate the personalities of certain individuals involved, internal politics, and other idiosyncracies, the goal of building a competitively capable organization usually is predominant in considering how to set up the organization chart.

> *There's no perfect or ideal organization structure.*

ORGANIZATIONAL STRUCTURES OF THE FUTURE

Many of today's companies are winding up the task of remodeling their traditional hierarchical structures once built around functional specialization and centralized authority. Such structures still make good strategic and organizational sense so long as (1) activities can be divided into simple, repeatable tasks that can be mastered quickly and then efficiently performed in mass quantity, (2) there are important benefits to deep functional expertise in each managerial discipline, and (3) customer needs are sufficiently standardized that it is easy to prescribe procedures for satisfying them. But traditional hierarchies are a liability in businesses where customer preferences are shifting from standardized products to custom orders and special features, product life cycles are growing shorter, custom mass-production methods are replacing standardized mass production techniques, customers want to be treated as individuals, the pace of technological change is accelerating, and market conditions are fluid. Multilayered management hierarchies and functionalized bureaucracies that require people to look upward in the organizational structure for answers tend to bog down in such environments. They can't deliver responsive customer service or adapt fast enough to changing conditions. Functional silos, task-oriented work, process fragmentation, layered management hierarchies, centralized decision making, big functional and middle-management bureaucracies, lots of checks and controls, and long response times undermine competitive success in fluid or volatile environments. Success in fast-changing markets depends on strategies built around such valuable competencies and organizational capabilities as quick response to shifting customer preferences, short design-to-market cycles, make-it-right-the-first-time quality, custom-order and multiversion production, expedited delivery, personalized customer service, accurate order filling, rapid assimilation of new technologies, creativity and innovativeness, and speedy reactions to external competitive developments.

> *During the past decade, new strategic priorities and rapidly shifting competitive conditions have triggered revolutionary changes in how companies are organizing the work effort.*

These new components of business strategy have been driving a revolution in corporate organization for the past decade.[40] Much of the corporate downsizing movement was and is aimed at busting up functional and middle-management bureaucracies and recasting authoritarian pyramidal organizational structures into flatter, decentralized structures. The latest organizational designs for matching structure to strategy feature fewer layers of management authority, small-scale business units, reengineered work processes to cut back on fragmentation across functional department lines,[41] the development of stronger competencies and organizational capabilities and the creation of new ones as needed, collaborative partnerships with outsiders, empowerment of firstline supervisors and nonmanagement employees, lean staffing of corporate support functions, open communications vertically and laterally (via e-mail), computers and telecommunications technologies to provide fast access to and dissemination of information, and accountability for results rather than emphasis on activity. The new organizational themes are lean, flat, agile, responsive, and innovative. The new tools of organizational design are managers and workers empowered to act on their own judgments, reengineered work processes, self-directed work teams, and networking with outsiders to improve existing organizational capabilities and create new ones. The new organization-building challenge is to outcompete rivals on the basis of superior organizational capabilities and resource strengths.

The command-and-control paradigm of vertically layered structures assumes that the people actually performing work have neither the time nor the inclination to monitor and control it and that they lack the knowledge to make informed decisions about how best to do it; hence, the need for prescribed procedures, close supervision, and managerial control of decision making. In flat, decentralized structures, the assumptions are that people closest to the scene are capable of making timely, responsible decisions when properly trained and when provided with access to the needed information. There is a strong belief that decentralized decision making shortens response times and spurs new ideas, creative thinking, innovation, and greater involvement on the part of subordinate managers and employees. Hence, jobs are defined more broadly; several tasks are integrated into a single job where possible. People operate in a more self-directed fashion. Decision-making authority is pushed down to the lowest level capable of taking competent, responsible action in a timely fashion. Fewer managers are needed because deciding how to do things becomes part of each person's or team's job and because electronic technology makes information readily available and communications instantaneous.

The organizations of the future will have several new characteristics:

- Fewer boundaries between different vertical ranks, between functions and disciplines, between units in different geographic locations, and between the company and its suppliers, distributors/dealers, strategic allies, and customers.

---

[40]Evidence to this effect is contained in the scores of examples reported in Tom Peters, *Liberation Management* (New York: Alfred A. Knopf, 1992); Quinn, *Intelligent Enterprise;* and Hammer and Champy, *Reengineering the Corporation.*

[41]However, it sometimes takes more than reengineering and process organization structures to eliminate the old functional mind-sets of employees; in particular, managers also have to work at instilling a collaborative culture and fostering a collective sense of responsibility among the members of the process team. Collective responsibility can be ingrained by basing rewards on group performance, rotating assignments among the process team members, holding periodic unitwide meetings to discuss process improvements, and designing process procedures that promote a high degree of collaboration among employees doing different pieces of the process. See Ann Majchrzak and Qianwei Wang, "Breaking the Functional Mind-set in Process Organizations," *Harvard Business Review* 74, no. 5 (September–October 1996), pp. 93–99.

ILLUSTRATION CAPSULE 34   Organizational Approaches for International and Global Markets

A 1993 study of 43 large U.S.-based consumer products companies conducted by McKinsey & Co., a leading management consulting firm, identified internal organizational actions with the strongest and weakest links to rapidly growing sales and profits in international and global markets.

Organizational Actions Strongly Linked to International Success

- Centralizing international decision making in every area except new product development.
- Having a worldwide management development program and more foreigners in senior management posts.
- Requiring international experience for advancement into top management.
- Linking global managers with videoconferencing and electronic mail.
- Having product managers of foreign subsidiaries report to a country general manager.
- Using local executives to head operations in foreign countries (however, this is rapidly ceasing to distinguish successful companies

because nearly everyone has implemented such a practice).

Organizational Actions Weakly Linked to International Success

- Creating global divisions.
- Forming international strategic business units.
- Establishing centers of excellence (where a single company facility takes global responsibility for a key product or emerging technology (too new to evaluate pro or con).
- Using cross-border task forces to resolve problems and issues.
- Creating globally-integrated management information systems.

However, the lists of organizational dos and don'ts are far from decisive. In general, the study found that internal organizational structure "doesn't matter that much" as compared to having products with attractive prices and features. It is wrong to expect good results just because of good organization. Moreover, certain organizational arrangements, such as centers of excellence, are too new to determine whether they positively affect sales and profit growth.

Source: Based on information reported by Joann S. Lublin, "Study Sees U.S. Businesses Stumbling on the Road to Globalization," *The Wall Street Journal*, March 22, 1993, p. B4B.

- A capacity for change and rapid learning.
- Collaborative efforts among people in different functional specialities and geographic locations—essential to create organization competencies and capabilities.
- Extensive use of digital technology—personal computers, wireless telephones, videoconferencing, and other state-of-the-art electronic products.

Illustration Capsule 34 reports the results of a study of trends in organizational arrangements in multinational and global companies.

KEY POINTS

The job of strategy implementation is to convert strategic plans into actions and good results. The test of successful strategy implementation is whether actual organization performance matches or exceeds the targets spelled out in the strategic plan. Shortfalls in performance signal weak strategy, weak implementation, or both.

In deciding how to implement strategy, managers have to determine what internal conditions are needed to execute the strategic plan successfully. Then they must create these conditions as rapidly as practical. The process of implementing and executing strategy involves

- Building an organization with the competencies, capabilities, and resource strengths to carry out the strategy successfully.

- Developing budgets to steer ample resources into those value chain activities critical to strategic success.
- Establishing strategy-supportive policies and procedures.
- Instituting best practices and pushing for continuous improvement in how value chain activities are performed.
- Installing information, communication, and operating systems that enable company personnel to carry out their strategic roles successfully day in and day out.
- Tying rewards and incentives to the achievement of performance objectives and good strategy execution.
- Creating a strategy-supportive work environment and corporate culture.
- Exerting the internal leadership needed to drive implementation forward and to keep improving on how the strategy is being executed.

The strategy-implementing challenge is to create a series of tight fits (1) between strategy and the organization's competencies, capabilities, and structure, (2) between strategy and budgetary allocations, (3) between strategy and policy, (4) between strategy and internal support systems, (5) between strategy and the reward structure, and (6) between strategy and the corporate culture. The tighter the fits, the more powerful strategy execution becomes and the more likely targeted performance can actually be achieved.

Implementing strategy is not just a top-management function; it is a job for the whole management team. *All managers function as strategy implementers* in their respective areas of authority and responsibility. *All managers* have to consider what actions to take in their areas to achieve the intended results—they each need an action agenda.

The three major organization-building actions are (1) filling key positions with able people, (2) building the core competencies, resource strengths, and organizational capabilities needed to perform its value chain activities proficiently, and (3) structuring the internal work effort and melding it with the collaborative efforts of strategic allies. Selecting able people for key positions tends to be one of the earliest strategy implementation steps because it takes a full complement of capable managers to get changes in place and functioning smoothly.

Building strategy-critical core competencies and competitive capabilities not easily imitated by rivals is one of the best ways to outexecute rivals with similar strategies and gain a competitive advantage. Core competencies emerge from skills and activities performed at different points in the value chain that, when linked, create unique organizational capability. The key to leveraging a company's core competencies into long-term competitive advantage is to concentrate more effort and more talent than rivals do on strengthening and deepening organizational competencies and capabilities. The multiskill, multiactivity character of core competencies and capabilities makes achieving dominating depth an exercise in (1) managing human skills, knowledge bases, and intellect and (2) coordinating and networking the efforts of different work groups, departments, and collaborative allies. It is a task that senior management must lead and be deeply involved in chiefly because it is senior managers who are in the best position to guide and enforce the necessary networking and cooperation among individuals, groups, departments, and external allies.

Building organizational capabilities is more than just an effort to strengthen what a company already does, however. There are times when management has to be *proactive* in developing *new* competencies and capabilities to complement the company's existing resource base and promote more proficient strategy execution. It is useful here to think of companies as a bundle of evolving competencies and capabilities, with the organization-building challenge being one of developing new capabilities and strengthening existing ones in a fashion calculated to achieve competitive advantage through superior strategy execution.

One capability-building issue is whether to develop the desired competencies and capabilities internally or whether it makes more sense to outsource them by partnering with key suppliers or forming strategic alliances. Decisions about whether to outsource or develop in-house capability often turn on the issues of (1) what can be safely delegated to outside suppliers versus what internal capabilities are key to the company's long-term success and (2) whether noncritical activities can be outsourced more effectively or efficiently than they can be performed internally. Either way, though, implementation actions are called for. Outsourcing means launching initiatives to identify the most attractive providers and to establish collaborative relationships. Developing the capabilities in-house means hiring new personnel with skills and experience relevant to the desired organizational competence/capability, then linking the individual skills/know-how to form organizational capability.

Matching structure to strategy centers around making strategy-critical activities the main organizational building blocks, finding effective ways to bridge organizational lines of authority and coordinate the related efforts of separate internal units and individuals, and effectively networking the efforts of internal units and external collaborative partners. Other big considerations include what decisions to centralize and what decisions to decentralize.

All organization structures have strategic advantages and disadvantages; *there is no one best way to organize*. Functionally specialized organization structures have *traditionally* been the most popular way to organize single-business companies. Functional organization works well where strategy-critical activities closely match discipline-specific activities and minimal interdepartmental cooperation is needed. But it has significant drawbacks: functional myopia and empire building, interdepartmental rivalries, excessive process fragmentation, and vertically layered management hierarchies. In recent years, process organization has been used to circumvent many of the disadvantages of functional organization.

Geographic organization structures are favored by enterprises operating in diverse geographic markets or across expansive geographic areas. SBU structures are well-suited to companies pursuing related diversification. Decentralized business-unit structures are well-suited to companies pursuing unrelated diversification. Matrix structures work well for companies that need separate lines of authority and managers for each of several strategic dimensions (products, buyer segments, functional departments, projects or ventures, technologies, core business processes, geographic areas) yet also need close cooperation between these managers to coordinate related value chain activities, share or transfer skills, and perform certain related activities jointly.

Whatever formal organization structure is chosen, it usually has to be supplemented with interdisciplinary task forces, incentive compensation schemes tied to measures of joint performance, empowerment of cross-functional teams to perform and unify fragmented processes and strategy-critical activities, special project and venture teams, self-contained work teams, contact managers, relationship managers, and special efforts to knit the work of different individuals and groups into valuable competitive capabilities. Building core competencies and competitive capabilities emerge from establishing and nurturing collaborative working relationships between individuals and groups in different departments and between a company and its external allies, not from how the boxes are arranged on an organization chart.

New strategic priorities like short design-to-market cycles, multiversion production, and personalized customer service are promoting a revolution in organization building featuring lean, flat, horizontal structures that are responsive and innovative. Such designs for matching structure to strategy involve fewer layers of management authority, small-scale business units, reengineering work processes to reduce fragmentation across departmental lines, the creation of process departments and cross-functional work groups, managers and workers empowered to act on their own judgments, collaborative partnerships with outsiders (suppliers, distributors/dealers, companies with complementary products/services, and even select competitors), increased outsourcing of noncritical activities, lean staffing of internal support functions, and use of computers and telecommunications technologies to provide fast access to information.

SUGGESTED READINGS

Aaker, David A. "Managing Assets and Skills: The Key to a Sustainable Competitive Advantage." *California Management Review* 31 (Winter 1989), pp. 91–106.

Bartlett, Christopher A., and Sumantra Ghoshal. "Matrix Management: Not a Structure, a Frame of Mind." *Harvard Business Review* 68, no. 4 (July–August 1990), pp. 138–45.

Hall, Gene, Jim Rosenthal, and Judy Wade. "How to Make Reengineering Really Work." *Harvard Business Review* 71, no. 6 (November–December 1993), pp. 119–31.

Hambrick, Donald C. "The Top Management Team: Key to Strategic Success." *California Management Review* 30, no. 1 (Fall 1987), pp. 88–108.

Hammer, Michael, and James Champy. *Reengineering the Corporation*. New York: HarperBusiness, 1993, chaps. 2 and 3.

Howard, Robert. "The CEO as Organizational Architect: An Interview with Xerox's Paul Allaire." *Harvard Business Review* 70, no. 5 (September–October 1992), pp. 107–19.

Kanter, Rosabeth Moss. "Collaborative Advantage: The Art of the Alliance." *Harvard Business Review* 72, no. 4 (July–August 1994), pp. 96–108.

Katzenbach, Jon R., and Douglas K. Smith. "The Discipline of Teams." *Harvard Business Review* 71, no. 2 (March–April 1993), pp. 111–24.

Larson, Erik W., and David H. Gobeli. "Matrix Management: Contradictions and Insights." *California Management Review* 29, no. 4 (Summer 1987), pp. 126–27.

Markides, Constantinos C. and Peter J. Williamson. "Corporate Diversification and Organizational Structure: A Resource-Based View." *Academy of Management Journal* 39, no. 2 (April 1996), pp. 340–67.

Pfeffer, Jeffrey. "Producing Sustainable Competitive Advantage through the Effective Management of People." *Academy of Management Executive* 9, no. 1 (February 1995), pp. 55–69.

Powell, Walter W. "Hybrid Organizational Arrangements: New Form or Transitional Development?" *California Management Review* 30, no. 1 (Fall 1987), pp. 67–87.

Prahalad, C. K., and Gary Hamel. "The Core Competence of the Corporation." *Harvard Business Review* 68 (May–June 1990), pp. 79–93.

Rackham, Neil, Lawrence Friedman, and Richard Ruff. *Getting Partnering Right: How Market Leaders Are Creating Long-Term Competitive Advantage*. New York: McGraw-Hill, 1996.

Quinn, James Brian. *Intelligent Enterprise*. New York: Free Press, 1992, chaps. 2 and 3.

Stalk, George, Philip Evans, and Lawrence E. Shulman. "Competing on Capabilities: The New Rules of Corporate Strategy." *Harvard Business Review* 70, no. 2 (March–April 1992), pp. 57–69.

Yip, George S. *Total Global Strategy: Managing for Worldwide Competitive Advantage*. Englewood Cliffs, N.J.: Prentice-Hall, 1992, chap. 8.

10 IMPLEMENTING STRATEGY: BUDGETS, POLICIES, BEST PRACTICES, SUPPORT SYSTEMS, AND REWARDS

I n the previous chapter we emphasized the importance of building organization capabilities and structuring the work effort so as to perform strategy-critical activities in a coordinated and competent manner. In this chapter we discuss five additional strategy-implementing tasks:

1. Reallocating resources to match the budgetary and staffing requirements of the new strategy.
2. Establishing strategy-supportive policies and procedures.
3. Instituting best practices and mechanisms for continuous improvement.
4. Installing support systems that enable company personnel to carry out their strategic roles day in and day out.
5. Employing motivational practices and incentive compensation methods that enhance commitment to good strategy execution.

LINKING BUDGETS TO STRATEGY

Implementing strategy forces a manager into the budget-making process. Organizational units need big enough budgets to carry out their parts of the strategic plan. There has to be ample funding of efforts to strengthen existing competencies and capabilities and/or to develop new ones. Organizational units, especially those charged with performing strategy-critical activities, have to be staffed with enough of the right kinds of people, be given enough operating funds to do their work proficiently, and have the funds to invest in

. . . Winning companies know how to do their work better.

Michael Hammer and James Champy

If you talk about change but don't change the reward and recognition system, nothing changes.

Paul Allaire
CEO, Xerox Corporation

If you want people motivated to do a good job, give them a good job to do.

Frederick Herzberg

. . . You ought to pay big bonuses for premier performance . . . be a top payer, not in the middle or low end of the pack.

Lawrence Bossidy
CEO, AlliedSignal

needed operating systems, equipment, and facilities. Strategy implementers must screen subordinates' requests for new capital projects and bigger operating budgets, distinguishing between what would be nice and what can make a cost-effective contribution to strategy execution and enhanced competitive capabilities. Moreover, implementers have to make a persuasive, documented case to superiors on what additional resources and competitive assets, if any, it will take to execute their assigned pieces of company strategy.

How well a strategy implementer links budget allocations to the needs of strategy can either promote or impede the implementation process. Too little funding slows progress and impedes the ability of organizational units to execute their pieces of the strategic plan. Too much funding wastes organizational resources and reduces financial performance. Both outcomes argue for the strategy implementer to be deeply involved in the budgeting process, closely reviewing the programs and budget proposals of strategy-critical organization units.

Implementers must also be willing to shift resources from one area to another to support new strategic initiatives and priorities. A change in strategy nearly always calls for budget reallocations. Units important in the old strategy may now be oversized and overfunded. Units that now have a bigger and more critical role may need more people, different support systems, new equipment, additional facilities, and above-average increases in their operating budgets. Strategy implementers need to be active and forceful in shifting resources, downsizing some areas, upsizing others, and amply funding activities with a critical role in the new strategy. They have to exercise their power to allocate resources to make things happen and make the tough decisions to kill projects and activities that are no longer justified. The funding requirements of the new strategy *must* drive how capital allocations are made and the size of each unit's operating budgets. Underfunding units and activities pivotal to strategic success can defeat the whole implementation process.

Aggressive resource reallocation can have a positive strategic payoff. For example, at Harris Corporation, where the strategy was to quickly transfer new research results to organizational units that could turn them into areas commercially viable products, top management regularly shifted groups of engineers out of research projects and moved them (as a group) into new commercial venture divisions. Boeing used a similar approach to reallocating ideas and talent; according to one Boeing officer, "We can do it (create a big new unit) in two weeks. We couldn't do it in two years at International Harvester."[1] Forceful actions to reallocate funds and move people into new units signal a strong commitment to implementing strategic change and are frequently needed to catalyze the implementation process and give it credibility.

Fine-tuning the implementation of a company's existing strategy seldom requires big movements of people and money. The needed adjustments can usually be accomplished through above-average budget increases to units where new initiatives are contemplated and below-average increases (or even small cuts) for the remaining units. The chief exception occurs where a prime ingredient of corporate/business strategy is to create altogether new competencies/capabilities or to generate fresh, new products and business opportunities within the existing budget. Then, as propos-

> **Strategic Management Principle**
>
> *Depriving strategy-critical groups of the funds needed to execute their pieces of the strategy can undermine the implementation process.*
>
> *New strategies usually call for significant budget reallocations.*

---

[1]Thomas J. Peters and Robert H. Waterman, Jr., *In Search of Excellence* (New York: Harper & Row, 1980), p. 125.

als and business plans worth pursuing bubble up from below, decisions have to be made about where the needed capital expenditures, operating budgets, and personnel will come from. Companies like 3M, GE, and Boeing shift resources and people from area to area on an as-needed basis to support the launch of new products and new business ventures. They empower "product champions" and small bands of would-be entrepreneurs by giving them financial and technical support and by setting up organizational units and programs to help new ventures blossom more quickly. Microsoft is quick to disband some project teams and create others to pursue fresh software projects or new ventures like MSN.

CREATING STRATEGY-SUPPORTIVE POLICIES AND PROCEDURES

Changes in strategy generally call for some changes in work practices and how operations are conducted. Asking people to alter established procedures and behavior always upsets the internal order of things. It is normal for pockets of resistance to develop and for people to exhibit some degree of stress and anxiety about how the changes will affect them, especially when the changes may eliminate jobs. Questions are also likely to arise over what activities need to be done in rigidly prescribed fashion and where there ought to be leeway for independent action.

Prescribing policies and operating procedures aids the task of implementing strategy in several ways:

1. New or freshly revised policies and procedures provide top-down guidance to operating managers, supervisory personnel, and employees about how certain things now need to be done and what behavior is expected, thus establishing some degree of regularity, stability, and dependability in how management has decided to try to execute the strategy and operate the business on a daily basis.

2. Policies and procedures help align actions and behavior with strategy throughout the organization, placing limits on independent action and channeling individual and group efforts along the intended path. Policies and procedures counteract tendencies for some people to resist or reject common approaches—most people refrain from violating company policy or ignoring established practices without first gaining clearance or having strong justification.

3. Policies and standardized operating procedures help enforce needed consistency in how particular strategy-critical activities are performed in geographically scattered operating units. Eliminating significant differences in the operating practices and procedures of units performing common functions is necessary to avoid sending mixed messages to internal personnel and to customers who do business with the company at multiple locations.

4. Because dismantling old policies and procedures and instituting new ones alter the character of the internal work climate, strategy implementers can use the policy-changing process as a powerful lever for changing the corporate culture in ways that produce a stronger fit with the new strategy.

Company managers, therefore, need to be inventive in devising policies and practices that can provide vital support to effective strategy implementation. McDonald's policy manual, in an attempt to steer "crew members" into stronger quality and service behavior patterns, spells out such detailed procedures as "Cooks must turn, never flip, hamburgers. If they haven't been purchased, Big Macs must be discarded

ILLUSTRATION CAPSULE 35   Nike's Manufacturing Policies and Procedures

When Nike decided on a strategy of outsourcing 100 percent of its athletic footwear from independent manufacturers (that, for reasons of low cost, all turned out to be located in Taiwan, South Korea, Thailand, Indonesia, and China), it developed a series of policies and production practices to govern its working relationships with its "production partners" (a term Nike carefully nurtured because it implied joint responsibilities):

- Nike personnel were stationed on-site at all key manufacturing facilities; each Nike representative tended to stay at the same factory site for several years to get to know the partner's people and processes in detail. They functioned as liaisons with Nike headquarters, working to match Nike's R&D and new product design efforts with factory capabilities and to keep monthly orders for new production in line with the latest sales forecasts.

- Nike instituted a quality assurance program at each factory site to enforce up-to-date and effective quality management practices.

- Nike endeavored to minimize ups and downs in monthly production orders at factory sites making Nike's premium-priced top-of-the-line models (volumes typically ran 20,000 to 25,000 pairs daily); the policy was to keep month-to-month variations in order quantity under 20 percent. These factories made Nike footwear exclusively and were expected to co-develop new models and to co-invest in new technologies.

- Factory sites that made mid-to-low-end Nike products in large quantities (usually 70,000 to 85,000 pairs per day), known as "volume producers," were expected to handle most ups and downs in monthly orders themselves; these factories usually produced shoes for five to eight other buyers, giving them the flexibility to juggle orders and stabilize their production.

- It was strict Nike policy to pay its bills from production partners on time, providing them with predictable cash flows.

Source: Based on information in James Brian Quinn, *Intelligent Enterprise* (New York: Free Press, 1992), pp. 60–64.

in 10 minutes after being cooked and french fries in 7 minutes. Cashiers must make eye contact with and smile at every customer." Caterpillar Tractor has a policy of guaranteeing its customers 24-hour parts delivery anywhere in the world; if it fails to fulfill the promise, it supplies the part free. Hewlett-Packard requires R&D people to make regular visits to customers to learn about their problems, talk about new product applications, and, in general, keep the company's R&D programs customer-oriented. Mrs. Fields' Cookies has a policy of establishing *hourly* sales quotas for each store outlet; furthermore, it is company policy for cookies not sold within two hours after being baked to be removed from the case and given to charitable organizations. Illustration Capsule 35 describes Nike's manufacturing policies in some detail.

Well-conceived policies and procedures aid implementation; out-of-sync policies are barriers.

Thus there is a definite role for new and revised policies and procedures in the strategy implementation process. Wisely constructed policies and procedures help enforce strategy implementation by channeling actions, behavior, decisions, and practices in directions that improve strategy execution. When policies and procedures aren't strategy-supportive, they become a barrier to the kinds of changes in attitude and behavior strategy implementers are trying to promote. Often, people opposed to certain elements of the strategy or certain implementation approaches will hide behind or vigorously defend long-standing policies and operating procedures in an effort to stall implementation or divert the approach to implementation along a different route. Anytime a company alters its strategy, managers should review existing policies and operating procedures, revise or discard those that are out of sync, and formulate new ones.

None of this implies that companies need thick policy manuals to guide strategy implementation and daily operations. Too much policy can be as stifling as wrong policy or as chaotic as no policy. There is wisdom in a middle approach: prescribe enough policies to give organizational members clear direction and to place desirable boundaries on their actions, then empower them to do act within these boundaries however they think makes sense. Such latitude is especially appropriate when individual creativity and initiative are more essential to good strategy execution than standardization and strict conformity.[2] Creating a strong, supportive fit between strategy and policy can therefore mean more policies, fewer policies, or different policies. It can mean policies that require things to be done a certain way or policies that give employees leeway to do activities the way they think best.

INSTITUTING BEST PRACTICES AND A COMMITMENT TO CONTINUOUS IMPROVEMENT

Identifying and implementing best practices is a journey, not a destination.

If value-chain activities are to be performed as effectively and efficiently as possible, each department and unit needs to benchmark how it performs specific tasks and activities against best-in-industry or best-in-world performers. A strong commitment to searching out and adopting best practices is integral to effective strategy implementation—especially for strategy-critical and big-dollar activities where better quality or lower costs impact bottom-line performance.[3]

The benchmarking movement to search out, study, and implement best practices has stimulated greater management awareness of the strategy-implementing importance of reengineering (the redesign of business processes), total quality management (TQM), and other continuous improvement programs. TQM is a philosophy of managing and set of business practices that emphasizes continuous improvement in all phases of operations, 100 percent accuracy in performing activities, involvement and empowerment of employees at all levels, team-based work design, benchmarking, and fully satisfying customer expectations. A 1991 survey by The Conference Board showed 93 percent of manufacturing companies and 69 percent of service companies had implemented some form of quality improvement program.[4] Another survey found that 55 percent of American executives and 70 percent of Japanese executives used quality improvement information at least monthly as part of their assessment of overall performance.[5] An Arthur D. Little study reported that 93 percent of the 500 largest U.S. firms had adopted TQM in some form as of 1992. Analysts have attributed the quality of many Japanese products to dedicated application of TQM principles. Indeed, *quality improvement processes have now become a globally pervasive part of the fabric of implementing strategies keyed to defect-free manufacture, superior product quality, superior customer service, and total customer satisfaction.*

Management interest in quality improvement programs typically originates in a company's production areas—fabrication and assembly in manufacturing enterprises, teller transactions in banks, order picking and shipping at catalog firms, or customer-contact interfaces in service organizations. Other times, interest begins with executives who hear TQM presentations, read about TQM, or talk to people in other companies that have benefited from total quality programs. Usually, interested man-

---

[2]Ibid., p. 65.

[3]For a discussion of the value of benchmarking in implementing strategy, see Yoshinobu Ohinata, "Benchmarking: The Japanese Experience," *Long Range Planning* 27, no. 4 (August 1994), pp. 48–53.

[4]Judy D. Olian and Sara L. Rynes, "Making Total Quality Work: Aligning Organizational Processes, Performance Measures, and Stakeholders," *Human Resource Management* 30, no. 3 (Fall 1991), p. 303.

[5]Ibid.

TABLE 10-1   Components of Popular TQM Approaches and 1992 Baldridge Award Criteria

DEMING'S 14 POINTS	THE JURAN TRILOGY	CROSBY'S 14 QUALITY STEPS
1. Constancy of purpose 2. Adopt the philosophy 3. Don't rely on mass inspection 4. Don't award business on price 5. Constant improvement 6. Training 7. Leadership 8. Drive out fear 9. Break down barriers 10. Eliminate slogans and exhortations 11. Eliminate quotas 12. Pride of workmanship 13. Education and retraining 14. Plan of action	1. *Quality Planning* • Set goals • Identify customers and their needs • Develop products and processes 2. *Quality control* • Evaluate performance • Compare to goals and adapt 3. *Quality improvement* • Establish infrastructure • Identify projects and teams • Provide resources and training • Establish controls	1. Management commitment 2. Quality improvement teams 3. Quality measurement 4. Cost of quality evaluation 5. Quality awareness 6. Corrective action 7. Zero-defects committee 8. Supervisor training 9. Zero-defects day 10. Goal-setting 11. Error cause removal 12. Recognition 13. Quality councils 14. Do it over again

THE 1992 BALDRIDGE AWARD CRITERIA (1000 points total)

1. *Leadership* (90 points)
   • Senior executive
   • Management for quality
   • Public responsibility
2. *Information and analysis* (80 points)
   • Scope and management of quality and performance data
   • Competitive comparisons and benchmarks
3. *Strategic quality planning* (60 points)
   • Strategic quality and planning process
   • Quality and performance plans
4. *Human resource development and management* (150 points)
   • Human resource management
   • Employee involvement
   • Employee education and training
   • Employee performance and recognition
   • Employee well-being and morale

5. *Management of process quality* (140 points)
   • Design and introduction of products and services
   • Process management—production and delivery
   • Process management—business and support
   • Supplier quality
   • Quality assessment
6. *Quality and operational results* (180 points)
   • Product and service quality
   • Company operations
   • Business process and support services
   • Supplier quality
7. *Customer focus and satisfaction* (300 points)
   • Customer relationships
   • Commitment to customers
   • Customer satisfaction determination
   • Customer satisfaction results
   • Customer satisfaction comparisons
   • Future requirements and expectations

Source: As presented in Thomas C. Powell, "Total Quality Management as Competitive Advantage," *Strategic Management Journal* 16, no. 1 (January 1995) p. 18 and based on M. Walton, *The Deming Management Method* (New York: Pedigree, 1986); J. Juran, *Juran on Quality by Design* (New York: Free Press, 1992); Philip Crosby, *Quality Is Free: The Act of Making Quality Certain* (New York: McGraw-Hill, 1979); and S. George, *The Baldridge Quality System* (New York: Wiley, 1992).

agers have quality and customer-satisfaction problems they are struggling to solve. See Table 10-1 for the different kinds of features emphasized by the leading proponents of TQM and for the criteria employed in selected winners of the Malcolm Baldridge Award for Quality.

While TQM concentrates on the production of quality goods and the delivery of excellent customer service, to succeed it must extend organizationwide to employee efforts in all departments—HR, billing, R&D, engineering, accounting and records, and information systems—that may lack less-pressing customer-driven incentives to

TABLE 10–2   Twelve Aspects Common to TQM and Continuous Improvement Programs

1. Committed leadership: a near-evangelical, unwavering, long-term commitment by top managers to the philosophy, usually under a name something like Total Quality Management, Continuous Improvement (CI), or Quality Improvement (QI).

2. Adoption and communication of TQM: using tools like the mission statement, and themes or slogans.

3. Closer customer relationships: determining customers' (both inside and outside the firm) requirements, then meeting those requirements no matter what it takes.

4. Closer supplier relationships: working closely and cooperatively with suppliers (often sole-sourcing key components), ensuring they provide inputs that conform to customers' end-use requirements.

5. Benchmarking: researching and observing operating competitive practices.

6. Increased training: usually includes TQM principles, team skills, and problem-solving.

7. Open organization: lean staff, empowered work teams, open horizontal communications, and a relaxation of traditional hierarchy.

8. Employee empowerment: increased employee involvement in design and planning, and greater autonomy in decision-making.

9. Zero-defects mentality: a system in place to spot defects as they occur, rather than through inspection and rework.

10. Flexible manufacturing: (applicable only to manufacturers) can include just-in-time inventory, cellular manufacturing, design for manufacturability (DFM), statistical process control (SPC), and design of experiments (DOE).

11. Process improvement: reduced waste and cycle times in all areas through cross-departmental process analysis.

12. Measurement: goal-orientation and zeal for data, with constant performance measurement, often using statistical methods.

Source: Thomas C. Powell, "Total Quality Management as Competitive Advantage," *Strategic Management Journal* 16, no. 1 (January 1995) p. 19.

TQM entails creating a total quality culture bent on continuously improving the performance of every task and value-chain activity.

improve. This is because the institution of best practices and continuous improvement programs involves reforming the corporate culture and shifting to a total quality/continuous improvement philosophy that permeates the organization—see Table 10-2 for the features common to most TQM programs.[6] TQM aims at instilling enthusiasm and commitment to doing things right from top to bottom of the organization. It entails a restless search for continuing improvement, the little steps forward each day that the Japanese call *kaizen.* TQM is a race without a finish. The managerial objective is to kindle a burning desire in people to use their ingenuity and initiative to progressively improve on how tasks are performed. TQM preaches that there's no such thing as good enough and that everyone has a responsibility to

---

[6]For a discussion of the shift in work environment and culture that TQM entails, see Robert T. Amsden, Thomas W. Ferratt, and Davida M. Amsden, "TQM: Core Paradigm Changes," *Business Horizons* 39, no. 6 (November–December 1996), pp. 6–14.

ILLUSTRATION CAPSULE 36   Motorola's Approach to TQM and Teamwork

Motorola is rated as one of the best companies in measuring performance against its strategic targets and in promoting total quality practices that lead to continuous improvement. Motorola was selected in 1988 as one of the first winners of the Malcolm Baldrige Quality Award and has since improved on its own award-winning efforts. In 1993, the company estimated it was saving about $2.2 billion annually from its team-oriented approach to TQM and continuous improvement.

A central feature of Motorola's approach is a year-long contest highlighting the successes of employee teams from around the world in improving internal company practices, making better products, saving money, pleasing customers, and sharing best practices with other Motorola groups. The contest, known as the Total Customer Satisfaction Team Competition, in 1992 attracted entries from nearly 4,000 teams involving nearly

40,000 of Motorola's 107,000 employees. Preliminary judging eventually reduced the 1992 finalists to 24 teams from around the world, all of which were invited to Chicago in January 1993 to make a 12–minute presentation to a panel of 15 senior executives, including the CEO. Twelve teams were awarded gold medals and 12 silver medals. The gold medalists are listed below.

Motorola does not track the costs of the contest because "the benefits are so overwhelming." It has sent hundreds of videos about the contests to other companies wanting details. However, TQM consultants are skeptical whether other companies have progressed far enough in establishing a team-based quality culture to benefit from a companywide contest. The downsides to such elaborate contests, they say, are the added costs (preparation, travel, presentation, and judging) and the risks to the morale of those who don't win.

Gold Medal Teams	Work Location	Achievement
B.E.A.P. Goes On	Florida	Removed bottleneck in testing pagers by using robots.
The Expedition	Malaysia	Designed and delivered a new chip for Apple Computer in six months.
Operation Paging Storm	Singapore	
ET/EV=1	Illinois	Eliminated component alignment defect in papers.
The Mission	Arizona	Streamlined order process for auto electronics.
Class Act	Illinois	Developed quality system for design of iridium satellites.
Dyna-Attackers	Dublin	Cut training program from five years to two with better results.
Orient Express	Malaysia	Cut production time and defect rate on new battery part.
The Dandles	Japan	Cut response time on tooling orders from 23 days to 4.
Cool Blue Racers	Arizona	Improved efficiency of boiler operations.
IO Plastics Misload	Manila	Cut product development time in half to win IBM contract. Eliminated resin seepage in modulator assembly.

Source: Based on information reported in Barnaby J. Feder, "At Motorola, Quality Is a Team Sport," *New York Times*, January 21, 1993, pp. C1 and C6.

participate in continuous improvement—see Illustration Capsule 36 describing Motorola's approach to involving employees in the TQM effort.

Effective use of TQM/continuous improvement techniques is a valuable competitive asset—one that can produce important competitive capabilities (in product design, cost reduction, product quality, and customer service) and be a source of competitive advantage.[7] Not only do ongoing incremental improvements add up over time and strengthen organizational capabilities but TQM/continuous improvement

---

[7]Thomas C. Powell, "Total Quality Management as Competitive Advantage," *Strategic Management Journal* 16 (1995), pp. 15–37. See, also, Richard M. Hodgetts, "Quality Lessons from America's Baldrige Winners," *Business Horizons* 37, no. 4 (July–August 1994), pp. 74–79 and Richard Reed, David J. Lemak, and Joseph C. Montgomery, "Beyond Process: TQM Content and Firm Performance," *Academy of Management Review* 21, no. 1 (January 1996), pp. 173–202.

programs have hard-to-imitate aspects. While it is relatively easy for rivals to under-take benchmarking, process improvement, and quality training, it is much more difficult for them to implant a total quality culture, empower employees, and generate deep and genuine management commitment to TQM philoso-phy and practices. TQM requires a substantial investment of management time and effort; some managers and employees resist TQM, viewing it as ideological or faddish. It is expensive (in terms of training and meetings) and it seldom produces short-term results. The longer term payoff depends heavily on management's success in instilling a culture within which TQM philosophies and practices can thrive.

Having the capability to generate continuous improvements in important value-chain activities is a valuable competitive asset.

The Difference between TQM and Process Reengineering   Best practices, process reen-gineering, and continuous improvement efforts like TQM all aim at improved effi-ciency and reduced costs, better product quality, and greater customer satisfaction. *The essential difference between process reengineering and TQM is that reengineering aims at quantum gains on the order of 30 to 50 percent or more, whereas total quality programs stress incremental progress, striving for inch-by-inch gains again and again.* The two approaches to improved performance of value-chain activities are not mutually exclusive; it makes sense to use them in tandem. Reengineering can be used first to produce a good basic design that dramatically improves a business process. Total quality programs can then be used to work out bugs, perfect the process, and gradually improve both efficiency and effectiveness. Such a two-pronged approach to implementing organizational and strategic change is like a marathon race where you run the first four laps as fast as you can, then gradually pick up speed the remainder of the way.

Reengineering seeks one-time quantum improvement; TQM seeks ongoing incremental improvement.

Capturing the Potential Benefits   Research indicates that some companies benefit from reengineering and TQM and some do not.[8] Usually, the biggest beneficiaries are companies that view such programs not as ends in themselves but as tools for implementing and executing company strategy more effectively. The skimpiest payoffs from best practices, TQM, and reengineering occur when company managers seize them as something worth trying, novel ideas that could improve things; in most such instances, they result in strategy-blind efforts to simply manage better. There's an important lesson here. Best practices, TQM, and reengineering all need to be seen and used as part of a bigger-picture effort to execute strategy proficiently. Only strategy can point to which activities matter and what performance targets make the most sense. Absent a strategic framework, managers lack the context in which to fix things that really matter to business-unit performance and competitive success.

When best practices, reengineering, and TQM are not part of a wider-scale effort to improve strategy execution and business performance, they deteriorate into strategy-blind efforts to manage better.

To get the most from benchmarking, best practices, reengineering, TQM, and related tools for enhancing organizational competence in executing strategy, manag-ers have to start with a clear fix on the indicators of successful strategy execution—defect-free manufacture, on-time delivery, low overall costs, exceeding customers' expectations, faster cycle time, increased product innovation, or some other specific performance measure. Benchmarking most or all value-chain activities against best-

---

[8]See, for example, Gene Hall, Jim Rosenthal, and Judy Wade, "How to Make Reengineering Really Work," *Harvard Business Review* 71, no. 6 (November–December 1993), pp. 119–31.

in-industry and best-in-world performance provides a basis for setting internal performance milestones and longer-range targets.

Then comes the managerial task of building a total quality culture and instilling the necessary commitment to achieving the targets and performance measures that the strategy requires. The action steps managers can take include:[9]

1. Visible, unequivocal, and unyielding commitment to total quality and continuous improvement, including a quality vision and specific, measurable quality goals.

2. Nudging people toward TQ-supportive behaviors by initiating such organizational programs as
   - Screening job applicants rigorously and hiring only those with attitudes and aptitudes right for quality-based performance.
   - Quality training for most employees.
   - Using teams and team-building exercises to reinforce and nurture individual effort (expansion of a TQ culture is facilitated when teams become more cross-functional, multitask, and increasingly self-managed).
   - Recognizing and rewarding individual and team efforts regularly and systematically.
   - Stressing prevention (doing it right the first time) not inspection (instituting ways to correct mistakes).

3. Empowering employees so that authority for delivering great service or improving products is in the hands of the doers rather than the overseers.

4. Using on-line information systems to provide all parties with the latest best practices and actual experiences with them, thereby speeding the diffusion and adoption of best practices throughout the organization and also allowing them to exchange data and opinions about how to improve/upgrade the best practices.

5. Preaching that performance can, and must, be improved because competitors are not resting on past laurels and customers are always looking for something better.

If the targeted performance measures are appropriate to the strategy and if top executives, middle managers, professional staff, and line employees buy into the process of continuous improvement, then the work climate will promote proficient strategy execution and good bottom-line business performance.

INSTALLING SUPPORT SYSTEMS

Company strategies can't be implemented or executed well without a number of support systems for business operations. American, United, Delta, and other major airlines cannot hope to provide world-class service without a computerized reservation system, an accurate and fast baggage handling system, and a strong aircraft maintenance program. FedEx has a computerized parcel-tracking system that can instantly report the location of any given package in its transit-delivery process; it

---

[9]Olian and Rynes, "Making Total Quality Work," pp. 305–6 and 310–11 and Paul S. Goodman and Eric D. Darr, "Exchanging Best Practices Information through Computer-Aided Systems," *Academy of Management Executive* 10, no. 2 (May 1996), p. 7.

has communication systems that allow it to coordinate its 21,000 vans nationwide to make an average of 720,000 stops per day to pick up customer packages; and it has leading-edge flight operations systems that allow a single controller to direct as many as 200 FedEx aircraft simultaneously, overriding their flight plans should weather or special emergencies arise—all these operations essential to FedEx's strategy of next-day delivery of a package that "absolutely, positively has to be there."[10]

Otis Elevator has a sophisticated support system called OtisLine to coordinate maintenance nationwide.[11] Trained operators take all trouble calls, input critical information on a computer screen, and dispatch people directly via a beeper system to the local trouble spot. From the trouble-call inputs, problem patterns can be identified nationally and the information communicated to design and manufacturing personnel, allowing them to quickly alter design specifications or manufacturing procedures to correct recurring problems. Also, much of the information needed for repairs is provided directly from faulty elevators through internally installed microcomputer monitors, further lowering outage time.

Strategic Management Principle

Innovative, state-of-the-art support systems can be a basis for competitive advantage if they give a firm capabilities that rivals can't match.

Procter & Gamble codes the more than 900,000 call-in inquiries it receives annually on its toll-free 800 number to obtain early warning signals of product problems and changing tastes.[12] Arthur Andersen Worldwide has an electronic system linking more than 82,000 people in 360 offices in 76 countries; the system has data, voice, and video capabilities and includes an electronic bulletin board for posting customer problems, for organizing around a customer's problem using people from all over the world, as well as the capability to collect, index, and distribute files containing information on particular subjects, customers, solutions, and company resources.[13] Andersen's Knowledge Xchange system captures the lessons learned in the company's daily work and research and makes it available to Andersen personnel 24 hours a day. Wal-Mart's computers transmit daily sales data to Wrangler, a supplier of blue jeans; using a model that interprets the data and software applications that act on these interpretations, specific quantities of specific sizes and colors are then shipped to specific stores from specific warehouses—the system lowers logistics and inventory costs and leads to fewer stockouts.[14] Domino's Pizza has computerized systems at each outlet to help with ordering, inventory, payroll, cash flow, and work control functions, freeing managers to spend more time on supervision, customer service, and business development.[15] Most telephone companies, electric utilities, and TV broadcasting systems have on-line monitoring systems to spot transmission problems within seconds and increase the reliability of their services. Software companies need systems that allow them to distribute their products on the Internet. At Mrs. Fields' Cookies, computer systems monitor hourly sales and suggest product mix changes, promotional tactics, or operating adjustments to improve customer response—see Illustration Capsule 37. Many companies have installed software systems on their company intranets to catalog best practices

---

[10]James Brian Quinn, *Intelligent Enterprise* (New York: Free Press, 1992) pp. 114–15.

[11]Ibid., p. 186.

[12]Ibid., p. 111.

[13]James Brian Quinn, Philip Anderson, and Sydney Finkelstein, "Leveraging Intellect," *Academy of Management Executive* 10, no. 3 (November 1996), p. 9.

[14]Stephan H. Haeckel and Richard L. Nolan. "Managing by Wire," *Harvard Business Review* 75, no. 5 (September–October 1993), p. 129.

[15]Quinn, *Intelligent Enterprise,* p. 181.

ILLUSTRATION CAPSULE 37 Management Information and Control Systems at Mrs. Fields' Cookies, Inc.

Mrs. Fields' Cookies is one of the best known specialty foods companies with over 800 outlets in operation in malls, airports, and other high pedestrian-traffic locations around the world. The business concept for Mrs. Fields' Cookies, as articulated by Debbi Fields, the company's founder and CEO, is "to serve absolutely fresh, warm cookies as though you'd stopped by my house and caught me just taking a batch from the oven." The company promotes its products mainly by sampling; store employees walk around giving away cookie samples. Another is for Fields to make unannounced visits to her stores, where she masquerades as a casual shopper to test the enthusiasm and sales techniques of store crews, sample the quality of the cookies they are baking, and observe customer reactions.

In 1978 when Debbi Fields opened her second store in San Francisco, 45 miles away from the first store in Palo Alto, she confronted the logistical problems of maintaining hands-on management and control at remote locations. Debbi's husband Randy developed a software program to issue instructions and advice to store managers and to provide a way of exercising control over store operations. Each morning local managers enter information on their store PCs—the day of the week, the month (to pick up seasonal shopping patterns), special mall activities or local events expected to influence traffic patterns, and the weather forecast. Randy's software program analyzes this information, together with the store's recent performance history, and prints out a daily sales goal (broken down by the hour). With the hourly sales quotas also comes an hourly schedule of how many batches of cookies to mix and bake and when to offer free samples.

As the day progresses, store managers type in actual hourly sales figures and customer counts. If customer counts are up but sales are lagging, the computerized software system recommends more aggressive sampling or more suggestive selling. If it becomes obvious the day is going to be a bust for the store, the computer automatically revises the sales projections for the day, reducing hourly quotas and instructing how much to cut back cookie baking. To facilitate crew scheduling by the store manager, sales projections are also provided for two weeks in advance. If a store manager has a specific problem, it can be entered on the system and routed to the appropriate person. The system gives store managers more time to work with their crews and achieve sales quotas, as opposed to handling administrative chores.

When Mrs. Fields' Cookies began to expand into Europe and Asia, the company's information technology department modified the software to take into account the different shopping patterns, buyer preferences, labor laws, languages, and supplier arrangements being encountered in foreign countries. A second generation of software, called the Retail Operations Intelligence system, was also developed; ROI has modules for inventory control, interviewing and hiring, repair and maintenance, lease management, and e-mail. All job applicants must sit at the store's terminal and answer a computerized set of questions as part of the interview process; the questions help store managers identify candidates with aptitudes for warmth, friendliness, and the ability to have a good time giving away samples, baking fresh batches, and talking to customers during the course of a sale.

Because the day-to-day variations in the cookie business are fairly easy to model and employee turnover in retail outlets like Mrs. Fields' is high, having the capability to "manage-by-wire" and run basic store operations on autopilot much of the time is a valuable strategy-implementing, strategy-executing assist. Debbi Fields also uses the electronic system as a means of projecting her influence and enthusiasm into stores far more frequently than she can reach through personal visits.

Source: Developed from information in Mike Korologos, "Debbi Fields," *Sky Magazine*, July 1988, pp. 42–50 and Stephan H. Haeckel and Richard L. Nolan, "Managing by Wire," *Harvard Business Review* 75, no. 5 (September–October 1993), pp. 123–24.

information and promote faster best practices transfer and implementation organizationwide.[16] Companies everywhere are rushing to create on-line data systems, connect more employees to the Internet and company intranets, use electronic mail as a

---

[16]Such systems speed organizational learning by providing fast, efficient communication, creating an organizational memory for collecting and retaining best practice information, and permitting people all across the organization to exchange information and updated solutions. See Goodman and Darr, "Exchanging Best Practices Information through Computer-Aided Systems," pp. 7–17.

major means of internal and external communication, and build Web pages to participate in the rapidly expanding world of electronic commerce.

Well-conceived, state-of-the art support systems not only facilitate better strategy execution, they also can strengthen organizational capabilities enough to provide a competitive edge over rivals. For example, a company with a differentiation strategy based on superior quality has added capability if it has systems for training personnel in quality techniques, tracking product quality at each production step, and ensuring that all goods shipped meet quality standards. A company striving to be a low-cost provider is competitively stronger if it has a benchmarking system that identifies opportunities to drive costs out of the business. Fast-growing companies get an important assist from recruiting systems that help attract and hire qualified employees in large numbers. In businesses such as public accounting and management consulting where large numbers of professional staffers need cutting-edge technical know-how, companies can gain a competitive edge if they have superior systems for training and retraining employees regularly and keeping them supplied with up-to-date information. Companies that rely on empowered customer service employees to act promptly and creatively in pleasing customers have to have state-of-the-art information systems that put essential data at employees' fingertips and give them instantaneous communications capabilities. Young companies wanting to build a business spanning a wide geographic area, grow rapidly, go public, and achieve a prominent industry standing have to invest more in organizational systems and infrastructure than small companies content to build a single-location business at a cautious pace. In today's business environment, competitive advantage goes to those firms most able to mobilize information and create systems to use knowledge effectively.

Companies that have learned how to use e-mail and word-processing systems proficiently and pervasively are much less hierarchical and tend to respond much faster to developing events than companies relying on traditional communication methods. Avid users of e-mail become available to anybody and everybody, resulting in a more open and democratic way of operating; moreover, information doesn't get screened and filtered. Because information is quickly broadcast and many people in different geographical areas can communicate readily, companies can conduct debates and develop solutions more rapidly. Microsoft makes exceptionally strong use of e-mail to distribute information, debate issues, mobilize its responses to developing events, speedily put people to work on emerging issues, and redeploy its resources. Intel is another company that uses e-mail to boost its agility. Price Waterhouse utilizes an on-line word-processing system to create client proposals that can be enriched by contributions from personnel in any of its offices around the world.

Installing Adequate Information Systems, Performance Tracking, and Controls

Accurate information is an essential guide to action. Every organization needs systems for gathering and storing data, tracking key performance indicators, identifying and diagnosing problems, and reporting strategy-critical information. Telephone companies have elaborate information systems to measure signal quality, connection times, interrupts, wrong connections, billing errors, and other measures of reliability. To track and manage the quality of passenger service, airlines have information systems to monitor gate delays, on-time departures and arrivals, baggage-handling times, lost baggage complaints, stockouts on meals and drinks, overbookings, and maintenance delays and failures. Many companies have provided customer-contact personnel with instant electronic access to customer databases so that they can respond effectively to customer inquiries and personalize customer services. Companies that rely on empowered employees need measurement and feedback systems to monitor the performance of workers and guide them to act within specified limits so that unwelcome surprises are avoided.[17]

Accurate, timely information allows organizational members to monitor progress and take corrective action promptly.

Electronic information systems allow managers to monitor implementation initiatives and daily operations, steering them to a successful conclusion in case early steps don't produce the expected progress or things seem to be drifting off course. Information systems need to cover five broad areas: (1) customer data, (2) operations data, (3) employee data, (4) supplier/partner/collaborative ally data, and (5) financial performance data. All key strategic performance indicators have to be measured as often as practical. Many retail companies generate daily sales reports for each store and maintain up-to-the-minute inventory and sales records on each item. Manufacturing plants typically generate daily production reports and track labor productivity on every shift. Many retailers and manufacturers have on-line data systems connecting them with their suppliers that monitor inventories, process orders and invoices, and track shipments. Monthly profit-and-loss statements and statistical summaries, long the norm, are fast being replaced by daily statistical updates and even up-to-the-minute performance monitoring that electronic technology makes possible. Such diagnostic control systems allow managers to detect problems early, intervene when needed, and adjust either the strategy or how it is being implemented. Early experiences are sometimes difficult to assess, but they yield the first hard data and should be closely scrutinized as a basis for corrective action. Ideally, statistical reports should flag big or unusual variances from preset performance standards.

Effective companies use computer-aided electronic systems to share data and information at lightning speed.

Statistical information gives the strategy implementer a feel for the numbers; reports and meetings provide a feel for new developments and problems; and personal contacts add a feel for the people dimension. All are good barometers of overall performance and good indicators of which things are on and off track.

Exercising Adequate Controls over Empowered Employees   A major problem facing today's managers is how to ensure that the actions of empowered subordinates stay within acceptable bounds and don't expose the organization to excessive risk.[18] There are dangers to leaving employees to their own devices in meeting performance standards. The media is full of reports of employees whose decisions or behavior went awry, either costing the company huge sums in losses or causing embarrassing lawsuits. Managers can't spend all their time making sure that everyone's decisions and behavior are between the white lines, yet they have a clear responsibility to institute adequate checks and balances and protect against unwelcome surprises. One of the main purposes of diagnostic control systems to track performance is to relieve managers of the burden of constant monitoring and give them time for other issues. But diagnostic controls are only part of the answer. Another valuable lever of control

---

[17]For a discussion of the need for putting appropriate boundaries on the actions of empowered employees and possible control and monitoring systems that can be used, see Robert Simons, "Control in an Age of Empowerment," *Harvard Business Review* 73 (March–April 1995), pp. 80–88.

[18]Ibid. See, also, David C. Band and Gerald Scanlan, "Strategic Control through Core Competencies," *Long Range Planning* 28, no. 2 (April 1995), pp. 102–14.

is establishing clear boundaries on behavior without telling employees what to do. Strictly prescribed rules and procedures discourage initiative and creativity. It is better to set forth what *not* to do, allowing freedom of action within specified limits. Another control device is face-to-face meetings to review information, assess progress and performance, reiterate expectations, and discuss the next action steps.

DESIGNING STRATEGY-SUPPORTIVE REWARD SYSTEMS

Strategies can't be implemented and executed with real proficiency unless organizational units and individuals are committed to the task. Company managers typically try to enlist organizationwide commitment to carrying out the strategic plan by motivating people and rewarding them for good performance. A manager has to do more than just talk to everyone about how important new strategic practices and performance targets are to the organization's future well-being. No matter how inspiring, talk seldom commands people's best efforts for long. *To get employees' sustained, energetic commitment, management has to be resourceful in designing and using motivational incentives—both monetary and nonmonetary.* The more a manager understands what motivates subordinates and the more he or she relies on motivational incentives as a tool for implementing strategy, the greater will be employees' commitment to good day in, day out execution of their roles in the company's strategic plan.

The role of the reward system is to make it personally satisfying and economically beneficial for organizational members to help the company execute its strategy competently, please customers, and realize the company's vision.

While financial incentives (salary increases, performance bonuses, stock options, and retirement packages) are the core component of most companies' reward systems, managers normally make extensive use of such nonmonetary incentives as frequent words of praise (or constructive criticism), special recognition at company gatherings or in the company newsletter, more (or less) job security, interesting assignments, opportunities to transfer to attractive locations, increased (or decreased) job control and decision-making autonomy, and the carrot of promotion and the stick of being "sidelined" in a routine or dead-end job. Effective managers are further alert to the motivating power of giving people a chance to be part of something exciting, giving them an opportunity for greater personal satisfaction, challenging them with ambitious performance targets, and the intangible bonds of group acceptance. But the motivation and reward structure has to be used *creatively* and tied directly to achieving the performance outcomes necessary for good strategy execution.

One of the biggest strategy-implementing challenges is to employ motivational techniques that build wholehearted commitment and winning attitudes among employees.

Strategy-Supportive Motivational Practices

Successful strategy implementers inspire and challenge employees to do their best. They get employees to buy into the strategy and commit to making it work. They structure individual efforts into teams and work groups in order to facilitate an exchange of ideas and a climate of support. They allow employees to participate in making decisions about how to perform their jobs, and they try to make jobs interesting and satisfying. They devise strategy-supportive motivational approaches and use them effectively. Consider some actual examples:

- At Mars Inc. (best known for its candy bars), every employee, including the president, gets a weekly 10 percent bonus by coming to work on time each day that week. This on-time incentive is designed to minimize absenteeism and tardiness and maximize the amount of labor time available for operating high-speed candy-making equipment (utilizing each available minute of machine time to produce the greatest number of candy bars reduces costs significantly).[19]

- In a number of Japanese companies, employees meet regularly to hear inspirational speeches, sing company songs, and chant the corporate litany. In the United States, Tupperware conducts a weekly Monday night rally to honor, applaud, and fire up its salespeople who conduct Tupperware parties. Amway and Mary Kay Cosmetics hold similar inspirational get-togethers for their sales forces.[20]

- Nordstrom typically pays its retail salespeople an hourly wage higher than the prevailing rates paid by other department store chains, plus it pays them a commission on each sale. Spurred by a culture that encourages salespeople to go all out to satisfy customers, to exercise their own best judgment, and to seek out and promote new fashion ideas, Nordstrom salespeople often earn twice the average incomes of sales employees at competing stores.[21] Nordstrom's rules for employees are simple: "Rule #1: Use your good judgment in all situations. There will be no additional rules."

- Microsoft, realizing that software creation is a highly individualistic effort, interviews hundreds of propective programmers to find the few most suited to write code for its programs. It places new recruits onto three-to seven-person teams under experienced mentors to work on the next generation of software programs. While project team members can expect to put in 60-to 80-hour workweeks to meet deadlines for getting new programs to market, the best programmers seek out and stay with Microsoft largely because they believe that Microsoft will determine where the industry moves in the future and working for Microsoft will allow them to share in the excitement, challenge, and rewards of working on this frontier (and only partly because of Microsoft's very attractive pay scales and lucrative stock option program).[22]

- Lincoln Electric, a company deservedly famous for its piecework pay scheme and incentive bonus plan, rewards individual productivity by paying workers for each nondefective piece produced (workers have to correct quality problems on their own time—defects can be traced to the worker who caused them). The piecework plan motivates workers to pay attention to both quality and volume produced. In addition, the company sets aside a substantial portion of its profits above a specified base for worker bonuses. To determine the size of each worker's bonus Lincoln Electric rates each worker on four equally important performance measures: dependability, quality, output, and ideas and cooperation. The higher a worker's merit rating, the higher the incentive bonus earned; the highest rated workers in good profit years receive bonuses of as much as 110 percent of their piecework compensation.[23]

[19]Peters and Waterman, *In Search of Excellence*, p. 269.

[20]Ibid., p. xx.

[21]Jeffrey Pheffer, "Producing Sustainable Competitive Advantage through the Effective Management of People," *Academy of Management Executive* 9, no. 1 (February 1995), pp. 59–60.

[22]Quinn, Anderson, and Finkelstein, "Leveraging Intellect," p. 8.

[23]Pheffer, "Producing Sustainable Competitive Advantage through the Effective Management of People," p. 59.

- A California automobile assembly plant run by Toyota emphasizes symbolic egalitarianism. All employees (managers and workers alike) wear blue smocks, there are no reserved spaces in the employee parking lot, there's no executive dining room—everyone eats in the same plant cafeteria, and there are only two job classifications for skilled trades and only one job classification for all other workers.[24]

- Monsanto, FedEx, AT&T, Advanced Micro Devices, and many other companies have tapped into the motivational power of self-managed teams and achieved very good results. Teams work because of the peer monitoring and expectations of coworkers that are brought to bear on each team member.

- Several Japanese automobile producers, believing that providing employment security is a valuable contributor to worker productivity and company loyalty, elect not to lay off factory workers but instead put them out in the field to sell vehicles when business slacks off for a period. Mazda, for example, during a sales downturn in Japan in the 1980s, shifted factory workers to selling its models door-to-door, a common practice in Japan. At the end of the year, when awards were given out to the best salespeople, Mazda found its top ten salespeople were all factory workers, partly because they were able to explain the product effectively. When business picked up and the factory workers returned to the plant, their experiences in talking to customers yielded useful ideas in improving the features and styling of Mazda's product line.[25]

- At GE Medical Systems, a program called Quick Thanks! allows an employee to nominate any colleague to receive a $25 gift certificate redeemable at certain stores and restaurants in appreciation of a job well done. Employees often hand out the award personally to deserving coworkers (in a recent 12-month period over 10,000 Quick Thanks! awards were presented). Peers prove to be tougher than executives in praising colleagues; for the recipient, the approving acknowledgment of coworkers matters more than the $25.[26]

These motivational approaches accentuate the positive; others blend positive and negative features. Consider the way Harold Geneen, former president and chief executive officer of ITT, allegedly combined the use of money, tension, and fear:

> Geneen provides his managers with enough incentives to make them tolerate the system. Salaries all the way through ITT are higher than average—Geneen reckons 10 percent higher—so that few people can leave without taking a drop. As one employee put it: "We're all paid just a bit more than we think we're worth." At the very top, where the demands are greatest, the salaries and stock options are sufficient to compensate for the rigors. As someone said, "He's got them by their limousines."
>
> Having bound his [managers] to him with chains of gold, Geneen can induce the tension that drives the machine. "The key to the system," one of his [managers] explains, "is the profit forecast. Once the forecast has been gone over, revised, and agreed on, the managing director has a personal commitment to Geneen to carry it out. That's how he produces the tension on which the success depends." The tension goes through the company, inducing ambition, perhaps exhilaration, but always with some sense of fear: what happens if the target is missed?[27]

---

[24]Ibid., p. 63.

[25]Ibid., p. 62.

[26]Steven Kerr, "Risky Business: The New Pay Game," *Fortune*, July 22, 1996, p. 95.

[27]Anthony Sampson, *The Sovereign State of ITT* (New York: Stein and Day, 1973), p. 132.

Balancing Positive and Negative Motivational Considerations   If a strategy imple- menter's motivational approach and reward structure induces too much stress, inter- nal competitiveness, and job insecurity, the results can be counterproductive. The prevailing view is that a manager's push for strategy implementation should be more positive than negative because when cooperation is positively enlisted and rewarded, rather than strong-armed by a boss's orders, people tend to respond with more enthusiasm, effort, creativity, and initiative. Yet it is unwise to com- pletely eliminate pressure for performance and the anxiety it evokes. There is no evidence that a no-pressure work environment leads to superior strategy execution or sustained high performance. As the CEO of a major bank put it, "There's a deliberate policy here to create a level of anxiety. Winners usually play like they're one touchdown behind."[28] High-performing orga- nizations need ambitious people who relish the opportunity to climb the ladder of success, love a challenge, thrive in a performance-oriented environment, and find some competition and pressure useful to satisfy their own drives for personal recog- nition, accomplishment, and self-satisfaction. Unless compensation, career, and job satisfaction consequences are tied to successfully implementing strategic initiatives and hitting strategic performance targets, few people will attach much significance to the company's vision, objectives, and strategy.

Positive motivational approaches generally work better than negative ones.

Linking the Reward System to Strategically Relevant Performance Outcomes

The most dependable way to keep people focused on competent strategy execution and achieving company performance targets is to *generously* reward individuals and groups who achieve their assigned performance targets and deny rewards to those who don't. *The use of incentives and rewards is the single most powerful tool management has to win strong employee commitment to diligent, competent strategy execution.* Failure to use this tool wisely and powerfully weakens the entire implementation/execution process. Deci- sions on salary increases, incentive compensation, promotions, who gets which key assignments, and the ways and means of awarding praise and recognition are the strategy implementer's foremost devices to get attention and build commitment. Such decisions seldom escape the closest employee scrutiny, saying more about what is expected and who is considered to be doing a good job than any other factor. A company's system of incentives and rewards thus ends up being the way its strategy is emotionally ratified in the form of real commitment. Performance-based incentives make it in employees' self-interest to exert their best efforts to achieve performance targets and to execute the strategy competently[29]

Strategic Management Principle

A properly designed reward structure is management's most powerful strategy- implementing tool.

The key to creating a reward system that promotes good strategy execution is to make strategically relevant measures of performance *the dominating basis* for designing incentives, evaluating individual and group efforts, and handing out re- wards. Performance targets have to be established for every unit, every manager, every team or work group, and perhaps every employee—targets that measure whether implementation is on track. If the company's strategy is to be a low-cost provider, the incentive system must reward actions and achievements that result in

---

[28] As quoted in John P. Kotter and James L. Heskett, *Corporate Culture and Performance* (New York: Free Press, 1992), p. 91.

[29] For a countervailing view on the merits of incentives, see Alfie Kohn, "Why Incentive Plans Cannot Work," *Harvard Business Review* 71, no. 6 (November–December 1993), pp. 54–63.

lower costs. If the company has a differentiation strategy predicated on superior quality and service, the incentive system must reward such outcomes as zero defects, infrequent need for product repair, low numbers of customer complaints, and speedy order processing and delivery. If a company's growth requires new product innovation, incentives should be tied to factors such as the percentages of revenues and profits coming from newly introduced products.

Strategic Management Principle

The strategy implementer's standard for judging whether individuals, teams, and organizational units have done a good job must be whether they achieve performance targets consistent with effective strategy execution.

Some of the best performing companies—Banc One, Nucor Steel, Lincoln Electric, Electronic Data Systems, Wal-Mart, Remington Products, and Mary Kay Cosmetics—owe much of their success to incentives and rewards that induce people to do the things critical to good strategy execution and competing effectively. At Banc One (one of the 10 largest U.S. banks and also one of the most profitable banks in the world based on return on assets), producing consistently high levels of customer satisfaction makes a big difference in how well it fares against rivals; customer satisfaction ranks high on Banc One's list of strategic priorities. To enhance employee commitment to the task of pleasing customers, Banc One ties the pay scales in each branch office to that branch's customer satisfaction rating—the higher the branch's ratings, the higher that branch's pay scales. By shifting from a theme of equal pay for equal work to one of equal pay for equal performance, Banc One has focused the attention of branch employees on the task of pleasing, even delighting, their customers.

Nucor's strategy was (and is) to be *the* low-cost producer of steel products. Because labor costs are a significant fraction of total cost in the steel business, Nucor's low-cost strategy entails achieving lower labor costs per ton of steel than competitors'. Nucor management designed an incentive system to promote high worker productivity and drive labor costs per ton below rivals'. Management has organized each plant's workforce into production teams (each assigned to perform particular functions) and, working with the teams, has established weekly production targets for each team. Base pay scales are set at levels comparable to wages for similar manufacturing jobs in the areas where Nucor has plants, but workers can earn a 1 percent bonus for each 1 percent that their output exceeds target levels. If a production team exceeds its weekly production target by 10 percent, team members receive a 10 percent bonus in their next paycheck; if a team exceeds its quota by 20 percent, team members earn a 20 percent bonus. Bonuses are paid every two weeks based on the prior two weeks' actual production levels. The results of Nucor's piece-rate incentive plan are impressive. Nucor's labor productivity (in tons produced per worker) runs over 20 percent above the average of the unionized workforces of the industry's large, integrated steel producers like U.S. Steel and Bethlehem Steel. Nucor enjoys about a $30 to $60 per ton cost advantage (a substantial part of which comes from its lower labor costs), and Nucor workers are the highest-paid workers in the steel industry.

As the example in Illustration Capsule 38 demonstrates, compensating and rewarding organization members on criteria not directly related to successful strategy execution undermines organization performance and condones the diversion of time and energy in less strategically relevant directions.

The Importance of Basing Incentives on Achieving Results, Not on Performing Assigned Functions   To create a system of rewards and incentives that support strategy, emphasis has to be put on rewarding people for accomplishing results, not for dutifully performing assigned functions. Focusing jobholders' attention and energy on "what to achieve" as opposed to "what to do" makes the work environment *results-oriented*. It is flawed management to tie incentives and rewards to satisfactory performance of duties and

---

ILLUSTRATION CAPSULE 38 The Folly of the Reward System in the Claims Division of a
Large Insurance Company

The past reward practices of the health care claims division of a large insurance company demonstrate the folly of hoping for one behavior but rewarding another behavior. Seeking to encourage employees to be accurate in paying surgical claims, the company tracked the number of returned checks and letters of complaint filed by policyholders. However, employees in the claims department frequently found it hard to tell from physician filings which of two surgical procedures, with different allowable benefits, was performed, and writing for clarification greatly reduced the number of claims paid within two days of receipt (a performance standard the company stressed). Consequently, the workers' norm quickly became "when in doubt, pay it out."

This practice was made worse by the firm's reward system which called for merit increases of 5 percent for "outstanding" employees, 4 percent for "above average" employees (most employees not rated as outstanding were designated as above average), and 3 percent for all other employees. Many employees were indifferent to the potential of an extra 1 percent reward for avoiding overpayment errors and working hard enough to be rated as outstanding.

However, employees were not indifferent to a rule which stated that employees forfeited their entire merit raise at the next six-month merit review if they were absent or late for work three or more times in any six-month period. The company, while hoping for performance, was rewarding attendance. But the absent-lateness rule was not as stringent as it might seem because the company counted the number of "times" rather than the number of "days"—a one-week absence counted the same as a one-day absence. A worker in danger of getting a third absence within a six-month period could sometimes stay away from work during the second absence until the first absence was over six months old; the limiting factor was that after a certain number of days the worker was paid sickness benefits instead of his or her regular pay (for workers with 20 or more years of service, the company provided sickness benefits of 90 percent of normal salary tax-free!!!).

Source: Steven Kerr, "On the Folly of Rewarding A, While Hoping for B," *Academy of Management Executive* 9, no. 1 February 1995), p. 11.

---

activities in hopes that the by-products will be the desired business outcomes and achievements.[30] In any job, performing assigned tasks is not equivalent to achieving intended outcomes. Working hard, staying busy, and diligently attending to assigned duties do not guarantee results. (As any student knows, just because an instructor teaches doesn't mean students are learning. Teaching and learning are different things—the first is an activity and the second is a result. The enterprise of education would no doubt take on a different character if teachers were rewarded for the result of what is learned instead of the activity of teaching.)

Incentive compensation for top executives is typically tied to company profitability (earnings growth, return on equity investment, return on total assets, economic value added), the company's stock price performance, and perhaps such measures as market share, product quality, or customer satisfaction that indicate the company's market position, overall competitiveness, and future prospects have improved. However, incentives for department heads, teams, and individual workers are often tied to outcomes more closely related to their area of responsibility. In manufacturing, incentive compensation may be tied to unit manufacturing costs, on-time production and shipping, defect rates, the number and extent of work stoppages due to labor disagreements and equipment breakdowns, and so on. In marketing, there may be

It is folly to reward one outcome in hopes of getting another outcome.

The whats to accomplish—the performance measures on which rewards and incentives are based—must be tightly connected to the requirements of successful strategy execution and good company performance.

---

[30]See Steven Kerr, "On the Folly of Rewarding A While Hoping for B," *Academy of Management Executive* 9 no. 1 (February 1995), pp. 7–14; Kerr, "Risky Business: The New Pay Game," pp. 93–96; and Doran Twer, "Linking Pay to Business Objectives," *Journal of Business Strategy* 15, no. 4 (July–August 1994), pp. 15–18.

incentives for achieving dollar sales or unit volume targets, market share, sales penetration of each target customer group, the fate of newly introduced products, the frequency of customer complaints, the number of new accounts acquired, and customer satisfaction. Which performance measures to base incentive compensation on depends on the situation—the priority placed on various financial and strategic objectives, the requirements for strategic and competitive success, and what specific results are needed in different facets of the business to keep strategy execution on track.

Guidelines for Designing Incentive Compensation Systems   The concepts and company experiences discussed above yield the following guidelines for creating an incentive compensation system to help drive successful strategy execution:

1. *The performance payoff must be a major, not minor, piece of the total compensation package*—at least 10 to 12 percent of base salary. Incentives that amount to 20 percent or more of total compensation are big attention getters, likely to really drive individual effort; incentives amounting to less than 5 percent of total compensation have comparatively weak motivational impact. Moreover, the payoff for high performers must be substantially greater than the payoff for average performers and the payoff for average performers substantially bigger than for below average performers.

2. *The incentive plan should extend to all managers and all workers*, not just be restricted to top management. It is a gross miscalculation to expect that lower-level managers and employees will work their tails off to hit performance targets just so a few senior executives can get lucrative bonuses!

3. *The reward system must be administered with scrupulous care and fairness.* If performance standards are set too high or if individual/group performance evaluations are not accurate and well documented, dissatisfaction and disgruntlement with the system will overcome any positive benefits.

4. *The incentives must be tightly linked to achieving only those performance targets spelled out in the strategic plan* and not to any other factors that get thrown in because they are thought to be nice. Performance evaluation based on factors not tightly related to the strategy signal that either the strategic plan is incomplete (because important performance targets were left out) or management's real agenda is something other than what was stated in the strategic plan.

5. *The performance targets each individual is expected to achieve should involve outcomes that the individual can personally affect.* The role of incentives is to enhance individual commitment and channel behavior in beneficial directions. That won't happen when the performance measures an individual is judged by are outside his/her arena of influence.

6. *Keep the time between the performance review and payment of the reward short.* A lengthy interval between review and payment breeds discontent and works against reinforcing cause and effect.

7. *Make liberal use of nonmonetary rewards; don't rely solely on monetary rewards.* Money, when used properly, is a great motivator, but praise, special recognition, handing out plum assignments, and so on can be potent motivators as well.

8. *Skirting the system to find ways to reward nonperformers must be absolutely avoided.* It is debatable whether exceptions should be made for people who've tried hard, gone the extra mile, yet still come up short because of circumstances beyond their control—arguments can be made either way. The problem with making exceptions for unknowable, uncontrollable, or unforeseeable circumstances is that once "good" excuses start to creep into justifying rewards for nonperformers, the door is open for all kinds of "legitimate" reasons why actual performance failed to match targeted performance. In short, people at all levels have to be held accountable for carrying out their assigned parts of the strategic plan, and they have to know their rewards are based on their accomplishments.

Once the incentives are designed, they have to be communicated and explained. Everybody needs to understand how incentives are calculated and how individual/group performance targets contribute to organizationwide performance targets. Moreover, the reasons for anyone's failure or deviations from targets have to be explored fully to determine whether the causes are poor individual/group performance or circumstances beyond the control of those responsible. The pressure to achieve the targeted strategic and financial performance and continuously improve on strategy execution should be unrelenting. A "no excuses" standard has to prevail.[31] But with the pressure to perform must come deserving and meaningful rewards. Without an ample payoff, the system breaks down, and the strategy implementer is left with the unworkable option of barking orders and pleading for compliance.

A Few Cautions about Performance-Based Incentive Pay In some foreign countries, incentive pay runs counter to local customs and cultural norms. Professor Steven Kerr cites the time he lectured an executive education class on the need for more performance-based pay and a Japanese manager protested, "You shouldn't bribe your children to do their homework, you shouldn't bribe your wife to prepare dinner, and you shouldn't bribe your employees to work for the company."[32] Singling out individuals and commending them for unusually good effort can also be a problem; Japanese culture considers public praise of an individual an affront to the harmony of the group. In some countries, employees have a preference for nonmonetary rewards—more leisure time, important titles, access to vacation villages, and nontaxable perks.

A change in strategy nearly always calls for budget reallocations. Reworking the budget to make it more strategy-supportive is a crucial part of the implementation process because every organization unit needs to have the people, equipment, facilities, and other resources to carry out its part of the strategic plan (but no more than what it really needs!). Implementing a new strategy often entails shifting resources from one area to another—downsizing units that are overstaffed and overfunded, upsizing those more critical to strategic success, and killing projects and activities that are no longer justified.

KEY POINTS

[31]Tom Peters and Nancy Austin, *A Passion for Excellence* (New York: Random House, 1985), p. xix.
[32]Kerr, "Risky Business: The New Pay Game," p. 96. For a more general criticism of why performance incentives are a bad idea, see Kohn, "Why Incentive Plans Cannot Work," pp. 54–63.

Anytime a company alters its strategy, managers are well advised to review existing policies and operating procedures, deleting or revising those that are out of sync and deciding if additional ones are needed. Prescribing new or freshly revised policies and operating procedures aids the task of implementation (1) by providing top-down guidance to operating managers, supervisory personnel, and employees regarding how certain things need to be done; (2) by putting boundaries on independent actions and decisions; (3) by promoting consistency in how particular strategy-critical activities are performed in geographically scattered operating units; and (4) by helping to create a strategy-supportive work climate and corporate culture. Thick policy manuals are usually unnecessary. Indeed, when individual creativity and initiative are more essential to good execution than standardization and conformity, it is better to give people the freedom to do things however they see fit and hold them accountable for good results rather than try to control their behavior with policies and guidelines for every situation. Hence, creating a supportive fit between strategy and policy can mean many policies, few policies, or different policies.

Competent strategy execution entails visible, firm managerial commitment to best practices and continuous improvement. Benchmarking, instituting best practices, reengineering core business processes, and total quality management programs all aim at improved efficiency, lower costs, better product quality, and greater customer satisfaction. *All these techniques are important tools for learning how to execute a strategy more proficiently.* Benchmarking provides a realistic basis for setting performance targets. Instituting "best-in-industry" or "best-in-world" operating practices in most or all value-chain activities is essential to create a quality-oriented, high-performance work environment. Reengineering is a way to make quantum progress in being world class while TQM instills a commitment to continuous improvement. Effective use of TQM/continuous improvement techniques is a valuable competitive asset in a company's resource portfolio—one that can produce important competitive capabilities (in reducing costs, speeding new products to market, or improving product quality, service, or customer satisfaction) and be a source of competitive advantage.

Company strategies can't be implemented or executed well without a number of support systems to carry on business operations. Well-conceived, state-of-the-art support systems not only facilitate better strategy execution, they can also strengthen organizational capabilities enough to provide a competitive edge over rivals. In an age of computers, computerized monitoring and control systems, E-mail, the Internet, company intranets, and wireless communications capabilities, companies can't hope to outexecute their competitors without cutting-edge information systems and technologically sophisticated operating capabilities that enable fast, efficient, and effective organization action.

Strategy-supportive motivational practices and reward systems are powerful management tools for gaining employee buy-in and commitment. The key to creating a reward system that promotes good strategy execution is to make strategically relevant measures of performance *the dominating basis* for designing incentives, evaluating individual and group efforts, and handing out rewards. Positive motivational practices generally work better than negative ones, but there is a place for both. There's also a place for both monetary and nonmonetary incentives.

For an incentive compensation system to work well (1) the monetary payoff should be a major percentage of the compensation package, (2) the use of incentives should extend to all managers and workers, (3) the system should be administered with care and fairness, (4) the incentives should be linked to performance targets spelled out in the strategic plan, (5) each individual's performance targets should involve outcomes the person can personally affect, (6) rewards should promptly follow the determination of good performance, (7) monetary rewards should be supplemented with liberal use of nonmonetary rewards, and (8) skirting the system to reward nonperformers should be scrupulously avoided.

SUGGESTED READINGS

Denton, Keith D. "Creating a System for Continuous Improvement." *Business Horizons* 38, no. 1 (January–February 1995), pp. 16–21.

Grant, Robert M., Rami Shani, and R. Krishnan, "TQM's Challenge to Management Theory and Practice." *Sloan Management Review* (Winter 1994), pp. 25–35.

Haeckel, Stephan H. and Richard L. Nolan. "Managing by Wire." *Harvard Business Review* 75, no. 5 (September–October 1993), pp. 122–32.

Herzberg, Frederick. "One More Time: How Do You Motivate Employees?" *Harvard Business Review* 65, no. 4 (September–October 1987), pp. 109–20.

Kerr, Steven. "On the Folly of Rewarding A While Hoping for B." *Academy of Management Executive* 9 no. 1 (February 1995), pp. 7–14.

Kiernan, Matthew J. "The New Strategic Architecture: Learning to Compete in the Twenty-First Century." *Academy of Management Executive* 7, no. 1 (February 1993), pp. 7–21.

Kohn, Alfie. "Why Incentive Plans Cannot Work." *Harvard Business Review* 71, no. 5 (September–October 1993), pp. 54–63.

Olian, Judy D. and Sara L. Rynes, "Making Total Quality Work: Aligning Organizational Processes, Performance Measures, and Stakeholders," *Human Resource Management* 30, no. 3 (Fall 1991), pp. 303–33.

Ohinata, Yoshinobu. "Benchmarking: The Japanese Experience." *Long Range Planning* 27, no. 4 (August 1994), pp. 48–53.

Pfeffer, Jeffrey. "Producing Sustainable Competitive Advantage through the Effective Management of People." *Academy of Management Executive* 9, no. 1 (February 1995), pp. 55–69.

Quinn, James Brian. *Intelligent Enterprise*. New York: Free Press, 1992, chap. 4.

Shetty, Y. K. "Aiming High: Competitive Benchmarking for Superior Performance." *Long-Range Planning* 26, no. 1 (February 1993), pp. 39–44.

Simons, Robert. "Control in an Age of Empowerment." *Harvard Business Review* 73 (March–April 1995), pp. 80–88.

Wiley, Carolyn. "Incentive Plan Pushes Production." *Personnel Journal* (August 1993), pp. 86–91.

11 IMPLEMENTING STRATEGY: CULTURE AND LEADERSHIP

In the previous two chapters we examined six of the strategy implementer's tasks—building a capable organization, steering ample resources into strategy-critical activities and operating units, establishing strategy-supportive policies, instituting best practices and programs for continuous improvement, creating internal support systems to enable better execution, and employing appropriate motivational practices and compensation incentives. In this chapter we explore the two remaining implementation tasks: creating a strategy-supportive corporate culture and exerting the internal leadership needed to drive implementation forward.

BUILDING A STRATEGY-SUPPORTIVE CORPORATE CULTURE

Every company has its own unique culture—one made distinctive by its own business philosophy and principles, its own ways of approaching problems and making decisions, its own embedded patterns of "how we do things around here," its own lore (stories told over and over to illustrate company values and what they mean to employees), its own taboos and political don'ts, its own organizational personality. The bedrock of Wal-Mart's culture is dedication to customer satisfaction, zealous pursuit of low costs, a strong work ethic, Sam Walton's legendary frugality, the ritualistic Saturday morning headquarters meetings to exchange ideas and review problems, and company executives' commitment to visiting stores, talking to customers, and soliciting suggestions from employees. At McDonald's the constant message from management is the overriding importance of quality, service, cleanliness, and value; employees are drilled over and over on the need for attention to detail and perfection in every fundamental of the business. At Microsoft, there are stories of the long hours programmers put in, the emotional peaks and valleys in encountering and overcoming coding problems, the exhilaration of completing a complex program on schedule, the satisfaction of working on cutting-edge projects, and the rewards of being part of a

---

ILLUSTRATION CAPSULE 39 The Culture at Nordstrom

The culture at Nordstrom, a department store retailer noted for exceptional commitment to its customers, revolves around the company's motto: "Respond to Unreasonable Customer Requests." Living up to the company's motto is so strongly ingrained in behavior that employees learn to relish the challenges that some customer requests pose. Usually, meeting customer demands in pleasing fashion entails little more than gracious compliance and a little extra personal attention. But occasionally it means paying a customer's parking ticket when in-store gift wrapping takes longer than normal or hand-delivering items purchased by phone to the airport for a customer with an emergency need.

At Nordstrom, each out-of-the-ordinary customer request is seen as an opportunity for a "heroic" act by an employee and a way to build the company's reputation for great service. Nordstrom encourages these acts by pro-

moting employees noted for outstanding service, keeping scrapbooks of "heroic" acts, and basing the compensation of salespeople mainly on commission (it is not unusual for good salespeople at Nordstrom to earn double what they would at other department store retailers).

For go-getters who truly enjoy retail selling and pleasing customers, Nordstrom is a great company to work for. But the culture weeds out those who can't meet Nordstrom's demanding standards and rewards those who are prepared to be what Nordstrom stands for.

Nordstrom starts new employees, even those with advanced degrees, out on the sales floor. Promotion is strictly from within, and when a new store is opened, its key people are recruited from other stores around the country to help perpetuate Nordstrom's culture and values and to make sure the new store is run the Nordstrom way.

Source: Based on information in Tracy Goss, Richard Pascale, and Anthony Athos, "Risking the Present for a Powerful Future," *Harvard Business Review* 71, no. 6 (November–December 1993), pp. 101–2 and Jeffrey Pheffer, "Producing Sustainable Competitive Advantage through the Effective Management of People," *Academy of Management Executive* 9, no. 1 (February 1995), pp. 59–60 and 65.

team responsible for developing trailblazing software. Illustration Capsule 39 describes the culture at Nordstrom's.

Where Does Corporate Culture Come From?

Corporate culture refers to a company's values, beliefs, traditions, operating style, and internal work environment.

The taproot of corporate culture is the organization's beliefs and philosophy about how its affairs ought to be conducted—the reasons why it does things the way it does. A company's culture is manifested in the values and principles that management preaches and practices, in its ethical standards and official policies, in its stakeholder relationships (especially its dealings with employees, unions, stockholders, vendors, and the communities in which it operates), in its traditions, in its supervisory practices, in employees' attitudes and behavior, in the legends people repeat about happenings in the organization, in the peer pressures that exist, in the organization's politics, and in the "chemistry" and "vibrations" that permeate its work environment. All these forces, some of which operate quite subtly, combine to define an organization's culture.

Beliefs and practices that become embedded in a company's culture can originate anywhere: from one influential individual, work group, department, or division, from the bottom of the organizational hierarchy or the top.[1] Very often, many components of the culture are associated with a founder or other early leaders who articulated them as a company philosophy or as a set of principles the organization should rigidly adhere to or as company policies. Sometimes, elements of the culture spring from the company's vision, its strategic intent, and core components of its strategy (like obsessive emphasis on low cost or technological leadership or first-rate quality). Over time, these cultural underpinnings take root, become embedded in how the

---

[1] John P. Kotter and James L. Heskett, *Corporate Culture and Performance* (New York: Free Press, 1992), p. 7.

company conducts its business, come to be shared by company managers and employees, and then persist as new employees are encouraged to embrace them. Fast-growing companies risk creating a culture by chance rather than by design if they rush to hire employees mainly for their technical skills and credentials and neglect to screen out candidates whose values, philosophies, and personalities aren't compatible with the organizational character, vision, and strategy that management is trying to cultivate.

A company's culture is a product of internal social forces; it is manifested in the values, behavioral norms, and ways of operating that prevail across the organization.

Once established, company cultures can be perpetuated in many ways: continuity of leadership, screening and selecting new group members according to how well their values and personalities fit in (as well as on the basis of talents and credentials), systematic indoctrination of new members in the culture's fundamentals, the efforts of senior group members to reiterate core values in daily conversations and pronouncements, the telling and retelling of company legends, regular ceremonies honoring members who display cultural ideals, and visibly rewarding those who follow cultural norms and penalizing those who don't.[2] However, even stable cultures aren't static. Crises and new challenges evolve into new ways of doing things. Arrival of new leaders and turnover of key members often spawn new or different values and practices that alter the culture. Diversification into new businesses, expansion into different geographical areas, rapid growth that adds new employees, and the exploding use of the Internet, company intranets, and electronic mail can all cause a culture to evolve. Indeed, one of the most important business phenomena of the late 1990s is the historic impact that widespread use of PCs and information technology is having on corporate cultures and on how a company's internal and external business is conducted.

Although it is common to speak about corporate culture in the singular, companies typically have multiple cultures (or subcultures).[3] Values, beliefs, and practices can vary by department, geographic location, division, or business unit. Global companies are highly multicultural. A company's subcultures can clash, or at least not mesh well, if recently acquired business units have not yet been assimilated or if different units operate in different countries or have varying managerial styles, business philosophies, and operating approaches. The human resources manager of a global pharmaceutical company who took on an assignment in the Far East discovered, to his surprise, that one of his biggest challenges was to persuade his company's managers in China, Korea, Malaysia, and Taiwan to accept promotions—their cultural values were such that they did not believe in competing with their peers for career rewards or personal gain, nor did they relish breaking ties to their local communities to assume cross-national responsibilities.[4] Many companies that have merged with or acquired foreign companies have to deal with language and custom-based cultural differences.

The Power of Culture

The beliefs, vision, objectives, and business approaches and practices underpinning a company's strategy may be compatible with its culture or they may not. When they are, the culture becomes a valuable ally in strategy implementation and execution.

[2]Ibid., pp. 7–8.

[3]Ibid., p. 5.

[4]John Alexander and Meena S. Wilson, "Leading across Cultures: Five Vital Capabilities," in *The Organization of the Future,* Frances Hesselbein, Marshall Goldsmith, and Richard Beckard, (San Francisco: Jossey-Bass, 1997), pp. 291–92.

When they are not, a company usually finds it difficult to implement the strategy successfully.[5]

A culture grounded in values, practices, and behavioral norms that match what is needed for good strategy execution helps energize people to do their jobs in a strategy-supportive manner. For example, a culture where frugality and thrift are values widely shared by organizational members is very conducive to successful execution of a low-cost leadership strategy. A culture where creativity, embracing change, and challenging the status quo are pervasive themes is conducive to successful execution of a product innovation and technological leadership strategy. A culture built around such principles as listening to customers, encouraging employees to take pride in their work, and giving employees a high degree of decision-making responsibility is conducive to successful execution of a strategy of delivering superior customer service. When a company's culture is out of sync with what is needed for strategic success, the culture has to be changed as rapidly as can be managed; the more entrenched the culture, the greater the difficulty of implementing new or different strategies. A sizable and prolonged strategy-culture conflict weakens and may even defeat managerial efforts to make the strategy work.

An organization's culture is an important contributor (or obstacle) to successful strategy execution.

Strong cultures promote good strategy execution when there's fit with the strategy and hurt execution when there's little fit.

A tight culture-strategy alignment acts in two ways to channel behavior and influence employees do their jobs in a strategy-supportive fashion:[6]

1. *A work environment where the culture matches well with the conditions for good strategy execution provides a system of informal rules and peer pressures regarding how to conduct business and how to go about doing one's job.* Strategy-supportive cultures shape the mood, temperament, and motivation of the workforce, positively affecting organizational energy, work habits and operating practices, the degree to which organizational units cooperate, and how customers are treated. Culturally approved behavior thrives, while culturally disapproved behavior gets squashed and often penalized. In a company where strategy and culture are misaligned, ingrained values and operating philosophies don't cultivate strategy-supportive ways of operating; often, the very kinds of behavior needed to execute strategy successfully run afoul of the culture and attract criticism rather than praise and reward.

A deeply rooted culture well matched to strategy is a powerful lever for successful strategy execution.

2. *A strong strategy-supportive culture nurtures and motivates people to do their jobs in ways conducive to effective strategy execution; it provides structure, standards, and a value system in which to operate; and it promotes strong employee identification with the company's vision, performance targets, and strategy.* All this makes employees feel genuinely better about their jobs and work environment and the merits of what the company is trying to accomplish. Employees are stimulated to take on the challenge of realizing the company's vision, do their jobs competently and with enthusiasm, and collaborate with others to execute the strategy.

This says something important about the task of leading strategy implementation: *Anything so fundamental as implementing a strategic plan involves moving the organization's culture into close alignment with the requirements for proficient strategy execution.* The optimal condition is a work environment that energizes the organization in a strategy-supportive fashion, promoting "can-do" attitudes and

---

[5]Ibid.
[6]Ibid., pp. 15–16.

acceptance of change where needed, enlisting and encouraging people to perform strategy-critical activities in superior fashion, and breeding needed organizational competencies and capabilities. As one observer noted:

> It has not been just strategy that led to big Japanese wins in the American auto market. It is a culture that enspirits workers to excel at fits and finishes, to produce moldings that match and doors that don't sag. It is a culture in which Toyota can use that most sophisticated of management tools, the suggestion box, and in two years increase the number of worker suggestions from under 10,000 to over 1 million with resultant savings of $250 million.[7]

Strong versus Weak Cultures

Company cultures vary widely in the degree to which they are embedded in company practices and behavioral norms. A company's culture can be weak and fragmented in the sense that many subcultures exist, few values and behavioral norms are widely shared, and there are few traditions. In weak or fragmented culture companies, there's little cohesion and glue across units from a business principles and work climate perspective—top executives don't espouse any business philosophy or extol use of particular operating practices. Because of a lack of common values and ingrained business approaches, organizational members typically have no deeply felt sense of identity with the company's vision and strategy; instead, many employees view the company as a place to work and their job as a way to make a living. While they may have some bonds with and loyalty toward their department, their colleagues, their union, or their boss, the weak company culture breeds no strong employee allegiance to what the company stands for and no sense of urgency about pushing strategy execution along. As a consequence, weak cultures provide no strategy-implementing assistance.

Strong Culture Companies   On the other hand, a company's culture can be strong and cohesive in the sense that the company conducts its business according to a clear and explicit set of principles and values, that management devotes considerable time to communicating these principles and values and explaining how they relate to its business environment, and that the values are shared widely across the company—by senior executives and rank-and-file employees alike.[8] Strong culture companies typically have creeds or values statements, and executives regularly stress the importance of using these values and principles as the basis for decisions and actions taken throughout the organization. In strong culture companies values and behavioral norms are so deeply rooted that they don't change much when a new CEO takes over—although they can erode over time if the CEO ceases to nurture them.

In a strong culture company, values and behavioral norms are like crabgrass: deeply rooted and difficult to weed out.

Three factors contribute to the development of strong cultures: (1) a founder or strong leader who establishes values, principles, and practices that are consistent and sensible in light of customer needs, competitive conditions, and strategic requirements; (2) a sincere, long-standing company commitment to operating the business according to these established traditions; and (3) a genuine concern for the well-being of the organization's three biggest constituencies—customers, employees, and shareholders. Continuity of leadership, small group size, stable group membership,

---

[7]Robert H. Waterman, Jr., "The Seven Elements of Strategic Fit," *Journal of Business Strategy* 2, no. 3 (Winter 1982), p. 70.

[8]Terrence E. Deal and Allen A. Kennedy, *Corporate Cultures* (Reading, Mass.: Addison-Wesley, 1982), p. 22.

geographic concentration, and considerable organizational success all contribute to the emergence of a strong culture.[9]

During the time a strong culture is being implanted, there's nearly always a good strategy-culture fit (which partially accounts for the organization's success). Mismatches between strategy and culture in a strong culture company tend to occur when a company's environment undergoes rapid-fire change, prompting a drastic strategy revision that clashes with the entrenched culture. In such cases, a major culture-changing effort has to be launched. Both IBM and Apple Computer have been going through wrenching culture changes to adapt to the new computer industry environment now driven by the so-called Wintel standard—Microsoft (with its Windows operating systems for PCs and its Windows-based PC software programs) and Intel (with its successive generations of faster microprocessors for PCs). IBM's bureaucracy and mainframe culture clashed with the shift to a PC-dominated world. Apple's culture clash stemmed from strong company sentiment to continue on with internally developed Macintosh technology (incompatible with all other brands of computers) despite growing preferences for Wintel-compatible equipment and software.

A strong culture is a valuable asset when it matches the requirements for good strategy execution and a dreaded liability when it doesn't.

Low-Performance or Unhealthy Cultures

A number of unhealthy cultural characteristics can undermine a company's business performance.[10] One is a politicized internal environment that allows influential managers to operate their fiefdoms autonomously and resist needed change. In politically dominated cultures, many issues get resolved on the basis of turf, vocal support or opposition by powerful executives, personal lobbying by a key executive, and coalitions among individuals or departments with vested interests in a particular outcome. What's best for the company plays second fiddle to personal aggrandizement.

A second unhealthy cultural trait, one that can plague companies suddenly confronted with fast-changing business conditions, is hostility to change and to people who champion new ways of doing things. Executives who don't value managers or employees with initiative or new ideas dampen experimentation and efforts to improve the status quo. Avoiding risks and not screwing up become more important to a person's career advancement than entrepreneurial successes and innovative accomplishments. This trait is most often found in companies with multilayered management bureaucracies that have enjoyed considerable market success in years past but whose business environments have been hit with accelerating change. General Motors, IBM, Sears, and Eastman Kodak are classic examples; all four gradually became burdened by a stifling bureaucracy that rejected innovation. Now, they are struggling to reinvent the cultural approaches that caused them to succeed in the first place.

A third unhealthy characteristic is promoting managers who understand complex organization structures, problem solving, budgets, controls, and how to handle administrative detail better than they understand vision, strategies, competitive capabilities, inspiration, and culture building. While the former are adept at organizational maneuvering, if they ascend to senior executive positions, the company can find itself short of the entrepreneurial skills and leadership needed to introduce new strategies, reallocate resources, build new competitive capabilities, and fashion a new culture— a condition that ultimately erodes long-term performance.

---

[9]Vijay Sathe, *Culture and Related Corporate Realities* (Homewood, Ill.: Richard D. Irwin, 1985).

[10]Kotter and Heskett, *Corporate Culture and Performance*, chapter 6.

A fourth characteristic of low-performance cultures is an aversion to looking outside the company for superior practices and approaches. Sometimes a company enjoys such great market success and reigns as an industry leader for so long that its management becomes inbred and arrogant. It believes it has all the answers or can develop them on its own. Insular thinking, inward-looking solutions, and a must-be-invented-here syndrome often precede a decline in company performance. Kotter and Heskett cite Avon, BankAmerica, Citicorp, Coors, Ford, General Motors, Kmart, Kroger, Sears, Texaco, and Xerox as examples of companies that had low-performance cultures during the late 1970s and early 1980s.[11]

Changing problem cultures is very difficult because of the heavy anchor of deeply held values, habits, and the emotional clinging of people to the old and familiar. Sometimes executives succeed in changing the values and behaviors of small groups of managers and even whole departments or divisions, only to find the changes eroded over time by the actions of the rest of the organization. What is communicated, praised, supported, and penalized by the entrenched majority undermines the new emergent culture and halts its progress. Executives can revamp formal organization charts, announce new strategies, bring in managers from the outside, introduce new technologies, and open new plants, yet fail to change embedded cultural traits and behaviors because of skepticism about the new directions and covert resistance to them.

Once a culture is established, it is difficult to change.

Adaptive Cultures

In fast-changing business environments, the capacity to introduce new strategies and organizational practices is a necessity if a company is to perform well over long periods of time.[12] Strategic agility and fast organizational response to new conditions require a culture that quickly accepts and supports company efforts to adapt to environmental change rather than a culture that has to be coaxed and cajoled to change.

In adaptive cultures, members share a feeling of confidence that the organization can deal with whatever threats and opportunities come down the pike; they are receptive to risk-taking, experimentation, innovation, and changing strategies and practices whenever necessary to satisfy the legitimate interests of stakeholders—customers, employees, shareowners, suppliers, and the communities where the company operates. Hence, members willingly embrace a proactive approach to identifying issues, evaluating the implications and options, and implementing workable solutions—there's a spirit of doing what's necessary to ensure long-term organizational success *provided core values and business principles are upheld in the process.* Entrepreneurship is encouraged and rewarded. Managers habitually fund product development, evaluate new ideas openly, and take prudent risks to create new business positions. Strategies and traditional operating practices are modified as needed to adjust to or take advantage of changes in the business environment. The leaders of adaptive cultures are adept at changing the right things in the right ways, not changing for the sake of change and not compromising core values or business principles. Adaptive cultures are supportive of managers and employees at all ranks who propose or help initiate useful change; indeed, executives consciously seek, train, and promote individuals who display these leadership traits.

Adaptive cultures are a strategy implementer's best ally.

One outstanding trait of adaptive cultures is that top management, while orchestrating responses to changing conditions, demonstrates genuine care for the well-being of

---

[11]Ibid., p. 68.

[12]This section draws heavily from Kotter and Heskett, *Corporate Culture and Performance*, chapter 4.

all key constituencies—customers, employees, stockholders, major suppliers, and the communities where the company operates—and tries to satisfy all their legitimate interests simultaneously. No group is ignored, and fairness to all constituencies is a decision-making principle—a commitment often described as "doing the right thing."[13] Pleasing customers and protecting, if not enhancing, the company's long-term well-being is seen as the best way of looking out for the interests of employees, stockholders, suppliers, and communities where the company operates. Management concern for the well-being of employees is a big factor in gaining employee support for change—employees understand that changes in their job assignments are part of the process of adapting to new conditions and that their job security will not be threatened in the process of adapting to change, unless the company's business unexpectedly reverses direction. In cases where workforce downsizing becomes necessary, management concern for employees dictates that separation be handled in a humane fashion. Management efforts to make the process of adapting to change fair, keeping adverse impacts to a minimum, breeds acceptance of and support for change among all stakeholders.

In less-adaptive cultures where resistance to change is the norm, managers avoid risk-taking and prefer following to leading when it comes to technological change and new product innovation.[14] They believe in moving cautiously and conservatively, endeavoring not to make "mistakes" and making sure they protect or advance their own careers, the interests of their immediate work groups, or their pet projects.

Creating the Fit between Strategy and Culture

It is the *strategy maker's* responsibility to select a strategy compatible with the "sacred" or unchangeable parts of prevailing corporate culture. It is the *strategy implementer's* task, once strategy is chosen, to change whatever facets of the corporate culture hinder effective execution.

Changing a company's culture and aligning it with strategy are among the toughest management tasks—easier to talk about than do. The first step is to diagnose which facets of the present culture are strategy-supportive and which are not. Then, managers have to talk openly and forthrightly to all concerned about those aspects of the culture that have to be changed. The talk has to be followed swiftly by visible actions to modify the culture—actions that everyone will understand are intended to establish a new culture more in tune with the strategy.

Symbolic Actions and Substantive Actions   Managerial actions to tighten the culture-strategy fit need to be both symbolic and substantive. Symbolic actions are valuable for the signals they send about the kinds of behavior and performance strategy implementers wish to encourage. The most important symbolic actions are those that top executives take to serve as role models—leading cost reduction efforts by curtailing executive perks; emphasizing the importance of responding to customers' needs by requiring all officers and executives to spend a significant portion of each week talking with customers and understanding their requirements; and assuming a high profile in altering policies and practices that hinder the new strategy. Another category of symbolic actions includes the events to designate and honor people whose actions and performance exemplify what is called for in the new culture. Many universities give outstanding teacher awards each year to symbolize their esteem for instructors with exceptional classroom talents. Numerous businesses have

---

[13]Ibid., p. 52.
[14]Ibid., p. 50.

employee-of-the-month awards. The military has a long-standing custom of awarding ribbons and medals for exemplary actions. Mary Kay Cosmetics awards an array of prizes—from ribbons to pink automobiles—to its beauty consultants for reaching various sales plateaus.

The best companies and the best executives expertly use symbols, role models, ceremonial occasions, and group gatherings to tighten the strategy-culture fit. Low-cost leaders like Wal-Mart and Nucor are renowned for their spartan facilities, executive frugality, intolerance of waste, and zealous control of costs. Executives sensitive to their role in promoting strategy-culture fits make a habit of appearing at ceremonial functions to praise individuals and groups that "get with the program." They honor individuals who exhibit cultural norms and reward those who achieve strategic milestones. They participate in employee training programs to stress strategic priorities, values, ethical principles, and cultural norms. Every group gathering is seen as an opportunity to implant values, praise good deeds, reinforce cultural norms, and promote changes that assist strategy implementation. Sensitive executives make sure that organizational members will construe current decisions and policy changes as consistent with and supportive of the company's new strategic direction.[15]

Awards ceremonies, role models, and symbols are a fundamental part of a strategy implementer's culture-shaping effort.

In addition to being out front personally and symbolically, leading the push for new behaviors and communicating the reasons for new approaches, strategy-implementers have to convince all those concerned that the effort is more than cosmetic. Talk and plans have to be complemented by substantive actions and real movement. The actions taken have to be credible, highly visible, and indicative of management's commitment to new strategic initiatives and the associated cultural changes. There are several ways to accomplish this. One is to engineer some quick successes that highlight the benefits of strategy-culture changes, thus making enthusiasm for the changes contagious. However, instant results are usually not as important as having the will and patience to create a solid, competent team committed to pursuing the strategy. The strongest signs that management is truly committed to creating a new culture include: replacing old-culture managers with "new breed" managers, changing long-standing policies and operating practices that are dysfunctional or that impede new initiatives, undertaking major reorganizational moves that bring structure into better alignment with strategy, tying compensation incentives directly to the new measures of strategic performance, and shifting substantial resources from old-strategy projects and programs to new-strategy projects and programs.

At the same time, chief strategy-implementers must be careful to *lead by example*. For instance, if the organization's strategy involves a drive to become the industry's low-cost producer, senior managers must display frugality in their own actions and decisions: Inexpensive decorations in the executive suite, conservative expense accounts and entertainment allowances, a lean staff in the corporate office, scrutiny of budget requests, and so on. The CEO of SAS Airlines, Jan Carlzon, symbolically reinforced the primacy of quality service for business customers by flying coach instead of first class and by giving up his seat to waitlisted travelers.[16]

Senior executives must personally lead efforts to align culture with strategy.

[15]Judy D. Olian and Sara L. Rynes, "Making Total Quality Work: Aligning Organizational Processes, Performance Measures, and Stakeholders," *Human Resource Management* 30, no. 3 (Fall 1991), p. 324.
[16]Ibid.

Implanting the needed culture-building values and behavior depends on a sincere, sustained commitment by the chief executive coupled with persistence in reinforcing the culture at every opportunity through both word and deed. Neither charisma nor personal magnetism are essential. However, personally talking to many groups about the reasons for change *is* essential; cultural changes are seldom accomplished successfully from an office. Moreover, creating and sustaining a strategy-supportive culture is a job for the whole management team. Major cultural change requires many initiatives from many people. Senior officers, department heads, and middle managers have to reiterate values, "walk the talk," and translate the desired cultural norms and behavior into everyday practice. In addition, strategy implementers must enlist the support of firstline supervisors and employee opinion leaders, convincing them of the merits of practicing and enforcing cultural norms at the lowest levels in the organization. Until a big majority of employees joins the new culture and shares a commitment to its basic values and norms, there's considerably more work to be done in both instilling the culture and tightening the culture-strategy fit.

The task of making culture supportive of strategy is not a short-term exercise. It takes time for a new culture to emerge and prevail; it's unrealistic to expect an overnight transformation. The bigger the organization and the greater the cultural shift needed to produce a culture-strategy fit, the longer it takes. In large companies, changing the corporate culture in significant ways can take three to five years at minimum. In fact, it is usually tougher to reshape a deeply ingrained culture that is not strategy-supportive than it is to instill a strategy-supportive culture from scratch in a brand-new organization.

Building Ethical Standards and Values into the Culture

A strong corporate culture founded on ethical business principles and moral values is a vital force behind continued strategic success. Many executives are convinced that a company must care about how it does business; otherwise a company's reputation, and ultimately its performance, is put at risk. Corporate ethics and values programs are not window dressing; they are undertaken to create an environment of strongly held values and convictions and to make ethical conduct a way of life. Morally upstanding values and high ethical standards nurture the corporate culture in a very positive way—they connote integrity, "doing the right thing," and genuine concern for stakeholders.

An ethical corporate culture has a positive impact on a company's long-term strategic success; an unethical culture can undermine it.

Companies establish values and ethical standards in a number of ways.[17] Companies steeped in tradition with a rich folklore to draw on rely on word-of-mouth indoctrination and the power of tradition to instill values and enforce ethical conduct. But many companies today set forth their values and codes of ethics in written documents. Table 11–1 indicates the kinds of topics such statements cover. Written statements have the advantage of explicitly stating what the company intends and expects, and they serve as benchmarks for judging both company policies and actions and individual conduct. They put a stake in the ground and define the company's position. Value statements serve as a cornerstone for culture building; a code of ethics serves as a cornerstone for developing a corporate conscience.[18] Illustration Capsule 40

---

[17]The Business Roundtable, *Corporate Ethics: A Prime Asset*, February 1988, pp. 4–10.

[18]For a discussion of the strategic benefits of formal statements of corporate values, see John Humble, David Jackson, and Alan Thomson, "The Strategic Power of Corporate Values," *Long Range Planning* 27, no. 6 (December 1994), pp. 28–42. For a study of the status of formal codes of ethics in large U. S. corporations,

TABLE 11-1   Topics Generally Covered in Value Statements and Codes of Ethics

Topics Covered in Values Statements	Topics Covered in Codes of Ethics
• Importance of customers and customer service • Commitment to quality • Commitment to innovation • Respect for the individual employee and the duty the company has to employees • Importance of honesty, integrity, and ethical standards • Duty to stockholders • Duty to suppliers • Corporate citizenship • Importance of protecting the environment	• Honesty and observance of the law • Conflicts of interest • Fairness in selling and marketing practices • Using inside information and securities trading • Supplier relationships and purchasing practices • Payments to obtain business/Foreign Corrupt Practices Act • Acquiring and using information about others • Political activities • Use of company assets, resources, and property • Protection of proprietary information • Pricing, contracting, and billing

presents the Johnson & Johnson Credo, the most publicized and celebrated code of ethics and values among U.S. companies. J&J's CEO calls the credo "the unifying force for our corporation." Illustration Capsule 41 presents the pledge that Bristol-Myers Squibb makes to all of its stakeholders.

Once values and ethical standards have been formally set forth, they must be ingrained in the company's policies, practices, and actual conduct. Implementing the values and code of ethics entails several actions:

Values and ethical standards must not only be explicitly stated but they must also be ingrained into the corporate culture.

- Incorporating the statement of values and the code of ethics into employee training and educational programs.
- Explicit attention to values and ethics in recruiting and hiring to screen out applicants who lack compatible character traits.
- Communication of the values and ethics code to all employees and explaining compliance procedures.
- Management involvement and oversight, from the CEO down to firstline supervisors.
- Strong endorsements by the CEO.
- Word-of-mouth indoctrination.

In the case of codes of ethics, special attention must be given to sections of the company that are particularly sensitive and vulnerable—purchasing, sales, and political lobbying.[19] Employees who deal with external parties are in ethically sensitive positions and often are drawn into compromising situations. Procedures for enforcing ethical standards and handling potential violations have to be developed.

---

see Patrick E. Murphy, "Corporate Ethics Statements: Current Status and Future Prospects," *Journal of Business Ethics* 14 (1995), pp. 727–40.

[19]Ibid., p. 7.

ILLUSTRATION CAPSULE 40   The Johnson & Johnson Credo

- We believe our first responsibility is to the doctors, nurses, and patients, to mothers and all others who use our products and services.
- In meeting their needs everything we do must be of high quality.
- We must constantly strive to reduce our costs in order to maintain reasonable prices.
- Customers' orders must be serviced promptly and accurately.
- Our suppliers and distributors must have an opportunity to make a fair profit.
- We are responsible to our employees, the men and women who work with us throughout the world.
- Everyone must be considered as an individual.
- We must respect their dignity and recognize their merit.
- They must have a sense of security in their jobs.
- Compensation must be fair and adequate, and working conditions clean, orderly, and safe.
- Employees must feel free to make suggestions and complaints.
- There must be equal opportunity for employment, development, and advancement for those qualified.

- We must provide competent management, and their actions must be just and ethical.
- We are responsible to the communities in which we live and work and to the world community as well.
- We must be good citizens—support good works and charities and bear our fair share of taxes.
- We must encourage civic improvements and better health and education.
- We must maintain in good order the property we are privileged to use, protecting the environment and natural resources.
- Our final responsibility is to our stockholders.
- Business must make a sound profit.
- We must experiment with new ideas.
- Research must be carried on, innovative programs developed, and mistakes paid for.
- New equipment must be purchased, new facilities provided, and new products launched.
- Reserves must be created to provide for adverse times.
- When we operate according to these principles, the stockholders should realize a fair return.

Source: 1982 Annual Report.

The compliance effort must permeate the company, extending into every organizational unit. The attitudes, character, and work history of prospective employees must be combined. Every employee must receive adequate training. Line managers at all levels must give serious and continuous attention to the task of explaining how the values and ethical code apply in their areas. In addition, they must insist that company values and ethical standards become a way of life. In general, instilling values and insisting on ethical conduct must be looked on as a continuous culture-building, culture-nurturing exercise. Whether the effort succeeds or fails depends largely on how well corporate values and ethical standards are visibly integrated into company policies, managerial practices, and actions at all levels.

Building a Spirit of High Performance into the Culture

A results-oriented culture that inspires people to do their best is conducive to superior strategy execution.

An ability to instill strong individual commitment to strategic success and to create an atmosphere in which there is constructive pressure to perform is one of the most valuable strategy-implementing skills. When an organization performs consistently at or near peak capability, the outcome is not only more success but also a culture permeated with a spirit of high performance. Such a spirit of performance should not be confused with whether employees are "happy" or "satisfied" or whether they "get along well together." An organization with a spirit of high performance emphasizes achievement and excellence. Its culture is results-

---

ILLUSTRATION CAPSULE 41   The Bristol-Myers Squibb Pledge

To those who use our products . . .

We affirm Bristol-Myers Squibb's commitment to the highest standards of excellence, safety, and reliability in everything we make. We pledge to offer products of the highest quality and to work diligently to keep improving them.

To our employees and those who may join us . . .

We pledge personal respect, fair compensation, and equal treatment. We acknowledge our obligation to provide able and humane leadership throughout the organization, within a clean and safe working environment. To all who qualify for advancement, we will make every effort to provide opportunity.

To our suppliers and customers . . .

We pledge an open door, courteous, efficient, and ethical dealing, and appreciation for their right to a fair profit.

To our shareholders . . .

We pledge a companywide dedication to continued profitable growth, sustained by strong finances, a high level of research and development, and facilities second to none.

To the communities where we have plants and offices . . .

We pledge conscientious citizenship, a helping hand for worthwhile causes, and constructive action in support of civic and environmental progress.

To the countries where we do business . . .

We pledge ourselves to be a good citizen and to show full consideration for the rights of others while reserving the right to stand up for our own.

Above all, to the world we live in . . .

We pledge Bristol-Myers Squibb to policies and practices which fully embody the responsibility, integrity, and decency required of free enterprise if it is to merit and maintain the confidence of our society.

Source: 1990 Annual Report.

---

oriented, and its management pursues policies and practices that inspire people to do their best.[20]

Companies with a spirit of high performance typically are intensely people-oriented, and they reinforce their concern for individual employees on every conceivable occasion in every conceivable way. They treat employees with dignity and respect, train each employee thoroughly, encourage employees to use their own initiative and creativity in performing their work, set reasonable and clear performance expectations, use the full range of rewards and punishment to enforce high-performance standards, hold managers at every level responsible for developing the people who report to them, and grant employees enough autonomy to stand out, excel, and contribute. To create a results-oriented culture, a company must make champions out of the people who turn in winning performances:[21]

- At Boeing, General Electric, and 3M Corporation, top executives make a point of honoring individuals who believe so strongly in their ideas that they take it on themselves to hurdle the bureaucracy, maneuver their projects through the system, and turn them into improved services, new products, or even new businesses. In these companies, "product champions" are given high visibility, room to push their ideas, and strong executive support.

---

[20]For a more in-depth discussion of what it takes to create a climate and culture that nurtures success, see Benjamin Schneider, Sarah K. Gunnarson, and Kathryn Niles-Jolly, "Creating the Climate and Culture of Success," *Organizational Dynamics* (Summer 1994), pp. 17–29.

[21]Thomas J. Peters and Robert H. Waterman, Jr., *In Search of Excellence* (New York: Harper & Row, 1982), pp. xviii, 240, and 269, and Thomas J. Peters and Nancy Austin, *A Passion for Excellence* (New York: Random House, 1985), pp. 304–7.

Champions whose ideas prove out are usually handsomely rewarded; those whose ideas don't pan out still have secure jobs and are given chances to try again.

- Some companies upgrade the importance and status of individual employees by referring to them as Cast Members (Disney), crew members (McDonald's), or associates (Wal-Mart and J. C. Penney). Companies like Mary Kay Cosmetics, Tupperware, and McDonald's actively seek out reasons and opportunities to give pins, buttons, badges, and medals for good showings by average performers—the idea being to express appreciation and give a motivational boost to people who stand out doing "ordinary" jobs.

- McDonald's has a contest to determine the best hamburger cooker in its entire chain. It begins with a competition to determine the best hamburger cooker in each store. Store winners go on to compete in regional championships, and regional winners go on to the "All-American" contest. The winners get trophies and an All-American patch to wear on their shirts.

- Milliken & Co. holds Corporate Sharing Rallies once every three months; teams come from all over the company to swap success stories and ideas. A hundred or more teams make five-minute presentations over a two-day period. Each rally has a major theme—quality, cost reduction, and so on. No criticisms and negatives are allowed, and there is no such thing as a big idea or a small one. Quantitative measures of success are used to gauge improvement. All those present vote on the best presentation and several ascending grades of awards are handed out. Everyone, however, receives a framed certificate for participating.

What makes a spirit of high performance come alive is a complex network of practices, words, symbols, styles, values, and policies pulling together that produces extraordinary results with ordinary people. The drivers of the system are a belief in the worth of the individual, strong company commitment to job security and promotion from within, managerial practices that encourage employees to exercise individual initiative and creativity in doing their jobs, and pride in doing the "itty-bitty, teeny-tiny things" right.[22] A company that treats its employees well generally benefits from increased teamwork, higher morale, and greater employee loyalty.

While emphasizing a spirit of high performance nearly always accentuates the positive, there are negative reinforcers too. Managers whose units consistently perform poorly have to be removed. Aside from the organizational benefits, weak-performing managers should be reassigned for their own good—people who find themselves in a job they cannot handle are usually frustrated, anxiety-ridden, harassed, and unhappy.[23] Moreover, subordinates have a right to be managed with competence, dedication, and achievement. Unless their boss performs well, they themselves cannot perform well. In addition, weak-performing workers and people who reject the cultural emphasis on dedication and high performance have to be weeded out. Recruitment practices need to aim at hiring only motivated, ambitious applicants whose attitudes and work habits mesh well with a results-oriented corporate culture.

---

[22]Jeffrey Pheffer, "Producing Sustainable Competitive Advantage through the Effective Management of People," *Academy of Management Executive* 9, no.1 (February 1995), pp. 55–69.

[23]Peter Drucker, *Management: Tasks, Responsibilities, Practices* (New York: Harper & Row, 1974), p. 457.

EXERTING STRATEGIC LEADERSHIP

The litany of good strategic management is simple enough: formulate a sound strategic plan, implement it, execute it to the fullest, win! But it's easier said than done. Exerting take-charge leadership, being a "spark plug," ramrodding things through, and getting things done by coaching others to do them are difficult tasks.[24] Moreover, a strategy manager has many different leadership roles to play: visionary, chief entrepreneur and strategist, chief administrator and strategy implementer, culture builder, resource acquirer and allocator, capabilities builder, process integrator, coach, crisis solver, taskmaster, spokesperson, negotiator, motivator, arbitrator, consensus builder, policy maker, policy enforcer, mentor, and head cheerleader.[25] Sometimes it is useful to be authoritarian and hard-nosed; sometimes it is best to be a perceptive listener and a compromising decision maker; sometimes a strongly participative, collegial approach works best; and sometimes being a coach and advisor is the proper role. Many occasions call for a highly visible role and extensive time commitments, while others entail a brief ceremonial performance with the details delegated to subordinates.

For the most part, major change efforts have to be vision driven and led from the top. Leading change has to start with diagnosing the situation and then deciding which way to handle it. Six leadership roles dominate the strategy implementer's action agenda:

1. Staying on top of what is happening and how well things are going.

2. Promoting a culture in which the organization is "energized" to accomplish strategy and perform at a high level.

3. Keeping the organization responsive to changing conditions, alert for new opportunities, bubbling with innovative ideas, and ahead of rivals in developing competitively valuable competencies and capabilities.

4. Building consensus, containing "power struggles," and dealing with the politics of crafting and implementing strategy.

5. Enforcing ethical standards.

6. Pushing corrective actions to improve strategy execution and overall organization performance.

Staying on Top of How Well Things Are Going

To stay on top of how well the implementation process is going, a manager needs to develop a broad network of contacts and sources of information, both formal and informal. The regular channels include talking with key subordinates, presentations and meetings, reviews of the latest operating results, talking to customers, watching the competitive reactions of rival firms, tapping into the grapevine, listening to rank-

---

[24]For an excellent survey of the problems and pitfalls in making the tranisition to a new strategy and to fundamentally new ways of doing business, see John P. Kotter, "Leading Change: Why Transformation Efforts Fail," *Harvard Business Review* 73, no. 2 (March–April 1995), pp. 59–67. See, also, Thomas M. Hout and John C. Carter, "Getting It Done: New Roles for Senior Executives," *Harvard Business Review* 73 no. 6 (November–December 1995), pp. 133–45 and Sumantra Ghoshal and Christopher A. Bartlett, "Changing the Role of Top Management: Beyond Structure to Processes," *Harvard Business Review* 73 no. 1 (January–February 1995), pp. 86–96.

[25]For a very insightful and revealing report on how one CEO leads the organizational change process, see Noel Tichy and Ram Charan, "The CEO as Coach: An Interview with Allied Signal's Lawrence A. Bossidy," *Harvard Business Review* 73, no. 2 (March–April 1995), pp. 68–78.

and-file employees, and observing the situation firsthand. However, some information is more trustworthy than the rest, and the views and perspectives offered by
different people can vary widely. Presentations and briefings by subordinates may represent "the truth but not the whole truth." Bad news or
problems may be minimized or in some cases not reported at all as subordinates delay conveying failures and problems in hopes that more time will
give them room to turn things around. Hence, strategy managers have to
make sure that they have accurate information and a "feel" for the existing
situation. One way this is done is by regular visits "to the field" and
talking with many different people at many different levels. The technique
of "managing by walking around" (MBWA) is practiced in a variety of styles:[26]

> *MBWA is one of the techniques effective leaders use to stay informed on how well strategy implementation and execution is proceeding.*

- At Hewlett-Packard, there are weekly beer busts in each division, attended by
  both executives and employees, to create a regular opportunity to keep in
  touch. Tidbits of information flow freely between down-the-line employees
  and executives—facilitated in part because "the HP Way" is for people at all
  ranks to be addressed by their first names. Bill Hewlett, one of HP's
  cofounders, had a companywide reputation for getting out of his office and
  "wandering around" the plant greeting people, listening to what was on their
  minds, and asking questions. He found this so valuable that he made MBWA
  a standard practice for all HP managers.

- McDonald's founder Ray Kroc regularly visited store units and did his own
  personal inspection on Q.S.C.&V. (Quality, Service, Cleanliness, and
  Value)—the themes he preached regularly. There are stories of his pulling
  into a unit's parking lot, seeing litter lying on the pavement, getting out of
  his limousine to pick it up himself, and then lecturing the store staff at
  length on the subject of cleanliness.

- The CEO of a small manufacturing company spends much of his time
  riding around the factory in a golf cart, waving to and joking with workers,
  listening to them, and calling all 2,000 employees by their first names. In
  addition, he spends a lot of time with union officials, inviting them to
  meetings and keeping them well informed about what is going on.

- Wal-Mart executives have had a long-standing practice of spending two to
  three days every week visiting Wal-Mart's stores and talking with store
  managers and employees. Sam Walton, Wal-Mart's founder, insisted, "The
  key is to get out into the store and listen to what the associates have to
  say. Our best ideas come from clerks and stockboys."

- Jack Welch, CEO of General Electric, not only spends several days each
  month personally visiting GE operations and talking with major customers
  but also arranges his schedule so that he can spend time talking with
  virtually every class of GE managers participating in courses at the
  company's famed leadership development center at GE's Crotonville, New
  York, headquarters. As Welch put it, "I'm here every day, or out into a
  factory, smelling it, feeling it, touching it, challenging the people."[27]

---

[26]Peters and Waterman, *In Search of Excellence,* pp. xx, 15, 120–23, 191, 242–43, 246–47, 287–90. For
an extensive discussion of the benefits of MBWA, see Peters and Austin, *A Passion for Excellence*, chapters 2, 3, and 19.

[27]As quoted in Ann M. Morrison, "Trying to Bring GE to Life," *Fortune*, January 25, 1982, p. 52.

- Some activist CEOs make a point of holding key meetings out in the field—at the premises of a major customer or at the facility of a business unit with a troublesome problem—to get their managers out of their comfort zones and create enough of a shared framework for constructive dialogue, disagreement and open debate, and collective solution.

Most managers attach great importance to spending time in the field, observing the situation firsthand and talking informally to many different people at different organizational levels. They believe it is essential to have a "feel" for situations, gathering their own firsthand information and not just relying on information gathered or reported by others. Successful executives are aware of the isolation of spending too much time in their offices or in meetings, the dangers of surrounding themselves with people who are not likely to offer criticism and different perspectives, and the risk of getting too much of their information secondhand, screened and filtered, and sometimes dated. As a Hewlett-Packard official expresses it in the company publication *The HP Way*:

Once a division or department has developed a plan of its own—a set of working objectives—it's important for managers and supervisors to keep it in operating condition. This is where observation, measurement, feedback, and guidance come in. It's our "management by wandering around." That's how you find out whether you're on track and heading at the right speed and in the right direction. If you don't constantly monitor how people are operating, not only will they tend to wander off track but also they will begin to believe you weren't serious about the plan in the first place. It has the extra benefit of getting you off your chair and moving around your area. By wandering around, I literally mean moving around and talking to people. It's all done on a very informal and spontaneous basis, but it's important in the course of time to cover the whole territory. You start out by being accessible and approachable, but the main thing is to realize you're there to listen. The second reason for MBWA is that it is vital to keep people informed about what's going on in the company, especially those things that are important to them. The third reason for doing this is because it is just plain fun.

Such contacts give the manager a feel for how things are progressing, and they provide opportunity to speak with encouragement, lift spirits, shift attention from the old to the new priorities, create some excitement, and project an atmosphere of informality and fun—all of which drive implementation forward in positive fashion and intensify the organizational energy behind strategy execution.

Fostering a Strategy-Supportive Climate and Culture

Strategy-implementers have to be out front in promoting a strategy-supportive organizational climate and culture. When major strategic changes are being implemented,

Successful culture changes have to be personally led by top management; it's a task that can't be delegated to others.

a manager's time is best spent *personally leading the changes* and promoting needed cultural adjustments. Gradual progress is often not enough. Conservative incrementalism seldom leads to major cultural adaptations; more usually, gradualism is defeated by the stubbornness of entrenched cultures and the ability of vested interests to thwart or minimize the impact of piecemeal change. Only with bold leadership and concerted action on many fronts can a company succeed in tackling so large and difficult a task as major cultural change. When only strategic fine-tuning is being implemented, it takes less time and effort to bring values and culture into alignment with strategy, but there is still a lead role for the manager to play in pushing ahead and prodding for continuous improvements.

The single most visible factor that distinguishes successful culture-change efforts from failed attempts is competent leadership at the top. Effective management action to match culture and strategy has several attributes:[28]

- A stakeholders-are-king philosophy that links the need to change to the need to serve the long-term best interests of all key constituencies.

- An openness to new ideas.

- Challenging the status quo with very basic questions: Are we giving customers what they really need and want? How can we be more competitive on cost? Why can't design-to-market cycle time be halved? What new competitive capabilities and resource strengths do we need? How can we grow the company instead of downsizing it? Where will the company be five years from now if it sticks with just its present business?

- Creating events where everyone in management is forced to listen to angry customers, dissatisfied stockholders, and alienated employees to keep management informed and to help them realistically assess the organization's strengths and weaknesses.

- Persuading individuals and groups to commit themselves to the new direction and energizing them to make it happen despite the obstacles.

- Repeating the new messages again and again, explaining the rationale for change, and convincing skeptics that all is not well and that fundamental changes in culture and operating practices are essential to the organization's long term well-being.

- Recognizing and generously rewarding those who exhibit new cultural norms and who lead successful change efforts—this helps expand the coalition for change.

Great power is needed to force major cultural change—to overcome the springback resistance of entrenched cultures—and great power normally resides only at the top. Moreover, the interdependence of values, strategies, practices, and behaviors inside organizations makes it difficult to change anything fundamental without simultaneous wider-scale changes. Usually the people with the power to effect change of that scope are those at the top.

Only top management has the power and organizational influence to bring about major cultural change.

Both words and deeds play a part in leading cultural change. Words inspire people, infuse spirit and drive, define strategy-supportive cultural norms and values, make clear the reasons for strategic and organizational change, legitimize new viewpoints and new priorities, urge and reinforce commitment, and arouse confidence in the new strategy. Deeds add credibility to the words, create strategy-supportive symbols, set examples, give meaning and content to the language, and teach the organization what sort of behavior is needed and expected.

Highly visible symbols and imagery are needed to complement actions. One General Motors manager explained how symbolism and managerial style accounted for the striking difference in performance between two large plants:[29]

> At the poorly performing plant, the plant manager probably ventured out on the floor once a week, always in a suit. His comments were distant and perfunctory. At South Gate, the better plant, the plant manager was on the floor all the time. He wore a baseball cap and a UAW jacket. By the way, whose plant do you think was spotless? Whose looked like a junkyard?

---

[28]Ibid., pp. 84, 144, and 148.

[29]As quoted in Peters and Waterman, *In Search of Excellence*, p. 262.

As a rule, the greater the degree of strategic change being implemented and the greater the shift in cultural norms needed to accommodate a new strategy, the more visible and clear the strategy implementer's words and deeds need to be. Moreover, the actions and images, both substantive and symbolic, have to be hammered out regularly, not just restricted to ceremonial speeches and special occasions. In such instances maintaining a high profile and "managing by walking around" are especially useful.

What the strategy leader says and does plants the seeds of cultural change and has a significant bearing on down-the-line strategy implementation and execution.

In global companies, leaders have to learn how to function effectively with diversity in cultures and behavioral norms and with the expectations of people who sometimes fervently insist on being treated as distinctive individuals or groups—a one-size-fits-all leadership approach won't work. Effective cross-cultural leadership requires sensitivity to cultural differences, discerning when diversity has to be accommodated and when differences can be and should be narrowed.[30]

Keeping the Internal Organization Responsive and Innovative

While formulating and implementing strategy is a manager's responsibility, the task of generating fresh ideas, identifying new opportunities, and responding to changing conditions cannot be accomplished by a single person. It is an organizationwide task, particularly in large corporations. One of the toughest parts of strategic leadership is generating fresh ideas from the rank and file, managers and employees alike, and promoting an entrepreneurial, opportunistic spirit that permits continuous adaptation to changing conditions. A flexible, responsive, innovative internal environment is critical in fast-moving high-technology industries, in businesses where products have short life cycles and growth depends on new product innovation, in companies with widely diversified business portfolios (where opportunities are varied and scattered), in markets where successful product differentiation depends on outinnovating the competition, and in situations where low-cost leadership hinges on continuous improvement and new ways to drive costs out of the business. Managers cannot mandate such an internal work climate by simply exhorting people to "be creative."

The faster a company's business environment changes, the more attention managers must pay to keeping the organization innovative and responsive.

Empowering Champions   One useful leadership approach is to take special pains to foster, nourish, and support people who are willing to champion new technologies, new operating practices, better services, new products, and new product applications and are eager to try carrying out their ideas. One year after taking charge at Siemens-Nixdorf Information Systems, Gerhard Schulmeyer produced the merged company's first profit after losing hundreds of millions of dollars annually since 1991; he credited the turnaround to the creation of 5,000 "change agents," almost 15 percent of the workforce, who volunteered for active roles in the company's change agenda while continuing to perform their regular jobs. As a rule, the best champions are persistent, competitive, tenacious, committed, and fanatic about the idea and seeing it through to success.

Identifying and empowering champions helps promote an environment of innovation and experimentation.

To promote a climate where champion innovators can blossom and thrive, strategy managers need to do several things. First, individuals and groups have to be encouraged to be creative, hold informal brainstorming sessions, let their imaginations fly in all

---

[30]For a discussion of this dimension of leadership, see Alexander and Wilson, "Leading across Cultures: Five Vital Capabilities," pp. 287–94.

directions, and come up with proposals. The culture has to nurture, even celebrate, experimentation and innovation. Everybody must be expected to contribute ideas, show initiative, and pursue continuous improvement. The trick is to keep a sense of urgency alive in the business so that people see change and innovation as a necessity. Second, people with maverick ideas or out-of-the-ordinary proposals have to be tolerated and given room to operate. Above all, would-be champions who advocate radical or different ideas must not be looked on as disruptive or troublesome. Third, managers have to promote lots of "tries" and be willing to tolerate mistakes and failures. Most ideas don't pan out, but the organization learns from a good attempt even when it fails. Fourth, strategy managers should be willing to use all kinds of organizational forms to support ideas and experimentation—venture teams, task forces, "performance shootouts" among different groups working on competing approaches, informal "boot-legged" projects composed of volunteers, and so on. Fifth, strategy managers have to see that the rewards for successful champions are large and visible and that people who champion an unsuccessful idea are encouraged to try again rather than be punished or sidelined. In effect, the leadership task is to create an adaptive, innovative culture that responds to changing conditions rather than fearing the new conditions or seeking to minimize them. Companies with innovative cultures include Sony, 3M, Motorola, and Levi Strauss. All four inspire their employees with strategic visions to excel and be world-class at what they do.

It's a constant organization-building challenge to broaden, deepen, or modify organization capabilities and resource strengths in response to ongoing customer-market changes.

Leading the Process of Developing New Capabilities   Often, effectively responding to changing customer preferences and competitive conditions requires top management intervention to establish new capabilities and resource strengths. Senior management usually has to lead the effort because core competencies and competitive capabilities typically come from the combined efforts of different work groups, departments, and collaborative allies. The tasks of managing human skills, knowledge bases, and intellect and then integrating them to forge competitively advantageous competencies and capabilities is best orchestrated by senior managers who appreciate their strategy-implementing significance and who have the clout to enforce the necessary networking and cooperation among individuals, groups, departments, and external allies.

The ideal leadership outcome is for senior management to proactively develop new competencies and capabilities to complement the company's existing resource base and promote more proficient strategy execution.

Effective company managers try to anticipate changes in customer-market requirements and proactively build new competencies and capabilities that offer a competitive edge over rivals. Senior managers are in the best position to see the need and potential of new capabilities and then to play a lead role in building capabilities and strengthening company resources. Building new competencies and capabilities ahead of rivals to gain a competitive edge is strategic leadership of the best kind, but strengthening the company's resource base in reaction to the newly developed capabilities of pioneering rivals is the most frequent occurrence.

Dealing with Company Politics

A manager can't effectively formulate and implement strategy without being perceptive about company politics and being adept at political maneuvering.[31] Politics virtually always comes into play in formulating the strategic plan. Inevitably, key

---

[31]For further discussion of this point see Abraham Zaleznik, "Power and Politics in Organizational Life," *Harvard Business Review* 48, no. 3 (May–June 1970), pp. 47–60; R. M. Cyert, H. A. Simon, and D. B.

individuals and groups form coalitions, and each group presses the benefits and potential of its own ideas and vested interests. Political considerations enter into decisions about which objectives take precedence and which lines of business have top priority in resource allocation. Internal politics is a factor in building a consensus for one strategic option over another.

As a rule, there is even more politics in implementing strategy than in formulating it. Typically, internal political considerations affect whose areas of responsibility get reorganized, who reports to whom, who has how much authority over subunits, what individuals should fill key positions and head strategy-critical activities, and which units will get the biggest budget increases. As a case in point, Quinn cites a situation where three strong managers who fought each other constantly formed a potent coalition to resist a reorganization scheme that would have coordinated the very things that caused their friction.[32]

Company politics presents strategy leaders with the challenge of building consensus for the strategy and how to implement it.

A strategy manager must therefore understand how an organization's power structure works, who wields influence in the executive ranks, which groups and individuals are "activists" and which are defenders of the status quo, who can be helpful and who may not be in a showdown on key decisions, and which direction the political winds are blowing on a given issue. When major decisions have to be made, strategy managers need to be especially sensitive to the politics of managing coalitions and reaching consensus. As the chairman of a major British corporation expressed it:

> I've never taken a major decision without consulting my colleagues. It would be unimaginable to me, unimaginable. First, they help me make a better decision in most cases. Second, if they know about it and agree with it, they'll back it. Otherwise, they might challenge it, not openly, but subconsciously.[33]

The politics of strategy centers chiefly around stimulating options, nurturing support for strong proposals and killing weak ones, guiding the formation of coalitions on particular issues, and achieving consensus and commitment. Successful executives rely upon the following political tactics:[34]

- Letting weakly supported ideas and proposals die through inaction.
- Establishing additional hurdles or tests for strongly supported ideas that the manager views as unacceptable but that are best not opposed openly.
- Keeping a low political profile on unacceptable proposals by getting subordinate managers to say no.
- Letting most negative decisions come from a group consensus that the manager merely confirms, thereby reserving personal veto for big issues and crucial moments.
- Leading the strategy but not dictating it—giving few orders, announcing few decisions, depending heavily on informal questioning, and seeking to probe and clarify until a consensus emerges.

Trow, "Observation of a Business Decision," *Journal of Business*, October 1956, pp. 237–48; and James Brian Quinn, *Strategies for Change: Logical Incrementalism* (Homewood, Ill.: Richard D. Irwin, 1980).
[32]Quinn, *Strategies for Change*, p. 68.
[33]Ibid., p. 65. This statement was made by Sir Alastair Pilkington, Chairman, Pilkington Brothers, Ltd.
[34]Ibid., pp. 128–45.

- Staying alert to the symbolic impact of one's actions and statements lest a false signal stimulate proposals and movements in unwanted directions.

- Ensuring that all major power bases within the organization have representation in or access to top management.

- Injecting new faces and new views into considerations of major changes to prevent those involved from coming to see the world the same way and then acting as systematic screens against other views.

- Minimizing political exposure on issues that are highly controversial and in circumstances where opposition from major power centers can trigger a "shootout."

The politics of strategy implementation is especially critical when it comes to introducing a new strategy against the resistance of those who support the old one. Except for crisis situations where the old strategy is plainly revealed as out-of-date, it is usually bad politics to push the new strategy by attacks on the old one.[35] Bad-mouthing old strategy can easily be interpreted as an attack on those who formulated it and those who supported it. The old strategy and the judgments behind it may have been well-suited to the organization's earlier circumstances, and the people who made these judgments may still be influential. In addition, the new strategy and/or the plans for implementing it may not have been the first choices of others, and lingering doubts may remain. Good arguments may exist for pursuing other actions. Consequently, in trying to surmount resistance, nothing is gained by knocking the arguments for alternative approaches. Such attacks often produce alienation instead of cooperation.

In short, to bring the full force of an organization behind a strategic plan, the strategy manager must assess and deal with the most important centers of potential support for and opposition to new strategic thrusts.[36] He or she needs to secure the support of key people, co-opt or neutralize serious opposition and resistance when and where necessary, learn where the zones of indifference are, and build as much consensus as possible. Political skills are a definite, maybe even necessary, managerial asset.

Enforcing Ethical Behavior

For an organization to display consistently high ethical standards, the CEO and those around the CEO must be openly and clearly committed to ethical and moral conduct.[37] In companies that strive hard to make high ethical standards a reality, top management communicates its commitment in a code of ethics, in speeches and company publications, in policies on the consequences of unethical behavior, in the deeds of senior executives, and in the actions taken to ensure compliance. Senior management repeatedly tells employees that it is not only their duty to observe ethical codes but also to report ethical violations. While such companies have provisions for disciplining violators, the main purpose of enforcement is to encourage compliance rather than administer punishment. Although the CEO leads the

---

[35]Ibid., pp. 118–19.

[36]Ibid., p. 205.

[37]The Business Roundtable, *Corporate Ethics*, pp. 4–10.

High ethical standards cannot be enforced without the open and unequivocal commitment of the chief executive.

enforcement process, all managers are expected to make a personal contribution by stressing ethical conduct with their subordinates and monitoring compliance with the code of ethics. "Gray areas" must be identified and openly discussed with employees, and procedures created for offering guidance when issues arise, for investigating possible violations, and for resolving individual cases. The lesson from these companies is that it is never enough to assume activities are being conducted ethically, nor can it be assumed that employees understand they are expected to act with integrity.

Managers can do several concrete things to exercise ethics leadership.[38] First and foremost, they must set an excellent ethical example in their own behavior and establish a tradition of integrity. Company decisions have to be seen as ethical— "actions speak louder than words." Second, managers and employees have to be educated about what is ethical and what is not; ethics training programs may have to be established and gray areas pointed out and discussed. Everyone must be encouraged to raise issues with ethical dimensions, and such discussions should be treated as a legitimate topic. Third, top management should regularly restate its clear support of the company's ethical code and take a strong stand on ethical issues. Fourth, top management must be prepared to act as the final arbiter on hard calls; this means removing people from a key position or terminating them when they are guilty of a violation. It also means reprimanding those who have been lax in monitoring and enforcing ethical compliance. Failure to act swiftly and decisively in punishing ethical misconduct is interpreted as a lack of real commitment.

A well-developed program to ensure compliance with ethical standards typically includes (1) an oversight committee of the board of directors, usually made up of outside directors; (2) a committee of senior managers to direct ongoing training, implementation, and compliance; (3) an annual audit of each manager's efforts to uphold ethical standards and formal reports on the actions taken by managers to remedy deficient conduct; and (4) periodically requiring people to sign documents certifying compliance with ethical standards.[39]

Leading the Process of Making Corrective Adjustments

No strategic plan and no scheme for strategy implementation can foresee all the events and problems that will arise. Making adjustments and midcourse corrections, as well as pushing for ever better execution is a normal and necessary part of leading the process of implementing and executing strategy. The *process* of deciding when to make adjustments and what adjustments to make varies according to the situation. In a crisis, the typical leadership approach is to have key subordinates gather information, identify options, and make recommendations, then personally preside over extended discussions of the proposed responses and try to build a quick consensus among members of the executive inner circle. If no consensus emerges and action is required immediately, the burden falls on the strategy manager to choose the response and urge its support.

Corrective adjustments in the company's approach to strategy implementation are normal and have to be made as needed.

When the situation allows managers to proceed more deliberately in deciding when to make changes and what changes to make, strategy managers seem to prefer

[38]Ibid.
[39]Ibid.

a process of gradually solidifying commitment to a particular course of action.[40] The process that managers go through in deciding on corrective adjustments is essentially the same for both proactive and reactive changes: They sense needs, gather information, broaden and deepen their understanding of the situation, develop options and explore their pros and cons, put forth action proposals, generate partial (comfort-level) solutions, build consensus, and finally formally adopt an agreed-on course of action.[41] The ultimate managerial prescription may have been given by Rene Mc-Pherson, former CEO at Dana Corporation. Speaking to a class of students at Stanford University, he said, "You just keep pushing. You just keep pushing. I made every mistake that could be made. But I just kept pushing."[42]

All this, once again, highlights the fundamental nature of strategic management: The job of formulating and implementing strategy is not one of steering a clear-cut course while carrying out the original strategy intact according to some preconceived plan. Rather, it is one of creatively (1) adapting and reshaping strategy to unfolding events and (2) drawing upon whatever managerial techniques are needed to align internal activities and behaviors with strategy. The process is interactive, with much looping and recycling to fine-tune and adjust visions, objectives, strategies, resources, capabilities, implementation approaches, and cultures to one another in a continuously evolving process. The best tests of good strategic leadership are improving business performance and a company that is agile, that is capable of adapting to multiple changes, and that is a good place to work.

KEY POINTS

Building a strategy-supportive corporate culture is important to successful implementation because it produces a work climate and organizational esprit de corps that thrive on meeting performance targets and being part of a winning effort. An organization's culture emerges from why and how it does things the way it does, the values and beliefs that senior managers espouse, the ethical standards expected of all, the tone and philosophy underlying key policies, and the traditions the organization maintains. Culture thus concerns the atmosphere and "feeling" a company has and the style in which it gets things done.

Very often, the elements of company culture originate with a founder or other early influential leaders who articulate certain values, beliefs, and principles the company should adhere to, which then get incorporated into company policies, a creed or values statement, strategies, and operating practices. Over time, these values and practices become shared by company employees and managers. Cultures are perpetuated as new leaders act to reinforce them, as new employees are encouraged to adopt and follow them, as legendary stories that exemplify them are told and retold, and as organizational members are honored and rewarded for displaying the cultural norms.

Company cultures vary widely in strength and in makeup. Some cultures are strongly embedded, while others are weak and fragmented in the sense that many subcultures exist, few values and behavioral norms are shared companywide, and there are few strong traditions. Some cultures are unhealthy, dominated by self-serving politics, resistant to change, and too inwardly focused; such cultural traits are

---

[40]Quinn, *Strategies for Change*, pp. 20–22.

[41]Ibid., p. 146.

[42]As quoted in Peters and Waterman, *In Search of Excellence*, p. 319.

often precursors to declining company performance. In fast-changing business environments, adaptive cultures are best because the internal environment is receptive to change, experimentation, innovation, new strategies, and new operating practices needed to respond to changing stakeholder requirements. One significant defining trait of adaptive cultures is that top management genuinely cares about the well-being of all key constituencies—customers, employees, stockholders, major suppliers, and the communities where it operates—and tries to satisfy all their legitimate interests simultaneously.

The philosophy, goals, and practices implicit or explicit in a new strategy may or may not be compatible with a firm's culture. A close strategy-culture alignment promotes implementation and good execution; a mismatch poses real obstacles. Changing a company's culture, especially a strong one with traits that don't fit a new strategy's requirements, is one of the toughest management challenges. Changing a culture requires competent leadership at the top. It requires symbolic actions (leading by example) and substantive actions that unmistakably indicate top management is seriously committed. The stronger the fit between culture and strategy, the less managers have to depend on policies, rules, procedures, and supervision to enforce what people should and should not do; rather, cultural norms are so well observed that they automatically guide behavior.

Healthy corporate cultures are also grounded in ethical business principles and moral values. Such standards connote integrity, "doing the right thing," and genuine concern for stakeholders and for how the company does business. To be effective, corporate ethics and values programs have to become a way of life through training, strict compliance and enforcement procedures, and reiterated management endorsements.

Successful strategy implementers exercise an important leadership role. They stay on top of how well things are going by spending considerable time outside their offices, wandering around the organization, listening, coaching, cheerleading, picking up important information, and keeping their fingers on the organization's pulse. They take pains to reinforce the corporate culture through the things they say and do. They encourage people to be creative and innovative in order to keep the organization responsive to changing conditions, alert to new opportunities, and anxious to pursue fresh initiatives. They support "champions" of new approaches or ideas who are willing to stick their necks out and try something innovative. They work hard at building consensus on how to proceed, on what to change and what not to change. They enforce high ethical standards. And they push corrective action to improve strategy execution and overall strategic performance.

A manager's action agenda for implementing and executing strategy is thus expansive and creative. As we indicated at the beginning of our discussion of strategy implementation (Chapter 9), eight bases need to be covered:

1. Building an organization capable of carrying out the strategy successfully.
2. Developing budgets to steer ample resources into those value-chain activities critical to strategic success.
3. Establishing strategically appropriate policies and procedures.
4. Instituting best practices and mechanisms for continuous improvement.
5. Installing support systems that enable company personnel to carry out their strategic roles successfully day in and day out.
6. Tying rewards and incentives tightly to the achievement of performance objectives and good strategy execution.

7. Creating a strategy-supportive work environment and corporate culture.

8. Leading and monitoring the process of driving implementation forward and improving on how the strategy is being executed.

Making progress on these eight tasks sweeps broadly across virtually every aspect of administrative and managerial work.

Because each instance of strategy implementation occurs under different organizational circumstances, a strategy implementer's action agenda always needs to be situation specific—there's no neat generic procedure to follow. And, as we said at the beginning, implementing strategy is an action-oriented, make-the-right-things-happen task that challenges a manager's ability to lead and direct organizational change, create or reinvent business processes, manage and motivate people, and achieve performance targets. If you now better understand the nature of the challenge, the range of available approaches, and the issues that need to be considered, we will look upon our discussion in these last three chapters as a success.

SUGGESTED READINGS

Badaracco, Joe and Allen P. Webb. "Business Ethics: A View from the Trenches." *California Management Review* 37, no. 2 (Winter 1995), pp. 8–28.

Clement, Ronald W. "Culture, Leadership, and Power: The Keys to Organizational Change." *Business Horizons* 37, no. 1 (January–February 1994), pp. 33–39.

Deal, Terrence E., and Allen A. Kennedy. *Corporate Cultures*. Reading, Mass.: Addison-Wesley, 1982, especially chaps. 1 and 2.

Eccles, Robert G. "The Performance Measurement Manifesto." *Harvard Business Review* 69 (January–February 1991), pp. 131–37.

Farkas, Charles M. and Suzy Wetlaufer, "The Ways Chief Executive Officers Lead," *Harvard Business Review* 74 no. 3 (May–June 1996), pp. 110–122.

Floyd, Steven W., and Bill Wooldridge. "Managing Strategic Consensus: The Foundation of Effective Implementation." *Academy of Management Executive* 6, no. 4 (November 1992), pp. 27–39.

Gabarro, J. J. "When a New Manager Takes Charge." *Harvard Business Review* 64, no. 3 (May–June 1985), pp. 110–23.

Ghoshal, Sumantra and Christopher A. Bartlett. "Changing the Role of Top Management: Beyond Structure to Processes." *Harvard Business Review* 73 no. 1 (January–February 1995), pp. 86–96.

Ginsburg, Lee and Neil Miller, "Value-Driven Management," *Business Horizons* (May–June 1992), pp. 25–27.

Green, Sebastian. "Strategy, Organizational Culture, and Symbolism." *Long Range Planning* 21, no. 4 (August 1988), pp. 121–29.

Heifetz, Ronald A. and Donald L. Laurie. "The Work of Leadership." *Harvard Business Review* 75, no. 1 (January–February 1997), pp. 124–34.

Humble, John, David Jackson, and Alan Thomson. "The Strategic Power of Corporate Values." *Long Range Planning* 27, no. 6 (December 1994), pp. 28–42.

Kirkpatrick, Shelley A., and Edwin A. Locke. "Leadership: Do Traits Matter?" *Academy of Management Executive* 5, no. 2 (May 1991), pp. 48–60.

Kotter, John P. "What Leaders Really Do." *Harvard Business Review* 68 no. 3 (May–June 1990), pp. 103–11.

———."Leading Change: Why Transformation Efforts Fail." *Harvard Business Review* 73, no. 2 (March–April 1995), pp. 59–67.

————, and James L. Heskett. *Corporate Culture and Performance*. New York: Free Press, 1992.

Miles, Robert H. *Corporate Comeback: The Story of Renewal and Transformation at National Semiconductor*. San Francisco: Jossey-Bass, 1997.

Murphy, Patrick E. "Corporate Ethics Statements: Current Status and Future Prospects." *Journal of Business Ethics* 14 (1995), pp. 727–40.

O'Toole, James. "Employee Practices at the Best-Managed Companies." *California Management Review* 28, no. 1 (Fall 1985), pp. 35–66.

Paine, Lynn Sharp. "Managing for Organizational Integrity." *Harvard Business Review* 72, no. 2 (March–April 1994), pp. 106–17.

Reimann, Bernard C., and Yoash Wiener. "Corporate Culture: Avoiding the Elitist Trap." *Business Horizons* 31, no. 2 (March–April 1988), pp. 36–44.

Schneider, Benjamin, Sarah K. Gunnarson, and Kathryn Niles-Jolly. "Creating the Climate and Culture of Success." *Organizational Dynamics* (Summer 1994), pp.17–29.

Scholz, Christian. "Corporate Culture and Strategy—The Problem of Strategic Fit." *Long Range Planning* 20 (August 1987), pp. 78–87.

II

READINGS IN
STRATEGIC
MANAGEMENT

BUILDING YOUR COMPANY'S VISION

James C. Collins
Jerry I. Porras

Collins and Porras suggest that building a visionary company involves discovering the company's core ideology and creating an envisioned future. Core ideology, the enduring character of the organization, consists of core values and core purpose, while the envisioned future is what the company aspires to become.

We shall not cease from exploration
And the end of all our exploring
Will be to arrive where we started
And know the place for the first time.
    T. S. Eliot
    Four Quartets

Companies that enjoy enduring success have core values and a core purpose that remain fixed while their business strategies and practices endlessly adapt to a changing world. The dynamic of preserving the core while stimulating progress is the reason that companies such as Hewlett-Packard, 3M, Johnson & Johnson, Procter & Gamble, Merck, Sony, Motorola, and Nordstrom became elite institutions able to renew themselves and achieve superior long-term performance. Hewlett-Packard employees have long known that radical changes in operating practices, cultural norms, and business strategies does not mean losing the spirit of the HP Way—the company's core principles. Johnson & Johnson continually questions its structure and revamps its processes while preserving the ideals embodied in its credo. In 1996, 3M sold off several of its large mature businesses—a dramatic move that surprised the business press—to refocus on its enduring core purpose of solving unsolved problems innovatively. We studied companies such as these in our research for *Built to Last: Successful Habits of Visionary Companies* and found that they have outperformed the general stock market by a factor of 12 since 1925.

Truly great companies understand the difference between what should never change and what should be open for change, between what is genuinely sacred and what is not. This rare ability to manage continuity and change—requiring a consciously practiced discipline—is closely linked to the ability to develop a vision.

FIGURE 1   Articulating a Vision

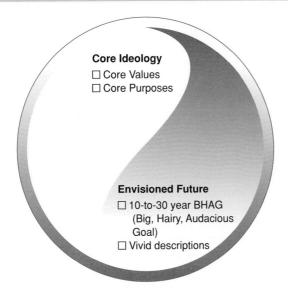

Vision provides guidance about what core to preserve and what future to stimulate progress toward. But *vision* has become one of the most overused and least understood words in the language, conjuring up different images for different people: of deeply held values, outstanding achievement, societal bonds, exhilarating goals, motivating forces, or raisons d'être. We recommend a conceptual framework to define vision, add clarity and rigor to the vague and fuzzy concept swirling around that trendy term, and give practical guidance for articulating a coherent vision within an organization. It is a prescriptive framework rooted in six years of research and refined and tested by our ongoing work with executives from a great variety of organizations around the world.

Truly great companies understand the difference between what should never change and what should be open for change, between what is genuinely sacred and what is not.

A well-conceived vision consists of two major components: *core ideology* and *envisioned future*. (See Figure 1, "Articulating a Vision.") Core ideology, the yin in our scheme, defines what we stand for and why we exist. Yin is unchanging and complements yang, the envisioned future. The envisioned future is what we aspire to become, to achieve, to create—something that will require significant change and progress to attain.

CORE IDEOLOGY

Core ideology defines the enduring character of an organization—a consistent identity that transcends product or market life cycles, technological breakthroughs, management fads, and individual leaders. In fact, the most lasting and significant contribution of those who build visionary companies is the core ideology. As Bill Hewlett said about his longtime friend and business partner David Packard upon Packard's death not long ago, "As far as the company is concerned, the greatest thing he left behind him was a code of ethics known as the HP Way." HP's core ideology, which has guided the company since its inception more than 50 years ago, includes a deep respect for the individual, a dedication to affordable quality and reliability, a commitment to community responsibility (Packard himself bequeathed his $4.3 billion of Hewlett-Packard stock to a charitable foundation), and a view that the company exists to make technical contributions for the advancement and welfare of humanity. Company builders such as David Packard, Masaru Ibuka of Sony, George Merck of Merck, William McKnight of 3M, and Paul Galvin of Motorola understood that it is more important to know who you are than where you are going, for where you are going will change as the world around you changes. Leaders die, products become obsolete, markets change, new technologies emerge, and management fads come and go, but core ideology in a great company endures as a source of guidance and inspiration.

Core ideology provides the glue that holds an organization together as it grows, decentralizes, diversifies, expands globally, and develops workplace diversity. Think of it as analogous to the principles of Judaism that held the Jewish people together for centuries without a homeland, even as they spread throughout the Diaspora. Or think of the truths held to be self-evident in the Declaration of Independence, or the enduring ideals and principles of the scientific community that bond scientists from every nationality together in the common purpose of advancing human knowledge. Any effective vision must embody the core ideology of the organization, which in turn consists of two distinct parts: core values, a system of guiding principles and tents; and core purpose, the organization's most fundamental reason for existence.

Core Values   Core values are the essential and enduring tenets of an organization. A small set of timeless guiding principles, core values require no external justification; they have *intrinsic* value and importance to those inside the organization. The Walt Disney Company's core values of imagination and wholesomeness stem not from market requirements but from the founder's inner belief that imagination and wholesomeness should be nurtured for their own sake. William Procter and James Gamble didn't instill in P&G's culture a focus on product excellence merely as a strategy for success but as an almost religious tenet. And that value has been passed down for more than 15 decades by P&G people. Service to the customer—even to the point of subservience—is a way of life at Nordstrom that traces its roots back to 1901, eight decades before customer service programs became stylish. For Bill Hewlett and David Packard, respect for the individual was first and foremost a deep personal value; they didn't get it from a book or hear it from a management guru. And Ralph S. Larsen, CEO of Johnson & Johnson, puts it this way: "The core values embodied in our credo might be a competitive advantage, but that is not *why* we have them. We have them because they define for us what we stand for, and we would hold them even if they became a competitive *dis*advantage in certain situations."

The point is that a great company decides for itself what values it holds to be core, largely independent of the current environment, competitive requirements, or management fads. Clearly, then, there is no universally right set of core values. A company need not have as its core value customer service (Sony doesn't) or respect for the individual (Disney doesn't) or quality (Wal-Mart Stores doesn't) or market focus (HP doesn't) or teamwork (Nordstrom doesn't). A company might have operating practices and business strategies around those qualities without having them at the essence of its being. Furthermore, great companies need not have likable or humanistic core values, although many do. The key is not *what* core values an organization has but that it has core values at all.

Companies tend to have only a few core values, usually between three and five. In fact, we found that none of the visionary companies we studied in our book had more

FIGURE 2 Core Values Are a Company's Essential Tenets

Merck
- Corporate social responsibility
- Unequivocal excellence in all aspects of the company
- Science-based innovation
- Honesty and integrity
- Profit, but profits from work that benefits humanity

Nordstrom
- Service to the customer above all else
- Hard work and individual productivity
- Never being satisfied
- Excellence in reputation; being part of something special

Philip Morris
- The right to freedom of choice
- Winning—beating others in a good fight
- Encouraging individual initiative

- Opportunity based on merit; no one is entitled to anything
- Hard work and continuous self-improvement

Sony
- Elevation of the Japanese culture and national status
- Being a pioneer—not following others; doing the impossible
- Encouraging individual ability and creativity

Walt Disney
- No cynicism
- Nurturing and promulgation of "wholesome American values"
- Creativity, dreams, and imagination
- Fanatical attention to consistency and detail
- Preservation and control of the Disney magic

than five: most had only three or four. (See Figure 2 "Core Values Are a Company's Essential Tenets.") And, indeed, we should expect that. Only a few values can be truly *core*—that is, so fundamental and deeply held that they will change seldom, if ever.

To identify the core values of your own organization, push with relentless honesty to define what values are truly central. If you articulate more than five or six, chances are that you are confusing core values (which do not change) with operating practices, business strategies, or cultural norms (which should be open to change). Remember, the values must stand the test of time. After you've drafted a preliminary list of the core values, ask about each one, If the circumstances changed and *penalized* us for holding this core value, would we still keep it? If you can't honestly answer yes, then the value is not core and should be dropped from consideration.

A high-technology company wondered whether it should put quality on its list of core values. The CEO asked, "Suppose in 10 years quality doesn't make a hoot of difference in our markets. Suppose the only thing that matters is sheer speed and horsepower but not quality. Would we still want to put quality on our list of core values?" The members of the management team looked around at one another and finally said no. Quality stayed in the *strategy* of the company, and quality-improvement programs remained in place as a mechanism for stimulating progress; but quality did not make the list of core values.

The same group of executives then wrestled with leading-edge innovation as a core value. The CEO asked, "Would we keep innovation on the list as a core value, no matter how the world around us changed?" This time, the management team gave a resounding yes. The managers' outlook might be summarized as, "We always want to do leading-edge innovation. That's who we are. It's really important to us and always will be. No matter what, And if our current markets don't value us, we will find markets that do." Leading-edge innovation went on the list and will stay there. A company should not change its core values in response to market changes; rather, it should change markets, if necessary, to remain true to its core values.

Who should be involved in articulating the core values varies with the size, age, and geographic dispersion of the company, but in many situations we have recommended what we call a *Mars Group*. It works like this: Imagine that you've been asked to re-create the very best attributes of your organization on another planet but you have seats on the rocket ship for only five to seven people. Whom should you send? Most likely, you'll choose the people who have a gut-level understanding of your core values, the highest level of credibility with their peers, and the highest levels of competence. We'll often ask people brought together to work on core values to nominate a Mars Group of five to seven individuals (not necessarily all from the assembled group). Invariably, they end up selecting highly credible representatives who do a super job of articulating the core values precisely because they are exemplars of those values—a representative slice of the company's genetic code.

Even global organizations composed of people from widely diverse cultures can identify a set of shared core values. The secret is to work from the individual to the organization. People involved in articulating the core values need to answer several questions: What core values do you personally bring to your work? (These should be so fundamental that you would hold them regardless of whether or not they were rewarded.) What would you tell your children are the core values that you hold at work and that you hope *they* will hold when they become working adults? If you awoke tomorrow morning with enough money to retire for the rest of your life, would you continue to live those core values? Can you envision their being as valid for you 100 years from now as they are today? Would you want to hold those core values, even if at some point one or more of them became a competitive *dis*advantage? If you were to start a new organization tomorrow in a different line of work, what core values would you build into the new organization regardless of its industry? The last three questions are particularly important because they make the crucial distinction between enduring core values that should not change and practices and strategies that should be changing all the time.

Core Purpose   Core purpose, the second part of core ideology, is the organization's reason for being. An effective purpose reflects people's idealistic motivations for doing the company's work. It doesn't just describe the organization's output or target customers; it captures the soul of the organization. (See Figure 3, "Core Purpose Is a Company's Reason for Being.") Purpose, as illustrated by a speech David Packard gave to HP employees in 1960, gets at the deeper reasons for an organization's existence beyond just making money. Packard said,

> I want to discuss why a company exists in the first place. In other words, why are we here? I think many people assume, wrongly, that a company exists simply to make money. While this is an important result of a company's existence, we have to go deeper and find the real reasons for our being. As we investigate this, we inevitably come to the conclusion that a group of people get together and exist as an institution that we call a company so they are able to accomplish something collectively that they could not accomplish separately—they make a contribution to society, a phrase which sounds trite but is fundamental. . . . You can look around [in the general business world and] see people who are interested in money and nothing else, but the underlying drives come largely from a desire to do something else: to make a product, to give a service—generally to do something which is of value.[1]

FIGURE 3   Core Purpose Is a Company's Reason for Being

3M: To solve unsolved problems innovatively

Cargill: To improve the standard of living around the world

Fannie Mae: To strengthen the social fabric by continually democratizing home ownership

Hewlett-Packard: To make technical contributions for the advancement and welfare of humanity

Lost Arrow Corporation: To be a role model and a tool for social change

Pacific Theatres: To provide a place for people to flourish and to enhance the community

Mary Kay Cosmetics: To give unlimited opportunity to women

McKinsey & Company: To help leading corporations and governments be more successful

Merck: To preserve and improve human life

Nike: To experience the emotion of competition, winning, and crushing competitors

Sony: To experience the joy of advancing and applying technology for the benefit of the public

Telecare Corporation: To help people with mental impairments realize their full potential

Wal-Mart: To give ordinary folk the chance to buy the same things as rich people

Walt Disney: To make people happy

Purpose (which should last at least 100 years) should not be confused with specific goals or business strategies (which should change many times in 100 years). Whereas you might achieve a goal or complete a strategy, you cannot fulfill a purpose; it is like a guiding star on the horizon—forever pursued but never reached. Yet although purpose itself does not change, it does inspire change. The very fact that purpose can never be fully realized means that an organization can never stop stimulating change and progress.

Whereas you might achieve a goal or complete a strategy, you cannot fulfill a purpose; it is like a guiding star on the horizon—forever pursued but never reached.

In identifying purpose, some companies make the mistake of simply describing their current product lines or customer segments. We do not consider the following statement to reflect an effective purpose: "We exist to fulfill our government charter and participate in the secondary mortgage market by packaging mortgages into investment securities." The statement is merely descriptive. A far more effective statement of purpose would be that expressed by the executives of the Federal National Mortgage Association, Fannie Mae: "To strengthen the social fabric by continually democratizing home ownership." The secondary mortgage market as we know it might not even exist in 100 years, but strengthening the social fabric by continually democratizing home ownership can be an enduring purpose, no matter how much the world changes. Guided and inspired by this purpose, Fannie Mae launched in the early 1990s a series of bold initiatives, including a program to develop new systems for reducing mortgage and underwriting costs by 40 percent in five years; programs to eliminate discrimination in the lending process (backed by $5 billion in underwriting experiments); and an audacious goal to provide, by the year 2000, $1 trillion targeted at 10 million families that had traditionally been shut out of home ownership—minorities, immigrants, and low-income groups.

Similarly, 3M defines its purpose not in terms of adhesives and abrasives but as the perpetual quest to solve unsolved problems innovatively—a purpose that is always leading 3M into new fields. McKinsey & Company's purpose is not to do management consulting but to help corporations and governments be more success-ful: in 100 years, it might involve methods other than consulting. Hewlett-Packard doesn't exist to make electronic test and measurement equipment but to make technical contributions that improve people's lives—a purpose that has led the company far afield from its origins in electronic instruments. Imagine if Walt Disney had conceived of his company's purpose as to make cartoons, rather than to make people happy; we probably wouldn't have Mickey Mouse, Disneyland, EPCOT Center, or the Anaheim Mighty Ducks hockey team.

One powerful method for getting to the purpose is the *five whys*. Start with the descriptive statement, We make X products, or We deliver X services, and then ask, Why is that important? five times. After a few whys, you'll find that you're getting down to the fundamental purpose of the organization.

We used this method to deepen and enrich a discussion about purpose when we worked with a certain market-research company. The executive team first met for several hours and generated the following statement of purpose for their organiza-tion: To provide the best market-research data available. We then asked the following question: Why is it important to provide the best market-research data available? After some discussion, the executives answered in a way that reflected a deeper sense of their organization's purpose: To provide the best market-research data available so that our customers will understand their markets better than they could otherwise. A further discussion let team members realize that their sense of self-worth came not just from helping customers understand their markets better but also from making a *contribution* to their customers' success. This introspection eventually led the com-pany to identify its purpose as: To contribute to our customers' success by helping them understand their markets. With this purpose in mind, the company now frames its product decisions not with the question Will it sell? but with the question Will it make a contribution to our customers' success?

The five whys can help companies in any industry frame their work in a more meaningful way. An asphalt and gravel company might begin by saying, We make gravel and asphalt products. After a few whys, it could conclude that making asphalt and gravel is important because the quality of the infrastructure plays a vital role in people's safety and experience; because driving on a pitted road is annoying and dangerous; because 747s cannot land safely on runways built with poor workmanship or inferior concrete; because buildings with substandard materials weaken with time and crumble in earthquakes. From such introspection may emerge this purpose: To make people's lives better by improving the quality of man-made structures. With a sense of purpose very much along these lines, Granite Rock Company of Wat-sonville, California, won the Malcolm Baldrige National Quality Award—not an easy feat for a small rock quarry and asphalt company. And Granite Rock has gone on to be one of the most progressive and exciting companies we've encountered in *any* industry.

Notice that none of the core purposes fall into the category "maximize share-holder wealth." A primary role of core purpose is to guide and inspire. Maximizing shareholder wealth does not inspire people at all levels of an organization, and it provides precious little guidance. Maximizing shareholder wealth is the standard off-the-shelf purpose for those organizations that have not yet identified their true core purpose. It is a substitute—and a weak one at that.

When people in great organizations talk about their achievements, they say very little about earnings per share. Motorola people talk about impressive quality im-provements and the effect of the products they create on the world. Hewlett-Packard people talk about their technical contributions to the marketplace. Nordstrom people talk about heroic customer service and remarkable individual performance by star salespeople. When a Boeing engineer talks about launching an exciting and revolutionary new aircraft, she does not say, "I put my heart and soul into this project because it would add 37 cents to our earnings per share."

One way to get at the purpose that lies beyond merely maximizing shareholder wealth is to play the "Random Corporate Serial Killer" game. It works like this: Suppose you could sell the company to someone who would pay a price that everyone inside and outside the company agrees is more than fair (even with a very generous set of assumptions about the expected future cash flows of the company). Suppose further that this buyer would guarantee stable employment for all employees at the same pay scale after the purchase but with no guarantee that those jobs would be in the same industry. Finally, suppose the buyer plans to kill the company after the purchase—its products or services would be discontinued, its operations would be shut down, its brand names would be shelved forever, and so on. The company would utterly and completely cease to exist. Would you accept the offer? Why or why not? What would be lost if the company ceased to exist? Why is it important that the company continue to exist? We've found this exercise to be very powerful for helping hard-nosed, financially focused executives reflect on their organization's deeper reasons for being.

Another approach is to ask each member of the Mars Group, How could we frame the purpose of this organization so that if you woke up tomorrow morning with enough money in the bank to retire, you would nevertheless keep working here? What deeper sense of purpose would motivate you to continue to dedicate your precious creative energies to this company's efforts?

As they move into the twenty-first century, companies will need to draw on the full creative energy and talent of their people. But why should people give full measure? As Peter Drucker has pointed out, the best and most dedicated people are ultimately volunteers, for they have the opportunity to do something else with their lives. Confronted with an increasingly mobile society, cynicism about corporate life, and an expanding entrepreneurial segment of the economy, companies more than ever need to have a clear understanding of their purpose in order to make work meaningful and thereby attract, motivate, and retain outstanding people.

DISCOVERING CORE IDEOLOGY

You do not create or set core ideology. You *discover* core ideology. You do not deduce it by looking at the external environment. You understand it by looking inside. Ideology has to be authentic. You cannot fake it. Discovering core ideology is not an intellectual exercise. Do not ask, What core values should we hold? Ask instead, What core values do we truly and passionately hold? You should not confuse values that you think the organization ought to have—but does not—with authentic core values. To do so would create cynicism throughout the organization. ("Who're they trying to kid? We all know that isn't a core value around here!") Aspirations are more appropriate as part of your envisioned future or as part of your strategy, not as part of the core ideology. However, authentic core values that have weakened over time can be considered a legitimate part of the core ideology—as long as you acknowledge to the organization that you must work hard to revive them.

Also be clear that the role of core ideology is to guide and inspire, not to differentiate. Two companies can have the same core values or purpose. Many companies could have the purpose to make technical contributions, but few live it as passionately as Hewlett-Packard. Many companies could have the purpose to preserve and improve human life, but few hold it as deeply as Merck. Many companies could have the core value of heroic customer service, but few create as intense a culture around that value as Nordstrom. Many companies could have the core value of innovation, but few create the powerful alignment mechanisms that stimulate the innovation we see at 3M. The authenticity, the discipline, and the consistency with which the ideology is lived—not the content of the ideology—differentiate visionary companies from the rest of the pack.

Core ideology needs to be meaningful and inspirational only to people inside the organization; it need not be exciting to outsiders. Why not? Because it is the people inside the organization who need to commit to the organizational ideology over the long term. Core ideology can also play a role in determining who *is* inside and who is not. A clear and well-articulated ideology attracts to the company people whose personal values are compatible with the company's core values; conversely, it repels those whose personal values are incompatible. You cannot impose new core values or purpose on people. Nor are core values and purpose things people can buy into. Executives often ask, How do we get people to share our core ideology? You don't. You can't. Instead, find people who are predisposed to share your core values and purpose; attract and retain those people; and let those who do not share your core values go elsewhere. Indeed, the very process of articulating core ideology may cause some people to leave when they realize that they are not personally compatible with the organization's core. Welcome that outcome. It is certainly desirable to retain within the core ideology a diversity of people and viewpoints. People who share the same core values and purpose do not necessarily all think or look the same.

Don't confuse core ideology itself with core-ideology statements. A company can have a very strong core ideology without a formal statement. For example, Nike has not (to our knowledge) formally articulated a statement of its core purpose. Yet, according to our observations, Nike has a powerful core purpose that permeates the entire organization: to experience the emotion of competition, winning, and crushing competitors. Nike has a campus that seems more like a shrine to the competitive spirit than a corporate office complex. Giant photos of Nike heroes cover the walls, bronze plaques of Nike athletes hang along the Nike Walk of Fame, statues of Nike athletes stand alongside the running track that rings the campus, and buildings honor champions such as Olympic marathoner Joan Benoit, basketball superstar Michael Jordan, and tennis pro John McEnroe. Nike people who do not feel stimulated by the competitive spirit and the urge to be ferocious simply do not last long in the culture. Even the company's name reflects a sense of competition: Nike is the Greek goddess of victory. Thus, although Nike has not formally articulated its purpose, it clearly has a strong one.

Identifying core values and purpose is therefore not an exercise in wordsmithery. Indeed, an organization will generate a variety of statements over time to describe the core ideology. In Hewlett-Packard's archives, we found more than half a dozen distinct versions of the HP Way, drafted by David Packard between 1956 and 1972. All versions stated the same principles, but the words used varied depending on the era and the circumstances. Similarly, Sony's core ideology has been stated many different ways over the company's history. At its founding, Masaru Ibuka described two key elements of Sony's ideology: "We shall welcome technical difficulties and focus on highly sophisticated technical products that have great usefulness for society regardless of the quantity involved; we shall place our main emphasis on ability, performance, and personal character so that each individual can show the best in ability and skill."[2] Four decades later, this same concept appeared in a statement of core ideology called Sony Pioneer Spirit: "Sony is a pioneer and never intends to follow others. Through progress, Sony wants to serve the whole world. It shall be always a seeker of the unknown. . . . Sony has a principle of respecting and encouraging one's ability . . . and always tries to bring out the best in a person. This is the vital force of Sony."[3] Same core values, different words.

You should therefore focus on getting the content right—on capturing the essence of the core values and purpose. The point is not to create a perfect statement but to gain a deep understanding of your organization's core values and purpose, which can then be expressed in a multitude of ways. In fact, we often suggest that once the core has been identified, managers should generate their own statements of the core values and purpose to share with their groups.

Finally, don't confuse core ideology with the concept of core competence. Core competence is a strategic concept that defines your organization's capabilities—what you are particularly good at—whereas core ideology captures what you stand for and why you exist. Core competencies should be well aligned with a company's core ideology and are often rooted in it; but they are not the same thing. For example, Sony has a core competence of miniaturization—a strength that can be strategically applied to a wide array of products and markets. But it does not have a core *ideology* of miniaturization. Sony might not even have miniaturization as part of its strategy in 100 years, but to remain a great company, it will still have the same core values described in the Sony Pioneer Spirit and the same fundamental reason for being—namely, to advance technology for the benefit of the general public. In a visionary company like Sony, core competencies change over the decades, whereas core ideology does not.

Once you are clear about the core ideology, you should feel free to change absolutely *anything* that is not part of it. From then on, whenever someone says something should not change because "it's part of our culture" or "we've always done it that way" or any such excuse, mention this simple rule: If it's not core, it's up for change. The strong version of the rule is, *If it's not core, change it!* Articulating core ideology is just a starting point, however. You also must determine what type of progress you want to stimulate.

ENVISIONED FUTURE

The second primary component of the vision framework is *envisioned future*. It consists of two parts: a 10-to-30-year audacious goal plus vivid descriptions of what it will be like to achieve the goal. We recognize that the phrase *envisioned future* is somewhat paradoxical. On the one hand, it conveys concreteness—something visible, vivid, and real. On the other hand, it involves a time yet unrealized—with its dreams, hopes, and aspirations.

A true BHAG is clear and compelling, serves as a unifying focal point of effort, and acts as a catalyst for team spirit.

Vision-Level BHAG　We found in our research that visionary companies often use bold missions—or what we prefer to call *BHAGs* (pronounced BEE-hags and shorthand for Big, Hairy, Audacious Goals)—as a powerful way to stimulate progress. All companies have goals. But there is a difference between merely having a goal and becoming committed to a huge, daunting challenge—such as climbing Mount Everest. A true BHAG is clear and compelling, serves as a unifying focal point of effort, and acts as a catalyst for team spirit. It has a clear finish line, so the organization can know when it has achieved the goal; people like to shoot for finish lines. A BHAG engages people—it reaches out and grabs them. It is tangible, energizing, highly focused. People get it right away; it takes little or no explanation. For example, NASA's 1960s moon mission didn't need a committee of wordsmiths to spend endless hours turning the goal into a verbose, impossible-to-remember mission statement. The goal itself was so easy to grasp—so compelling in its own right—that it could be said 100 different ways yet be easily understood by everyone. Most corporate statements we've seen do little to spur forward movement because they do not contain the powerful mechanism of a BHAG.

Although organizations may have many BHAGs at different levels operating at the same time, vision requires a special type of BHAG—a vision-level BHAG that applies to the entire organization and requires 10 to 30 years of effort to complete. Setting the BHAG that far into the future requires thinking beyond the current capabilities of the organization and the current environment. Indeed, inventing such a goal forces an executive team to be visionary, rather than just strategic or tactical. A BHAG should not be a sure bet—it will have perhaps only a 50 percent or 70 percent probability of success—but the organization must believe that it can reach the goal anyway. A BHAG should require extraordinary effort and perhaps a little luck. We have helped companies create a vision-level BHAG by advising them to think in terms of four broad categories: target BHAGs, common-enemy BHAGs, role-model BHAGs, and internal-transformation BHAGs. (See Figure 4, "Big, Hairy, Audacious Goals Aid Long-Term Vision.")

Vivid Description   In addition to vision-level BHAGs, an envisioned future needs what we call *vivid description*—that is, a vibrant, engaging, and specific description of what it will be like to achieve the BHAG. Think of it as translating the vision from words into pictures, of creating an image that people can carry around in their heads. It is a question of painting a picture with your words. Picture painting is essential for making the 10-to-30-year BHAG tangible in people's minds.

For example, Henry Ford brought to life the goal of democratizing the automobile with this vivid description: "I will build a motor car for the great multitude. . . . It will be so low in price that no man making a good salary will be unable to own one and enjoy with his family the blessing of hours of pleasure in God's great open spaces. . . . When I'm through, everybody will be able to afford one, and everyone will have one. The horse will have disappeared from our highways, the automobile will be taken for granted . . . [and we will] give a large number of men employment at good wages."

The components-support division of a computer-products company had a general manager who was able to describe vividly the goal of becoming one of the most sought-after divisions in the company: "We will be respected and admired by our peers. . . . Our solutions will be actively sought by the end-product divisions, who will achieve significant product 'hits' in the marketplace largely because of our technical contribution. . . . We will have pride in ourselves. . . . The best up-and-coming people in the company will seek to work in our division. . . . People will give unsolicited feedback that they love what they are doing. . . . [Our own] people will walk on the balls of their feet. . . . [They] will willingly work hard because they want to. . . . Both employees and customers will feel that our division has contributed to their life in a positive way."

In the 1930s, Merck had the BHAG to transform itself from a chemical manufacturer into one of the preeminent drug-making companies in the world, with a research

---

FIGURE 4   Big, Hairy, Audacious Goals Aid Long-Term Vision

Target BHAGs can be quantitative or qualitative

- Become a $125 billion company by the year 2000 (Wal-Mart, 1990)
- Democratize the automobile (Ford Motor Company, early 1900s)
- Become the company most known for changing the worldwide poor-quality image of Japanese products (Sony, early 1950s)
- Become the most powerful, the most serviceable, the most far-reaching world financial institution that has ever been (City Bank, predecessor to Citicorp, 1915)
- Become the dominant player in commercial aircraft and bring the world into the jet age (Boeing, 1950)

Common-enemy BHAGs involve David-versus-Goliath thinking

- Knock off RJR as the number one tobacco company in the world (Philip Morris, 1950s)
- Crush Adidas (Nike, 1960s)
- *Yamaha wo tsubusu!* We will destroy Yamaha! (Honda, 1970s)

Role-model BHAGs suit up-and-coming organizations

- Become the Nike of the cycling industry (Giro Sport Design, 1986)
- Become as respected in 20 years as Hewlett-Packard is today (Watkins-Johnson, 1996)
- Become the Harvard of the West (Stanford University, 1940s)

Internal-transformation BHAGs suit large, established organizations

- Become number one or number two in every market we serve and revolutionize this company to have the strengths of a big company combined with the leanness and agility of a small company (General Electric Company, 1980s)
- Transform this company from a defense contractor into the best diversified high-technology company in the world (Rockwell, 1995)
- Transform this division from a poorly respected internal products supplier to one of the most respected, exciting, and sought-after divisions in the company (Components Support Division of a computer products company, 1989)

---

capability to rival any major university. In describing this envisioned future, George Merck said at the opening of Merck's research facility in 1993, "We believe that research work carried on with patience and persistence will bring to industry and commerce new life; and we have faith that in this new laboratory, with the tools we have supplied, science will be advanced, knowledge increased, and human life will win ever a greater freedom from suffering and disease. . . . We pledge our every aid that this enterprise shall merit the faith we have in it. Let your light so shine—that those who seek the Truth, that those who toil that this world may be a better place to live in, that those who hold aloft that torch of science and knowledge through these social and economic dark ages, shall take new courage and feel their hands supported."

Passion, emotion, and conviction are essential parts of the vivid description. Some managers are uncomfortable expressing emotion about their dreams, but that's what motivates others. Churchill understood that when he described the BHAG facing Great Britain in 1940. He did not just say, "Beat Hitler." He said, "Hitler knows he will have to break us on this island or lose the war. If we can stand up to him, all Europe may be free, and the life of the world may move forward into broad, sunlit uplands. But if we fail, the whole world, including the United States, including all we have known and cared for, will sink into the abyss of a new Dark Age, made more sinister and perhaps more protracted by the lights of perverted science. Let us therefore brace ourselves to our duties and so bear ourselves that if the British Empire and its Commonwealth last for a thousand years, men will still say, 'This was their finest hour.'"

A Few Key Points   Don't confuse core ideology and envisioned future. In particular, don't confuse core purpose and BHAGs. Managers often exchange one for the other, mixing the two together or failing to articulate both as distinct items. Core purpose—not some specific goal—is the reason why the organization exists. A BHAG is a clearly articulated goal. Core purpose can never be completed, whereas the BHAG is reachable in 10 to 30 years. Think of the core purpose as the star on the horizon to be chased forever; the BHAG is the mountain to be climbed. Once you have reached its summit, you move on to other mountains.

Identifying core ideology is a discovery process, but setting the envisioned future is a creative process. We find that executives often have a great deal of difficulty coming up with an exciting BHAG. They want to analyze their way into the future. We have found, therefore, that some executives make more progress by starting first with the vivid description and backing from there into the BHAG. This approach involves starting with questions such as, We're sitting here in 20 years; what would we love to see? What should this company look like? What should it feel like to employees? What should it have achieved? If someone writes an article for a major business magazine about this company in 20 years, what will it say? One biotechnology company we worked with had trouble envisioning its future. Said one member of

> *Identifying core ideology is a discovery process, but setting the envisioned future is a creative process.*

the executive team, "Every time we come up with something for the entire company, it is just too generic to be exciting—something banal like 'advance biotechnology worldwide.'" Asked to paint a picture of the company in 20 years, the executives mentioned such things as "on the cover of *Business Week* as a model success story . . . the *Fortune* most admired top-ten list . . . the best science and business graduates want to work here . . . people on airplanes rave about one of our products to seatmates . . . 20 consecutive years of profitable growth . . . an entrepreneurial culture that has spawned half a dozen new divisions from within . . . management gurus use us as an example of excellent management and progressive thinking," and so on. From this, they were able to set the goal of becoming as well respected as Merck or as Johnson & Johnson in biotechnology.

It makes no sense to analyze whether an envisioned future is the right one. With a creation—and the task is creation of a future, not prediction—there can be no right answer. Did Beethoven create the right *Ninth Symphony*? Did Shakespeare create the right *Hamlet*? We can't answer these questions; they're nonsense. The envisioned future involves such essential questions as Does it get our juices flowing? Do we find it stimulating? Does it spur forward momentum? Does it get people going? The envisioned future should be so exciting in its own right that it would continue to keep the organization motivated even if the leaders who set the goal disappeared. City Bank, the predecessor of Citicorp, had the BHAG, "to become the most powerful, the most serviceable, the most far-reaching world financial institution that has ever been"—a goal that generated excitement through multiple generations until it was achieved. Similarly, the NASA moon mission continued to galvanize people even though President John F. Kennedy (the leader associated with setting the goal) died years before its completion.

To create an effective envisioned future requires a certain level of unreasonable confidence and commitment. Keep in mind that a BHAG is not just a goal; it is a Big,

FIGURE 5   Putting It All Together: Sony in the 1950s

Core Ideology

Core Values

- Elevation of the Japanese culture and national status
- Being a pioneer—not following others; doing the impossible
- Encouraging individual ability and creativity

Purpose

To experience the sheer joy of innovation and the application of technology for the benefit and pleasure of the general public

Envisioned Future

BHAG

Become the company most known for changing the worldwide poor-quality image of Japanese products

Vivid Description

We will create products that become pervasive around the world. . . . We will be the first Japanese company to go into the U.S. market and distribute directly. . . . We will succeed with innovations that U.S. companies have failed at—such as the transistor radio. . . . Fifty years from now, our brand name will be as well known as any in the world . . . and will signify innovation and quality that rival the most innovative companies anywhere. . . . "Made in Japan" will mean something fine, not something shoddy.

Hairy, Audacious Goal. It's not reasonable for a small regional bank to set the goal of becoming "the most powerful, the most serviceable, the most far-reaching world financial institution that has ever been," as City Bank did in 1915. It's not a tepid claim that "we will democratize the automobile," as Henry Ford said. It was almost laughable for Philip Morris—as the sixth-place player with 9 percent market share in the 1950s—to take on the goal of defeating Goliath RJ Reynolds Tobacco Company and becoming number one. It was hardly modest for Sony, as a small, cash-strapped venture, to proclaim the goal of changing the poor-quality image of Japanese products around the world. (See Figure 5, "Putting It All Together: Sony in the 1950s.") Of course, it's not only the audacity of the goal but also the level of commitment to the goal that counts. Boeing didn't just envision a future dominated by its commercial jets; it bet the company on the 707 and, later, on the 747. Nike's people didn't just talk about the idea of crushing Adidas; they went on a crusade to fulfill the dream. Indeed, the envisioned future should produce a bit of the "gulp factor": when it dawns on people what it will take to achieve the goal, there should be an almost audible gulp.

But what about failure to realize the envisioned future? In our research, we found that the visionary companies displayed a remarkable ability to achieve even their most audacious goals. Ford did democratize the automobile; Citicorp did become the most far-reaching bank in the world; Philip Morris did rise from sixth to first and beat RJ Reynolds worldwide; Boeing did become the dominant commercial aircraft company; and it looks like Wal-Mart will achieve its $125 billion goal, even without Sam Walton. In contrast, the comparison companies in our research frequently did not achieve their BHAGs, if they set them at all. The difference does not lie in setting easier goals: the visionary companies tended to have even more audacious ambitions. The difference does not lie in charismatic, visionary leadership: the visionary companies often achieved their BHAGs without such larger-than-life leaders at the helm. Nor does the difference lie in better strategy: the visionary companies often realized their goals more by an organic process of "let's try a lot of stuff and keep what works" than by well-laid strategic plans. Rather, their success lies in building the strength of their organization as their primary way of creating the future.

Why did Merck become the preeminent drugmaker in the world? Because Merck's architects built the best pharmaceutical research and development organization in the world. Why did Boeing become the dominant commercial aircraft company in the world? Because of its superb engineering and marketing organization, which had the ability to make projects like the 747 a reality. When asked to name the most important decisions that have contributed to the growth and success of Hewlett-Packard, David Packard answered entirely in terms of decisions to build the strength of the organization and its people.

Finally, in thinking about the envisioned future, beware of the We've Arrived Syndrome—a complacent lethargy that arises once an organization has achieved one BHAG and fails to replace it with another. NASA suffered from that syndrome after the successful moon landings. After you've landed on the moon, what do you do for an encore? Ford suffered from the syndrome when, after it succeeded in democratizing the automobile, it failed to set a new goal of equal significance and gave General Motors the opportunity to jump ahead in the 1930s. Apple Computer suffered from the syndrome after achieving the goal of creating a computer that nontechies could use. Start-up companies frequently suffer from the We've Arrived Syndrome after going public or after reaching a stage in which survival no longer seems in question. An envisioned future helps an organization only as long as it hasn't yet been achieved. In our work with companies, we frequently hear executives say, "It's just not as exciting around here as it used to be; we seem to have lost our momentum." Usually, that kind of remark signals that the organization has climbed one mountain and not yet picked a new one to climb.

Many executives thrash about with mission statements and vision statements. Unfortunately, most of those statements turn out to be a muddled stew of values, goals, purposes, philosophies, beliefs, aspirations, norms, strategies, practices, and descriptions. They are usually a boring, confusing, structurally unsound stream of words that evoke the response "True, but who cares?" Even more problematic, seldom do these statements have a direct link to the fundamental dynamic of visionary companies: preserve the core and stimulate progress. That dynamic, not vision or mission statements, is the primary engine of enduring companies. Vision simply provides the context for bringing this dynamic to life. Building a visionary company requires 1 percent vision and 99 percent alignment. When you have superb alignment, a visitor could drop in from outer space and infer your vision from the operations and activities of the company without ever reading it on paper or meeting a single senior executive.

Creating alignment may be your most important work. But the first step will always be to recast your vision or mission into an effective context for building a visionary company. If you do it right, you shouldn't have to do it again for at least a decade.

ENDNOTES

1. David Packard, speech given to Hewlett-Packard's training group on March 8, 1960; courtesy of Hewlett-Packard Archives.
2. See Nick Lyons, *The Sony Vision* (New York: Crown, 1976). We also used a translation by our Japanese student Tsuneto Ikeda.
3. Akio Morita, *Made in Japan* (New York: E. P. Dutton, 1986), p. 147.

ONE MORE TIME: WHAT BUSINESS ARE YOU IN?

Ron McTavish

The author states that scope is the fundamental starting point for strategic planning and that a company should analyze "what is" and "what has happened" before deciding "what should happen." Through analysis of cases, McTavish has developed a multidimensional definition of scope based on four key factors: technology, customer function, market segments, and value chain position.

Companies everywhere are adjusting to newer, harsher economic realities. Stories of downsizing, cost-cutting, flattening of organizational structures, and layoffs, while still disconcerting, no longer cause the astonishment they once did.

During painful adjustments many companies, in the interests of becoming "lean and mean," are "rediscovering" their core businesses. Frequently they are urged to do so as the only hope of survival. Acquisitions made in more comfortable times must meet harsher criteria or be dropped.

This is not to say that companies are no longer alert to diversification opportunities, or to deny that core businesses themselves can be severely threatened. But what is evident is that an ability to clearly define or, more significantly, redefine the company's scope is becoming an increasing preoccupation in boardrooms, even in the most substantial organizations. For example, IBM's former Chairman, John F. Akers, speaks of the need to "redefine the IBM company," and Sears has curtailed its involvement in activities such as financial brokerage and even catalog trading in order to concentrate on their core retailing business.[1]

Such decisions bear directly on the question of company scope. They are not taken easily and will demand thorough analysis of numerous factors. This article discusses an approach to this problem based on categorizing the key factors and presenting them in an analytical framework. The suggested framework cannot by itself answer the fundamental question about company scope. But it is managerially useful because a display of all relevant criteria ensures that they are at least put on the table and taken into account. Too much emphasis on one or two factors, as implied by the idea

Source: *Long Range Planning* 28, no. 2 (1995), pp. 49–60. Copyright © 1995 Elsevier Science Ltd. Printed in Great Britain.

of product-market scope, needs to give way to a broader perspective which includes all pertinent influencing factors. A portrayal of key factors also provides a useful focus and integrating device for managerial discussion.

Before presenting the framework, the article first of all looks briefly at the limitations of some approaches to scope definition, and uses case studies to highlight the practical difficulties of formulating such a definition. The framework is then presented as a means of clarifying these definitional issues and a detailed case described. The article finally suggests some important managerial guidelines.

COMPANY ATTITUDE TO SCOPE DEFINITION

While strategic planning is well established in companies generally, it is a moot point whether questions of company scope are raised very frequently unless overwhelming pressures demand it. This is partly because the thrust of the business, once established, may be thought immutable for long periods of time. For example, Dow Chemicals' essential scope—to be a large-volume producer of commodity chemicals—was first developed some 50 years ago and has served the company well for several decades. However, Dow has lately focused more on specialty chemicals and higher-margin products. Another example is Crown, Cork and Seal who, until 1977, pursued a strategy of being a differentiated, low-cost producer of steel cans, crown bottle tops, and related container machinery for the beer, soft drink, food, and aerosol markets. Crown's scope, however, also required major adjustments when some of its key markets were threatened, in part by aluminum can makers. These examples suggest that definitions of scope are durable and hence probably do not command regular or on-going strategic attention. Yet they do not last forever and need periodic reassessment.

When organizations do decide to pay attention to the fundamental issues of business definition, the idea of scope can readily be supplemented by a miscellany of additional concepts. "Vision," "role," "mission," "focus," "strategic thrust," and others come to mind. If not a cause of confusion, such concepts can help in thinking about scope, but their limitations should be borne in mind.

A case in point is the idea of defining company role, first popularized by Theodore Levitt: firms are blinkered if they see themselves as "goods producing" not "market satisfying."[2] The example of the buggywhip company, redefining and broadening its scope to embrace transportation generally, entered marketing mythology and influenced the thinking of countless companies.[3]

Now this thinking seems rather dated. Companies cannot go so far in the direction of markets that they ignore their resources, or vice versa. What is needed is an approach which goes beyond simply seeing can makers as packaging companies, or telephone companies as being in communications. Such thinking may be revealing up to a point, but it fails to take into account the many dimensions of the firm's capabilities and markets which must be allowed for in any comprehensive definition of scope. It is such a multidimensional approach which will be described here.

Inattention to defining company scope is surprising, given its acknowledged position as the starting point of strategic planning.[4] When clarity exists, benefits flow to all parts of the organization: product strategy is more focused; there is a clearer definition of target markets; positioning strategy becomes clearer; R&D receives more specific direction, and there is an improved ability to pick out relevant and exploitable opportunities in new market developments. In contrast, when clarity is absent, firms lack a sense of purpose and direction and find forward planning difficult.

PRACTICAL PROBLEMS

Companies pondering fundamental issues of business definition and scope are essentially struggling to find a strategic vision—a shared understanding of what the firm should be and how it must change. The newly emerging school of strategy called the "resource-based" view is one approach to answering such questions.[5] A comparison of this approach with the one suggested in this article may be helpful.

A Comparison with the "Resource-Based" View

Proponents of the resource-based approach view the successful firm as a bundle of somewhat unique resources and capabilities. If the firm's core capabilities are scarce, durable, defensible, or hard to imitate, and can be closely aligned with the key success factors of target markets, they can form the basis of sustainable competitive advantage and profit. The central focus of the approach is on developing those core capabilities that will be effective in various possible market segments and in several different possible futures.

Following from this, the methodology of the approach involves building a four-step framework. The first three steps, generating broad future scenarios, conducting competitive and market segment analysis, and analyzing company and competitive core capabilities, are used to assist managers to develop a strategic vision and identify strategy options (Step 4). The process has been employed by, for example, Apple Computers as well as several other companies.[6]

Although this approach is multidimensional and addresses fundamental corporate concerns, its main focus is on company resources and their alignment with future markets rather than on scope as such. Of course the approach has strong implications for scope issues, particularly the "vision statements" which emerge from the process. For example, the major part of one possible vision for Apple is to become "a consumer-oriented electronics company focused on communication and information products."[6] Such a vision clearly calls for continued emphasis on software development, or an enlargement of technological scope. Moreover, the rather general statement has specific implications for scope in terms of markets, products, and customer functions to be served.

But to pursue the Apple example, the main concern of the resource-based view is to seek compatibility between the vision and the company's core capabilities. Scope considerations are implicit rather than explicit. In contrast, the major concern of the approach proposed here *is* scope. Of course, there are common elements: both approaches are concerned with target market emphasis and product selection, for example.

However, the suggested approach is distinctive in its development of a four-dimensional model to clarify scope rather than a two-part one (as implied by the idea of product-market scope); in its conceptualization of some of the scope dimensions themselves (for example, customer functions and value chain position, to be explained below); and in its emphasis on display techniques to assist managerial decision taking. Both operate as aids to management decision taking and do not claim to usurp the decision taking role.

Company Experiences

Let us now turn to the question of scope. As in the case of the resource-based view, this, too, requires a systematic analysis, but case experience suggests that this may not be an orderly process: it can be thrown off course by unplanned-for events, for example, new knowledge gained from a novel application, or changes in buyer motivational priorities. Also the process may not be entirely within management's control. The familiar necessity to cope with both controllable and uncontrollable forces is present in the scope decision too.

These points are illustrated using three case studies, below. The study of these cases suggests the factors which need to be brought into a decision framework (described in subsequent sections) but also highlights the more imponderable external factors at work which, if they cannot be controlled, should at least be understood.

Xerox

In Xerox's case, a far-reaching change in scope is under way.[7] In part the change has been dictated by changing markets and technology. The company has had to understand and respond to these changes, illustrating the need for constant attention to the scope question.

The situation facing Xerox can be briefly summarized as follows: the company's business in light-lens copiers and duplicators has been threatened by the evolution of digital technology. In effect the light-lens element in a copier can now be replaced with a scanning device that digitizes the information, and allows the performance of various other functions such as editing and color change. But more significantly, electronic information coming from a personal computer or mainframe can be merged with paper information creating complex, digital document systems.

Faced with this new technological environment and changing customer behaviour, Xerox found it inappropriate to go on seeing themselves as sellers of "stand-alone" copying devices. Instead, as the worlds of paper-based information and digital information merge, the company is now moving to a newer focus: "the document." The contrast between the old—making and selling "boxes"—and the new—designing innovative business systems to improve customer productivity—is dramatic, with widespread implications for the firm and its future scope.

Reliance Electric

Reliance Electric illustrates how limited sales potential in a firm's traditional product-market can be the impetus for a change in scope.[8] Faced with a mature market for their motor products, Reliance over a period of years redefined its scope to include the mechanical drive linkage and systems that connected the motor to the machine. This rethinking more than doubled the company's potential market and opened the door to a whole range of combined electrical-mechanical developments. These eliminated many of the interface problems and costs that occurred when the products were designed by different manufacturers.

The Chairman of Reliance credits subsequent profit growth to "getting the right market focus." In this case the breakthrough came from detailed study of the product's application and its use with associated equipment, in effect an analysis of part of the Reliance customer's value chain.

Nike

While both Xerox and Reliance Electric have been influenced by, and responded to, different technological and market changes, it is a paradox that a company's own marketing activities may constrict its scope opportunities. In other words, companies generally face the problem that the sheer fact of offering a product to the market over a period of time sets up market expectations about the product's quality and appropriate usage to which the firm's name is associated. When a strong brand name is established, this problem of customer perception is particularly acute. In the scope equation, brand perceptions must be understood.

An illustrative case is Nike.[9] From the outset the market perception was: here is a running shoe, Nike is a running shoe company, and the brand name stands for excellence in track and field. However, the company did not immediately appreciate the limitations on its scope set by this perception. Faced with a slowing-down of the running shoe market in the early 1980s, partly as a result of competition from Reebok, Nike entered the casual shoe market. The reasoning was that customers in any case used their Nike shoes for several purposes, and the company was good at producing shoes.

But Nike failed badly. The experience forced the company to define what the Nike brand really meant. It was concluded that the early running shoe brand sent a clear message, but casual shoes a confusing one. Ultimately, the company redefined its scope more narrowly as a sports and fitness company. Understanding the market's brand perception, the formation of which was a function of Nike's own brand promotion, thus fundamentally influenced the company's scope options.

Lessons Learned

Such examples do not exhaust the difficulties of scope definition. For example, a redefined or enlarged scope, as in the cases of Reliance Electric and Xerox, will lead to the development of newer products to "fill" the new scope. These newer products might induce a search for newer applications, which in turn might broaden the scope farther. So scope definition is not a lock-step process but a dynamic one with much interaction between market, technological, customer application, product, and brand perception factors. Managements face the dilemma that change is probably inevitable, that if nothing is done external forces will greatly restrict their area of discretion, and that if they choose a proactive course they will face difficult decisions with far-reaching consequences.

> *Scope definition is not a lock-step process but a dynamic one with much interaction between market, technological, customer application, product, and brand perception factors.*

APPROACHING SCOPE DEFINITION

Let us now suggest a decision framework to aid management analysis of such scope problems. As a preliminary, it is as well to remember that there is no single "right" way to go about this. Two companies may coexist and both be successful although they define their scope in two different ways. We have noted the evolving conception of scope favored by Xerox. But the company faces competition in the newer digital world not only from organizations such as Canon, but also from firms now in the printing or computer systems business. It is unlikely that all will view scope in an identical way.

Another point is that much depends on the key motivating forces of the business, its "drivers." Some "high tech" companies are product and technology driven, for example, while many examples of market-driven companies can be pointed out in consumer goods. It is true that companies with single drivers run the risk of oversimplifying company strategy, also that management may not agree on what single force should be dominant. Whatever the merits of these arguments the existence of dominant driving forces is bound to exert a key influence on scope decisions.

Having said this, the framework proposed here is based on the belief that ideally the firm should pay attention to all relevant factors bearing on the company's scope. The factors would then be considered explicitly and balanced in any given situation.

What factors, then, best describe the key dimensions of the firm's scope? Abell[10] argues that scope is frequently conceptualized along two main dimensions, either in terms of the firm's served markets, or in terms of the products and services it offers. However, taken together, these encompass three dimensions: *who* is being served (the firm's market segments); *what needs* are being satisfied (in other words, what customer functions do the products satisfy); and *how* are customer functions satisfied (what technologies are used).

In practice, it is usually necessary for the firm to define its scope in terms of its "product-market" strategy rather than in terms of either products or served markets alone. But product descriptions are usually in terms of technology and customer functions performed; and descriptions of served markets are typically in terms of market segments and functions served.

Thus, according to Abell, neither description alone typically gives a complete three-dimensional definition of scope in terms of segments, functions, and technologies. The relevance to scope of these three factors is also clear from the case studies, as is a fourth factor-stage in the value chain. According to this analysis, therefore, what is needed is a breaking out from the restricted two-dimensional model to one incorporating four key factors. These are outlined briefly below.

Customer Functions

Here we are referring to the customer functions which the supplier seeks to perform, or help to perform, through the sale of appropriate products to the customer. (This reflects, in part, the idea of the product as a "bundle of benefits," not just a physical entity.) In Xerox's case, the simple customer function of copying is perceived to encompass the user's desire for "business systems productivity." This has led the company to develop newer products, for example PaperWorks, a software packaging that allows users to access their personal computers from any fax machine in the world. Xerox's scope is broadening by introducing new products to address these changing customer functions.

Technology Dimension

Xerox, too, illustrates the point that strategic scope must also be thought of in terms of the range and mix of technologies used to produce final products and services. In effect, technologies describe the alternative ways in which a particular function can be performed for a customer. In the case of PaperWorks, cited above, this emerged out of research on advanced image processing at the firm's Palo Alto Research Center, which gave birth to a variety of new technologies.[11] Success in the copier market also requires competence in other technologies such as control hardware and software, and panel displays. Innovation in mechanical paper movement and optics, important a decade ago, and still relevant, needs to be supplemented by newer technologies and broader technological scope to keep offering customers products with more refined problem solutions.

Customer Segment Dimension

The scope of the firm in terms of markets served is an obvious factor to consider, for example, Reliance Electric's deliberate decision to seek out new product-markets.

Stage in the Value Chain

Porter's familiar value chain[12] suggests that we should also view scope in terms of stages in the chain from raw materials to completed product. For example, a characteristic of minicomputer makers is the forward definition of their business scope to incorporate company operation of retail outlets. In the case of Reliant Electric, a similar principle is at work except that here we need to "decompose" the plant operations segment of the chain into its component parts. Then the electric motor can be thought of as being at one stage of the plant's operations, the connecting mechanism to the machine at another, the output of the machine at another, and so on.

A Note on Information Gathering

Firms can use various techniques to collect appropriate information about these scope dimensions. For example, information on customer functions and value chain position can be obtained through customer tracking methods, applications research, and information from the field, for example salesforce feedback. This can be supplemented by internal document appraisal, for example quotations and order analysis, which, allied with market research, can be used to throw light on existing and emerging customers and market segments. In addition, a "technology portfolio" might be useful to portray how a firm is distributing its mix of technologies (not products), and where these technologies stand in development, market exploitation, and competitive strength.[13]

CASE EXAMPLE OF A MULTIDIMENSIONAL FRAMEWORK

We can now portray the above factors in a descriptive framework as a management aid to strategic thinking. This is done in Figure 1, using an actual case (a manufacturer of industrial valves). The case studies described above remind us of the different factors impinging on scope. A case study is used to emphasize the variety of these factors and their interrelationships, the importance of considering external factors such as demand changes and competitive pressures, and the key role of understanding the company's core competencies and historical evolution. Moreover, a case study is useful to "go behind" the static framework and illustrate the practical problems and managerial lessons learned in grappling with the factors and reaching a conclusion.

The top half of Figure 1 describes the early scope dimensions of Northern Valves, a small but very successful U.S.-based competitor in the highly fragmented industrial valve market. The company's specialty is a valve product variously described as a "double dump," "flapgate," or "tipping" valve, first developed by the firm in the mid-1960s as an outgrowth of many years' experience making highly durable cast alloy products for severely abrasive applications in the mining industry. (See Figure 2 for further description of the valve.)

Figure 1 shows the scope of the firm at that time. From the viewpoint of technology the firm possessed a captive foundry, capable of producing the hard-wearing cast alloy parts needed for the new valve. In addition the firm possessed a number of patents for this flap or "pivoting" valve, indicating the key principle of operation, namely the opening and shutting by a pivot of a door or flap. The valve essentially functioned as an "air lock," allowing material to pass through an opening where

FIGURE 1   Evaluation of Company Scope: Northern Valves Inc.

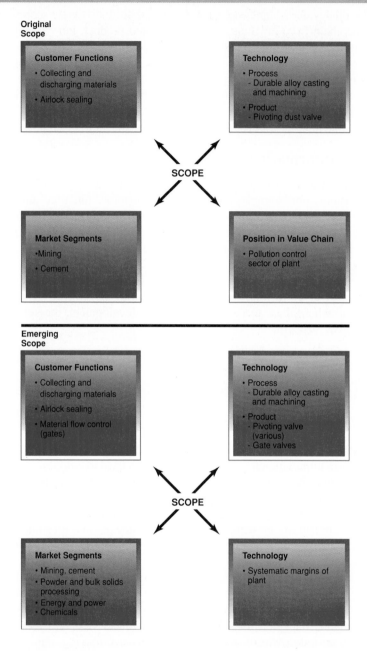

there are different pressures on either side. Binding all of this together were core competencies in mechanical engineering design and in devising engineering solutions for severely abrasive process-flow applications, especially in mining.

Looking now from the technology to the customer functions box at the top of Figure 1, we see the technology employed to achieve specific customer functions— collecting, discharging, sealing—through the valve. At this point, the company described the valve as a "dust valve" to be employed mainly for the feed and discharge control of dust, dry bulk products, and waste.

FIGURE 2   Operation of a Flap Valve

A flap valve functions as an air lock allowing material to pass through an opening where there are different pressures (positive or negative) on either side of the valve. The valve has two connecting chambers. In a positive pressure situation (greater pressure above the valve) the flap valve receives a volume of material in the top chamber, the door (or flap) opens, discharging the material into the bottom chamber. That door then closes and seals, maintaining pressure, and the door in the bottom chamber opens, allowing the material to fall out for a final removal from the site. In a negative pressure situation the valve operates similarly, except that in this case it is the closing of the bottom door which maintains pressure by preventing air from blowing back into the valve. The valves are manufactured in various sizes to accommodate different volumes of material that pass through. The larger sizes weigh 2–3 tons (cast alloy construction) and are 5–6 feet in height.

The customer segments part of the figure point to the limited market scope at that time—focus on mining and minerals, and cement markets. Finally, the value chain box shows an emphasis on the air pollution control "end" of the user's plant operations, under filter baghouse dust collectors to deal with product and "nuisance" dust.

The early scope of this company can therefore be seen to be quite limited: a single product technology (pivoting gate) underlying a limited product line (dust valves) sold to restricted markets in restricted applications. Let us now look at how this has changed (see Figure 3 for a summary of the main changes).

NORTHERN VALVES: EMERGING SCOPE

Looking now at the bottom half of Figure 1, we are able to describe the emerging scope of the company, and to highlight some of the factors leading to change. The points discussed below result from a recent review by the company of its scope, and therefore reflect the impact on scope of management thinking and various strategic and other moves taken in the years following the dust valve's introduction.

Position in the Value Chain

As the company gained experience in the application of the valve—a process taking place over several years—specialization in the pollution control of dust emissions was more and more realized to be too restrictive, especially as the valve was used increasingly for non-dust materials, for example, ash. (In the case of ash in a waste-to-energy plant, this might take several forms and "show up" at different points in the plant as a by-product of different processes.)[14] There was therefore need for a different, broader conception of how the product could be used at different points in the production value chain, not simply at "the end" to collect dust.

It was only after prolonged thought that the broader concept of "systemic margins" emerged in the company, i.e., the idea that the valve was essentially used at the "doors" or "margins" of a customer plant, the points at which materials passed from one processing phase to another, or were collected, metered or discharged. Using this concept, the company began to envision customer plants not simply as potential dust valve applications, but as total flow process systems with internal "margins," but also with external ones, i.e., where for example allowable waste material is dis-

FIGURE 3   Summary of Scope Changes (Northern Valves Inc.)

Scope Dimension	Direction of Change
1. Customer functions	
A. Historic	Unchanged
(Material collection, discharge, airlock sealing)	
B. Evolving view	Broader
(material "gates")	
2. Market segments	Broader
3. Position in value chain	Broader
4. Technologies	
A. Process	Unchanged
B. Product	Broader

charged into the atmosphere. How this broader conception of scope has impacted other aspects of the firm's operations is outlined below.

Customer Segments

Figure 1 shows a clear broadening of the company's spectrum of market segments, including an area which the company describes as "powder and bulk processing" (which includes chemicals), energy production (including utilities, waste-to-energy and recycling plants), and the customary areas of mining and cement. However, this is only partly the result of deliberate management strategy in recognizing and pursuing new non-dust opportunities. It also reflects action by the market itself in seeking to apply a product so well proven in abrasive applications. In effect, knowledgeable purchasing and engineering managers will make it their business to seek out competent suppliers with good quality reputations, thereby effectively extending the market opportunities of the latter, and their potential scope.

This point should be stressed because it illustrates the willingness of the market to "allow" the supplier to broaden its scope, though this can apply in the opposite direction as the Nike case shows. The Northern Valves experience illustrates the idea that the market can be a function of the product and that it is difficult to be sure in advance how newer market segments will perceive a new product and apply it.[15] In fact, Northern continues to be surprised by the emergence of newer applications (e.g. in photographic toner, gypsum, ceramics and glass plants, to give some examples). As these applications are studied, it has been found to add a richness to the comprehension of the systematic margin idea, but also to add a deeper understanding of customer functions.

Customer Functions

The customer function aspect speaks to the functions the valve performs for the customer, or the benefits the customer seeks. Looking at Figure 1, we can see that the airlock or sealing function, by which the integrity of associated systems is maintained, has not changed fundamentally. It remains the company's unique and enduring market focus. What has changed, however, is the richness of the product mix dedicated to solving this problem. The original dust valve is now available in numerous sizes, capacities, and drives with various optional features and construction materials indicating a considerable product development effort over the years.

However, a much broader expansion of the product line is now under way. This flows from a newer conception of the customer's basic need, born of prolonged thinking about the fundamental function of the valve in countless applications. This is that the customer basically needs a "gate" or "door" to shut off or permit material flow as needed. In this we see an extension of the "systematic margin" thinking. Traditionally the company has supplied a pivoting gate for dry materials handling. But thinking about "gates" in general leads one to think about other forms of gate valving, for example, "slide-gates," by which technology the gate slices through the material flow, cutting it off, rather than pivoting to an open or closed position.

Of great significance to the company, however, is that it is led by this thinking to "knife-gates" (which are used in liquid applications) and the realization that the company's scope might be broadened beyond traditional dry materials to include liquid and gas applications.

The company movement in this broader direction is reflected in its promotion of itself as a "gate valve company" and the offer of a much broader range of "gate-related" products, not solely the pivoting gate line.

Technology Dimension

An enduring feature of the company's technological capability is the retention of a captive foundry as a fundamental core competence and a long-term development of pivoting-valve technology. This underlies the vastly developed product line now available for addressing dry materials flow problems where a strong seal or airlock is needed. Therefore Northern shows a very limited technological scope in the sense that it does not possess a wide mix of technologies, but applies a given technology intensely in a specified area.

However, as the newer gate valve concept takes hold, the company faces the problem of pushing their technological capabilities in newer, less familiar areas, for example in knife-gates for liquid applications. Moreover, if the systematic gate idea leads to diversification into products with which the valve is associated (e.g. pneumatic conveying systems), further technologies will have to be contemplated.

Implications

What has Northern's management learned from this exercise? First, as Figure 1 shows, the scope review permits a clear view of the main changes taking place, and clarifies possible strategic options for the future. Second, as shown in Table 1, the broadening or otherwise of the firm's scope can be studied along each dimension, and an overall view taken.

A notable feature is that the customer function (of airlock sealing) has not broadened in any significant way, though the newer "gate" concepts may change this in the future. On the other hand, the company has broadened its product range considerably, by introducing numerous variants on the pivoting valve theme, has substantially broadened its market scope, and has a much broader view of its position in the value chain. This has been accompanied by concentration on existing technological capability.

Therefore, although broadening its scope in some directions, Northern has maintained a consistent focus on familiar dry material processing problems. This is significant in the light of recent research into more than 40 companies which concludes that companies that have taken leadership positions in their industries in the last decade have typically done so "by narrowing their business focus, not broadening it."[16] Northern continues to enjoy a leadership position in its historic niche. This finding will undoubtedly influence its thinking as it contemplates new markets and technologies (e.g. liquids) for the future.

This company's experience also throws light on the dynamics of the decision process, in particular the interaction of controllable and uncontrollable factors and the limitations of management discretion. Thus in Northern's case, broadening of the market scope was as much a matter of market initiative as it was of conscious management choice, though one would have to credit management for creative thinking about the core benefits of the valve. Again, prolonged and laudable attention to product quality produced unforeseen sales in unfamiliar applications, which in turn prompted close analysis of what the valve was used for.

A Cautionary Note

A word of caution is, however, needed. It must always be stressed that scope definition is essentially the starting point of strategic planning. Northern still faces a variety of agonizing choices and implementation issues: moving into newer valve areas means confronting newer, specialized, competitors; technological development of newer products (e.g. rotary valves) is not easy for a pivoting valve specialist; newer markets may have limited abrasion and temperature problems (in which Northern specializes); and technological problems of material transfer at "systemic margins" will not always be compatible with Northern's products, so newer technologies and products may have to be considered.

How these problems will be resolved and what avenues Northern will ultimately pursue are matters for the judgment of the company's management and will depend on an array of factors such as time frames, risk levels, growth prospects, and competitors.

However, borrowing from the resource-based view, it is clear that Northern would be wise to build on its substantial core competencies in flap-gate valve design and cast alloy technology. It is in such areas that the company has enjoyed substantial experience over many years and which can be looked to for sources of competitive advantage. Venturing into newer product technologies and markets is a more demanding proposition and will call for a detailed and frank appraisal of existing skills and their flexibility in newer roles. Such an appraisal might form part of the familiar SWOT analysis so that capabilities might be viewed in terms of the opportunities and threats of the marketplace.

As Northern appraises its product-market opportunities, a product portfolio analysis is likely to be helpful.[17] Decisions will have to be taken on the appropriateness of the current portfolio and whether and how it is to be upgraded. Continuation of present strategies for the existing flap-gate line appears appropriate in order to maintain market share, for example, but aggressive support of new entries (e.g. in liquid applications) might be needed to ensure substantial market penetration. Such decisions will be aided by the methodology of portfolio analysis and creative displays of data.

Lastly, Northern faces the problem of determining marketing mix and positioning strategies for new products in order to achieve durable competitive advantages. Here knowledge of industry norms over a wide area—costs, product designs, service levels, quality standards—will be needed to determine the feasibility of market entry. Such information might be acquired as part of a market attractiveness/business position analysis.

The Impacts of Scope Thinking

Despite these problems, the immediate impact of the newer scope thinking has been to galvanize the company and give it a greater sense of purpose and direction:

- The "gate" idea has fostered a newer, integrative conception of product strategy—a "layered" strategy—in which newer products are seen as mutually supporting, leading to an ever-widening customer base ("layered market strategy").
- Sales promotion and advertising are focused on the "gate" theme: the company presents itself as a full-service provider of gate valve solutions and is increasingly recognized as such. (Contrast the early dust valve orientation.)
- Engineering is encouraged to innovate consistently fresh new designs with the "gate" theme in mind.
- New product search activity is more clearly focused on areas of high potential, namely at the points of materials transfer in customer plants, with special attention to products with which the valve is synergistically associated (baghouses, cyclones, discharge hoppers).
- Sales engineering looks beyond dust applications to the total functioning of the customer's plant so that "gate" problems are recognized anywhere they occur. This in turn has led to greater customer acceptance of the firm as a problem-solver, and has enhanced customer relationships.
- Market research is better able to single out new markets for study because it is easier to comprehend where the most exploitable opportunities lie. (For example, the company has achieved a significant market penetration in waste-to-energy plants by realizing the transferability of its core capabilities to this field.)

MANAGERIAL GUIDELINES

Based on the experience of Northern Valves and the other company cases described in this article, the following management guidelines are suggested. A theme running through these proposals is the need to "take hold" of the scope issue proactively and to anticipate the impact of different external forces.

- Discuss the scope issue at frequent intervals, even when the market seems to be going well.
- Make scope planning an integral part of the strategic planning process.
- Favor a multidimensional approach.
- Utilize "displays" of key influencing factors to aid perception and promote discussion.
- Understand the meaning to the market of the company's brand. Recognize that the market will develop a perception of the product whether the company likes it or not. This might help, but could restrict scope options. Use frequent brand awareness and similar studies to keep track of market attitude.
- Stay close to the customer. This is becoming a cliché, but it is critical to understand how the customer is applying the product and the changing benefits he seeks from it.
- Experiment with newer concepts of customer functions and benefits sought (the "gate" concept; the "document") and review current thinking accordingly.

- Keep abreast of technological trends impacting on customers. These can fundamentally influence the customer's product needs and hence the supplier's potential product scope (Xerox). Use appropriate means to assess scenarios of innovation diffusion patterns in key markets.[18]

- As new concepts of scope emerge, review the firm's markets, and assess new markets with these in mind (e.g. Northern Valves' conception of "systematic gate for material processing" suggests broader applications than dust alone, such as ash handling in power plants and processing of powders and chemicals).

- Appreciate that there is no intrinsic merit in either a broad scope or a narrow one. Either is justifiable depending on the strategic objectives sought. In addition, the chosen focus of the company can be consistent with either a broad or narrow scope. (For example, one industrial distributor carries 12 pages of water heaters in its catalog to appeal to a market segment which ascribes value to a service according to how closely it appears to be designed just for them: a focus on "customer intimacy" is thus achieved by a very broad product scope).[19]

CONCLUSION

Decisions on company scope are of great importance to the firm yet are probably not given the attention they deserve, especially in happy economic times. However, harsher economic circumstances are forcing companies to realize that they must regularly think about their essential purposes, and regularly ask themselves "deceptively simple questions."[20] In this context, how are companies to go about defining, or redefining their scope?

First of all, it is crucial to rediscover the key point that scope *is* a fundamental starting point of strategic planning and should be treated as such. Therefore discussions on scope should emerge and be examined regularly as part of the strategic planning process.

With scope firmly established in planning, the firm is better placed to guard against the less predictable external forces which constrict scope, and is therefore better placed to dictate its own destiny. Discussions of "the external environment," which are a feature of any strategic plan, should always prompt a review of the scope issue.

With scope firmly established in planning, the firm is better placed to guard against the less predictable external forces which constrict scope, and is therefore better placed to dictate its own destiny.

Lastly, the firm should analyze scope decisions formally. This article recommends using a multidimensional approach with all significant dimensions clearly displayed. Discussion can then be focused on such factors—customer functions, technology, market segments, and value chain position. In addition, discussion should note any interactions between the factors, the impact on them of external forces, and the core skills and historical trend of the company.

In effect, the company should analyze "what is" and "what has happened" as a prelude to deciding "what should happen." The latter calls for difficult strategic choices, but these will be facilitated in companies where the scope issue has received consistent attention, and where prolonged thinking about the fundamental nature of the product, the core benefits sought, and the impact of external factors has led to enduring concepts of the nature of the firm and its fundamental purposes.

ENDNOTES

1. "Hardware and Tear," *The Economist*, December 19, 1992, pp. 61–62.
2. T. Levitt, "Marketing Myopia," *Harvard Business Review*, July–August 1960, pp. 45–56.
3. K. Simmonds, "Removing the Chains from Product Strategy," *Journal of Management Studies* 5, no. 1 (1968), pp. 29–40.
4. Derek F. Abell, *Defining the Business: The Starting Point of Strategic Planning* (Englewood Cliffs, NJ: Prentice-Hall, 1980).
5. J. B. Barney, "Firm Resources and Sustained Competitive Advantage," *Journal of Management* 17 no. 1 (1991), pp. 99–120.
6. Paul J. H. Schoemaker, "How to Link Strategic Vision to Core Capabilities," *Sloan Management Review*, Fall 1992, pp. 67–81.
7. Robert Howard, "The CEO as Organizational Architect: An Interview with Xerox's Paul Allaire," *Harvard Business Review*, September–October 1992, pp. 106–21.
8. Quoted in B. Charles Ames and James D. Hlavacek, *Managerial Marketing for Industrial Firms* (New York: Random House, 1984).
9. Geraldine E. Willigan, "High-Performance Marketing: An Interview with Nike's Phil Knight," *Harvard Business Review*, July–August 1992, pp. 90–101.
10. Abell, *Defining the Business*.
11. Howard, "The CEO."
12. Michael Porter, *Competitive Advantage: Creating and Sustaining Superior Performance*. (New York: Free Press, 1985).
13. Noel Capon and Rashi Glazer, "Marketing and Technology: A Strategic Coalignment," *Journal of Marketing* 51 (July 1987), pp. 1–14.
14. Manzoor Alam and David J. Schlotthauer, "Planning for Successful Ash Handling," *Solid Waste and Power*, August 1990, pp. 30–36.
15. Raymond Odioso, "An R and D Executive Looks at Marketing," *Research Management* 28, no. 5 (1985), pp. 20–25.
16. Michael Treacy and Fred Wiersema, "Customer Intimacy and Other Value Disciplines," *Harvard Business Review*, January–February 1993, pp. 84–93.
17. George Day, "Diagnosing the Product Portfolio," *Journal of Marketing*, April 1977, pp. 29–38.
18. See, for example, the annual *R and D Scoreboard* published by *Business Week* indicating R and D spending by industry sector and by numerous individual companies.
19. Treacy and Wiersema, "Customer Intimacy."
20. "To Save Big Blue," *The Economist*, January 16, 1993, pp. 18–19.

READING 3

STRATEGY AS REVOLUTION

Gary Hamel

Working from the premise that revolutionary companies are attempting to rewrite the rules of competition and shake up the industry, Hamel states that companies must revolutionize their strategic planning process or surrender to the revolutionaries. He suggests 10 ways of thinking about the challenge of creating strategy that can help a company liberate its revolutionary spirit.

Let's admit it. Corporations around the world are reaching the limits of incrementalism. Squeezing another penny out of costs, getting a product to market a few weeks earlier, responding to customers' inquiries a little bit faster, ratcheting quality up one more notch, capturing another point of market share—those are the obsessions of managers today. But pursuing incremental improvements while rivals reinvent the industry is like fiddling while Rome burns.

Look at any industry and you will see three kinds of companies. First are the rule makers, the incumbents that built the industry. IBM, CBS, United Airlines, Merrill Lynch, Sears, Coca-Cola, and the like are the creators and protectors of industrial orthodoxy. They are the oligarchy. Next are the rule takers, the companies that pay homage to the industrial "lords." Fujitsu, ABC, U.S. Air, Smith Barney, J. C. Penney, and numerous others are those peasants. Their life is hard. Imagine working at Fujitsu for 30 years trying to catch IBM in the mainframe business, or being McDonnell Douglas to Boeing, or Avis to Hertz. We Try Harder may be a great advertising slogan, but it's depressingly futile as a strategy. What good will it do to work harder to follow the rules when some companies are rewriting them? IKEA, the Body Shop, Charles Schwab, Dell Computer, Swatch, Southwest Airlines, and many more are the rule breakers. Shackled neither by convention nor by respect for precedent, these companies are intent on overturning the industrial order. They are the malcontents, the radicals, the industry revolutionaries.

Never has the world been more hospitable to industry revolutionaries and more hostile to industry incumbents. The fortifications that protected the industrial oligarchy are crumbling under the weight of deregulation, technological upheaval, globalization, and social change. But it's not just the forces of change that are overturning old industrial structures—it's the actions of companies that harness those forces for the cause of revolution. (See Figure 1, "Nine Routes to Industry Revolution.")

The fortifications that protected the industrial oligarchy are crumbling under the weight of deregulation, technological upheaval, globalization, and social change.

What if your company is more ruling class than revolutionary? You can either surrender the future to revolutionary challengers or revolutionize the way your company creates strategy. What is required is not a little tweak to the traditional planning process but a new philosophical foundation: strategy *is* revolution; everything else is tactics.

The following ten principles can help a company liberate its revolutionary spirit and dramatically increase its chances of discovering truly revolutionary strategies. Companies in industries as diverse as personal care products, information services, food processing, insurance, and telecommunications have internalized and acted on these principles. Every organization, however, must interpret and apply them in its own way. These are not a set of step-by-step instructions but a way of thinking about the challenge of creating strategy—the challenge of becoming an industry revolutionary.

Principle 1: Strategic Planning Isn't Strategic Consider your company's planning process. Which describes it best—column A, on the left, or column B, on the right?

A	B
Ritualistic	Inquisitive
Reductionist	Expansive
Extrapolative	Prescient
Positioning	Inventing
Elitist	Inclusive
Easy	Demanding

Unless your company is truly exceptional, you've probably admitted that the words in column A are more fitting than those in column B. In the vast majority of companies, strategic planning is a calendar-driven ritual, not an exploration of the potential for revolution. The strategy-making process tends to be reductionist, based on simple rules and heuristics. It works from today forward, not from the future back, implicitly assuming, whatever the evidence to the contrary, that the future will be more or less like the present. Only a tiny percentage of an industry's conventions are ever challenged, rendering strategy making largely extrapolative. An industry's boundaries are taken as a given; thus the question is how to position products and services within those boundaries rather than how to invent new, uncontested competitive space. Further, the planning process is generally elitist, harnessing only a small proportion of an organization's creative potential.

Perhaps most disturbing, strategy making is often assumed to be easy, especially in comparison with implementing strategy. But of course strategy making is easy when the process limits the scope of discovery, the breadth of involvement, and the amount of intellectual effort expended. Of course the process is easy when its goal is something far short of revolution. How often has strategic planning produced true

FIGURE 1   Nine Routes to Industry Revolution

Unless you are an industry leader with an unassailable position—a status that, given the lessons of history, not even Microsoft would be wise to claim—you probably have a greater stake in staging a revolution than in preserving the status quo. The opportunities for revolution are many and mostly unexplored. How should a would-be revolutionary begin? By looking for ways to redefine products and services, market space, and even the entire structure of an industry.

Reconceiving a Product or Service

1. Radically Improving the Value Equation. In every industry, there is a ratio that relates price to performance: X units of cash buy Y units of value. The challenge is to improve that value ratio and to do so radically—500 percent or 1,000 percent, not 10 percent or 20 percent. Such a fundamental redefinition of the value equation forces a reconception of the product or service.

Fidelity Investments, for instance, wondered why a person couldn't invest in foreign equity markets for tens or hundreds of dollars rather than thousands. On a recent flight, I heard one flight attendant say to another, "I just moved some of my investments from the Europe Fund to the Pacific Basin Fund." Such a comment would have been inconceivable a decade or two ago, but Fidelity and other mutual-fund revolutionaries have redefined the industry's value equation. Hewlett-Packard's printer business and IKEA are other value revolutionaries.

. 2. Separating Function and Form. Another way to challenge the existing concept of a product or service is to separate core benefits (function) from the ways in which those benefits are currently embodied in a product or service (form). Any organization that is able to distinguish form from function and then reconceive one or both has the opportunity to create an industry revolution.

Consider credit cards, which perform two functions. First, a credit card inspires a merchant to trust that you are who the card says you are: your name is embossed on the front, your signature appears on the back, and your photo may even appear in the corner. Nevertheless, credit card fraud is a rapidly escalating problem. In what form will "trust" be delivered in the future? Probably through biometric data: a handprint, voiceprint, or retinal scan. Any credit card maker that is not investing in those technologies today may be surprised by interlopers. Second, a credit card gives

you permission to charge up to your credit limit. What new opportunities appear if you distinguish permission as a general function from the particular case of permission to charge? In many hotels, a card with a magnetic stripe gives guests "permission" to enter their rooms. Did credit card makers see the opportunity to use the cards in this way? No, the card security market is owned largely by newcomers.

3. Achieving Joy of Use. We live in a world that takes ease of use for granted. The new goal is joy of use. We want our products and services to be whimsical, tactile, informative, and just plain fun. Any company that can wrap those attributes around a mundane product or service has the chance to be an industry revolutionary.

What's the most profitable food retailer per square foot in the United States? Probably Trader Joe's, a cross between a gourmet deli and a discount warehouse, which its CEO, John Shields, calls a "fashion food retailer." Essentially without competition, its 74 stores were averaging annual sales of $1,000 per square foot in 1995—twice the rate of conventional supermarkets and more than three times that of most specialty food shops. Customers shop Trader Joe's as much for entertainment as for sustenance. The store stocks dozens of offbeat foods—jasmine fried rice, salmon burgers, and raspberry salsa—as well as carefully selected, competitively priced staples. By turning shopping from a chore into a culinary treasure hunt, Trader Joe's has more than doubled its sales over the last five years to $605 million.

Redefining Market Space

4. Pushing the Bounds of Universality. Every company has an implicit notion of its served market: the types of individuals and institutions that are—and are not—customers. Revolutionary companies, however, focus not just on their served market but on the total imaginable market.

A few years back, who would have considered children a likely market for 35-millimeter film? Would you have given your $500 Nikon to an eight-year-old? Probably not. Parents today, however, think nothing of giving a disposable camera to a child for a day at the beach, a birthday party, or the family's vacation. The single-use camera has made access to photography virtually universal. In 1995, the single-use-camera market reached 50 million units, worth close to $1 billion at retail. From class to mass, adult to child,

FIGURE 1(continued) Nine Routes to Industry Revolution

professional to consumer, and national to global, the traditional boundaries of market space are being redefined by revolutionary companies.

5. Striving for Individuality. No one wants to be part of a mass market. We'll all buy the same things—but only if we have to. Deep in our need to be ourselves, to be unique, are the seeds of industry revolution.

A woman who wants a perfect-fitting pair of jeans, for example, can now get measured at one of Levi Strauss's Personal Pair outlets, and a computer will pick out exactly the right size. The woman's specifications are sent to Levi's by computer, and her made-to-order jeans arrive a few days later. The price? Just about $10 more than an off-the-shelf pair. Levi's plans to introduce the Personal Pair system to nearly 200 stores in the United States by the end of the decade. The company is counting on its revolutionary approach to put a considerable dent in the growing market for private-label jeans.

6. Increasing Accessibility. Most market spaces have temporal and geographic bounds: customers must go to a specific store at a specific location between certain hours. But market space is becoming cyberspace, and every day industry revolutionaries are resetting consumers' expectations about accessibility.

Consider First Direct, a bank that can be reached only by telephone. The fastest-growing bank in Great Britain, First Direct was opening 10,000 new accounts per month in mid-1995—the equivalent of two or three branches. The professionals and workaholics who make up First Direct's half million customers carry, on average, a balance that's ten times higher than the average balance at Midland Bank, First Direct's parent, while overall costs per client are 61 percent less. One of the first U.S. banks to experiment with so-called direct banking estimates that it will ultimately be able to close at least half of its branches.

Redrawing Industry Boundaries

7. Rescaling Industries. As industry revolutionaries seek out and exploit new national and global economies of scale, industries around the world—even office cleaning and haircutting—are consolidating at a fearsome pace. Any industry that was local, such as consumer banking, is becoming national. Any industry that was national, such as the airline business, is becoming global.

Every minute and a half, Service Corporation International buries or cremates someone, somewhere in the world. Performing 320,000 funerals per year, SCI has become the world's largest funeral operator in an industry that traditionally has been very fragmented. Most funeral operators have been family businesses. By buying up small operators, SCI has reaped economies of scale in purchasing, capital utilization (sharing hearses among operators, for example), marketing, and administration.

Of course, an industry can be scaled down as well as up. Bed-and-breakfast inns, microbreweries, local bakeries, and specialty retailers are the result of industries that have scaled down to serve narrow or local customer segments more effectively.

8. Compressing the Supply Chain. The cognoscenti use the word *disintermediation* in its literal sense: the removal of intermediaries. Wal-Mart, for instance, essentially turned the warehouse into a store, thus disintermediating the traditional small-scale retailer. And Xerox hopes to reinvent the way companies distribute printed documents by disintermediating trucking companies from the printing business. Why, Xerox asks, should annual reports, user manuals, catalogs, employee handbooks, and other printed matter be hauled across the country in trucks? Why not send the information digitally and print it close to where it is needed? Xerox is working with a variety of partners to stage this revolution.

9. Driving Convergence. Revolutionaries not only radically change the value-added structure within industries but also blur the boundaries between industries. Deregulation, the ubiquity of information, and new customer demands give revolutionaries the chance to transcend an industry's boundaries.

For example, a consumer can now get a credit card from General Motors, a mortgage from Prudential or GE Capital, a retirement account at Fidelity Investments, and a checkbook from Charles Schwab. Innovative hospitals "capitate" lives, guaranteeing to provide an individual with a full range of health services for a fixed sum per year. Insurance companies, such as Aetna, respond by refashioning themselves into health care providers. Boston Market offers hot family-style meals for takeout, and supermarkets respond by offering an ever wider selection of prepared foods, further blurring the boundary between the grocery and fast-food industries.

Industry revolutionaries don't ask what industry they are in. They know that an industry's boundaries today are about as meaningful as borders in the Balkans.

strategic innovation? No wonder that in many organizations, corporate planning departments are being disbanded. No wonder that consulting firms are doing less and less "strategy" work and more and more "implementation" work.

The essential problem in organizations today is a failure to distinguish *planning* from *strategizing*.[1] Planning is about programming, not discovering. Planning is for technocrats, not dreamers. Giving planners responsibility for creating strategy is like asking a bricklayer to create Michelangelo's *Pietà*.

Most executives know a strategy when they see one. Wal-Mart has a clear strategy; so does Federal Express. But recognizing a strategy that already exists is not enough. Where do strategies come form? How are they created? Strategizing is not a rote procedure—it is a quest. Any company that believes that planning can yield strategy will find itself under the curse of incrementalism while freethinking newcomers lead successful insurrections.

> *Any company that believes that planning can yield strategy will find itself under the curse of incrementalism while freethinking newcomers lead successful insurrections.*

Principle 2: Strategy Making Must Be Subversive   Galileo challenged the centrality of Earth and man in the cosmos. The American colonists challenged the feudal dependencies and inherited privileges of European society. Picasso and other modernists challenged representational art. Einstein challenged Newtonian physics. Revolutionaries are subversive, but their goal is not subversion. What the defenders of orthodoxy see as subversiveness, the champions of new thinking see as enlightenment.

If there is to be any hope of industry revolution, the creators of strategy must cast off industrial conventions. For instance, Anita Roddick, the founder of the Body Shop, turned Charles Revson's hope-in-a-bottle formula on its head. Instead of assuming, as the cosmetics industry always had, that women lack self-confidence and will pay inflated prices for simple formulations if they believe that they will make them more attractive, Roddick assumed that women have self-esteem and just want lighthearted, environmentally responsible products. Roddick wasn't kidding when she said, "I watch where the cosmetics industry is going and then walk in the opposite direction."

Identify the 10 or 20 most fundamental beliefs that incumbents in your industry share. What new opportunities present themselves when you relax those beliefs? Consider the hotel industry's definition of a day, which begins when you check in and ends at noon, when you must check out. But if you check in at 1 AM after a grueling journey, why should you have to check out at the same time or pay the same amount as the person who arrived at 5 o'clock the previous afternoon? If a rental-car company can manage a fleet of cars on a rotating 24-hour basis, why can't a hotel do exactly the same with a fleet of rooms?

Rule makers and rule takers are the industry. Rule breakers set out to redefine the industry, to invent the new by challenging the old. Ask yourself, What are the fundamental conventions we have examined and abandoned in our company? Can you think of more than one or two? Can you think of any at all? If not, why not? As a senior executive, are you willing to embrace a subversive strategy-making process?

Principle 3: The Bottleneck Is at the Top of the Bottle   In most companies, strategic orthodoxy has some very powerful defenders: senior managers. Imagine an organizational pyramid with senior managers at the apex. (It has become fashionable to draw the pyramid with customers at the top and senior managers at the bottom. But as long as senior managers retain their privileges—corporate aircraft, spacious suites, and so on—I prefer to leave the pointy end at the top.) Where are you likely to find people with the least diversity of experience, the largest investment in the past, and the greatest reverence for industrial dogma? At the top. And where will you find the people responsible for creating strategy? Again, at the top.

The organizational pyramid is a pyramid of experience. But experience is valuable only to the extent that the future is like the past. In industry after industry, the terrain is changing so fast that experience is becoming irrelevant and even dangerous. Unless the strategy-making process is freed from the tyranny of experience, there is little chance of industry revolution. If you're a senior executive, ask yourself these questions: Has a decade or two of experience made me more willing or less willing to challenge my industry's conventions? Have I become more curious or less curious about what is happening beyond the traditional boundaries of my industry? Be honest. As Ralph Waldo Emerson wrote, "There are always two parties, the party of the past and the party of the future; the establishment and the movement." To which party do you belong?

Principle 4: Revolutionaries Exist in Every Company   It is often said that you cannot find a pro-change constituency in a successful company. I disagree. It is more accurate to say that in a successful company you are unlikely to find a pro-change constituency among the top dozen or so officers.

Make no mistake: there are revolutionaries in your company. If you go down and out into your organization—out into the ranks of much maligned middle managers, for instance—you will find people straining against the bit of industrial orthodoxy. All too often, however, there is no process that lets those revolutionaries be heard. Their voices are muffled by the layers of cautious bureaucrats who separate them from senior managers. They are isolated and impotent, disconnected from others who share their passions. So, like economic refugees seeking greater opportunity in new lands, industry revolutionaries often abandon their employers to find more imaginative sponsors.

Like economic refugees seeking greater opportunity in new lands, industry revolutionaries often abandon their employers to find more imaginative sponsors.

No one doubts that Jack Welch of General Electric, Percy Barnevik of ABB Asea Brown Boveri, and Ray Smith of Bell Atlantic are pro-change leaders. But rather than celebrating the exceptions—the few truly transformational executives who populate every tome on leadership—isn't the greater challenge to help the pro-change constituency that exists in every company find its voice? Sure, there are some radical corporate leaders out there. But weren't they always revolutionaries at heart? Why couldn't they have had a much greater impact on their companies earlier in their careers? Perhaps they, too, found it difficult to challenge the combined forces of precedence, position, and power. It would be sad to conclude that a company can fully exploit the emotional and intellectual energy of a revolutionary only if he or she succeeds in navigating the tortuous route to the top. How many revolutionaries will wait patiently for such a chance?

As a corporate leader, do you know where the revolutionaries are in your own organization? Have you given them a say in the strategy-making process? One thing is certain: if you don't let the revolutionaries challenge you from within, they will eventually challenge you from without in the marketplace.

Principle 5: Change Is Not the Problem; Engagement Is   Senior executives assume two things about change that squelch revolutionary strategies. The first assumption is that "people"—that is, middle managers and all the rest—are against change. The second assumption follows from the first: only a hero-leader can force a timid and backward-looking organization into the future. All too often, change epics portray the chief executive dragging the organization kicking and screaming into the twenty-first century. Enough of top-management grandstanding. Humankind would not have accomplished what it has over the past millennium if it was ambivalent about change or if the responsibility for change was vested in the socially or politically elite.

Imagine that I coax a flatlander to the top of a snow-covered mountain. After strapping two well-waxed skis onto the flatlander's feet, I give the nervous and unprepared nonskier a mighty push. He or she goes screaming over a precipice; I'm booked for murder. One could well understand how the novice might not appreciate the "change" I sought to engineer. Now imagine that the nonskier takes lessons for a few days. The now fledgling skier may ascend the same mountain and, though full of caution, voluntarily point the skis downhill. What has changed? Even with a bit of training, skiing is not without risks. But in the second scenario, the skier has been given a modicum of control—an ability to influence speed and direction.

All too often, when senior managers talk about change, they are talking about fear-inducing change, which they plan to impose on unprepared and unsuspecting employees. All too often, *change* is simply a code word for something nasty: a wrenching restructuring or reorganization. This sort of change is not about opening up new opportunities but about paying for the past mistakes of corporate leaders.

The objective is not to get people to support change but to give them responsibility for engendering change, some control over their destiny. You must engage the revolutionaries, wherever they are in your company, in a dialogue about the future. Does your strategy-making process do this? Do you secretly believe that change is better served by a more compliant organization than by a more vociferous one? When senior managers engage their organization in a quest for revolutionary strategies, they are invariably surprised to find out just how big the pro-change constituency actually is.

Principle 6: Strategy Making Must Be Democratic   Despite years of imploring people to bring their brains to work, to get involved in quality circles, process reengineering, and the like, senior managers have seldom urged them to participate in the process of strategy creation. But if senior managers can't address the challenge of operational improvements by themselves—witness their reliance on quality circles, suggestion systems, and process-improvement task forces—why would they be able to take on the challenge of industry revolution? After all, what do a company's top 40 or 50 executives have to learn from one another? They've been talking at one another for years. Their positions are well rehearsed, and they can finish one another's sentences. In fact, there is often a kind of intellectual incest among the top officers of a large company.

The capacity to think creatively about strategy is distributed widely in an enterprise. It is impossible to predict exactly where a revolutionary idea is forming; thus the net must be cast wide. In many of the companies I work with, hundreds and sometimes thousands of people get involved in crafting strategy. They are asked to look deeply into potential discontinuities, help define and elaborate the company's core competencies, ferret out corporate orthodoxies, and search for unconventional strategic options. In one company, the idea for a multimillion-dollar opportunity came from a twenty-something secretary. In another company, some of the best ideas about the organization's core competencies came from a forklift operator.

To help revolutionary strategies emerge, senior managers must supplement the hierarchy of experience with a hierarchy of imagination. This can be done by dramatically extending the strategy franchise. Three constituencies that are usually underrepresented in the strategy-making process must have a disproportionate say. The first constituency is young people—or, more accurately, people with a youthful perspective. Of course, some 30-year-olds are "young fogies," but most young people live closer to the future than people with gray hair. It is ironic that the group with the biggest stake in the future is the most disenfranchised from the process of strategy creation.

My definition of success in a strategy-creation process is exemplified by an executive committee spending half a day learning something new from a 25-year-old. Recently, a young technical employee in an accounting company explained the implications of virtual reality to the senior partners. His pitch went like this: "Think about a complex set of corporate accounts. How easily and quickly can you uncover the subtle relationships among the numbers that might point to a problem or opportunity? Virtual reality will allow you to 'fly' over a topography of corporate accounts. That big black hole over there is a revenue shortfall, and that red mountain is unsold inventory. A few small companies are already working on applying virtual reality to financial accounts. Are we going to get on board or risk getting left behind?" The partners actually learned something new that day. When was the last time a Generation-X employee in your company exchanged ideas with the executive committee?

The people at an organization's geographic periphery are the second constituency that deserves a larger say in strategy making. The capacity for strategic innovation increases proportionately with each mile you move away from headquarters. For a U.S. company, the periphery might be India, Singapore, Brazil, or even the West Coast. For a Japanese company, it might be Indonesia or the United States. At the periphery of an organization, people are forced to be more creative because they usually have fewer resources, and they are exposed to ideas and developments that do not conform to the company's orthodoxies. Remember the old Chinese defense of local exceptions to central rule: The emperor is far away and the hills are high. But again, in many companies the periphery has little say in the strategy-making process. If a company aims to generate 40 percent or 50 percent of its revenues in international markets, international voices should have a say in the strategy-making process to match.

The third constituency that deserves a disproportionate say is newcomers, people who have not yet been co-opted by an industry's dogma. Perhaps you've looked outside your company or industry for senior executives with fresh perspectives. But how systematically have you sought the advice of newcomers at all levels who have not yet succumbed to the dead hand of orthodoxy? Think about last year's strategic-planning process. How many new voices were heard? How hard did you work to create the opportunity to be surprised?

Inviting new voices into the strategy-making process, however, is not enough. Senior executives must ensure that they don't drown out people who are overly inclined to deference. In one company, the young representative of a strategy-creation team presented the group's findings to the management committee. When the anxious young employee showed up at the appointed place and hour, he was confronted by a daunting spectacle: 12 executives, most with more than 20 years of seniority, ensconced in high-backed leather chairs arranged around an enormous boardroom table. The brave young manager never stood a chance. Less than five minutes into the four-hour talk, he was being pelted with disbelief and skepticism. The management committee demonstrated its capacity for (unwitting) intimidation and learned little.

After this fiasco, the people attempting to facilitate the dialogue saw to it that the setting for the next meeting was very different. First, it was held off-site on neutral territory. Second, all 25 members of the strategy-creation team were invited; thus they outnumbered the executives. Third, the management committee sat in ordinary chairs arranged in a semicircle—they had no table behind which to hide. Finally, the management committee was asked to hold all comments during the presentation. Afterward, each member of the management committee was assigned two members of the team for a four-hour discussion that focused on how the team had arrived at its conclusions. The next morning, the executives were willing to admit that they had learned a lot, and they were able to give helpful advice to the team members about where they should deepen and expand their work.

That is strategy making as a democratic process. People should have a say in their destiny, a chance to influence the direction of the enterprise to which they devote their energy. The idea of democracy has become so enervated, and the individual's sense of responsibility to the community so feeble, that they can both be summarized in the slogan One Person, One Vote. That notion represents not the full ideal of democracy but its minimal precondition. If one exercises the rights of citizenship only once every 1,461 days, can one claim to be a citizen in any meaningful sense? In the corporate sphere, suggestion schemes and town hall meetings are but the tender shoots of a pluralistic process. Democracy is not simply about the right to be heard; it is about the opportunity to influence opinion and action. It is about being impatient and impassioned, informed and involved. The real power of democracy is that not only the elite can shape the agenda. One's voice can be bigger than one's vote. Susan B. Anthony, Martin Luther King, Jr., Ralph Nader, Rush Limbaugh, and Jesse Jackson have all had an influence on political thought and action that has gone far beyond a single vote.

That which is imposed is seldom embraced. An elitist approach to strategy creation engenders little more than compliance.

What percentage of the employees in your company have ever seen a copy of the corporate strategy, much less participated in its creation? No wonder that what passes for strategy is usually sterile and uninspiring. Saul Alinsky, one of the most effective social revolutionaries in the United States this century, wrote this about the output of top-down, elitist planning: "It is not a democratic program but a monumental testament to lack of faith in the ability and intelligence of the masses of people to think their way through to the successful solution of their problems . . . the people will have little to do with it." That which is imposed is seldom embraced. An elitist approach to strategy creation engenders little more than compliance.

Principle 7: Anyone Can Be a Strategy Activist   Perhaps senior managers are reluctant to give up their monopoly on the creation of strategy. After all, how often has the monarch led the uprising? What can so-called ordinary employees do to ensure that their company becomes or remains the author of industry revolution? Plenty. They can become strategy activists. Today frontline employees and middle managers are inclined to regard themselves more as victims than as activists. They have lost confidence in their ability to shape the future of their organizations. They have forgotten that from Gandhi to Mandela, from the American patriots to the Polish shipbuilders, the makers of revolutions have not come from the top. Notwithstanding all the somber incantations that change must start at the top, is it realistic to expect that, in any reasonable percentage of cases, senior managers will start an industry revolution? No.

In one large company, a small group of middle managers who were convinced that their company was in danger of forfeiting the future to less conventional rivals established what they called a "delta team." The managers, none of whom was a corporate officer, had no mandate to change the company and asked no one for permission to do so. Over several months, they worked quietly and persistently to convince their peers that it was time to rethink the company's basic beliefs. This conviction gradually took root among a cross-section of managers, who started asking senior executives difficult questions about whether the company was actually in control of its destiny. Did the company have a unique and compelling view of its future? Was the company ahead of or behind the industry's change curve? Was it at the center or on the periphery of the coalitions that were reshaping the industry? Ultimately, senior managers conceded that they could not answer those questions. The result was a concerted effort, spanning several months and hundreds of employees, to find opportunities to create industry revolution. Out of this effort came a fundamental change in the company's concept of its mission, a score of new and unconventional business opportunities, and a doubling of revenues over the next five years.

Activists are not anarchists. Their goal is not to tear down but to reform. They know that an uninvolved citizenry deserves whatever fate befalls it, as do cautious and cringing middle managers. People who care about their country—or their organization—don't wait for permission to act. Activists don't shape their opinions to fit the prejudices of those they serve. They are patriots intent on protecting the enterprise from mediocrity, self-interest, and mindless veneration of the past. Not every activist ends up a hero. Shortly after he became president of the Supreme Soviet, Nikita Khrushchev gave a speech to a large group of Communist Party leaders in which he denounced the excesses of Stalin. During a pause, a voice rang out from the back of the hall, "You were there. Why didn't you stop him?" Taken aback by such impertinence, Khrushchev thundered, "Who said that?" The questioner slunk low in his seat and was silent. After a long, uncomfortable minute in which his eyes raked the audience, Khrushchev replied, "Now you know why." It is often safer to be silent. The corporate equivalent of Lubyanka is an office without a telephone or a window. Dissenters aren't shot for treason; they're asked to take a "lateral career move."

Listen to Thomas Paine: "Let them call me rebel and welcome, I feel no concern from it; but I should suffer the misery of devils, were I to make a whore of my soul." In a corporate context, this sounds like hyperbole. But think of the great companies that have fallen hopelessly behind the change curve because middle managers and first-level employees lacked the courage to speak up. To be an activist, one must care more for one's community than for one's position in the hierarchy. The goal is not to leave senior executives behind. The goal is not to stage a palace coup. But when senior managers are distracted, when planning has supplanted strategizing, and when more energy is being devoted to protecting the past than to creating the future, activists must step forward.

Principle 8: Perspective Is Worth 50 IQ Points[2]   Without enlightenment, there can be no revolution. To discover opportunities for industry revolution, one must look at the world in a new way, through a new lens. It is impossible to make people smarter, but you can help them see with new eyes. Remember when you took your first economics course? I do. It didn't make me any smarter, but it gave me a new lens through which to look at the world. Much that had been invisible—the link between savings and investment, between interest rates and exchange rates, and between supply and demand—suddenly became visible.

A view of the corporation as a bundle of core competencies rather than a collection of business units is a new perspective. A view of discontinuities as levers for change rather than threats to the status quo is a new perspective. A view that imagination rather than investment determines an organization's capacity to be strategic is a new perspective.

Any company intent on creating industry revolution has four tasks. First, the company must identify the unshakable beliefs that cut across the industry—the industry's conventions. Second, the company must search for discontinuities in technology, lifestyles, working habits, or geopolitics that might create opportunities to rewrite the industry's rules. Third, the company must achieve a deep understanding of its core competencies. Fourth, the company must use all this knowledge to identify the revolutionary ideas, the unconventional strategic options, that could be put to work in its competitive domain. What one sees from the mountaintop is quite different from what one sees from the plain. There can be no innovation in the creation of strategy without a change in perspective.

Principle 9: Top-Down and Bottom-Up Are Not the Alternatives   The creation of strategy is usually characterized as either a top-down or bottom-up process. Strategy either emerges as a grand design at the top—think of Jack Welch's famous "three circles," which defined GE's future business focus—or bubbles up from lone entrepreneurs, such as the man who invented Post-It Notes at 3M. But all too often, top-down strategies are dirigiste rather than visionary. And in all too many companies, the entrepreneurial spark is more likely to be doused by a flood of corporate orthodoxy than fanned by resources and the support of senior executives. In my experience, new-venture divisions, skunk works, and the musings of research fellows are no more likely to engender an industry revolution than is an annual planning process.

Just as a political activist who fails to influence those with legislative authority will make little lasting difference, a strategy activist who fails to win senior managers' confidence will achieve nothing. Senior managers may not have a monopoly on imagination, but they do have a board-sanctioned monopoly on the allocation of resources. To bankroll the revolution, senior executives must believe, both intellectually and emotionally, in its aims. So although the revolution doesn't need to start at the top, it must ultimately be understood and endorsed by the top. In the traditional model of strategy creation, the thinkers are assumed to be at the top and the doers down below. In reality, the thinkers often lie deep in the organization, and senior managers simply control the means of doing.

To achieve diversity of perspective and unity of purpose, the strategy-making process must involve a deep diagonal slice of the organization. A top-down process often achieves unity of purpose: the few who are involved come to share a conviction about the appropriate course of action and can secure some degree of compliance from those below. A bottom-up process can achieve diversity of perspective: many voices are heard and many options are explored. But unity without diversity leads to dogma, and diversity without unity results in competing strategy agendas and the fragmentation of resources. Only a strategy-making process that is deep and wide can achieve both diversity and unity.

Bringing the top and bottom together in the creation of strategy will help bypass the usually painful and laborious process whereby a lowly employee champions an idea up the chain of command. Managers, many of whom may be more intent on protecting their reputations for prudence than on joining the ranks of the lunatic fringe, are likely to shoot down any revolutionary idea that reaches them. There are many ways of linking those on the bottom with those in the officer corps. Senior executives can sponsor a process of deep thinking about discontinuities, core competencies, and new rules that involves a cross section of the organization. Senior managers can participate as team members—together with secretaries, salespeople, and first-level engineers—in the search for revolutionary opportunities. An executive committee can devote one week per month to keeping up to speed with the revolutionary ideas that are gestating deep in the organization.

What senior executives must not do is ask a small, elite group or the "substitute brains" of a traditional strategy-consulting firm to go away and plot the company's future. With neither senior managers nor a substantial cross-section of the organization involved, the output will likely be considered a bastard by all except those who created it.

Of course, senior managers must ultimately make hard choices about which revolutionary strategies to support and what resources to commit, but they must avoid the temptation to judge prematurely. In the quest for revolutionary strategies, a senior executive must be more student than magistrate. In one company, the CEO believed that the strategy-making team was responsible for convincing him that it had come up with the right answers. That is the wrong attitude. It is the CEO's responsibility to stay close enough to the organization's learning process that he or she can share employees' insights and understand their emerging convictions. In the traditional planning process, outcomes are likely to cluster closely around senior managers' prejudices; the gap between recommendations and preexisting predilections is likely to be low. But that is not the case in a more open-ended process of strategic discovery. If the goal is to ensure that the resource holders and the revolutionaries end up at the same place at the same time, senior executives must engage in a learning process alongside those at the vanguard of industry revolution.

Principle 10: You Can't See the End from the Beginning   A strategy-making process that involves a broad cross-section of the company, delves deeply into discontinuities and competencies, and encourages employees to escape an industry's conventions will almost inevitably reach surprising conclusions. At EDS, such a process convinced many in the organization that it was not enough to be a business-to-business company. As the dividing line between professional life and personal life was blurring, EDS realized that it had to become capable of serving individuals as well as businesses. After an open and creative strategy-making process, EDS installed automated teller machines in many 7-Eleven stores. Months earlier, few would have anticipated, much less credited, such a move.

Not everyone enjoys surprises. Senior managers cannot predict where an open-ended strategy-making process will lead, but they cannot go only part of the way to industry revolution. If nervous executives open up a dialogue and then ignore the outcome, they will poison the well. In one company, senior managers articulated their reluctance to staff a strategy-making team with a cohort of young, out-of-the-box employees. The CEO was convinced that he needed to set clear boundaries on the work of the eager revolutionaries. Defending his desire to impose prior restraint on the strategy-creation process, he asked, "What if the team comes back with dumb ideas?" The response: "If that is the case, you have a bigger problem—dumb managers." Senior managers should be less worried about getting off-the-wall suggestions and more concerned about failing to unearth the ideas that will allow their company to escape the curse of incrementalism.

Though it is impossible to see the end from the beginning, an open-ended and inclusive process of strategy creation substantially lessens the challenge of implementation. Implementation is often more difficult than it need be because only a handful of people have been involved in the creation of strategy and only a few key executives share a conviction about the way forward. Too often, the planning process ends with the challenge of getting "buy-in," of getting what is in the heads of the bosses into the heads of the worker bees. But when several hundred employees share the task of identifying and synthesizing a set of unconventional strategic options, the conclusions take on an air of inevitability. In such a process, senior managers' task is less to "sell" the strategy than to ensure that the organization acts on the convictions that emerge. How often does the planning process start with senior executives asking what the rest of the organization can teach them about the future? Not often enough.

To invite new voices into the strategy-making process, to encourage new perspectives, to start new conversations that span organizational boundaries, and then to help synthesize unconventional options into a point of view about corporate direction—those are the challenges for senior executives who believe that strategy must be revolution.

ENDNOTES

1. Thanks to James Scholes, my colleague at Strategos, for suggesting this distinction.
2. I owe this aphorism to Alan Kay, a research fellow at Apple Computer. Kay's point that new thinking depends more on perspective than on raw intelligence is as apropos to strategy innovation as it is to new-product innovation.

USING CORE CAPABILITIES TO CREATE COMPETITIVE ADVANTAGE

Carl Long
Mary Vickers-Koch

This article examines the origins of the concept of core capabilities and how it has reemerged as a powerful strategic thinking tool. The authors distinguish between core capabilities and core competencies and identify types of capabilities. They suggest that a clear strategic vision backed by capability-based strategies provides the best possibility for long-term success.

The traditional approach to strategic planning has taken some hard hits of late. Many companies are dismantling their large, formal planning departments, and Henry Mintzberg devotes five of the six chapters of his new book, *The Rise and Fall of Strategic Planning*, to the weaknesses inherent in how companies have managed strategy and how academics have written about it. In a *Harvard Business Review* article with the more optimistic title of "The Fall and Rise of Strategic Planning," Mintzberg summarizes these weaknesses, pointing out that strategic planning often spoils strategic thinking by "causing managers to confuse real vision with the manipulation of numbers." He concludes that successful strategies tend to be visions, not plans.

Mintzberg's insight highlights an emerging paradox: Even as many companies abandon the elaborate planning procedures they used in the 1970s and 1980s, they show increasing interest in *strategic visioning* as a means of creating meaning and direction, and in *strategic thinking* as a means of creating value for customers. To appreciate the discrepancies, consider that, while Mintzberg was carefully documenting the fall of strategic planning, Gary Hamel and C. K. Prahalad were writing a book that reframes "what it means to be strategic—and successful."

What is happening to our understanding and use of strategy? What is driving these paradoxical movements?

Source: *Organizational Dynamics*, Summer 1995.

Examining how businesses traditionally developed their strategies, and comparing it with the way some innovative firms have begun to plan, reminds us of the change in many companies' approach to quality. Quality was traditionally associated with inspectors assuring quality after the fact—after parts were made—rather than getting everyone down the line involved in building in quality in the first place, as eventually happened through the total quality management movement.

We believe a similar trend is emerging in the field of strategy. Traditionally, many companies regarded strategy development as an exercise in which specialists "programmed" the right products and services into existing markets. But as global competition grows more complex and volatile, and as information technology revolutionizes organizational structure and decision making, we are seeing responsive, flexible, and innovative organizational designs displace hierarchical, command-and-control structures. This is putting strategy as a planning-by-the-numbers process on the same road to obsolescence as the notion that we can create quality by setting tolerance standards and manning inspection stations.

More and more companies are beginning to view strategy as a process involving a broad spectrum of management to identify and develop the *core capabilities* the company can use to create unique levels of value for selected customers and other stakeholder groups.

The basic concept of core capabilities has existed for some time, and writers like Gary Hamel and C. K. Prahalad have given a great deal of attention to the concept. But the *application* of core capabilities as a key component of strategy is relatively new, and there is still much to learn about the application process.

In this article, we examine the origins of the concept of core capabilities, how it remained dormant for a number of years, and why it has reemerged as a powerful strategic concept. Most importantly, we examine how it can be applied as a valuable strategic thinking tool.

We do not intend to present an exhaustive review of the strategy literature. At least two excellent books have already done so. The first of these, *Strategy Formulation: Analytical Concepts*, by Charles Hofer and Dan Schendel, appeared in 1978 when strategy was at the height of its popularity in the business world. The second, by Henry Mintzberg (cited earlier), appeared in 1994, when the traditional views of strategy were being reconsidered. Mintzberg's work views historical developments from that perspective.

Indeed, looking back at the development of strategy can help us place the concept of core capabilities or competencies in context.

PRODUCT AND MARKET FOCUS IN EARLY STRATEGY WRITINGS

We often think of the word *strategy*, from the Greek word *strategia*, meaning "generalship," as a long-standing part of our management vocabulary. But the word did not appear in the English-speaking world until the beginning of the 19th century. It was first used to refer to the science and art of employing political, economic, military, and other forces to support the policies of a nation or group of nations. It eventually came to be most strongly associated with the deployment of military forces in support of an overall goal.

The word doesn't surface in management literature until the 1950s. As with so many other management ideas, Peter Drucker appears to be one of the first to talk about strategy in a business context. However, he spoke about it in 1954 only in terms of answering the questions: "What is our business? And what should it be?" He had little else to say about it.

The term *distinctive competence* was first used by Philip Selznick in 1957 to refer to what a firm does especially well in relation to its competitors. *The Encyclopedia of Management*, published in 1963 and edited by Carl Heyel, has no entries labeled *strategy* or *strategic*, although it does have an entry for long-range planning.

In 1962, Alfred Chandler was one of the first to offer an explicit definition of strategy: "the determination of the basic long-term goals and objectives of an enterprise, and the adoption of courses of action and the allocation of resources necessary for carrying out these goals." But the first writers to focus on the concept of strategy in terms of its development and implementation were Kenneth Andrews and Igor Ansoff, who independently introduced such concepts in 1965.

In that same year, Ansoff first used the term *capabilities* to describe a company's ability to deal with different combinations of competitive environments and levels of "entrepreneurial turbulence." He spoke of the different *managerial* capabilities needed to deal with stable, reactive, or anticipatory environments, and of *functional* capabilities—the firm's skill level in functions such as R&D, purchasing, and marketing. But he did not describe capabilities as components of strategy. In fact, he saw strategy development and capability development as separate, competing demands for limited resources. When a company needed both a strategy change and a capability transformation, he recommended a fairly elaborate priority-setting exercise to choose between them. However, he left no doubt which should come first in a pinch, saying, "In such cases, strategy transformation must be given first priority."

Within the strategy arena, he gave more attention and emphasis to external appraisals and action plans centered on products and markets. Indeed, Ansoff said, "The end product of strategic decisions is deceptively simple; a combination of products and markets is selected for the firm."

It was not until 1978 that writers and managers began to consider competence and capability as integral components of strategy. Although Hofer and Schendel use the terms only as alternate ways of referring to resource deployments, they clearly saw the components as specific means of creating competitive advantage:

> We have included resource deployments (distinctive competences) as a strategy component, however, because it is clear that no actions or goal achievements can take place unless some basic skills are created and resources obtained and deployed in ways that cannot be duplicated easily by others. Second, resource deployments and competitive advantages are not only very fundamental aspects of strategy, but they also may be more important than scope in determining success. This claim is contrary to much of the current literature in the policy field, most of which assumes that scope is the predominate and, in some instances, the only component of strategy.

Most other writers saw the creation of competitive advantage and shareholder value only in relation to the selection of products and markets. These writers tended to think of a company as owning a portfolio of individual businesses, each with its own set of products, services, and markets. It became general practice to break companies into discrete components called strategic business units (SBUs). Some SBUs grew and needed lots of resources; others leveled off but generated lots of cash; some were on their way out. Strategic planners following this practice went on to develop formulas for identifying each unit's contribution to the company's overall stock price. This approach—called "value-based planning"—led to an intense concentration on moving portfolio components around to affect the stock price. Not coincidentally, the symbol often chosen to represent the conventional view of strategy was a chess board, with products as the pieces and markets as the squares.

THE CONSEQUENCES OF STRATEGY AS PORTFOLIO PLANNING

As a legal entity, the corporation was created to have a separate existence from the individuals who run it. Theoretically, a corporate form of organization could exist in perpetuity, unfettered by the biological limitations of human life spans. Yet a study reported by Richard Hodgetts, Fred Luthans, and Sang Lee in the Winter 1994 issue of *Organizational Dynamics* ranked the 100 largest U.S. industrial firms as of 1980 and followed them for 12 years, until 1992. Only about half (56 percent) of the firms were still in the top 100 at the end of the study, and only 18 percent had managed to improve their ranking. In other words, 82 percent of the companies either declined in performance or disappeared from the list over that period.

The study suggests that even some of the biggest and best companies have had serious problems maintaining a competitive advantage over time. What has been the role of strategy in this ongoing struggle?

Strategy, when viewed as portfolio planning, often puts management into the role of bankers or traders, expected to buy and sell or manipulate financial resource allocations between SBUs to inflate stock prices, all in the name of increasing shareholder value. This type of strategic planning focuses extreme attention on what companies do for one constituency (shareholders) and very little directly on how, or if, they are creating value for customers, employees, and other stakeholder groups. Robert Reich, former Secretary of Labor, once called this focus on short-term profits for selected investors through legal and financial maneuvering "paper entrepreneurialism." Another executive said, "Paying attention only to share price is like trying to play tennis by keeping your eye on the scoreboard rather than on the ball."

The preoccupation with stock price as the definition of value and the SBU as the unit of competition has several unfortunate results. It tends to pit one SBU against another in competition for the firm's resources and blocks the sharing of core capabilities across units within the firm. It also defines value from the shareholder's point of view, rather than from the customer's. It places more emphasis on financial resource allocation and balancing the portfolio than on growing the company as a whole and achieving synergy by sharing core capabilities across the company. The focus is on increasing productivity by reducing the denominator of the "production v investment = productivity" equation, rather than by increasing the numerator.

The consequences of this one-track focus are clearly shown in a series of studies John Kotter and James Heskett conducted and wrote about a few years ago in *Corporate Culture and Performance*. From the more than 200 companies in their studies, they compared 12 firms that had what they called "performance-enhancing cultures" to 20 firms without such cultures. The differences were striking. Over the 11-year period covered by the study (1977–1988), the firms with performance-enhancing cultures increased their revenues four times as much as the other firms and increased their stock price by 12 times as much. They raised their net income 700 percent, compared with an average of 1 percent for the other firms.

These are astonishing differences. In trying to understand what distinguished the high-performing firms from the others, the authors pinpointed several interdependent characteristics that interacted with great synergy. The high-performers had cultures that were:

1. "Strong," with shared values and practices that promoted and supported those core competencies (skills, knowledge, attitudes, and know-how) that were most important to their efforts to serve the firm's stakeholders.

2. "Strategically appropriate," with strategies that matched the business context of the firm (core capabilities effectively linked to strategic targets).

3. "Adaptive," with strong leadership focused on serving the needs of *all* key stakeholder groups and on developing processes that delivered the attributes they most valued.

CAPABILITIES REDISCOVERED

The approach to strategy taken by the high-performing firms in the Kotter and Heskett study places core capabilities at the center of the company's strategic resources. These firms focus on their distinctive, hard-to-imitate core capabilities, rather than on portfolios of products and markets, and their strategic vision determines the scope of the strategy.

> *Capability-based organizations take the traditional strategic task of finding the best fit between a firm's resources and existing business conditions and markets to a new level.*

Capability-based organizations take the traditional strategic task of finding the best fit between a firm's resources and existing business conditions and markets to a new level. They define their resources in terms of the capabilities they have developed for adding value for their customers and other stakeholders.

These companies don't just ask, "What businesses are we in?" and "What businesses should we be in, given the competitive landscape and forecasts for future changes?" Instead, they pay more attention to the question, "What *capabilities* do we need to develop and nurture to take full advantage of those changes?" They are rediscovering the importance of organizational competencies or capabilities as strategic resources—an insight that was largely ignored for a number of years, as companies searched for quicker, more direct means of affecting share price.

When the focus is exclusively on shareholders, it reinforces the vertical orientation of the organization and strengthens the tendency to create functional silos. However, focusing on customers as the arbiters of value shifts attention to the processes that run horizontally through organizations to meet the needs and expectations of customers. This emphasis on cross-functional (and cross-SBU) process improvement causes companies to think differently about how they add value. It broadens their perspectives on who their stakeholders are and causes them to ask, "What special skills, knowledge, abilities, and processes do we use to meet the needs of our stakeholders and to create whatever competitive advantage we now enjoy? And how can we use these capabilities as a foundation for building future competitive advantage?"

The very leadership agenda of many companies has been affected. Instead of being based on the "paper entrepreneurialism" Robert Reich spoke about, more and more companies are basing their leadership agenda on:

- Vision
- Opportunity identification
- Capability assessment

In these companies, the vision represents a set of targeting parameters that defines major stakeholder groups and how the company can best add value for them. Dynamic rather than static, the vision is based on an ongoing effort to identify emerging opportunities in the external environment and assess the firm's core capabilities and how these can be applied to create value.

KEY TERMS IN CAPABILITY-BASED STRATEGIC THINKING

As the thinking about strategy developed, planners began to use the terms *core competence* and *core capability* more or less interchangeably. However, George Stalk, Philip Evans, and Lawrence Shulman, writing in the March–April 1992 issue of *Harvard Business Review*, took a different position:

> Competencies and capabilities represent two different but complementary dimensions of an emerging paradigm for corporate strategy. Both concepts emphasize "behavioral" aspects of strategy in contrast to the traditional structural model. But whereas core competence emphasizes technological and production expertise at specific points along the value chain, capabilities are more broadly based, encompassing the entire value chain.

We have illustrated our own distinctions in Figure 1: *Competencies* relate to the skills, knowledge, and technological know-how that give a special advantage at specific points of the value chain, which in combination with the *strategic processes* that link the chain together, form *core capabilities*.

Competencies relate to the skills, knowledge, and technological know-how that give a special advantage at specific points of the value chain, which in combination with the strategic processes *that link the chain together, form* core capabilities.

We find it useful to distinguish between competencies and processes in a firm's capabilities because each requires different kinds of decisions and actions. The decisions and actions required to improve a firm's competence usually revolve around the people and technology needed to improve skills and abilities—those necessary to add value to products and services. A different set of decisions and actions are required to improve or redesign the processes used to deliver those products and services in ways that customers and other stakeholders most value. Yet only when these two aspects are successfully brought together can the firm display the full measure of its capabilities.

FIGURE 1   Defining Core Capabilities

Core competencies:
the special knowledge, skills, and technological know-how that distinguish you from other firms.

+   **=**   **Core capabilities:**

Strategic processes:
the business processes you use to deliver your special know-how in the form of products, services, and other results that have high value to customers and other stakeholders.

the most critical and most distinctive resources a company possesses, and the most difficult to copy when effectively linked with appropriate strategic targets in a value chain that begins and ends with the company's key stakeholders.

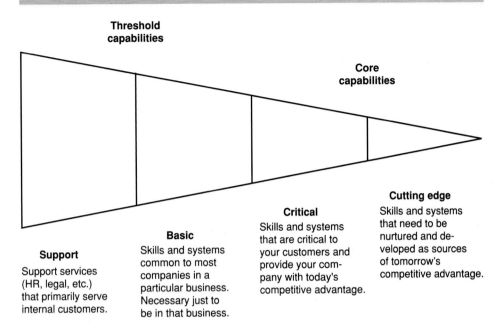

FIGURE 2   Types of Core Capabilities

Threshold capabilities

Core capabilities

Cutting edge
Skills and systems that need to be nurtured and developed as sources of tomorrow's competitive advantage.

Critical
Skills and systems that are critical to your customers and provide your company with today's competitive advantage.

Basic
Skills and systems common to most companies in a particular business. Necessary just to be in that business.

Support
Support services (HR, legal, etc.) that primarily serve internal customers.

For example, a company like Honda emphasizes core competencies consisting of skills and knowledge to design and build small, smooth-running engines and power trains. However, much of Honda's success is due to the business processes it has developed for training and supporting its dealer network system. The merchandising, selling, floor planning, and service management all exist to provide customers with the attributes they most value. We must look at both of these aspects to fully understand Honda's competitive advantage.

Another example is Wal-Mart. It has developed core competencies related to selecting good sites and to creating a culture of service excellence that extends from suppliers to customers. And it has invested heavily in strategic processes such as "cross-docking." Goods are continuously delivered to warehouses where they are selected, repacked, and dispatched to stores with minimal or no time in inventory. The process requires a variety of interlocked support systems and continuous contact between suppliers, distribution centers, and points of sale; a dedicated satellite communication system supports these systems. Cross-docking helps Wal-Mart maintain low costs and make the right goods available as needed. Its service-oriented employees get reliable products to sell at low prices, and in the styles and colors customers want.

THRESHOLD CAPABILITIES AND CORE CAPABILITIES

While it is always a combination of competencies and processes that makes up a capability, there are various types of capabilities, as Figure 2 illustrates. First, there are *threshold capabilities*, necessary just to be in the game. These include services to support internal customers (human resources, legal, and accounting skills and processes, for example) as well as those skills and systems that are conditions for doing business in the company's industry.

This is not to say that they cannot make a huge difference in a firm's success, depending on how well they are used. However, they are typically not the capabilities that account for the firm's real competitive advantage in its chosen field.

The capabilities a business relies on for its competitive advantage are the ones we think of as *core capabilities*. Here we make a distinction between those competencies and processes that provide today's competitive advantage, called *critical core capabilities*, and those competencies and processes that will provide tomorrow's competitive advantage—*cutting edge core capabilities*.

The recent decision by Mead Corporation to sell its Mead Data Central Division represents an interesting example of a company changing its mind about where its cutting edge capabilities lie. Mead Data Central, with its Lexis, Nexis, and other on-line services, has been a huge success for Mead. When Mead purchased the company 20 years ago, it saw itself as entering a business that would replace paper in the future (a "what business are we in?" issue).

Although Mead's vision of storing information in computers instead of on paper is still valid, technology has changed the landscape. Cutting edge capabilities now reside in the creation of software to search out precise slices of data and distribute the desired information to PCs, rather than in the ability to store large amounts of data in a mainframe and sell access to it in bulk form.

Despite Data Central's high growth and profitability, it represents only about 12 percent of Mead's total annual revenues. As one analyst put it, "The demands for information today go beyond what a company like Mead can do with the business." To keep up would divert too many resources from its core businesses—paper, pulp, and other forest products.

Two days after the Mead decision to divest Data Central was announced in *The New York Times* (May 21, 1994), another story appeared about a company that made what appeared to be the opposite kind of decision. The Williams Companies, one of the nation's largest processors and transporters of natural gas, had rejected an offer of $2 billion from LDDS Communications to buy Wiltel, the Williams telecommunications unit that has become the nation's fourth-largest fiber optic network.

At first glance, natural gas processing and transmission seem to have little in common with fiber optics. Natural gas is a fairly staid, highly regulated business—a universe apart from the glitz of a fiber optic network's cargo of video, audio, and movie signals carrying the latest in entertainment products.

Yet the expertise in maintaining a transmission network and the electronic monitoring and switching systems capabilities associated with natural gas transmission turns out to be a cutting edge capability in the fiber optics business. Williams also discovered that its abandoned pipelines were perfect for carrying fiber optic cables; they go for miles and miles without requiring a splice. And even where pipelines are still in use, the cables can be placed beside them in the rights of way already owned by the Williams Companies. Moreover, the equipment is more secure because backhoe operators who sometimes rip up the cables by accident tend to be more careful around gas pipelines.

So, two businesses that seem quite different on the surface turn out to share a need for some similar capabilities. What were critical capabilities in the gas transmission business turn out to be cutting edge capabilities in the fiber optic network business. It's a telling example of how a company can link core capabilities with appropriate, though not obvious strategic targets to leverage value.

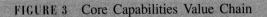

FIGURE 3 Core Capabilities Value Chain

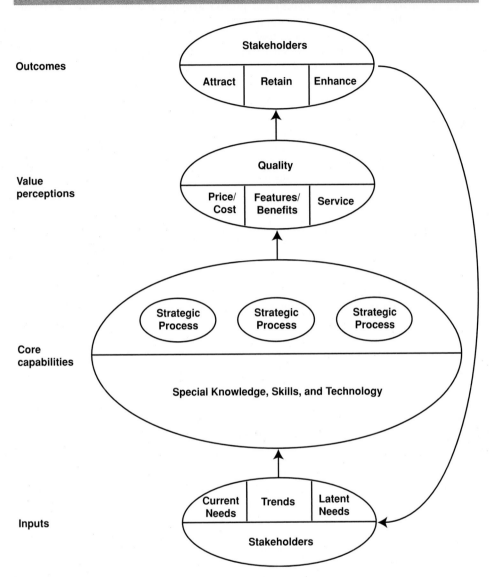

CREATING A CORE CAPABILITIES VALUE CHAIN

To become capability based, organizations need to explore their value chain in two ways. First, they must search for the specific points along the value chain where the margins are greatest between the value stakeholders' place on what is added and the cost of adding it. Through the search, a company learns what special skills, knowledge, or technology it possesses that give it an advantage at these points of its value chain. Second, they need to learn how to fashion a series of business processes into feedback loops that begin and end with the needs of the customer and other stakeholders, thereby determining what special capabilities are critical to meeting the needs of their key stakeholder groups. (See Figure 3.)

Viewing the two sets of information as complementary allows businesses to make operating decisions that create greater synergy. Creating value at specific points by applying core competencies, and creating value throughout the value chain by linking it together with more effective processes, greatly leverages the total amount of value that can be created.

Creating value at specific points by applying core competencies, and creating value throughout the value chain by linking it together with more effective processes, greatly leverages the total amount of value that can be created.

If a company focuses only on the specific points in its value chain where it has superior technology or skills, it will be tempted to subcontract to the lowest bidder those activities it thinks others can perform better or cheaper. However, if the company also concentrates on the value that comes from effectively linking the processes that create and deliver the valued product or service, it is more likely to try to improve its own strategic processes or to form close alliances and partnership with favored suppliers in order to maintain better control over its critical chains of processes.

This focus on adding value through processes will also increase the company's interest in breaking down functional barriers and relying more extensively on cross-functional teams and structures. Unlike a portfolio of SBUs, which are often pitted against one another to compete for resources, capability-based organizations search for innovative ways to apply their core capabilities across functions and units. They emphasize practices and processes rather than the structuring of existing product categories and market segments—the usual focus of traditional strategies. Capability-based organizations seek to create maximum value by developing as broad an array of products and services as possible from the core capabilities they have developed over time.

It is important not to confuse activity-based management (ABM) with the concept of core capabilities. Some writers have equated the *activities* the firm performs better than its competitors (and which are critical to its end products or services) with its core competencies. However, by drawing attention to activities, ABM keeps us focused on the present. We end up rearranging the portfolio of current activities, instead of examining the potential the underlying capabilities have for new activities, products, and services.

Instead of seeing the firm as a portfolio of activities, capability-based organizations look beyond activities to understand the underlying skills and know-how that give the firm the ability to perform certain activities better than others. By taking this deeper view, they free their thinking to see new and different applications of their underlying capabilities.

As we saw in the Williams Companies example, the expertise used in maintaining the transmission network and switching system required for natural gas provided a cutting edge capability that allowed the company to move into the fiber optics network business. It is not at all clear if the company would have been able to leap to that conclusion if it had operated only as a portfolio of current activities.

REARRANGING PORTFOLIOS DOES NOT NECESSARILY CREATE VALUE

Strategy planning that depends on making structural changes in a company's portfolio of products and markets to create value can be very misleading. It overlooks the difficulty of redesigning key business processes and of acquiring the skills, knowledge, technology, and know-how that will be required to create a true competitive edge in whatever new domain a company has chosen.

From a portfolio perspective, a company like Kodak might consider expanding into the emerging area of electronic image processing. On paper, this may look attractive: Kodak knows some of the markets, and electronic imaging will likely be a rapidly growing field, as home-made images increasingly become part of the home entertainment business.

However, deciding whether to create a portfolio of businesses that process and convert images does not answer whether Kodak has the *capabilities* to be a leader in both chemical and electronic imaging. Thinking in terms of core capabilities helps focus attention on the importance of this question. The current business requires competencies and business processes that involve chemists and film processing, while the new area requires competencies and processes associated with electronics and electronic imaging and manipulation processes.

After several brief, tentative forays into electronics, Kodak recently seems to have made a firmer commitment to the broader strategy. In June 1994, chairman George M. C. Fisher went on record that electronic image handling and manipulation was a key area of growth for the company. To give weight to his words, he hired John Sculley, ex-chief of Apple Computer, to "help Kodak develop a more aggressive marketing approach" in this area. The senior vice president to whom Sculley will report said they will first decide how they should be positioned, "then we will go segment by segment through the imaging chain" to determine how individual products fit within the broader categories.

It will be interesting to see whether Kodak will be able to develop the core capabilities it needs to establish a competitive advantage and succeed in its new business arena, while trying to sustain its leadership position in its current business.

John Sculley, while still chief executive officer of Apple Computer, figured in another, possibly fateful decision involving core capabilities. In 1989, according to *The Wall Street Journal*, he had a contract in hand that needed only his signature to license Apple's user-friendly operating software to other PC makers. He chose not to sign. Instead of capitalizing on its core capability of designing operating systems that were far easier to use than others at the time, Apple chose to remain a self-contained computer maker. Unlike Microsoft, which allowed its operating system to be cloned, thereby becoming the industry standard, Apple operating systems remain only a small percentage of the market. As a result, the large majority of applications software produced each year is designed for the Microsoft system, making Microsoft even more attractive to potential customers.

Just recently, Michael Spindler, Sculley's successor as CEO of Apple, announced Apple's plans to allow IBM to clone Macintosh software. Linley Gwennap, editor of the newsletter *Microprocess Report*, summed up the opportunity lost as a result of the delay: "There's no question Macintosh could be where Windows is today if they had done this [licensing] five years ago."

USING CORE CAPABILITIES TO CREATE COMPETITIVE DISTINCTIONS

Customers differ in their willingness or ability to pay for certain types of benefits, depending on the value they place on each benefit and on their own resources. Interestingly, both the TQM movement and a number of individual writers, including Michael Porter and Michael Treacy, have come up with similar lists of ways companies can add value. In one way or another, they suggest that companies tend to choose between (1) meeting basic requirements at the best price; (2) providing the best product features and quality; and (3) focusing on each customer's needs and providing special services.

All companies tend to gravitate toward one or another of these primary ways of creating value. That in itself will not provide much of a competitive advantage. Instead, each company needs to look inward to understand its own specific capabilities and outward to identify its special opportunities in the world around it. Competitive advantage results from the company's ability to bring its capabilities and its opportunities into balance.

To understand how companies with the same value discipline can use core capabilities to create distinctive value, consider two highly successful regional banks. Wachovia and Banc One both create value primarily by being "customer intimate," to use Treacy's term. Yet they have created very different competitive advantages by emphasizing different core competencies and processes to create their own unique core capabilities.

Wachovia focuses on its ability to create competencies and systems that provide customer intimacy at the individual customer level, while Banc One focuses on being customer intimate at the community level as well as on backing up its service with a strong dose of "operational excellence" from headquarters.

Wachovia's concentration on serving the needs of individual customers requires the company to hire and train large numbers of front-line employees to provide personal banking service to individuals. Wachovia has developed special processes that help each front-line employee serve about 1,200 customers with personalized service. As a result, this bank has the highest "cross sell ratio" (average number of products per customer) of any bank.

Banc One, on the other hand, has concentrated on responding to the needs of entire communities. The company hires and trains affiliated bank presidents who have deep roots in their local communities. Banc One's competencies lie not in its front-line employees, but in its local top-management personnel. The organization gives local bank presidents lots of autonomy, as well as access to a highly centralized headquarters group that gathers information about best practices and makes systems and processes available based on the findings. The company trains local bank officials to tailor those processes to their own banking communities.

Wachovia has developed core capabilities that allow it to generate very high returns from each customer it serves compared to other banks. But its growth is limited because of the time it takes to hire and train large numbers of front-line employees to provide personal banking services on a mass scale.

Banc One's core capabilities were developed to help it "out-local the national banks and out-national the local banks." Maintaining close ties with local communities and the sophisticated procedures and systems from headquarters will clearly help the bank expand and grow. However, Banc One will probably never be able to realize the same level of profits from each customer that Wachovia achieves.

LINKING CORE CAPABILITIES TO STRATEGIC TARGETS

The best way for a company to find the most beneficial balance between internal capabilities and external opportunities comes from involving key line managers in the effort. Including them in the process of identifying the company's core capabilities, in conjunction with assessing its economic and competitive environment, provides an important source of information for profiling the company's strategic targets. This can help resolve thorny resource allocation decisions, align the workforce with a clear customer focus, and identify process redesign needs. Helping people understand their organization's core capabilities helps them understand its purpose and direction. Developing and nurturing core capabilities can then be embraced by everyone in the organization, not just a select few.

To find the balance, an organization must discover and operate from its greatest sources of inherent strength (areas of special knowledge, skills, and technology), and design business processes that deliver the mix of attributes that its stakeholders value most. This development process places primary importance on the firm's ability to meet the critical needs of customers and the other stakeholder groups at a value-to-cost ratio better than its competitors. Highlights of this strategic targeting include:

- Validating the historical milestones of the organization and establishing a vision of the future that defines, shapes, and gives meaning to the organization's strategic purpose.

- Discovering which capabilities the company has depended upon to create whatever competitive advantage it has attained.

- Identifying unique opportunities among the company's customer groups and market segments to create the greatest possible value through the use of the company's core capabilities.

- Determining which current capabilities need to be nurtured and which future capabilities need to be developed to continue to add value in the eyes of the customers and market segments selected.

- Establishing priorities for resource allocation and the timing of critical moves necessary to build those capabilities and to meet the needs and expectations of targeted customers.

- Developing feedback mechanisms that support continuous learning and rapid responses to maintain the optimum balance between core capabilities and strategic targets.

This balance can be achieved at several levels. At the simplest level, the company can examine existing core capabilities and market segments and identify opportunities to use those capabilities to create new products and services for blank areas in those market segments. Then, the company can explore existing market segments to determine what new core capabilities could be developed to protect its position in those existing markets. Or it can create new products and services by redeploying or recombining existing core capabilities to satisfy new market segments. In the highest level of innovation, a company can search out the most promising new market segments and try to develop new core capabilities to participate there.

At any level, core capabilities are the most critical and most distinctive resources a company possesses. They are difficult for competitors to copy because they are based on knowledge, skills, and processes developed over time into workable combinations within the context of a particular organizational setting. For the same reason they are also difficult to change suddenly. This makes it extremely important for a company to clearly identify and understand its core capabilities in relation to its market opportunities.

THE FUTURE OF CORE CAPABILITIES

Many of the factors contributing to the increasing interest in core capabilities are the same forces that have changed our thinking about hierarchical structures, the roles of managers and leaders, and decision making. Information technology, combined with TQM's emphasis on the customer, process improvement, and employee involvement, will have considerable influence in redirecting companies' attention toward examining how they add value and toward capabilities as the focal point of strategy.

As businesses rethink how they add value, individuals in organizations are feeling the impact of these changes as well. The cover story of the September 19, 1994, issue of *Fortune* magazine was titled "The End of the Job." It was simply reporting a conclusion that has been reached by many students of large organizations: that jobs as we know them will disappear. Instead of being a job holder, a person will become "a package of capabilities, drawn upon variously in different project-based situations." Such "packages" will coalesce into teams around an emerging issue, deal with the issue, then regroup into other team configurations around other issues.

The key integrating mechanism at both the individual level and the organizational level will be a shared strategic vision—one with both insight into emerging opportunities and an understanding of current and potential core capabilities. This form of strategy development will differ greatly from the analytical planning exercises used in traditional strategy planning departments. It will engage a much broader spectrum of employees and will seek continuous feedback from both the internal and external environments to fuel strategic thinking as an ongoing learning experience.

A clear strategic vision back by capability-based strategies will provide the critical integrating focus for an organization's competitive efforts. William Davidson, writing in the *IBM Systems Journal* in 1993, suggested that many reengineering projects fail to deliver promised results because of their focus. He warned that companies "that become focused on near-term operating performance and financial results may be led to pursue a variety of unrelated re-engineering projects. Each project may offer seemingly impressive results, but a fragmented approach to operations improvement may limit the company's ability to realize its full growth potential." Uncoordinated reengineering projects that do not support the company's core capabilities will not add maximum value for its stakeholders.

Companies need a clear focus, but it is important that they focus on those things that add the greatest value. Robert Tomasko, in *Rethinking the Corporation: The Architecture of Change*, pointed out that companies need to give priority "to investments that strengthen critical capabilities that will, in turn, provide returns leveraged through all the products and businesses that can make use of them." To develop this strategy, a company must understand the full range of its capabilities, the dynamics of their interactions, and how its mix of capabilities matches the current and emerging needs of its stakeholders.

As markets continue to fragment and proliferate and product cycles move at ever faster speeds, it will become increasingly important for businesses to compete as core capability builders rather than as share price manipulators. The ability to develop core capabilities that add value to products and services and to exploit emerging opportunities through accurate strategic targeting is the true competitive advantage that will prevail.

BIBLIOGRAPHY

For a recent, critical overview of strategy development in business organizations, see Henry Mintzberg, *The Rise and Fall of Strategic Planning* (New York: Free Press, 1994). He outlines the many shortcomings he sees in the way strategies were developed in organizations in years past. Mintzberg further elaborates on the weaknesses of the traditional strategic planning process in "The Fall and Rise of Strategic Planning," *Harvard Business Review*, January–February 1994. In this article, however, he also outlines a continuing role for the professional strategic planner as the emphasis shifts from strategic planning to strategic thinking. Mintzberg suggests that, instead of developing strategies, the planner's role should be confined to "programming" the implementation of management's strategic thinking.

For a broader look at where strategy development seems to be headed, see Gary Hamel and C. K. Prahalad, *Competing for the Future* (Boston: Harvard Business School Press, 1994). This book elaborates on the authors' earlier articles in the *Harvard Business Review*: "The Core Competence of the Corporation," May–June 1990; "Strategic Intent," May–June 1989; and "Strategy as Stretch and Leverage," March–April 1993.

Readers wanting an overview of the key contributors to the early development of strategy concepts will find Charles W. Hofer and Dan Schendel, *Strategy Formulation: Analytical Concepts* (St. Paul, MN: West, 1978) to be of special interest. This book includes a matrix comparing 13 authors' concepts of strategy and the strategy formulation process.

Those interested in a more direct encounter with the thinking of early contributors to and influencers of the development of concepts of strategy and its formulation should see Peter Drucker, *The Practice of Management* (New York: Harper & Row, 1954); Philip Selznick, *Leadership in Administration* (Evanston, IL: Row, Peterson, 1957); Alfred Chandler, *Strategy and Structure: Chapters in the History of American Industrial Enterprise* (Cambridge, MA: M.I.T. Press, 1962); Kenneth Andrews, Edmund Learned, C. Roland Christensen, and William Guth, *Business Policy: Texts and Cases* (Burr Ridge, IL: Richard D. Irwin, 1965); and Igor H. Ansoff, *Corporate Strategy: An Analytic Approach to Business Policy for Growth and Expansion* (New York: McGraw-Hill, 1965).

To sample the work of one of the most influential writers to develop the line of thinking started by these early contributors, see Michael E. Porter, *Competitive Advantage: Creating and Sustaining Superior Performance* (New York: Free Press, 1985).

Among those reporting evidence that many firms were failing to sustain a lasting competitive advantage were Richard M. Hodgetts, Fred Luthans, and Sang M. Lee, "New Paradigm Organizations: From Total Quality to Learning to World Class," *Organizational Dynamics*, Winter 1994. Insight into this failure and evidence of the strong relationship between corporate culture and performance and the benefits organizations derive from focusing on all their major stakeholders is provided by John Kotter and James Heskett, *Corporate Culture and Performance* (New York: Free Press, 1992). An early warning of the dangers of an exclusive focus on manipulating share price for certain shareholders as a measure of value creation is found in Robert B. Reich, *The Next American Frontier* (New York: Penguin, 1983). The Hodgetts, Luthans, and Lee article outlined the paradigm shift that is influencing the way people think about strategy.

LOOKING INSIDE FOR COMPETITIVE ADVANTAGE

Jay B. Barney

Creating sustained competitive advantage depends on the unique resources and capabilities that a firm brings to competition in its environment. To discover these resources and capabilities, managers must look inside their firm for valuable, rare, and costly-to-imitate resources, and then exploit these resources through their organization.

The history of strategic management research can be understood as an attempt to "fill in the blanks" created by the SWOT framework; i.e., to move beyond suggesting that strengths, weaknesses, opportunities, and threats are important for understanding competitive advantage to suggest models and frameworks that can be used to analyze and evaluate these phenomena.[1] Michael Porter and his associates have developed a number of these models and frameworks for analyzing environmental opportunities and threats.[2] Porter's work on the "five forces model," the relationship between industry structure and strategic opportunities, and strategic groups can all be understood as an effort to unpack the concepts of environmental opportunities and threats in a theoretically rigorous, yet highly applicable way.

However, the SWOT framework tells us that environmental analysis—no matter how rigorous—is only half the story. A complete understanding of sources of competitive advantage requires the analysis of a firm's internal strengths and weaknesses as well.[3] The importance of integrating internal with environmental analyses can be seen when evaluating the sources of competitive advantage of many firms. Consider, for example,

- Wal-Mart, a firm that has, for the last 20 years, consistently earned a return on sales twice the average of its industry.
- Southwest Airlines, a firm whose profits continued to increase, despite losses at other U.S. airlines that totaled almost $10 billion from 1990 to 1993.
- Nucor Steel, a firm whose stock price continued to soar through the 1980s and 90s, despite the fact that the market value of most steel companies has remained flat or fallen during the same time period.[4]

Source: *Academy of Management Executive* 9, no. 4 (1995).

These firms, and many others, have all gained competitive advantages—despite the unattractive, high-threat, low-opportunity environments within which they operate. Even the most careful and complete analysis of these firms' competitive environments cannot, by itself, explain their success. Such explanations must also include these firms' internal attributes—their strengths and weaknesses—as sources of competitive advantage. Following more recent practice, internal attributes will be referred to as *resources* and *capabilities* throughout the following discussion.[5]

A firm's resources and capabilities include all of the financial, physical, human, and organizational assets used by a firm to develop, manufacture, and deliver products or services to its customers. Financial resources include debt, equity, retained earnings, and so forth. Physical resources include the machines, manufacturing facilities, and buildings firms use in their operations. Human resources include all the experience, knowledge, judgment, risk-taking propensity, and wisdom of individuals associated with a firm. Organizational resources include the history, relationships, trust, and organizational culture that are attributes of groups of individuals associated with a firm, along with a firm's formal reporting structure, explicit management control systems, and compensation policies.

> *A firm's resources and capabilities include all of the financial, physical, human, and organizational assets used by a firm to develop, manufacture, and deliver products or services to its customers.*

In the process of filling in the "internal blanks" created by SWOT analysis, managers must address four important questions about their resources and capabilities: (1) the question of value, (2) the question of rareness, (3) the question of imitability, and (4) the question of organization.

THE QUESTION OF VALUE

To begin evaluating competitive implications of a firm's resources and capabilities, managers must first answer the question of value: Do a firm's resources and capabilities add value by enabling it to exploit opportunities and/or neutralize threats?

The answer to this question, for some firms, has been yes. Sony, for example, has a great deal of experience in designing, manufacturing, and selling miniaturized electronic technology. Sony has used these resources to exploit numerous market opportunities, including portable tape players, portable disc players, portable televisions, and easy-to-hold 8mm video cameras. 3M has used its skills and experience in substrates, coatings, and adhesives, along with an organizational culture that rewards risk taking and creativity, to exploit numerous market opportunities in office products, including invisible tape and Post-It™ Notes. Sony's and 3M's resources—including their specific technological skills and their creative organizational cultures—made it possible for these firms to respond to, and even create, new environmental opportunities.

Unfortunately, for other firms, the answer to the question of value has been no. For example, USX's long experience in traditional steel-making technology and the traditional steel market made it almost impossible for USX to recognize and respond to fundamental changes in the structure of the steel industry. Because they could not recognize new opportunities and threats, USX delayed its investment in, among other opportunities, thin-slab continuous casting steel manufacturing technology. Nucor Steel, on the other hand, was not shackled by its experience, made these investments early, and has become a major player in the international steel industry. In a similar way, Sears was unable to recognize or respond to changes in the retail market that had been created by Wal-Mart and specialty retail stores. In a sense, Sears's historical success, along with a commitment to stick with a traditional way of doing things, led it to miss some significant market opportunities.[6]

Although a firm's resources and capabilities may have added value in the past, changes in customer tastes, industry structure, or technology can render them less valuable in the future. General Electric's capabilities in transistor manufacturing became much less valuable when semiconductors were invented. American Airlines' skills in managing their relationship with the Civil Aeronautics Board (CAB) became much less valuable after airline deregulation. IBM's numerous capabilities in the mainframe computing business became less valuable with the increase in power, and reduction in price, of personal and minicomputers. One of the most important responsibilities of strategic managers is to constantly evaluate whether or not their firm's resources and capabilities continue to add value, despite changes in the competitive environment.

One of the most important responsibilities of strategic managers is to constantly evaluate whether or not their firm's resources and capabilities continue to add value, despite changes in the competitive environment.

Some environmental changes are so significant that few, if any, of a firm's resources remain valuable in any environmental context.[7] However, this kind of radical environmental change is unusual. More commonly, changes in a firm's environment may reduce the value of a firm's resources in their current use, while leaving the value of those resources in other uses unchanged. Such changes might even *increase* the value of those resources in those other uses. In this situation, the critical issue facing managers is: How can we use our traditional strengths in new ways to exploit opportunities and/ or neutralize threats?

Numerous firms have weathered these environmental shifts by finding new ways to apply their traditional strengths. AT&T had developed a reputation for providing high-quality long distance telephone service. It moved rapidly to exploit this reputation in the newly competitive long distance market by aggressively marketing its services against MCI, Sprint, and other carriers. Also, AT&T had traditional strengths in research and development with its Bell Labs subsidiary. To exploit these strengths in its new competitive context, AT&T shifted Bell Labs' mission from basic research to applied research, and then leveraged those skills by forming numerous joint ventures, acquiring NCR, and other actions. Through this process, AT&T has been able to use some of its historically important capabilities to try to position itself as a major actor in the global telecommunications and computing industry.

Another firm that has gone through a similar transformation is the Hunter Fan Company. Formed in 1886, Hunter Fan developed the technology it needed to be the market share leader in ceiling fans used to cool large manufacturing facilities. Unfortunately, the invention of air conditioning significantly reduced demand for industrial fans, and Hunter Fan's performance deteriorated rapidly. However, in the 1970s, rising energy prices made energy conservation more important to home owners. Since ceiling fans can significantly reduce home energy consumption, Hunter Fan was able to move quickly to exploit this new opportunity. Of course, Hunter Fan had to develop some new skills as well, including brass-plating capabilities and new distribution networks. However, by building on its traditional strengths in new ways, Hunter Fan has become a leader in the home ceiling fan market.[8]

By answering the question of value, managers link the analysis of internal resources and capabilities with the analysis of environmental opportunities and threats.

By answering the question of value, managers link the analysis of internal resources and capabilities with the analysis of environmental opportunities and threats. Firm resources are not valuable in a vacuum, but rather are valuable only when they exploit opportunities and/or neutralize threats. The models developed by Porter and his associates can be used to isolate potential opportunities and threats that the resources a firm controls can exploit or neutralize.

Of course, the resources and capabilities of different firms can be valuable in different ways. This can be true, even if firms are competing in the same industry. For example, while both Rolex and Timex manufacture watches, they exploit very different valuable resources. Rolex emphasizes its quality manufacturing, commitment to excellence, and high-status reputation in marketing its watches. Timex emphasizes its high-volume, low-cost manufacturing skills and abilities. Rolex exploits its capabilities in responding to demand for very expensive watches; Timex exploits its resources in responding to demand for practical, reliable, low-cost timekeeping.

THE QUESTION OF RARENESS

That a firm's resources and capabilities are valuable is an important first consideration in understanding internal sources of competitive advantage. However, if a particular resource and capability is controlled by numerous competing firms, then that resource is unlikely to be a source of competitive advantage for any one of them. Instead, valuable but common (i.e., not rare) resources and capabilities are sources of competitive parity. For managers evaluating the competitive implications of their resources and capabilities, these observations lead to the second critical issue: How many competing firms already possess these valuable resources and capabilities?

Consider, for example, two firms competing in the global communications and computing industries: NEC and AT&T. Both these firms are developing many of the same capabilities that are likely to be needed in these industries over the next decade. These capabilities are clearly valuable, although—since at least these two firms, and maybe others, are developing them—they may not be rare. If they are not rare, they cannot—by themselves—be sources of competitive advantage for either NEC or AT&T. If either of these firms is to gain competitive advantages, they must exploit resources and capabilities that are different from the communication and computing skills they are *both* cited as developing. This may be part of the reason why AT&T recently restructured its telecommunications and computer businesses into separate firms.[9]

While resources and capabilities must be rare among competing firms in order to be a source of competitive advantage, this does not mean that common, but valuable, resources are not important. Indeed, such resources and capabilities may be essential for a firm's survival. On the other hand, if a firm's resources are valuable and rare, those resources may enable a firm to gain at least a temporary competitive advantage. Wal-Mart's skills in developing and using point-of-purchase data collection to control inventory have given it a competitive advantage over Kmart, a firm that until recently has not had access to this timely information. Thus, for many years, Wal-Mart's valuable point-of-purchase inventory control systems were rare, at least relative to its major U.S. competitor, Kmart.[10]

THE QUESTION OF IMITABILITY

A firm that possesses valuable and rare resources and capabilities can gain, at least, a temporary competitive advantage. If, in addition, competing firms face a cost disadvantage in imitating these resources and capabilities, firms with these special abilities can obtain a sustained competitive advantage. These observations lead to the question of imitability: Do firms without a resource or capability face a cost disadvantage in obtaining it compared to firms that already possess it?

Obviously, imitation is critical to understanding the ability of resources and capabilities to generate sustained competitive advantages. Imitation can occur in at least two ways: duplication and substitution. Duplication occurs when an imitating firm builds the same kinds of resources as the firm it is imitating. If one firm has a competitive advantage because of its research and development skills, then a duplicating firm will try to imitate that resource by developing its own research and development skills. In addition, firms may be able to substitute some resources for other resources. If these substitute resources have the same strategic implications and are no more costly to develop, then imitation through substitution will lead to competitive parity in the long run.

So, when will firms be at a cost disadvantage in imitating another's resources and capabilities, either through duplication or substitution? While there are numerous reasons why some of these internal attributes of firms may be costly to imitate, most of these reasons can be grouped into three categories: the importance of history in creating firm resources; the importance of numerous "small decisions" in developing, nurturing, and exploiting resources; and the importance of socially complex resources.

The Importance of History

As firms evolve, they pick up skills, abilities, and resources that are unique to them, reflecting their particular path through history. These resources and capabilities reflect the unique personalities, experiences, and relationships that exist in only a single firm. Before World War II, Caterpillar was one of several medium-sized firms in the heavy construction equipment industry struggling to survive intense competition. Just before the outbreak of war, the Department of War (now the Department of Defense) concluded that, in order to pursue a global war, they would need one worldwide supplier of heavy construction equipment to build roads, air strips, army bases, and so forth. After a brief competition, Caterpillar was awarded this contract and, with the support of the Allies, was able to develop a worldwide service and supply network for heavy construction equipment at very low cost.

After the war, Caterpillar continued to own and operate this worldwide service and supply network. Indeed, Caterpillar management still advertises their ability to deliver any part, for any piece of Caterpillar equipment, to any place in the world, in under two days. By using this valuable capability, Caterpillar was able to become the dominant firm in the heavy construction equipment industry. Even today, despite recessions and labor strife, Caterpillar remains the market share leader in most categories of heavy construction equipment.[11]

Consider the position of a firm trying to duplicate Caterpillar's worldwide service and supply network, at the same cost as Caterpillar. This competing firm would have to receive the same kind of government support that Caterpillar received during World War II. This kind of government support is very unlikely.

It is interesting to note that at least one firm in the heavy construction equipment industry has begun to effectively compete against Caterpillar: Komatsu. However, rather than attempting to duplicate Caterpillar's service and supply network, Komatsu has attempted to exploit its own unique design and manufacturing resources by building machines that do not break down as frequently. Since Komatsu's machines break down less frequently, Komatsu does not require as extensive a worldwide service and supply network as Caterpillar. In this sense, Komatsu's special design and manufacturing skills in building machines that break down less frequently may be a strategic substitute for Caterpillar's worldwide service and supply network.[12]

In general, whenever the acquisition or development of valuable and rare resources depends upon unique historical circumstances, those imitating these resources will be at a cost disadvantage building them. Such resources can be sources of sustained competitive advantage.

The Importance of Numerous Small Decisions

Strategic managers and researchers are often enamored with the importance of "Big Decisions" as determinants of competitive advantage. IBM's decision to bring out the 360 series of computers in the 1960s was a "Big Decision" that had enormous competitive implications until the rise of personal computers. General Electric's decision to invest in the medical imaging business was a "Big Decision" whose competitive ramifications are still unfolding. Sometimes such "Big Decisions" are critical in understanding a firm's competitive position. However, more and more frequently, a firm's competitive advantage seems to depend on numerous "small decisions" through which a firm's resources and capabilities are developed and exploited. Thus, for example, a firm's competitive advantage in quality does not depend just upon its announcing that it is seeking the Malcolm Baldrige Quality Award. It depends upon literally hundreds of thousands of decisions made each day by employees in the firm—small decisions about whether or not to tighten a screw a little more, whether or not to share a small idea for improvement, or whether or not to call attention to a quality problem.[13] From the point of view of sustaining a competitive advantage, "small decisions" have some advantages over "Big Decisions." In particular, small decisions are essentially invisible to firms seeking to imitate a successful firm's resources and capabilities. "Big Decisions," on the other hand, are more obvious, easier to describe, and, perhaps, easier to imitate. While competitors may be able to observe the consequences of numerous little decisions, they often have a difficult time understanding the sources of the advantages.[14] A case in point is The Mailbox, Inc., a very successful firm in the bulk mailing business in the Dallas–Ft. Worth market. If there was ever a business where it seems unlikely that a firm would have a sustained competitive advantage, it is bulk mailing. Firms in this industry gather mail from customers, sort it by postal code, and then take it to the post office to be mailed. Where is the competitive advantage here? And yet, The Mailbox has enjoyed an enormous market share advantage in the Dallas–Ft. Worth area for several years. Why?

When asked, managers at The Mailbox have a difficult time describing the sources of their sustained advantages. Indeed, they can point to *no* "Big Decisions" they have made to generate this advantage. However, as these managers begin to discuss their firm, what becomes clear is that their success does not depend on doing a few big things right, but on doing lots of little things right. The way they manage accounting, finance, human resources, production, or other business functions, separately, is not exceptional. However, to manage all these functions so well, and so consistently over time is truly exceptional. Firms seeking to compete against The Mailbox will not have to imitate just a few internal attributes; they will have to imitate thousands, or even hundreds of thousands of such attributes—a daunting task indeed.[15]

The Importance of Socially Complex Resources

A final reason that firms may be at a cost disadvantage in imitating resources and capabilities is that these resources may be socially complex. Some physical resources (e.g., computers, robots, and other machines) controlled by firms are very complex. However, firms seeking to imitate these physical resources need only purchase them, take them apart, and duplicate the technology in question. With just a couple of exceptions (including the pharmaceutical and specialty chemicals industries), patents provide little protection from the imitation of a firm's physical resources.[16] On the other hand, socially complex resources and capabilities—organizational phenomena like reputation, trust, friendship, teamwork, and culture—while not patentable, are much more difficult to imitate. Imagine the difficulty of imitating Hewlett-Packard's (HP) powerful and enabling culture. One of the most important components of HP's culture is that it supports and encourages teamwork and cooperation, even across divisional boundaries. HP has used this socially complex capability to enhance the compatibility of its numerous products, including printers, plotters, personal computers, minicomputers, and electronic instruments. By cooperating across these product categories, HP has been able to almost double its market value, all without introducing any radical new products or technologies.[17]

In general, when a firm's resources and capabilities are valuable, rare, and socially complex, those resources are likely to be sources of sustained competitive advantage. One firm that apparently violates this assertion is Sony. Most observers agree that Sony possesses some special management and coordination skills that enable it to conceive, design, and manufacture high-quality, miniaturized consumer electronics. However, it appears that every time Sony brings out a new miniaturized product, several of its competitors quickly duplicate that product, through reverse engineering, thereby reducing Sony's technological advantage. In what way can Sony's socially complex miniaturization skills be a source of sustained competitive advantage, when most of Sony's products are quickly imitated?

The solution to this paradox depends on shifting the unit of analysis from the performance of Sony's products over time to the performance of Sony over time. After it introduces each new product, Sony experiences a rapid increase in sales and profits associated with that product. However, this leads other firms to reverse engineer the Sony product and introduce their own version. Increased competition leads the sales and profits associated with the new product to be reduced. Thus, at the level of individual products introduced by Sony, Sony apparently enjoys only very short-lived competitive advantages.

However, by looking at the total returns earned by Sony across all of its new products over time, the source of Sony's sustained competitive advantage becomes clear. By exploiting its capabilities in miniaturization, Sony is able to constantly introduce new and exciting personal electronics products. No one of these products generates a sustained competitive advantage. However, over time, across several such product introductions, Sony's capability advantages do lead to a sustained competitive advantage.[18]

THE QUESTION OF ORGANIZATION

A firm's competitive advantage potential depends on the value, rareness, and imitability of its resources and capabilities. However, to fully realize this potential, a firm must also be organized to exploit its resources and capabilities. These observations lead to the question of organization: Is a firm organized to exploit the full competitive potential of its resources and capabilities?

A firm's competitive advantage potential depends on the value, rareness, and imitability of its resources and capabilities.

Numerous components of a firm's organization are relevant when answering the question of organization, including its formal reporting structure, its explicit management control systems, and its compensation policies. These components are referred to as *complementary* resources because they have limited ability to generate competitive advantage in isolation. However, in combination with other resources and capabilities, they can enable a firm to realize its full competitive advantage.[19]

Much of Caterpillar's sustained competitive advantage in the heavy construction industry can be traced to its becoming the sole supplier of this equipment to Allied forces in World War II. However, if Caterpillar's management had not taken advantage of this opportunity by implementing a global formal reporting structure, global inventory and other control systems, and compensation policies that created incentives for its employees to work around the world, then Caterpillar's potential for competitive advantage would not have been fully realized. These attributes of Caterpillar's organization, by themselves, could not be a source of competitive advantage; i.e., adopting a global organizational form was only relevant for Caterpillar because it was pursuing a global opportunity. However, this organization was essential for Caterpillar to realize its full competitive advantage potential.

In a similar way, much of Wal-Mart's continuing competitive advantage in the discount retailing industry can be attributed to its early entry into rural markets in the southern United States. However, to fully exploit this geographic advantage, Wal-Mart needed to implement appropriate reporting structures, control systems, and compensation policies. We have already seen that one of these components of Wal-Mart's organization—its point-of-purchase inventory control system—is being imitated by Kmart, and thus, by itself, is not likely to be a source of sustained competitive advantage. However, this inventory control system has enabled Wal-Mart to take full advantage of its rural locations by decreasing the probability of stockouts and by reducing inventory costs.

While a complementary organization enabled Caterpillar and Wal-Mart to realize their full competitive advantage, Xerox was prevented from taking full advantage of some of its most critical valuable, rare, and costly-to-imitate resources and capabilities because it lacked such organizational skills. Through the 1960s and early 1970s, Xerox invested in a series of very innovative technology development research efforts. Xerox managed this research effort by creating a stand-alone research laboratory (Xerox PARC, in Palo Alto, California), and by assembling a large group of highly creative and innovative scientists and engineers to work there. Left to their own devices, these scientists and engineers developed an amazing array of technological innovations, including the personal computer, the "mouse," windows-type software, the laser printer, the "paperless office," ethernet, and so forth. In retrospect, the market potential of these technologies was enormous. Moreover, since these technologies were developed at Xerox PARC, they were rare. Finally, Xerox may have been able to gain some important first mover advantages if they had been able to translate these technologies into products, thereby increasing the cost to other firms of imitating these technologies.

Unfortunately, Xerox did not have an organization in place to take advantage of these resources. For example, no structure existed whereby Xerox PARC's innovations could become known to managers at Xerox. Indeed, most Xerox managers—even many senior managers—were unaware of these technological developments through the mid-1970s. Once they finally became aware of them, very few of the innovations survived Xerox's highly bureaucratic product development process—a process where product development projects were divided into hundreds of minute tasks, and progress in each task was reviewed by dozens of large committees. Even those innovations that survived the product development process were not exploited by Xerox managers. Management compensation at Xerox depended almost exclusively on maximizing current revenue. Short-term profitability was relatively less important in compensation calculations, and the development of markets for future sales and profitability was essentially irrelevant. Xerox's formal reporting structure, its explicit management control systems, and its compensation policies were all inconsistent with exploiting the valuable, rare, and costly-to-imitate resources developed at Xerox PARC. Not surprisingly, Xerox failed to exploit any of these potential sources of sustained competitive advantage.[20]

This set of questions can be applied in understanding the competitive implications of phenomena as diverse as the "cola wars" in the soft drink industry and competition among different types of personal computers.

THE COMPETITIVE IMPLICATIONS OF THE "COLA WARS"

Almost since they were founded, Coca-Cola, Inc., and PepsiCo, Inc., have battled each other for market share in the soft drink industry. In many ways, the intensity of these "cola wars" increased in the mid-1970s with the introduction of PepsiCo's "Pepsi Challenge" advertising campaign. While significant advertising and other marketing expenditures have been made by both these firms, and while market share has shifted back and forth between them over time, it is not at all clear that these efforts have generated competitive advantages for either Coke or Pepsi.

Obviously, market share is a very valuable commodity in the soft drink industry. Market share translates directly into revenues, which, in turn, has a large impact on profits and profitability. Strategies pursued by either Coke or Pepsi designed to acquire market share will usually be valuable.

But are these market share acquisition strategies rare or does either Coca-Cola or Pepsi have a cost advantage in implementing them? Both Coca-Cola and PepsiCo are marketing powerhouses; both have enormous financial capabilities and strong management teams. Any effort by one to take share away can instantly be matched by the other to protect that share. In this sense, while Coke's and Pepsi's share acquisition strategies may be valuable, they are not rare, nor does either Coke or Pepsi have a cost advantage in implementing them. Assuming that these firms are appropriately organized (a reasonable assumption), then the cola wars should be a source of competitive parity for these firms.

This has, apparently, been the case. For example, Pepsi originally introduced its "Pepsi Challenge" advertising campaign in the Dallas–Ft. Worth market. After six months of the Pepsi Challenge—including price discounts, coupon campaigns, numerous celebrity endorsements, and so on—Pepsi was able to double its share of the Dallas–Ft. Worth market from 7 percent to 14 percent. Unfortunately, the retail price of Pepsi's soft drinks, after six months of the Pepsi Challenge, was approximately one-half the prechallenge level. Thus Pepsi doubled its market share, but cut its prices in half—exactly the result one would expect in a world of competitive parity.[21]

It is interesting to note that both Coca-Cola and Pepsi are beginning to recognize the futility of going head to head against an equally skilled competitor in a battle for market share to gain competitive advantages. Instead, these firms seem to be altering both their market share and other strategies. Coke, through its Diet Coke brand name, is targeting older consumers with advertisements that use personalities from the 50s, 60s, and 70s (e.g., Elton John and Gene Kelly). Pepsi continues its focus on attracting younger drinkers with its "choice of a new generation" advertising campaigns. Coke continues its traditional focus on the soft drink industry, while Pepsi has begun diversifying into fast-food restaurants and other related businesses. Coke has extended its marketing efforts internationally, whereas Pepsi focuses mostly on the market in the United States (although it is beginning to alter this strategy). In all these ways, Coke and Pepsi seem to be moving away from head-to-head competition for market share, and moving toward exploiting *different* resources.

THE COMPETITIVE POSITION OF THE MACINTOSH COMPUTER

Building on earlier research conducted by Xerox PARC, Apple Computer developed and marketed the first user-friendly alternative to DOS-based personal computers, the Macintosh. Most Macintosh users have a passion for their computers that is usually reserved for personal relationships. Macintosh users shake their heads and wonder why DOS-based computer users don't wake up and experience the "joy of Macintosh."

The first step in analyzing the competitive position of the Macintosh is to evaluate whether or not "user friendliness" in a personal computer is valuable; i.e., does it exploit an environmental opportunity and/or neutralize an environmental threat? While user friendliness is not a requirement of all personal computer users, it is not unreasonable to conclude that many of these computer users, other things being equal, would prefer working on a user-friendly machine compared with a user-unfriendly machine. Thus, the Macintosh computer does seem to respond to a real market opportunity.

When the Macintosh was first introduced, was user friendliness rare? At that time, DOS-based machines were essentially the only alternative to the Macintosh, and DOS-based software, in those early days, was anything but user friendly. Thus, the Macintosh was apparently both valuable and rare, and thus a source of at least a temporary competitive advantage for Apple.

Was the user friendliness of the Macintosh costly to imitate? At first, it seemed likely that user-friendly software would rapidly be developed for DOS-based machines, and thus that the user-friendly Macintosh would enjoy only a temporary competitive advantage. However, history has shown that user friendliness was not easy to imitate.

Imitation of the user-friendly Macintosh by DOS-based machines was slowed by a combination of at least two factors. First, the Macintosh hardware and software system had originally been developed by teams of software, hardware, and production engineers all working in Apple Computer. The teamwork, trust, commitment, and enthusiasm that these Apple employees enjoyed while working on Macintosh technology were difficult for other computer firms to duplicate, since most of those firms specialized either in hardware design and manufacturing (e.g., IBM) or software development (e.g., Microsoft, Lotus). In other words, the socially complex resources that Apple was able to bring to bear in the Macintosh project were difficult to duplicate in vertically nonintegrated computer hardware and software firms.

Second, Apple management had a different conception of the personal computer and its future than did managers at IBM and other computer firms. At IBM, for example, computers had traditionally meant mainframe computers, and mainframe computers were expected to be complicated and difficult to operate. User friendliness was never an issue in IBM mainframes (users of IBM's JCL know the truth of that assertion!), and thus was not an important concern when IBM entered into the personal computer market. However, at Apple, computers were Jobs's and Wozniak's toys—a hobby, to be used for fun. If management's mindset is that "computers are supposed to be fun," then it suddenly becomes easier to develop and build user-friendly computers.

Obviously, these two mindsets—IBM's "computers are complex tools run by technical specialists" versus Apple's "computers are toys for everyone"—were deeply embedded in the cultures of these two firms, as well as those firms that worked closely with them. Such mindsets are socially complex, slow to change, and difficult to imitate. It took some time before the notion that a computer should be (or even could be) easy to use came to prominence in DOS-based systems.[22] Only recently, after almost 10 years (an eternity in the rapidly changing personal computer business), has user-friendly software for DOS-based machines been developed. With the introduction of Windows by Microsoft, the rareness of Macintosh's user friendliness has been reduced, as has been the competitive advantage that Macintosh had generated.

Interestingly, just as Windows software was introduced, Apple began to radically change its pricing and product development strategies. First Apple cut the price of the Macintosh computer, reflecting the fact that user friendliness was not as rare after Windows as it was before Windows. Second, Apple seems to have recognized the need to develop new resources and capabilities to enhance their traditional user-friendly strengths. Rather than only competing with other hardware and software companies, Apple has begun developing strategic alliances with several other computer firms, including IBM and Microsoft. These alliances may help Apple develop the resources and capabilities they need to remain competitive in the personal computer industry over the next several years.

THE MANAGEMENT CHALLENGE

In the end, this discussion reminds us that sustained competitive advantage cannot be created simply by evaluating environmental opportunities and threats, and then conducting business only in high-opportunity, low-threat environments. Rather, creating sustained competitive advantage depends on the unique resources and capabilities that a firm brings to competition in its environment. To discover these resources and capabilities, managers must look inside their firm for valuable, rare, and costly-to-imitate resources, and then exploit these resources through their organization.

ENDNOTES

1. The original SWOT framework was proposed and developed by E. Learned, C. Christiansen, K. Andrews, and W. Guth in *Business Policy* (Burr Ridge, IL: Richard D. Irwin, 1969). Though the field of strategic management has evolved a great deal since then, this fundamental SWOT framework, as an organizing principle, has remained unchanged. See for example Michael Porter. "The Contributions of Industrial Organization to Strategic Management," *Academy of Management Review* 6 (1981), pp. 609–20; and Jay Barney, "Firm Resources and Sustained Competitive Advantage," *Journal of Management* 17 (1991), pp. 99–120.

2. Porter's work is described in detail in M. Porter, *Competitive Strategy* (New York: Free Press, 1980), and M. Porter, *Competitive Advantage* (New York: Free Press, 1985).

3. A variety of different authors have begun to explore the competitive implications of a firm's internal strengths and weaknesses. Building on some seminal insights by Edith Penrose, *The Theory of the Growth of the Firm* (New York: Wiley, 1959), this work has come to be known as the Resource-Based View of the Firm. Resource-based scholarly work includes: Birger Wernerfelt, "A Resource-Based View of the Firm," *Strategic Management Journal* 5 (1984), pp. 171–80; Richard Rumelt, "Toward a Strategic Theory of the Firm," in R. Lamb, ed., *Competitive Strategic Management* (Englewood Cliffs, NJ: Prentice-Hall, 1984), pp. 556–70; Jay Barney, "Strategic Factor Markets," *Management Science* 41 (1980), pp. 1231–41; and Jay Barney, "Organizational Culture: Can It Be A Source of Sustained Competitive Advantage?" *Academy of Management Review* 11 (1986), pp. 791–800. The framework developed in this article draws most closely from Jay Barney, "Firm Resources and Sustained Competitive Advantage."

4. For more detailed discussions of the internal resources and capabilities of these firms, see Pankaj Ghemewat, "Wal-Mart Stores' Discount Operations," Case No. 9-387-018 (Harvard Business School, 1986); S. Chakravarty, "Hit 'Em Hardest with the Mostest," *Forbes* 148 (September 16, 1991), pp. 48–54; and Pankaj Ghemewat, "Nucor at a Crossroad," Case No. 9-793-039 (Harvard Business School, 1992).

5. Different terms have been used to describe these internal phenomena, including core competencies (C. K. Prahalad and Gary Hamel, "The Core Competence of the Organization," *Harvard Business Review* 90 (1990), pp. 79–93), firm resources (Birger Wernerfelt "A Resource-Based View," and Jay Barney, "Firm Resources and Sustained Competitive Advantage") and firm capabilities (George Stalk, Phillip Evans, and Lawrence Shulman, "Competing on Capabilities: The New Rules of Corporate Strategy," *Harvard Business Review*, March–April, 1992, pp. 57–69). While distinctions among these terms can be drawn, for our purposes they can, and will, be used interchangeably.

6. For details, see B. Schlender, "How Sony Keeps the Magic Going," *Fortune* 125 (February 24, 1992), pp. 76–84; L. Krogh, J. Praeger, D. Sorenson, and J. Tomlinson, "How 3M Evaluates Its R&D Programs," *Research Technology Management* 31 (November–December, 1988), pp. 10–14; Richard Rosenbloom, "Continuous Casting Investments at USX Corporation," Case No. 9-392-232 (Harvard Business School, 1990); and Cynthia Montgomery, "Sears, Roebuck and Co. in 1989," Case No. 9-391-147 (Harvard Business School, 1989).

7. This kind of environmental or technological shift is called a Schumpeterian revolution, and firms in this setting have little systematic hope of gaining competitive advantages, unless the competitive environment shifts again, although they can be lucky. See Jay B. Barney, "Types of Competitors and the Theory of Strategy: Toward an Integrative Framework." *Academy of Management Review*, 1986, pp. 791–800.

8. For a discussion of AT&T's attempt to develop new resources and capabilities, see D. Kirkpatrick, "Could AT&T Rule the World?" *Fortune*, May 17, 1993, pp. 54–56. Hunter Fan's experience was described through personal communication with managers there, and in a publication celebrating Hunter Fan's 100th anniversary in 1986.

9. Prahalad and Hamel's 1990 discussion of NEC's attempt to develop the resources needed to compete in the global telecommunications and computer industry is insightful, especially in comparison to Kirkpatrick's discussion of AT&T's efforts in *Fortune*.

10. Wal-Mart's point of purchase inventory control system and the impact of Wal-Mart's rural stores on its performance, are described in Ghemewat, "Wal-Mart Stores Discount Operations." Kmart's inventory control response to Wal-Mart is described in L. Steven's "Front Line Systems," *Computerworld* 26 (1992), pp. 61–63.

11. See M. G. Rukstad and J. Horn, "Caterpillar and the Construction Equipment Industry in 1988," Case No. 9-389-097 (Harvard Business School, 1989).

12. Komatsu's response to Caterpillar's competitive advantage is described in C. A. Bartlett and U.S. Rangan, "Komatsu Ltd.," Case No. 9-385-277 (Harvard Business School, 1985).

13. See Richard Blackburn and Benson Rosen, "Total Quality and Human Resources Management: Lessons Learned from Baldrige Award-Winning Companies," *Academy of Management Executive* 7 (1993), pp. 49–66.

14. These invisible assets have been described by H. Itami, *Mobilizing Invisible Assets* (Cambridge, MA: Harvard University Press, 1987).

15. Personal communication.

16. See E. Mansfield, "How Rapidly Does New Industrial Technology Leak Out?" *Journal of Industrial Economics* 34 (1985), pp. 217–23; and E. Mansfield, M. Schwartz, and S. Wagner, "Imitation Costs and Patents: An Empirical Study," *Economic Journal* 91 (1981), pp. 907–18.

17. See S. K. Yoder, "A 1990 Reorganization at Hewlett-Packard Already Is Paying Off," *The Wall Street Journal*, July 22, 1991, p. A1. This is not to suggest that socially complex resources and capabilities do not change and evolve in an organization. They clearly do. Nor does this suggest that managers can never radically alter a firm's socially complex resources and capabilities. Such transformational leaders do seem to exist, and do have an enormous impact on these resources in a firm. Managers such as the late Mike Walsh at Tenneco, Lee Iacocca at Chrysler, and Jack Welch at General Electric apparently have been such leaders. However, this kind of leadership is a socially complex phenomenon, and thus very difficult to imitate. Even if a leader in one firm can transform its socially complex resources and capabilities, it does not necessarily mean that other firms will be able to imitate this feat at the same cost. The concept of transformational leaders is discussed in N. Tichy, *The Transformational Leader* (New York: Wiley, 1986).

18. See Schlender, "How Sony Keeps the Magic."

19. See Raphael Amit and Paul Schoemaker, "Strategic Assets and Organizational Rent," *Strategic Management Journal* 14 (1993), pp. 33–46;

David Teece, "Profiting From Technological Innovation," *Research Policy* 15 (1986), pp. 285–305; and Ingemar Dierickx and Karel Cool, "Asset Stock Accumulation and Sustainability of Competitive Advantage," *Management Science* 35 (1989), pp. 1504–11, for a discussion of complementary resources and capabilities. Of course, complementary organizational resources are part of a firm's overall resource and capability base, and thus the competitive implications of these resources could be evaluated using the questions of value, rareness, and imitability. However, the question of organization is included in this discussion to emphasize the particular importance of complementary organizational resources in enabling a firm to fully exploit its competitive advantage potential.

20. Xerox's organizational problems with Xerox PARC are described, in detail, in David T. Kearns and David A. Nadler, *Prophets in the Dark* (New York: Harper Collins, 1992); Douglas K. Smith and Robert C. Alexander, *Fumbling the Future* (Now York: William Morrow, 1988); and L. Hooper, "Xerox Tries to Shed Its Has Been Image with a Big New Machine," *The Wall Street Journal*, September 20, 1990, p. A1.

21. See A. E. Pearson and C. L. Irwin, "Coca-Cola vs. Pepsi-Cola (A)," Case No. 9-387-108 (Harvard Business School, 1988), for a discussion of the cola wars, and their competitive implications for Coke and Pepsi.

22. See D. B. Yoffie, "Apple Computer—1992," Case No. 9-792-081 (Harvard Business School, 1992), for a complete discussion of Apple, IBM, and Apple's new strategies for the 1990s.

WHAT IS STRATEGY?

Michael E. Porter

Porter suggests that companies that focus myopically on improving organizational effectiveness jeopardize long-term success when they fail to develop a sustainable strategy. He states that the essence of strategy is choosing to perform activities differently than rivals do and that companies must consider strategic positioning and strategic fit when crafting strategies.

OPERATIONAL EFFECTIVENESS IS NOT STRATEGY

For almost two decades, managers have been learning to play by a new set of rules. Companies must be flexible to respond rapidly to competitive and market changes. They must benchmark continuously to achieve best practice. They must outsource aggressively to gain efficiencies. And they must nurture a few core competencies in the race to stay ahead of rivals.

Positioning—once the heart of strategy—is rejected as too static for today's dynamic markets and changing technologies. According to the new dogma, rivals can quickly copy any market position, and competitive advantage is, at best, temporary.

But those beliefs are dangerous half-truths, and they are leading more and more companies down the path of mutually destructive competition. True, some barriers to competition are falling as regulation eases and markets become global. True, companies have properly invested energy in becoming leaner and more nimble. In many industries, however, what some call *hypercompetition* is a self-inflicted wound, not the inevitable outcome of a changing paradigm of competition.

The root of the problem is the failure to distinguish between operational effectiveness and strategy. The quest for productivity, quality, and speed has spawned a remarkable number of management tools and techniques: total quality management, benchmarking, time-based competition, outsourcing, partnering, reengineering, change management. Although the resulting operational improvements have often been dramatic, many companies have been frustrated by their inability to translate those gains into sustainable profitability. And bit by bit, almost imperceptibly, man-

FIGURE 1   Operational Effectiveness versus Strategic Positioning

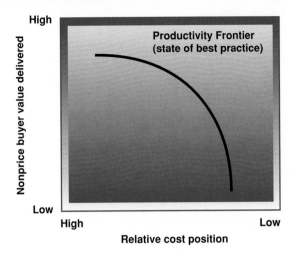

agement tools have taken the place of strategy. As managers push to improve on all fronts, they move farther away from viable competitive positions.

Operational Effectiveness: Necessary but Not Sufficient

Operational effectiveness and strategy are both essential to superior performance, which, after all, is the primary goal of any enterprise. But they work in very different ways. (See Figure 1.)

A company can outperform rivals only if it can establish a difference that it can preserve. It must deliver greater value to customers or create comparable value at a lower cost, or do both. The arithmetic of superior profitability then follows: delivering greater value allows a company to charge higher average unit prices; greater efficiency results in lower average unit costs.

Ultimately, all differences between companies in cost or price derive from the hundreds of activities required to create, produce, sell, and deliver their products or services, such as calling on customers, assembling final products, and training employees. Cost is generated by performing activities, and cost advantage arises from performing particular activities more efficiently than competitors. Similarly, differentiation arises from both the choice of activities and how they are performed. Activities, then, are the basic units of competitive advantage. Overall advantage or disadvantage results from all a company's activities, not only a few.[1]

A company can outperform rivals only if it can establish a difference that it can preserve.

Operational effectiveness (OE) means performing similar activities *better* than rivals perform them. Operational effectiveness includes but is not limited to efficiency. It refers to any number of practices that allow a company to better utilize its inputs by, for example, reducing defects in products or developing better products faster. In contrast, strategic positioning means performing *different* activities from rivals' or performing similar activities in *different ways*.

Differences in operational effectiveness among companies are pervasive. Some companies are able to get more out of their inputs than others because they eliminate wasted effort, employ more advanced technology, motivate employees better, or have greater insight into managing particular activities or sets of activities. Such differences in operational effectiveness are an important source of differences in profitability among competitors because they directly affect relative cost positions and levels of differentiation.

Differences in operational effectiveness were at the heart of the Japanese challenge to Western companies in the 1980s. The Japanese were so far ahead of rivals in operational effectiveness that they could offer lower cost and superior quality at the same time. It is worth dwelling on this point, because so much recent thinking about competition depends on it. Imagine for a moment a *productivity frontier* that constitutes the sum of all existing best practices at any given time. Think of it as the maximum value that a company delivering a particular product or service can create at a given cost, using the best available technologies, skills, management techniques, and purchased inputs. The productivity frontier can apply to individual activities, to groups of linked activities such as order processing and manufacturing, and to an entire company's activities. When a company improves its operational effectiveness, it moves toward the frontier. Doing so may require capital investment, different personnel, or simply new ways of managing.

The productivity frontier is constantly shifting outward as new technologies and management approaches are developed and as new inputs become available. Laptop computers, mobile communications, the Internet, and software such as Lotus Notes, for example, have redefined the productivity frontier for salesforce operations and created rich possibilities for linking sales with such activities as order processing and after-sales support. Similarly, lean production, which involves a family of activities, has allowed substantial improvements in manufacturing productivity and asset utilization.

For at least the past decade, managers have been preoccupied with improving operational effectiveness. Through programs such as TQM, time-based competition, and benchmarking, they have changed how they perform activities in order to eliminate inefficiencies, improve customer satisfaction, and achieve best practice. Hoping to keep up with shifts in the productivity frontier, managers have embraced continuous improvement, empowerment, change management, and the so-called learning organization. The popularity of outsourcing and the virtual corporation reflect the growing recognition that it is difficult to perform all activities as productively as specialists.

As companies move to the frontier they can often improve on multiple dimensions of performance at the same time. For example, manufacturers that adopted the Japanese practice of rapid changeovers in the 1980s were able to lower cost and improve differentiation simultaneously. What were once believed to be real trade-offs—between defects and costs, for example—turned out to be illusions created by poor operational effectiveness. Managers have learned to reject such false trade-offs.

Constant improvement in operational effectiveness is necessary to achieve superior profitability. However, it is not usually sufficient. Few companies have competed successfully on the basis of operational effectiveness over an extended period, and staying ahead of rivals gets harder every day. The most obvious reason for that is the rapid diffusion of best practices. Competitors can quickly imitate management techniques, new technologies, input improvements, and superior ways of meeting customers' needs. The most generic solutions—those that can be used in multiple settings—diffuse the fastest. Witness the proliferation of OE techniques accelerated by support from consultants.

OE competition shifts the productivity frontier outward, effectively raising the bar for everyone. But although such competition produces absolute improvement in operational effectiveness, it leads to relative improvement for no one. Consider the

FIGURE 2   Japanese Companies Rarely Have Strategies

The Japanese triggered a global revolution in operational effectiveness in the 1970s and 1980s, pioneering practices such as total quality management and continuous improvement. As a result, Japanese manufacturers enjoyed substantial cost and quality advantages for many years.

But Japanese companies rarely developed distinct strategic positions of the kind discussed in this article. Those that did—Sony, Canon, and Sega, for example—were the exception rather than the rule. Most Japanese companies imitate and emulate one another. All rivals offer most if not all product varieties, features, and services; they employ all channels and match one anothers' plant configurations.

The dangers of Japanese-style competition are now becoming easier to recognize. In the 1980s, with rivals operating far from the productivity frontier, it seemed possible to win on both cost and quality indefinitely. Japanese companies were all able to grow in an expanding domestic economy and by penetrating global markets. They appeared unstoppable. But as the gap in operational effectiveness narrows, Japanese companies are increasingly caught in a trap of their own making. If they are to escape the mutually destructive battles now ravaging their performance, Japanese companies will have to learn strategy.

To do so, they may have to overcome strong cultural barriers. Japan is notoriously consensus oriented, and companies have a strong tendency to mediate differences among individuals rather than accentuate them. Strategy, on the other hand, requires hard choices. The Japanese also have a deeply ingrained service tradition that predisposes them to go to great lengths to satisfy any need a customer expresses. Companies that compete in that way end up blurring their distinct positioning, becoming all things to all customers.

Source: This discussion of Japan is drawn from the author's research with Hirotaka Takeuchi, with help from Mariko Sakakibara.

$5 billion-plus U.S. commercial-printing industry. The major players—R.R. Donnelley & Sons Company, Quebecor, World Color Press, and Big Flower Press—are competing head to head, serving all types of customers, offering the same array of printing technologies (gravure and web offset), investing heavily in the same new equipment, running their presses faster, and reducing crew sizes. But the resulting major productivity gains are being captured by customers and equipment suppliers, not retained in superior profitability. Even industry-leader Donnelley's profit margin, consistently higher than 7 percent in the 1980s, fell to less than 4.6 percent in 1995. This pattern is playing itself out in industry after industry. Even the Japanese, pioneers of the new competition, suffer from persistently low profits. (See Figure 2, "Japanese Companies Rarely Have Strategies.")

The second reason that improved operational effectiveness is insufficient—competitive convergence—is more subtle and insidious. The more benchmarking companies do, the more they look alike. The more that rivals outsource activities to efficient third parties, often the same ones, the more generic those activities become. As rivals imitate one another's improvements in quality, cycle times, or supplier partnerships, strategies converge and competition becomes a series of races down identical paths that no one can win. Competition based on operational effectiveness alone is mutually destructive, leading to wars of attrition that can be arrested only by limiting competition.

Competition based on operational effectiveness alone is mutually destructive, leading to wars of attrition that can be arrested only by limiting competition.

The recent wave of industry consolidation through mergers makes sense in the context of OE competition. Driven by performance pressures but lacking strategic vision, company after company has had no better idea than to buy up its rivals. The competitors left standing are often those that outlasted others, not companies with real advantage.

After a decade of impressive gains in operational effectiveness, many companies are facing diminishing returns. Continuous improvement has been etched on managers' brains. But its tools unwittingly draw companies toward imitation and homogeneity. Gradually, managers have let operational effectiveness supplant strategy. The result is zero-sum competition, static or declining prices, and pressures on costs that compromise companies' ability to invest in the business for the long term.

STRATEGY RESTS ON UNIQUE ACTIVITIES

Competitive strategy is about being different. It means deliberately choosing a different set of activities to deliver a unique mix of value.

Southwest Airlines Company, for example, offers short-haul, low-cost, point-to-point service between midsize cities and secondary airports in large cities. Southwest avoids large airports and does not fly great distances. Its customers include business travelers, families, and students. Southwest's frequent departures and low fares attract price-sensitive customers who otherwise would travel by bus or car, and convenience-oriented travelers who would choose a full-service airline on other routes.

Most managers describe strategic positioning in terms of their customers: "Southwest Airlines services price- and convenience-sensitive travelers," for example. But the essence of strategy is in the activities—choosing to perform activities differently or to perform different activities than rivals. Otherwise, a strategy is nothing more than a marketing slogan that will not withstand competition.

A full-service airline is configured to get passengers from almost any point A to any point B. To reach a large number of destinations and serve passengers with connecting flights, full-service airlines employ a hub-and-spoke system centered on major airports. To attract passengers who desire more comfort, they offer first-class or business-class service. To accommodate passengers who must change planes, they coordinate schedules and check and transfer baggage. Because some passengers will be traveling for many hours, full-service airlines serve meals.

Southwest, in contrast, tailors all its activities to deliver low-cost, convenient service on its particular type of route. Through fast turnarounds at the gate of only 15 minutes, Southwest is able to keep planes flying longer hours than rivals and provide frequent departures with fewer aircraft. Southwest does not offer meals, assigned seats, interline baggage checking, or premium classes of service. Automated ticketing at the gate encourages customers to bypass travel agents, allowing Southwest to avoid their commissions. A standardized fleet of 737 aircraft boosts the efficiency of maintenance.

Southwest has staked out a unique and valuable strategic position based on a tailored set of activities. On the routes served by Southwest, a full-service airline could never be as convenient or as low cost.

Ikea, the global furniture retailer based in Sweden, also has a clear strategic positioning. Ikea targets young furniture buyers who want style at low cost. What turns this marketing concept into a strategic positioning is the tailored set of activities that make it work. Like Southwest, Ikea has chosen to perform activities differently from its rivals. (See Figure 3.)

FIGURE 3   Finding New Positions: The Entrepreneurial Edge

Strategic competition can be thought of as the process of perceiving new positions that woo customers from established positions or draw new customers into the market. For example, superstores offering depth of merchandise in a single product category take market share from broad-line department stores offering a more limited selection in many categories. Mail-order catalogs pick off customers who crave convenience. In principle, incumbents and entrepreneurs face the same challenges in finding new strategic positions. In practice, new entrants often have the edge.

Strategic positionings are often not obvious, and finding them requires creativity and insight. New entrants often discover unique positions that have been available but simply overlooked by established competitors. Ikea, for example, recognized a customer group that had been ignored or served poorly. Circuit City Stores' entry into used cars, CarMax, is based on a new way of performing activities—extensive refurbishing of cars, product guarantees, no-haggle pricing, sophisticated use of in-house customer financing—that has long been open to incumbents.

New entrants can prosper by occupying a position that a competitor once held but has ceded through years of imitation and straddling. And entrants coming from other industries can create new positions because of distinctive activities drawn from their other business. CarMax borrows heavily from Circuit City's expertise in inventory management, credit, and other activities in consumer electronics retailing.

Most commonly, however, new positions open up because of change. New customer groups or purchase occasions arise; new needs emerge as societies evolve; new distribution channels appear; new technologies are developed; new machinery or information systems become available. When such changes happen, new entrants, unencumbered by a long history in the industry, can often more easily perceive the potential for a new way of competing. Unlike incumbents, newcomers can be more flexible because they face no trade-offs with their existing activities.

Consider the typical furniture store. Showrooms display samples of the merchandise. One area might contain 25 sofas; another will display five dining tables. But those items represent only a fraction of the choices available to customers. Dozens of books displaying fabric swatches or wood samples or alternate styles offer customers thousands of product varieties to choose from. Salespeople often escort customers through the store, answering questions and helping them navigate this maze of choices. Once a customer makes a selection, the order is relayed to a third-party manufacturer. With luck, the furniture will be delivered to the customer's home within six to eight weeks. This is a value chain that maximizes customization and service but does so at high cost.

In contrast, Ikea serves customers who are happy to trade off service for cost. Instead of having a sales associate trail customers around the store, Ikea uses a self-service model based on clear, in-store displays. Rather than rely solely on third-party manufacturers, Ikea designs its own low-cost, modular, ready-to-assemble furniture to fit its positioning. In huge stores, Ikea displays every product it sells in roomlike settings, so customers don't need a decorator to help them imagine how to put the pieces together. Adjacent to the furnished showrooms is a warehouse section with the products in boxes on pallets. Customers are expected to do their own pickup and delivery, and Ikea will even sell you a roof rack for your car that you can return for a refund on your next visit.

Although much of its low-cost position comes from having customers "do it themselves," Ikea offers a number of extra services that its competitors do not.

In-store child care is one. Extended hours are another. Those services are uniquely aligned with the needs of its customers, who are young, not wealthy, likely to have children (but no nanny), and, because they work for a living, have a need to shop at odd hours.

The Origins of Strategic Positions

Strategic positions emerge from three distinct sources, which are not mutually exclusive and often overlap. First, positioning can be based on producing a subset of an industry's products or services. I call this *variety-based positioning* because it is based on the choice of product or service varieties rather than customer segments. Variety-based positioning makes economic sense when a company can best produce particular products or services using distinctive sets of activities.

Jiffy Lube International, for instance, specializes in automotive lubricants and does not offer other car repair or maintenance services. Its value chain produces faster service at a lower cost than broader line repair shops, a combination so attractive that many customers subdivide their purchases, buying oil changes from the focused competitor, Jiffy Lube, and going to rivals for other services.

The Vanguard Group, a leader in the mutual fund industry, is another example of variety-based positioning. Vanguard provides an array of common stock, bond, and money market funds that offer predictable performance and rock-bottom expenses. The company's investment approach deliberately sacrifices the possibility of extraordinary performance in any one year for good relative performance in every year. Vanguard is known, for example, for its index funds. It avoids making bets on interest rates and steers clear of narrow stock groups. Fund managers keep trading levels low, which holds expenses down; in addition, the company discourages customers from rapid buying and selling because doing so drives up costs and can force a fund manager to trade in order to deploy new capital and raise cash for redemptions. Vanguard also takes a consistent low-cost approach to managing distribution, customer service, and marketing. Many investors include one or more Vanguard funds in their portfolio, while buying aggressively managed or specialized funds from competitors.

The people who use Vanguard or Jiffy Lube are responding to a superior value chain for a particular type of service. A variety-based positioning can serve a wide array of customers, but for most it will meet only a subset of their needs.

A second basis for positioning is that of serving most or all the needs of a particular group of customers. I call this *needs-based positioning*, which comes closer to traditional thinking about targeting a segment of customers. It arises when there are groups of customers with differing needs, and when a tailored set of activities can serve those needs best. Some groups of customers are more price sensitive than others, demand different product features, and need varying amounts of information, support, and services. Ikea's customers are a good example of such a group. Ikea seeks to meet all the home furnishing needs of its target customers, not just a subset of them.

A variant of needs-based positioning arises when the same customer has different needs on different occasions or for different types of transactions. The same person, for example, may have different needs when traveling on business than when traveling for pleasure with the family. Buyers of cans—beverage companies, for example—will likely have different needs from their primary supplier than from their secondary source.

It is intuitive for most managers to conceive of their business in terms of the customers' needs they are meeting. But a critical element of needs-based positioning is not at all intuitive and is often overlooked. Differences in needs will not translate into meaningful positions unless the best set of activities to satisfy them *also* differs. If that were not the case, every competitor could meet those same needs, and there would be nothing unique or valuable about the positioning.

In private banking, for example, Bessemer Trust Company targets families with a minimum of $5 million in investable assets who want capital preservation combined with wealth accumulation. By assigning one sophisticated account officer for every 14 families, Bessemer has configured its activities for personalized service. Meetings, for example, are more likely to be held at a client's ranch or yacht than in the office. Bessemer offers a wide array of customized services, including investment management and estate administration, oversight of oil and gas investments, and accounting for racehorses and aircraft. Loans, a staple of most private banks, are rarely needed by Bessemer's clients and make up a tiny fraction of its client balances and income. Despite the most generous compensation of account officers and the highest personnel cost as a percentage of operating expenses, Bessemer's differentiation with its target families produces a return on equity estimated to be the highest of any private banking competitor.

Citibank's private bank, on the other hand, serves clients with minimum assets of about $250,000 who, in contrast to Bessemer's clients, want convenient access to loans—from jumbo mortgages to deal financing. Citibank's account managers are primarily lenders. When clients need other services, their account manager refers them to other Citibank specialists, each of whom handles prepackaged products. Citibank's system is less customized than Bessemer's and allows it to have a lower manager-to-client ratio of 1:125. Biannual office meetings are offered only for the largest clients. Both Bessemer and Citibank have tailored their activities to meet the needs of a different group of private banking customers. The same value chain cannot profitably meet the needs of both groups.

The third basis for positioning is that of segmenting customers who are accessible in different ways. Although their needs are similar to those of other customers, the best configuration of activities to reach them is different. I call this *access-based positioning*. Access can be a function of customer geography or customer scale—or of anything that requires a different set of activities to reach customers in the best way.

Segmenting by access is less common and less well understood than the other two bases. Carmike Cinemas, for example, operates movie theaters exclusively in cities and towns with populations under 200,000. How does Carmike make money in markets that are not only small but also won't support big-city ticket prices? It does so through a set of activities that result in a lean cost structure. Carmike's small-town customers can be served through standardized, low-cost theater complexes requiring fewer screens and less sophisticated projection technology than big-city theaters. The company's proprietary information system and management process eliminate the need for local administrative staff beyond a single theater manager. Carmike also reaps advantages from centralized purchasing, lower rent and payroll costs (because of its locations), and rock-bottom corporate overhead of 2 percent (the industry average is 5 percent). Operating in small communities also allows Carmike to practice a highly personal form of marketing in which the theater manager knows patrons and promotes attendance through personal contacts. By being the dominant if not the only theater in its markets—the main competition is often the high school

FIGURE 4   The Connection with Generic Strategies

In *Competitive Strategy* (Free Press, 1985), I introduced the concept of generic strategies—cost leadership, differentiation, and focus—to represent the alternative strategic positions in an industry. The generic strategies remain useful to characterize strategic positions at the simplest and broadest level. Vanguard, for instance, is an example of a cost leadership strategy, whereas Ikea, with its narrow customer group, is an example of cost-based focus. Neutrogena is a focused differentiator. The bases for positioning—varieties, needs, and access—carry the understanding of those generic strategies to a greater level of specificity. Ikea and Southwest are both cost-based focusers, for example, but Ikea's focus is based on the needs of a customer group, and Southwest's is based on offering a particular service variety.

The generic strategies framework introduced the need to choose in order to avoid becoming caught between what I then described as the inherent contradictions of different strategies. Trade-offs between the activities of incompatible positions explain those contradictions. Witness Continental Lite, which tried and failed to compete in two ways at once.

football team—Carmike is also able to get its pick of films and negotiate better terms with distributors.

Rural versus urban-based customers are one example of access driving differences in activities. Serving small rather than large customers or densely rather than sparsely situated customers are other examples in which the best way to configure marketing, order processing, logistics, and after-sale service activities to meet the similar needs of distinct groups will often differ.

Positioning is not only about carving out a niche. A position emerging from any of the sources can be broad or narrow. (See Figure 4.) A focused competitor, such as Ikea, targets the special needs of a subset of customers and designs its activities accordingly. Focused competitors thrive on groups of customers who are overserved (and hence overpriced) by more broadly targeted competitors, or underserved (and hence underpriced). A broadly targeted competitor—for example, Vanguard or Delta Air Lines—serves a wide array of customers, performing a set of activities designed to meet their common needs. It ignores or meets only partially the more idiosyncratic needs of particular customer groups.

Whatever the basis—variety, needs, access, or some combination of the three—positioning requires a tailored set of activities because it is always a function of differences on the supply side; that is, of differences in activities. However, positioning is not always a function of differences on the demand, or customer, side. Variety and access positionings, in particular, do not rely on *any* customer differences. In practice, however, variety or access differences often accompany needs differences. The tastes—that is, the needs—of Carmike's small-town customers, for instance, run more toward comedies, Westerns, action films, and family entertainment. Carmike does not run any films rated NC-17.

Strategy is the creation of a unique and valuable position, involving a different set of activities.

Having defined positioning, we can now begin to answer the question, "What is strategy?" Strategy is the creation of a unique and valuable position, involving a different set of activities. If there were only one ideal position, there would be no need for strategy. Companies would face a simple imperative—win the race to discover and preempt it. The essence of strategic positioning is to choose activities that are different from rivals'. If the same set of activities were best to produce all varieties, meet all needs, and access all customers, companies could easily shift among them and operational effectiveness would determine performance.

A SUSTAINABLE STRATEGIC POSITION REQUIRES TRADE-OFFS

Choosing a unique position, however, is not enough to guarantee a sustainable advantage. A valuable position will attract imitation by incumbents, who are likely to copy it in one of two ways.

First, a competitor can reposition itself to match the superior performer. J. C. Penney, for instance, has been repositioning itself from a Sears clone to a more upscale, fashion-oriented, soft-goods retailer. A second and far more common type of imitation is straddling. The straddler seeks to match the benefits of a successful position while maintaining its existing position. It grafts new features, services, or technologies onto the activities it already performs.

For those who argue that competitors can copy any market position, the airline industry is a perfect test case. It would seem that nearly any competitor could imitate any other airline's activities. Any airline can buy the same planes, lease the gates, and match the menus and ticketing and baggage handling services offered by other airlines.

Continental Airlines saw how well Southwest was doing and decided to straddle. While maintaining its position as a full-service airline, Continental also set out to match Southwest on a number of point-to-point routes. The airline dubbed the new service Continental Lite. It eliminated meals and first-class service, increased departure frequency, lowered fares, and shortened turnaround time at the gate. Because Continental remained a full-service airline on other routes, it continued to use travel agents and its mixed fleet of planes and to provide baggage checking and seat assignments.

But a strategic position is not sustainable unless there are trade-offs with other positions. Trade-offs occur when activities are incompatible. Simply put, a trade-off means that more of one thing necessitates less of another. An airline can choose to serve meals—adding cost and slowing turnaround time at the gate—or it can choose not to, but it cannot do both without bearing major inefficiencies.

Trade-offs create the need for choice and protect against repositioners and straddlers. Consider Neutrogena soap. Neutrogena Corporation's variety-based positioning is built on a "kind to the skin," residue-free soap formulated for pH balance. With a large detail force calling on dermatologists, Neutrogena's marketing strategy looks more like a drug company's than a soap maker's. It advertises in medical journals, sends direct mail to doctors, attends medical conferences, and performs research at its own Skincare Institute. To reinforce its positioning, Neutrogena originally focused its distribution on drugstores and avoided price promotions. Neutrogena uses a slow, more expensive manufacturing process to mold its fragile soap.

In choosing this position, Neutrogena said no to the deodorants and skin softeners that many customers desire in their soap. It gave up the large-volume potential of selling through supermarkets and using price promotions. It sacrificed manufacturing efficiencies to achieve the soap's desired attributes. In its original positioning, Neutrogena made a whole raft of trade-offs like those, trade-offs that protected the company from imitators.

Trade-offs arise for three reasons. The first is inconsistencies in image or reputation. A company known for delivering one kind of value may lack credibility and confuse customers—or even undermine its reputation—if it delivers another kind of value or attempts to deliver two inconsistent things at the same time. For example, Ivory soap, with its position as a basic, inexpensive everyday soap would have a hard time reshaping its image to match Neutrogena's premium "medical" reputation. Efforts to create a new image typically cost tens or even hundreds of millions of dollars in a major industry—a powerful barrier to imitation.

Second, and more important, trade-offs arise from activities themselves. Different positions (with their tailored activities) require different product configurations, different equipment, different employee behavior, different skills, and different management systems. Many trade-offs reflect inflexibilities in machinery, people, or systems. The more Ikea has configured its activities to lower costs by having its customers do their own assembly and delivery, the less able it is to satisfy customers who require higher levels of service.

However, trade-offs can be even more basic. In general, value is destroyed if an activity is overdesigned or underdesigned for its use. For example, even if a given salesperson were capable of providing a high level of assistance to one customer and none to another, the salesperson's talent (and some of his or her cost) would be wasted on the second customer. Moreover, productivity can improve when variation of an activity is limited. By providing a high level of assistance all the time, the salesperson and the entire sales activity can often achieve efficiencies of learning and scale.

Finally, trade-offs arise from limits on internal coordination and control. By clearly choosing to compete in one way and not another, senior management makes organizational priorities clear. Companies that try to be all things to all customers, in contrast, risk confusion in the trenches as employees attempt to make day-to-day operating decisions without a clear framework.

Positioning trade-offs are pervasive in competition and essential to strategy. They create the need for choice and purposefully limit what a company offers.

Positioning trade-offs are pervasive in competition and essential to strategy. They create the need for choice and purposefully limit what a company offers. They deter straddling or repositioning, because competitors that engage in those approaches undermine their strategies and degrade the value of their existing activities.

Trade-offs ultimately grounded Continental Lite. The airline lost hundreds of millions of dollars, and the CEO lost his job. Its planes were delayed leaving congested hub cities or slowed at the gate by baggage transfers. Late flights and cancellations generated a thousand complaints a day. Continental Lite could not afford to compete on price and still pay standard travel-agent commissions, but neither could it do without agents for its full-service business. The airline compromised by cutting commissions for all Continental flights across the board. Similarly, it could not afford to offer the same frequent-flier benefits to travelers paying the much lower ticket price for Lite service. It compromised again by lowering the rewards of Continental's entire frequent-flier program. The results: angry travel agents and full-service customers.

Continental tried to compete in two ways at once. In trying to be low cost on some routes and full service on others, Continental paid an enormous straddling penalty. If there were no trade-offs between the two positions, Continental could have succeeded. But the absence of trade-offs is a dangerous half-truth that managers must unlearn. Quality is not always free. Southwest's convenience, one kind of high quality, happens to be consistent with low costs because its frequent departures are facilitated by a number of low-cost practices—fast gate turnarounds and automated ticketing, for example. However, other dimensions of airline quality—an assigned seat, a meal, or baggage transfer—require costs to provide.

In general, false trade-offs between cost and quality occur primarily when there is redundant or wasted effort, poor control or accuracy, or weak coordination. Simultaneous improvement of cost and differentiation is possible only when a company begins far behind the productivity frontier or when the frontier shifts outward. At the frontier, where companies have achieved current best practice, the trade-off between cost and differentiation is very real indeed.

After a decade of enjoying productivity advantages, Honda Motor Company and Toyota Motor Corporation recently bumped up against the frontier. In 1995, faced with increasing customer resistance to higher automobile prices, Honda found that the only way to produce a less-expensive car was to skimp on features. In the United States, it replaced the rear disk brakes on the Civic with lower-cost drum brakes and used cheaper fabric for the back seat, hoping customers would not notice. Toyota tried to sell a version of its best-selling Corolla in Japan with unpainted bumpers and cheaper seats. In Toyota's case, customers rebelled, and the company quickly dropped the new model.

For the past decade, as managers have improved operational effectiveness greatly, they have internalized the idea that eliminating trade-offs is a good thing. But if there are no trade-offs companies will never achieve a sustainable advantage. They will have to run faster and faster just to stay in place.

As we return to the question, What is strategy? we see that trade-offs add a new dimension to the answer. Strategy is making trade-offs in competing. The essence of strategy is choosing what *not* to do. Without trade-offs, there would be no need for choice and thus no need for strategy. Any good idea could and would be quickly imitated. Again, performance would once again depend wholly on operational effectiveness.

FIT DRIVES BOTH COMPETITIVE ADVANTAGE AND SUSTAINABILITY

Positioning choices determine not only which activities a company will perform and how it will configure individual activities but also how activities relate to one another. While operational effectiveness is about achieving excellence in individual activities, or functions, strategy is about *combining* activities. (See Figure 5.)

Southwest's rapid gate turnaround, which allows frequent departures and greater use of aircraft, is essential to its high-convenience, low-cost positioning. But how does Southwest achieve it? Part of the answer lies in the company's well-paid gate and ground crews, whose productivity in turnarounds is enhanced by flexible union rules. But the bigger part of the answer lies in how Southwest performs other activities. With no meals, no seat assignment, and no interline baggage transfers, Southwest avoids having to perform activities that slow down other airlines. It selects airports and routes to avoid congestion that introduces delays. Southwest's strict limits on the type and length of routes make standardized aircraft possible: every aircraft Southwest turns is a Boeing 737.

What is Southwest's core competence? Its key success factors? The correct answer is that everything matters. Southwest's strategy involves a whole system of activities, not a collection of parts. Its competitive advantage comes from the way its activities fit and reinforce one another.

Fit locks out imitators by creating a chain that is as strong as its *strongest* link. As in most companies with good strategies, Southwest's

Fit locks out imitators by creating a chain that is as strong as its strongest link.

FIGURE 5   Mapping Activity Systems

Activity-system maps, such as this one for Ikea, show how a company's strategic position is contained in a set of tailored activities designed to deliver it. In companies with a clear strategic position, a number of higher-order strategic themes (in dark blue) can be identified and implemented through clusters of tightly linked activities (in light blue).

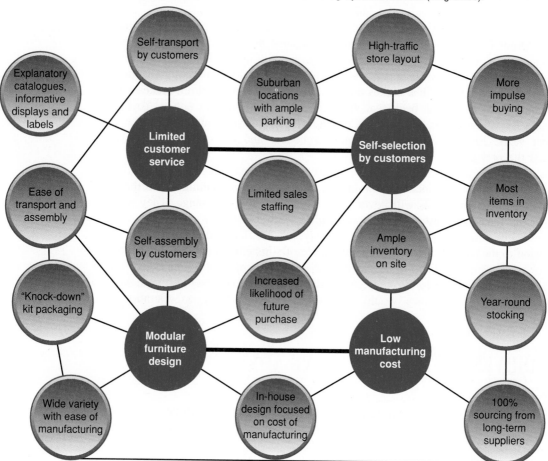

activities complement one another in ways that create real economic value. One activity's cost, for example, is lowered because of the way other activities are performed. Similarly, one activity's value to customers can be enhanced by a company's other activities. That is the way strategic fit creates competitive advantage and superior profitability.

Types of Fit

The importance of fit among functional policies is one of the oldest ideas in strategy. Gradually, however, it has been supplanted on the management agenda. Rather than seeing the company as a whole, managers have turned to "core" competencies, "critical" resources, and "key" success factors. In fact, fit is a far more central component of competitive advantage than most realize.

Fit is important because discrete activities often affect one another. A sophisticated salesforce, for example, confers a greater advantage when the company's product embodies premium technology and its marketing approach emphasizes customer assistance and support. A production line with high levels of model variety is more valuable when combined with an inventory and order processing system that minimizes the need for stocking finished goods, a sales process equipped to explain and encourage customization, and an advertising theme that stresses the benefits of product variations that meet a customer's special needs. Such complementarities are pervasive in strategy. Although some fit among activities is generic and applies to many companies, the most valuable fit is strategy-specific because it enhances a position's uniqueness and amplifies trade-offs.[2] (See Figures 6 and 7.)

There are three types of fit, although they are not mutually exclusive. First-order fit is *simple consistency* between each activity (function) and the overall strategy. Vanguard, for example, aligns all activities with its low-cost strategy. It minimizes portfolio turnover and does not need highly compensated money managers. The company distributes its funds directly, avoiding commissions to brokers. It also limits advertising, relying instead on public relations and word-of-mouth recommendations. Vanguard ties its employees' bonuses to cost savings.

Consistency ensures that the competitive advantages of activities cumulate and do not erode or cancel themselves out. It makes the strategy easier to communicate to customers, employees, and shareholders, and improves implementation through single-mindedness in the corporation.

Second-order fit occurs when *activities are reinforcing*. Neutrogena, for example, markets to upscale hotels eager to offer their guests a soap recommended by dermatologists. Hotels grant Neutrogena the privilege of using its customary packaging while requiring other soaps to feature the hotel's name. Once guests have tried Neutrogena in a luxury hotel, they are more likely to purchase it at the drugstore or ask their doctor about it. Thus Neutrogena's medical and hotel marketing activities reinforce one another, lowering total marketing costs.

In another example, Bic Corporation sells a narrow line of standard, low-priced pens to virtually all major customer markets (retail, commercial, promotional, and giveaway) through virtually all available channels. As with any variety-based positioning serving a broad group of customers, Bic emphasizes a common need (low price for an acceptable pen) and uses marketing approaches with a broad reach (a large sales force and heavy television advertising). Bic gains the benefits of consistency across nearly all activities, including product design that emphasizes ease of manufacturing, plants configured for low cost, aggressive purchasing to minimize material costs, and in-house parts production whenever the economics dictate.

Yet Bic goes beyond simple consistency because its activities are reinforcing. For example, the company uses point-of-sale displays and frequent packaging changes to stimulate impulse buying. To handle point-of-sale tasks, a company needs a large salesforce. Bic's is the largest in its industry, and it handles point-of-sale activities better than its rivals do. Moreover, the combination of point-of-sale activity, heavy television advertising, and packaging changes yields far more than impulse buying of any activity in isolation could.

Third-order fit goes beyond activity reinforcement to what I call *optimization of effort*. The Gap, a retailer of casual clothes, considers product availability in its stores a critical element of its strategy. The Gap could keep products either by holding store inventory or by restocking from warehouses. The Gap has optimized its effort across these activities by restocking its selection of basic clothing almost daily out of three warehouses, thereby minimizing the need to carry large in-store inventories. The emphasis is on restocking because The Gap's merchandising strategy sticks to basic

FIGURE 6   Vanguard's Activity System

Activity-system maps can be useful for examining and strengthening strategic fit. A set of basic questions should guide the process. First, is each activity consistent with the overall positioning — the varieties produced, the needs served, and the type of customers accessed? Ask those responsible for each activity to identify how other activities within the company improve or detract from their performance. Second, are there ways to strengthen how activities and groups of activities reinforce one another? Finally, could changes in one activity eliminate the need to perform others?

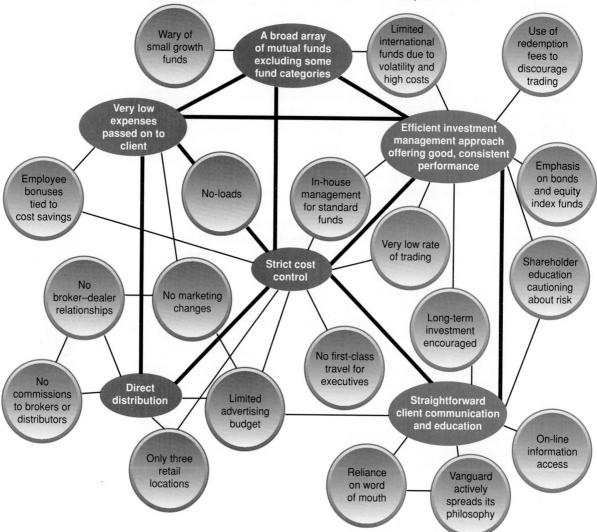

items in relatively few colors. While comparable retailers achieve turns of three to four times per year, The Gap turns its inventory seven and a half times per year. Rapid restocking, moreover, reduces the cost of implementing The Gap's short model cycle, which is six to eight weeks long.[3]

Coordination and information exchange across activities to eliminate redundancy and minimize wasted effort are the most basic types of effort optimization. But there are higher levels as well. Product design choices, for example, can eliminate the need

FIGURE 7   Southwest Airlines' Activity System

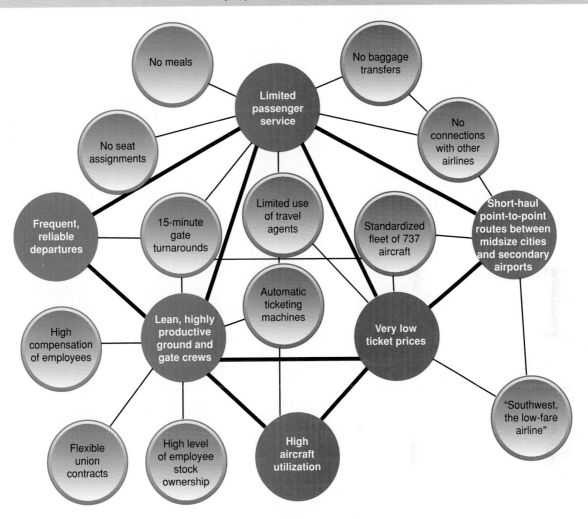

for after-sale service or make it possible for customers to perform service activities themselves. Similarly, coordination with suppliers or distribution channels can eliminate the need for some in-house activities, such as end-user training.

In all three types of fit, the whole matters more than any individual part. Competitive advantage grows out of the *entire system* of activities. The fit among activities substantially reduces cost or increases differentiation. Beyond that, the competitive value of individual activities—or the associated skills, competencies, or resources—cannot be decoupled from the system or the strategy. Thus in competitive companies it can be misleading to explain success by specifying individual strengths, core competencies, or critical resources. The list of strengths cuts across many functions, and one strength blends into others. It is more useful to think in terms of themes that pervade many activities, such as low cost, a particular notion of customer service, or a particular conception of the value delivered. These themes are embodied in nests of tightly linked activities.

Fit and Sustainability

Strategic fit among many activities is fundamental not only to competitive advantage but also to the sustainability of that advantage. It is harder for a rival to match an array of interlocked activities than it is merely to imitate a particular salesforce approach, match a process technology, or replicate a set of product features. Positions built on systems of activities are far more sustainable than those built on individual activities. (See Figure 8.)

Consider this simple exercise. The probability that competitors can match any activity is often less than one. The probabilities then quickly compound to make matching the entire system highly unlikely ($.9 \times .9 = .81$; $.9 \times .9 \times .9 \times .9 = .66$, and so on). Existing companies that try to reposition or straddle will be forced to reconfigure many activities. And even new entrants, though they do not confront the trade-offs facing established rivals, still face formidable barriers to imitation.

The more a company's positioning rests on activity systems with second- and third-order fit, the more sustainable its advantage will be. Such systems, by their very nature, are usually difficult to untangle from outside the company and therefore hard to imitate. And even if rivals can identify the relevant interconnections, they will have difficulty replicating them. Achieving fit is difficult because it requires the integration of decisions and actions across many independent subunits.

A competitor seeking to match an activity system gains little by imitating only some activities and not matching the whole. Performance does not improve; it can decline. Recall Continental Lite's disastrous attempt to imitate Southwest.

Finally, fit among a company's activities creates pressures and incentives to improve operational effectiveness, which makes imitation even harder. Fit means that poor performance in one activity will degrade the performance in others, so that weaknesses are exposed and more prone to get attention. Conversely, improvements in one activity will pay dividends in others. Companies with strong fit among their activities are rarely inviting targets. Their superiority in strategy and in execution only compounds their advantages and raises the hurdle for imitators.

When activities complement one another, rivals will get little benefit from imitation unless they successfully match the whole system. Such situations tend to promote winner-take-all competition. The company that builds the best activity

---

FIGURE 8   Alternative Views of Strategy

The Implicit Strategy Model of the Past Decade	Sustainable Competitive Advantage
• One ideal competitive position in the industry	• Unique competitive position for the company
• Benchmarking of all activities and achieving best practice	• Activities tailored to strategy
• Aggressive outsourcing and partnering to gain efficiencies	• Clear trade-offs and choices vis-à-vis competitors
• Advantages rest on a few key success factors, critical resources, core competencies	• Competitive advantage arises from fit across activities
• Flexibility and rapid responses to all competitive and market changes	• Sustainability comes from the activity system, not the parts
	• Operational effectiveness a given

system—Toys R Us, for instance—wins, while rivals with similar strategies—Child World and Lionel Leisure—fall behind. Thus finding a new strategic position is often preferable to being the second or third imitator of an occupied position.

The most viable positions are those whose activity systems are incompatible because of trade-offs. Strategic positioning sets the trade-off rules that define how individual activities will be configured and integrated. Seeing strategy in terms of activity systems only makes it clearer why organizational structure, systems, and processes need to be strategy-specific. Tailoring organization to strategy, in turn, makes complementarities more achievable and contributes to sustainability.

One implication is that strategic positions should have a horizon of a decade or more, not of a single planning cycle. Continuity fosters improvements in individual activities and the fit across activities, allowing an organization to build unique capabilities and skills tailored to its strategy. Continuity also reinforces a company's identity.

Conversely, frequent shifts in positioning are costly. Not only must a company reconfigure individual activities, but it must also realign entire systems. Some activities may never catch up to the vacillating strategy. The inevitable result of frequent shifts in strategy, or of failure to choose a distinct position in the first place, is "me-too" or hedged activity configurations, inconsistencies across functions, and organizational dissonance.

What is strategy? We can now complete the answer to this question. Strategy is creating fit among a company's activities. The success of a strategy depends on doing many things well—not just a few—and integrating among them. If there is no fit among activities, there is no distinctive strategy and little sustainability. Management reverts to the simpler task of overseeing independent functions, and operational effectiveness determines an organization's relative performance.

REDISCOVERING STRATEGY

The Failure to Choose

Why do so many companies fail to have a strategy? Why do managers avoid making strategic choices? Or, having made them in the past, why do managers so often let strategies decay and blur?

Commonly, the threats to strategy are seen to emanate from outside a company because of changes in technology or the behavior of competitors. Although external changes can be the problem, the greater threat to strategy often comes from within. A sound strategy is undermined by a misguided view of competition, by organizational failures, and, especially, by the desire to grow.

Managers have become confused about the necessity of making choices. When many companies operate far from the productivity frontier, trade-offs appear unnecessary. It can seem that a well-run company should be able to beat its ineffective rivals on all dimensions simultaneously. Taught by popular management thinkers that they do not have to make trade-offs, managers have acquired a macho sense that to do so is a sign of weakness.

Unnerved by forecasts of hypercompetition, managers increase its likelihood by imitating everything about their competitors. Exhorted to think in terms of revolution, managers chase every new technology for its own sake.

The pursuit of operational effectiveness is seductive because it is concrete and actionable. Over the past decade, managers have been under increasing pressure to deliver tangible, measurable performance improvements. Programs in operational effectiveness produce reassuring progress, although superior profitability may remain elusive. Business publications and consultants flood the market with information about what other companies are doing, reinforcing the best-practice mentality. Caught up in the race for operational effectiveness, many managers simply do not understand the need to have a strategy.

Companies avoid or blur strategic choices for other reasons as well. Conventional wisdom within an industry is often strong, homogenizing competition. Some managers mistake "customer focus" to mean they must serve all customer needs or respond to every request from distribution channels. Others cite the desire to preserve flexibility.

Organizational realities also work against strategy. Trade-offs are frightening, and making no choice is sometimes preferred to risking blame for a bad choice. Companies imitate one another in a type of herd behavior, each assuming rivals know something they do not. Newly empowered employees, who are urged to seek every possible source of improvement, often lack a vision of the whole and the perspective to recognize trade-offs. The failure to choose sometimes comes down to the reluctance to disappoint valued managers or employees.

The Growth Trap

Among all other influences, the desire to grow has perhaps the most perverse effect on strategy. Trade-offs and limits appear to constrain growth. Serving one group of customers and excluding others, for instance, places a real or imagined limit on revenue growth. Broadly targeted strategies emphasizing low price result in lost sales with customers sensitive to features or service. Differentiators lose sales to price-sensitive customers.

Managers are constantly tempted to take incremental steps that surpass those limits but blur a company's strategic position. Eventually, pressures to grow or apparent saturation of the target market lead managers to broaden the position by extending product lines, adding new features, imitating competitors' popular services, matching processes, and even making acquisitions. For years, Maytag Corporation's success was based on its focus on reliable, durable washers and dryers, later extended to include dishwashers. However, conventional wisdom emerging within the industry supported the notion of selling a full line of products. Concerned with slow industry growth and competition from broad-line appliance makers, Maytag was pressured by dealers and encouraged by customers to extend its line. Maytag expanded into refrigerators and cooking products under the Maytag brand and acquired other brands—Jenn-Air, Hardwick Stove, Hoover, Admiral, and Magic Chef—with disparate positions. Maytag has grown substantially from $684 million in 1985 to a peak of $3.4 billion in 1994, but return on sales has declined from 8 percent to 12 percent in the 1970s and 1980s to an average of less than 1 percent between 1989 and 1995. Cost cutting will improve this performance, but laundry and dishwasher products still anchor Maytag's profitability.

Neutrogena may have fallen into the same trap. In the early 1990s, its U.S. distribution broadened to include mass merchandisers such as Wal-Mart Stores. Under the Neutrogena name, the company expanded into a wide variety of products—eye-makeup remover and shampoo, for example—in which it was not unique and which diluted its image, and it began turning to price promotions.

Compromises and inconsistencies in the pursuit of growth will erode the competitive advantage a company had with its original varieties or target customers. At-

---

FIGURE 9　Reconnecting with Strategy

Most companies owe their initial success to a unique strategic position involving clear trade-offs. Activities once were aligned with that position. The passage of time and the pressures of growth, however, led to compromises that were, at first, almost imperceptible. Through a succession of incremental changes that each seemed sensible at the time, many established companies have compromised their way to homogeneity with their rivals.

The issue here is not with the companies whose historical position is no longer viable; their challenge is to start over, just as a new entrant would. At issue is a far more common phenomenon: the established company achieving mediocre returns and lacking a clear strategy. Through incremental additions of product varieties, incremental efforts to serve new customer groups, and emulation of rivals' activities, the existing company loses its clear competitive position. Typically, the company has matched many of its competitors' offerings and practices and attempts to sell to most customer groups.

A number of approaches can help a company reconnect with strategy. The first is a careful look at what it already does. Within most well-established companies is a core of uniqueness. It is identified by answering questions such as the following:

- Which of our product or service varieties are the most distinctive?
- Which of our product or service varieties are the most profitable?
- Which of our customers are the most satisfied?
- Which customers, channels, or purchase occasions are the most profitable?
- Which of the activities in our value chain are the most different and effective?

Around this core of uniqueness are encrustations added incrementally over time. Like barnacles, they must be removed to reveal the underlying strategic positioning. A small percentage of varieties or customers may well account for most of a company's sales and especially its profits. The challenge, then, is to refocus on the unique core and realign the company's activities with it. Customers and product varieties at the periphery can be sold or allowed through inattention or price increases to fade away.

A company's history can also be instructive. What was the vision of the founder? What were the products and customers that made the company? Looking backward, one can reexamine the original strategy to see if it is still valid. Can the historical positioning be implemented in a modern way, one consistent with today's technologies and practices? This sort of thinking may lead to a commitment to renew the strategy and may challenge the organization to recover its distinctiveness. Such a challenge can be galvanizing and can instill the confidence to make the needed trade-offs.

---

tempts to compete in several ways at once create confusion and undermine organizational motivation and focus. Profits fall, but more revenue is seen as the answer. Managers are unable to make choices, so the company embarks on a new round of broadening and compromises. Often, rivals continue to match each other until desperation breaks the cycle, resulting in a merger or downsizing to the original positioning. For a discussion of "reconnecting with strategy," see Figure 9.

Profitable Growth

Many companies, after a decade of restructuring and cost-cutting, are turning their attention to growth. Too often, efforts to grow blur uniqueness, create compromises, reduce fit, and ultimately undermine competitive advantage. In fact, the growth imperative is hazardous to strategy. (See Figure 10.)

FIGURE 10   Emerging Industries and Technologies

Developing a strategy in a newly emerging industry or in a business undergoing revolutionary technological changes is a daunting proposition. In such cases, managers face a high level of uncertainty about the needs of customers, the products and services that will prove to be the most desired, and the best configuration of activities and technologies to deliver them. Because of all this uncertainty, imitation and hedging are rampant: unable to risk being wrong or left behind, companies match all features, offer all new services, and explore all technologies.

During such periods in an industry's development, its basic productivity frontier is being established or reestablished. Explosive growth can make such times profitable for many companies, but profits will be temporary because imitation and strategic convergence will ultimately destroy industry profitability. The companies that are enduringly successful will be those that begin as early as possible to define and embody in their activities a unique competitive position. A period of imitation may be inevitable in emerging industries, but that period reflects the level of uncertainty rather than a desired state of affairs.

In high-tech industries, this imitation phase often continues much longer than it should. Enraptured by technological change itself, companies pack more features—most of which are never used—into their products while slashing prices across the board. Rarely are trade-offs even considered. The drive for growth to satisfy market pressures leads companies into every product area. Although a few companies with fundamental advantages prosper, the majority are doomed to a rat race no one can win.

Ironically, the popular business press, focused on hot, emerging industries, is prone to presenting these special cases as proof that we have entered a new era of competition in which none of the old rules are valid. In fact, the opposite is true.

What approaches to growth preserve and reinforce strategy? Broadly, the prescription is to concentrate on deepening a strategic position rather than broadening and compromising it. One approach is to look for extensions of the strategy that leverage the existing activity system by offering features or services that rivals would find impossible or costly to match on a stand-alone basis. In other words, managers can ask themselves which activities, features, or forms of competition are feasible or less costly to them because of complementary activities that their company performs.

Deepening a position involves making the company's activities more distinctive, strengthening fit, and communicating the strategy better to those customers who should value it. But many companies succumb to the temptation to chase "easy" growth by adding hot features, products, or services without screening them or adapting them to their strategy. Or they target new customers or markets in which the company has little special to offer. A company can often grow faster—and far more profitably—by better penetrating needs and varieties where it is distinctive than by slugging it out in potentially higher growth arenas in which the company lacks uniqueness. Carmike, now the largest theater chain in the United States, owes its rapid growth to its disciplined concentration on small markets. The company quickly sells any big-city theaters that come to it as part of an acquisition.

Globalization often allows growth that is consistent with strategy, opening up larger markets for a focused strategy. Unlike broadening domestically, expanding globally is likely to leverage and reinforce a company's unique position and identity.

Companies seeking growth through broadening within their industry can best contain the risks to strategy by creating stand-alone units, each with its own brand name and tailored activities. Maytag has clearly struggled with this issue. On the one hand, it has organized its premium and value brands into separate units with different strategic positions. On the other, it has created an umbrella appliance company for all its brands to gain critical mass. With shared design, manufacturing, distribution, and customer service, it will be hard to avoid homogenization. If a given business unit attempts to compete with different positions for different products or customers, avoiding compromise is nearly impossible.

The Role of Leadership

The challenge of developing or reestablishing a clear strategy is often primarily an organizational one and depends on leadership. With so many forces at work against making choices and trade-offs in organizations, a clear intellectual framework to guide strategy is a necessary counterweight. Moreover, strong leaders willing to make choices are essential.

In many companies, leadership has degenerated into orchestrating operational improvements and making deals. But the leader's role is broader and far more important. General management is more than the stewardship of individual function. Its core is strategy: defining and communicating the company's unique position, making trade-offs, and forging fit among activities. The leader must provide the discipline to decide which industry changes and customer needs the company will respond to, while avoiding organizational distractions and maintaining the company's distinctiveness. Managers at lower levels lack the perspective and the confidence to maintain a strategy. There will be constant pressures to compromise, relax trade-offs, and emulate rivals. One of the leader's jobs is to teach others in the organization about strategy—and to say no.

Strategy renders choices about what not to do as important as choices about what to do. Indeed, setting limits is another function of leadership. Deciding which target group of customers, varieties, and needs the company should serve is fundamental to developing a strategy. But so is deciding not to serve other customers or needs and not to offer certain features or services. Thus strategy requires constant discipline and clear communication. Indeed, one of the most important functions of an explicit, communicated strategy is to guide employees in making choices that arise because of trade-offs in their individual activities and in day-to-day decisions.

Improving operational effectiveness is a necessary part of management, but it is *not* strategy. In confusing the two, managers have unintentionally backed into a way of thinking about competition that is driving many industries toward competitive convergence, which is in no one's best interest and is not inevitable.

Managers must clearly distinguish operational effectiveness from strategy. Both are essential, but the two agendas are different.

The operational agenda involves continual improvement everywhere there are no trade-offs. Failure to do this creates vulnerability even for companies with a good strategy. The operational agenda is the proper place for constant change, flexibility, and relentless efforts to achieve best practice. In contrast, the strategic agenda is the right place for defining a unique position, making clear trade-offs, and tightening fit. It involves the continual search for ways to reinforce and extend the company's position. The strategic agenda demands discipline and continuity; its enemies are distraction and compromise.

Strategic continuity does not imply a static view of competition. A company must continually improve its operational effectiveness and actively try to shift the productivity frontier; at the same time there needs to be ongoing effort to extend its uniqueness while strengthening the fit among its activities. Strategic continuity, in fact, should make an organization's continual improvement more effective.

A company may have to change its strategy if there are major structural changes in its industry. In fact, new strategic positions often arise because of industry changes, and new entrants unencumbered by history often can exploit them more easily. However, a company's choice of a new position must be driven by the ability to find new trade-offs and leverage a new system of complementary activities into a sustainable advantage.

ENDNOTES

1. I first described the concept of activities and its use in understanding competitive advantage in *Competitive Advantage* (New York: Free Press, 1985). The ideas in this article build on and extend that thinking.

2. Paul Milgrom and John Roberts have begun to explore the economics of systems of complementary functions, activities, and functions. Their focus is on the emergence of "modern manufacturing" as a new set of complementary activities, on the tendency of companies to react to external changes with coherent bundles of internal responses, and on the need for central coordination—a strategy—to align functional managers. In the latter case, they model what has long been a bedrock principle of strategy. See Paul Milgrom and John Roberts, "The Economics of Modern Manufacturing: Technology, Strategy, and Organization," *American Economic Review* 80 (1990), pp. 511–28; Paul Milgrom, Yingyi Qian, and John Roberts, "Complementarities, Momentum, and Evolution of Modern Manufacturing," *American Economic Review* 81 (1991), pp. 84–88; and Paul Milgrom and John Roberts, "Complementarities and Fit: Strategy, Structure, and Organizational Changes in Manufacturing," *Journal of Accounting and Economics* 19 (March–May 1995), pp. 179–208.

3. Material on retail strategies is drawn in part from Jan Rivkin, "The Rise of Retail Category Killers," unpublished working paper, January 1995. Nicolaj Siggelkow prepared the case study on The Gap.

COPING WITH HYPERCOMPETITION: UTILIZING THE NEW 7S's FRAMEWORK[1]

Richard A. D'Aveni

Hypercompetition results from the dynamics of strategic maneuvering among global and innovative combatants. It creates an environment in which sustainable competitive advantage is difficult, if not impossible. To help managers deal with hypercompetition, D'Aveni offers a framework that can be used to analyze industries and competitors and to identify a firm's strengths and weaknesses.

We have seen giants of American industry, such as General Motors and IBM, shaken to their cores. Their competitive advantages, once considered unassailable, have been ripped and torn in the fierce winds of competition. Technological wonders appear overnight. Aggressive global competitors arrive on the scene. Organizations are restructured. Markets appear and fade. The weathered rule books and generic strategies once used to plot our strategies no longer work as well in this environment.

The traditional sources of advantages no longer provide long-term security. Both GM and IBM still have economies of scale, massive advertising budgets, the best distribution systems in their industries, cutting-edge R&D, deep pockets, and many other features that give them power over buyers and suppliers and that raise barriers to entry that seem impregnable. But these are not enough any more. Leadership in price and quality is also not enough to assure success. Being first is not always the same as being best. Entry barriers are trampled down or circumvented. Goliaths are brought down by clever Davids with slingshots. Welcome to the world of hypercompetition.

Source: © *Academy of Management Executive* 9, no. 3 (1995).

HYPERCOMPETITION

In hypercompetition the frequency, boldness, and aggressiveness of dynamic movement by the players accelerates to create a condition of constant disequilibrium and change.

Hypercompetition results from the dynamics of strategic maneuvering among global and innovative combatants. It is a condition of rapidly escalating competition based on price-quality positioning, competition to create new know-how and establish first-mover advantage, competition to protect or invade established product or geographic markets, and competition based on deep pockets and the creation of even deeper-pocketed alliances. In hypercompetition the frequency, boldness, and aggressiveness of dynamic movement by the players accelerates to create a condition of constant disequilibrium and change. Market stability is threatened by short product life cycles, short product design cycles, new technologies, frequent entry by unexpected outsiders, repositioning by incumbents, and radical redefinitions of market boundaries as diverse industries merge. In other words, environments escalate toward higher and higher levels of uncertainty, dynamism, heterogenity of the players, and hostility.

It is not just fast-moving, high-tech industries, such as computers, or industries shaken by deregulation, such as the airlines, that are facing this aggressive competition. There is evidence that competition is heating up across the board, even in what once seemed the most sedate industries. From software to soft drinks, from microchips to corn chips, from packaged goods to package delivery services, there are few industries that have escaped hypercompetition. As Jack Welch, CEO of General Electric, commented. "It's going to be brutal. When I said a while back that the 1980s were going to be a white-knuckle decade and the 1990s would be even tougher, I may have understated how hard it's going to get."[2]

There are few industries and companies that have escaped this shift in competitiveness. Even such seemingly comatose industries as hot sauces or such commodity strongholds as U.S. grain production have been jolted awake by the icy waters of hypercompetition.

MOVEMENT TOWARD, BUT FAILURE TO REACH, PERFECT COMPETITION

American corporations have traditionally sought established markets wherein profits were attainable. They have done so by looking for low or moderate levels of competition (see Figure 1). Low- and moderate-intensity competition occurs if a company has a monopoly (or quasi-monopoly protected by entry barriers) or if competitors implicitly or explicitly collude, allowing each other to "sustain" an advantage in one or more industries or market segments. Collusion or cooperation, while it can be useful in limiting aggressiveness, is limited because there is incentive to cheat on the collusive agreement and gain advantage. Entry and mobility barriers are destroyed by firms seeking the profit potential of industries or segments with low or moderate levels of competition. Gentlemanly agreements to stay out of each other's turf fall apart as firms learn how to break the barriers inexpensively. As competition shifts toward higher intensity, companies begin to develop new advantages rapidly and attempt to destroy competitors' advantages. This leads to a further escalation of competition into hypercompetition, at which stage companies actively work to string together a series of temporary moves that undermine competitors in an endless cycle of jockeying for position. Just one hypercompetitive player (often from abroad) is enough to trigger this cycle.

FIGURE 1 Different Levels of Competition within an Industry

Low-Intensity Competition	⇒	Moderate Competition	⇒	High-Intensity Competition	⇒	Extreme Competition

No Competition

- Monopoly.
- Legal monopoly through patents.
- Excessive profits are sustainable for years.

Competition Avoidance

- Firms position around each other but not directly against each other.
- Segmentation of markets occurs so there is only one player in each segment.
- Barriers to entry are used to limit entry of markets by competitors.
- If some small degree of segment/niche overlap occurs, firms tacitly cooperate to restrict this overlap or restrain competitive behavior.
- Long-term sustainable advantage and profits are possible, but only as long as all the competitors cooperate or respect the entry barriers.

Hypercompetition

- Firms aggressively position against one another by attempting to disadvantage opponents.
- Firms create new competitive advantages which make obsolete or match opponents' advantages in one or more of the four arenas.
- Firms attempt to stay ahead of their competitors in one or more of the arenas.
- Firms create new competitive advantages that make the opponents' advantages irrelevant by moving to compete in another arena.
- Temporary advantage and short periods of profit are achievable until competitors catch up with or outmaneuver the aggressor's last competitive move.

Perfect Competition

- All four of the traditional competitive advantages have been eliminated so the players are equal in all four arenas.
- Firms compete on price until no one makes abnormal profits.
- Normally, perfect competition is not preferred over lower levels of competition because lower levels of competition lead to more opportunity for profits.

The Trends

Monopoly	⇑ ⇑	Oligopoly	⇑ ⇑	Dynamic Competition	⇑ ⇑	Perfect Competition
(one player)		(small number of players)		(several players)		(many players)
Excessive Profits		Sustainable Profits		Intermittent or Low Profits		No Abnormal Profits

At each point firms press forward to gain new advantages or tear down those of their rivals. This movement, however, takes the industry to faster and more intense levels of competition. The most interesting aspect of this movement is that, as firms maneuver and outmaneuver each other, they are constantly pushing toward perfect competition, where no one has an advantage. However, while firms push toward perfect competition, they must attempt to avoid it because abnormal profits are not at all possible in perfectly competitive markets. In hypercompetitive markets it is possible to make temporary profits. Thus, even though perfect competition is treated as the "equilibrium" state in static economic models, it is neither a desired nor a sustainable state from the perspective of corporations seeking profits. They would prefer low and moderate levels of competition but often settle for hypercompetitive markets because the presence of a small number of aggressive foreign corporations won't cooperate enough to allow the old, more genteel levels of competition that existed in the past.

THE NEW 7S's

Paraphrasing George Bernard Shaw, while reasonable people adapt to the world, the unreasonable ones persist in trying to adapt the world to themselves. Thus, all progress depends upon the unreasonable person. In hypercompetition the reasonable strategies that focus on sustaining advantages do not lead to progress. It is not enough to merely adapt to the environment. Companies make progress in hypercompetition by the unreasonable approach of actively disrupting advantages of others to adapt the world to themselves. These strategies are embodied in the New 7S's.[3]

The new framework is designed to sustain the momentum through a series of initiatives rather than structure the firm to achieve internal fit or fit with today's external environment.

My studies of successful and unsuccessful companies in hypercompetitive environments reveal seven key elements of a dynamic approach to strategy. Unlike the old 7S framework, originally developed by McKinsey and Company, the new framework is based on a strategy of finding and building temporary advantages through market disruption rather than sustaining advantage and perpetuating an equilibrium. It is designed to sustain the momentum through a series of initiatives rather than structure the firm to achieve internal fit or fit with today's external environment, as if today's external conditions will persist for a long period of time.

The New 7S's are:

- Superior stakeholder satisfaction.
- Strategic soothsaying.
- Positioning for speed.
- Positioning for surprise.
- Shifting the rules of the game.
- Signaling strategic intent.
- Simultaneous and sequential strategic thrusts.

Because of the nature of the hypercompetitive environment, the New 7S's are not presented as a series of generic strategies or a recipe for success. Instead, these are key approaches that can be used to carry the firm in many different directions. They are focused on disrupting the status quo through a series of temporary advantages rather than maintaining equilibrium by sustaining advantages. The exact strategic actions formulated under this system will depend on many variables within the industry and the firm. Many types of strategic initiatives can be carried out using the New 7S's, and there are many variations.

FIGURE 2   Disruption and the New 7S's

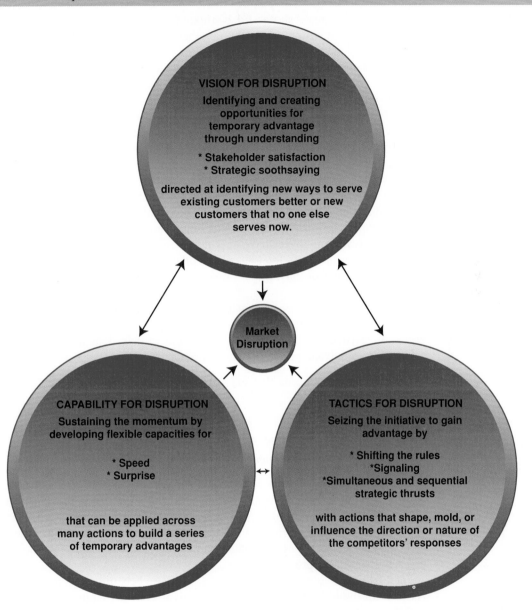

As shown in Figure 2, the New 7S's encompass three factors for effective delivery of a series of market disruptions: vision, capabilities, and tactics. What is being called for is an increased emphasis on the first two levels (vision and capabilities) and more creative approaches to the last level (tactics) than many firms currently use.

VISION FOR DISRUPTION: THE FIRST TWO S's

Successful firms learn how to disrupt the status quo. A key to their choice of a disruption is the realization that not all disruptions are good. The disruptions are those that involve the first S—the creation of a temporary ability to serve the customer better than competitors can.

Successful firms learn how to disrupt the status quo.

To create this type of disruption, successful firms prioritize customers as the most important stakeholder. This implies that employees and investors are prioritized less highly. Thus, to create successful disruptions, the firm must find a way to satisfy employees and investors even though their interests have been subordinated to customers.

Before the Pentium chip, Intel rarely asked customers what they wanted, but now they have instituted a process of concurrent engineering to get customers (and internal manufacturing) involved as early as possible. Now, when designing new chips, Intel designers visit every major customer and major software houses to ask them what they want in a chip. Intel has also provided early software simulations of its new chips to computer makers, allowing them to get a jump on designing their new machines, and has produced software compilers to help software companies use the new chip.

CEO Andrew Grove holds regular meetings with employees from all parts of the organization to brainstorm about the future, competitive challenges, and customer needs. Employees are motivated and empowered to serve customers' priorities above their own. Employees have a right to demand AR—"action required"—of any executive. Over the years Intel has also worked to avoid layoffs through asking staff to put in overtime or cut back on hours, so employees remain motivated to serve customers.

Disruptions that satisfy current customer needs are not enough. Constantly improving customer satisfaction is now so standard that firms that once led the pack on customer satisfaction find themselves without any lead at all. Thus, the key to achieving real advantage from customer satisfaction is to

- Identify customer needs that even the customer cannot articulate for him/herself.
- Find new, previously unserved customers to serve.
- Create customer needs that never existed before.
- Predict changes in customer needs before they happen.

To do this, firms are now engaging in the second S, strategic soothsaying. This allows firms to see and create *future* needs that they can serve better than any competitor does, even if only temporarily. The ability to see and create these future needs depends upon the firm's ability to predict future trends, to control the development of key technologies and other know-how that will shape the future, and to create self-fulfilling prophecies.

Intel CEO Grove has quipped that the company bets millions on science fiction.[4] As pressure builds from clonemakers and rival systems, engineers are brought together to consider the emerging technological capabilities and the performance needed to keep ahead of competitors. Intel has also expanded into other areas such as supercomputers, flash memories, video chips, and networking boards. Its sales in these areas are climbing at an average rate of 68 percent per year.[5] It has gained 85 percent of the emerging market for flash memory chips and practically owns one-third of the market for massively parallel computers. This experience provides knowledge that Intel can then apply to standard chips, adding features such as video.

The second S, strategic soothsaying, is concerned with understanding the future evolution of markets and technology that will proactively create new opportunities to serve existing or new customers. This also contributes to the firm's vision of where the next advantage will be discovered and where the company should focus its disruption.

CAPABILITIES FOR DISRUPTION: THE NEXT TWO S's

To act on this vision, companies need two key capabilities: speed and surprise. As in fencing, speed and surprise are key factors in gaining an advantage before competitors are able to do so and in delaying competitor reactions to the new advantage.

If two companies recognize the opportunity to create a new advantage at the same time, the company that can create the advantage faster will win. Because success depends on the creation of a series of temporary advantages, a company's ability to move quickly from one advantage to the next is crucial. Speed allows companies to maneuver to disrupt the status quo, erode the advantage of competitors, and create new advantages before competitors are able to preempt these moves.

> *Speed allows companies to maneuver to disrupt the status quo, erode the advantage of competitors, and create new advantages before competitors are able to preempt these moves.*

Intel used to bring out one or two new chips each year and a new microprocessor family every three or four years. In 1992 it drove out nearly 30 new variations on its 486 chip and introduced the next generation of chip, the Pentium. To stay ahead of clonemakers, Intel plans to create new families of chips every year or two throughout the 1990s.[6] Instead of waiting until the current generation of chip is rolled out before working on the next one, Intel now develops several generations of chips at once. It is already working on making its chips obsolete before they have even hit the market. Intel has created design-automation software that allows it to add two or three times the transistors to each new chip design with no increase in development time. It also has achieved a breakthrough in modeling systems that promises to cut the four-year product-development cycle by six months. The new Quickturn system will allow Intel to perform engineering tests up to 30,000 times faster.

If a competitor is unaware of the opportunity to create a new advantage, surprise can maintain that lack of awareness. While this is not a source of sustainable advantage (once the competitor recognizes the advantage, it can usually move quickly to duplicate it), surprise allows the company to create the advantage and to extend the period in which the advantage is unique. Surprise also allows companies to act to undermine competitor advantages before the competitors can take defensive actions.

Intel's multiple capabilities—with strengths in microprocessors, other chips, flash memories, personal computers, and supercomputers—keep competitors guessing about its next move. Since its early days, it has often pursued a strategy of simultaneously pursuing alternative technology, and it currently has its own versions of the competing RISC-based chip (Reduced Instruction-Set Computing) although it continues to defend its stronghold of CISC (Complex Instruction-Set Computing), which offers more software. Not wanting to compete with its customers, Intel hasn't entered the personal computer market under its own name, but it has developed the capabilities to do so as the only supplier to computer manufacturers with a brand name—so competitors never know when it might decide to enter the PC market.

Intel has used advances in modeling and design of new chips to surprise competitors. Its new modeling system gave it a strategic victory over a competing RISC-based chip. At a technology forum in 1991, an Intel executive demonstrated a working model of the Pentium chip, using a link to the model, before an actual chip was ready. In what may have been a response to Intel's signal, six months later Compaq Computer Corporation canceled plans to launch a RISC-based personal computer.[7] And it is still unclear whether new research efforts in RISC chips will surprise Intel.

Intel also maintains a flexible workforce, shifting employees to different projects and keeping operations lean. Despite its continued growth in revenues, the number of Intel employees declined between 1984 and 1992 to maintain flexibility.

Capabilities for speed and surprise are therefore key elements for successfully disrupting the status quo and creating temporary advantages. These capabilities are flexible in that they can be deployed across a wide range of specific actions.

TACTICS FOR DISRUPTION: THE LAST THREE S's

The final three S's—shifting the rules of the game, signaling, and simultaneous and sequential strategic thrusts—are concerned with the tactics used in delivering a company's disruptions, especially tactics that influence the flow of future dynamic strategic interactions among competitors. These three S's follow the vision developed by the first two S's and use the potential for speed and surprise from the third and fourth S's.

In contrast to static approaches to strategy, these final three S's are concerned with a dynamic process of actions and interactions. Most planning is concerned with the company's next move to gain advantage. It usually analyzes potential competitive responses but doesn't shape those responses to its advantage.

The view presented here is a set of tactics designed to disrupt the status quo and create temporary advantage. Tactics such as actions that shift the rules of competition create a sudden and discontinuous move in the industry, reshaping the competitive playing field and confusing the opponent.

Intel's move into new areas such as supercomputers, interactive digital video, and flash memory has helped shift the rules of competition. Flash memory provides an alternative to the standard memory market, where Intel lost out to Japanese competitors. Intel is adding ancillary products, such as networking circuit boards and graphic chips, that make it easier for computer makers to add these features. It has also designed a personal computer with workstation power, the Panther, which it is licensing to computer makers. This shifts the rules by creating a machine that Intel is not marketing itself. The purpose of the design is to take full advantage of Intel's Pentium chip.

Signaling can delay or dampen the competitor's actions to create advantage, throw the competitor off balance, or create surprise. Grove has signaled Intel's intent to fight the clonemakers "with everything we've got."[8] It has also stated a vision of making the company the center of all computing, from palmtops to supercomputers. Its precise strategy for doing this is less visible. Although it has clearly revealed that it has 686 and 786 chips in the works, what these chips will be able to do is still open to speculation. As discussed, Intel used signaling to shift the rules of competition by transforming computer chips from a hidden commodity to a marketing asset through its Intel Inside campaign. By making the chip visible and using branding in marketing PCs, it made major gains in its battle against the clones. But the brand is only as powerful as the computer chip behind it.

A company might feint a move in one direction and then move forcefully in another direction, creating surprise and temporary advantage from the misdirection of the opponent.

Competitive thrusts in this environment are rapid—either a sequence of moves or a set of simultaneous actions—to upset the equilibrium of the industry, disrupt the status quo, and open opportunities for new advantage. As an example of a set of simultaneous thrusts, a company might feint a move in one direction and then move forcefully in another direction, creating surprise and temporary advantage from the misdirection of the opponent. One can think of sequential thrusts as being akin to the sequence of plays used in a football game. One team may run the ball several times until the defense is conditioned to expect a run play. Then the offense switches to the long bomb at a time that should call for a run. The sequence of actions creates surprise and temporary advantage, since once the play is used, the defense will watch out for the long bomb in future plays.

Intel has used a variety of simultaneous and sequential strategic thrusts to seize the initiative. In the late 1970s, struggling with its 8086 microprocessor chip. Intel launched an all-out assault—code-named Operation Crush—against Motorola and other competitors. Intel set up war rooms to work toward making the 8086 the industry standard. It was this effort to simultaneously attack several segments of the market that helped lead to IBM's decision to adapt the 8088 as the center of its personal computer.[9] Intel rode the wave of the PC's growth to dominance in the microprocessor industry.

Intel also participated in both the memory and microprocessor markets at various points in time. In a way, Intel's retreat from the memory chip market and return with flash memory might be seen as a sequential set of moves akin to a strategic retreat followed by regrouping and counterattack. It has used multiple exploratory attacks to develop a variety of know-how and technology capabilities and gauge competitor and customer reactions (for example, its simultaneous development of RISC and CISC technology). It has also explored promising markets (such as video and massively parallel computing) and moved into those with the highest potential for growth. It has built its businesses by using a sequential strategy, moving from memory chips to microprocessors, to boards, to building personal computers (although not marketing them).

These three tactics reflect the increasing speed and intensity of hypercompetition. Although these actions sometimes push companies into the gray areas of antitrust because the behaviors could be construed as exclusionary or anticompetitive actions, companies are increasingly seeing them as necessary for competitive survival.

PUTTING ALL THE S's TOGETHER

Figure 2 illustrates how the New 7S's work together to develop a vision, capabilities, and tactics for disruption.

As suggested earlier, while the traditional 7S's are concerned with capitalizing on creating a static strategic fit among internal aspects of the organization, the New 7S's are concerned with four key goals that are based on understanding dynamic strategic interactions over long periods of time.

1. *Disrupting the status quo.* Competitors disrupt the status quo by identifying new opportunities to serve the customer, signaling, shifting the rules, and attacking through sequential and simultaneous thrusts. These moves end the old pattern of competitive interaction between rivals. This requires speed and surprise; otherwise, the company's competitors simply change at the same rate.

2. *Creating Temporary advantage.* Disruption creates temporary advantages. These advantages are based on better knowledge of customers, technology, and the future. They are derived from customer orientation and employee empowerment throughout the entire organization. These advantages are short-lived, eroded by fierce competition.

3. *Seizing the initiative.* By moving aggressively in each arena, acting to create a new advantage or undermine a competitor's old advantage, the company seizes the initiative. This throws the opponent off balance and puts it at a disadvantage for a while. The opponent is forced to play catch-up, reacting rather than shaping the future with its own actions to seize the initiative. The initiator is proactive, while competitors are forced to be reactive.

4. *Sustaining the momentum.* Several actions in a row to seize the initiative create momentum. The company continues to develop new advantages and doesn't wait for competitors to undermine them before launching the next initiative. For example, while U.S. manufacturers are doing remedial work in quality improvement, Japanese manufacturers are now building key advantages in flexibility. This succession of actions sustains the momentum. This is the only source of sustainable competitive advantage in hypercompetitive environments.

In slower and less aggressive competitive environments, companies could concentrate primarily on making great swords. In hypercompetition, they have been forced to concentrate much more on the skills of fencing.

In hypercompetition it is not enough to build a static set of competencies. Good resources are not enough. They must be used effectively. This is precisely why successful firms pay attention to tactics as well as capabilities and vision in an environment of traditional competition and to competencies in an environment of hypercompetition. In slower and less aggressive competitive environments, companies could concentrate primarily on making great swords. In hypercompetition, they have been forced to concentrate much more on the skills of fencing. It is these dynamic skills that are the most significant competencies of the firm. Thus, a company's success depends equally upon its swords and its fencing skills, and the New 7S's are intended to guide firms toward making the right swords, learning how to fence, and pointing them in the right direction.

SOME TRADE-OFFS

One final analysis can be done using the New 7S's. In choosing which to concentrate on, companies are forced to make trade-offs among them. This makes it difficult for companies to do all seven equally well. Companies choose among the seven to confront different challenges and opportunities that present themselves.

Thus, it is possible to analyze a competitor (or one's own company) to see what types of trade-offs have been made. Once these are identified, the weakness of the competitor (or one's own company) is apparent. Furthermore, the trade-off means that the competitor can't plug the weakness without giving up something else. Thus, it is possible to identify weakness, which, if attacked, forces the competition to be slow to respond or to give up some other strength in order to respond. Either way the competitor loses.

Among the trade-offs implied by the New 7S's are the following:

- *Trade-offs at the expense of stakeholder satisfaction (S-1)* can be undermined by speed (S-3), as companies may sacrifice product or service quality to gain speed or push employees to work harder and faster. Speeding products to market with little testing could also reduce customer satisfaction. Similarly surprise (S-4), shifting the rules (S-5), signaling (S-6), and simultaneous and sequential strategic thrusts (S-7) also have the potential to confuse customers, employees, and shareholders as well as competitors.

- *Trade-offs at the expense of future orientation/soothsaying.* Strategic soothsaying (S-2) can be hurt by speed (S-3), which often leaves little time for reflecting on what lies ahead, and surprise (S-4), which is sudden and unpredictable enough to make prognostication irrelevant or impossible. Shifting the rules (S-5) often reshapes competition in a way that unpredictably changes future opportunities so that soothsaying becomes difficult. To the extent that competitor reactions are not anticipated, simultaneous and sequential strategic thrusts (S-7) sometimes make soothsaying more difficult.

- *Trade-offs at the expense of speed.* Speed (S-3) can be eroded through the slowness of decision making in an organization such as the ones used to increase stakeholder satisfaction (S-1). Also, strategic alliances used to shift the rules (S-5) sometimes reduce speed because of negotiations. Shifting the rules of competition (S-5) may require a trade-off with speed. It can temporarily reduce speed (S-3), for example, because of the confusion and time it takes to regroup and retool to create the new rules. Simultaneous and sequential strategic thrusts (S-7) can reduce speed (S-3) because they require more effort than single thrusts.

- *Trade-offs at the expense of surprise.* The flexibility and stealth of surprise (S-4) can be eroded by strategies to increase capabilities for speed. For example, just-in-time systems could decrease the company's flexibility while increasing speed. Alliances to shift the rules sometimes also decrease surprise because the alliances are usually public. Signaling can also reduce the element of surprise because it often involves revealing the strategic intent of the company. Sequential thrusts can reduce surprise (S-4) by committing the company to a clear set of actions.

These trade-offs mean that firms can't always do all of the New 7S's equally well, even if they are above a reasonable threshold on each one of them. Thus, a competitor can do a trade-off analysis to identify the maneuvers it can do through use of the S's that the opponent can't do well because the opponent can't respond without depleting its strength in one of the other S's. Other firms will creatively switch among the New 7S's to shift the rules of competition, sometimes focusing on the opponent's weaker S's, sometimes using several in concert.

Moreover, firms have limited resources, so they can't acquire all seven of the New S's at once. They must prioritize them and make trade-offs. Thus, it will be rare that a firm is equally good at all of the New 7S's. This will create opportunities for a new type of hypercompetitive behavior whereby firms use the resource investment trade-offs made by a competitor to determine which of the New 7S's should be invested in first. Finally, truly hypercompetitive firms, like Intel, will find ways to eliminate the trade-offs. Trade-offs exist only if firms believe that trade-offs are necessities and stop looking for ways to do both alternatives. After all, it was once said that firms could not achieve low cost and high quality at the same time. Now it is not just a reality but a necessity for survival in many industries.

WILL ADVANTAGES FROM USING THE NEW 7S's EVENTUALLY ERODE?

Like all know-how, knowledge of how to use the New 7S's might eventually be expected to erode as it becomes widely assimilated. As knowledge of these approaches becomes increasingly widespread and all competitors begin using them—this is already taking place—one might expect that any advantage would be neutralized. In particular, this erosion may be seen in the temporary advantages of a customer focus. As customer focus (a central part of S-1) has been driven through U.S. organizations by the total quality movement and other forces, it has become less of an advantage and more of a requisite to succeed in business.

While the impact of the New 7S's may be diminished somewhat by their widespread adoption, there are several factors that promise to continue to make them a source of advantage even after they are widely used. First, the New 7S's have some inherent flexibility so that different companies using the New 7S's can take very different strategies. The use of simultaneous and sequential strategic thrusts (S-7) presents a wide range of options and variations. There are many other thrusts that can be designed for specific opportunities, making it difficult for firms to exactly replicate a competitor's use of the New 7S's.

Second, the New 7S's are dynamic. Companies use them in different ways over time. Stakeholder satisfaction changes, competitive opportunities change, sources of temporary advantage change. The New 7S's and their goals of creating disruption and seizing the initiative remain constant, but the method companies use to achieve these goals constantly change. In this way, even if competitors in an industry are using the New 7S's, their moves will continue to be unpredictable.

Third, companies usually cannot use all of the New 7S's at once because of inherent trade-offs among the S's. Companies perform a balancing act in weighing these trade-offs. This adds to the unpredictability of competitive moves, because companies can use any of the New 7S's in developing their next strategic move, and the trade-offs may make it difficult to respond.

As more competitors focus on disrupting the status quo and seizing the initiative, this intent may become fairly predictable. Companies will know that their competitors will be actively working on their next competitive move. But this intent does little to reveal the actual strategies of competitors. All it does is make it clear that the company will not pursue one strategy, namely, sustaining its current advantage. This leaves every action other than that one open.

The one certain impact is that as the New 7S's become more widespread, competition will become more aggressive. Instead of having one or two competitors seeking to disrupt the status quo, every competitor will be looking for the next source of temporary advantage. With this further intensification of hypercompetition, one might expect an increased interest in alliances and other forms of cooperation to dampen the intensity of competition (as has already been seen). Ultimately, however, the only way out of this dilemma is for companies to become more aggressive in seizing the initiative. Cooperative attempts to end this cycle of aggression will be seen as either illegal (collusive antitrust violations), or futile, since it is like shoveling sand against the tide. Leading firms will be wary of cooperative efforts that ask them to be less aggressive and give up their temporary advantage. Lagging firms with the fire in their bellies to be number one will not be satisfied with their permanent status as second-class citizens. So the New 7S's will be used more aggressively and more frequently in the future world of hypercompetition.

The one certain impact is that as the New 7S's become more widespread, competition will become more aggressive.

While the New 7S's will continue to be important, especially with the intensifying competition of the future, there may be even newer S's that emerge as keys to competitive success. Hypercompetitive companies will continue to monitor and define these new strategic approaches in new attempts to provide temporary advantages and sustain momentum with a series of successful short-term advantages.

ENDNOTES

1. Adapted from: R. A. D'Aveni, *Hypercompetition: Managing the Dynamics of Strategic Maneuvering* (New York: Free Press, 1994).

2. Strateford Sherman, "How to Prosper in the Value Decade," *Fortune*, Nov. 30, 1992, p. 91.

3. This title is derived from McKinsey's original 7S's framework. See especially, R. Waterman, T. Peters, and J. Phillips, "Structure Is Not Organization," *Business Horizons*, June 1980, pp. 14–26; James Brian Quinn and Henry Mintzberg, "Dealing with Structure and Systems," *The Strategy Process* (Englewood Cliffs, NJ: Prentice Hall, 1988), pp. 270–76.

4. Robert D. Hof, "Inside Intel," *Business Week*, June 1, 1992, p. 88.

5. Ibid., p. 90.

6. Ibid., pp. 86–94.

7. Ibid., p. 89.

8. Ibid., p. 87.

9. Ashish Nanda and Christopher A. Bartlett, "Intel Corporation—Leveraging Capabilities for Strategic Renewal," working paper, Graduate School of Business, Harvard University, November 25, 1992, p. 3.

WHY DIVERSIFY? FOUR DECADES OF MANAGEMENT THINKING

Michael Goold, *Ashridge Strategic Management Centre*

Kathleen Luchs, *Ashridge Strategic Management Centre*

This article traces the chronological history of corporate diversification strategies, from the rise of conglomerates in the 1950s and 1960s to the development of synergistic portfolios built around sharing core competencies that is the school of thought in the 1990s.

Large, diversified corporations have been under critical scrutiny for many years. In 1951 the prevailing view in America was summarized in an article in the *Harvard Business Review:*

> The basic presumption is that a company turning from one type of activity to another is up to no good, especially if in the process it has become "big business."[1]

Such companies were accused of being too powerful, and, in particular, of cross-subsidizing their different businesses to force competitors from the field. They were therefore seen as anticompetitive.

Today, diversified companies are also regarded by many commentators as being "up to no good," but for just the opposite reason; they are now charged with being uncompetitive. The problem is not that they are over-mighty competitors, but that they add no value to their businesses. In 1987, Michael Porter wrote of the failure of many corporate strategies:

> I studied the diversification records of 33 large, prestigious U.S. companies over the 1950–1986 period and found that most of them had divested many more acquisitions than they had kept. The corporate strategies of most companies have dissipated instead of created shareholder value. . . . By taking over companies and breaking them up, corporate raiders thrive on failed corporate strategies.[2]

Source: *Academy of Management Executive* 7, no. 3 (1993), pp. 7–25.

How has thinking about the rationale for diversified companies evolved during this period of time? Why has fear of the power of diversified companies been replaced with skepticism about their results? What have we learned, both about diversification strategies that work and those that don't work? There have been relatively few influential ideas about what constitutes a successful strategy for a diversified company. This article explores the development of these ideas, and examines current thinking about corporate-level strategy.

DIVERSIFICATION AND CORPORATE STRATEGY IN THE 1950s AND 1960s

An important and enduring justification for the diversified company is the argument that the managers of these companies possess general management skills that contribute to the overall performance of a company. Kenneth Andrews argued that there had been a steady growth of executive talent in America, equal to the task of managing diversity. The establishment of business schools in the early twentieth century created the basis for the education of professional managers, and the divisionalized structure of large corporations provided the opportunities for younger managers to gain the requisite experience.[3]

General Management Skills

The idea that professional managers possessed skills that could be put to good use across different businesses rested on the assumption that different businesses nevertheless required similar managerial skills. This assumption received support from management theory. During the 1950s and 1960s much scholarly attention focused on identifying basic principles of management, useful to all managers and applicable to all kinds of enterprises. Peter Drucker argued that "intuitive" management was no longer sufficient. He encouraged managers to study the principles of management and to acquire knowledge and analyze their performance systematically.[4]

The interest in investigating and analyzing underlying management principles continued into the 1960s. Harold Koontz wrote of the "deluge of research and writing from the academic halls." According to Koontz, it was the management process school, which aimed to identify universal principles of management, that held the greatest promise for advancing the practice of management.[5]

Theorists such as Koontz and Drucker naturally emphasized the issues and problems which were common across different types of businesses, since their aim was to help all managers improve their skills and the performance of their businesses. Though they did not explicitly claim that professional managers could manage any business, it was not a great leap to conclude that, if all managers face similar problems, professional managers might be able to use their skills in different businesses. Simple observation, as well as theory, supported this idea. Robert Katz noted, "We are all familiar with those 'professional managers' who are becoming the prototypes of our modern executive world. These men shift with great ease, and with no apparent loss in effectiveness, from one industry to another. Their human and conceptual skills seem to make up for their unfamiliarity with the new job's technical aspects."[6] There was widespread respect for management skills, and business people were encouraged to apply their general management skills to improve the effectiveness of charities, universities, and government.[7]

In Europe, too, there was interest in general management skills. The founding of business schools in the U.K. and in France during the 1960s, and the growing interest in management training, was in part motivated by the perceived need to provide European managers with the same kind of general management skills as their U.S. competitors. Indeed, there was concern in Europe that the management skills of U.S. companies were so powerful that Americans would take over large chunks of European industry.[8]

Rise of Conglomerates

During the 1960s, the growth of conglomerates, with their numerous acquisitions of unrelated businesses across different industries, provided almost laboratory conditions in which to test out the idea that professional managers could apply their skills to many different businesses. Conglomerates such as Textron, ITT, and Litton not only grew rapidly, but also profitably, and top managers of these companies perceived themselves as breaking new ground. For example, David Judleson of Gulf & Western claimed, "Without the high degree of sophistication, skill, and effectiveness that management has developed only in the last two decades, the conglomerate could not exist. These management techniques provide the necessary unity and compatibility among a diversity of operations and acquisitions."[9] Harold Geneen used a system of detailed budgets, tight financial control, and face-to-face meetings among his general managers to build ITT into a highly diversified conglomerate.[10] In 1967, Royal Little, who masterminded Textron's broad diversification, explained that the company succeeded because, "we are adding that intangible called business judgement."[11] Textron had common financial controls, budgetary systems, and capital allocation procedures across its many businesses, but it provided few central services and had only a very small corporate office. The group vice presidents, who were responsible for a number of divisions, were appointed from outside the company. They acted as overseers and consultants to the divisions.

These new American conglomerates were admired abroad. In the U.K., one writer wrote glowingly of Litton Industries and its spectacular growth across high-tech industries, claiming that the company was " . . . a technological achievement of its own, an operation in the technology of management as much as the management of technology."[12] Several British companies, such as Slater Walker, embarked upon a strategy of conglomerate diversification during the 1960s and 1970s. The emphasis in Britain, however, was more on identifying and buying companies whose assets were worth more than their stock market price and less on the application of sound, underlying general management principles by the top management group.[13]

Did the conglomerates add value to their numerous businesses across different industries? The practices of at least some conglomerates such as Textron held up well under academic scrutiny. Normal Berg argued that corporate executives in such companies were fulfilling new roles as "managers of managers." While he admitted that it was too early to draw firm conclusions about the long-term success of conglomerates, Berg suggested that corporate strategies based on improving the performance of a diverse collection of businesses would have important implications for the practice of management and also for public policy.[14]

Faith in general management skills seemed to justify a kind of virtuous circle of corporate growth and diversification.

For more than 20 years, faith in general management skills seemed to justify a kind of virtuous circle of corporate growth and diversification. Andrews summarized the basic premise, arguing that, "successful diversification—because it always means successful surmounting of formidable administrative problems—develops know-how which further diversification will capitalize and extend."[15] The conglomerate movement of the 1960s, involving extensive diversification across a wide variety of industries, seemed to demonstrate that the specialized skills and practices of corporate general managers enabled them to manage ever greater complexity and diversity.

Conglomerates and Performance Problems

There was little reason to question the belief that general management skills provided a sufficient rationale for diversified companies while such corporations were performing well and growing profitably. But by the late 1960s, conglomerates were encountering performance problems. In early 1969, the stock prices of conglomerates such as Litton, Gulf & Western, and Textron fell as much as 50 percent from their highs a year earlier, compared to a 9 percent decline in the Dow Jones Industrial Average over the period, and one observer foresaw a round of conglomerate divestitures if such companies were to survive. Even ITT's consistent record of increased quarterly earnings over 58 quarters during the 1960s and 1970s was broken in 1974.[16]

What became apparent was that sound principles of organization and financial control, coupled with a corporate objective of growth, were not, alone, sufficient to ensure satisfactory performance in highly diversified companies. Indeed, General Electric, a leader in the development of sophisticated techniques and principles for the management of a diverse portfolio of businesses, found by the early 1970s that its management approach had resulted in an extended period of what GE called "profitless growth." For example, the company's sales increased 40 percent from 1965 to 1970, while its profits actually fell.[17]

By the late 1960s, there was an increasing awareness that a new approach to the management of diversity was needed.

DIVERSIFICATION AND CORPORATE STRATEGY IN THE 1970s

As a response to the increasing recognition that large and diversified companies present particular management problems, increasing attention was devoted to the question of the issues on which general managers should focus their efforts.

The Concept of Strategy

One theme that emerged with increasing force during the 1960s and 1970s was the need for senior managers to focus their attention on the "strategies" of their companies. Strategy was more than long-range planning or objective setting; it was a way of deciding the basic direction of the company and preparing it to meet future challenges.[18]

C. Roland Christensen, one of the creators of the business policy course at Harvard during the 1960s, argued that the concept of strategy made it possible to simplify the complex tasks of top managers.[19] A focus on strategy prevented senior executives from meddling in operating details and day-to-day issues which should be left to more junior managers with direct responsibility for them. It allowed them to concentrate on the most important issues facing their companies—and it simplified management by providing a framework for decisions.

CEOs readily accepted that strategy should be their main and unique responsibility. During the late 1960s and 1970s many companies established formal planning systems, and the appropriate structure and uses of such systems received much attention from academics.[20] In the early 1970s, Louis Gerstner remarked on how quickly strategic planning had been adopted by companies, noting, "Writer after writer has hailed this new discipline as the fountainhead of all corporate progress."[21]

The strategic frameworks, models, and tools being developed by academics and consultants focused mainly on strategic issues at the business-unit level, and they were, therefore, less relevant in helping to define an overall strategy for companies with many different businesses. Andrews, however, defined the main task of corporate-level strategy as identifying the businesses in which the firm would compete, and this became the accepted understanding of corporate strategy.[22] This general concept of corporate strategy, though, did not provide much practical guidance for some of the problems managers of diversified companies confronted. In particular, it did not help managers decide how resources should be allocated among businesses, especially when investment proposals were being put forward by a large number of disparate businesses, each with its own strategy. This problem was exacerbated when the aggregate demand for resources exceeded what was available.

Problems with Resource Allocation

Resource allocation decisions in diversified companies are a key part of corporate strategy, but they present particular difficulties.

Resource allocation decisions in diversified companies are a key part of corporate strategy, but they present particular difficulties. Corporate management must grasp the relative merits of investment proposals coming from a range of businesses in different sectors, with different time horizons, competitive positions, and risk profiles, not to mention management teams with differing credibilities. This can be complex. In the early 1970s, for example, a company such as ITT had to allocate resources among businesses that included telecommunications, insurance, rental cars, bakeries, and construction. With many divisions competing for funds, how could a company be sure it was investing in the best projects for future growth?[23]

Joseph Bower explored in detail how a large, diversified firm allocated resources. His research highlighted the gulf between financial theory, which saw the manager's task as choosing projects with the highest returns, and corporate reality, where all proposed projects showed at least the return required by the corporate hurdle rate for investment. In practice, divisional managers only proposed projects with acceptable forecast returns, and corporate-level managers had little basis on which to choose among projects.

Bower argued that investment decisions should not be made on a project-by-project basis, but had to be integrally related to a business's strategic product and market decisions.[24] During the 1970s, the new techniques of portfolio planning that were introduced by the Boston Consulting Group and others gained wide acceptance because they helped corporate executives to resolve practical problems of capital allocation in the context of an overall corporate strategy.[25]

Portfolio Planning

Portfolio planning provided corporate managers with a common framework to compare many different businesses. The industry attractiveness/business position matrix developed at GE, the Boston Consulting Group's growth/share matrix, and variations developed at other consultancies were used to classify businesses in terms of their strategic position and opportunities. These classifications helped managers to set both appropriate objectives and resource allocation strategies for different businesses, and to determine the overall cash requirements and cash generation of the corporate portfolio.[26]

The helicopter view provided by portfolio planning techniques was widely perceived as useful. For example, one CEO explained:

> Portfolio planning became relevant to me as soon as I became CEO. I was finding it very difficult to manage and understand so many different products and markets. I just grabbed at portfolio planning, because it provided me with a way to organize my thinking about our businesses, and the resource allocation issues facing the total company. I became and still am very enthusiastic. I guess you could say that I went for it hook, line, and sinker.[27]

During the 1970s, more and more corporations adopted portfolio planning, with the largest diversified companies being among the earliest adherents. One survey showed that by 1979, 45 percent of the Fortune 500 companies were using some form of portfolio planning.[28]

In many companies, portfolio planning techniques became more than analytical tools to help chief executives direct corporate resources towards the most profitable opportunities: they became the basis of corporate strategy itself. The key concept here was the idea of a balanced portfolio: made up of businesses whose profitability, growth, and cash flow characteristics would complement each other, and add up to a satisfactory overall corporate performance. Imbalance could be caused, for example, either by excessive cash generation with too few growth opportunities or by insufficient cash generation to fund the growth requirements elsewhere in the portfolio.[29] Often, the first step towards balancing the corporate portfolio was to identify businesses that were a drain on corporate resources. Monsanto, for example, used portfolio planning to restructure its portfolio, divesting low-growth commodity chemicals businesses and acquiring businesses in higher-growth industries such as biotechnology.[30]

Portfolio planning reinforced the virtuous circle of corporate growth and diversification that had been originally founded on general management skills. It helped corporate-level managers correct past diversification mistakes, leading to divestiture of weak businesses, and it encouraged them to invest in a mix of businesses, with different strategic (and cash) characteristics to balance their corporate portfolios and ensure future growth.

Problems with Portfolio Management

Even as an increasing number of corporations turned to portfolio planning, problems emerged in managing balanced portfolios.[31] Companies discovered that while certain businesses appeared to meet all the economic requirements of the corporate portfolio, they did not fit easily into the corporate family. It turned out to be extremely difficult, for example, for corporate managers with long experience of managing mature businesses in a particular industry sector to manage effectively their acquired growth businesses in new, dynamic, and unfamiliar sectors.

Research on how companies actually used portfolio planning confirmed the difficulties of managing businesses with different strategic characteristics, missions, or mandates. Philippe Haspeslagh investigated whether companies adjusted their systems of financial planning, capital investment appraisal, incentive compensation, or strategic planning to fit the requirements of their different businesses. The focus of his study was on the role played by general management, rather than on specific business-level strategies. He found that companies made few changes in their formal corporate-level systems, but corporate-level managers in successful companies did make informal attempts to adapt these systems to their businesses.[32] In another study on the effectiveness of portfolio planning techniques, the authors discovered that cash cows performed better in an organizational context of autonomy while fast-growing businesses benefited from more control. They concluded that the administrative context was an important variable in explaining business performance, and that many companies were taking the wrong approach to some of their businesses.[33]

> *The recognition that different types of businesses had to be managed differently undermined the argument that general management skills, buttressed by the common frameworks of strategy and portfolio planning, provided the rationale for diversified companies.*

The recognition that different types of businesses had to be managed differently undermined the argument that general management skills, buttressed by the common frameworks of strategy and portfolio planning, provided the rationale for diversified companies. Many companies discovered that common systems and approaches, when applied to different kinds of businesses, could minimize value from those businesses. Portfolio planning helped corporate executives sort out the contribution of each of their businesses to the corporate portfolio, but it did not answer the other critical question confronting a diversified company: what contribution should the corporation make to each of its businesses?

DIVERSIFICATION AND CORPORATE STRATEGY IN THE 1980s

During the 1980s, there was widespread skepticism about the ability of companies to manage and add value to diverse, conglomerate portfolios. Raiders such as Carl Icahn and T. Boone Pickens demonstrated that they could acquire even the largest companies, break them up, and realize huge profits. The takeover activity of the 1980s prompted a rethinking of both the role of corporate management in large companies, and of the kinds of strategies which were appropriate for diversified companies.

Cost Cutting at Headquarters

What seemed most obvious about the corporate level in many companies was not its contribution, but it cost. Thus, attention shifted to cutting headquarters costs. Some companies turned central services into profit centers, charged with selling their services to the business units, while other companies disbanded some central functions altogether. The pruning of corporate staffs often meant devolving more authority to line managers in decentralized units.[34]

Cost cutting and the downsizing of corporate staffs, however, were not alone sufficient to demonstrate that corporate management could add value to their businesses, and the overall performance of large, diversified corporations also came under increasing scrutiny. Michael Porter published a study showing the high rate of divestiture of acquisitions among American corporations, arguing that the diversification strategies of many companies had failed to create value.[35] Also, the wave of takeovers caused executives to pay increasing attention to their company's stock price as analysts and raiders identified "value gaps," or the difference between the current stock market price of a company and its breakup value.[36]

Value-Based Planning

Faced with the threat from raiders and the criticism of academics such as Porter, chief executives devoted themselves increasingly to the task of creating shareholder value. Managers were encouraged to evaluate corporate performance in the same terms as the stock market (and raiders), using economic rather than accounting measures, and to take whatever actions were necessary to improve their company's stock price. Value-based planning, using the financial tools of discounted cash flow, ROE spreads, and hurdle rates, provided corporate managers with a fresh perspective on the link between stock prices and competitive strategy.[37]

A company's stock price, according to proponents of value-based planning, is determined by the value of the strategies of its businesses. However, it can be very difficult for managers to assess the strategies of dissimilar businesses: ". . . corporate level planners facing a portfolio of four, ten, dozens, or dozens and dozens of units do not know—probably cannot know—enough about each unit's competitive position, industry, rivals, and customers to make this determination."[38] One of the appeals of value-based planning is that, like portfolio planning, it offers corporate-level executives a means of evaluating many different businesses using a common framework. The corporate level can require business units to make strategic choices on the basis of economic returns, and doing this systematically across all units, it is argued, provides corporate management with the basis for making decisions on capital allocation.

Value-based planning techniques gained many adherents, especially among American corporations. In 1987 an article in *Fortune* described how "managements have caught the religion. At first reluctant, they pound at the door of consultants who can teach them the way to a higher stock price—a price so high it would thwart even the most determined raider."[39]

But value-based planning also has limitations as a guide to corporate strategy. It can help corporate managers to focus on the goal of increasing shareholder wealth and to understand the criteria that must be met to do so. It does not, however, provide much insight into the kind of corporate strategies that should be pursued to meet these criteria. A higher stock price is a reward for creating value. But the key question remains: how *can* corporations add value to diverse business portfolios? Perhaps the most influential view on this vital topic to have emerged during the 1980s is that they should "stick to the knitting."

Stick to the Knitting

The concept of corporate success based on core businesses, or stick to the knitting, gained popularity in 1982 with the publication of Peters and Waterman's *In Search of Excellence*. Successful corporations, they observed, did not diversify widely. They tended to specialize in particular industries and focused intently on improving their knowledge and skills in the areas they knew best.[40]

Stick-to-the-knitting advice was also a reaction against the analytical techniques and impersonal approach of much of strategic and portfolio planning. Bob Hayes and Bill Abernathy voiced these concerns in their article "Managing Our Way to Economic Decline." In their view, too many American corporations were being run by "pseudoprofessional" managers, skilled in finance and law, but lacking in technological expertise or in-depth experience in any particular industry. They warned that portfolios diversified across different industries and businesses were appropriate for stocks and bonds, but not for corporations.[41] The need for experience and deep knowledge of a business was also emphasized by Henry Mintzberg, who criticized the "thin and lifeless" strategies that result from treating businesses as mere positions on a portfolio matrix. He argued that instead of broad diversity, we need "focused organizations that understand their missions, 'know' the people they serve, and excite the ones they employ; we should be encouraging thick management, deep knowledge, healthy competition and authentic social responsibility."[42]

> *The widespread conviction that companies should stick to the knitting increased skepticism about the ability of corporations to manage and add value to diverse portfolios.*

The widespread conviction that companies should stick to the knitting increased skepticism about the ability of corporations to manage and add value to diverse portfolios. It reinforced the practical pressures created by the corporate raiders and contributed to a wave of retrenching. From the mid-1980s onwards, a goal for many corporations has been to rationalize their portfolios to overcome the perceived disadvantages of broad diversification.

Corporate Restructuring

Restructuring (whether voluntary or not) has frequently led to the disposal of corporate assets. In 1985, for example, General Mills announced its intention to focus on its core businesses of consumer foods and restaurants, and the company sold off its toy and fashion businesses.[43] More recently, General Signal embarked on a strategy of "back to the basics," retreating from its earlier major investments in high-tech businesses to focus on its traditional "boring" products such as industrial mixers.[44]

Restructuring has been widely regarded as a salutary correction to the excesses of broad diversification. Michael Jensen has argued that corporate breakups, divisional sell-offs, and LBOs are critical developments that can prevent the wasteful use of capital by managers of large public corporations, and other recent academic studies support the view that restructuring does help improve the performance of corporations.[45] But restructuring implies a sense of which businesses a company should retain and which it should divest. How should the core businesses be selected?

One answer is that companies should restructure to limit their businesses to one, or a few, closely related industries. In this way, managers stick to what they know well, and are best able to exploit corporate expertise. This approach is consistent with stick-to-the-knitting advice, but it is not a complete answer. Successful companies such as GE, Hanson, and Cooper Industries nevertheless have businesses in many different industries. Furthermore, sticking to a single industry does not necessarily limit complexity or ensure that companies expand into areas they "know." During the 1980s, companies such as Prudential and Merrill Lynch sought to combine different types of financial services businesses. They discovered that businesses such as insurance, stockbroking, and banking, though all in the financial services industry, nonetheless required very different approaches, resources, and skills.[46]

Another reservation about a stick-to-the-knitting strategy based on limiting diversification to closely related businesses is that, despite extensive research, empirical evidence on the performance of companies pursuing more and less related diversification strategies is ambiguous and contradictory. Many studies have compared the performance of single-product firms, companies that diversify into related products, markets, or technologies, and unrelated conglomerates, but no firm relationship between different diversification strategies and performance has been discovered.[47]

Some concept of what constitutes a "core portfolio"—or the corporate "knitting"—is required, though, if restructuring is to result in long-term improvement in corporate performance.

DIVERSIFICATION AND CORPORATE STRATEGY IN THE 1990s

The main issues for corporate strategy in the 1990s have therefore emerged as how to identify the businesses that should form a core portfolio for a corporation, and how to find ways of adding value to those businesses.

Three main alternative answers to these questions have received support in current management thinking:

1. Diversification should be limited to those businesses with synergy.

2. The corporate focus should be on exploiting core competences across different businesses.

3. Successful diversification depends on building a portfolio of businesses which fits with the managerial "dominant logic" of top executives and their management style.

Synergy

Synergy occurs when the performance of a portfolio of businesses adds up to more than the sum of its parts. The concept of synergy is based in part on economies of scale; two or more businesses can lower their costs if they can combine manufacturing facilities, use a common salesforce, or advertise jointly, and in this way the combined businesses are worth more than they would be on a stand-alone basis.[48]

In much of the current management literature, synergy has become virtually synonymous with corporate-level strategy. Michael Porter views the management of interrelationships between businesses as the essence of corporate-level strategy, arguing that without synergy a diversified company is little more than a mutual fund.[49] Rosabeth Moss Kanter, too, argues that the achievement of synergy is the only justification for a multibusiness company.[50] In a review of the literature on mergers, Friedrich Trautwein, a German academic, found that managers almost always justified diversification moves in terms of the synergies available, and that most of the advice in the management literature on diversification was based on the concept of realizing synergies.[51]

In practice, however, many companies have found it very difficult to gain benefits from a corporate strategy based on synergy.[52] Acquisitions aimed at realizing synergies can be especially risky; for example, two academic commentators have noted that anticipated synergy benefits " . . . show an almost unshakeable resolve not to appear when it becomes time for their release."[53] Quantitative evidence appears to support the observation that synergies are hard to achieve; a recent study on takeovers concluded that most gains arise from asset disposals and restructuring rather than from synergy.[54]

Those who view synergy as the essence of corporate-level strategy, including Porter and Kanter, acknowledge that companies find it difficult to gain synergy benefits and that the failure rate is high. Much of the current literature, therefore, focuses on implementation—what companies have to do to gain benefits from sharing skills or activities across businesses. Porter, for instance, discusses the need for the evolution of a new organizational form, which he calls the "horizontal organization." These organizations facilitate interrelationships across different businesses by overlaying horizontal structures, systems, and managerial approaches onto the vertical relationships which currently characterize the ties between business units and corporate management.[55] Kanter describes the emergence of the "post-entrepreneurial corporation," which aims to create the relationships and management processes required for cross-business cooperation.[56] Christopher Bartlett and Sumantra Ghoshal argue a similar case for the complex problems facing multinationals attempting to make the most of their businesses in different countries. In their view, multinationals need to develop new organizational capabilities so that components, products, resources, people, and information can flow freely among interdependent units. Bartlett and Ghoshal describe such an integrated network as a "transnational organization."[57]

Transnational or horizontal or postentrepreneurial organizations, by definition, capture many synergy benefits because they have the organizational capabilities to manage complex interrelationships across businesses. There are, however, very few examples of companies that represent these new kinds of organizations, at least in full-fledged form. Consequently, much of the advice on synergy remains theoretical and prescriptive.

There is evidence, furthermore, that managing complex interrelationships to create synergies across businesses is not the only means of creating value. Michael Goold and Andrew Campbell, in their study of strategic management styles, found that companies such as Hanson and Courtaulds, which placed very little emphasis on synergy as a source of corporate value added, performed at least as well as companies that placed more emphasis on linkages across businesses.[58] These findings are reinforced by successful multibusiness companies such as KKR, the leveraged buyout specialists, and Berkshire Hathaway, managed by the renowned investor Warren Buffet, which are collections of independent businesses, and whose strategies are not based on exploiting synergies across their businesses. The assumption that synergy is the only rationale for a group of companies does not fit the available evidence, and this suggests that not all corporations need to focus their efforts on constructing and managing portfolios of interrelated businesses.

Synergy remains a powerful concept in our understanding of corporate strategy, but it is difficult to accept that it is the "one best way" to create value in a multibusiness company. For some companies, the advantages of managing stand-alone businesses may outweigh the long-term investment required to create linkages among those businesses, and the potential for synergy may simply not exist in some corporate portfolios. We need to discover more about when synergy is an appropriate corporate strategy, and we need to learn more about how companies successful at managing interrelationships across businesses go about it.

Core Competences

Another approach to corporate strategy stresses building on the core competences of the corporation. This can be seen as a particular case of synergy, with corporate value creation dependent on exploiting unique skills and capabilities across a portfolio of businesses. Gary Hamel and C. K. Prahalad focus on technological competences. They argue that the corporate portfolio should not be perceived simply as a group of businesses, but also as a collection of such competences. In managing the corporate portfolio, managers must ensure that each part draws on and contributes to the core competences the corporation is seeking to build and exploit. Even a poorly performing business may be contributing to an important core competence, and if managers divest such businesses they may also be discarding some of their competences. If corporations are unable to transfer a core competence from one

In managing the corporate portfolio, managers must ensure that each part draws on and contributes to the core competences the corporation is seeking to build and exploit.

business to another, then they are wasting their resources. According to Prahalad and Hamel, many of the current management approaches of Western corporations, including SBUs, decentralization, and resource allocation practices, undermine the ability of corporations to build core competences, since autonomous businesses seldom have the resources or vision to build world-class competences.[59]

Hiroyuki Itami, a Japanese academic, focuses on building the corporation's "invisible assets," such as expertise in a particular technology, brand names, reputation, or customer information. Such assets, he argues, can be employed throughout the firm without being used up, and they are the only sustainable source of competitive advantage.[60] Philippe Haspeslagh and David Jemison, authors of a recent study on acquisitions, support a capabilities-based view of corporate value creation, defining core capabilities as managerial and technological skills gained mainly through experience. Such capabilities can be applied across the corporation's businesses and make an important contribution to customer benefits.[61] It can be difficult to define a corporation's capabilities objectively, but understanding what they are can provide important insights into its sources of competitive advantage and the strategic options of the firm.[62]

The work on core skills, capabilities, or resources has generated much interest. Walter Kiechel, in *Fortune* magazine, describes how some executives are perceiving their role, and that of corporate management, as guardians and promoters of the company's core skills, and sums up the current understanding of these concepts: "To the extent that such skills can be exploited by each of the company's businesses, they represent a reason for having all those businesses under one corporate umbrella—a much better reason, the experts add, than the fabled synergies that multibusiness companies of yore were supposed to realize but seldom did."[63]

But corporations which do base their strategy on core competences have to be careful that the overall competence-based strategy does not become an excuse for poor performance or poor judgment. IBM, for example, acquired Rolm to gain access to the smaller company's expertise in PBX systems. Five years later, however, following heavy losses, IBM sold a majority stake in Rolm to Siemens. Some commentators think that IBM was too optimistic about Rolm's competences and potential and not sufficiently knowledgeable about changes under way in the PBX market or within Rolm.[64] It can be difficult to judge when an investment in a business is justified in terms of building a core competence, particularly if it means suspending normal profitability criteria and if the investment is in an unfamiliar business area.

Another danger with the competence approach to corporate strategy is that businesses may require similar core competences, but demand different overall strategies and managerial approaches. Texas Instruments, for example, attempted to exploit the core competence it had developed in its semiconductors business in areas such as calculators, watches, and home computers. It failed in these new areas not because it lacked the core semiconductor competence, but because its top management had no experience in managing such consumer-oriented businesses.[65] Similarly, Procter and Gamble applied its skills in product innovation and consumer promotion to a soft drinks business, Crush, but eventually divested the business because it ran into unfamiliar problems managing the local bottlers who largely control distribution of soft drinks.[66] Core competences may add value in specific areas in a variety of different businesses, but this is no guarantee that, overall, a company will be able to manage those different businesses successfully.

The work on core competences and capabilities broadens our understanding of a corporation's resources, and points out the important role of corporate management in building such resources and ensuring that they are used to the best advantage. As with synergy, however, it is difficult to accept that this is the only way to add value to a corporate portfolio. Corporate executives are concerned not only with building skills and competences in their businesses, but also with allocating resources to them, approving their plans and strategies, and monitoring and controlling their results. These important "shareholder" functions can also be a source of added value, if done well. Some companies such as Berkshire Hathaway and Hanson lay far more stress on these shareholder functions than on competence building; and, in all companies, the shareholder functions occupy a vital place, even where the management of core competences is also a focus of attention.

Dominant Logic and Management Style

A third approach to corporate success focuses on how corporate management adds value to a portfolio of businesses, in particular in its shareholder role. C. K. Prahalad and Richard Bettis argue that the more diverse a firm, the more complex the problems in managing it. Diversity, however, cannot be defined simply in terms of the number of products or markets in which a firm competes; the strategic variety of the firm's businesses is a more significant measure of its diversity. With firms in strategically similar businesses, executives can use common methods and approaches, using a single managerial dominant logic: "A dominant general management logic is defined as the way in which managers conceptualize the business and make critical resource allocation decisions—be it in technologies, product development, distribution, advertising, or in human resource management."[67]

When managerial dominant logic does not match the needs of the business, tensions and problems arise. Corporate management is liable to appoint the wrong managers to the business, to sanction inappropriate plans and investments, to control against the wrong targets and to interfere unproductively in the managing of the business.

Goold and Campbell's work on strategic management styles shows how dominant logic works in specific companies. In their research on large, diversified companies they identified different types of strategic management styles, with the main styles being Financial Control, Strategic Control, and Strategic Planning. The different styles each added value, but in different ways and to businesses with different characteristics and requirements. Financial Control companies, for example, have distinctive administrative and control systems, emphasizing the setting and meeting of annual budget targets. Although they may invest in a wide variety of industries, the portfolios of businesses of successful Financial Control companies share common characteristics.[68] Hanson is a good example: "The company's strategy is to focus on mature, stable businesses: 'We avoid areas of very high technology. We do not want to be in businesses which are highly capital intensive, where decision making has to be centralized or which rely on huge and sometimes expensive research with a prospect of a return sometime or never.'"[69]

In this view, the dominant logic or management style of the corporate management group is central to the performance of a diversified firm, and a group of businesses is best managed when the dominant logic of top managers matches the strategic characteristics and requirements of the businesses. The importance of the "fit" between top managers and the businesses in the corporate portfolio has also been emphasized by executives. Orion Hoch of Litton, for example, has explained the reasons for Litton's extensive divestments and restructuring: "Our aim was to go back to businesses that we could be comfortable with . . . We want to get back to doing what we were good at doing."[70] Gary Roubos, CEO of Dover Corporation, argues that the company is a successful conglomerate because it invests only in businesses in which it has considerable management "feel," even though these businesses are highly diverse: "Automatic lifts and toggle clamps are different—but they have much more in common than, say, investment banking and selling soap."[71]

Dominant logic may help to explain why conglomerate diversification can succeed, and also why diversification based on synergy or core competences can fail. If conglomerate diversification, such as that of Hanson, is based on businesses with a similar strategic logic, then it is possible for corporate management to take a common approach and to add value to those businesses. On the other hand, businesses with opportunities for sharing activities or skills, or ones requiring the same core competence, may nonetheless have different strategic logics. This makes it difficult for corporate management to realize synergy or exploit a core competence across the businesses. Oil companies that diversified into other extractive, energy or natural resource businesses in pursuit of synergies or core competences tended to find that the benefits they sought were overwhelmed by the problems caused by dissimilarities in strategic logic between the new businesses and the core oil businesses.

The concepts of dominant logic and management style offer some promising insights into both successful and unsuccessful diversification efforts, but there are unanswered questions.[72] Should diversified corporations aim to build portfolios of strategically related businesses, to ensure that top management and corporate systems and approaches do add value? Or should corporations seek to differentiate their approaches—develop "multiple dominant logics"—to manage businesses with different strategic characteristics successfully?

Goold and Campbell discovered that companies tend to adopt a particular strategic management style, even though the style was usually implicit, and that it was difficult for managers to cope with a variety of approaches or styles. They argued that CEOs should aim to focus their portfolios on the kinds of businesses which would gain benefits from their strategic management style.[73] On the other hand, authorities on multinationals argue that the increasing complexities of globally spread businesses and international competition require corporations to develop new capabilities to manage businesses facing different strategic issues. C. K. Prahalad and Yves Doz maintain that the winners in the struggle for global competitive advantage will be those companies that can develop differentiated structures, management processes, and systems, appropriate to the wide variety of their businesses.[74] Bartlett and Ghoshal describe how the "administrative heritage" of companies emphasizes a particular approach to issues such as coordination across businesses, but they argue that the idealized transnational company should be able to combine different approaches and develop "a full arsenal of coordinating processes, practices, and tools, and to use those mechanisms in the most effective and efficient manner."[75]

The question of whether it is possible to differentiate your management approaches to add value to many different kinds of businesses remains open. Bartlett and Ghoshal found evidence that some companies were seeking ways to encompass much more variety, but none had yet become a true transnational. We need more research to establish when it is appropriate to differentiate your management approaches to encompass the needs of diverse kinds of businesses, and when it is reasonable to adjust the corporate portfolio to a particular management style, or to a single managerial dominant logic. Work is also needed to clarify how to operationalize the concepts of dominant logic and strategic relatedness. We do not yet know how the limits of a dominant logic should be defined, how managers and corporations develop a new strategic management style, or if this is even possible.

THE CHALLENGE OF DIVERSIFICATION

During the last four decades, managers and academics have sought both to understand the basis of successful diversification, and to address the problems created by it. Figure 1 summarizes the evolution of thinking and practice during this time.

From the 1950s onwards, the development of management principles and the professional education of managers led to the belief that general management skills provided the justification for diversification. Diversified companies and conglomerates were seen to add value through the skills of their professional top managers, who applied modern management techniques and generalized approaches to a wide variety of businesses across different industries. During the late 1960s, however, the performance of many conglomerates weakened, and a new approach to corporate management of diversity was sought. The concepts of strategy and strategic management provided a new focus for senior management's attention during the 1970s, but soon proved unable to resolve many of the choices and trade-offs involved in resource allocation in the multibusiness firm. Portfolio planning techniques helped

FIGURE 1   Evolution of Thinking on Corporate Strategy and Diversification

	Basis of Corporate Value Added		Diversification Approaches and Issues
1950s / 1960s	General management skills	▶▶▶▶▶▶▶▶▶▶▶▶	Rise of conglomerates
			Performance problems with conglomerates
1970s	Strategy concept	▶▶▶▶▶▶▶▶▶▶▶▶	Strategic management of diversity
	Portfolio planning techniques	◀◀◀◀◀◀◀◀◀◀◀	Resource allocation problems
			Balanced portfolio management
1980s	Value based planning concepts		Manageability problems
			Restructuring
1990s	Synergy Core Competencies Dominant logic and management style	◀◀◀◀◀◀ / ▶▶▶▶▶▶▶▶▶▶▶	Core portfolios

many companies improve capital allocation across businesses with different strategic positions, and led to the idea of balanced portfolio management. But such analytical approaches overlooked the problem of manageability. Many companies found it difficult to manage businesses facing different strategic issues, and during the 1980s poor corporate performance again became a critical issue. Raiders, executives, and academics realized that many diversified corporations were not creating shareholder value, and there was a wave of takeovers, corporate breakups, and restructuring. The main themes of corporate strategy during the 1980s became restructuring back to core businesses and a resolve to stick to the knitting.

As we move into the 1990s, it has, however, become increasingly clear that there is no consensus on what sticking to the knitting in practice implies, or on how companies should be adding value to their remaining core businesses. Among the currently popular themes, the search for synergy and the building of core competences each have significant followings. But both views need to be complemented with some account of how the corporation can discharge its shareholder functions well. Here the concept of understanding the dominant strategic logic of a portfolio, and its compatibility with the approaches of top management, seems promising.

In our view, it is probable that a full account of corporate strategy and of diversification will need to draw on several of the strands of thought we have reviewed. Ultimately, diversity can only be worthwhile if corporate management adds value in some way and the test of a corporate strategy must be that the businesses in the portfolio are worth more under the management of the company in question than they would be under any other ownership.[76] To achieve this goal with a diverse group of businesses, it may be necessary to restructure portfolios to allow more uniformity in dominant logic and management style, more effective means of realizing synergies, and more sharing of core competences.

ENDNOTES

1. Kenneth R. Andrews, "Product Diversification and the Public Interest," *Harvard Business Review,* July 1951, p. 94.

2. M. E. Porter, "From Competitive Advantage to Corporate Strategy," *Harvard Business Review,* May–June 1987, p. 43.

3. Andrews, "Product Diversification," pp. 91–107; "Toward Professionalism in Business Management," *Harvard Business Review,* March–April 1969, pp. 49–60.

4. Peter Drucker, *The Practice of Management* (New York, 1955; re-issued Pan Books, 1968), p. 21.

5. Harold Koontz, "The Management Theory Jungle," *Academy of Management Journal* 4, no. 3 (December 1961), p. 175.

6. Robert L. Katz, "Skills of an Effective Administrator," *Harvard Business Review,* January–February 1955, p. 37.

7. Arthur B. Langlie, "Top Management's Responsibility for Good Government," and Thomas Roy Jones, "Top Management's Responsibility to the Community," both in H. B. Maynard, ed., *Top Management Handbook* (New York: McGraw-Hill, 1960); Andrews, "Product Diversification"; Y. K. Shetty and Newman S. Perry, Jr., "Are Top Executives Transferable across Companies?" *Business Horizons,* June 1976, pp. 23–28.

8. Richard Whitley, Alan Thomas, and Jane Marceau, *Masters of Business? Business Schools and Business Graduates in Britain and France* (London: Tavistock, 1981); J.-J. Servan-Schreiber, *The American Challenge,* translated by Ronald Steel (London: Hamish Hamilton, 1968).

9. David N. Judelson, "The Conglomerate—Corporate Form of the Future," *Michigan Business Review,* July 1969, pp. 8–12; reprinted in John W. Bonge, and Bruce P. Coleman, *Concepts for Corporate Strategy* (New York: Macmillan, 1972), p. 458.

10. Harold Geneen, with Alvin Moscow, *Managing* (New York: Doubleday, 1984).

11. Norman Berg, "Textron, Inc.," HBS Case Study 373-337, 1973, p. 16.

12. R. Heller, "The Legend of Litton," *Management Today,* October 1967; reprinted in Igor Ansoff, ed., *Business Strategy* (New York: Penguin Books, 1969), p. 378.

13. Jim Slater, *Return to Go: My Autobiography* (London: Weidenfield and Nicolson, 1977), p. 91.

14. Norman A. Berg, "What's Different about Conglomerate Management?" *Harvard Business Review,* November–December 1969, pp. 112–20.

15. Andrews, "Product Diversification," p. 98.

16. Robert S. Attiyeh, "Where Next for Conglomerates?" *Business Horizons,* December 1969, pp. 39–44; reprinted in Bonge and Coleman, *Concepts for Corporate Strategy;* Geneen, *Managing,* p. 43.

17. Michael Goold and John Quinn, *Strategic Control* (Hutchinson and Economist Publications, 1990); Richard G. Hamermesh, *Making Strategy Work* (New York: John Wiley & Sons, 1986), p. 3; William K. Hall, "SBUs: Hot, New Topic in the Management of Diversification," *Business Horizons,* February 1978, p. 17.

18. Peter Drucker, "Long-Range Planning: Challenge to Management Science," *Management Science* 5, no. 3 (1959), pp. 238–49; Igor Ansoff, *Corporate Strategy* (New York: McGraw-Hill, 1965); Alfred P. Sloan, *My Years with General Motors* (New York: Doubleday, 1963; reissued by Penguin Books, 1986); Alfred D. Chandler, Jr., *Strategy and Structure* (Cambridge, MA: MIT, 1962; reissued 1982); Myles L. Mace, "The President and Corporate Planning," *Harvard Business Review,* January–February 1965, pp. 49–62.

19. C. Roland Christensen, et al., *Business Policy: Text and Cases* (Burr Ridge, IL: Richard D. Irwin, 1965).

20. R. F. Vancil and P. Lorange, "Strategic Planning in Diversified Companies," *Harvard Business Review,* January–February 1975, pp. 81–90; Peter Lorange and Richard F. Vancil, *Strategic Planning Systems* (Englewood Cliffs, NJ: Prentice-Hall, 1977); K. A. Ringbakk, "Organized Planning in Major U.S. Companies," *Long Range Planning* 2, no. 2 (December 1969), pp. 46–57; Norman A. Berg, "Strategic Planning in Conglomerate Companies," *Harvard Business Review,* May–June 1965, pp. 79–92.

21. Louis V. Gerstner, "Can Strategic Management Pay Off?" *Business Horizons* 15, no. 6 (December 1972), p. 5.

22. Kenneth R. Andrews, *The Concept of Corporate Strategy* (Burr Ridge, IL: Richard D. Irwin, 1980), p. 35.

23. Berg, "What's Different?"

24. Joseph L. Bower, *Managing the Resource Allocation Process* (Boston, MA: Harvard Business School Press, 1970; Harvard Business School Classics Edition, 1986).

25. Bower, *Resource Allocation;* Hamermesh, *Moving Strategy.*

26. Hall, "SBUs, pp. 17–25; George S. Day, "Diagnosing the Product Portfolio," *Journal of Marketing,* April 1977, pp. 29–38.

27. Hamermesh, *Making Strategy,* p. 30.

28. Philippe Haspeslagh, "Portfolio Planning: Uses and Limits," *Harvard Business Review,* January–February 1982, pp. 58–73.

29. Barry Hedley, "Strategy and the 'Business Portfolio,'" *Long Range Planning,* February 1977, pp. 9–15; Charles W. Hofer and Dan Schendel, *Strategy Formulation: Analytical Concepts* (New York: West, 1978).

30. Hamermesh, *op. cit.,* p. 71.

31. Richard A. Bettis and William K. Hall, "The Business Portfolio Approach—Where It Falls Down in Practice," *Long Range Planning* 16, no. 2, April 1983, pp. 95–104.

32. Haspeslagh, *Making Strategy.*

33. Richard G. Hamermesh and Roderick E. White, "Manage beyond Portfolio Analysis," *Harvard Business Review,* January–February 1984, pp. 103–9.

34. Rosabeth Moss Kanter, *When Giants Learn to Dance* (London: Simon & Schuster, 1989), p. 94; Thomas More, "Goodbye, Corporate Staff," *Fortune,* December 21, 1987.

35. Porter, "From Competitive Advantage."

36. David Young and Brigid Sutcliffe, "Value Gaps—The Raiders, the Market or the Managers?" research paper, Ashridge Strategic Management Centre, January 1990.

37. Alfred Rappaport, *Creating Shareholder Value: The New Standard for Business Performance* (New York: Free Press, 1986); Bernard C. Reimann, *Managing for Value* (Oxford: Basic Blackwell, 1987).

38. William W. Alberts and James M. McTaggart, "Value Based Strategic Investment Planning," *Interfaces,* January–February 1984, pp. 138–51; see also Enrique R. Arzac, "Do Your Business Units Create Shareholder Value?" *Harvard Business Review,* January–February 1986, pp. 121–26.

39. John J. Curran, "Are Stocks Too High?" *Fortune,* September 28, 1987, p. 24.

40. Thomas J. Peters and Robert H. Waterman, *In Search of Excellence* (New York: Free Press, 1982).

41. Bob Hayes and Bill Abernathy, "Managing Our Way to Economic Decline," *Harvard Business Review,* July–August 1980, pp. 67–77.

42. Henry Mintzberg, *Mintzberg on Management* (New York: Free Press, 1989), p. 373.

43. Michael E. Porter, "General Mills, Inc.: Corporate Strategy," HBS Case Study 9-388-123, 1988.

44. Seth Lubove, "Dog with Bone," *Fortune,* April 13, 1992, p. 106.

45. Michael Jensen, "The Eclipse of the Public Corporation," *Harvard Business Review,* September–October 1989, pp. 61–74; S. Chatterjee, "Sources of Value in Takeovers: Synergy or Restructuring—Implications for Target and Bidder Firms," *Strategic Management Journal* 13, no. 4 (May 1992), pp. 267–86; S. Bhagat, A. Shleifer, R. Vishny, "Hostile Takeovers in the 1980s: The Return to Corporate Specialization," Brookings Paper on Economic Activity: Microeconomics, 1990.

46. Robert M. Grant, "On 'Dominant Logic,' Relatedness and the Link Between Diversity and Performance," *Strategic Management Journal* 9, no. 6 (November–December 1988), pp. 639–42; Robert M. Grant, "Diversification in the Financial Services Industry," in Andrew Campbell and Kathleen Luchs, *Strategic Synergy* (London: Butterworth Heinemann, 1992).

47. There is an extensive literature on this topic. See Richard P. Rumelt, *Strategy, Structure and Economic Performance* (Boston, MA: Harvard Business School Press, 1974); Richard P. Rumelt, "Diversification Strategy and Profitability," *Strategic Management Journal* 3 (1982) pp. 359–69; Richard A. Bettis, "Performance Differences in Related and Unrelated Diversified Firms," *Strategic Management Journal* 2 (1981), pp. 379–93; Kurt H. Christensen and Cynthia A. Montgomery, "Corporate Economic Performance: Diversification Strategy versus Market Structure," *Strategic Management Journal* 2 (1981), pp. 327–43; Gerry Johnson and Howard Thomas, "The Industry Context of Strategy, Structure and Performance: The U.K. Brewing Industry," *Strategic Management Journal* 8 (1987), pp. 343–61; Anju Seth, "Value Creation in Acquisitions: A Re-Examination of Performance Issues," *Strategic Management Journal* 11 (1990), pp. 99–115.

48. Ansoff, *Corporate Strategy.*

49. Michael E. Porter, *Competitive Advantage* (New York: Free Press, 1985).

50. Kanter, *When Giants,* p. 90.

51. Friedrich Trautwein, "Merger Motives and Merger Prescriptions," *Strategic Management Journal* 11 (1990), pp. 283–95.

52. Vasudevan Ramanujam and P. Varadarajan, "Research on Corporate Diversification: A Synthesis," *Strategic Management Journal* 10 (1989), pp. 523–51; Campbell and Luchs, *Strategic Synergy.*

53. Richard Reed and George A. Luffman, "Diversification: the Growing Confusion," *Strategic Management Journal* 7 (1986), p. 34.

54. Chatterjee, "Sources of Value," pp. 267–86.

55. Porter, *Competitive Advantage.*

56. Kanter, *When Giants.*

57. Christopher A. Bartlett and Sumantra Ghoshal, *Managing across Borders: The Transnational Solution* (Boston, MA: Harvard Business School Press, 1989).

58. Michael Goold and Andrew Campbell, *Strategies and Styles* (Oxford: Basil Blackwell, 1987).

59. C. K. Prahalad and Gary Hamel, "The Core Competence of the Corporation," *Harvard Business Review,* May–June 1990, pp. 79–91; Gary Hamel and C. K. Prahalad, "Strategic Intent," *Harvard Business Review,* May–June 1989, pp. 63–76.

60. Hiroyuki Itami, *Mobilizing Invisible Assets* (Cambridge, MA: Harvard University Press, 1987).

61. Philippe Haspeslagh and David B. Jemison, *Managing Acquisitions* (New York: Free Press, 1991), p. 23.

62. Robert M. Grant, "The Resource-Based Theory of Competitive Advantage: Implications for Strategy Formulation," *California Management Review,* Spring 1991, pp. 114–35; Andrew Campbell, "Building Core Skills," in Campbell and Luchs, *Strategic Synergy;* George Stalk, Philip Evans, and Laurence E. Shulman, "Competing on Capabilities," *Harvard Business Review,* March–April 1992, pp. 57–69.

63. Walter Kiechel, "Corporate Strategy for the 1990s," *Fortune,* February 29, 1988, p. 20.

64. Robert D. Hof and John J. Keller, "Behind the Scenes at the Fall of Rolm," *Business Week,* July 10, 1989, pp. 82–84.

65. C. K. Prahalad and R. A. Bettis, "The Dominant Logic: A New Linkage between Diversity and Performance," *Strategic Management Journal* 7 (1986), p. 495.

66. Patricia Winters, "Crush Fails to Fit on P&G Shelf," *Advertising Age,* July 10, 1989.

67. Prahalad and Bettis, "Dominant Logic," p. 490.

68. Goold and Campbell, *Strategies and Styles.*

69. Andrew Campbell, Marion Devine, and David Young, *A Sense of Mission* (London: Hutchinson, 1990), p. 242.

70. *Barron's,* May 20, 1991.

71. F. J. Aguilar, "Groen: A Dover Industries Company," HBS Case 9-388-055, 1988.

72. Michael Goold and Andrew Campbell, "Brief Case: From Corporate Strategy to Parenting Advantage," *Long Range Planning* 24, no. 1 (February 1991), pp. 115–17.

73. Goold and Campbell, *op. cit.*

74. C. K. Prahalad and Yves L. Doz, *The Multinational Mission* (London: Free Press, 1987), p. 261.

75. Bartlett and Ghoshal, *Managing across Borders,* p. 166.

76. Michael Goold and Andrew Campbell, "Corporate Strategy and Parenting Skills," research report, Ashridge Strategic Management Centre, 1991.

COLLABORATING ACROSS LINES OF BUSINESS FOR COMPETITIVE ADVANTAGE

Jeanne M. Liedtka, *University of Virginia*

Successful collaboration requires the development of new skills, mindsets, and corporate architecture. Based on interviews with a set of professional service firms known for their ability to collaborate successfully, the author has identified the factors associated with turning collaboration into competitive advantage.

Asked to describe the essence of the advantage that a leading investment bank enjoyed, a senior executive offered the following comment on this competitor's superior capacity for internal cooperation:

> They are the team to beat. Why? They don't slow themselves down with the clutter of bureaucracy—they let them swarm. They are gang tacklers who overwhelm the problem. That could yield inefficiency, but it doesn't. They are smart, quick, and they work seamlessly together.

As his comment reflects, the art of building and sustaining collaborative relationships is a fundamental prerequisite for competitive success in many industries. Major initiatives aimed at reengineering, outsourcing, and global supply chain management all seek to create value through a process of dismantling traditional barriers between functions and firms and have been much discussed. Collaboration across lines of business-based divisions has been strangely underrepresented in these discussions; yet it can have profound strategic significance in particular industry contexts. This article explores what those contexts look like, the value that collaborative approaches contribute, and the practices characterizing a set of high-performing firms that have succeeded based upon their capacity to achieve collaborative outcomes. The article begins by linking collaboration with current thinking in the field of strategy about competitive advantage.

Source: ©*Academy of Management Executive* 10, no. 2 (1996).

COLLABORATION AS A SOURCE OF COMPETITIVE ADVANTAGE

The path to sustaining competitive advantage has been a central concern of the field of strategy since its inception. For much of this time, advantage has been viewed as a function of industry selection and of positioning within an industry. Recent writing in the strategy field, though, has given increased attention to the development of a distinctive set of organizational capabilities.[1] Capabilities consist of skills and knowledge, linked together through business processes that produce outcomes in the marketplace. Here, the essence of advantage focuses on the identification and development of processes rather than on particular products or markets. In this way of thinking, today's product is no more than a temporary solution to today's customer problem—it offers no hope for sustaining advantage. Therefore, the ability to develop an ongoing flow of products provides the best advantage in today's fast-placed environment.

In increasing numbers of industries, sustaining competitive advantage relies upon the development of a broad-based and portable set of capabilities. Bankers, for example, can no longer afford to focus on the sale of a mortgage, the opening of a checking account, or the issuance of a credit card as discrete and independent activities. Instead, competitive advantage in the future will go to those organizations that can build profitable relationships with customers across a broad range of financial services. Service needs evolve continuously, requiring the disparate functional groups of old to speak to the customer with a single voice and deliver their products in a seamless way.

Only certain processes confer advantage, however. Processes are strategically significant to the extent that they provide superior value to customers, are hard to imitate, and render the organization more adaptable to change.[2] This third condition is particularly challenging, as the processes that fulfill conditions one and two are often highly resistant to change and impede a firm's ability to prosper in the long-term. The ability to *continuously build new capabilities* is at the heart of competitive advantage in industries characterized by rapid change. This requires what we call meta-capabilities, the skills and knowledge that underlie the process of capability building itself. Meta-capabilities enable the continuous re-creation of specific business-related capabilities over time.

Learning is one example of a meta-capability. In fact, the ability to learn new sets of skills on an ongoing basis may be the *only* sustainable source of advantage for the future. As Eric Hoffer noted:

> In a world of change, the learners shall inherit the Earth; while the learned shall find themselves perfectly suited for a world that no longer exists.[3]

Increased interest, in both academic and practitioner circles, in the theory and practice of learning organizations,[4] offers strong support for the relevance of Hoffer's view to today's business environment.

Collaboration is a second meta-capability. For our purposes, we define collaboration as a process of decision making among interdependent parties; it involves joint ownership of decisions and collective responsibility for outcomes.[5] Collaboration allows organizations to work and learn across the silos that have characterized organizational structures. The boundaries that we are interested in here are those formed by lines of business, usually represented by separate divisions under a larger corporate umbrella. This multidivi-

Collaboration allows organizations to work and learn across the silos that have characterized organizational structures.

sional form, despite being criticized as a fossil by some, remains the most common form of organizational structure in the developed world.[6] Firms form lines of business to break down the functional silos and achieve focus and responsiveness to particular market segments. Increasingly, however, the environment that gave rise to the demand for lines of business is itself changing, in different ways in different contexts, creating new demands on the line of business structure.

One major environmental change is the disintegration of the traditional industry boundaries that formed the foundation of lines of business. Some leading strategic thinkers have announced the end of industry as we have known it.[7] Consider the case of financial services, where the collapse of barriers between the banking, insurance, and securities businesses is reshaping the competitive landscape. Similarly, the new realm that we have come to call multimedia, forming out of the convergence of telecommunications, computers, cable, and entertainment, develops with astonishing speed. As boundaries have fallen, new entrants, equipped with different capability sets, make it difficult for large, previously entrenched competitors to maintain market share and growth. Focused providers, like Schwab in securities and Geico in auto insurance, have proven themselves to be adept at cherry-picking the most attractive customers away from market leaders. These rapidly growing competitors have rewritten the rules of competition and have cost structures—largely technology-driven rather than bricks-and mortar-based—that their larger, more established competitors cannot hope to copy. Strategic options in these converging areas appear to be narrowing, and providing superior value to customers becomes possible in one of only two ways. The first is through specialization that provides focused and cost-effective, albeit narrow, solutions to customers. These customers create their own packages of products and services, using multiple vendors. The second available strategy is to be a provider of a full range of services—one-stop shopping. This range of desired services, however, increasingly crosses lines of business. What many market leaders in banking today call full service means offering customers the opportunity to wade through the bureaucratic maze of the bank's internal structure to create their own packages—often paying a price premium to do so. For many so-called full-service firms, then, achieving superior profitability means developing a new capability to create solutions that cross lines of business effectively and efficiently in a way that is invisible to customers. Operating out of today's silos is no longer an option.

In other industries, such as professional services, current competitors rather than new entrants drive changes that increase the need for collaboration across lines of business. These competitors create relationship-based package solutions to offset the increasing commoditization of current products and services. They search for customer groups that can be shared profitably across divisions. In public accounting, for instance, the Big 6 have witnessed the continuing erosion of margins as clients have come to view the audit as an undifferentiated product, with greatly reduced switching costs. In response to this erosion, a number of accounting firms seek to position themselves as the leading providers of a board range of professional services—financial, tax and consulting—across traditional business lines.

In yet a third context, pressures for simultaneous centralization and decentralization drive the need for enhanced collaboration. Escalated demand for responsiveness to increasingly sophisticated customer needs continues to argue for a line of business decision-making locus close to the customer. At the same time, the need to obtain economies of scale in operations and to achieve critical mass in investments in areas like information technology increases the need for centralization.

Take, for example, the credit card industry from the perspective of a regional retail bank. Increasing economies of scale in processing and customer service necessitate highly centralized management of these functions. Banks today cannot afford the luxury of autonomous, geographically scattered, small-scale operations in these areas. Yet the most attractive credit card holders are those for whom credit cards are just one product in a broader relationship with their local bank. In an industry characterized by ever increasing mailbox clutter in the search for new accounts, local customers tend to be more loyal and less price sensitive. It requires entrepreneurial spirit at the local level to find and nurture these loyalty-based relationships. Yet how can local managers who see themselves as retail bankers, with little affinity for the credit card folks and no control over the level of service their customer receives, be engaged to do this? And what happens when the picture is further complicated by a need to also move other types of financial products—securities or insurance, for instance—with similar operating economics, through that same local market? Only through collaboration across lines of business can the organization, as a whole, present a seamless face to its customers.

Despite the emergence of the myriad new organizational forms we read so much about, the boxes and lines on an organization chart are a poor match for the dilemmas raised by eroding industry barriers, increasing commoditization, and simultaneous pressures for centralization and decentralization. Any design reflects a compromise that inevitably leaves important things undone. The multidivisional form, especially when operated cooperatively, has a long and distinguished history and offers the best prospect, demonstrated empirically, for producing above average returns in firms with distinct but related businesses.[8] Its success in shifting environments, however, depends on a capability for effective collaboration.

Like other fundamental shifts in management thinking, effective collaboration is difficult to achieve in a climate of business as usual, as it relies on qualities not present in most organizations. Successful collaboration requires the development of new skills, mindsets and corporate architectures. The quality of many attempts at collaboration today is discouraging, as any time-stressed, meeting-saturated manager will testify. The risks and effort involved in working across lines of business often seem to outweigh the benefits in organizations where turf protection has been the norm and where competition for corporate funding has been the only reminder of interdependence. In banking, for example, branch personnel routinely urge their best customers to seek their mortgages elsewhere, bypassing their own mortgage companies. In accounting, audit partners breathe a sigh of relief as a new consulting project goes to another firm, rather than to their own consulting practice. In major medical centers, physicians threaten to secede from hospital physical associations, rather than expand cooperative decision making with fellow physicians in other specialities. Concerns about the existence of internal silos have a new urgency, as the difficulty of achieving meaningful cooperation across lines of business becomes apparent.

Successful collaboration requires the development of new skills, mindsets and corporate architectures.

The risks and effort involved in working across lines of business often seem to outweigh the benefits in organizations where turf protection has been the norm and where competition for corporate funding has been the only reminder of interdependence.

In examining firms that excel at producing value through collaboration, we have observed a set of skills, a way of thinking, and a variety of organizational supports in place that other firms lack. This is not surprising. Collaboration calls upon *skills* that have rarely been rewarded in most organizations—listening with an open mind to the proposals of others versus selling one's own solutions harder; acknowledging and using conflict productively versus suppressing and ignoring it; leading by supporting and facilitating versus managing through authority or fiat; and designing new end-to-end value systems rather than tinkering with incremental fixes to current processes.

Pressures to operate lines of business while achieving collaboration present new dilemmas for today's managers that are insoluble within their current *ways of thinking*. Managers have become comfortable with accepting responsibility for *outcomes;* collaboration often demands that they give up their authority over the *functions that are necessary to achieving these outcomes*. They have been asked to take *ownership;* collaboration insists that they forfeit *control*. "How can I own what I don't control?" is a central question underlying much of the struggle produced by attempts at collaboration. Yet the success of collaboration cannot rely on organizational charts or corporate mandates; it depends far more on the capabilities and commitment of the working partners in the field than on the directives issued from divisional or corporate headquarters. Collaboration requires commitment, not compliance. And although its potential value is measured along the value chain and through the eyes of customers, the reality of its success is contingent on the ability of individuals, scattered within and across organizations, to build meaningful relationships.

This commitment cannot be generated or sustained by the field itself, however. Commitment requires an architecture that compensates for the inadequacy of the structure itself, whatever that structure may be. The architecture consists of the larger values, systems, and processes that provide the infrastructure to support collaboration.

To understand the best practices in collaboration, we studied firms with a long history of significant and successful collaboration—a set of high-performing professional partnerships—and compared and contrasted these with a set of struggling partnerships.[9] Although the high-performing firms are partnerships in a legal sense of the word, as we better understood their sources of advantages we came to see the legal partnership form as playing only a part in their success. Other factors, potentially present in organizations of all legal forms, contributed more significantly to their ability to achieve collaborative outcomes of real strategic value. These factors included:

- A partnering mindset.
- A partnering skillset.
- A supportive context that provides commitment, processes, and resources to facilitate collaboration.

All three elements were critical in the creation of positive partnership outcomes. In learning from these firms, the concept of partnering itself came to provide a language well-suited to capturing the essence of what a collaborative capability should look like. We came to believe that the professional partnerships we studied in law, health care, accounting, and investment banking had much to teach all firms interested in developing a capability for collaboration.

The remainder of this article examines the three factors cited above (summarized in Figure 1), at a more detailed level. Working partners from these firms, some struggling and some succeeding, speak in their own words about the factors causing the success or failure of their partnerships.

FIGURE 1   Components of Effective Partnering

Partnering Mindset

A view of partnership as opportunity
A sense of at-stakeness
A level of trust among partners
A readiness to learn from each other

Partnering Skillset

Creating shared goals and realistic
   expectations
Using conflict productively
Redesigning systems

Supporting Organizational Architecture

- A belief in honest communication
- Committed leadership
- Joint planning and budgeting processes
- Congruent measurement and reward systems
- Resource availability

CONTRIBUTORS TO PARTNERSHIP SUCCESS: THE PARTNERING MINDSET

Perhaps the most striking quality of the successful partnerships studied was the partners' ways of thinking, the mindset with which the partners approached their relationship with the firm, its customers, and each other. This partnering mindset was characterized by (1) a view of partnering as representing opportunity, rather than loss of control, (2) a sense of what we will call *at-stakeness,* both for themselves and the organization, (3) a level of trust among partners, and (4) a readiness to learn from each other.

A View of Partnership as Reflecting Opportunity

I could have been in a practice where I would have been a solo pediatrician. Coming out of a residency that is not a real comfortable position to be in . . . To be a partner here is to belong to an organization that I'm very proud of . . . it's kind of a community. It's gotten so large now that it feels even more like a community because we have so many people who work here . . . To me that's not an uncomfortable feeling. I know that some people would have difficulty not knowing the names of everybody they work with, but I'm more focused on the quality it represents and the care that we're able to provide at a very high level.

That is how a physician at one of the largest and most successful private physician practice groups in the United States described her decision to join the firm. Although a member of a profession known for the long-cherished autonomy that it has enjoyed, this physician did not view the partnership as an infringement on her ability to make her own choices. Rather she saw it as a rich source of possibilities not available if she were acting independently.

Charles Handy argues that managers today need three senses to ward off the "disorientation and rudderlessness" that the pace of change around us inevitably fosters. These include a sense of continuity, a sense of connection, and a sense of direction.[10] Collaboration played an important role in providing all three of these senses for partners in the high-performing firms studied. Partnership was seen by these managers as *enhancing,* rather than reducing control, as they expanded their capability base through the larger capability base that partnering created.

This was rarely the case in struggling partnerships. What we found instead was that at corporate headquarters the benefits of the collaboration were generally well understood. To the field managers, however, what was often most apparent were the risks. This disproportion became serious as the field was asked to implement initiatives for which the risks were clear, but for which the benefits, even at a firmwide level, were dimly visible to them. Too often, those who had done the evaluation of whether to partner assumed that their logic was clear, meaningful, and shared by all. This was frequently not the case. Consider, for instance, the initiatives on the part of major CPA firms to sell a wider variety of services—consulting expertise, for example—to their major corporate clients, surely a winning strategy with clear benefits to all. To headquarters the incremental revenues were very attractive on the margin. The consulting partners were enthusiastic. The audit partners, however, had invested years in carefully nurturing client relationships amid an increasingly competitive environment, and the calculus looked quite different to them. The potential downside to the audit relationship of a consulting project gone bad (that he or she had no control over) far outweighed the incremental revenue potential of any given consulting project. Not surprisingly, corporate encouragement to cross-sell produced few results. Until that audit partner's calculus changes, the likelihood of a successful partnership between the Audit and Consulting lines of business is small. In successful partnerships, partners saw clear and tangible benefits available only through joint action, benefits that exceeded the risks they entailed.

> *In successful partnerships, partners saw clear and tangible benefits available only through joint action, benefits that exceeded the risks they entailed.*

A Sense of At-Stakeness

> The key is that you have to assume that the person is going to be there for you. Meaning that if you ask for a certain effort from someone . . . If you feel that the person's going to do it and do it properly . . . then you've got the makings, in my view, of a real partnership. If you have a sense that when you go to your colleague . . . they will say yes for reasons of compensation or power or whatever, but they will do it in as minimal a way as they can . . . you have completely the opposite. You have the sense that you're alone, you're isolated, you're working for yourself.

In successful partnerships, the result of collaborative efforts *matter.* They matter, first of all, to the organization. Partners have a clear sense of the firm's strategic direction and the pivotal role that collaboration plays in achieving it. Individuals also see themselves as having a personal stake in partnership outcomes (as the manager quoted above, a partner in a highly successful investment bank notes). One group of partners labeled this attribute "skin in the game." These partners committed to their relationship, not because they were told to, but because it held the promise of producing an outcome that they cared deeply about. Successful partners felt too much at stake to allow disbelief or discomfort to undermine their commitment to making the partnership work. Such personal at-stakeness was easily distinguished from the more distant wait-and-see attitude prevalent among struggling partners.

> *Successful partners felt too much at stake to allow disbelief or discomfort to undermine their commitment to making the partnership work.*

Partnerships may look like marriages made in heaven to the senior management, but to those in the trenches they can feel more like shotgun weddings. Of relevance, therefore, is how to gain a sense of at-stakeness when the relationship starts off under duress. One of the crucial steps is the passage from token acceptance of the partnership into "private acceptance."[11] Private acceptance involves moving beyond compliance to a directive from above to seeing oneself as primarily responsible for making the relationship work. In struggling partnerships, the very notion of the concept of partnership itself undermined managers' at-stakeness. Here, the essence of the partnership was seen as the business units' linkage, usually through headquarters, from which the policies, procedures, and pronouncements that governed the shape of the relationship were issued. This limited view of the partnership relations as owned by headquarters created dependency in the field, rather than at-stakeness, as lower-level managers were encouraged to look upward and not inward for the solutions to problems.[12] In order for partnering across lines to succeed, partnership must be conceived of as *both* an organizational relationship at the business-unit level and as a personal relationship between individuals in the field. Driven from a strategic vision, this latter relationship is both *part of* and *separate from* the headquarters relationship.

Such at-stakeness was nurtured, in high-performing firms, through a process of involvement at every stage and in all significant decisions relating to the partnership. Involvement did not imply democracy or consensus decision making at every turn. Max DePree described it as meaning a "voice not a vote."[13] To one Regional Head of a retail bank it meant that "you have to be sure that *nothing* happens in your partner's marketplace that they had no voice in." Both partners must have a meaningful role in determining their fate.

> *In struggling partnerships, trust was demanded; in successful ones, it was earned. In effective partnerships, trust was an outcome created over time, based on a track record of performance.*

Level of Trust among Partners

> I use a phrase, a "foxhole friend" . . . In this environments, you'd like to have foxhole lawyers. People you could be in the foxhole with and count on so that you can go to sleep when you're on their watch . . . You entrust yourself to them.

Not surprisingly, trust was a much discussed topic in all of our partnership discussions, as it was in the above conversation with a partner in a highly regarded New York law firm. In struggling partnerships, trust was demanded; in successful ones, it was earned. In effective partnerships, trust was an *outcome* created over time, based on a track record of performance. Such trust had two distinct elements. The first was an absolute faith in the technical competency of partners. As another partner is the same firm noted:

> I left a partnership because I simply could not, in good conscience, say to the people who were my clients, that I was responsible for, come to me with work in areas that I don't do, whether that be tax or corporate or trusts and estates or whatever it was, outside my area of expertise. Because I know that you'll get a good performance. I couldn't say that, I was not happy with the quality of my other partners or their diligence . . . Here, I'm busting to say that to people . . . And that's something that you have at your core, or it's not really a good partnership.

The premise behind partnership formation is that each party brings a skill that the other lacks—thus creating a set of possibilities acting *jointly* that do not exist acting independently. While the best partnerships viewed their process as one of learning together, a partner's basic competency was non-negotiable. Those partnerships that relied initially on a level of expertise beyond current partner capabilities experienced difficulty from the start. High-performing partnerships exhibited a sense of pride founded upon a belief in the technical excellence of their partners.

In addition to competence, equity plays a significant role in partnership trust formation.[14] Thus, partners must trust each other's *intentions,* as well as each other's *ability to deliver.* Either alone was insufficient. Increasing performance levels did not build trust where partners questioned motives; nor were good intentions sufficient when delivery on promises faltered.

An important part of the development of trust was a willingness to forgive, which one partner described as "giving up all hope of a better yesterday." Early stumbles were a reality in most partnerships. Partnerships got stuck when individuals responded by distancing themselves and watching their partners twist in the wind when things went wrong. Conversely, partnerships moved forward when they acknowledged problems, put the past in perspective, and were willing to begin again. Struggling partnership publicly ignored, then privately remembered, failures; successful ones acknowledge failures, then forgave them.

Readiness to Learn from Each Other

All of us as individuals who work with a particular customer know that we don't have all of the answers. All of us have to depend on each other to make sure that we get the right answer for the customer . . . Customers' problems have become more complex so they do demand input and expertise from different people within the firm and I think one is just evidencing common sense and intelligence to say, "I don't have to come up with all the answers.

The most successful partnerships were not composed of people who arrived at the table with all of the answers. They came with important *questions* whose answers drew on the wisdom of all. Each believed he or she had important things left to learn. Similarly, those who saw themselves as fully capable of acting alone were poor prospects for making a partnering relationship work. Though each partner comes, as we have said, with his or her own particular expertise, the benefits of partnership accrued as they *educated each other* and, in the process, developed new capabilities that neither had before. The best partnerships did much more than merely compensate for each other's areas of ignorance by filling in the gaps; they enlarged each other's competency base and that of the firm as a whole. A lawyer offered an example from his recent experiences that illustrated the benefits of collaborative learning:

We had an experience last week where we were contacted by an investor in the United Kingdom . . . I worked with one of my litigation partners to put together a quick outline of what we felt the issues would be that the client would have to face. We consulted with a number of partners in the firm to reduce all of that to four or five pages, so that we could make a pitch to the client. We made that pitch and it was successful—in part, because we had brought all of those resources together and focused them on one person, as opposed to sending over to the U.K. a team of six people—which all of our competition did.

MECHANISMS FOR MANAGING THE PARTNERSHIP RELATIONSHIP: THE PARTNERING SKILLSET

Creating Shared Goals and Realistic Expectations

The entire culture of this firm is built around putting the customer's interests first. If the customer's interests are served, then ours will follow . . . There's somebody running every product, there's somebody running every region and there's somebody running every industry. And there's a lot of confusion about who's really the boss, so to speak. But that's not important. What's important is what does the customer need and how do we deliver it.

Without shared goals, partnerships were forced to rely on the mutual pursuit of individual self-interest. Self-interest was an important factor in sustaining all partnerships; alone, it did not provide an adequate basis for long-term success. The dynamic of expediency that it created offered little incentive to keep plugging when the going got rough—as it usually did at some point in all the firms. Collaboration, for many managers, was initially an unnatural act. Achieving it required that they locate a common ground on which to build the relationship. Almost without exception, it was the customer who provided the common focus around which high-performing partnerships found meaning.

If shared goals provided the end point, clear and realistic expectations for each partner's contribution were the markers that shaped members' *perception* of success along the journey. These were arrived at in multiple ways. Some partnerships found a contract useful for defining the obligations and responsibilities of each party. The proponents of a contractual agreement argued for the clarity it provided. Detractors saw that same specificity as interfering with the give and take of a high-performing partnership, whose basis is trust and whose greatest asset is its flexibility. Both sides agreed that a *process of negotiation of expectations* must occur.[15] This was often, but not always, facilitated by the development of a document. The key issue was that expectations be *joint* and that there be a process through which each party made explicit its original expectations, which were then adjusted through discussion to a joint set of expectations. External benchmarks were often an important input into the expectations-setting discussion. In high-performing partnerships, the other party was never treated as a "captive market"—an excuse to underperform outside sources.

Using Conflict Productivity

There's an importance in the way that you deal with each other that we maintain civility and that we're able to debate and discuss things together without getting emotional and angry about it. Very, very important that people here respect each other's opinion, consider it and that they work towards consensus and that things don't get polarized.

On important issues, successful partnerships were able to work through points of conflict to achieve consensus, in a process that one partner described as "almost like steering the Titanic—it doesn't move very fast." This process of addressing and resolving conflicting opinions harnessed and leveraged the creative potential inherent in the diversity of partners' views. Struggling partnerships, on the other hand, had less patience and were more likely to suppress conflict and to substitute compromise for consensus. The process of watering down each party's best solution produced compromise that perpetuated mediocrity and indifference, not excellence or commitment. Successful partnerships learned to move over time from common ground to a higher ground. The search for higher ground often involved using the tension created by opposing views to explore alternatives. As Eric Hoffer noted:

The most gifted members of the human species are at their creative best when they cannot have their way.[16]

Struggling partnerships were more likely to reward their managers for selling solutions than for engaging in dialogue; for talking rather than listening. Peter Senge has referred to this communication style as advocacy and argues that it needs to be balanced with a spirit of inquiry for conflict to produce learning.[17] Addressing conflict through a process of advocacy, he asserts, tends to lead to escalation of the conflict and further polarization of the parties. Using inquiry, on the other hand, managers can break out of the loop of repeatedly making their cases ever more vehemently and begin a process in which each partner questions his or her own generalizations, makes explicit the assumptions upon which his or her viewpoint is based, and attempts to bring the same understanding to the perspective of his or her partners. Next comes a willingness to test those assumptions by looking for gaps in logic, envisioning data that could be brought to bear to support or refute assumptions, and exploring what would be necessary to change each other's views. The outcome of a successful process of dialogue is both better decisions and a renewed sense of ownership for all members of the partnership.

Redesigning Systems

The most exciting thing that is happening in our institution right now is that we are learning together by first describing and appreciating what our system is—basically applying systems theory to our practice . . . And learning where our part fits into the whole with our colleagues . . . Asking how do we redesign that thing to fit the customers' needs even better. That large system diagram has become an important element in the organization for learning. Because what we're learning about is not just the vague nature of our interdependencies, but the process links that make up those interdependencies . . . The central focus of learning in our organization in the future is going to be our process literacy and how to interpret and analyze what's happening in our processes.

The most dramatic collaborative outcomes occurred in high-performing partnerships that combined a strong set of shared values, skill at bridging diverse viewpoints, and an ability to analyze and redesign processes—and used the combination to create new integrated systems. The breakthroughs achieved were impressive. A physician described the outcome of a collaborative redesign of the process for diagnosing and treating a breast lump in a patient:

We formulated a team. It included a surgeon and it included radiologists. It included also representatives of the adult primary care practice, family practice, and ob-gyn . . . We involved administration and nursing and x-ray techs. And by grabbing this process we were better able to create a set of chain reactions that occurs when a woman presents with symptomatic breast problems . . . It's had two effects. The first effect was that in January 1992, before we instituted these guidelines, we saw that 78 percent of our breast cancers were detected in stages zero, one, and two—the most treatable forms . . . By the first quarter of 1993, in excess of 96 percent of our cancers were caught in stages zero, one, and two. But it's not because the surgeons are biopsying better. Not because the radiologists are imaging better and it's not because the primary care physicians are recognizing the problems earlier. The other effect that is has had is that for patients, who were experiencing undue stress from knowing that there was something in their breast that had to be evaluated. We've reduced something that used to take weeks to a matter of hours. And that's how an integrated system works.

THE LARGER CONTEXT FOR PARTNERSHIP SUCCESS ————

Supported by Organizational Architecture

Successful partners did not create the mindsets, goals, processes, and outcomes that we have talked about thus far by themselves. They were supported by a larger organizational architecture that valued what they were striving for and that gave them the resources to succeed. In borrowing the term from Nadler and his associates,[18] we use their definition of organizational architecture as including all of the elements of design of the social and work systems, including formal structure, the design of work practices, operating styles, and processes for selection, socialization, development, and reward. A special emphasis on nurturing a collaborative capacity was present in all of these areas of the high-performance firms. The physician practice group deliberately set entry salary levels just below market rates to discourage those recruits more interested in personal income than in organizational values. Mentoring was a highly valued activity in all the high performers. Senior partners were keenly aware of their need to model appropriate behaviors. Among the aspects of larger context, the most prominent for high-performance partnerships were a culture steeped in honesty, committed leadership, congruent processes for measurement, reward and budgeting, and the provision of time and information.

A Belief in Honest Communication

It has to be safe to be honest . . . if you have an environment where it's safe to be honest, you will get more innovation and you will get more creative thinking and willingness to speak up.

In struggling partnerships, concerns about the political costs of honesty enhanced the difficulty of collaboration since these concerns deprived the coopera-tive effort of an essential ingredient, namely, accurate information. Return-ing to our earlier CPA firm example, we might ask what would it take to bring the calculus of corporate, audit, and consulting partners into align-ment? To begin the process, a forthright acknowledgment from the audit partners that they do not trust the consulting partners with their clients might prompt an examination of the assumptions and data supporting the lack of trust. As long as the issue remains closed to discussion, we can predict the scenario that results: consulting partners continue to push for access; corporate continues to needle the audit partners to accede; the audit partners continue to plead whatever plausible excuse saves their client relationships. They breathe a sigh of relief when another consulting firm is hired, preserving the safety of their own audit relationships. The dance around the issue of substance continues.

> *In struggling partnerships, concerns about the political costs of honesty enhanced the difficulty of collaboration since these concerns deprived the cooperative effort of an essential ingredient, namely, accurate information.*

What, then, will encourage the audit partner to speak the truth about his or her reluctance? Only a climate where support exists to bring substantive issues to the surface, however awkward and politically charged they may be.

Committed Leadership

I've got to believe, as it is with most organizations . . . that it has to flow from the top. That is, if the leaders of the firm evidence that they cooperate on a day-to-day basis with each other and if they do not permit turf warfare to break out and if they do no permit politicking or individual-oriented behavior to exist, those things don't exist . . . People around here have been rewarded who have put the customer first, who have put the firm first and their own success and their own career development would follow. And again, I think that happens at the top. If the senior people in the firm are not living that day in and day out, then they're going to send signals to the organization that is going to create different behavior.

Active, visible senior management support for partnership endeavors was clearly essential. Senior management sensed the need to speak the strategic purpose the partnership served clearly and frequently. Equally importantly, senior management held each partner accountable for performance. Noncooperative behavior was confronted and dealt with. Successful partnerships, as we have already noted, were characterized by a willingness to forgive; the corollary to this was a willingness to monitor compliance and respond. Senior managers who failed to keep their commitment to the partnership, or to hold others to their commitments, sent a message that subverted the partnership process and eroded commitment. Talk is not cheap where partnerships are concerned. Talk that was not backed up by action was, in fact, quite expensive in the long term. It cost both leaders and the partnership itself credibility.

Joint Planning and Budgeting Process

> We have all kinds of so-called partnerships around here. Yet, in setting the annual plan we had absolutely no input.

Partners owned only commitments that they had a voice in creating. Given that most commitments in organizations are crystallized during formal planning and budgeting processes, these processes represented critical opportunities to recognize and incorporate input from all partners. High-performing partnerships took such involvement as given and rarely discussed the importance of these processes. Disillusioned partners pointed to them frequently as a sore spot. Few things were as damaging to partnerships as the unilateral insertion of performance goals into a joint plan by one partner (often at the insistence of corporate). So long as actual performance was on budget, the other partner's resentment merely simmered. When budget was missed, it exploded.

Congruent Measurement and Reward Systems

> Each partner (here) shares in the overall pot of profits. A system like this is different than a lot of places. A lot of firms today have evolved toward a system where you kind of eat what you kill. And that kind of system, I think, is counter to collegiality, is counter to cooperativeness, is counter to the kind of devotion to the body as a whole.

We have known for a long time that people do what we reward them for, not what we ask them to. Partnerships based solely on each individual's financial self-interest faced a far greater obstacle than those that designed incentives linking individual and partnership success. The successful organizations studied chose a variety of different compensation systems to motivate collaborative behavior. Some utilized only organizationwide measures of performance, as in the firm whose executive was quoted above. Others relied on a double-counting approach:

> Everything from an accounting standpoint would be double or triple counted, so that people would all get full credit . . . That is a way to keep people from arguing about whether they contributed more than someone else. Because it's not serving any customer's best interest to be sitting around haggling about how a dollar gets sliced up around the firm.

Thus, the question of how to divide the pie was not seen as trivial; nor was it allowed to consume the lion's share of partners' attention. It was a discussion that worked much better when the partnership was seen as producing the kind of solutions that increased the size of the pie for all.

Resource Availability

An important part of senior management's keeping its commitment to the partnership was providing the necessary resources to ensure its success: (1) education in the mindshift and skills that partnering requires, (2) investments in infrastructure, especially in the area of information technology to make information available real-time, to support the learning process and decrease coordination costs, and (3) time to allow the relationships to develop. Time often seemed, in fact, to be the major resource constraint that most struggling partnerships dealt with. Pressures to move quickly to market damaged partnerships at their most vulnerable stage—their infancy. Early stumbles that resulted from pushing product out, in advance of working the process out, became cognitive anchors that left a lingering legacy of ill will in their wake. The high-performing partnerships emphasized speed on *tactical* decisions; on strategic choices they were willing to invest the time in a process that yielded a response that partners were comfortable with—even if it meant being slower to market than competitors.

CONCLUSION

Talking about partnership is easy; making partnership work is difficult. The surge in partnering activity of all kinds has arisen in response to the new environmental demands that today's organizations face. The strategic imperative for boundary busting collaboration in industries as diverse as retail banking, health care, law, and accounting is clear. As the Medical Director of one farsighted clinic explained:

> If people can't cooperate and work as a system, they can't be efficient. They can't create processes that work smoothly. They can't get rid of variation . . . I think that is going to be our primary sustainable advantage—our capacity to integrate across all specialties. A systems-oriented medical staff that is willing to subordinate the prima donna ego kind of stuff in order for the system as a whole to succeed. I think it's a practical business strategy.

This kind of partnering cannot be grafted onto yesterday's ways of thinking and behaving. Nor can it be achieved through structure alone. The capability for collaboration develops as part of a new way of managing and designing organizations that includes many other issues under discussion in business today—continuous improvement, employee empowerment, organizational learning, and innovation. Gaining the strategic benefits of partnering requires a transformation, at both corporate and field levels, in the way we think about managerial control, organizational architecture, and even the very sources of competitive advantage. At the field level, it requires a mindset that seeks ownership and sees opportunity and a skillset that fosters dialogue and system redesign.

Those who fail to develop a capability for collaboration may find themselves as disadvantaged in the competitive marketplace of the future as those burdened by obsolete physical plant or technologies. An executive of the firm described at the beginning of this article offered a description of his favored competitors:

> Where people lock their doors. Where people protect their clients. Where people only worry about their own career. That is a firm that I like to compete against. Because I know that I may not be as good as the individuals I'm competing against one up, but our firm is a lot better than any individual that we compete with.

ENDNOTES

1. There has been much discussion of this new view of strategy, beginning with G. Hamel and C. K. Prahalad, "Strategic Intent," *Harvard Business Review,* May–June 1989, pp. 63–76. Also see G. Stalk, P. Evans, and

L. Shulman, "Competing on Capabilities: The New Rules of Corporate Strategy," *Harvard Business Review,* March–April 1992, pp. 57–69; and G. Day, "The Capabilities of Market-Driven Organizations," *Journal of Marketing,* October 1994, pp. 37–52.

2. See Day, "Capabilities."

3. From Eric Hoffer, *The Ordeal of Change* (New York: Harper & Row, 1963).

4. See Peter Senge, *The Fifth Discipline: The Art and Practice of the Learning Organization* (New York: Doubleday, 1990).

5. This is taken from B. Gray, *Collaborating* (San Francisco: Jossey-Bass, 1991), p. 227.

6. For a detailed discussion of the history and theory behind the multidivisional form, see R. Hoskisson, C. Hill and H. Kim, "The Multidivisional Structure: Organizational Fossil or Source of Value?" *Journal of Management* 19, no. 2, pp. 269–98.

7. See James Moore, "Predators and Prey: A New Ecology of Competition," *Harvard Business Review,* May–June 1993, pp. 76–86.

8. See Hoskisson et al., "Multidivisional Structure."

9. All of the firms that participated in these discussions requested that we preserve their anonymity in sharing our findings with a wider audience. Accordingly, we refer only to their industry. Similarly, the names of the partners quoted are not used. All quotes, however, are taken directly from the transcripts of one-on-one discussions with these partners, without altering them in any way. The high-performance firms were recommended for inclusion by industry experts and are widely regarded in their respective fields as leaders, in terms of the outcomes that they produce through their collaboration across lines of business.

10. See Charles Hardy, *The Age of Paradox* (Boston: Harvard Business School Press, 1994).

11. K. Reardon and R. Spekman, "Starting Out Right: Negotiation Lessons for Domestic and Cross-Cultural Business Alliances," *Business Horizons,* January–February 1994, pp. 71–79.

12. G. Pinchot and E. Pinchot, *The End of Bureaucracy and the Rise of the Intelligent Organization* (San Francisco: Berrett-Koehler, 1993).

13. Max DePree, *Leadership Is an Art* (New York: Dell, 1989).

14. P. Ring and A. Van de Ven, "Developmental Processes of Cooperative Interorganizational Relationships," *Academy of Management Review* 19, no. 1, pp. 90–118.

15. J. Mohr and R. Spekman, "Characteristics of Partnership Attributes, Communication Behavior and Conflict Resolution Techniques," *Strategic Management Journal* 15 (1994), pp. 135–52.

16. Eric Hoffer, *Ordeal of Change.*

17. See Peter Senge, "Mental Models," *Planning Review,* March–April 1992.

18. See D. Nadler, M. Gerstein, R. Shaw, and Associates, *Organizational Architecture* (San Francisco: Jossey-Bass).

THE HORIZONTAL CORPORATION

John A. Byrne, *Journalist*

To produce significant increases in productivity, firms must concentrate on managing across the organization as opposed to up and down. Performance increases begin with a restructuring of the hierarchical organization chart by organizing around the core processes fundamental to performance goals and creating teams from different departments to manage them.

WANTED: Bureaucracy basher, willing to challenge convention, assume big risks, and rewrite the accepted rules of industrial order.

It's a job description that says nothing about your skills in manufacturing, finance, or any other business discipline. And as seismic changes continue to rumble across the corporate landscape, it's the kind of want ad the twenty-first century corporation might write.

Skeptical? No matter where you work, it's likely that your company has been, in today's vernacular, "downsized" and "delayered." It has chopped out layers of management and supposedly empowered employees with greater responsibility. But you're still bumping up against the same entrenched bureaucracy that has held you back before. The engineers still battle manufacturing. Marketing continues to slug it out with sales. And the financial naysayers fight everyone.

That's because, despite the cutbacks, you probably still work in the typical vertical organization, a company in which staffers look up to bosses instead of out to customers. You and your colleagues feel loyalty and commitment to the functional fiefdoms in which you work, not to the overall corporation and its goals. And even after all the cutting, too many layers of management still slow decision making and lead to high coordination costs.

Mere downsizing, in other words, does little to change the fundamental way that work gets done in a corporation. To do that takes a different organizational model, the horizontal corporation. Already, some of Corporate America's biggest names, from American Telephone & Telegraph and DuPont to General Electric and

Source: *Business Week*, December 20, 1993, pp. 76–81.

FIGURE 1   Seven of the Key Elements of the Horizontal Corporation

Simple downsizing didn't produce the dramatic rises in productivity many companies hoped for. Gaining quantum leaps in performance requires rethinking the way work gets done. To do that, some companies are adopting a new organization model. Here's how it might work:

1. **Organize around process, not task**. Instead of creating a structure around functions or departments, build the company around its three to five "core processes," with specific performance goals. Assign an "owner" to each process.

2. **Flatten hierarchy**. To reduce supervision, combine fragmented tasks, eliminate work that fails to add value, and cut the activities within each process to a minimum. Use as few teams as possible to perform an entire process.

3. **Use teams to manage everything**. Make teams the main building blocks of the organization. Limit supervisory roles by making the team manage itself. Give the team a common purpose. Hold it accountable for measurable performance goals.

4. **Let customers drive performance**. Make customer satisfaction—not stock appreciation or profitability—the primary driver and measure of performance. The profits will come and the stock will rise if the customers are satisfied.

5. **Reward team performance**. Change the appraisal and pay systems to reward team results, not just individual performance. Encourage staffers to develop multiple skills rather than specialized know-how. Reward them for it.

6. **Maximize supplier and customer contact**. Bring employees into direct, regular contact with suppliers and customers. Add supplier or customer representatives as full working members of in-house teams when they can be of service.

7. **Inform and train all employees**. Don't just spoon-feed sanitized information on a "need to know" basis. Trust staffers with raw data, but train them in how to use it to perform their own analyses and make their own decisions.

Motorola, are moving toward the idea. In the quest for greater efficiency and productivity, they're beginning to redraw the hierarchical organization charts that have defined corporate life since the Industrial Revolution. (See Figure 1.)

"WAVE OF THE FUTURE"

Some of these changes have been under way for several years under the guise of "total quality management" efforts, reengineering, or business-process redesign. But no matter which buzzword or phrase you choose, the trend is toward flatter organizations in which managing across has become more critical than managing up and down in a top-heavy hierarchy.

The trend is toward flatter organizations in which managing across has become more critical than managing up and down in a top-heavy hierarchy.

The horizontal corporation, though, goes much further than these previous efforts: It largely eliminates both hierarchy and functional or departmental boundaries. In its purest state, the horizontal corporation might boast a skeleton group of senior executives at the top in such traditional support functions as finance and human resources. But virtually everyone else in the organization would work together in multidisciplinary teams that perform core processes, such as product development or sales generation. The upshot: The organiza-

---

FIGURE 2 Companies Moving toward the Horizontal Model

- **AT&T:** Network Systems Division reorganized its entire business around processes; now sets budgets by process and awards bonuses to employees based on customer evaluations.
- **Eastman Chemical:** Kodak unit has over 1,000 teams; ditched senior V-Ps for administration, manufacturing, and R&D in favor of self-directed teams.
- **General Electric:** Lighting business scrapped vertical structure, adopting horizontal design with more than 100 processes and programs.
- **Lexmark International:** Former IBM division axed 60 percent of managers in manufacturing and support in favor of cross-functional teams worldwide.
- **Motorola:** Government Electronics group redesigned its supply management organization as a process with external customers at the end; team members are now evaluating peers.
- **Xerox:** Develops new products through multidisciplinary teams that work in a single process, instead of vertical functions or departments.

Source: *Business Week*, McKinsey & Co.

tion might have only three or four layers of management between the chairman and the staffers in a given process.

If the concept takes hold, almost every aspect of corporate life will be profoundly altered. Companies would organize around process—developing new products, for example—instead of around narrow tasks, such as forecasting market demand for a given new product. Self-managing teams would become the building blocks of the new organization. Performance objectives would be linked to customer satisfaction rather than profitability or shareholder value. And staffers would be rewarded not just for individual performance but for the development of their skills and for team performance.

For most companies, the idea amounts to a major cultural transformation—but one whose time may be at hand. "It's a wave of the future," declares M. Anthony Burns, chairman of Ryder System Inc., the truck-leasing concern. "You just can't summarily lay off people. You've got to change the process and drive out the unnecessary work, or it will be back tomorrow." Such radical changes hold the promise for dramatic gains in productivity, according to Lawrence A. Bossidy, chairman of AlliedSignal Inc. "There's an awful lot more productivity you're going to see in the next few years as we move to horizontally organized structures with a focus on the customer," says Bossidy.

How so? Just as a light bulb wastes electricity to produce unwanted heat, a traditional corporation expends a tremendous amount of energy running its own internal machinery—managing relations among departments or providing information up and down the hierarchy, for example.

A horizontal structure eliminates most of those tasks and focuses almost all of a company's resources on its customers. That's why proponents of the idea say it can deliver dramatic improvements in efficiency and speed. "It can get you from 100 horsepower to 500 horsepower," says Frank Ostroff, a McKinsey & Co. consultant. With colleague Douglas Smith, he coined the term "the horizontal organization" and developed a series of principles to define the new corporate model. (See Figures 2 and 3.)

FIGURE 3 How to Create a Horizontal Corporation

- Identify strategic objectives.
- Analyze key competitive advantages to fulfill objectives.
- Define core processes, focusing on what's essential to accomplish your goals.
- Organize around processes, not functions. Each process should link related tasks to yield a product or service to a customer.
- Eliminate all activities that fail to add value or contribute to the key objectives.
- Cut function and staff departments to a minimum, preserving key expertise.
- Appoint a manager or team as the "owner" of each core process.
- Create multidisciplinary teams to run each process.
- Set specific performance objectives for each process.
- Empower employees with authority and information to achieve goals.
- Revamp training, appraisal, pay, and budgetary systems to support the new structure and link it to customer satisfaction.

Source: McKinsey & Co., *Business Week*.

The idea is drawing attention in corporate and academic circles. In the past year, Ostroff has given talks on the horizontal organization before sizable gatherings of corporate strategic planners, quality experts, and entrepreneurs. He has also carried the message to MBAs and faculty at the University of Pennsylvania and Yale University, and he boasts invitations from Harvard University and several leading European business schools.

PROCESS AND PAIN

But this is much more than just another abstract theory making the B-school lecture rounds. Examples of horizontal management abound, though much of the movement is occurring at lower levels in organizations. Some AT&T units are now doing annual budgets based not on functions or departments but on processes such as the maintenance of a worldwide telecommunications network. They're even dishing out bonuses to employees based on customer evaluations of the teams performing those processes. Du Pont Co. has set up a centralized group this year to nudge the chemical giant's business units into organizing along horizontal lines. Chrysler Corp. used a process approach to turn out its new Neon subcompact quickly for a fraction of the typical development costs. Xerox Corp. is employing what it calls "microenterprise units" of employees that have beginning-to-end responsibility for the company's products.

In early December, nearly two dozen companies—including such international giants as Boeing, British Telecommunications, Stockholm-based L. M. Ericsson, and Volvo Europe—convened in Boston under the auspices of Mercer Management Consulting, another consulting shop peddling the idea, to swap stories on their efforts to adopt horizontal management techniques. Indeed, nearly all of the most prominent consulting firms are now raking in 10s of millions of dollars in revenues by advising companies to organize their operations horizontally.

What those consultants' clients are quickly discovering, however, is that eliminating the neatly arranged boxes on an organization chart in favor of a more horizontal structure can often be a complex and painful ordeal. Indeed, simply defining the processes of a given corporation may prove to be a mind-boggling and time-consuming exercise. Consider AT&T. Initially, the company's Network Services Division, which has 16,000 employees, tallied up some 130 processes before it narrowed them down to 13 core ones.

Eliminating the neatly arranged boxes on an organization chart in favor of a more horizontal structure can often be a complex and painful ordeal.

After that comes the challenge of persuading people to cast off their old marketing, finance, or manufacturing hats and think more broadly. "This is the hardest damn thing to do," says Terry M. Ennis, who heads up a group to help Du Pont's businesses organize along horizontal lines. "It's very unsettling and threatening for people. You find line and function managers who have been honored and rewarded for what they've done for decades. You're in a white-water zone when you change."

Some management gurus, noting the fervor with which corporate chieftains embrace fads, express caution. "The idea draws together a number of fashionable trends and packages them in an interesting way," says Henry Mintzberg, a management professor at McGill University. "But the danger is that an idea like this can generate too much enthusiasm. It's not for everyone." Mintzberg notes that there is no one solution to every organization's problems. Indeed, streamlined vertical structures may suit some mass-production industries better than horizontal ones.

Already, consultants say, some companies are rushing to organize around processes without linking them to the corporation's key goals. Before tinkering with its organization chart, Ostroff says, a company must understand the markets and the customers it wants to reach and complete an analysis of what it will take to win them. Only then should the company begin to identify the most critical core processes to achieve its objectives—whether they're lowering costs by 30 percent or developing new products in half the time it normally required.

DIFFERENT CLIMATE

In the days when business was more predictable and stable, companies organized themselves in vertical structures to take advantage of specialized experts. The benefits are obvious: Everyone has a place, and everyone understands his or her task. The critical decision-making power resides at the top. But while gaining clarity and stability, such organizations make it difficult for anyone to understand the task of the company as a whole and how to relate his or her work to it. The result: Collaboration among different departments was often a triumph over formal organization charts.

To solve such problems, some companies turned to so-called matrix organizations in the 1960s and 1970s. The model was built around specific projects that cut across departmental lines. But it still kept the hierarchy intact and left most of the power and responsibility in the upper reaches of the organization.

Heightened global competition and the ever-increasing speed of technological change have since altered the rules of the game and have forced corporate planners to seek new solutions. "We were reluctant to leave the command-and-control structure because it had worked so well," says Philip Engel, president of CNA Corp., the Chicago-based insurance company that is refashioning its organization. "But it no longer fits the realities."

Many companies are moving to this new form of corporate organization after failing to achieve needed productivity gains by simple streamlining and consolidation.

Indeed, many companies are moving to this new form of corporate organization after failing to achieve needed productivity gains by simple streamlining and consolidation. "We didn't have another horse to ride," says Kenneth L. Garrett, a senior vice-president at AT&T's Network

Systems Division. "We weren't performing as well as we could, and we had already streamlined our operations."

In all cases, the objective of the horizontal corporation is to change the narrow mind-sets of armies of corporate specialists who have spent their careers climbing a vertical hierarchy to the top of a given function. As Du Pont's Terry Ennis puts it: "Our goal is to get everyone focused on the business as a system in which the functions are seamless." Du Pont executives are trying to do away with what Ennis calls the "disconnects" and "handoffs" that are so common between functions and departments. "Every time you have an organizational boundary, you get the potential for a disconnect," Ennis says. "The bigger the organization, the bigger the functions, and the more disconnects you get."

SPEEDIER CYCLES

The early proponents of the horizontal corporation are claiming significant gains. At General Electric Co., where Chairman John F. Welch Jr. speaks of building a "boundaryless" company, the concept has reduced costs, shortened cycle times, and increased the company's responsiveness to its customers. GE's $3 billion lighting business scrambled a more traditional structure for its global technology organization in favor of one in which a senior team of 9 to 12 people oversees nearly 100 processes or programs worldwide, from new product design to improving the yield on production machinery. In virtually all the cases, a multidisciplinary team works together to achieve the goals of the process.

The senior leadership group—composed of managers with "multiple competencies" rather than narrow specialists—exists to allocate resources and ensure coordination of the processes and programs. "They stay away from the day-to-day activities, which are managed by the teams themselves," explains Harold Giles, manager of human resources in GE's lighting business.

The change forced major upheavals in GE's training, appraisal, and compensation systems. To create greater allegiance to a process, rather than a boss, the company has begun to put in place so-called "360-degree appraisal routines" in which peers and others above and below the employee evaluate the performance of an individual in a process. In some cases, as many as 20 people are now involved in reviewing a single employee. Employees are paid on the basis of the skills they develop rather than merely the individual work they perform.

Ryder System is another convert. The company had been organized by division—each with its own functions—based on product. But it wanted an organization that would reduce overhead while being more responsive to customers. "We were reaching the end of the runway looking for cost efficiencies, as most companies have," says J. Ernie Riddle, senior vice-president for marketing. "So we're looking at processes from front to back."

To purchase a vehicle for leasing, for instance, required some 14 to 17 handoffs as the documents wended their way from one functional department to another at a local, and then a national level. "We passed the baton so many times that the chances of dropping it were great," says Riddle. By viewing this paperwork flow as a single process from purchasing the vehicle to providing it to a customer, Ryder has reduced the handoffs to two from five. By redesigning the work, weeding out unnecessary approvals, and pushing more authority down the organization, the company cut its purchasing cycle by a third, to four months.

"A CLEAN SHEET"

Some start-ups have opted to structure themselves as horizontal companies from the get-go. One such company is Astra/Merck Group, a new stand-alone company formed to market antiulcer and high-blood-pressure drugs licensed from Sweden's Astra. Instead of organizing around functional areas, Astra/Merck is structured around a half-dozen "market-driven business processes," from drug development to product sourcing and distribution. "We literally had a clean sheet of paper to build the new model company," says Robert C. Holmes, director of strategic planning. "A functional organization wasn't likely to support our strategic goals to be lean, fast, and focused on the customer."

Some fairly small companies are also finding the model appealing. Consider Modicon Inc., a North Andover (Massachusetts) maker of automation-control equipment with annual revenues of $300 million. Instead of viewing product development as a task of the engineering function, President Paul White defined it more broadly as a process that would involve a team of 15 managers from engineering, manufacturing, marketing, sales, and finance.

By working together, Modicon's team avoided costly delays from disagreements and misunderstandings. "In the past," says White, "an engineering team would have worked on this alone with some dialogue from marketing. Manufacturing wouldn't get involved until the design was brought into the factory. Now, all the business issues are right on the table from the beginning."

TEAM HATS

The change allowed Modicon to bring six software products to market in one-third the time it would normally take. The company, a subsidiary of Germany's Daimler Benz, still has a management structure organized by function. But many of the company's 900 employees are involved in up to 30 teams that span several functions and departments. Predicts White: "In five years, we'll still have some formal functional structure, but people will probably feel free enough to spend the majority of their time outside their functions."

So far, the vast majority of horizontal experimentation has been at the lower levels of organization. Increasingly, however, corporations are overhauling their entire structures to bear a closer resemblance to the horizontal model defined by consultants Ostroff and others. Eastman Chemical Co., the $3.5 billion unit of Eastman Kodak Co. to be spun off as a stand-alone company on January 1, replaced several of its senior vice-presidents in charge of the key functions with "self-directed work teams." Instead of having a head of manufacturing, for example, the company uses a team consisting of all its plant managers. "It was the most dramatic change in the company's 70-year history," maintains Ernest W. Deavenport Jr., president of Eastman Chemical. "It makes people take off their organizational hats and put on their team hats. It gives people a much broader perspective and forces decision making down at least another level."

In creating the new organization, the 500 senior managers agreed that the primary role of the functions was to support Eastman's business in chemicals, plastics, fibers, and polymers. "A function does not and should not have a mission of its own," insists Deavenport. Common sense? Of course. But over the years, the functional departments had grown strong and powerful, as they have in many organizations, often at the expense of the overall company as they fought to protect and build turf.

FIGURE 4   Horizontal Organization

Congratulations, You're Moving to a New Pepperoni

If the 21st century corporation goes horizontal, what will its organization chart look like? That's right, organization charts—those dull, lifeless templates that reduce power relationships to a confusing mass of boxes and arrows. As a growing number of planners try to turn a management abstraction into a pragmatic reality, organization charts are beginning to look stranger and stranger.

Consider Eastman Chemical Co., the Eastman Kodak Co. division to be spun off as a separate company in January. "Our organization chart is now called the pizza chart because it looks like a pizza with a lot of pepperoni sitting on it," says Ernest W. Deavenport Jr., who as president is the pepperoni at the center of the pie. "We did it in circular form to show that everyone is equal in the organization. No one dominates the other. The white space inside the circles is more important than the lines."

Each pepperoni typically represents a cross-functional team responsible for managing a business, a geographic area, a function, or a "core-competence" in a specific technology or area such as innovation. The white space around them is where the collaborative interaction is supposed to occur.

Eastman Chemical's pizza isn't the only paper representation of the horizontally inclined corporation. PepsiCo flipped its pyramidal organization chart upside-down. To help focus on customers, Pepsi put its field reps at the top. Chief Executive Craig Weatherup now calls Pepsi-Cola, the huge beverage unit of PepsiCo, "the right-side-up company." Astra/Merck Group—nearly a pure horizontal company—boasts a chart with a stack of six elongated rectangles, each representing a core process of the pharmaceutical start-up. Across the top are a series of functional boxes, or "skill centers," that drive down through the processes with arrows.

Wild Shamrocks

For its own conceptual model of what the horizontal organization should look like, McKinsey & Co., the consulting firm, came up with a fairly abstract rendering of three boxes floating above a trio of core processes. Each process is represented by a bar with three circles on the surface. The circles symbolize the multidisciplinary teams in charge of a specific process.

Now, virtually all of the company's managers work on at least one cross-functional team, and most work on two or more on a daily basis. For example, Tom O. Nethery, a group vice-president, runs an industrial-business group. But he also serves on three other teams that deal with such diverse issues as human resources, cellulose technology, and product-support services. (See Figure 4.)

These changes in the workplace are certain to dramatically alter titles, career paths, and the goals of individuals, too. At AT&T's Network Systems Division, each of 13 core processes boasts an "owner" and a "champion." While the owners focus on the day-to-day operations of a process, the champions ensure that the process remains linked with overall business strategies and goals. Through it all, collaboration is key. "An overriding challenge is how you get marketing people to talk to finance people when they've thrown rocks at each other for decades," says Gerald Ross, cofounder of ChangeLab International, a consulting firm that specializes in cultural transformation. "Your career will be dependent on your ability to work across boundaries with others very different from you."

Don't rush to write the obituary for functional management, however. No companies have completely eliminated functional specialization. And even advocates of the new model don't envision the end of managers who are experts in manufacturing,

FIGURE 4 (continued) Horizontal Organization

This is not the first time organizational theorists have tried to come up with a workable alternative to the vertical structure that has dominated business for a century or more. Some have been as wild as the shamrock image promoted by Charles Handy, a lecturer at the London Business School. Its three leaves symbolize the joining forces of core employees, external contractors, and part-time staffers. James Brian Quinn, a Dartmouth B-school prof, thought up the starburst to reflect the company that splits off units like shooting stars.

But these experimental designs are really just metaphors for the 21st century corporation, not pragmatic structures that any company has actually adopted. And for every upside-down pyramid, you'll still find thousands of conventional charts.

Just browse through the Conference Board's repository of organization charts, a collection that features the latest diagrams of 450 corporations, from Advance Bank Australia to Xerox. The New York–based organization has been selling charts, at $14 apiece, for nearly a decade. Over that time, the organizational diagrams have gotten flatter, with fewer reporting levels, and they've become more decentralized, too. More recently, in response to heightened concern over corporate governance, some companies such as Mobil Oil Corp. and Ford Motor Co. have put shareholders and the board of directors in boxes above the top dog. But they still favor the old vertical, command-and-control hierarchy.

All of the Conference Board's best-sellers—BankAmerica, Ford, General Electric, IBM, and Motorola—are pretty much what you would expect: plenty of boxes connected by lines in steep pyramids. Indeed, under Ford's office of the chief executive, there are a mind-boggling 59 boxes of divisions, departments, and functions.

Only a few of the charts reflect the trend toward horizontal organization. Why? For one thing, it's simply too early. "Organization charts lag what's happening," says Douglas Smith, a consultant who helped develop the horizontal idea. "And a lot of people can't figure out how to draw it any other way." For another, most of the more dramatic changes along horizontal lines are occurring at divisional or subsidiary levels. That's where—at PepsiCo and Eastman Kodak, at least—those pizzas and inverted pyramids are symbols that the business-as-usual days are long gone.

finance, and the like. "It's only the rarest of organizations that would choose to be purely vertical or horizontal," says consultant Douglas Smith. "Most organizations will be hybrids."

Still, the horizontal corporation is an idea that's gaining currency and one that will increasingly demand people who think more broadly and thrive on change, who manage process instead of people, and who cherish teamwork as never before.

RETHINKING ORGANIZATIONAL DESIGN

Robert W. Keidel

This article groups organizational design approaches into three categories: restructuring, reengineering, and rethinking. Unlike restructuring (which reconfigures organization units) or reengineering (which tends to be tactical rather than strategic), rethinking attempts to understand the link between the way managers think and the way they design organizations. Organizational rethinking means incorporating character, constituencies, and capabilities into the design of organizations.

Corporate managers are being bombarded by one salvo after another of organizational design "solutions." The latter include (in alphabetical order):

- Delayering
- Downsizing
- Process innovation
- Process management
- Process redesign
- Reengineering
- Restructuring
- Rightsizing

Indeed, one consulting client sarcastically likened the subject of organizational design to a Rorschach test—10 inkblots that, as he put it, "could mean anything to anyone—it's all subjective interpretation."

The premise of this article is that organizational design initiatives often fail to achieve their objectives because they trivialize the concept. Especially problematic is *restructuring*—which includes downsizing, rightsizing, and delayering—because its only intent is to increase shareholder well-being. By contrast, *reengineering*—a covering label for process management, process innovation, and process redesign—considers both shareholder and customer concerns; however, it tends to ignore organizational effects on employees. A third approach, *rethinking*, explicitly

Source: *Academy of Management Executive* 8, no. 4 (1994).

addresses all three perspectives. Consequently, it offers special promise as a long-term methodology.

Restructuring amounts to manipulating units represented by the organization chart; reengineering involves revising organizational processes; and rethinking is concerned with the way in which organizational issues and decisions are patterned. More precisely, restructuring is a reduction in any one or a mix of the following: (1) overall organizational size, as defined by the number of employees; (2) number of organizational units; (3) size of organizational units; and (4) number of hierarchical levels. According to Edward Bowman and Harbir Singh, *organizational* restructuring "is intended to increase the efficiency and effectiveness of management teams through significant changes in organizational structure, often accompanied by downsizing."[1]

Reengineering is a reconfiguration of work to better serve customers (and as a consequence, to benefit shareholders). In the words of bestselling authors Michael Hammer and James Champy, reengineering entails the "radical redesign of business processes to achieve dramatic improvements in critical contemporary measures of performance, such as cost, quality, service, and speed."[2]

Rethinking is an attempt to probe beneath organizational structures (restructuring) and processes (reengineering) in order to understand the link between the way managers think and the way they design organizations.

Rethinking is an attempt to probe beneath organizational structures (restructuring) and processes (reengineering) in order to understand the link between the way managers think and the way they design organizations. Rethinking seeks to identify the logic that connects cognitive patterns and organizational patterns.

Summary contrasts among restructuring, reengineering, and rethinking are presented in Figure 1.

RESTRUCTURING

This is the most rudimentary category of understanding organizational design. *Design* equals *structure* equals *organization chart*—administrative groupings and reporting relations; therefore, redesign amounts to little more than altering boxes and lines. Such a perspective is what Henry Mintzberg may have had in mind when he disparagingly referred to "a management whose knowledge consists of black symbols on white paper."[3]

Restructuring typically means reconfiguring organizational units, often large ones.

Restructuring typically means reconfiguring organizational units, often large ones. For example, whole divisions or business units may be combined, disaggregated, or spun off. Or business functions—such as engineering, operations, information systems, and distribution—may be melded together, folded into business units, or precipitated out. Restructuring—which almost always implies job loss—is often called *rightsizing* or *downsizing*; the former term is usually no more than a euphemism for the latter, which itself is a euphemism for layoffs. Another form of restructuring is *delayering*, which means reducing the number of layers, or hierarchical levels, in the organization—that is, the "distance" between the top manager (chief executive officer/president) and those at the bottom, or operating level.

Restructuring approaches, especially when they are layoff-driven, are numerical exercises grounded in economics. The rationale may be survival: a company is *in extremis,* and its continued existence is at risk. Or the impetus may be the need for increased growth and/or profitability.[4] In any case, the chief beneficiaries are shareholders because the overriding performance criterion is efficiency. Customers may or

FIGURE 1   Three Approaches to Organizational Design

	Restructuring (Organization Units)	Reengineering (Organization Processes)	Rethinking (Organization Cognition)
Metaphors:	Downsizing Rightsizing Delayering	Process management Process innovation Process redesign	Framing Patterning Learning
Target:	Organizational units and hierarchical levels	Business functions and work systems	Individual, group, and organizational mindsets
Nature:	Numerical	Technical	Conceptual
Rationale:	Survival or repositioning	Tactical competitiveness	Strategic advantage
Beneficiaries:	Shareholders	Shareholders and customers	Shareholders, customers, and employees
Performance criteria:	Efficiency	Efficiency and customer satisfaction	Efficiency, customer satisfaction, and employee development
Organizational variables addressed:	Control	Control and autonomy	Control, autonomy, and cooperation
Method:	Computing ratios	Flow-charting work processes (interdependencies)	Modeling organization as a balance of multiple perspectives
Upside:	Reduced costs	Simpler, faster work processes	Richer planning, decision-making, and innovation capabilities
Downside:	Organizational trauma	Organizational anxiety	Organizational frustration

may not be better served. In certain instances (especially when delayering takes place), customer service may improve as a result of a new, less cumbersome and hierarchical process. At other times, however, those who remain in the recharted organization wind up on overload, and customer service is likely to deteriorate. For example, many small companies have complained of inferior service from major accounting firms after the latter had merged and subsequently cut staff.[5]

The primary technique used in restructuring is simple arithmetic: the computation of ratios. Several ratios may come into play—such as headcount to sales volume, corporate staff to operating employees, and managerial "span of control" (that is, the number of people reporting to a given individual). Benchmarking exercises have sometimes led to dramatic restructuring programs, as firms discover that their productivity (however defined) is out of line with that of competitors. For example, earlier this year Digital Equipment Corp. CEO Robert Palmer justified massive job cuts by contrasting DEC's revenue per employee with more favorable ratios at Hewlett-Packard and IBM.[6]

The upside of restructuring is, paradoxically, cost reduction—which may translate into an economically viable future. Clearly, bulging bureaucracies cannot weather global competition, and many such organizations have had no alternative than to take draconian measures. Thus between spring 1991 and spring 1994, 27 corporations announced job reductions that totaled more than 630,000—an average of over 23,000.[7] For more than a few of these firms, survival was (is) at stake. One company on the list is Sears, Roebuck—which announced cutbacks of 50,000 employees.

Sears's retrenchment is a sensible antidote to prior excesses that included diversification across real estate (Coldwell Banker), insurance (Allstate), and financial investments (Dean Witter).

Restructuring's downside, however, tends to be severe. To begin with, there is no guarantee that such measures will work. A study by Kim Cameron of 150 companies that had downsized found that 75 percent of this number ended up in worse shape.[8] (Of course, one never knows whether such firms might have become even more distressed had no restructuring taken place.)

Moreover, restructuring may lead to organizational *trauma*, a psychiatric condition defined by *Webster's* as "a painful emotional experience, or shock, often producing a lasting psychic effect and, sometimes, a neurosis." Even when restructuring appears to succeed, the real question may be, "for how long?" How can those who survive a seismic layoff, much less a succession of jolts, not feel guilty that their own hides were spared and anxious that they might be next on the hit list? And how can one expect much in the way of discretionary energy—in the form of imagination, commitment, and teamwork (as opposed to simply "doing time")—for the sake of an organization that can no longer be trusted?

REENGINEERING

Reengineering, under whatever label, is the current vogue. Michael Hammer and James Champy's book, *Reengineering the Corporation*, remained on *The New York Times* bestseller list from June until December 1993, and then reappeared for several weeks in 1994. Whereas restructuring is concerned with moving, shrinking, or eliminating organizational units ("boxes"), reengineering has to do with changing the way work is carried on. The argument for reengineering, at its most basic, goes as follows. Too many corporations (and other organizations) historically have been organized vertically, by functions—research and development (R&D), manufacturing, marketing, finance, and so on. As a consequence, employees' mind-sets have become defined by their particular function—or "silo" or "chimney" or "stovepipe," as some have put it.

Customers could care less, however, about internal organizational design. All that matters to them is composite output—in terms of quality, cost, and time. The challenge, therefore, is to improve on current competitiveness by reorganizing into work processes that make the most sense from the customer's point of view. This change is typically described as moving to a horizontal flow of tasks that cuts across the various functions. The new arrangement, ideally, is a work system comprising a set of business processes—each with a definable beginning and ending—such as new product development, customer acquisition, and order fulfillment.

Reengineering tends to be tactical, rather than strategic, because (1) it focuses on operational processes, as opposed to organizational purposes (which include the choice of product/market domain); (2) its improvement time frame is relatively near term; and (3) this activity tends not to consider human development as a source of continuous competitive advantage.

Reengineering tends to be tactical, rather than strategic.

Yet unlike classical industrial engineering, which also concerned itself with workflow, reengineering explicitly identifies customers (along with shareholders) as beneficiaries, and imaginatively uses information technology to streamline and simplify organization.[9] Proponents of reengineering advocate starting with a "blank sheet of paper." In other words, assume that nothing presently exists. What is the best way to arrange work in order to delight the customer? Determining this pattern requires flow-charting the entire work process.

Much of reengineering comes down to recasting what organizational theorists call task *interdependencies*.[10] In *pooled* interdependence, organizational parts (individuals or units, such as salespersons and salesforces) are relatively independent of each other; each provides a discrete contribution to the whole. In *sequential* interdependence, the parts interact in series, as in an assembly line; each renders a cumulative contribution to the whole. In *reciprocal* interdependence, the parts interact in a back-and-forth manner and make joint contributions to the whole. To oversimplify somewhat, the reengineering challenge often amounts to *decreasing* sequential interdependence (by minimizing the need for "handoffs" between different functions or departments), and *increasing* both pooled interdependence (by decentralizing authority) and reciprocal interdependence (by organizing in a way that brings resources together not sequentially, but simultaneously—as exemplified by "simultaneous engineering" in the automobile industry).

The upside to organizational reengineering is obvious. The work systems of many corporations are dysfunctional remnants of a less complicated, less dynamic, less competitive day and age. Moreover, all organizations tend to bureaucratize over time—as routines become entrenched, turf becomes delineated and defended, and politics takes precedence over performance. In short, the interests of organizational parts assert themselves over the interests of the whole.

Reengineering can change a firm's work orientation and, in so doing, produce quantifiable results. AT&T designed a new, autonomous business telephone systems (PBX) salesforce that, among other things, reduced the number of project handoffs between the time of a sale and final installation from 12 to 3, increased customer readiness to repurchase from 53 percent to 82 percent, and increased invoices paid within 30 days of installation from 31 percent to 71 percent.[11]

Although reengineering's time frame is typically less than long term, there are compelling examples of extended performance improvements. Over a three-year period, Union Carbide reduced fixed costs by $400 million.[12] And from the early 1980s to the early 1990s, Taco Bell raised its restaurant peak capacity from $400 per hour to $1,500 per hour—while simultaneously reducing prices.[13]

But reengineering has a serious downside: its tendency to arouse organizational *anxiety*, defined by *Webster's* as "a state of being uneasy, apprehensive, or worried about what may happen . . . " At best, reengineering offers (some) employees the prospect of hope and increased influence over their future. At worst, reengineering verges on restructuring, and anxiety is replaced by trauma. Indeed, the term *reengineering*, as applied to organizations, is unfortunate; it is mechanistic and utterly devoid of human content.

Michael Hammer has estimated that some 50 to 70 percent of all reengineering initiatives fail to achieve their objectives. Ironically, Hammer's observations about what it takes for reengineering to work also provide clues as to why such initiatives often fail. Hammer talks about the need to "break some glass," and he has been quoted as saying that to succeed at reengineering, a manager must be, among other things, "a leg breaker."[14] Where, then, are the positives for most people? To the extent that reengineering is a top-down proposition (as Hammer advocates), then where are the opportunities for employees to influence decisions that affect them? It is quite possible that, as far as downside is concerned, restructuring and reengineering differ only in degree, not in kind.

RETHINKING

Organizational design may be a mirror image of our cognitions. Therefore, to redesign the organization, we need to redesign the way we think. The increasing use of such expressions as "intellectual capital," "core competencies," and "organizational learning" suggests just such an approach to organizational design and change, an approach that is qualitatively unlike the previous two categories. Our organizational arrangements are a projection of our mental patterns, whether or not we know it. Fred Kofman and Peter Senge contrast organizational cognition and organizational processes as follows:

> [M]any companies are trying to "reengineer" themselves away from stovepipe structures and toward horizontal business processes that cut across traditional functions and power hierarchies. While potentially significant, such changes often prove difficult to implement and those that are implemented only "reap the low-hanging fruit."
>
> The reason is that the walls that exist in the physical world are reflections of our mental walls. The separation between the different functions is not just geographic, it lives in the way we think. Redesigns that "throw down the walls" between different functions may have little enduring effect unless they also change the fragmentary mental models that created the walls in the first place.[15]

The target of "re-cognition" or rethinking is neither organizational units nor organizational processes. It is individual and collective mind-sets, or ways of making sense of the world.[16] Organizational cognition is conceptual, not numerical or technical, and it is a concern rarely pursued for immediate or even moderate-term ends. Rather, cognition is seen as the source of strategic advantage.

Organizational rethinking means incorporating character, constituencies, and capabilities into the design of organizations.

Organizational rethinking, as used in this article, means conceptualizing design in a manner that incorporates organizational identity, or *character*—who we are, and what we stand for; organizational purpose, or *constituencies*—for whose benefit we exist; and organizational methods, or *capabilities*—how we satisfy customers/consumers.

To "rethink" organizational design is to consider the following kinds of questions when making a design/change decision:

- Is the proposed action true to our essential character? Does it fit the kind of organization that we are (want to be)?

- What impact will this action have on our various constituencies? How are the latter likely to respond?

- Will this action exploit, and hopefully enhance, our distinctive capabilities? In what ways?

Most basically, rethinking relates design decisions to a systematic mental model. One such model is triangular: organizations can be understood as a balance of hierarchical *control*, individual/unit *autonomy*, and spontaneous *cooperation*, as depicted by Figure 2.[17] The challenge is threefold. Every organization and unit within it must *prioritize* control, autonomy, and cooperation so that necessary trade-offs are made; *integrate* these variables because all three are essential and interdependent; and *focus* on whichever variable(s) require attention at any given time, regardless of their priority.

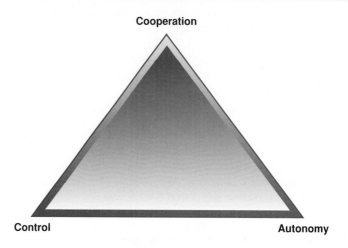

FIGURE 2   Organizational Design as Balance

This triad applies to all system levels—from the "micro" (pair of individuals or small group) to the "macro" (corporation, industry, sector, and beyond)—and capsulizes a wide range of trade-offs.[18] Consider, for example, organizational constituencies. Shareholders have a control charter: boards of directors that represent them are legally authorized and expected to control or "direct" their organizations to ensure that shareholders' interests are safeguarded. Customers exercise the most autonomy because, at least in a free marketplace, they can either take a company's products/ services or leave them. Employees, to be effective, must cooperate—with each other, with management, and with the aims of the enterprise as a whole.

These constituencies are also complementary. Over time, shareholder needs will be met only if customer needs are met; the latter, in turn, will be served only if employees are motivated to do so. Consequently, satisfied employees imply satisfied customers, who in turn imply satisfied shareholders.

With my assistance, a large retail food company created what it called the "performance food chain" (Figure 3) to demonstrate the process that had to occur in order for the firm to achieve its financial targets. This graphic depicts a triangle within a triangle. Organization was conceptualized as a balance of formal structure (control), individual competence (autonomy), and teamwork (cooperation). An effective organization produces customer satisfaction, which in turn results in the desired financial performance (which leads to further investment in the organization).

This image became a staple that unified a series of managerial teambuilding seminars across the company. In fact the food chain idea embodied three key properties of a cognitive approach to organizational design and change: it was sensible, communicable, and portable. This representation was sensible because it revealed logical connections that everyone could grasp and verify as important. It was communicable in large part because it was a picture, with familiar icons, that laid bare a complex set of dynamics. Finally, it was portable because its value was not dependent on any particular organizational setting or change program; managers could take the visual with them, wherever they might go within (and outside) the firm.

The upside of organizational rethinking is more sophisticated planning and decision-making— and innovation—capability. The downside is the difficulty and frustration that accompany "thinking about thinking."

The upside of organizational rethinking is more sophisticated planning and decision-making—and innovation—capability. The downside is the difficulty

FIGURE 3 Performance Food Chain

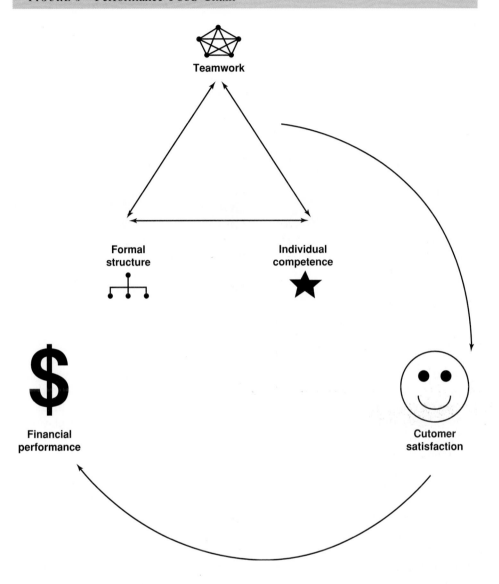

and frustration that accompany "thinking about thinking." Our egos and self-images are closely aligned with the way we perceive and interpret reality. Any criticism of established patterns is bound to provoke discomfort.[19] Even more significant is the difficulty that many individuals have in "juggling more than two variables," as one manager put it. Yet the consequences of *not* doing so may be severe.

THE THREE APPROACHES IN PERSPECTIVE

An obvious advantage of *restructuring* is its clear economic impact. Such action produces explicit and immediate results—financial savings that go right to the bottom line. The presumed payoff from *reengineering* is also easy to comprehend—although this process does not produce the direct hit that restructuring does. Effects

FIGURE 4   Alternative Leverage Points

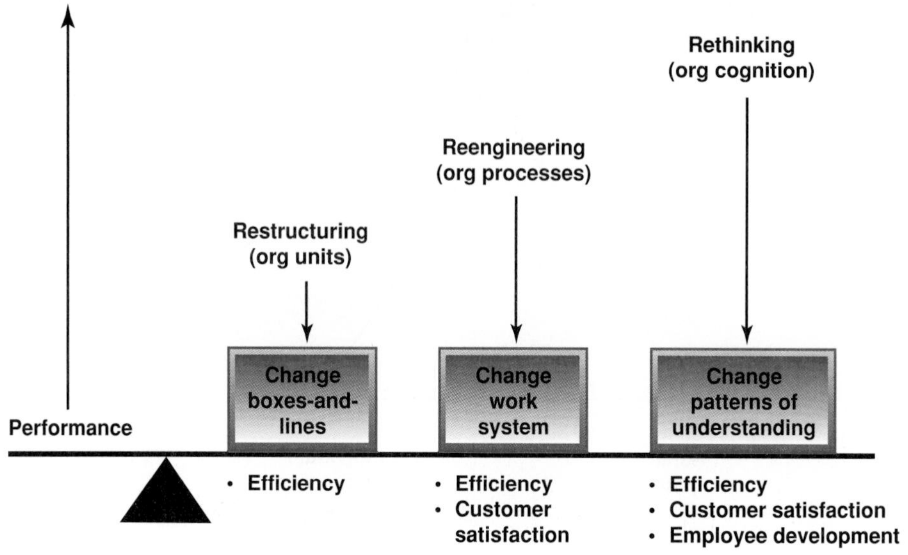

are explicit but deferred. A major problem with *rethinking* is the complex causal chain involved; positive impact is implicit and deferred.

Moreover, with rethinking—as David Garvin has pointed out with respect to learning—an overlapping, three-step process is involved: cognitive change produces behavioral change, which then leads to performance improvement.[20] Indeed, for rethinking to "take," an organization may have to create what Fred Kofman and Peter Senge call a *practice field*—an offline setting in which people can play with ideas, confront otherwise taboo topics, and generally open up their minds.[21]

Organizational rethinking would make little sense, of course, if it did not promise value at least commensurate with its difficulty. The potential leverage is significant, as suggested by Figure 4. The rationale for this leverage is what systems theory calls the *law of requisite variety*: an organization must be able to match whatever variety (complexity) its environment confronts it with. Or in sports terms, if your opponent can score in three different ways, you had better be able to defend against all three. Organizational issues are overwhelmingly triadic, as Ian Mitroff and Harold Linstone imply by their advocacy of "unbounded systems thinking"—that is, conceptualizing simultaneously through three lenses: *technical* (control), *personal* (autonomy), and *organizational* (cooperation).[22] Organizations that can respond effectively to such challenges will have a "cognitive edge" over those that cannot.[23]

Rethinking is a broader category than reengineering; conceptually it includes reengineering, just as the latter includes restructuring. To recap, *restructuring* is based on one variable: shareholders [= efficiency = control]; *reengineering* is based on two variables: shareholders + customers [= customer satisfaction = autonomy]. *Rethinking* adds a third variable: employees [= employee development = cooperation].

Philosophically and practically, cooperation has been in relatively short supply in the West.[24] The hierarchical, functional bureaucracies that Hammer and Champy criticize require little in the way of spontaneous cooperation because behavioral patterns are prescribed at the top. What these organizations really need from the majority of their employees is compliance within narrow charters, departments, and roles. And that is precisely what people have given, in return for the implied promise of a permanent job. But although Hammer and Champy advocate "cross-divisional teams," their model of decision making remains authoritarian, and largely ignores the organizational *context* in which reengineering projects take place.

Context has to do first with integrating the entire set of business processes that are being redesigned, and matching the latter with organizational resources. Second, context includes corporate policies, plans, and practices that impinge on process redesign—especially those that relate to senior managers' behavior. Third and perhaps most essential, context refers to the organization's emotional tenor—present and future. As an increasing number of managers are learning the hard way, eliminate 20 percent of your workforce, and you have permanently scarred much of the remaining 80 percent. This dynamic may help to explain why reengineering so often fails.

SITUATIONAL GUIDELINES

Even though the three design options can be considered "nested" (with restructuring a subset of reengineering, and the latter a subset of rethinking), each has its time and place. *Business Week*'s John Byrne acknowledges that "downsizing [restructuring] is . . . not a strategy, and it is not a panacea for poor management . . . But the idea that downsizing can't sometimes be an effective way for bloated, uncompetitive companies to cut costs is pure nonsense."[25] Similarly, reengineering may be a *sine qua non* for historically bureaucratic, inflexible firms to recapture competitiveness—irrespective of the fallout for certain employees.

Restructuring makes the most sense when a firm has little choice but to reduce costs quickly; that is, to "cut its losses." Under such conditions, employee commitment may be irrelevant: if the company goes under, no employees will remain. Abstractly, reengineering occupies a middle ground between restructuring and rethinking—and may actually approximate either of these extremes. But based on widely reported failure rates, reengineering in practice more often resembles restructuring than rethinking.

> *Restructuring makes the most sense when a firm has little choice but to reduce costs quickly.*

Rethinking requires slack time for learning about and "playing with" individual and organizational cognitive patterns. Many privately held firms are prime candidates because they need not impress Wall Street with a strong next quarter or even next year. Public corporations require enough financial cushion—and discipline—so that the long term is not sacrificed for the short term. The best candidates for rethinking, whether private or public, are firms that are financially and culturally able to defer their return on investment.[26]

> *Rethinking requires slack time for learning about and "playing with" individual and organizational cognitive patterns.*

Realistically, every company can expect to encounter pressures, at various times, for all three forms of organizational design. Just as no firm can remain "excellent" indefinitely, so should no corporation expect to be forever exempt from the need to cut staff, or to reconfigure operations. But a long-term perspective that encompasses both restructuring and reengineering should explicitly build in a concern for human development. For today's employees will almost certainly play a crucial role in determining the corporate tomorrow.[27]

Thomas Davenport presents a hopeful perspective on reengineering (and perhaps, restructuring) that explicitly addresses employees and the need for discretionary teamwork: "firms should strive to use reengineering not to eliminate jobs, but to increase the desirability of their products and services in the marketplace. This is the only way to employ the reengineering concept and preserve employee morale and loyalty, and to successfully enlist employee ideas for better processes."[28]

To expand on Davenport's point, the logic for organizations to care about employees is threefold. First, human development is intrinsically right. As Norwegian social scientist P. G. Herbst observed nearly 20 years ago, ultimately "the product of work is people."[29] Second, a humanistic orientation is instrumentally sensible from the corporation's standpoint. Strategic advantage clearly depends on capable, committed, *empowered* employees in all areas, at all levels. Finally, productive employment is essential to the economic health of society as a whole: the more people out of work, the fewer consumers able to buy new products and services; hence, even more people out of work. And so on.

NINE REDESIGN RECOMMENDATIONS

Granted, the individual must take responsibility for his or her working future. Government clearly also has a role—in providing reeducation and retraining support, if nothing else. An enormous void remains, however, that business can and should address. Here are nine recommendations for redesign—whether the spin is restructuring, reengineering, or otherwise. The first three suggestions have to do with minimizing negatives; the second three, with maximizing positives; and the third three, with challenging the way in which redesign is comprehended.

1. *Consider* all *cost-reduction alternatives*. There are other costs than people costs (such as those associated with buildings, machines, and materials). But even within the human realm, cutting staff is not the only possible action. In late 1993, Volkswagen AG reduced its workweek to four days and thereby saved 30,000 jobs. Companies such as Honeywell Home & Building Control (HBC) and Hewlett-Packard have pared expenses by reconfiguring tasks and organizations—and reassigning people—with virtually no loss of jobs. Indeed Hewlett-Packard, by combining organizational change with voluntary early retirement and severance packages, reassigned some 5 percent of its workforce between 1990 and 1994.[30]

    Other firms such as New United Motor Manufacturing (NUMMI)—the Fremont, California-based joint venture between General Motors and Toyota—have used slack production periods as an opportunity to train workers and carry out maintenance.[31] Harman International Industries, Inc., a California-based consumer electronics firm, has initiated a program that it calls "Off-Line Employment," or "Olé" for short.[32] Workers who would otherwise be laid off during a downturn are put to work on ancillary but productive tasks (such as making parts that had previously been purchased from outside vendors) until market conditions improve, and they can return to their regular jobs.

2. *Front-end-load any sizable layoffs*. Whenever major staff reductions are absolutely necessary, the smart organizational move is to downsize first, and only afterwards to mount a systematic development effort. This sequence is consistent with a psychological principle called *force field theory*: reduce the negatives (restraining forces) in a situation before significantly increasing the positives (driving forces); otherwise, the contradiction between the two forces will confuse people and undermine change. Such a tack appears to be what IBM chief executive Louis Gerstner had in mind in July 1993, when he

announced plans to cut 35,000 jobs in one fell swoop, rather than drag out the layoff process: "we have got to get behind us this Chinese water torture we've been going through quarter after quarter."[33]

3. *Spread the pain.* When pay cuts are the order of the day, the negative impact is generally more palatable if misery is spread throughout the company—and everyone knows this. Consider the experience of a firm that, because of financial difficulties, imposed a 10-week, 15 percent pay cut on two of its facilities.[34] In the first plant, managers announced the decision but did not explain why it was necessary. In the second plant, managers discussed the reasons for the reduction, indicated that everyone was taking a pay hit, and suggested that such action was an alternative to layoffs. In the first plant, thefts by employees increased by a factor of three; in the second plant, thefts barely rose at all and then fell back to their historical level.

   Nucor Corporation has a "Share the Pain" program in which percentage pay cuts actually increase with hierarchical standing. According to CEO Ken Iverson, "management should take the biggest drop in pay because they have the most responsibility."[35] In Japan, such a pattern is widespread. Thus when Fujitsu Ltd. struggled in 1992, executives lost more than one-third of their compensation.[36]

4. *Leverage human development.* So much for managing the minuses. Robust strategies lie elsewhere. The essential question is, are employees resources or constraints? Those familiar with the pharmaceutical industry know that the quickest route to an impressive bottom line is to gut R&D staff. The full impact of such action will not become visible until a firm's patent protection has expired. At that point, of course, the company itself may expire. This is *negative* leverage.

   The intelligent tack in any industry is to "overinvest" in human R&D. 3M, for example, has long had an informal policy that permits scientists and engineers to spend 15 percent of their paid time on business-related research projects of their own choosing. Hence paradoxically, a stream of serendipitous successes like Post-it™ notes is almost predictable.

   Applied Manufacturing and Engineering Technology (AMET), an Austin, Texas-based division of Applied Materials, Inc., has instituted a similar practice for all its employees. AMET, which makes machines that produce computer chips, expects managers and workers alike to devote 20 percent of their time to improving existing products and work processes. People are literally encouraged to invent their way out of current jobs—with the promise that they will be rewarded with better jobs.[37]

5. *Create—and reward—shared wins.* Most corporations have abundant opportunities for linking micro pay to macro performance. Profit sharing can make a difference—as Chrysler demonstrated dramatically in early 1994 by paying 81,000 workers bonuses that averaged $4,300. Scanlon plans, Rucker plans, and other "gainsharing" programs have also proven useful. So has the practice of extending stock options to *everyone* in the corporation—as has been done at Du Pont, Merck, PepsiCo, Pfizer, Silicon Graphics, and Tandem Computers.

   Overall, however, American firms have barely scratched the surface. Wyatt Co., a consulting firm, surveyed 531 companies in order to learn about the effects of organizational restructuring.[38] Among its most significant findings:

pay freezes and diminished pay increases were of only marginal value. These measures, while instituted by more than 50 percent of the firms surveyed, were deemed "very effective" by only 20 percent. Far more useful, according to respondents, was the practice of connecting employees' pay to corporate goals. Yet fewer than one-third of the firms polled had done so.

6. *Let everyone know what the score is.* Although it continues to reduce staff in certain areas, AT&T is exploring other ways to economize than by knocking and chopping heads. In particular, AT&T is sharing the big picture more widely than ever before. That firm is moving away from an adversarial, "line-of-scrimmage" labor relations posture that encourages the unions to dig in for job security. Instead, AT&T is involving labor officials in joint corporate planning and is giving union members the opportunity to compete for jobs with offshore sites. Thus an AT&T unit in Atlanta, by devising high-quality, low-cost production methods, won back communications refurbishing work that had been carried out in Matamoros, Mexico.[39]

   Perhaps the most impressive example of information sharing in all of American industry is Springfield ReManufacturing Corporation (SRC) under president Jack Stack. SRC, which rebuilds truck engines, practices what it calls "open-book management"—a policy in which virtually all information about performance is visible to all. Everyone in that firm receives a weekly income statement, has been trained in analyzing this information, and can see how his or her performance contributed to or detracted from the company's performance.

7. *Beware of fetishes.* Restructuring or reengineering (or indeed, rethinking) can easily degenerate into a fetish, or fix, that is regarded as an all-purpose solution. Techniques (the *how*) may overshadow the nature of design/change (the *what*) and its purpose (the *why*). Eric Trist, the father of sociotechnical systems theory, noted (in 1983) exactly this tendency with respect to an analytical procedure that he and Fred Emery had developed: "the nine-step model, which has become something of a fetish with a number of practitioners, was never intended as a universally applicable methodology . . ."[40]

   To guard against such regression, it is useful to address three questions: (1) what is the *root* organizational issue or concern or problem? (2) what are plausible alternative approaches, and their respective strengths and weaknesses? and (3) what are the long-term consequences, in addition to short-term results, of taking a given path?

8. *Identify and integrate multiple perspectives.* Any nontrivial organizational design initiative will affect shareholders *and* customers *and* employees—even if the focus is only one or two of these parties. Managers who can appreciate all three points of view will likely outperform others who cannot because they will anticipate, and be able to resolve, more difficulties. Such managers will resemble savvy trial lawyers and negotiators who grasp, and imaginatively synthesize, not only conflicting interests but the "game" as a whole.

9. *Take time out to reflect.* A busyness ethic pervades American business. We are action-driven, perpetually in motion. Managers are praised, not for being deep thinkers but for being *quick studies*—as in *quick on the draw* wild west style. The good news is a constitutional resistance to paralysis by analysis.

The bad news is a tendency to pull the trigger before aiming the gun.

If there is truth to the Pareto principle—that 20 percent of all activities produces 80 percent of the value added—then most corporations would benefit from increasing the time they devote to reflection. An index of the current state is how readily a manager or professional (or other employee) can afford to be seen reading or discussing a business-related book or article during "working hours." In my experience, the typical answer is "hardly at all."

THE POWER OF MENTAL MODELS

The quality of organizational design will always be a function of the way in which issues, options, and implications are framed. The frames we use express our underlying mental models. The model elaborated in this article calls for balancing three perspectives—shareholders', customers', and employees'—that mirror, respectively, three organizational variables: control, autonomy, and cooperation. My approach is unusual among organizational design discourses in the attention that it pays to employees/cooperation. But there is mounting evidence that such attention pays off. Financially successful firms as disparate as large/high-tech Motorola and small/low-tech Marsh Furniture Co. have demonstrated the multiplier effect of human commitment. Under the leadership of George Fisher (now Kodak's chairman), a struggling Motorola rejected conventional slash-and-burn alternatives and instead transformed itself into a wireless communications world beater.

Entrepreneur David Marsh, who founded the 45-person, Houston-based company that bears his name, also chose the high road. His philosophy for managing people is simple yet profound: "what you do because you love it is your best investment in yourself, and your best chance at success."[41] It is a sentiment that more corporations ought to embrace.

ENDNOTES

1. Edward H. Bowman and Harbir Singh, "Corporate Restructuring: Reconfiguring the Firm," *Strategic Management Journal* 14 (Summer 1993), p. 6. Bowman and Singh distinguish two other forms of restructuring, *portfolio* and *financial*, that are conceptually distinct, yet interactive. Portfolio and financial restructuring are beyond the scope of this article, although, like organizational restructuring, their overriding concern is shareholder well-being.

2. Michael Hammer and James Champy, *Reengineering the Corporation: A Manifesto for Business Revolution* (New York: HarperBusiness, 1993), p. 32.

3. Henry Mintzberg, *Mintzberg on Management* (New York: Free Press, 1989), p. 354.

4. The line between *organizational* restructuring and *portfolio* restructuring is often difficult to draw. Challenging economic times force most companies to determine rigorously, and sometimes ruthlessly, in which businesses they will and will not compete. The most famous portfolio approach is the Boston Consulting Group's two-dimensional grid, market growth × relative market share, which defines four categories: *dogs, cash cows, question marks*, and *stars*. See John S. Hammond and Gerald B. Allan, *Note on the*

Boston Consulting Group Concept of Competitive Analysis and Corporate Strategy (Boston, MA: Harvard Business School, 1975).

5. Lee Berton, "Big Accounting Firms, Striving to Cut Costs, Irritate Small Clients," *The Wall Street Journal*, April 21, 1994, pp. A1, A8.

6. John R. Wilke, "Digital Plans at Least 20,000 More Job Cuts," *The Wall Street Journal*, May 6, 1994, p. A3.

7. Robert Rosenstein, "Where Did All the People Go?" *Forbes*, April 25, 1994, pp. 242–43.

8. Kim S. Cameron, cited in Richard A. Melcher, "How Goliaths Can Act like Davids," *Business Week/Enterprise*, 1993, p. 193.

9. Modern industrial engineering (IE) may effectively exploit available information technology, but IE still appears to regard customer needs as of only secondary importance. The current *Handbook of Industrial Engineering* contains 2,780 pages, yet its index references only 21 pages for all customer-related categories. See Gavriel Salvendy, ed., *Handbook of Industrial Engineering*, 2d ed. (New York: Wiley-Interscience, 1992).

10. The three forms of interdependence are discussed at length in James D. Thompson, *Organizations in Action* (New York: McGraw-Hill, 1967).

11. Gene Hall, Jim Rosenthal, and Judy Wade, "How to Make Reengineering *Really* Work," *Harvard Business Review*, November–December 1993, pp. 119–31.

12. Thomas A. Stewart, "Reengineering: The Hot New Managing Tool," *Fortune*, August 23, 1993, pp. 41–48.

13. Hammer and Champy, "Reengineering the Corporation," 177.

14. Hammer, quoted in Stewart, *Reengineering*, p. 42.

15. Fred Kofman and Peter M. Senge, "Communities of Commitment: The Heart of Learning Organizations," *Organizational Dynamics*, Autumn 1993, p. 8.

16. There are numerous ways to characterize individual/organizational thinking; several approaches that differ from the methodology elaborated in this article are nonetheless compatible with it. To wit: Elliott Jacques, *Requisite Organization* (Arlington, VA: Cason Hall, 1989), uses *time-span*; that is, individuals' temporal horizons, to capture differences in thinking capacity; his range is from one day to 50 years. Others focus on *causality* and distinguish between linear and nonlinear causal processes. See, for example, Magoroh Maruyama, "The Second Cybernetics: Deviation-Amplifying Mutual Causal Processes," *American Scientist* 51 (1963), pp. 164–79; Karl Weick, *The Social Psychology of Organizing*, 2d ed. (Reading, MA: Addison-Wesley, 1979); and Peter Senge, *The Fifth Discipline: The Art & Practice of The Learning Organization* (New York: Doubleday, 1990). A third, often implicit approach to understanding cognition is to gauge the sophistication of *metaphors* that are commonly applied. Useful discussions of metaphor include George Lakoff and Mark Johnson, *Metaphors We Live By* (Chicago, IL: University of Chicago Press, 1980); Peter K. Manning, "Metaphors of the Field: Varieties of Organizational Discourse," *Administrative Science Quarterly* 25, no. 1 (1979), pp. 102–19; Gareth Morgan, *Images of Organization* (Beverly Hills, CA: Sage, 1986); and Gareth Morgan, *Imagination: The Art of Creative Management* (Newbury

Park, CA: Sage, 1993). A fourth, catchall category may be loosely called *creative problem solving*. It is exemplified by such concepts as *synectics* [W. J. Gordon, *Synectics* (New York: Harper & Row, 1961)]; *lateral thinking* [Edward de Bono, *Lateral Thinking* (New York: Harper & Row, 1970)]; *excursions* [George M. Prince, *The Practice of Creativity* (New York: Collier Books, 1970)]; and *conceptual blockbusting* [James L. Adams, *Conceptual Blockbusting* (Reading, MA: Addison-Wesley, 1974)].

17. For earlier treatments of the control/autonomy/cooperation triad, see Robert W. Keidel, *Corporate Players: Designs for Working and Winning Together* (New York: Wiley, 1988); Robert W. Keidel, "Triangular Design: A New Organizational Geometry," *Academy of Management Executive*, November 1990, pp. 21–37; and Robert W. Keidel, *A Concept of Organizational Design* (Washington, DC: The World Bank, Organization & Management Series, Occasional Paper #1, May 1993). Similar frameworks are William E. Smith's triadic concept of power, as described in "Planning for the Electricity Sector in Colombia," in Marvin E. Weisbord et al., *Discovering Common Ground* (San Francisco, CA: Berrett-Koehler, 1992), pp. 171–86; and Kenneth R. Slocum/SENCORP's triad of *business management responsibilities*, as outlined in *The SENCORP Management Model*, Strategic Management Society, 13th Annual Conference, Chicago, September 13, 1993).

18. The control/autonomy/cooperation triad is *self-similar*, to use a term from *fractal* geometry; in other words, this triad expresses the same dynamics at multiple system levels. For a technical discussion of fractal geometry, see Benoit B. Mandelbrot, *The Fractal Character of Nature* (New York: W. H. Freeman, 1983); Mandelbrot's work has been popularized in James Gleick, *Chaos: Making a New Science* (New York: Viking, 1987). Robert W. Keidel's *Seeing Organizational Patterns: A New Theory and Language of Organizational Design* (San Francisco, CA: Berrett-Koehler, forthcoming) contains a theoretical appendix of more than two-hundred triads (primarily from the management/organizational literatures) that parallel control, autonomy, and cooperation.

19. The frustration that accompanies organizational rethinking is not unlike that often associated with *total quality management* (TQM), which also calls for a systemic (multiperspective) reappreciation of organizational purposes. See, for example, Robert M. Grant, Rami Shani, and R. Krishnan, "TQM's Challenge to Management Theory and Practice," *Sloan Management Review*, Winter 1994, pp. 25–35.

20. David A. Garvin, "Building a Learning Organization," *Harvard Business Review*, July–August 1993, pp. 78–91.

21. Kofman and Senge, *Communities,*" p. 22.

22. Ian I. Mitroff and Harold A. Linstone, *The Unbounded Mind: Breaking the Chains of Traditional Business Thinking* (New York: Oxford University Press, 1993).

23. Fifteen years ago, Richard Walton (in "Work Innovations in the United States," *Harvard Business Review*, July–August 1979, pp. 88–98) argued that quality of worklife programs with joint human and productivity objectives seem to do better on both counts than those with single

objectives. The logic here is similar, although with respect to *three* objectives (constituencies).

24. Michael Schrage, in *Shared Minds: The New Technologies of Collaboration* (New York: Random House, 1990, p. 44) argues, "The Western tradition of intellectual thought doesn't embrace collaboration as a vital creative behavior. You don't find collaboration as part of Aristotelian or Platonic thought (which is ironic, given the role of dialogue in creating enlightenment). Nor is collaboration a part of the Judeo-Christian ethic of community. Adam Smith talked about the 'division of labor,' not collaboration: Marx heralded the 'labor theory of value,' yet left the collaborative processes that yield this value virtually unexamined. Similarly, the nascent sciences of human thought and behavior give collaboration short shrift. Pavlov, John B. Watson, B. F. Skinner, and the behaviorist school scarcely touch collaboration as a social process. Freud brilliantly explored and described the inner beyonds of the human psyche, but not in the context of the way people create shared understandings."

25. John A. Byrne, "There Is an Upside to Downsizing," *Business Week*, May 9, 1994, p. 69.

26. A troubling aspect of this line of argument is the "rich get richer" syndrome. Those organizations most in need of serious rethinking may be least able (and least likely) to move in that direction. Hence, the gap between healthy and nonhealthy may only widen. This dynamic, of course, plays out at all societal levels. As Gary Becker has pointed out in "Why the Third World Should Stress the Three R's," *Business Week*, May 2, 1994, p. 16, many third world nations are stunting their future by depriving poor children of elementary education.

27. At issue here is *long-term* trust and cooperation. A parallel exists with the human interaction pattern called *tit-for-tat*, as articulated by Robert Axelrod in *The Evolution of Cooperation* (New York: Basic Books, 1984). Axelrod shows that tit-for-tat—starting out collaboratively and thereafter responding in kind—is highly effective in encouraging and sustaining cooperative behavior. By analogy, an organization's "cooperating" with employees in the present improves the probability that employees will reciprocate in the future.

28. Thomas H. Davenport, review of *Reengineering the Corporation*, in *Sloan Management Review*, Fall 1993, p. 103. Davenport is the author of *Process Innovation: Reengineering Work through Information Technology* (Boston, MA: Harvard Business School Press, 1993).

29. Phillip G. Herbst, "The Product of Work is People," Epilogue in Louis E. Davis and Albert B. Cherns, eds., *The Quality of Working Life, Volume One: Problems, Prospects, and the State of the Art* (New York: Free Press, 1975).

30. Ronald Henkoff, "Getting Beyond Downsizing," *Fortune*, January 10, 1994, pp. 58–60, 62, 64.

31. Jeffrey Pfeffer, *Competitive Advantage through People* (Boston, MA: Harvard Business School Press, 1994).

32. Robert Kuttner, "Talking Marriage and Thinking One-Night Stand," *Business Week*, October 18, 1993, p. 16.

33. Louis V. Gerstner, Jr., quoted in Michael Miller and Laurie Hays, "IBM Posts $8.4 Billion 2nd-Period Loss, Halves Dividend, Plans 35,000 Job Cuts." *The Wall Street Journal*, July 28, 1993, p. A3.

34. The following account is taken from Jerald Greenberg in *Security*; cited in *Boardroom*, May 15, 1991, p. 2.

35. Ken Iverson, quoted in "Face-to-Face," *Inc.,* April 1986, p. 44.

36. Robert Neff, "What Do Japanese CEOs *Really* Make?" *Business Week*, April 26, 1993, pp. 60–61.

37. Personal communication with Steven C. Taylor, Austin Corporate Relations Manager, AMET, November 16, 1993.

38. *Best Practices in Corporate Restructuring: Wyatt's 1993 Survey of Corporate Restructuring* (Chicago, IL: The Wyatt Company, 1993).

39. Personal communication with Burke Stinson, AT&T Corporate Media Relations Manager, January 21, 1994.

40. Eric L. Trist, *Afterword*, in Calvin Pava, *Managing New Office Technology: An Organizational Strategy* (New York: Free Press, 1983), p. 173.

41. David Marsh, quoted in Toni Mack, "Idealist Makes Good," *Forbes*, December 6, 1993, p. 102.

BRAIN POWER: WHO OWNS IT ... HOW THEY PROFIT FROM IT

Thomas A. Stewart, *Journalist*

This article suggests that intellectual capitalism has changed both the strategic architecture and the ownership structure of companies competing in the information age. Because thinking and inventing, rather than machinery and processes, are the assets upon which knowledge works and knowledge companies depend, the careful management of human capital is critical for successful strategy implementation.

The logic of capitalism was simple. Mr. Moneybags got an idea for a business. He turned his money, plus some from a bank, into fixed assets—a factory, machines, offices. He hired a Man in a Gray Flannel Suit to manage the assets. The manager, in turn, hired workers to operate the machines. Moneybags paid them—hourly wages to the easily replaceable workers, annual salaries to the managers, a reflection of their longer-term value. Moneybags kept all the profits; he was also responsible for paying the bank, maintaining the machines, and buying new ones. He might offer the public a chance to share ownership with him; occasionally he gave managers the option to buy a piece too. He almost never let the workers in on the action, though in good years he gave them a goose for Christmas.

In the middle of the last century, Karl Marx noted that the industrial worker, unlike the craftsman and the small farmer, no longer owned the tools of his trade or the product of his labor. Marx was wrong about many things, but not about this, which he called the "alienation of labor." Henry Ford owned everything needed to make cars and owned the cars themselves, until he sold them. Then the customer took sole possession.

Intellectual capitalism is different. In knowledge-intensive companies, it's not clear who owns the company, its tools, or its products. Moneybags's modern-day descendant starts with seed money from a Silicon Valley venture

> *In knowledge-intensive companies, it's not clear who owns the company, its tools, or its products.*

Source: *Fortune* March 17, 1997.

capitalist. He leases office space in some Edge City corporate village and doesn't own a factory; a company in Taiwan manufactures his products. The only plant and equipment the company owns are computers, desks, and a 1950s Coke machine someone picked up at auction. Whereas Moneybags bought the assets of his company, it is unclear who makes the investments on which intellectual capitalism depends, the investments in people. The manager—the Man in the Ralph Lauren Polo Shirt—paid his own way through business school. The worker is shelling out for an electronics course she takes at night, though the company will reimburse her for half the cost when she completes it. Every manager and worker receives stock options—as a group they may own as much stock as the capitalists.

Many jobs still and always will require big, expensive machines bought by someone else. But in the age of intellectual capital, the most valuable parts of those jobs are the human tasks: sensing, judging, creating, building relationships. Far from being alienated from the tools of his trade and the fruit of his labor, the knowledge worker carries them between his ears. If I write a story, *Fortune* owns the copyright but I still own whatever knowledge is in it; if you buy the magazine, you don't get sole possession of the knowledge. I have it; *Fortune* has it; and hundreds of thousands of others have it too. Employees, companies, and customers share joint and several ownership of the assets and output of knowledge work.

This change upsets the nature and governance of corporations. Look at Cordiant, the advertising agency that used to be known as Saatchi & Saatchi. In December 1994 institutional investors, unhappy at what they viewed as the arrogance and fecklessness of CEO Maurice Saatchi, forced the board of directors to dismiss him. Protesting, several other executives left too, and some large accounts—first Mars, the candymaker, and later British Airways—defected. As far as the balance sheet was concerned, Saatchi's dismissal was a nonevent. Nevertheless the stock, which had been trading on the New York Stock Exchange at 8⅝, immediately fell to 4. The moral of the story: The shareholders thought they owned Saatchi & Saatchi; in fact they owned less than half of it. Most of the value of the company was human capital, embodied in Saatchi.

There's lots of evidence of the value of human capital. Why, then, do companies manage it so haphazardly? One reason is that they have a hard time distinguishing between the cost of paying people and the value of investing in them. At the same time, compensation systems and governance structures fail to recognize who owns intellectual assets.

Human capital is, to quote Yeats out of context, the place where all the ladders start: the wellspring of innovation, the home page of insight. Money talks, but it does not think; machines perform, often better than any human being can, but they do not invent. Thinking and invention, however, are the assets upon which knowledge works and knowledge companies depend.

The point bears emphasizing: Routine, low-skill work, even if it's done manually, does not generate or employ human capital for the organization. Often the work involved in such jobs can be automated, which is why these are the jobs most at risk nowadays; when it cannot be automated, the worker, contributing and picking up little in the way of skill, can easily be replaced if he leaves—he is a hired hand, not a hired mind.

I'm not saying such workers lack skill or talent. They might have a jeroboam of brains, but it is private stock; the employer doesn't get any. Pull a first novel off the shelf at a bookstore and read the author's biography: John Doe, it says, a graduate of the University of Chicago, has sheared sheep in Montana, tended bar in Fort Worth, loaded cargo on the docks of Baltimore, and worked as an orderly in a Rangoon mental hospital. If the listening skills he learned as a bartender made him a better worker in Rangoon, that was happenstance; he has been picking up human capital to put in his novel, not to offer to his employers.

The question for companies is how to acquire as much human capital as they can use profitably.

Our point of view must be organizational, not individual: The question for companies is how to acquire as much human capital as they can use profitably. Human capital grows two ways: when the organization uses more of what people know and when more people know more stuff that is useful to the organization.

The first, unleashing the human capital already in the organization, requires minimizing mindless tasks, meaningless paperwork, unproductive infighting. The Taylorized workplace squandered human assets in such activities. Frank Ostroff, a fellow at Perot Systems, realized the extent of the waste when as a college student he took a summer job at a tiremaking factory in Ohio: "We'd spend eight hours a day doing something completely mindless like applying glue to rubber to tire after tire, all day long. And then these same people would go home and spend their evenings and weekends rebuilding entire cars from scratch or running volunteer organizations." The company got eight hours' work from those people but no benefit from their minds.

In the Information Age no one can use human capital so inefficiently. With competition fierce, says GE's Chairman Jack Welch, "the only ideas that count are the A ideas. There is no second place. That means we have to get everybody in the organization involved. If you do that right, the best ideas will rise to the top." To use more of what people know, companies need to create opportunities for private knowledge to be made public and tacit knowledge to be made explicit. GE's Work-Out program—a never-ending series of town meetings in which employees propose changes in work processes and bosses are required to approve or reject them on the spot—is one proven way to begin the process of getting at the ideas of more people. Some companies are setting up electronic networks and other knowledge-sharing systems. But every company already has informal networks and forums where tips are exchanged and ideas are generated, and which at their best become powerful learning forums.

Second, to get more people to know more useful stuff, leaders need to focus and amass talent where it is needed. The link to strategy is essential. Kodak, for example, a great company built on the silver-halide chemistry that underlies the photography business, is struggling to build the human capital it needs as digital photography threatens to erode the chemistry-based business. As the 1990s began, task forces all over Kodak were busy trying to find ways to use digital imaging in its product line. The effort led nowhere, though the company in a decade had invested $5 billion in digital-photography R&D.

Kodak's problem was one of scale and focus: The small groups were imprisoned in the divisional boxes that created them; the boundaries made it difficult for them to collaborate or share their knowledge—at one point there were 23 different groups working to develop digital scanners. Kodak had a few teams of snipers; it needed a corps.

Recognizing the problem when he became CEO in 1993, Kodak's George Fisher dismantled the departmental task forces, putting most of them into a new digital and applied imaging division. Its sales (of such products as "smart" film, which stores shutter speed and other data to allow better photo-processing, and a CopyPrint station, now set up in many photo stores, which uses digital technology to make on-the-spot enlargements of ordinary prints) totaled $500 million in 1994 and an estimated $1 billion in 1996. There's a lesson in Kodak's early experience with digital imaging: Human capital is easily dissipated. It needs to be massed and concentrated. Intelligence, like any asset, needs to be cultivated in the context of action. Random hiring of Ph.D.s won't cut it.

Human capital is easily dissipated. It needs to be massed and concentrated. Intelligence, like any asset, needs to be cultivated in the context of action.

There aren't many companies that, like Kodak, face the likelihood that their entire business might become based on a completely different science. For most, the challenge, no less important, is to find and enhance talents that truly are assets—for not all skills are created equal—and turn them to advantage by making them, in some sense, company property.

Some knowledge can, of course, be owned outright and protected by intellectual-property laws. Some can be codified in processes, procedures, manuals, databases, files, knowledge-management systems, decision-support software, and other intellectual assets that the company indisputably owns—what has come to be known as structural intellectual capital.

People themselves, however, can be rented, but not owned. Ceding "ownership" of human capital to a corporation has to be voluntary. The short but not simple way to do this: Create a sense of cross-ownership between employee and company. Says management thinker Charles Handy: "I believe that corporations should be membership communities . . . In order to hold people inside the corporation, we can't really talk about their being employees anymore . . . There has to be some kind of continuity and some sense of belonging."

A fundamental paradox lies at the heart of the Information Age organization: At the same time that employers have weakened the ties of job security and loyalty, they more than ever depend on human capital. For their part, knowledge workers, because they bring to their work not only their bodies but their minds—even their souls—are far more loyal to their work (though not to their employer) than those tiremakers whose first love was for the hobbies that waited for them at home. Compounding the problem is the fact that the most valuable knowledge workers are also best able to leave their employers, taking their talent and their work with them.

The most valuable knowledge workers are also best able to leave their employers, taking their talent and their work with them.

Community . . . belonging . . . If it sounds like Dr. Spock, don't worry. Organizations can help create bonds of ownership in both implicit and explicit ways that are thoroughly adult. An adversarial relationship with employees, like one with suppliers and customers, may save or make a few dollars in the short run but at the expense of destroying wealth.

The implicit way is to foster intellectual communities in areas that are central to competitive advantage—that is, in hard-to-replace, high-value activities like marketing if you're Nike or engine design if you're Ford. To create human capital, a company needs to foster teamwork, communities of practice, and other social forms of learning. Individual talent is great, but it walks out the door. Interdisciplinary teams capture, formalize, and capitalize talent; it becomes less dependent on any individual. A vibrant learning community gives the company an ownership stake: if Sally leaves, three other people know what she knows—and though Sally has left, she will probably remain unofficially part of the group. Chances are, employees already, consciously or not, define themselves by such communities. They are chemists (currently working for Du Pont), managers (whose paycheck says General Electric), human resources professionals (once at Procter & Gamble, now with Intel, thinking of going out on their own). If the community's heart is in your shop, they'll want to stay. But if their professional satisfaction comes from learning about cheese, you won't keep them if you offer only the chance to build a better mousetrap.

There are also explicit ways to forge the company-employee bond—namely, to treat employees like the capitalists they are. Says shareholder activist Robert A. B. Monks: "I would never invest one nickel of passive capital in a service firm where the value added is done by people who go out the door at 5 P.M." But what if you can capture the value of that knowledge or make sure the people don't walk?

It's no accident that employee stock ownership is widespread in knowledge-intensive businesses. Nor is it surprising that incentive pay has become more popular. Says MIT's Erik Brynjolfsson: "When employees have information not available to their employers . . . the employer can get the employee to choose actions that will make them both better off only by giving him a share of the profits and losses."

The knowledge worker is as much an investor as the shareholder. Says Michael Brown, CFO of Microsoft: "Fifteen or 20 years ago a person was either an employee or he was unemployed. Now look around: People are owners, managers, and employees—sometimes all three in the same hour." Only by recognizing this fact can companies protect their intellectual assets. Says Brown: "Employee ownership is a profound example of how the Information Age has changed the nature of the corporation."

Microsoft's capital structure exemplifies the change. Microsoft has never needed other people's money. It's been pay as you go since Bill Gates and Paul Allen founded the company in 1975: $85.5 billion in market value, all generated by internal cash flow; the company has never had a dime in long-term debt.

Why, then, did Gates and Allen bother to incorporate, which they did in 1981? And why did they take the company public in 1986, if they didn't need to raise capital? Part of the reason was to limit liability—not even Bill Gates can risk taking on America's tort lawyers. But that wasn't the major factor. Says Brown: "For pure Information Age companies, the principal barrier to entry is the ability to concentrate intellectual property. When these companies go public, they don't do it to raise proceeds to build plants. They do it to monetize the value of their employee ownership programs. Microsoft was incorporated to create a vehicle to share ownership, not to ramp up production. And the principal reason we went public was to monetize the value."

Let's play that back. Gates and Allen incorporated because they needed a vehicle to share ownership. With whom? With employees. Why? Because they created the company's key property—line upon line of software code—and owned its most important asset—the knowledge of how to write more code. Forming a corporation and taking it public gave them an incentive to keep their assets working for Microsoft, rather than take them elsewhere. Today, ownership of Microsoft is split roughly fifty-fifty between people who invested financial capital in the company—outside shareholders—and people who invested human capital—employees and founders.

Even traditional companies, which depend on huge factories and need to reward the shareholders who put up the money to acquire them, can take a leaf from the books of Microsoft and companies like them. General Electric now gives stock options to 22,000 employees versus just 200 in the 1980s; but stock ownership isn't the only way to compensate employees for the fact that they own part of the company even if they own no shares. Other companies offer gain-sharing bonuses; they are, in effect, dividends paid to employees for investing human capital. They recognize the fact, as Peter Drucker says, that "in the knowledge society the most probable assumption for organizations—and certainly the assumption on which they have to conduct their affairs—is that they need knowledge workers far more than knowledge workers need them."

When individuals are able to capture for themselves almost all the value of their human capital, they often become independent contractors. For most of us, though, there is some economic value that is created by our being part of an organization, a reason why the work we do together is worth more than the sum of our individual efforts. The organization has a legitimate claim on that human capital. But not an exclusive one.

READING
13

STRATEGIC OUTSOURCING

James Brian Quinn, *Dartmouth College*

Frederick G. Hilmer, *University of New South Wales*

By strategically outsourcing and emphasizing a company's core competencies, managers can leverage their firms' skills and resources for increased competitiveness. The authors suggest ways to determine what those core competencies are and which activities are better performed externally.

Two new strategic approaches, when properly combined, allow managers to leverage their companies' skills and resources well beyond levels available with other strategies:

- Concentrate the firm's own resources on a set of "core competencies" where it can achieve definable preeminence and provide unique values for customers.[1]

- Strategically outsource other activities—including many traditionally considered integral to any company—for which the firm has neither a critical strategic need nor special capabilities.[2]

The benefits of successfully combining the two approaches are significant. Managers leverage their company's resources in four ways. First, they maximize returns on internal resources by concentrating investments and energies on what the enterprise does best. Second, well-developed core competencies provide formidable barriers against present and future competitors that seek to expand into the company's areas of interest, thus facilitating and protecting the strategic advantages of market share. Third, perhaps the greatest leverage of all is the full utilization of external suppliers' investments, innovations, and specialized professional capabilities that would be prohibitively expensive or even impossible to duplicate internally. Fourth, in rapidly changing marketplaces and technological situations, this joint strategy decreases risks, shortens cycle times, lowers investments, and creates better responsiveness to customer needs.

Two examples from our studies of Australian and U.S. companies illustrate our point:

Source: *Sloan Management Review*, Summer 1994.

- Nike, Inc., is the largest supplier of athletic shoes in the world. Yet it outsources 100 percent of its shoe production and manufactures only key technical components of its "Nike Air" system. Athletic footwear is technology- and fashion-intensive, requiring high flexibility at both the production and marketing levels. Nike creates maximum value by concentrating on preproduction (research and development) and postproduction activities (marketing, distribution, and sales) linked together by perhaps the best marketing information system in the industry. Using a carefully developed, on-site "expatriate" program to coordinate its foreign-based suppliers, Nike even outsourced the advertising component of its marketing program to Wieden & Kennedy, whose creative efforts drove Nike to the top of the product recognition scale. Nike grew at a compounded 20 percent growth rate and earned a 31 percent ROE for its shareholders through most of the past decade.

- Knowing it could not be the best at making chips, boxes, monitors, cables, keyboards, and so on for its explosively successful Apple II, Apple Computer outsourced 70 percent of its manufacturing costs and components. Instead of building internal bureaucracies where it had no unique skills, Apple outsourced critical items like design (to Frogdesign), printers (to Tokyo Electric), and even key elements of marketing (to Regis McKenna, which achieved a "$100 million image" for Apple when it had only a few employees and about $1 million to spend). Apple focused its internal resources on its own Apple DOS (disk operating system) and the supporting macro software to give Apple products their unique look and feel. Its open architecture policy stimulated independent developers to write the much-needed software that gave Apple II's customers uniquely high functionality. Apple thus avoided unnecessary investments, benefited from its vendors' R&D and technical expertise, kept itself flexible to adopt new technologies as they became available, and leveraged its limited capital resources to a huge extent. Operating with an extremely flat organization, Apple enjoyed three times the capital turnover and the highest market value versus fixed investment ratio among major computer producers throughout the 1980s.[3]

How can managers combine core competency concepts and strategic outsourcing for maximum effectiveness? To achieve benefits like Nike's or Apple's requires careful attention to several difficult issues, each of which we discuss in turn:

1. What exactly is a "core competency"? Unfortunately, most of the literature on this subject is tautological—"core" equals "key" or "critical" or "fundamental." How can managers analytically select and develop the core competencies that will provide the firm's uniqueness, competitive edge, and basis of value creation for the future?

2. Granting that the competencies defining the firm and its essential reasons for existence should be kept in-house, should all else be outsourced? In most cases, common sense and theory suggest a clear "no." How then can managers determine strategically, rather than in a short-term or ad hoc fashion, which activities to maintain internally and which to outsource?

3. How can managers assess the relative risks and benefits of outsourcing in particular situations? And how can they contain critical risks—especially the potential loss of crucial skills or control over the company's future directions—when outsourcing is desirable?

CORE COMPETENCY STRATEGIES

The basic ideas behind core competencies and strategic outsourcing have been well supported by research extending over a 20-year period.[4] In 1974, Rumelt noted that neither of the then-favored strategies—unrelated diversification or vertical integration—yielded consistently high returns.[5] Since then, other carefully structured research has indicated the effectiveness of disaggregation strategies in many industries.[6] Noting the failures of many conglomerates in the 1960s and 1970s, both financial theorists and investors began to support more focused company concepts. Generally this meant "sticking to your knitting" by cutting back to fewer product lines. Unfortunately, this also means a concomitant increase in the systematic risk these narrowed markets represented.

However, some analysts noted that many highly successful Japanese and American companies had very wide product lines, yet were not very vertically integrated.[7] Japanese companies, like Sony, Mitsubishi, Matsushita, or Yamaha, had extremely diverse product offerings, as did 3M or Hewlett-Packard in the United States. Yet they were not conglomerates in the normal sense. They were first termed "related conglomerates," redeploying certain key skills from market to market.[8] At the same time, these companies also contracted our significant support activities. Although frequently considered vertically integrated, the Japanese auto industry, for example, was structured around "mother companies" that primarily performed design and assembly, with a number of independent suppliers and alliance partners—without ownership bonds to the mother companies—feeding into them.[9] Many other Japanese high-tech companies, particularly the more innovative ones like Sony and Honda, used comparable strategies leveraging a few core skills against multiple markets through extensive outsourcing.

The term "core competency strategies" was later used to describe these and other less diversified strategies developed around a central set of corporate skills.[10] However, there has been little theory or consistency in the literature about what "core" really means. Consequently, many executives have been understandably confused about the topic. They need not be if they think in terms of the specific skills the company has or must have to create unique value for customers. However, their analyses must go well beyond looking at traditional product or functional strategies to the fundamentals of what the company can do better than anyone else.[11]

For example, after some difficult times, it was easy enough for a beer company like Foster's to decide that it should not be in the finance, forest products, and pastoral businesses into which it had diversified. It has now divested these peripheral businesses and is concentrating on beer. However, even within this concept, Foster's true competencies are in brewing and marketing beer. Many of its distribution, transportation, and can production activities, for example, might actually be more effectively contracted out. Within individual functions like production, Foster's could further extend its competitive advantage by outsourcing selected activities—such as maintenance or computing—where it has no unique capabilities.

The Essence of Core Competencies

What then is really "core"? And why? The concept requires that managers think much more carefully about which of the firm's activities really do—or could—create unique value and which activities managers could more effectively buy externally. Careful study of both successful and unsuccessful corporate examples suggests that effective core competencies are:

1. **Skill or knowledge sets, not products or functions.** Executives need to look beyond the company's products to the intellectual skills or management systems that actually create a maintainable competitive edge. Products, even those with valuable legal protection, can be too easily back-engineered, duplicated, or replaced by substitutes. Nor is a competency typically one of the traditional functions such as production, engineering, sales, or finance, around which organizations were formed in the past. Instead, competencies tend to be sets of skills that cut across traditional functions. This interaction allows the organization to consistently perform an activity better than functional competitors and to continually improve on the activity as markets, technology, and competition evolve. Competencies thus involve activities such as product or service design, technology creation, customer service, or logistics that tend to be based on knowledge rather than on ownership of assets or intellectual property per se. Knowledge-based activities generate most of the value in services and manufacturing. In services, which account for 79 percent of all jobs and 76 percent of all value added in the United States, intellectual inputs create virtually all of the value added. Banking, financial services, advertising, consulting, accounting, retailing, wholesaling, education, entertainment, communications, and health care are clear examples. In manufacturing, knowledge-based activities—like R&D, product design, process design, logistics, marketing research, marketing, advertising, distribution and customer service—also dominate the value-added chain of most companies (see Figure 1).

   Executives need to look beyond the company's products to the intellectual skills or management systems that actually create a maintainable competitive edge.

2. **Flexible, long-term platforms—capable of adaptation or evolution.** Too many companies try to focus on the narrow areas where they currently excel, usually on some product-oriented skills. The real challenge is to consciously build dominating skills in areas that the customer will continue to value over time, as Motorola is doing with its focus on "superior quality, portable communications." The uniqueness of Toys "R" Us lies in its powerful information and distribution systems for toys, and that of State Street Boston in its advanced information and management systems for large custodial accounts. Problems occur when managers choose to concentrate too narrowly on products (as computer companies did on hardware) or too inflexibly on formats and skills that no longer match customer needs (as FotoMat and numerous department stores did). Flexible skill sets and constant, conscious reassessment of trends are hallmarks of successful core competency strategies.

   The real challenge is to consciously build dominating skills in areas that the customer will continue to value over time.

3. **Limited in number.** Most companies target two or three (not one and rarely more than five) activities in the value chain most critical to future success. For example, 3M concentrates on four critical technologies in great depth and supports these with a peerless innovation system. As work becomes more complex, and the opportunities to excel in many detailed activities proliferate, managers find they cannot be best in every activity in the value chain. As they go beyond three to five activities or skill sets, they are unable to match the performance of their more focused competitors or suppliers. Each skill set requires intensity and management dedication that cannot tolerate dilution. It is hard to imagine Microsoft's top managers taking their enthusiasm and skills in software into, say, chip design or even large-scale training in

FIGURE 1   Make or Buy?

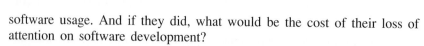

software usage. And if they did, what would be the cost of their loss of attention on software development?

4. **Unique sources of leverage in the value chain.** Effective strategies seek out places where there are market imperfections or knowledge gaps that the company is uniquely qualified to fill and where investments in intellectual resources can be highly leveraged. Raychem and Intel concentrate on depth-in-design and on highly specialized test-feedback systems supporting carefully selected knowledge-based products—not on volume production of standardized products—to jump over the experience curve advantages of their larger competitors. Morgan Stanley, through its TAPS system, and Bear Stearns, through its integrated bondtrading programs, have developed in-depth

knowledge bases creating unique intellectual advantages and profitability in their highly competitive markets.

5. **Areas where the company can dominate.** Companies consistently make more money than their competitors only if they can perform some activities—which are important to customers—more efficiently than anyone else. True focus in strategy means the capacity to bring more power to bear on a selected sector than any competitor can. Once, this meant owning and managing all the elements in the value chain supporting a specific product or service in a selected market position. Today, however, some outside supplier, by specializing in the specific skills and technologies underlying a single element in the value chain, can become more proficient at that activity than virtually any company spreading its efforts over the whole value chain. In essence, each company is in competition with all potential suppliers of each activity in its value chain. Hence, it must benchmark its selected core competencies against all other potential suppliers of that activity and continue to build these core capabilities until it is demonstrably best. Thus the basic nature of strategic analysis changes from an industry analysis perspective to a horizontal analysis of capabilities across all potential providers of an activity regardless of which industry the provider might be in (see Figure 1).

6. **Elements important to customers in the long run.** At least one of the firm's core competencies should normally relate directly to understanding and serving its customers—i.e., the right half of the value chain in Figure 1. High-tech companies with the world's best state-of-the-art technology often fail when they ignore this caveat. On the other hand, Merck matches its superb basic research with a prescription drug marketing know-how that is equally outstanding. By aggressively analyzing its customers' value chains, a company can often identify where it can specialize and provide an activity at lower cost or more effectively to the customer. Such analyses have created whole new industries, like the specialized mortgage broker, syndication, secondary market, transaction-processing, escrow, title search, and insurance businesses that have now taken over these risks and functions for banks and have disaggregated the entire mortgage industry.

By aggressively analyzing its customers' value chains, a company can often identify where it can specialize and provide an activity at lower cost or more effectively to the customer.

7. **Embedded in the organization's systems.** Maintainable competencies cannot depend on one or two talented stars—such as Steven Jobs and Stephen Wozniak at Apple or Herbert Boyer and Arthur D. Riggs at Genentech—whose departure could destroy a company's success. Instead the firm must convert these into a corporate reputation or culture that outlives the stars. Especially when a strategy is heavily dependent on creativity, personal dedication, and initiative or on attracting top-flight professionals, core competencies must be captured within the company's systems—broadly defined to include its values, organization structures, and management systems. Such competencies might include recruiting (McKinsey, Goldman Sachs), training (McDonald's, Disney), marketing (Procter & Gamble, Hallmark), innovation (Sony, 3M), motivation systems (ServiceMaster), or control of remote and diverse operating sites within a common framework and philosophy (Exxon, CRA, Inc.). These systems are often at the heart of consistent superior performance; in many cases, a firm's systems become its core competencies.[12]

Preeminence: The Key Strategic Barrier

Managers should consciously develop their core competencies to strategically block competitors and avoid outsourcing these or giving suppliers access to the knowledge bases or skills critical to their core competencies.

For its selected core competencies, the company must ensure that it maintains absolute preeminence. It may also need to surround these core competencies with defensive positions, both upstream and downstream. In some cases, it may have to perform some activities where it is not best-in-world, just to keep existing or potential competitors from learning, taking over, eroding, or bypassing elements of its special competencies. In fact, managers should consciously develop their core competencies to strategically block competitors and avoid outsourcing these or giving suppliers access to the knowledge bases or skills critical to their core competencies. Honda, for example, does all its engine R&D in-house and makes all the critical parts for its small motor design core competency in closely controlled facilities in Japan. It will consider outsourcing any other noncritical elements in its products but builds a careful strategic block around this most essential element for all its businesses.[13]

Most important, as a company's preeminence in selected fields grows, its knowledge-based core competencies become ever harder to overtake. Knowledge bases tend to grow exponentially in value with investment and experience. Intellectual leadership tends to attract the most talented people, who then work on and solve the most interesting problems. The combination in turn creates higher returns and attracts the next round of outstanding talent. In addition to the examples we have already cited, organizations as diverse as Bechtel, AT&T Bell Labs, Microsoft, Boeing, Intel, Merck, Genentech, McKinsey, Arthur Andersen, Sony, Nike, Nintendo, Bankers Trust, and Mayo Clinic have found this to be true.

Some executives regard core activities as those the company is continuously engaged in, while peripheral activities are those that are intermittent and therefore can be outsourced. From a strategic outsourcing viewpoint, however, core competencies are the activities that offer long-term competitive advantage and thus must be rigidly controlled and protected. Peripheral activities are those not critical to the company's competitive edge.

STRATEGIC OUTSOURCING

If supplier markets were totally reliable and efficient, rational companies would outsource everything except those special activities in which they could achieve a unique competitive edge, i.e., their core competencies. Unfortunately, most supplier markets are imperfect and do entail some risks for both buyer and seller with respect to price, quality, time, or other key terms. Moreover, outsourcing entails unique transaction costs—searching, contracting, controlling, and recontracting—that at times may exceed the transaction costs of having the activity directly under management's in-house control.

To address these difficulties, managers must answer three key questions about any activity considered for outsourcing. First, what is the potential for obtaining competitive advantage in this activity, taking account of transaction costs? Second, what is the potential vulnerability that could arise from market failure if the activity is outsourced? Conceptually, these two factors can be arrayed in a simple matrix (see Figure 2). Third, what can we do to alleviate our vulnerability by structuring arrangements with suppliers to provide appropriate controls yet provide for necessary flexibilities in demand?

FIGURE 2   Competitive Advantage versus Strategic Vulnerability

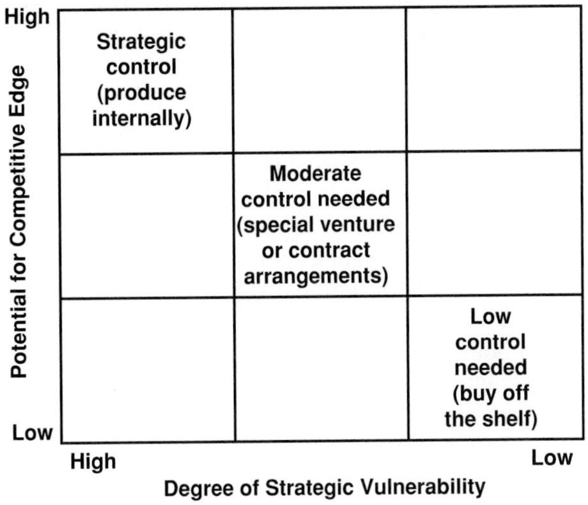

The two extremes on the matrix in Figure 2 are relatively straightforward. When the potentials for both competitive edge and strategic vulnerability are high, the company needs a high degree of control, usually entailing production internally or through joint ownership arrangements or tight long-term contracts (explicit or implicit). For example, Marks & Spencer is famous for its network of tied suppliers, which create the unique brands and styles that underpin its value reputation. Spot suppliers would be too unreliable and unlikely to meet the demanding standards that are Marks & Spencer's unique consumer franchise. Hence, close control of product quality, design, technology, and equipment through contracts and even financial support is essential. The opposite case is perhaps office cleaning where little competitive edge is usually possible and there is an active and deep market of supplier firms. In between, there is a continuous range of activities requiring different degrees of control and strategic flexibility.

At each intervening point, the question is not just whether to make or buy, but how to implement a desired balance between independence and incentives for the supplier versus control and security for the buyer. Most companies will benefit by extending outsourcing first in less critical areas—or in parts of activities, like payroll, rather than all of accounting. As they gain experience, they may increase profit opportunities greatly by outsourcing more critical activities to noncompeting firms that can perform them more effectively. In a few cases, more complex alliances with competitors may be essential to garner specialized skills that cannot be obtained in other ways. At each level, the company must isolate and rigorously control strategically critical relationships between its suppliers and its customers.

The key strategic issue in insourcing versus outsourcing is whether a company can achieve a maintainable competitive edge by performing an activity internally—usually cheaper, better, in a more timely fashion, or with some unique capability—on a continuing basis.

Competitive Edge

The key strategic issue in insourcing versus outsourcing is whether a company can achieve a maintainable competitive edge by performing an activity internally—usually cheaper, better, in a more timely fashion, or with some unique capability—on a continuing basis. If one or more of these dimensions is critical to the customer and if the company can perform that function uniquely well, the activity should be kept in-house. Many companies unfortunately assume that because they have performed an activity internally, or because it seems integral to their business, the activity should be insourced. However, on closer investigation and with careful benchmarking, its internal capabilities may turn out to be significantly below those of best-in-world suppliers.

For example, Ford Motor Company found that many of its internal suppliers' quality practices and costs were nowhere near those of external suppliers when it began its famous "best in class" worldwide benchmarking studies on 400 subassemblies for the new Taurus-Sable line. A New York bank with extensive worldwide operations investigated why its Federal Express costs were soaring and found that its internal mail department took two more days than Federal Express to get a letter or package from the third floor to the fortieth floor of its building. In interviews with top operating managers in both service and manufacturing companies concerning benchmarking, we frequently encountered a paraphrase of, "We thought we were best in the world at many activities. But when we benchmarked against the best external suppliers, we found we were not even up to the worst of the benchmarking cases."

Transaction Costs

In all calculations, analysts must include both internal transaction costs and those associated with external sourcing. If the company is to produce the item or service internally on a long-term basis, it must back up its decision with continuing R&D, personnel development, and infrastructure investments that at least match those of the best external supplier. Otherwise, it will lose its competitive edge over time. Managers often tend to overlook such backup costs, as well as the losses from laggard innovation and nonresponsiveness of internal groups that know they have a guaranteed market. Finally, there are the headquarters and support costs of constantly managing the insourced activity. One of the great gains of outsourcing is the decrease in executive time for managing peripheral activities—freeing top management to focus more on the core of its business.

Various studies have shown that, when these internal transaction costs are thoroughly analyzed, they can be extremely high.[14] Since it is easier to identify the explicit transaction costs of dealing with external suppliers, these generally tend to be included in analyses. Harder-to-identify internal transaction costs are often not included, thus biasing results.

Vulnerability

When there are many suppliers (with adequate but not dominating scale) and mature market standards and terms, a potential buyer is unlikely to be more efficient than the best available supplier. If, on the other hand, there is not sufficient depth in the market, overly powerful suppliers can hold the company ransom. Conversely, if the number of suppliers is limited or individual suppliers are too weak, they may be unable to supply innovative products or services as well as a much larger buyer could by performing the activity in-house. While the activity or product might not be one of its core competencies, the company might nevertheless benefit by producing internally rather than undertaking the training, investment, and codesign expenses necessary to bring weak suppliers up to needed performance levels.

Another form of vulnerability is the lack of information available in the marketplace or from individual suppliers; for example, a supplier may secretly expect labor disruptions or raw material problems but hide these until it is too late for the customer to go elsewhere. A related problem occurs when a supplier has unique information capabilities; for example, large wholesalers or retailers, market research firms, software companies, or legal specialists may have information or fact-gathering systems that would be impossible for the buyer or any other single supplier to reproduce efficiently. Such suppliers may be able to charge what are essentially monopoly prices, but this could still be less costly than reproducing the service internally. In other cases, there may be many capable suppliers (e.g., R&D or software), but the costs of adequately monitoring progress on the suppliers' premises might make outsourcing prohibitive.

Sometimes the whole structure of information in an industry will militate for or against outsourcing. Computing, for example, was largely kept in-house in its early years because the information available to a buyer of computing services and its ability to make judgments about such services were very different for the buying company (which knew very little) than for the supplier (which had excellent information). Many buyers lacked the competency to either assess or monitor sellers and feared loss of vital information. A company can outsource computing more easily today in part because buyers' computer, technical management, and software know-how are sufficient to make informed judgments about external suppliers.

In addition to information anomalies, Stuckey and White note three types of "asset specificity" that commonly create market imperfections, calling for controlled sourcing solutions rather than relying on efficient markets.[15] These are: (1) site specificity, where sellers have located costly fixed assets in close proximity to the buyer, thus minimizing transport and inventory costs for a single supplier; (2) technical specificity, where one or both parties must invest in equipment that can be used only by the parties in conjunction with each other and has low value in alternative uses; and (3) human capital specificity, where employees must develop in-depth skills that are specific to a particular buyer or customer relationship.

Stuckey and White explain the outsourcing implications of information and specificity problems in the case of a bauxite mine and an alumina refiner. Refineries are usually located close to mines because of the high cost of transporting bauxite, relative to its value. Refineries in turn are tuned to process the narrow set of physical properties associated with the particular mine's bauxite. Different and highly specialized skills and assets are needed for refining versus mining. Access to information further compounds problems; if an independent mine expects a strike, it is unlikely to share that information with its customers, unless there are strong incentives. As a result, the aluminum industry has moved toward vertical integration or strong bilateral joint ventures, as opposed to open outsourcing of bauxite supplies—despite the apparent presence of a commodity product and many suppliers and sellers. In this case, issues of both competitive advantage and potential market failure dictate a higher degree of sourcing control.

Degree of Sourcing Control

In deciding on a sourcing strategy for a particular segment of their business, managers have a wide range of control options (see Figures 3 and 4 for the most basic). Where there is a high potential for vulnerability and a high potential for competitive edge, tight control is indicated (as in the bauxite case). At the opposite end is, say, office cleaning. Between these extremes are opportunities for developing special incentives or more complex oversight contracts to balance intermediate levels of

FIGURE 3   Range of Outsourcing Options

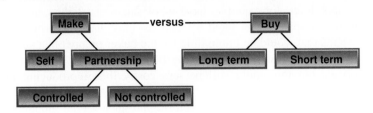

vulnerability against more moderate prospects for competitive edge. Nike's multitier strategy offers an interesting example (see Figure 5).

The practice and law of strategic alliances are rapidly developing new ways to deal with common control issues—by establishing specified procedures that permit direct involvement in limited stages of a partner's activities without incurring the costs of ownership arrangements or the loss of control inherent in arm's-length transactions. As they work their way through the available options, managers should ask themselves a series of strategic questions:

1. Do we really want to produce the good or service internally in the long run? If we do, are we willing to make the back-up investments necessary to sustain a best-in-world position? Is it critical to defending our core competency? If not,

2. Can we license technology or buy know-how that will let us be best on a continuing basis? If not,

3. Can we buy the item as an off-the-shelf product or service from a best-in-world supplier? Is this a viable long-term option as volume and complexity grow? If not,

4. Can we establish a joint development project with a knowledgeable supplier that ultimately will give us the capability to be best at this activity? If not,

5. Can we enter into a long-term development or purchase agreement that gives us a secure source of supply and a proprietary interest in knowledge or other property of vital interest to us and the supplier? If not,

6. Can we acquire and manage a best-in-world supplier to advantage? If not, can we set up a joint venture or partnership that avoids the shortcomings we see in each of the above? If so,

7. Can we establish controls and incentives that reduce total transaction costs below those of producing internally?

Flexibility versus Control

One of the main purposes of outsourcing is to have the supplier assume certain classes of investments and risks, such as demand variability.

Within this framework, there is a constant trade-off between flexibility and control. One of the main purposes of outsourcing is to have the supplier assume certain classes of investments and risks, such as demand variability. To optimize costs, the buying company may want to maintain its internal capacity at relatively constant levels despite highly fluctuating sales demands. Under these circumstances, it needs a surge strategy.

For example, McDonald's, with $8 billion in sales and 10.1 percent growth per year, needs to call in part-time and casual workers to handle extensive

FIGURE 4   Potential Contract Relationships

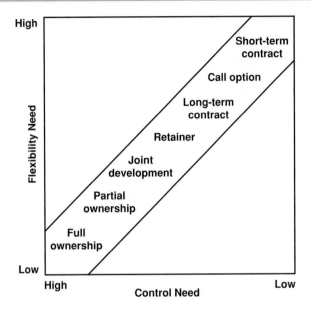

daily variations yet be able to select its future permanent or managerial personnel from these people. IBM has had the opposite problem; since its core demand has been declining, the company has had to lay off employees. Yet it needs surge capacity for: (1) quick access to some former employees' basic skills; (2) available production capacity without the costs of supporting facilities full time; and (3) the ability to exploit strong outside parties' specialized capabilities through temporary consortia—for example, in applications software, microprocessors, network development, or factory automation. Strategically, McDonald's has created a pool of people available on "call options," while IBM—through spinouts of factories with baseload commitments to IBM, guaranteed consulting employment for key people, flexible joint ventures, and strategic alliances—has created "put options" to handle surge needs as it downsizes and tries to turn around its business.

There is a full spectrum of outsourcing arrangements, depending on the company's control and flexibility needs (see Figure 4). The issue is less whether to make or buy an activity than it is how to structure internal versus external sourcing on an optimal basis. Companies are outsourcing much more of what used to be considered either integral elements of their value chains or necessary staff activities. Because of greater complexity, higher specialization, and new technological capabilities, outside suppliers can now perform many such activities at lower cost and with higher value added than a fully integrated company can. In some cases, new production technologies have moved manufacturing economies of scale toward the supplier. In others, service technologies have lowered transaction costs substantially, making it possible to specify, transport, store, and coordinate inputs from external sources so inexpensively that the balance of benefits has shifted from insourcing to outsourcing. In certain specialized niches, outside companies have grown to such size and sophistication that they have developed economies of scale, scope, and knowledge intensity so formidable that neither smaller nor more integrated producers can effectively compete with them (e.g., ADP Services in payroll, and ServiceMaster in

FIGURE 5   Nike's Multitier Partner Strategy

Nike, Inc., has a three-tier strategy of "production partners." *Developed partners* produce Nike's latest and most expensive "statement products," which can absorb higher production costs. These companies usually produce lower volumes, codevelop products, and coinvest in new technologies.

Volume producers are above-average in size (making 70,000 to 85,000 units a day, compared to 20,000 to 25,000 units for developed partners). They generally produce a specific type of footwear (say, basketball shoes) and are vertically integrated. Nike does no development work with them because each company may produce for seven or eight other buyers to keep up its volume. Although Nike tries very hard to stabilize volumes for its developed partners, volume partners are expected to handle most surges in volume themselves.

Developing sources are attractive primarily because of their low labor costs and their capacity to diversify assembly locations. All produce exclusively for Nike, which has a strong "tutelage" program to develop them into higher-level suppliers. To help both parties, Nike tries to link developing sources (through joint ventures) with its developed partners. The latter assist by providing needed training, helping to finance some operations, and moving some of their own labor-intensive activities to these units.

In addition to its first tier of assembly units, Nike supports a complex network of second-tier suppliers for materials, components, and subassemblies. In Nike's third tier, some of the more specialized and technical components are made in supplier companies that Nike totally controls—i.e., for some of its patented features like the Nike Airsole.® Nike manages its external suppliers through its "expatriate" program. Nike expatriates become permanent personnel in each factory producing Nike footwear, functioning as liaisons with corporate R&D, headquarters, and worldwide quality assurance and product development efforts. Nike's own R&D group participates in design, its corporately owned component factories give it a second window on production, and its corporate offices constantly scan new suppliers for better techniques.

maintenance). To the extent that knowledge about a specific activity is more important than knowledge about the end product itself, specialized suppliers can often produce higher value added at lower cost for that activity than almost any integrated company.

STRATEGIC BENEFITS VERSUS RISKS

Too often companies look at outsourcing as a means to lower only short-term direct costs. However, through strategic outsourcing, companies can lower their long-term capital investments and leverage their key competencies significantly, as Apple and Nike have done. They can also force many types of risk and unwanted management problems onto suppliers.

For example, Gallo, the largest producer and distributor of wines in the United States, outsources most of its grapes, pushing the risks of weather, land prices, and labor problems onto its suppliers. Argyle Diamonds, one of the world's largest diamond producers, outsources virtually all aspects of its operation except the crucial steps of separation and sorting of diamonds. It contracts all its huge earth-moving operations (to avoid capital and labor risks), its housing and food services for workers (to avoid confrontations on nonoperating issues), and much of its distribution (to De Beers to protect prices, to finance inventories, and to avoid the complications of worldwide distribution). By outsourcing to best-in-class suppliers in each case, it further ensures the quality and image of its operations.

Important Strategic Benefits

Strategically, outsourcing can provide the buyer with greater flexibility, especially in the purchase of rapidly developing new technologies, fashion goods, or the myriad components of complex systems. It decreases the company's design-cycle times, as multiple best-in-class suppliers work simultaneously on individual components of the system. Each supplier can both have more personnel depth and sophisticated technical knowledge about its specific area and also support more specialized facilities for higher quality than the coordinating (buyer) company might possibly achieve alone. In the same vein, strategic outsourcing spreads the company's risk for component and technology developments among a number of suppliers. The company does not have to undertake the full failure risks of all component R&D programs or invest in and constantly update production capabilities for each component system. Further, the buyer is not limited to its own innovative capabilities; it can tap into a stream of new product and process ideas and quality improvement potentials it could not possibly generate itself.

Strategic outsourcing spreads the company's risk for component and technology developments among a number of suppliers.

In the world's advanced economies, increased affluence has forced much greater attention to new product ideas, to quality details, and to customization. Because small specialized suppliers' often offer greater responsiveness, and new technologies have decreased the size needed to achieve economies of scale, the average size of industrial firms has decreased since the late 1960s, and subcontracting constitutes an ever greater portion of most producers' costs.[16] Outsourcing has become a major strategy to leverage internal technical capabilities and to tap the rapid response and innovative capabilities of small enterprises. Richard Leibhaber, chief strategy and technology officer at MCI, commented:

> MCI constantly seeks to grow by finding and developing associations with small companies having interesting services they can hang onto the MCI network. Although we employ only about 1,000 professional technical personnel internally, 19,000 such personnel work directly for us through contracts . . . Now we do about 60 percent of our software development work internally, but we manage [in detail] the other 40 percent in contractors' hands. We do all the specification, process rating, operational procedures, and system testing inside our company. We design the system. We control the process. Then we let others do what they can do best.[17]

Boston Consulting Group, which has studied more than 100 major companies doing extensive outsourcing, has concluded that most Western companies outsource primarily to save on overhead or short-term costs.[18] The result is a piecemeal approach that "results in patches of overcapacity scattered at random throughout the company's operation . . . [These companies] end up with large numbers of subcontractors, which are more costly to manage than in-house operations that are individually less efficient."[19] Worse still, the buying companies, by not providing adequate monitoring and technical backup, often lose their grip on key competencies they may need in the future. The Japanese, by contrast, outsource primarily to improve the efficiency and quality of their own processes, focus on a very few sources, build close interdependent relationships, and hold on tightly to high value-added activities that are crucial to quality. For those systems they contract out, Japanese companies advise closely on manufacturing and cooperate in process and product R&D on the suppliers' premises.

Strategic Risks

Outsourcing complete or partial activities creates great opportunities but also new types of risks. Management's main strategic concerns are (1) loss of critical skills or developing the wrong skills, (2) loss of cross-functional skills, and (3) loss of control over a supplier.

- **Loss of critical skills or developing the wrong skills.** Unfortunately, many U.S. companies outsourced manufacture of what, at the time, seemed to be only minor components, like semiconductor chips or a bicycle frame, and taught suppliers how to build them to needed quality standards. Later these companies found their suppliers were unable or unwilling to supply them as required. By then, the buying company had lost the skills it needed to reenter manufacture and could not prevent its suppliers from either assisting competitors or entering downstream markets on their own. In some cases, by outsourcing a key component, the company lost its own strategic flexibility to introduce new designs when it wanted, rather than when the vendor permitted a change. For example, few manufacturers can afford to design a new laser-printer engine to obtain a slight timing edge, rather than wait for Canon (with its 84 percent market share in such engines) to move.[20] The activity share that Canon has in the design function for this field or that Matsushita now has in drives for CD players gives each company such an overwhelming competitive advantage that it can control other characteristics of its industry, limiting the strategic options of others. The dual strategy framework we propose prevents such bypassing and helps managers explicitly address both needed long-term competencies and strategic vulnerabilities before embarking on outsourcing.

- **Loss of cross-functional skills.** The interactions among skilled people in different functional activities often develop unexpected new insights or solutions. Companies fear outsourcing will make such cross-functional serendipity less likely. However, if the company consciously ensures that its remaining employees interact constantly and closely with its outsourced experts, its employees' knowledge base can be much higher than if production were in-house, and the creativity benefits can be even greater. For example, companies using Texas Instrument's or Intel's design capabilities can have these suppliers' designers—with their much greater technical expertise and access to support technologies—codesign chips in-house with their own design teams during development. In such circumstances, the buyer's employees are in contact with much more skilled integrated circuit people than the firm could possibly have itself.

  In a number of industries studied, two-thirds of all innovation occurred at the customer-supplier interface.[21] By definition, outsourcing increases the buyer's own participation (as the customer) in such interfaces. Consequently, if managed properly, the practice often can increase total innovation potentials substantially (through leveraging multiple supplier relationships).

  However, having outsourced expertise at many different locations may make close cross-functional teamwork more difficult. To guard against this, in entering long-term outsourcing relationships that may involve future innovation, many managers specify that an outsource partner's personnel may be "seconded" to the buying company for special development projects. They then ensure that close personal relationships are developed between the supplier companies and their own technical personnel at the bench and operating levels. Contractual prearrangements are usually necessary to ensure that critical personnel from the outsource partner are available when needed. But the buying company must be close enough to its partner to evaluate and name the specific people it wants. Otherwise the provision may be useless when needed.

- **Loss of control over a supplier.** Real problems can occur when the supplier's priorities do not match the buyer's. The most successful outsourcers find it absolutely essential to have both close personal contact and rapport at the floor level and political clout and understanding with the supplier's top management. For this reason, Nike both has full-time "production expatriates" on its suppliers' premises and frequently brings the suppliers' top people to its Beaverton, Oregon, headquarters to exchange details about future capabilities and prospects. When conflicts occur, both the supplier's CEO and key operating personnel can be pressured directly to break the logjam. Even then, serious difficulties can occur if the buyer does not have sufficient market power relative to the seller. Some buying companies go to the extreme of owning key pieces of equipment the seller uses to make the components they are purchasing. If priorities conflict too badly, the buyer can remove its equipment and shut down the seller's whole line. These buyers say that such arrangements "ensure we can get the seller's attention when we need it."

  Real problems can occur when the supplier's priorities do not match the buyer's.

  Nevertheless, unless the buyer's core competency is a true block to the marketplace, some suppliers, after building up their expertise with the buyer's support, will attempt to bypass the buyer directly in the marketplace, as Giant Manufacturing of Taiwan, a supplier of bicycle frames, did to Schwinn. Alternatively, the seller may learn as much as possible from the buyer and its engineering groups and then attempt to resell this knowledge in different product configurations to the buyer's competitors, as Toshiba did with submarine propeller technology. Careful definition, limitation, and implementation of means to remedy such external conflicts are critical in any but the most routine outsourcing arrangements. Companies that outsource extensively have generally found satisfactory legal and operational ways to deal with the problem—and are often willing to share useful techniques with those outside their industry.

New Management Approaches

Most large companies have very sophisticated techniques for the traditional purchasing of parts, subassemblies, supplies, equipment, construction, or standard services. And models from the natural resources, real estate/construction, and finance/insurance industries—where joint ventures have been common for years—can provide useful guides for more complex partnering relationships. In addition to seeking out these experiences, the main managerial adjustments for most companies are those needed for coping with the increased scale, diversity, and service-oriented nature of the activities potentially outsourced. These center on: (1) a much more professional and highly trained purchasing and contract management group (as compared with the lowly purchasing groups of the past); and (2) a greatly enhanced logistics-information system (to track and evaluate vendors, coordinate transportation activities, and manage service transactions and materials movements from the vendors' hands to the customers'). There is vast electronic document interchange (EDI) and materials requirements planning (MRP) literature on such logistics management for products and components.

Now, similar concepts are needed for the management of knowledge and service-based activities. A number of companies are establishing direct computer connections between their service suppliers and the top managers controlling that function, as Apple has done with its consulting and public relations groups. It is increasingly easier to implement software interfaces that allow continuous electronic monitoring and executive interactions for the design, financial, advertising, public relations, R&D, real estate, or personnel-search activities as well as manufacturing, being performed at remote locations. To manage more extended outsourcing effectively, contracting and logistics activities generally need to be elevated to corporate strategic levels. So should the development of the much more sophisticated knowledge-based systems needed to capture and analyze essential details about the company's own internal processes and those of vendors. Most companies' systems need improving in this respect, but some interesting developments are under way.

For example, a consortium headed by Digital Equipment, Ford, Texas Instruments, US West, Carnegie Group, and Alcorp is developing a next-generation software tool called Initiative for Managing Knowledge Assets (IMKA). Built around the proven knowledge-based systems of DEC and TI, IMKA uses many features found in object-oriented programs that allow collection and comparison of knowledge from a variety of different end nodes, inside and outside the company. For example, it can compare each supplier plant throughout the world for its capability to meet a given subsystem's circuit performance, manufacturing, design, interconnection, weight, cost, or power requirement parameters—for any of 100,000 different objects—against the capabilities of other possible supplier plants. In milliseconds, it can coordinate and check the production dynamics necessary to ensure that parts are produced in optimum locations at lowest cost and to specification throughout the world.

Many companies fear they may not be able to maintain sufficient knowledge internally to manage their specialist suppliers, a real problem if not attacked systematically. Successful outsourcers upgrade both their top management talent and their information systems for this purpose. When they move aggressively, many companies have found that they actually improve their knowledge bases through strategic outsourcing, as Ford did with its best-in-class program. By actively riding circuit on the best outside suppliers and experts, they obtain more stimulation and insights than any insider group could possibly offer, unless that group represents the core competence of the company.

Further, when executives continuously interact with the very best talent in the world, not just the best in the next office, they are considerably more likely to stay at the top of their professions. As a side benefit of outsourcing, they can pressure internal supply groups to compete with the best external companies, question subordinates more knowledgeably, and keep internal groups more competitive.

CONCLUSION

Most companies can substantially leverage their resources through strategic outsourcing by: (1) developing a few well-selected core competencies of significance to customers and in which the company can be best-in-world; (2) focusing investment and management attention on them; and (3) strategically outsourcing many other activities where it cannot be or need not be best. There are always some inherent risks in outsourcing, but there are also risks and costs of insourcing. When approached within a genuinely strategic framework, using the variety of outsourcing options available and analyzing the strategic issues developed here, companies can overcome many of the costs and risks. When intelligently combined, core competency and extensive outsourcing strategies provide improved returns on capital, lowered risk, greater flexibility, and better responsiveness to customer needs at lower costs.

ENDNOTES

1. J. B. Quinn, T. L. Doorley, and P. C. Paquette, "Technology in Services: Rethinking Strategic Focus," *Sloan Management Review*, Winter 1990, pp. 79–87.

2. J. B. Quinn, "Leveraging Knowledge and Service Based Strategies through Outsourcing," in *Intelligent Enterprise* (New York: Free Press, 1992), pp. 71–97.

3. M. Moritz, *The Little Kingdom: The Private Story of Apple Computer* (New York: Morrow, 1984); W. Davidson, "Apple Computer, Inc.," University of Virginia, Darden Research Foundation, Case UVA-BP219, 1984.

4. R. Coase, "The Nature of the Firm," *Economica*, November 1937, pp. 386–405; O. Williamson, *Markets and Hierarchies, Analysis and Antitrust Implications* (New York: Free Press, 1975).

5. R. Rumelt, *Strategy, Structure and Economic Performance* (Cambridge, MA: Harvard University Press, 1974).

6. R. D'Aveni and A. Illinich, "Complex Patterns of Vertical Integration in the Forest Products Industry," *Academy of Management Journal* 35 (1992), pp. 596–625; P. Y. Batteyri, "The Concept of Impartition Policies: A Different Approach to Vertical Integration Strategies," *Strategic Management Journal* 9 (1988), pp. 507–20.

7. G. J. Maloney, "The Choice of Organizational Form . . . ," *Strategic Management Journal* 13 (1992), pp. 559–84; R. Miles and C. Snow, "Organizations, New Concepts and New Forms," *California Management Review*, Spring 1986, pp. 62–73.

8. Rumelt, *Strategy, Structure and Economic Performance*.

9. W. Davidson, *The Amazing Race, Winning the Technorivalry with Japan* (New York: John Wiley, 1983).

10. C. Prahalad and G. Hamel, "The Core Competence of the Corporation," *Harvard Business Review*, May–June 1990, pp. 79–91.

11. J. B. Quinn, T. L. Doorley, and P. C. Paquette, "Beyond Products: Service-Based Strategies," *Harvard Business Review*, March–April 1990, pp. 58–68.

12. D. Turner and M. Crawford, "Managing Current and Future Competitive Performance: The Role of Competence," University of New South Wales, Australian Graduate School of Management, Center for Corporate Change, 1992.

13. H. Mintzberg and J. B. Quinn, "Honda Motor Co.," in *The Strategy Process* (Englewood Cliffs, NJ: Prentice Hall, 1993), pp. 140–55.

14. R. D'Aveni and D. Ravenscraft, "Economies of Integration vs. Bureaucracy Costs: Does Vertical Integration Improve Performance?" *Academy of Management Journal*, forthcoming; H. Mintzberg, *The Nature of Managerial Work* (New York: Harper & Row, 1973).

15. J. Stuckey and D. White, "When and When *Not* to Vertically Integrate," *Sloan Management Review*, Spring 1993, pp. 71–83.

16. "The Incredible Shrinking Company," *The Economist*, December 15, 1990, pp. 65–66; "Costing the Factory of the Future," *The Economist*, March 3, 1990, pp. 61–62.

17. Interview with J. B. Quinn, March 1992.

18. "Manufacturing: The Ins and Outs of Outing," *The Economist*, August 31, 1991, pp. 54 and 56.

19. M. F. Blaxill and T. M. Hout, "The Fallacy of the Overhead Quick Fix," *Harvard Business Review*, July–August 1991, pp. 93–101.

20. R. Reich, "Who Is Us?" *Harvard Business Review*, January–February 1990, pp. 53–64.

21. E. von Hippel, *The Sources of Innovation* (New York: Oxford University Press, 1988).

PRODUCING SUSTAINABLE COMPETITIVE ADVANTAGE THROUGH THE EFFECTIVE MANAGEMENT OF PEOPLE

Jeffrey Pfeffer, *Stamford University*

This article suggests that firms that view their workforce as a source of competitive advantage, rather than a cost to be minimized or avoided, are more likely to successfully outmaneuver and outperform their rivals. The author points to 13 practices that characterize companies that are effective in achieving competitive success through the management of their people.

Suppose that in 1972, someone asked you to pick the five companies that would provide the greatest return to stockholders over the next 20 years. And suppose that you had access to books on competitive success that were not even written. How would you approach your assignment? In order to earn tremendous economic returns, the companies you picked should have some sustainable competitive advantage, something that (1) distinguishes them from their competitors, (2) provides positive economic benefits, and (3) is not readily duplicated.

Conventional wisdom then (and even now) would have you begin by selecting the right industries. After all, "not all industries offer equal opportunity for sustained profitability, and the inherent profitability of its industry is one essential ingredient in determining the profitability of a firm."[1] According to Michael Porter's now famous framework, the five fundamental competitive forces that determine the ability of firms in an industry to earn above-normal returns are "the entry of new competitors, the threat of substitutes, the bargaining power of buyers, the bargaining power of suppliers, and the rivalry among existing competitors.[2] You should find industries with barriers to entry, low supplier and buyer bargaining power, few ready substi-

Source: Adapted from Jeffrey Pfeffer. *Competitive Advantage through People* (Boston: Harvard Business School Press, 1994).

tutes, and a limited threat of new entrants to compete away economic returns. Within such industries, other conventional analyses would urge you to select firms with the largest market share, which can realize the cost benefits of economies of scale. In short you would probably look to industries in which patent protection of important product or service technology could be achieved and select the dominant firms in those industries.

You would have been very successful in selecting the five top-performing firms from 1972 to 1992 if you took this conventional wisdom and turned it on its head. The top five stocks, and their percentage returns, were (in reverse order): Plenum Publishing (with a return of 15,689 percent), Circuit City (a video and appliance retailer; 16,410 percent), Tyson Foods (a poultry producer; 18,118 percent), Wal-Mart (a discount chain; 19,807 percent), and Southwest Airlines (21,775 percent).[3] Yet during this period, these industries (retailing, airlines, publishing, and food processing) were characterized by massive competition and horrendous losses, widespread bankruptcy, virtually no barriers to entry (for airlines after 1978), little unique or proprietary technology, and many substitute products or services. And in 1972, none of these firms was (and some still are not) the market share leader, enjoying economies of scale or moving down the learning curve.

The point here is not to throw out conventional strategic analysis based on industrial economics but simply to note that the source of competitive advantage has always shifted over time. What these five successful firms tend to have in common is that for their sustained advantage, they rely not on technology, patents, or strategic position, but on how they manage their workforce.

THE IMPORTANCE OF THE WORKFORCE AND HOW IT IS MANAGED

As other sources of competitive success have become less important, what remains as a crucial, differentiating factor is the organization, its employees, and how they work. Consider, for instance, Southwest Airlines, whose stock had the best return from 1972 to 1992. It certainly did not achieve that success from economies of scale. In 1992, Southwest had revenues of $1.31 billion and a mere 2.6 percent of the U.S. passenger market.[4] People Express, by contrast, achieved $1 billion in revenues after only 3 years of operation, not the almost 20 it took Southwest. Southwest exists not because of regulated or protected markets but in spite of them. "During the first three years of its history, no Southwest planes were flown."[5] Southwest waged a battle for its very existence with competitors who sought to keep it from flying at all and, failing that, made sure it did not fly out of the newly constructed Dallas–Fort Worth international airport. Instead, it was restricted to operating out of the close-in Love Field, and thus was born its first advertising slogan, "Make Love, Not War." Southwest became the "love" airline out of necessity, not choice.

In 1978, competitors sought to bar flights from Love Field to anywhere outside Texas. The compromise Southwest wrangled permitted it to fly from Love to the four states contiguous to Texas.[6] Its competitive strategy of short-haul, point-to-point flights to close-in airports (it now flies into Chicago's Midway and Houston's Hobby airports) was more a product of its need to adapt to what it was being permitted to do than a conscious, planned move—although, in retrospect, the strategy has succeeded brilliantly. Nor has Southwest succeeded because it has had more access to lower-cost capital—indeed, it is one of the least leveraged airlines in the United States.

Southwest's planes, Boeing 737s, are obviously available to all its competitors. It isn't a member of any of the big computerized reservation systems; it uses no unique process technology and sells essentially a commodity product—low-cost, low-frills airline service at prices its competitors have difficulty matching.

Much of its cost advantage comes from its very productive, very motivated, and, by the way, unionized workforce. Compared to the U.S. airline industry, according to 1991 statistics, Southwest has fewer employees per aircraft (79 versus 131), flies more passengers per employee (2,318 versus 848), and has more available seat miles per employee (1,891,082 versus 1,339,995).[7] It turns around some 80 percent of its flights in 15 minutes or less, while other airlines on average need 45 minutes, giving it an enormous productivity advantage in terms of equipment utilization.[8] It also provides an exceptional level of passenger service. Southwest has won the airlines' so-called triple crown (best on-time performance, fewest lost bags, and fewest passenger complaints—in the same month) *nine* times. No competitor has achieved that even once.[9]

What is important to recognize is why success, such as that achieved at Southwest, can be sustained and cannot readily be imitated by competitors. There are two fundamental reasons. First, the success that comes from managing people effectively is often not as visible or transparent as to its source. We can see a computerized information system, a particular semiconductor, a numerically controlled machine tool. The culture and practices that enable Southwest to achieve its success are less obvious. Even when they are described, as they have been in numerous newspaper articles and even a segment on "60 Minutes," they are difficult to really understand. Culture, how people are managed, and the effects of this on their behavior and skills are sometimes seen as the "soft" side of business, occasionally dismissed. Even when they are not dismissed, it is often hard to comprehend the dynamics of a particular company and how it operates because the way people are managed often fits together in a system. It is easy to copy one thing but much more difficult to copy numerous things. This is because the change needs to be more comprehensive and also because the ability to understand the system of management practices is hindered by its very extensiveness.

Thus, for example, Nordstrom, the department store chain, has enjoyed substantial success both in customer service and in sales and profitability growth over the years. Nordstrom compensates its employees in part with commissions. Not surprisingly, many of its competitors, after finally acknowledging Nordstrom's success, and the fact that it was attributable to the behavior of its employees, instituted commission systems. By itself, changing the compensation system did not fully capture what Nordstrom had done, nor did it provide many benefits to the competition. Indeed, in some cases, changing the compensation system produced employee grievances and attempts to unionize when the new system was viewed as unfair or arbitrary.

THIRTEEN PRACTICES FOR MANAGING PEOPLE

Contrary to some academic writing and to popular belief, there is little evidence that effective management practices are (1) particularly faddish (although their implementation may well be), (2) difficult to understand or to comprehend why they work, or (3) necessarily contingent on an organization's particular competitive strategy. There are interrelated practices—I enumerate 13, but the exact number and how they are defined are somewhat arbitrary—that seem to characterize companies that are effective in achieving competitive success through how they manage people.

The following policies and practices emerge from extensive reading of both the popular and academic literature, talking to numerous people in firms in a variety of industries, and the application of some simple common sense. The particular way of subdividing the terrain is less important than considering the entire landscape, so the reader should realize that the division into categories is somewhat arbitrary. The themes, however, recur repeatedly in studies of organizations. It is important to recognize that the practices are interrelated—it is difficult to do one thing by itself with much positive result.

Employment Security

Security of employment signals a long-standing commitment by the organization to its workforce. Norms of reciprocity tend to guarantee that this commitment is repaid. However, conversely, an employer that signals through word and deed that its employees are dispensable is not likely to generate much loyalty, commitment, or willingness to expend extra effort for the organization's benefit. New United Motor Manufacturing (NUMMI), the Toyota-GM joint venture in California, guaranteed workers' jobs as part of the formal labor contract in return for a reduction in the number of job classifications and an agreement not to strike over work standards. This commitment was met even in the face of temporarily slow demand, and many observers believe that as a result, trust between employees and the organization increased substantially.

An employer that signals through word and deed that its employees are dispensable is not likely to generate much loyalty, commitment, or willingness to expend extra effort for the organization's benefit.

Taking on people not readily eliminated exerts pressure to be careful and selective in hiring. Moreover, "employment security enhances employee involvement because employees are more willing to contribute to the work process when they need not fear losing their own or their co-workers' jobs. Employment security contributes to training as both employer and employee have greater incentives to invest in training,"[10] because there is some assurance that the employment relationship will be of sufficient duration to earn a return on the time and resources expended in skill development.

Selectivity in Recruiting

Security in employment and reliance on the workforce for competitive success mean that one must be careful to choose the right people, in the right way. Studies covering populations ranging from machine operators, typists, and welders to assembly workers—all in self-paced jobs so that individual differences mattered—indicate that the most productive employees were about twice as good as the least productive.[11] Southwest Airlines worries a lot about hiring the right people. In fact, it flies some of its best customers to Dallas and involves them in the flight attendant hiring process, believing that those who are in contact with the front-line employees probably know best what makes a good employee. At Lincoln Electric, hiring is done very carefully based on the desire to succeed and the capacity for growth.[12]

One of the practices of many of the Japanese automobile-manufacturing plants opened in the United States that proved especially newsworthy was their extensive screening of employees. Some of this was undoubtedly done to weed out those who were likely to be pro-union, but much of the screening was to find those people who could work best in the new environment, could learn and develop, and needed less supervision. There was little screening for particular skills, under the assumption that these could be readily learned. Nordstrom, the very effective specialty retailer whose sales per square foot are about double the industry average, tends to recruit sales clerks who are young and college-educated, seeking a career in retailing.[13]

Besides getting the right people in the door, recruiting has an important symbolic aspect. If someone goes through a rigorous selection process, the person feels that he or she is joining an elite organization. High expectations for performance are created, and the message sent is that people matter.

High Wages

If you want to recruit outstanding people, and want them to stay with the organization, paying more is helpful, although not absolutely necessary. High wages tend to attract more applicants, permitting the organization to be more selective in finding people who are going to be trainable and who will be committed to the organization. Perhaps most important, higher wages send a message that the organization values its people. Particularly if these wages are higher than required by the market, employees can perceive the extra income as a gift and work more diligently as a result.[14] Nordstrom typically pays its people an hourly wage higher than the prevailing rate for retail clerks at comparable stores. Coupled with incentive pay for outstanding work, Nordstrom salespeople often earn twice the average retail income.

> *Higher wages send a message that the organization values its people.*

Companies sometimes believe that lowering labor costs is essential for competitive success. This is not invariably the case, even in cost-competitive businesses, because in many organizations, labor costs are a small fraction of the total costs. Furthermore, even if labor costs (let alone labor rates) are higher, it may be that enhanced service, skill, and innovation more than compensate by increasing the level of overall profit. For instance, the CEO of Wendy's, facing declining company profitability, decided that the best way to become the customer's restaurant of choice was to become the employer of choice.[15] This entailed improving both benefits and base compensation, instituting a quarterly bonus, and creating an employee stock option plan. The results were dramatic: "Our turnover rate for general managers fell to 20 percent in 1991 from 39 percent in 1989, while turnover among co- and assistant managers dropped to 37 percent from 60 percent—among the lowest in the business. With a stable—and able—workforce, sales began to pick up as well."[16]

Incentive Pay

There has been a tendency to overuse money in an effort to solve myriad organizational problems. People are motivated by more than money—things like recognition, security, and fair treatment matter a great deal. Nevertheless, if people are responsible for enhanced levels of performance and profitability, they will want to share in the benefits. Consider the alternative—if all the gains from extra ingenuity and effort go just to top management or to shareholders (unless these are also employees), people will soon view the situation as unfair, become discouraged, and abandon their efforts. Thus, many organizations seek to reward performance with some form of contingent compensation.

Lincoln Electric is deservedly famous for its piecework and incentive bonus plan. Contrary to first impressions, the plan does much more than merely reward individual productivity. Although the factory workforce is paid on a piecework basis, it is paid only for good pieces—workers correct quality problems on their own time.

Moreover, defects can be traced to the individual who produced them. Quality is emphasized as well as productivity. Additionally, piecework is only a part of the employee's compensation. Bonuses, which often constitute 100 percent of regular salary, are based on the company's profitability—encouraging employees to identify with the whole firm. They are also based on the individual's merit rating, and that rating is, in turn, based on four equally important aspects of performance: dependability, quality, output, and ideas and cooperation.[17] This broader evaluation mitigates the pernicious tendencies of simplistic incentive systems to go awry.

Employee Ownership

Employee ownership offers two advantages. Employees who have ownership interests in the organizations for which they work have less conflict between capital and labor—to some degree they are both capital and labor. Employee ownership, effectively implemented, can align the interests of employees with those of shareholders by making employees shareholders, too. Second, employee ownership puts stock in the hands of people, employees, who are more inclined to take a long-term view of the organization, its strategy, and its investment policies and less likely to support hostile takeovers, leveraged buyouts, and other financial maneuvers. Of course, to the extent that one believes this reduced risk of capital market discipline inhibits efficiency, significant employee shareholding is a disadvantage. However, the existing evidence largely contradicts this negative view.

It is probably no coincidence that all five of the companies mentioned as providing the best shareholder returns from 1972 to 1992 appear on The Employee Ownership 1000, a listing of "1000 companies in which employees own more than 4% of the stock of a corporation" traded on the New York or American stock exchanges or the over-the-counter market.[18] Although employee ownership is no panacea, and its effects depend largely on how it is implemented, the existing evidence is consistent with the view that employee ownership has positive effects on firm performance.[19]

Information Sharing

If people are to be a source of competitive advantage, clearly they must have the information necessary to do what is required to be successful.

If people are to be a source of competitive advantage, clearly they must have the information necessary to do what is required to be successful. At the Advanced Micro Devices submicron development center, there are computer terminals throughout the plant that every employee has been trained to use in order to obtain information about product yields, development progress, production rates, or any other aspect of the operation. One reason sometimes given for not disclosing information to large numbers of employees is that it may leak to competitors. When Robert Beck was head of human resources for the Bank of America, he perceptively told the management committee, reluctant to disclose the bank's strategy and other information to its employees, that the competitors almost certainly knew the information already; typically, the only people in the dark are the firm's own employees.

Participation and Empowerment

Sharing information is a necessary precondition to another important feature found in many successful work systems: encouraging the decentralization of decision making and broader worker participation and empowerment in controlling their own work process. At Nordstrom, the written philosophy states:

We also encourage you to present your own ideas. Your buyers have a great deal of autonomy, and are encouraged to seek out and promote new fashion directions at all times . . . Nordstrom has a strong open-door policy and we encourage you to share your concerns, suggestions and ideas . . .

Nordstrom Rules:

Rule #1: Use your good judgment in all situations. There will be no additional rules.[20]

The evidence is that participation increases both satisfaction and employee productivity.[21] Autonomy is one of the most important dimensions of jobs and was the focus of many job-redesign efforts undertaken as part of the quality of working life movement in the 1960s and 1970s.[22] The fundamental change involves moving from a system of hierarchical control and coordination of activity to one in which lower-level employees, who may have more or better information, are permitted to do things to enhance performance. At a Levi Strauss jeans factory, when it was time to purchase new forklift trucks, the drivers themselves got involved. They determined specifications, negotiated with suppliers, and made the final purchase decision, in the process saving the company money as well as obtaining equipment more appropriate for that plant. At Eaton, a unionized manufacturer, workers tired of fixing equipment that broke down suggested that they build two new automated machines themselves. They did it for less than a third of what outside vendors would have charged and doubled the output of the department in the first year.[23]

Self-Managed Teams

Organizations that have tapped the power of teams have often experienced excellent results. Monsanto, a large chemical company, implemented work organization based on self-managed teams at its chemical and nylon complex near Pensacola, Florida. Teams of workers were responsible for hiring, purchasing, job assignments, and production.[24] Management was reduced from seven levels to four, and the plant experienced increases in both profitability and safety. At a 318-person submarine systems plant owned by AT&T, costs were reduced more than 30 percent through the use of teams.[25] Federal Express uses teams in its back-office operation with great success—service problems fell 13 percent in 1989 after the company's 1,000 clerical workers were organized in teams and given additional training and authority.[26] One of the more dramatic examples of the benefits of using teams occurred at Johnsonville Sausage. In 1986, a manufacturer asked Johnsonville to produce private-label sausage. The president was about to decline the new business, because he believed that the plant was already at capacity and could not handle the additional workload. However,

before deciding, he assembled his 200 production workers, who are organized in teams of five to 20, and asked them to decide . . . After . . . ten days, they came back with an answer: "We can do it" . . . The teams decided how much new machinery they would need and how many new people; they also made a schedule of how much to produce per day. Since Johnsonville took on the new project, productivity has risen over 50 percent in the factory.[27]

Teams work because of the peer monitoring and expectations of co-workers that are brought to bear to both coordinate and monitor work.

Teams work because of the peer monitoring and expectations of co-workers that are brought to bear to both coordinate and monitor work. Indeed, even critics of the team concept often argue that the problem with teams as a substitute for hierarchy is not that this approach doesn't work but that it works too well. Thus, a dissident union leader in the NUMMI plant noted: "[W]hen the team's under pressure, people try to meet the team's expectations and under peer pressure, they end up pushing themselves too hard . . . The team concept is a nice idea, but when you put the teams under pressure, it becomes a damn effective way to divide workers."[28]

Training and Skill Development

An integral part of most new work systems is a greater commitment to training and skill development. Note, however, that this training will produce positive returns only if the trained workers are then permitted to employ their skills. One mistake many organizations make is to upgrade the skills of both managers and workers but not change the structure for work in ways that permit people to do anything different. Under such circumstances, it is little wonder that training has no apparent effect.

At Advanced Micro Devices' submicron development facility, some 70 percent of the technicians came from older facilities at AMD. In keeping with AMD's emphasis on employment stability, as old facilities were closed, people were evaluated with respect to their basic skills. If accepted, they were put through a seven-month program at Mission College—at full pay and at company expense—and then went to work in the new facility. This training not only demonstrated the firm's commitment to its employees, which was then reciprocated, but also ensured that the facility would be staffed with highly qualified people who had been specifically trained for their new jobs.

At a Collins and Aikman carpet plant in Georgia, more than a third of the employees were high school dropouts, and some could neither read nor write. When the firm introduced computers to increase productive efficiency, however, it chose not to replace its existing workforce but to upgrade its skills. After spending about $1,200 per employee on training, including lost job time, the company found that the amount of carpet stitched increased 10 percent. Moreover, quality problems declined by half. The employees, with more skills and better morale, submitted some 1,230 suggestions, and absenteeism fell by almost half.[29]

Cross-Utilization and Cross-Training

Having people do multiple jobs has a number of potential benefits. The most obvious is that doing more things can make work more interesting—variety is one of the core job dimensions that affect how people respond to their work. Variety in jobs permits a change in pace, a change in activity, and potentially even a change in the people with whom one comes in contact, and each of these forms of variety can make work life more challenging. Beyond its motivational effects, having people do multiple jobs has other important benefits. One is keeping the work process both transparent and as simple as possible. If people are expected to shift to new tasks readily, the design of those tasks has to be straightforward enough so they can be learned quickly. A second, somewhat related benefit is the potential for newcomers to a job to see things that can be improved that experienced people don't see, simply because they have come to take the work process so much for granted.

Multiskilling is also a useful adjunct to policies that promise employment security. After all, it is easier to keep people at work if they have multiple skills and can do different things. By the same token, maintaining employment levels sometimes compels organizations to find new tasks for people, often with surprising results. When Mazda, the Japanese automobile manufacturer, suffered a decline in business in the 1980s, rather than laying off factory workers, it put them to work selling cars, which, in Japan, are often sold door to door. At the end of the year, when awards were presented to the best salespeople, the company discovered that the top 10 were all former factory workers. They could explain the product effectively, and of course, when business picked up, the fact that factory workers had experience talking to customers yielded useful ideas about product characteristics.

At Lechmere, a retail chain owned by Dayton-Hudson, the company experimented with cross-training and utilization of employees at a new store in Sarasota, Florida. The store offered the workers raises based on the number of jobs they learned to perform, a variant of a pay-for-skill plan. The workforce, composed of 60 percent full-time employees rather than the 30 percent typical for the chain, was substantially more productive than in other stores. "Cashiers are encouraged to sell records and tapes. Sporting goods salesmen get tutoring in forklifts. That way Lechmere can quickly adjust to changes in staffing needs simply by redeploying existing workers. The pay incentives, along with the prospect of a more varied and interesting work-day, proved valuable lures in recruiting."[30]

Symbolic Egalitarianism

One important barrier to decentralizing decision making, using self-managed teams, and eliciting employee commitment and cooperation is the symbols that separate people from each other. Consequently, it is not surprising that many of the firms that are known for achieving competitive advantage through people have various forms of symbolic egalitarianism—ways of signaling to both insiders and outsiders that there is comparative equality and it is not the case that some think and others do. At NUMMI, the executive dining room was eliminated, and everyone eats in the same cafeteria. Everyone wears a blue smock. There are no reserved places in the em-ployee parking lot.

Communication across levels is greatly enhanced by the opportunity to interact and meet in less formal settings. This means that senior management is more likely to know what is actually going on and be able to communicate its ideas more directly to everyone in the facility. The reduction in the number of social categories tends to decrease the salience of various subdivisions in the organization, diminishes "us" versus "them" thinking, and provides more of a sense of everyone working toward a common goal. This egalitar-ianism makes cross-movement easier because there are fewer status dis-tinctions to be overcome. At NUMMI, there is only one classification for Division 1 personnel compared to more than 80 previously. The number of skilled trades classifications shrank from 18 under the old General Motors systems to 2.[31]

Egalitarianism makes cross-movement easier because there are fewer status distinctions to be overcome.

Egalitarian symbols come in many forms. In some organizations, it is dress—few who have worked in a manufacturing facility have not heard the phrase "the suits are coming" when people from headquarters, typically more formally dressed, arrive. Physical space is another way in which common fate can be signaled, or not. The CEO of Solectron, a contract manufacturer that won the Malcolm Baldrige award, does not have a private office, and neither does the chairman. In contrast, John DeLorean's graphic description of the 14th-floor headquarters for General Motors was one of hushed, quiet offices reached by a private elevator that was secured—in other words, executives cut off from the rest of the organization.[32]

Although symbolic egalitarianism would seem easy to implement, the elimination of status symbols is often one of the most difficult things for a company to do. A friend bemoaned the fact that just as he had reached a managerial level that entitled him to use a private dining room, have preferential parking, and occupy a larger office, his employer embarked on a total quality movement and eliminated all of these perquisites.

Wage Compression

Although issues of wage compression are most often considered in terms of hierarchical compression, and particularly CEO pay relative to that of others, there is a horizontal aspect to wage compression as well. It can have a number of efficiency-enhancing properties for organizations.

It is important to remember that wage compression is distinct from incentive pay. Incentive pay simply means that people are rewarded, either individually or in groups, for their performance. These rewards can be large, producing wide variation in salaries, or small, producing substantially less variation. It is also important to recognize that incentive pay—particularly applied to larger units such as work groups, departments, or the entire organization—can either reduce or increase the wage dispersion that would otherwise exist. Most gain-sharing and profit-sharing programs actually reduce pay dispersion, although they need not do so.

When tasks are somewhat interdependent and cooperation is helpful for accomplishing work, pay compression, by reducing interpersonal competition and enhancing cooperation, can lead to efficiency gains.[33] Furthermore, large differences in the allocation of organizational rewards can motivate people to achieve these rewards. Although increased motivation can produce greater efforts, large differences in rewards can as readily result in excessive time and energy spent on ingratiating oneself with one's supervisor or trying to affect the criteria for reward allocation.[34] By this reasoning, a more compressed distribution of salaries can actually produce higher overall performance, as there is less incentive for individuals to waste their time on gaming the system.

To the extent that wages are compressed, pay is likely to be deemphasized in the reward system and in the organization's culture. This has some obvious economic benefits—people are not constantly worrying about whether they are compensated appropriately and attempting to rebargain their salaries. A deemphasis on pay can also focus attention on the other advantages of organizational membership such as good colleagues and work that is interesting and meaningful. There is a literature in psychology that suggests we attempt to figure out why we are doing what we are by looking at ourselves as an outside observer would.[35] If we see we are very well paid, perhaps on a contingent basis, for what we do, we are likely to attribute our behavior to the economic rewards. If, however, we are not particularly well paid, or if pay is less salient, and if it is distributed on a less contingent basis (which will make it less salient), then we are likely to attribute our behavior to other, more intrinsic factors such as the inherent enjoyment of the work. In other words, being paid in a contingent fashion for what we do can actually undermine our intrinsic interest in and satisfaction with that activity.[36] Thus, pay compression, by helping to deemphasize pay, can enhance other bases of satisfaction with work and build a culture that is less calculative in nature.

Promotion from Within

Promotion from within is a useful adjunct to many of the practices described. It encourages training and skill development because the availability of promotion opportunities within the firm binds workers to employers and vice versa. It facilitates decentralization, participation, and delegation because it helps promote trust across hierarchical levels; promotion from within means that supervisors are responsible for coordinating the efforts of people whom they probably know quite well. By the same token, those being coordinated personally know managers in higher positions. This contact provides social bases of influence so that formal position can loom less important. Promotion from within also offers an incentive for performing well, and although tied to monetary rewards, promotion is a reward that also has a status-based, nonmonetary component. Perhaps most important, it provides a sense of fairness and justice in the workplace. If people do an outstanding job but outsiders are being brought in over them, there will be a sense of alienation from the organization. One other advantage of promotion from within is that it tends to ensure that people in management positions actually know something about the business, the technology, and the operations they are managing. There are numerous tales of firms managed by those with little understanding of the basic operations, often with miserable results. David Halberstam's history of Ford Motor tells how finance took control of the company. Not only were these people not "car men," they knew little about automobiles, technology, production processes, or the market—anything that could not be conveyed via statistics—and had little interest in learning.[37] The problem with managing only through statistics is that without some understanding of the underlying processes that produce the measures, it is likely that managers will either focus on inappropriate measures or fail to fully comprehend what they mean.

> *Promotion from within tends to ensure that people in management positions actually know something about the business, technology, and the operations they are managing.*

By contrast, at Lincoln Electric, almost everyone who joins the company learns to weld—Lincoln's main product is, after all, arc welding equipment. Graduation from the welding program requires coming up with some innovation to the product. At Nordstrom, even those with advanced degrees start on the sales floor. Promotion is strictly from within, and when Nordstrom opens a new store, its key people are recruited from other stores around the country. This helps perpetuate the Nordstrom culture and values but also provides assurance that those running the store know what they are doing and have experience doing it the Nordstrom way.

TAKING THE LONG VIEW

The bad news about achieving some competitive advantage through the workforce is that it inevitably takes time to accomplish. By contrast, a new piece of equipment can be quickly installed: a new product technology can be acquired through a licensing agreement in the time it takes to negotiate the agreement; and acquiring capital only requires the successful conclusion of negotiations. The good news, however, is that once achieved, competitive advantage obtained through employment practices is likely to be substantially more enduring and more difficult to duplicate. Nevertheless, the time required to implement these practices and start seeing results means that a long-term perspective is needed. It also takes a long time horizon to execute many of these approaches. In the short term, laying off people is probably more profitable compared to trying to maintain employment security; cutting training is a quick way to maintain short-term profits; and cross-training and cross-utilization may provide insights and innovation in time, but initially, the organization forgoes the advantages of more narrow specialization and the immediate proficiency achieved thereby.

What determines an organization's time horizon is an important issue, but one outside the scope of this article. In general, however, there is some evidence that family ownership, employee ownership, or other forms of organization that lessen the immediate pressures for quick earnings to please the securities market are probably helpful. Lincoln Electric is closely held, and the Nordstrom family retains a substantial fraction of the ownership of that retailer. NUMMI has Toyota as one of the joint venture partners, and Toyota's own plans for the facility virtually dictate that it take a long-term view, which is consistent with its culture and tradition. Again, the Walton family's ownership position in Wal-Mart helps ensure that the organization takes a long view of its business processes.

It is almost inconceivable that a firm facing immediate short-term pressure would embark on activities that are apparently necessary to achieve some competitive advantage through people. This provides one explanation for the limited diffusion of these practices. If the organization is doing well, it may feel no need to worry about its competitive position. By the same token, if the organization is in financial distress, the immediate pressures may be too severe to embark on activities that provide productivity and profit advantages, but only after a longer, and unknown period of time.

MEASUREMENT OF THE PRACTICES

Measurement is a critical component in any management process, and this is true for the process of managing the organization's workforce. Measurement serves several functions. First, it provides feedback as to how well the organization is implementing various policies. For example, many organizations espouse a promotion from within policy but don't fulfill this objective. Often, this is because there is no systematic collection and reporting of information such as what percentage of the positions at given levels have been filled internally. A commitment to a high-wage policy obviously requires information as to where in the relevant labor market the organization's wages fall. A commitment to training is more likely to be fulfilled if data are collected, not only on the total amount spent on training but also on what types of employees have received training and what sorts of training are being delivered.

Second, measurement ensures that what is measured will be noticed. "Out of sight, out of mind" is a principle that applies to organizational goals and practices as well as to people. One of the most consistent findings in the organizational literature is that measures affect behavior.[38] Most people will try to succeed on the measures even if there are no direct, immediate consequences. Things that are measured get talked about, and things that are not don't.

Things that are measured get talked about, and things that are not don't.

It is no accident that companies seriously committed to achieving competitive advantage through people make measurement of their efforts a critical component of the overall process. Thus, for example, at Advanced Micro Devices' submicron development facility, management made how people were managed a priority and measured employee attitudes regularly to see whether they were "achieving the vision." One survey asked questions such as: How many teams are you on in your own department and with members of other departments? How many hours per week do you spend receiving training and training others? The survey also asked the extent to which people agreed or disagreed with statements such as: there is problem solving at all levels in my work group; people in my work group are encouraged to take the initiative; a spirit of teamwork exists in our work group.

In a world in which financial results are measured, a failure to measure human resource policy and practice implementation dooms this to second-class status, oversight, neglect, and potential failure. The feedback from the measurements is essential to refine and further develop implementation ideas as well as to learn how well the practices are actually achieving their intended results.

FIGURE 1   New versus Old Paradigms at Levi Strauss

Old Paradigm	New Paradigm
Economy of *scale* as basis for improvement logic	Economy of *time* as basis for improvement logic
Quality involves trade-offs	Quality is a "religion"; no compromise
Doers are separate from thinkers	Doers must also be thinkers
Assets are things	Assets are people
Profit is the primary business goal	Customer satisfaction is the primary business goal
Hierarchical organization; goal is to please the boss	Problem-solving network organization; goal is to please the internal or external customer
Measure to judge operational results	Measure to help people make operational improvements

Source: Presentation by Peter Thigpen at the Stanford School of Business, February 26, 1991.

OVERARCHING PHILOSOPHY

Having an overarching philosophy or view of management is essential. It provides a way of connecting the various individual practices into a coherent whole and also enables people in the organization to persist and experiment when things don't work out immediately. Moreover, such a philosophy makes it easier to explain what the organization is doing, justify it, and mobilize support from internal and external constituencies. Most simply put, it is hard to get somewhere if you don't know where you are going. In a similar fashion, practices adopted without a deeper understanding of what they represent and why they are important to the organization may not add up to much, may be unable to survive internal or external problems, and are likely to produce less than stellar results.

Many companies that seek competitive success through their people and practice a number of approaches really began with some underlying principles or else developed them early in the process. Levi Strauss's quality enhancement process began with the understanding that "manufacturing for quality and speed meant breaking the old paradigms," turning the culture upside down and completely reorienting the parameters of the business.[39] The company and its manufacturing senior vice president explicitly articulated the underlying assumptions of the old way of thinking and the new, as illustrated in Figure 1.

SOME WORDS OF CAUTION

It would be difficult to find a single company that does all of these things or that does them all equally well. Some successful firms have tended to do a higher percentage, and it is useful to grade one's own company against the overall list. Nevertheless, there are few companies that do everything. Which practice is most critical does depend in part on the company's particular technology and market strategy.

A second important caution is to recognize that it is possible for a company to do all of these things and be unprofitable and unsuccessful, or to do few or none of them and be quite successful. How? These factors are almost certainly related to a company's ability to achieve competitive success through its workforce. But although that may be an important basis of success, and one that is even increasing in importance, it is clearly not the *only* basis of success.

IBM, for instance, has done many of these things and has built a skilled and dedicated workforce. That in and of itself, however, could not overcome a product strategy that overemphasized large, mainframe computers. People Express, now defunct, also built a strong culture, selectively recruited, and used innovative compensation and work organization strategies to build flexibility and productivity in its operations. Indeed, it was one of the lowest-cost providers of airline services. But this cost advantage could not overcome other problems, such as the founder's edifice complex, which resulted in too-rapid expansion, acquisition of Frontier Airlines and becoming seriously financially overleveraged, and a growth rate that was not sustainable given the firm's fundamental human resource policies. In focusing on managing the workforce, I highlight only *one* dimension of the several that determine corporate performance.

A third word of caution is that these practices have potential downsides as well as benefits and are not necessarily easy to implement, particularly in a one-at-a-time fashion. One obvious problem is that they all necessarily entail more involvement and responsibility on the part of the workforce. There are many employees who would rather work only with their bodies and check their minds at the door—particularly if that is what they have become accustomed to—and instituting work practices that entail more effort and involvement may force turnover. These practices may be resisted by others in the company as well. The reader is cautioned that implementation issues loom large, regardless of how sensible the practices may be.

ENDNOTES

1. Michael E. Porter, *Competitive Advantage* (New York: Free Press, 1985), p. 1.
2. Ibid., p. 4.
3. "Investment Winners and Losers," *Money*, October 1992, p. 133.
4. Bridget O'Brian, "Southwest Airlines Is a Rare Air Carrier: It Still Makes Money," *The Wall Street Journal*, October 26, 1992, p. A1.
5. James Campbell Quick, "Crafting an Organizational Culture: Herb's Hand at Southwest Airlines," *Organizational Dynamics* 21 (Autumn 1992), p. 47.
6. O'Brian, "Southwest Airlines," p. A7.
7. Quick, "Crafting," p. 50.
8. O'Brian, "Southwest Airlines," p. A1.
9. Ibid., p. A7.
10. Clair Brown, Michael Reich, and David Stern, "Becoming a High Performance Work Organization: The Role of Security, Employee Involvement, and Training," Working Paper 45, Institute of Industrial Relations (Berkeley, CA: University of California, 1992), p. 3.
11. Frank L. Schmidt and John E. Hunter, "Individual Differences in Productivity: An Empirical Test of Estimates Derived from Studies of Selection Procedure Utility," *Journal of Applied Psychology* 68 (1983), pp. 407–14.

12. Harry C. Handlin, "The Company Built upon the Golden Rule: Lincoln Electric," in Bill L. Hopkins and Thomas C. Mawhinney, eds., *Pay for Performance: History, Controversy, and Evidence* (New York: Haworth Press, 1992), p. 157.

13. Nordstrom: Dissension in the Ranks?" Harvard Business School Case 9-191-002 (1990), p. 7.

14. George Akerlof, "Gift Exchange and Efficiency Wage Theory," *American Economic Review* 74 (1984), pp. 79–83.

15. James W. Near, "Wendy's Successful 'Mop Bucket Attitude'," *The Wall Street Journal*, April 27, 1992, p. A16.

16. Ibid.

17. Handlin, "The Company," p. 159.

18. Joseph R. Blasi and Douglas L. Kruse, *The New Owners* (New York: Harper Business, 1991), p. 257.

19. Corey M. Rosen, Katherine J. Klein, and Karen M. Young, *Employee Ownership in America* (Lexington, MA: Lexington Books, 1986).

20. Richard T. Pascale, "Nordstrom, Inc.," unpublished case (San Francisco, CA: 1991), Exhibits 7 and 8.

21. David L. Levine and Laura D'Andrea Tyson, "Participation, Productivity, and the Firm's Environment," in Alan S. Blinder, ed., *Paying for Productivity: A Look at the Evidence* (Washington, DC: The Brookings Institution, 1990, pp. 183–243.

22. J. Richard Hackman and Greg R. Oldham, *Work Redesign* (Reading, MA: Addison-Wesley, 1980).

23. Thomas F. O'Boyle, "Working Together: A Manufacturer Grows Efficient by Soliciting Ideas from Employees," *The Wall Street Journal*, June 5, 1992, p. A4.

24. Barnaby Feder, "At Monsanto, Teamwork Works," *New York Times*, June 25, 1991, p. C1.

25. Barbara Presley Noble, "An Approach with Staying Power," *New York Times*, March 8, 1992, p. 23.

26. Brian Dumaine, "Who Needs a Boss?" *Fortune*, May 7, 1990, p. 54.

27. Ibid., p. 55.

28. Paul S. Adler, "The 'Learning Bureaucracy': New United Motor Manufacturing, Inc.," in Barry M. Staw and Larry L. Cummings, eds., *Research in Organizational Behavior* (Greenwich, CT: JAI Press, 1995), p. 32.

29. Helene Cooper, "Carpet Firm Sets Up an In-House School to Stay Competitive," *The Wall Street Journal* October 5, 1992, pp. A1, A6.

30. Norm Alster, "What Flexible Workers Can Do," *Fortune*, February 13, 1989, p. 62.

31. Adler, "Learning Bureaucracy," p. 17.

32. J. Patrick Wright, *On a Clear Day You Can See General Motors* (Grosse Pointe, MI: Wright Enterprises, 1979).

33. Edward P. Lazear, "Pay Equality and Industrial Politics," *Journal of Political Economy* 97 (1989), pp. 561–80.

34. Paul Milgrom and John Roberts, "An Economic Approach to Influence Activities in Organizations," *American Journal of Sociology* 94 (1988), pp. S154–79.

35. Daryl J. Bem, "Self-Perception Theory," in Leonard Berkowitz, ed., *Advances in Experimental Social Psychology*, vol. 6 (New York: Academic Press, 1972), pp. 1–62.

36. Mark R. Lepper and David Greene, "Turning Play into Work: Effects of Adult Surveillance and Extrinsic Rewards on Children's Intrinsic Motivation," *Journal of Personality and Social Psychology* 31 (1975), pp. 479–86.

37. David Halberstam, *The Reckoning* (New York: William Morrow, 1986).

38. See, for example, Peter M. Blau, *The Dynamics of Bureaucracy* (Chicago, IL: University of Chicago Press, 1955); and V. F. Ridgway, "Dysfunctional Consequences of Performance Measurement," *Administrative Science Quarterly* 1 (1956), pp. 240–47.

39. Presentation by Peter Thigpen at Stanford Graduate School of Business, February 26, 1991.

ON THE FOLLY OF REWARDING A, WHILE HOPING FOR B

Steven Kerr, *VP Corporate Mangement Development General Electric Co.*

The basic premise of this "classic[1]" article is that reward systems often reward the behavior that is discouraged while failing to reward the desired behavior. To make an impact on employees, reward systems must positively reinforce desired behaviors.

Whether dealing with monkeys, rats, or human beings, it is hardly controversial to state that most organisms seek information concerning what activities are rewarded, and then seek to do (or at least pretend to do) those things, often to the virtual exclusion of activities not rewarded. The extent to which this occurs of course will depend on the perceived attractiveness of the rewards offered, but neither operant nor expectancy theorists would quarrel with the essence of this notion.

Nevertheless numerous examples exist of reward systems that are fouled up in that the types of behavior rewarded are those which the rewarder is trying to discourage, while the behavior desired is not being rewarded at all.

Numerous examples exist of reward systems that are fouled up in that the types of behavior rewarded are those which the rewarder is trying to discourage, while the behavior desired is not being rewarded at all.

FOULED UP SYSTEMS

In Politics

Officials goals are "purposely vague and general and do not indicate . . . the host of decisions that must be made among alternative ways of achieving official goals and the priority of multiple goals. . . . "[2] They usually may be relied on to offend absolutely no one, and in this sense can be considered high-acceptance, low-quality goals. An example might be "All Americans are entitled to health care." Operative

Source: *Academy of Management Executive* no. 1 (1995).

goals are higher in quality but lower in acceptance, since they specify where the money will come from, and what alternative goals will be ignored.

The American citizenry supposedly wants its candidates for public office to set forth operative goals, making their proposed programs clear, and specifying sources and uses of funds. However, since operative goals are lower in acceptance, and since aspirants to public office need acceptance (from at least 50.1 percent of the people), most politicians prefer to speak only of official goals, at least until after the election. They of course would agree to speak at the operative level if "punished" for not doing so. The electorate could do this by refusing to support candidates who do not speak at the operative level. Instead, however, the American voter typically punishes (withholds support from) candidates who frankly discuss where the money will come from, rewards politicians who speak only of official goals, but hopes that candidates (despite the reward system) will discuss the issues operatively.

In War

If some oversimplification may be permitted, let it be assumed that the primary goal of the organization (Pentagon, Luftwaffe, or whatever) is to win. Let it be assumed further that the primary goal of most individuals on the front lines is to get home alive. Then there appears to be an important conflict in goals—personally rational behavior by those at the bottom will endanger goal attainment by those at the top.

But not necessarily! It depends on how the reward system is set up. The Vietnam war was indeed a study of disobedience and rebellion, with terms such as "fragging" (killing one's own command officer) and "search and evade" becoming part of the military vocabulary. The difference in subordinates' acceptance of authority between World War II and Vietnam is reported to be considerable and veterans of the Second World War were often quoted as being outraged at the mutinous actions of many American soldiers in Vietnam.

Consider, however, some critical differences in the reward system in use during the two conflicts. What did the GI in World War II want? To go home. And when did he get to go home? When the war was won! If he disobeyed the orders to clean out the trenches and take the hills, the war would not be won and he would not go home. Furthermore, what were his chances of attaining his goal (getting home alive) if he obeyed the orders compared to his chances if he did not? What is being suggested is that the rational soldier in World War II, whether patriotic or not, probably found it expedient to obey.

Consider the reward system in use in Vietnam. What did the soldier at the bottom want? To go home. And when did he get to go home? When his tour of duty was over! This was the case whether or not the war was won. Furthermore, concerning the relative chance of getting home alive by obeying orders compared to the chance if they were disobeyed, it is worth noting that a mutineer in Vietnam was far more likely to be assigned rest and rehabilitation (on the assumption that fatigue was the cause) than he was to suffer any negative consequence.

In his description of the "zone of indifference," Barnard stated that "a person can and will accept a communication as authoritative only when . . . at the time of his decision, he believes it to be compatible with his personal interests as a whole."[3] In light of the reward system used in Vietnam, wouldn't it have been personally irrational for some orders to have been obeyed? Was not the military implementing a system which rewarded disobedience, while hoping that soldiers (despite the reward system) would obey orders?

In Medicine

Theoretically, physicians can make either of two types of error, and intuitively one seems as bad as the other. Doctors can pronounce patients sick when they are actually well (a type 1 error), thus causing them needless anxiety and expense, curtailment of enjoyable foods and activities, and even physical danger by subjecting them to needless medication and surgery. Alternately, a doctor can label a sick person well (a type 2 error), and thus avoid treating what may be a serious, even fatal ailment. It might be natural to conclude that physicians seek to minimize both types of error.

Such a conclusion would be wrong. It has been estimated that numerous Americans have been afflicted with iatrogenic (physician *caused*) illnesses.[4] This occurs when the doctor is approached by someone complaining of a few stray symptoms. The doctor classifies and organizes these symptoms, gives them a name, and obligingly tells the patient what further symptoms may be expected. This information often acts as a self-fulfilling prophecy, with the result that from that day on the patient for all practical purposes is sick.

Why does this happen? Why are physicians so reluctant to sustain a type 2 error (pronouncing a sick person well) that they will tolerate many type 1 errors? Again, a look at the reward system is needed. The punishments for a type 2 error are real; guilt, embarrassment, and the threat of a malpractice suit. On the other hand, a type 1 error (labeling a well person sick) is a much safer and more conservative approach to medicine in today's litigious society. Type 1 errors also are likely to generate increased income and a stream of steady customers who, being well in a limited physiological sense, will not embarrass the doctor by dying abruptly. Fellow physicians and the general public therefore are really *rewarding* type 1 errors while *hoping* fervently that doctors will try not to make them.

A current example of rewarding type 1 errors is provided by Broward County, Florida, where an elderly or disabled person facing a competency hearing is evaluated by three court-appointed experts who get paid much more *for the same examination* if the person is ruled to be incompetent. For example, psychiatrists are paid $325 if they judge someone to be incapacitated, but earn only $125 if the person is judged competent. Court-appointed attorneys in Broward also earn more—$325 as opposed to $175—if their clients lose than if they win. Are you surprised to learn that, of 598 incapacity proceedings initiated and completed in the county in 1993, 570 ended with a verdict of incapacitation?[5]

In Universities

Society hopes that professors will not neglect their teaching responsibilities but rewards them almost entirely for research and publications. This is most true at the large and prestigious universities. Clichés such as "good research and good teaching go together" notwithstanding, professors often find that they must choose between teaching and research-oriented activities when allocating their time. Rewards for good teaching are usually limited to outstanding teacher awards, which are given to only a small percentage of good teachers and usually bestow little money and fleeting prestige. Punishments for poor teaching are also rare.

Society hopes that professors will not neglect their teaching responsibilities but **rewards them almost entirely for** *research and publications.*

Rewards for research and publications, on the other hand, and punishments for failure to accomplish these, are common. Furthermore, publication-oriented résumés usually will be well-received at other universities, whereas teaching credentials, harder to document and quantify, are much less transferable. Consequently, it is rational for university professors to concentrate on research, even to the detriment of teaching and at the expense of their students.

By the same token, it is rational for students to act based upon the goal displacement[6] which has occurred within universities concerning what they are rewarded for. If it is assumed that a primary goal of a university is to transfer knowledge from teacher to student, then grades become identifiable as a means toward that goal, serving as motivational, control, and feedback devices to expedite the knowledge transfer. Instead, however, the grades themselves have become much more important for entrance to graduate school, successful employment, tuition refunds, and parental respect, than the knowledge or lack of knowledge they are supposed to signify.

It therefore should come as no surprise that we find fraternity files for examinations, term paper writing services, and plagiarism. Such activities constitute a personally rational response to a reward system which pays off for grades rather than knowledge. These days, reward systems—specifically, the growing threat of lawsuits—encourage teachers to award students high grades, even if they aren't earned. For example:

> When Andy Hansen brought home a report card with a disappointing C in math, his parents . . . sued his teacher . . . After a year and six different appeals within the school district, another year's worth of court proceedings, $4,000 in legal fees paid by the Hansens, and another $8,500 by the district . . . the C stands. Now the student's father, auto dealer Mike Hansen, says he plans to take the case to the State Court of Appeals . . . "We went in and tried to make a deal: They wanted a C, we wanted an A, so why not compromise on a B?" Mike Hansen said. "But they dug in their heels, and here we are."[7]

In Consulting

It is axiomatic that those who care about a firm's well-being should insist that the organization get fair value for its expenditures. Yet it is commonly known that firms seldom bother to evaluate a new TQM, employee empowerment program, or whatever, to see if the company is getting its money's worth. Why? Certainly it is not because people have not pointed out that this situation exists; numerous practitioner-oriented articles are written each year on just this point.

One major reason is that the individuals (in human resources, or organization development) who would normally be responsible for conducting such evaluations are the same ones often charged with introducing the change effort in the first place. Having convinced top management to spend money, say, on outside consultants, they usually are quite animated afterwards in collecting rigorous vignettes and anecdotes about how successful the program was. The last thing many desire is a formal, revealing evaluation. Although members of top management may actually *hope* for such systematic evaluation, their reward systems continue to *reward* ignorance in this area. And if the HR department abdicates its responsibility, who is to step into the breach? The consultants themselves? Hardly! They are likely to be too busy collecting anecdotal "evidence" of their own, for use on their next client.

In Sports

Most coaches disdain to discuss individual accomplishments, preferring to speak of teamwork, proper attitude, and one-for-all spirit. Usually, however, rewards are distributed according to individual performance. The college basketball player who passes the ball to teammates instead of shooting will not compile impressive scoring statistics and is less likely to be drafted by the pros. The ballplayer who hits to right field to advance the runners will win neither the batting nor home run titles, and will be offered smaller raises. It therefore is rational for players to think of themselves first, and the team second.

In Government

Consider the cost-plus contract or its next of kin, the allocation of next year's budget as a direct function of this year's expenditures—a clear-cut example of a fouled-up reward system. It probably is conceivable that those who award such budgets and contracts really hope for economy and prudence in spending. It is obvious, however, that adopting the proverb "to those who spend shall more be given," rewards not economy, but spending itself.

In Business

The past reward practices of a group health claims division of a large Eastern insurance company provides another rich illustration. Attempting to measure and reward accuracy in paying surgical claims, the firm systematically kept track of the number of returned checks and letters of complaint received from policyholders. However, underpayments were likely to provoke cries of outrage from the insured, while overpayments often were accepted in courteous silence. Since it was often impossible to tell from the physician's statement which of two surgical procedures, with different allowable benefits, was performed, and since writing for clarifications would have interfered with other standards used by the firm concerning percentage of claims paid within two days of receipt, the new hire in more than one claims section was soon acquainted with the informal norm: "When in doubt, pay it out!"

This situation was made even worse by the firm's reward system. The reward system called for annual merit increases to be given to all employees, in one of the following three amounts:

1. If the worker was "outstanding" (a select category, into which no more than two employees per section could be placed): 5 percent.

2. If the worker was "above average" (normally all workers not "outstanding" were so rated): 4 percent.

3. If the worker committed gross acts of negligence and irresponsibility for which he or she might be discharged in many other companies: 3 percent.

Now, since the difference between the five percent theoretically attainable through hard work and the four percent attainable merely by living until the review date is small, many employees were rather indifferent to the possibility of obtaining the extra one percent reward. In addition, since the penalty for error was a loss of only one percent, employees tended to ignore the norm concerning indiscriminant payments.

However, most employees were not indifferent to a rule which stated that, should absences or latenesses total three or more in any six-month period, the entire four or five percent due at the next merit review must be forfeited. In this sense, the firm was *hoping* for performance, while *rewarding* attendance. What it got, of course, was attendance. (If the absence/lateness rule appears to the reader to be stringent, it really wasn't. The company counted "times" rather than "days" absent, and a ten-day

---

FIGURE 1   Common Management Reward Follies

We hope for . . .	But we often reward . . .
• Long-term growth; environmental responsibility	• Quarterly earnings
• Teamwork	• Individual effort
• Setting challenging "stretch" objectives	• Achieving goals; "making the numbers"
• Downsizing; rightsizing; delayering; restructuring	• Adding staff; adding budget; adding Hay points
• Commitment to total quality	• Shipping on schedule, even with defects
• Candor; surfacing bad news early	• Reporting good news, whether it's true or not; agreeing with the boss, whether or not (s)he's right

---

absence therefore counted the same as one lasting two days. A worker in danger of accumulating a third absence within six months merely had to remain ill—away from work—during a second absence until the first absence was more than six months old. The limiting factor was that at some point salary ceases, and sickness benefits take over. This was usually sufficient to get the younger workers to return, but for those with 20 or more years' service, the company provided sickness benefits of 90 percent of normal salary, tax-free! Therefore . . .).

Thanks to the U.S. government, even the reporting of wrongdoing has been corrupted by an incredibly incompetent reward system that calls for whistleblowing employees to collect up to 30 percent *of the amount of a fraud* without a stated limit. Thus prospective whistleblowers are encouraged to delay reporting a fraud, even to actively participate in its continuance, in order to run up the total and, thus, their percentage of the take.

I'm quite sure that by now the reader has thought of numerous examples in his or her own experience which qualify as "folly." However, just in case, Figure 1 presents some additional examples well worth pondering.

CAUSES

Many managers seek to establish simple, quantifiable standards against which to measure and reward performance. Such efforts may be successful in highly predictable areas within an organization, but are likely to cause goal displacement when applied anywhere else.

Extremely diverse instances of systems which reward behavior A although the rewarder apparently hopes for behavior B have been given. These are useful to illustrate the breadth and magnitude of the phenomenon, but the diversity increases the difficulty of determining commonalities and establishing causes. However, the following four general factors may be pertinent to an explanation of why fouled-up reward systems seem to be so prevalent.

1. Fascination with an "Objective" Criterion   Many managers seek to establish simple, quantifiable standards against which to measure and reward performance. Such efforts may be successful in highly predictable areas within an organization, but are likely to cause goal displacement when applied anywhere else.

2. Overemphasis on Highly Visible Behaviors   Difficulties often stem from the fact that some parts of the task are highly visible while other parts are not. For example, publications are easier to demonstrate than teaching, and scoring baskets and hitting home runs are more readily observable than feeding teammates and advancing base runners. Similarly, the adverse consequences of pronouncing a sick person well are more visible than those sustained by labeling a well person sick. Team-building and creativity are other examples of behaviors which may not be rewarded simply because they are hard to observe.

3. Hypocrisy   In some of the instances described the rewarder may have been getting the desired behavior, notwithstanding claims that the behavior was not desired. For example, in many jurisdictions within the United States, judges' campaigns are funded largely by defense attorneys, while prosecutors are legally barred from making contributions. This doesn't do a whole lot to help judges to be "tough on crime" though, ironically, that's what their campaigns inevitably promise.

4. Emphasis on Morality or Equity Rather than Efficiency   Sometimes consideration of other factors prevents the establishment of a system which rewards behavior desired by the rewarder. The felt obligation of many Americans to vote for one candidate or another, for example, may impair their ability to withhold support from politicians who refuse to discuss the issues. Similarly, the concern for spreading the risks and costs of wartime military service may outweigh the advantage to be obtained by committing personnel to combat until the war is over. The 1994 Clinton health plan, the Americans with Disabilities Act, and many other instances of proposed or recent governmental intervention provide outstanding examples of systems that reward inefficiency, presumably in support of some higher objective.

ALTERING THE REWARD SYSTEM

Managers who complain about lack of motivation in their workers might do well to consider the possibility that the reward systems they have installed are paying off for behavior other than what they are seeking. This, in part, is what happened in Vietnam, and this is what regularly frustrates societal efforts to bring about honest politicians and civic-minded managers.

A first step for managers might be to explore what types of behavior are currently being rewarded. Chances are excellent that these managers will be surprised by what they find—that their firms are not rewarding what they assume they are.

A first step for such managers might be to explore what types of behavior are currently being rewarded. Chances are excellent that these managers will be surprised by what they find—that their firms are not rewarding what they assume they are. In fact, such undesirable behavior by organizational members as they have observed may be explained largely by the reward systems in use.

This is not to say that all organizational behavior is determined by formal rewards and punishments. Certainly it is true that in the absence of formal reinforcement some soldiers will be patriotic, some players will be team oriented, and some employees will care about doing their job well. The point, however, is that in such cases the rewarder is not *causing* the behavior desired but is only a fortunate bystander. For an organization to *act* upon its members, the formal reward system should positively reinforce desired behavior, not constitute an obstacle to be overcome.

For an organization to act *upon its members, the formal reward system should positively reinforce desired behavior, not constitute an obstacle to be overcome.*

POSTSCRIPT

An irony about this article's being designated a management classic is that numerous people claim to have read and enjoyed it, but I wonder whether there was much in it that they didn't know. I believe that most readers already knew, and act on in their nonwork lives, the principles that underlie this article. For example, when we tell our daughter (who is about to cut her birthday cake) that her brother will select the first piece, or inform our friends *before* a meal that separate checks will be brought at the end, or tell the neighbor's boy that he will be paid five dollars for cutting the lawn *after* we inspect the lawn, we are making use of prospective rewards and punishments to cause other people to care about our own objectives. Organizational life may seem to be more complex, but the principles are the same.

ENDNOTES

1. Originally published in 1975, *Academy of Management Journal* 18, pp. 769–83.
2. Charles Perrow, "The Analysis of Goals in Complex Organizations," in A. Etzioni, ed., *Readings on Modern Organizations* (Englewood Cliffs, NJ: Prentice-Hall, 1969), p. 66.
3. Chester I. Barnard, *The Functions of the Executive* (Cambridge, MA: Harvard University Press, 1964), p. 165.
4. L. H. Garland, "Studies of the Accuracy of Diagnostic Procedures," *American Journal Roentgenological, Radium Therapy Nuclear Medicine* 82 (1959), pp. 25–38; and Thomas J. Scheff, "Decision Rules, Types of Error, and Their Consequences in Medical Diagnosis," in F. Massarik and P. Ratoosh, eds., *Mathematical Explorations in Behavioral Science* (Burr Ridge, IL: Irwin, 1965).
5. *Miami Herald*, May 8, 1994, pp. 1a, 10a.
6. Goal displacement results when means become ends in themselves and displace the original goals. See Peter M. Blau and W. Richard Scott, *Formal Organizations* (San Francisco, CA: Chandler, 1962).
7. *San Francisco Examiner*, reported in *Fortune*, February 7, 1994, p. 161.

CREATING THE CLIMATE AND CULTURE OF SUCCESS

Benjamin Schneider, *University of Maryland*

Sarah K. Gunnarson, *McManis Associates*

Kathryn Niles-Jolly, *U.S. Office of Personnel Management*

The authors suggest that organizations become more effective when they create, maintain, and, if needed, change climates and cultures to emphasize innovation, service, and organizational citizenship behaviors. Because climates are created by practices, procedures, and rewards, organizations can change climates, and indirectly cultures, through the selection and orientation of new employees, formal and informal reward structures, training, and allocation of resources.

If you wandered around 3M for awhile and asked some casual questions, you would soon sense what places this corporation at or near the top of *Fortune*'s "Most Admired Company" list year after year.

You couldn't help noticing, for example, the number of informal meetings in progress. At these meetings, representatives of 3M's sales, marketing, manufacturing, engineering, R&D, and even accounting departments discuss new product ideas and problems. Customers also may be part of the group, conveniently discussing their problems with people from different parts of the company, without ever having to leave the room.

You would see a striking amount of cooperation among 3M employees. Employees go out of their way to help each other—they volunteer to work on other employees' ideas by working long extra hours. Even when told to stop working on something that interests them, employees persist, working on it on their own time.

Chat with any of 3M's 40 division managers. They most likely will reveal that the unit achieved 25 percent of its sales income from products that are less than five years old. And the manager would probably credit this record to the way employees organize themselves into product development teams—each team made up of *volunteers* and chaired by a new product champion.

In effect, what 3M management has done is create and maintain a climate that fosters innovation, customer service, and "citizenship behavior"—i.e., employees voluntarily help, in various ways, to preserve and protect the organization. Managers in many organizations, from Marriott to Motorola, from Xerox to Ritz-Carlton, share 3M's belief that organizations must maintain these three aspects of climate simultaneously.

Some call this achievement "total quality management" Others call it a "systems approach." At 3M they call it "success."

DEFINING CLIMATE AND CULTURE

Climate is the atmosphere that employees perceive is created in their organization by practices, procedures, and rewards.

Climate—the "feeling in the air" one gets from walking around a company—may be difficult to define. But this doesn't make it any less real. Climate is the atmosphere that employees perceive is created in their organization by practices, procedures, and rewards. These perceptions are developed on a day-to-day basis. They are *not* based on what management, the company newsletter, or the annual report proclaim—rather, the perceptions are based on executives' behavior and the actions they reward.

Certain perceptions play heavily in the creation of the climate employees perceive. At a company like 3M, they include the following:

- Practices and procedures in this company encourage innovation.
- Employees in this company get rewarded for giving warm and friendly service.
- Employees cooperate for the organization's sake, rather than simply meeting the minimum requirements of their job descriptions.

Employees observe what happens to them (and around them) and then draw conclusions about their organization's priorities. They then set their own priorities accordingly. Thus, these perceptions provide employees with *direction* and *orientation* about where they should focus their energies and competencies. This, in turn, becomes a major factor in creating a climate.

Because organizations have numerous priorities, any organization can harbor many climates. For example, General Electric might have a climate that supports innovation in the R&D division and one that supports service in the 1-800 GE Answering Service division. These departments also might share an overall climate for organizational citizenship behavior (OCB).

Culture, on the other hand, refers to the broader pattern of an organization's mores, values, and beliefs.

Culture, on the other hand, refers to the broader pattern of an organization's mores, values, and beliefs. Again, the actions of senior managers strongly influence culture. By observing and interpreting these actions, employees are able to explain *why* things are the way they are, and *why* the organization focuses on certain priorities. Culture, then, stems from employees' interpretations of the assumptions, values, and philosophies that produce the climates they experience. For example, employees' cultural interpretations might be the following:

- Senior managers create a climate for innovation because they give high priority to competitiveness. They also value change, and they recognize the danger of complacency.
- Senior managers create a climate for service excellence because they value customer *and* employee satisfaction.

- Senior managers create a climate for citizenship behavior because they want employees to do more than just come to work. They value the extra effort it takes to preserve and promote organizational success.

Employees automatically make these attributions about what management values. The challenge for management is to act in ways that will lead employees to the kinds of attributions that result in commitment to management's most important values.

Culture is created and transmitted mainly through employees sharing their interpretations of events. ("They are bringing in computers so they can reduce head count"), or through storytelling ("One day there was a blizzard and the manager drove a customer home because the customer's car was buried in the snow"). Cultural characteristics attributed to the organization actually become the organization's characteristics when employees share their beliefs about management. The more employees talk about management's qualities, the more the qualities become organization characteristics.

> *Culture is created and transmitted mainly through employees sharing their interpretations of events.*

Thus, it is virtually impossible to have a service, innovative, or OCB culture unless employees attribute these values to management. Employees must first make these attributions, then share their attributions with other employees, for these aspects of culture to literally become part of the organization.

From our experience, an organization needs employees to perceive all three management values to be successful. No organization succeeds over the long run without attention to customer service, to innovation and change, and to the extra effort and energy that comes from employees' good will.

Readers might debate with us whether these are *the* three climates and cultures that must simultaneously exist for a business to be successful. These are the three we are betting on; contentious readers are free to choose their own three—or four or five—and conduct their own research. Even if we lose the bet, our major point still holds: that organizations must focus their employees' energies and competencies on multiple priorities simultaneously, and that it is through climate and culture that this focus happens.

Below, we consider each of the three requirements, giving special attention to management actions that can foster these climates, as well as employee attributions that create (or are) culture.

THE CLIMATE AND CULTURE FOR INNOVATION

Andre Delbecq and Peter Mills of the University of Santa Clara in California tried to identify the characteristics that distinguish highly innovative companies from companies that are less innovative. Their findings, based on studies of several hundred managers in high-technology and health service organizations, provide valuable insight into an innovative climate and culture. While Delbecq and Mills did not interpret their findings using the terminology of climate and culture, we will do so here.

The researchers defined innovation as the capacity to develop and effectively market innovations. We define innovation more broadly as an organization's capacity to change and to continuously reinvent itself.

Delbecq and Mills discovered that the practices and procedures shown in Figure 1 and discussed below were the major ways in which the highly innovative organizations differed from less innovative organizations:

FIGURE 1   Keys to Successful Innovators

- Top management commits emotional and financial support and provides an advocate for the innovation.
- Top management ensures there is a market for the planned innovation.
- The planned innovation has support from all levels of the organization.
- The planned innovation goes through several small, carefully evaluated steps prior to actual implementation.

- *Commitment from top management and sponsorship.* In organizations with low innovation, top management does not provide financial and/or emotional support to get the innovation project started. In contrast, organizations that promote innovation commit many resources to the project: They earmark special funds, they assign employees to find and promote innovations, and they make sure that each potential innovation has an assigned advocate or sponsor.

- *Emphasis on market analyses and customer sensitivity.* The low innovators relied on poor feasibility studies, or moved forward with no feasibility study. This left them with unrealistic assessments for the demand for the innovation, overly complex designs, and insufficient attention to the support (such as training or marketing) that success requires. High innovators, on the other hand, were "close to" and "in touch with" the average potential user, so they could accurately assess market demand and the support required to meet that demand.

- *Adoption procedures.* The low innovators lacked the organization's formal commitment, as well as the resources for implementation. High innovators, in contrast, received firm commitments from people throughout the organization. As a result, the innovations' advocates felt supported rather than alone and isolated.

- *Implementation.* Not only were low innovators under-resourced, they also had delusions of grandeur that prompted them to prematurely implement the innovations without adequate testing along the way. The high-innovation organizations took small steps, evaluating each throughout the process. They then made the necessary adjustments for market acceptance. In addition, the gradual rollout allowed the companies to realistically determine the resources required to sustain the innovation.

When an organization's practice and procedures are similar to the high innovators described by Delbecq and Mills, a company has a climate for innovation. No single practice or procedure shown in Figure 1 would suffice for such a climate; all of the differences between the way the high and low innovators function must first be in place. The reason is that climate perceptions are based on *aggregate* practices and procedures, not isolated practices or procedures. Climate perceptions are *global*; they are *summaries* of many experiences.

The contrasts that Delbecq and Mills present can be used to infer the beliefs employees might share about senior managers' implicit assumptions and values. Although Delbecq and Mills did not explicitly identify these, we will surmise what they might include. Employees might agree that *management* believes that:

- *Success in the marketplace comes from complete knowledge of, and input from, the end user.* Customer acceptance, not engineering sophistication, is what ultimately leads to successful innovation.

- *The quality of the idea is important, not the authority and power of the person behind the innovation.* Decisions should be based on information and data rather than politics and power.

- *Creative people need nurturing, support, and organizational commitment to succeed.* No matter how creative, these people cannot sustain the effort it takes to successfully innovate if left alone and unsupported.

- *Decisions should be made a step at a time.* This is slow but also the most effective path to success.

This last inference may seem to be counterintuitive: intuition, for example, suggests that innovative companies are quick actors. In fact, they *are* quick actors—but only after careful analysis and study. Innovative firms are the way they are because they *constantly* pursue innovative ideas; they are sticklers for detail; and they demonstrate commitment to innovation over time.

Our research and consulting show us that management creates a climate by what management *does*, not by what it says. Employees believe their company is an innovative company when they see things happening to them and around them that push them to be innovative and demand they pay attention to innovation. At 3M and elsewhere (for example, at the Procter & Gamble Co. and Hewlett-Packard) everything is set up to foster innovation—who gets hired, who is rewarded, how the organization is structured, what procedures and resources are available, and so on.

> *Employees believe their company is an innovative company when they see things happening to them and around them that push them to be innovative and demand they pay attention to innovation.*

It takes more than innovation to win in today's competitive national and international environment, however. Recall that the United States bred the concepts and early models of the compact disk and the video cassette recorder, only to see these innovations languish in research, not in development. Companies like 3M, Motorola, and Hewlett-Packard know that research is not enough; *development* of the product for market is required. More recently, another issue has become a key to success in the marketplace—service to the end-user consumer.

Perhaps researchers and consultants have focused so intently on customer satisfaction with products that they have overlooked the role of service in the world of consumer goods. Recently, however, various studies of service industries have shed new light on the role service plays in any business. The implications of these findings for goods-producing firms are becoming clear.

THE CLIMATE AND CULTURE FOR SERVICE EXCELLENCE

Service organizations need to think differently about their business, compared with those companies producing tangible products. This is true because of the ways in which services differ from goods:

- *Services are more intangible than goods.* Goods yield "things" while services yield "experiences." As a result, relationships between the consumer and the service deliverer are more significant in the evaluation of a service. Consider the "intangibility" of an experience in the theater. Once a play is over, the

---

FIGURE 2   Keys to Service Excellence

- Human resource practices promote employee well-being and a sense of community.
- There is active retention of existing customers.
- There is attention to details regarding the quality of staff and the resources needed to deliver excellent service.

---

participant is left only with the experience, not an object or product. Many services have some of this same intangibility.

- *Services often require consumer participation in the production of the service.* For example, airplane passengers provide information about where they want to go, what they want to eat, and where they want to sit. If the customer fails to do his or her part (i.e., arrive for departure), the airline cannot save that flight for another customer and recoup its costs.

- *Services tend to be produced and consumed simultaneously.* Due to intangibility and the need for consumer participation, services are usually produced and consumed in the presence of both an employee and a consumer. Thus, a cabin attendant in an airplane cannot deliver a service in the absence of a passenger. In contrast, a product can be manufactured at one place and point in time, then shipped, stored, inventoried, and ultimately delivered to a consumer at another place and time.

These differences between services and products exist on continua; they are not dichotomies. The more central that providing a service is to the business, however, the more important delivery becomes in determining an organization's effectiveness.

One of us (Schneider) and his colleagues have produced a series of studies and papers that reveal the kinds of practices and procedures that characterize a climate for service. Figure 2 summarizes these findings and shows the kinds of practices and procedures employees report exist when *customers* say they experience high quality service.

- *Human resources practices that promote employee well-being and a sense of community.* When *employees* view their organization's practices and procedures as "treating them well" and providing a sense of community at work, *customers* report they receive high-quality service.

- *Active retention of current customers.* When *customers* say a service organization delivers high service quality, *employees* describe their organization as being equally concerned with retaining current customers and attracting new consumers.

- *Attention to details regarding the quality of staff and availability of necessary resources.* In organizations that deliver service rated as superior by customers, employees say they are well trained, and that the equipment and supplies they work with are up-to-date and well-serviced. In general, the logistics of service excellence are very carefully thought out.

Because service quality is in the delivery, it is the interaction between the service deliverer and the consumer at the time of delivery that determines service quality for the consumer. Organizations can only indirectly control what has been called the "service encounter" because of the simultaneous nature of production and consumption. In the absence of direct control of the service encounter, it is the climate and culture that determine high-quality service. When the organization has practices and procedures that communicate service as a top priority, then service quality is usually the result.

When the organization has practices and procedures that communicate service as a top priority, then service quality is usually the result.

How does management communicate that service quality is a priority? Management sends this message through various facets of "how things are done" within the organization. When employees experience support for performing well (via staffing, training, and logistics support), when they feel they are personally treated well, and when the organization emphasizes excellence in the treatment of current customers, then employees experience a climate for service excellence. At Disneyland, for example, "cast members" go through an intensive selection process and a continuous socialization to the Disney way. This socialization includes education and experience in multiple functions so they can identify with how their "role" fits with the rest of the experience created for customers. But Disneyland does more than carefully select and train employees—it is impeccably maintained. Because management has made the collection and disposal of trash a high priority, customers are struck by the overall cleanliness of the facility. In general, the backstage activities (e.g., kitchen help in the restaurants) receive as much attention as the people who play the characters. Consequently, the total environment sends a service quality message, and this message leads to an unforgettable experience for the Disney guests.

The principles we have enumerated also apply to (*a*) internal service and (*b*) service to customers of goods-producing organizations. By internal service, we refer to relationships between employees and work groups within an organization—the relationship between sales and production, for example, or between marketing and human resources. When these functions treat each other as valued "customers," people working in the functions feel better about themselves and the organization *and* end-user consumers report they receive superior service. At hundreds of companies now (Xerox, to cite one example), project teams composed of employees from different functions are being used to solve problems. These teams break down the old walls separating functions—walls that resulted in poor service quality to each other, and ultimately to customers.

At Chrysler, a similar process seems to have led to improved products, such as the best-selling mini-vans and a new line of cars for 1993 that has received rave reviews. In this goods-producing environment, cross-functional project teams have improved internal communication and internal service to each other such that Chrysler has cut the amount of time required to produce a new line of automobiles from five years to three years (for the new Neon). Not only has internal communication and service improved, but Chrysler is also involving *dealer* sales and service people as partners in new ways of thinking about the production, delivery, sales, and service of Chrysler products. Total quality management is moving beyond customer satisfaction with the *product* to customer satisfaction with the entire *experience* of buying and owning a car.

When management creates and maintains a climate for service, employees are likely to attribute to management the following values:

- *People are the key to our success.* Both customers and employees are valuable resources and should be viewed as long-term investments in the future.

FIGURE 3   Keys to Organizational Citizenship Behavior

- Management is nonexploitative and trustworthy.
- There are norms of helpfulness and cooperation.
- There are fair reward systems based on broad and diverse contributions to organizational success.

- *Employees have a tendency to treat others as they have been treated.* Customer-contact employees who are treated as valuable persons by the organization will treat the organization's customers similarly. How employees get treated will be reflected in how customers get treated.
- *It is the little things that count.* Good service consists of many well-executed small details.
- *Work should offer employees a sense of community and belonging where employees treat each other like family.* Studies at Sears and Ryder, as well as studies reported by the FORUM Corporation, all support the following conclusion: When employees experience their organization as one that supports them as people and supports excellence in service delivery, customers report they receive superior service.

There is more to organizational effectiveness than service and innovation, however. Organizational effectiveness also requires that employees be committed to the organization's success. This commitment needs to take the form of cooperative, extra-role behaviors where employees are dedicated to the organization's long-term survival. In short, employees determine the success of an organization by their support of the organization. These kinds of supportive behaviors on the part of employees are called good citizenship.

THE CLIMATE AND CULTURE FOR CITIZENSHIP BEHAVIOR

For about a decade now, Dennis Organ and his colleagues at Indiana University (Bloomington) have studied the role that cooperative, extra-role behaviors play in facilitating organizational effectiveness. Organizational citizenship behavior (OCB) or prosocial organizational behavior (POB) consists of helpful, cooperative acts that are not directly required of employees. Examples include orienting new employees, using sick leave only when one is really sick, and helping a supervisor with a task without being asked. Taken as a whole, however, these behaviors quickly add up and greatly benefit the organization. The research suggests that three key issues (summarized in Figure 3) relate to a climate and culture for OCBs:

- *Perceptions of fairness and trust.* When employees perceive that a "just world" exists in their organization, supervisors report that employees display more OCBs. Fairness generates a sense of trust, and this trust yields employee behaviors supportive of organizational effectiveness. A just world is created for employees based on perceptions of fairness and equity, not only with regard to pay but also with regard to all forms of recognition and reward— benefits, respect, and opportunities for advancement.

- *Norms of helpfulness and cooperation.* When a senior manager is willing to pitch in on the assembly line or take over a teller's post during a crisis, this communicates the importance of cooperation. When employees see others "going beyond the call of duty" to benefit the organization as a whole, they tend to do the same. When a new employee observes these behaviors early in his or her tenure, this employee is more likely to see such action as the norm—what is expected.

- *Fair reward systems based on broad contributions.* Individually based piece-rate systems have the potential to depress the probability of OCBs. For example, if employees are rewarded only for very specific performance behaviors and nothing else (such as loyalty, tenure, courtesy, trying new ways of doing things), then they may conclude that the only behaviors of importance are those tied to the productivity on which the piece-rate system is based. When employees see co-workers being recognized for many different kinds of activities that promote organizational effectiveness, the probability increases that they, too, will display these other forms of OCB.

In summary, research shows that a climate for these cooperative and organizationally helpful behaviors is likely to exist when management is perceived to be fair and just, when newcomers see cooperative behavior on the part of co-workers and supervisors, and when reward systems are tied to more than job-specific, individually based piece-rate productivity. An organization with a climate for OCB might have employees who attribute to management the following values:

A climate for these cooperative and organizationally helpful behaviors is likely to exist when management is perceived to be fair and just, when newcomers see cooperative behavior on the part of co-workers and supervisors, and when reward systems are tied to more than job-specific, individually based piece-rate productivity.

- *Earning employees' trust is essential to employee commitment.* Workers who see themselves as exploited have little or no commitment. The employer-employee relationship is a reciprocal, two-way relationship.

- *An atmosphere of reciprocation and cooperation establishes a culture in which employees willingly go beyond their job descriptions.* Management must display cooperation and helpfulness if they expect employees to be cooperative and helpful.

- *Leaders must set trends for performance by doing the same kinds of things they expect from subordinates.* Leaders are not special. For example, if leaders expect employees to take a cut in pay, they should be willing to take a comparable salary reduction.

When employees attribute these assumptions to management, they create a culture for OCBs. We argue that this culture is likely only when the climate for OCBs exists. As we said about the climates and cultures for service and for innovation, it is the practice and procedures employees observe that yield the global climate perceptions. These perceptions, in turn, yield the attributions about management's assumptions, beliefs, and values.

IMPLICATIONS FOR ORGANIZATIONAL CHANGE

Managers can improve their organization's effectiveness by changing their organization's climate and culture, but the process for doing so is slow and difficult. This is because managers must modify the practices, procedures, and behavior by which they manage before there will be a change in the climate. And climate change precedes cultural change.

To complicate things, not only is it difficult for people to change their behavior, it can take a long time for the change to become noticeable. We change very slowly because we must overcome the inertia of our own behavior first; only after we overcome that inertia do we actually begin to change in ways that others can see. The whole process is somewhat like the launch of a space shuttle. The rocket motors, fighting against gravity, expend most of their fuel on the launch pad—producing no noticeable movement for a while. Similarly, managers can expend a lot of energy to change a climate and culture without having a lot to show for it—until inertia is overcome and the climate can get moving in new directions.

One risk of change is that the organization will operate *less* effectively for a while as the new climate is being created; when the practices and procedures are changing, employees become less certain about what management has as its priorities. This creates ambiguity, and ambiguity leads to stress.

One CEO with whom we have worked said that changing the climate of an organization is like changing a Boeing 727 into a Boeing 747 *in mid-flight*. On the one hand, the change seems worth the trouble, because the 747 will be a more effective transport vehicle. On the other hand, there will be a point where the craft is neither 727 nor 747—and the whole thing could crash!

But change, and the change process, have positive consequences, too. Change sensitizes people to what happens to them and around them. Consequently, the change process is a great opportunity for management to flood the environment with cues to the intended new priorities. The more consistent the messages are about the new priorities, and the more employees participate in the change, the more likely the change in climate is to happen. Also, the more visible the manifestations of the change are, the more likely employees will latch onto the new climate.

The new *culture* will emerge later as employees have opportunities to talk with each other about what is going on and why it is happening. They will begin to share their beliefs about the change and management's goals and priorities, and make attributions about management's values based on their experiences.

In general, management can more directly change climate than it can change culture.

In general, management can more directly change climate than it can change culture. But changing even climate is a demanding task—ask managers at General Motors or IBM or Sears.

Suppose the management of an organization wished to create a climate and culture for success by dealing with the three priorities we have outlined. How might management use our presentation as a framework? Here are some areas to consider.

1. New Employee Recruitment, Selection, and Orientation The *kinds* of employees recruited and selected and the *kinds* of orientation experiences provided for new employees send strong messages about organizational priorities. For example, human resources personnel can conduct job and organizational analyses to identify the characteristics important to consider in selection. Only people who are likely to have those personal attributes should be recruited and hired. You simply cannot hire and socialize new employees for only one priority; success requires competencies and energies directed at multiple simultaneous priorities.

2. Training The mere presence of formal training programs and what is emphasized in training sends powerful messages about an organization's priorities. Most organizations, if they have training at all, focus narrowly on job-specific skills. To our way of thinking, all employees require training for all of the organization's priorities. Every employee has responsibility for identifying opportunities to be innovative, for ensuring the service delivered both internally and externally is superior, and for finding opportunities to be helpful and to support the organization's progress.

Most employees possess *inclinations* or *predispositions* toward making greater contributions to the organization. Training gives them the *skills* that permit those inclinations and predispositions to become active. In other words, training transfers a motivation into a competency.

3. Formal and Informal Reward Systems   There are two key issues here: (1) which behaviors get rewarded and (2) whether rewards are dispensed fairly. Humans direct their energies and competencies toward rewards they value. Management must ensure that rewards reinforce behavior that maximizes the simultaneous attainment of multiple organizational priorities. Behaviors that are customer-oriented *and* innovation-oriented *and* put the spotlight on citizenship behavior should be rewarded. Valued rewards include not only pay and promotion but also recognition and other perquisites (cars, offices, and so forth).

4. Logistical Resources   Employees can experience their work world as one that either facilitates or inhibits the attainment of stated priorities. Organizations that state priorities but fail to support those priorities with resources will evoke appropriate cynicism. Employees pay attention to what management actually provides resources to accomplish—to where management puts its money, not where it puts its mouth. Money is usually required to support priorities, especially to support the attainment of service *and* innovation *and* OCB. Resources in the way of staff, technology, training to use new technology, and so forth are what really send the message about priorities.

The purpose of this list is to encourage managers to scrutinize every facet of their organization's practices, procedures, and rewards, and look for omissions and inconsistencies between what is being preached and what is actually happening. What is happening determines the climate and the attributions employees make about what management values.

CONCLUSION

Organizations become effective when they create, maintain, and sometimes change climates and cultures to emphasize the achievement of multiple priorities. In this environment, employees are able to interpret what happens to them and around them in ways that are consistent with their organization's goals and priorities—and set their own priorities accordingly.

Employees have thousands, if not millions, of seemingly isolated experiences as they go about their work. But these experiences do not remain isolated. The experiences are clustered according to the meaning employees give them. These clusters of events and experiences result in climate perceptions.

These climate perceptions, in turn, serve to illustrate for employees what management believes in and values. Figure 4 summarizes that employees may surmise management values in an organization that has climates for innovation, service, and OCB. The Figure shows that employees attribute to management a set of broadly

FIGURE 4   Key Cultural Assumptions Related to Innovation, Service, and OCB

	Innovation	Service	OCB
How We Solve Problems	Through gathering information, not power; slow but sure.	By attending to small details.	If you see something that needs doing, you do it.
How We Manage People	A creative mind needs nurturing and support.	With consideration; treat employees as you want them to treat customers.	By setting examples for employees; act as you want employees to act.
How We Succeed	Through customer acceptance.	By treating both employees and customers well.	Through both managers and employees going beyond their role requirements for the greater good of the organization.

focused values—values concerning how the organization solves problems, or how an organization manages people, or what an organization believes are the keys to success.

A look back at Figures 1, 2, and 3 reveals that the values summarized in Figure 4 are based on employees' climate perceptions. These perceptions, in turn, are based on employee experiences with the practices and procedures of the organization and the kinds of behaviors they see being rewarded.

In tandem with climate, the key to organizational effectiveness is for management to identify the values they hold about the nature of people and the way the world works. Managers need to identify their values because it is inevitable that the practices and procedures they establish and the behaviors they reward will reflect those values—and their employees will attribute values to them based on what they do—not what they say. Our experience is that many managers are unaware of the kinds of values they hold or, even worse, they espouse values that are inconsistent with their behavior and with the values their employees attribute to them.

Obviously, every service organization espouses good service, but how many managers hold the kinds of values that lead to the promotion of a climate for service excellence? Just as obviously, every organization would rather be a successful innovator than a failed innovator, but how many organizations create the kind of practices and procedures and reward the behaviors required to create a climate for innovation? According to Delbecq and Mills, most of the organizations they studied were failures at innovation. We believe this is true because most decision makers hold values about people and how to run a business that are inconsistent with success at innovation. And to be successful in an increasingly competitive and global environment, organizations must be simultaneously excellent in service *and* innovation. They must also create conditions that foster a willingness to expend extra effort on behalf of the organization.

Management cannot expect employees to focus their energies and competencies only on what management *says* is important. Instead, employees will focus on what management communicates through their behavior—through the decisions they make about the practices and procedures and rewards employees experience. Whether on purpose or by default, management is responsible for the climates and cultures created in the minds of employees. Ultimately, these are the climates and cultures that determine how successful an organization will be.

SELECTED BIBLIOGRAPHY

Some useful books on climate and culture include Benjamin Schneider, ed., *Organizational Climate and Culture* (San Francisco: Jossey-Bass, 1990); Harrison Trice and Jan Byers, *Organizational Culture* (Englewood Cliffs, NJ: Prentice-Hall, 1992); and Edgar Schein, *Organizational Culture and Leadership*, 2nd ed. (San Francisco: Jossey-Bass, 1992).

The information about 3M at the opening comes from Tom Peters and Robert Waterman, Jr., *In Search of Excellence: Lessons from America's Best-run Companies* (New York: Warner Books, 1982).

The materials on innovation used as a basis for this article are from Andre Delbecq and Peter Mills, "Managerial Practices that Enhance Innovation," *Organizational Dynamics*, Summer 1985, pp. 24–34. The materials on innovation throughout the article profited from a book by Louis Tornatzky and Mitchell Fleischer, *The Process of Technological Innovation* (New York: Lexington Books, 1990). The information about service climate comes from Benjamin Schneider and David Bowen, "Employee and Customer Perceptions of Service in Banks: Replication and Extension," *Journal of Applied Psychology*, August 1985, pp. 423–33. For additional information on service quality and human resources management, see Benjamin Schneider and David Bowen, "The Service Organization: Human Resources Is Crucial," *Organizational Dynamics*, Spring 1993. For a good treatise on management action for service quality and the FORUM Corporation's research, see Richard Whitely, *The Customer Driven Company: Moving From Talk to Action* (Reading, MA: Addison-Wesley, 1990). On organizational citizenship behavior, see Dennis Organ, *Organizational Citizenship Behavior: The Good Soldier Syndrome* (Lexington, MA: Lexington Books, 1986). On the importance of organizational reward systems, rather than management's words, for direct employee energies and competencies, see the seminal article by Steven Kerr, "On the Folly of Rewarding A, While Hoping for B," *Academy of Management Journal*, May 1975, pp. 769–83.

TEN COMMANDMENTS FOR CEOs SEEKING ORGANIZATIONAL CHANGE

James H. Reynierse, *President*
James H. Reynierse & Associates

This article suggests that organizational transformation or cultural change must be one of the CEO's top priorities. The author outlines 10 keys to success to help executives implement change and reshape their organization's directions.

In our ever-changing, fast-paced world, competitive relationships can shift quickly when companies respond too slowly to increased competition in their industry group. Succeeding in such a competitive and changing environment demands that CEOs reshape their organization to meet today's challenges and competitive realities.

But responding to change remains highly elusive because there is a natural resistance to change at all levels within the organization, including at the top. CEOs and other members of the executive suite need to take a hard look at their existing organization and culture, ask tough questions about its appropriateness for the current competitive environment, and take concrete, implemental steps to forge a preferred culture and drive it downward throughout the entire organization.

But therein lies the challenge, for few management teams both establish a comprehensive strategy for remaining competitive and take a hands-on approach to implement change internally. By not getting involved, they signal to employees that the change really isn't very important.

A key premise of this article is that cultural change or any organizational transformation is essentially a top-down activity. It cannot be delegated. If the CEO perceives the need for change, makes it a top priority, and gives it a great deal of time and attention, the organization will change. By the same token, if the CEO offers only limited lip service, needed changes just won't happen. This article outlines how the CEO can be an enthusiastic sponsor of change by paying enough attention to implementation to

If the CEO perceives the need for change, makes it a top priority, and gives it a great deal of time and attention, the organization will change.

Source: *Business Horizons*, 37, no. 1 (January–February 1994).

make the transformation take place. Reynierse and Leyden provide a case study incorporating these steps.[1]

1. STRATEGY-DRIVEN

The process I am advocating will be relatively ineffective without a strategic framework to provide competitive advantage. This process is not a substitute for such a strategy. Rather, the strategy is the starting point that establishes the context for all other steps. However, strategies will be relatively ineffective when management pays insufficient attention to their impact on the workforce—for ultimately it is the work force who will implement the strategy and make it succeed or fail. The point is that unless such a strategic plan is implemented and executed effectively, it will not be fully realized in the competitive marketplace. An overview of this process is depicted in Figure 1.

A company's business strategies, plans, and goals are the starting point—not the end—of this exercise. They formalize the CEO's vision, setting the tone and establishing direction for the company in both the long and short terms. They provide a context for all other activities and decisions, establishing the limits for making many choices along the way. In addition, they determine the direction and boundaries for building the new organizational culture, including molding employee expectations.

Resources are scarce in every organization, and management must accept the fact that it can't do everything. Strategic choices reflect judgment about where companies

FIGURE 1   Overview of the Change Process

think they have marketplace competitive advantage so that plans implemented here enable them to grow faster and earn more than their competitors in these market segments. Similarly, the resources dedicated to building the organization are determined by this strategic focus.

2. TOP-DOWN INVOLVEMENT

If something is important, a good rule of thumb is to have a top-down approach to getting it done. Ideally, then, the CEO must get involved. If the CEO attends to the organization, it will improve and gain competitive advantage. Conversely, if the CEO gives it scant time and attention, little organizational growth will occur. In short, the CEO who enthusiastically sponsors a broadly conceived program for building the company is more likely to succeed and reap the benefits down the road. A companywide initiative needs an enthusiastic and supportive CEO who does not hesitate to play a continuing role during the change process.

A companywide initiative needs an enthusiastic and supportive CEO who does not hesitate to play a continuing role during the change process.

But where is the top? And who is the CEO? Building organizations is often better served by dealing with chunk-sized bites rather than the whole company. Particularly for large companies, it often makes better sense to deal with natural strategic business units (SBUs) rather than the entire company. At one level, there are often unique problems or opportunities in a unit or company division. At another level, it is most meaningful for those involved to deal with issues that directly concern them and their business unit.

The approach I am advocating includes determining the firm's core values and mission. It is unlikely that every SBU or company division will share the same core values or mission. Individual business units often have unique customers, competitors, product maturity, strategies, and objectives. These units need the autonomy to develop their own focus. For such cases the division executive is functionally the CEO for that unit and can provide the vision, enthusiasm, and driving force for success.

Throughout, however, the CEO must remain interested and provide broad support for what is taking place., Even when the primary leadership role resides elsewhere, the CEO must be an advocate for change and reinforce actions taken at these lower levels.

3. ORGANIZATIONAL ASSESSMENT

Periodically, it is valuable to take an objective snapshot of the broader organization. This not only provides information about the company's strengths and limitations but can also identify how those strengths and limitations measure up to the mission and the core values. Effective organizations have employees who share these values, and a carefully conceived organizational assessment will identify pockets of agreement and resistance.

Several techniques, including surveys, interviews, and focus groups, are used for these organizational assessments. The organizational dynamics survey has been particularly effective, because it provides an objective measure of the underlying values that mold organizations.[2] For example, the survey's broad customer-orientation category taps a cultural value related to making customers a priority and satisfying their needs.

Surveys are particularly important because they get every employee involved; everyone has the chance to be heard. Surveys also provide an opportunity for management to pay attention to employees' concerns and to build their trust. This is achieved when management openly communicates with employees regarding key issues and responds to problems by taking timely, corrective action. At the same time, establishing trust is the first step in getting employees to "buy in" to management's broader vision.

4. CLARIFY CORE VALUES

Peters and Waterman[3] have "one all-purpose bit of advice for management . . . figure out your value system. Decide what your company stands for." Today many frequently echo this management theme. Identifying and clarifying core values are central to this approach as well. When they are integrated with a company's business strategies, core values help provide a focused mission. All too often, companies or their natural business units lack focus; their employees are confused about what the company stands for and what it is trying to achieve. However, when the focus and the mission are clear, they can drive the entire organization or SBU.

Mission statements ideally should be brief, concise, and to the point. They should identify primary business activities, integrate key strategies, and reflect the firm's core values. When we speak about core values we are dealing with many attractive virtues—McLaughlin, McLaughlin, and Lischick,[4] for example, identified more than 100—and it is tempting to include as many as possible. In my experience, however, an organization can give proper attention to only a few—say, three to five—clearly stated core values. Anything more will be too diffuse and will only confuse employees and dilute management's efforts. In other words, management has to make some hard choices, and established strategies provide the context for focus.

There are no shortcuts; there is no generic mission statement. To build a focused organization, the management team has to participate in the process. We use a value clarification exercise when working with top and senior management. This exercise consists of 30 corporate values that are relevant (and credible) for business and industry. Each is defined and serves as an effective probe, placing key issues on the table for discussion. Some representative examples are shown in Figure 2. Because many are presented with a different thrust or emphasis, they can generate a provocative and lively discussion.

This value-clarification process gains agreement for key priorities and direction, and fosters team-building through shared values and mission. Similarly, it lays the groundwork for resolving internal differences between functional groups that may

---

FIGURE 2   Representative Corporate Values

Shareholder Value	Creating increasing value and benefits for shareholders and safeguarding their investment.
Business Results Return/Profit	Maximizing financial results.
Commitment	Cultivating the desire and energy of people to identify with and buy into the success of the organization.
Competent People	Attracting and keeping knowledgeable, technically skilled, experienced, and capable people.
Customer Focus	Providing products and services of superior value to satisfy customers' needs.
Technological Leadership	Developing and using the most advanced "state-of-the-art" technologies available.

have varied goals or priorities. Finally, it sets the stage for driving the process downward through the entire workforce so other employees can "buy in" and share the focused mission as well.

The risk in all this, says Peters,[5] is that management does such a good job that these values become fixed, even though they no longer are appropriate. The necessary caveat here is to return to strategy and competitive marketplace reality. Very simply, if the strategy is no longer appropriate and requires change, the core values and focused mission probably need to be changed as well. They must therefore be revisited and modified as necessary to be congruent with any new strategies.

A case can be made that because clarifying core values is so central to this approach, it should occur earlier in the process. There are benefits, however, of having it follow the organizational assessment step because this gives management another opportunity to respond to the input and reactions of the workforce. Their perceptions of what the company really values are important and may indicate that changes are needed.

5. WORKFORCE INVOLVEMENT AND PARTICIPATION

One of the advantages of the employee survey approach to assessing an organization is that all employees have the opportunity to participate and express their opinion. In other words, at an early stage in the process they have the chance to level with management, provide an employee perspective, and establish an agenda for later stages.

While we begin the more intensive activities at the top with senior management, we involve lower-level employees, particularly lower levels of management, as quickly as possible. Although every situation will be different and will require different solutions, management should be vigilant for opportunities to involve new participants. A valuable tool is the use of focused task forces to address any priority issues that may have emerged from the organizational assessments or team-building sessions. This permits additional employee involvement at the problem-solving and solution-generating stages of the exercise.

The key to successful implementation, then, is the steps that are taken to drive the process downward—to downstream—so that all employees feel they are a part of this focused mission.

A fundamental assumption is that a focused organization requires a workforce that shares this focus. The key to successful implementation, then, is the steps that are taken to drive the process downward—to downstream—so that all employees feel they are a part of this focused mission. Implementing management's vision demands paying attention to employers, managing their expectations, and responding to their concerns.

Building the firm requires taking action steps that promote the core values and focused mission. I call these steps the "culture carriers." It is through them that senior management can reinforce values consistently and frequently. Put another way, the "culture carriers" provide direction for marketing the core values and mission with all employees. The five "culture carriers" we have identified are summarized in Figure 3 and will be discussed separately.

6. INSPIRATIONAL LEADERSHIP

Our studies of corporate culture indicate that there are two ways management stays in touch with what is going on in the company:

1. By visiting work areas and being visible to their employees. This is inspirational leadership at its best and is similar to the idea of "Managing by Walking Around" (MBWA), as developed by Peters and Waterman; and Peters and Austin.[6]

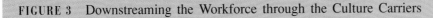

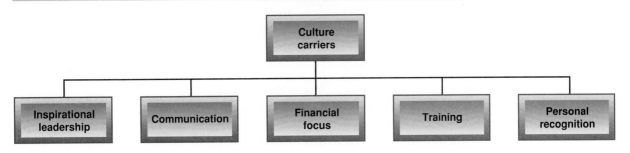

FIGURE 3   Downstreaming the Workforce through the Culture Carriers

2. Through the balance sheet and financial focus. In general, however, many top executives emphasize financial performance and focus to the extent that they neglect their leadership roles.

The broad process for organizational change outlined here provides structure for MBWA and for being a "cheerleader." Although executives tend to underestimate their leadership effectiveness, they in fact exert considerable power by virtue of their leadership position. As DePree[7] observed, "Leaders need to be concerned with the institutional value system." Each time they go out to a work area and talk to an employee or group of employees represents an opportunity to exercise influence and reinforce the company's mission and core values. This clearly communicates to employees what is important to the organization and what is expected of them. When the CEO or division head is leading the charge, everyone quickly picks up on it, and any ambiguity regarding what is taking place is quickly removed. The results are multiplied when this leadership role is being exercised by the entire management team.

When the CEO or division head is leading the charge, everyone quickly picks up on it, and any ambiguity regarding what is taking place is quickly removed. The results are multiplied when this leadership role is being exercised by the entire management team.

As an example, the management team of one of my client organizations "made a contract" with one another during a planning retreat to spend "15 minutes a day" walking around, getting to know employees, and talking with them in each of their subordinate organizations. Though initially they were ambivalent and self-conscious about their task, it soon became an accepted and high-priority activity. They would confront each other daily by asking, "Have you spent your 15 minutes walking around yet today?" This, together with several other steps, quickly led to a turnaround in an otherwise demoralized workforce. It was an important step for management to become informed, get on top of operations, get in touch with its people, and communicate direction.

7. COMMUNICATION

Put as simply as possible, employees cannot accept or implement top management's vision if they are unaware of it. Frequent formal and informal channels of communication are needed with all employees to introduce the focused mission and core values and reinforce them over a period of time. Executives must make liberal use of meetings, video presentations, posters, newspaper articles, brochures, and so on. If there is a rule of thumb, it is that you can't do too much in this area.

Some of our clients have successfully used "kick-off" meetings in which they celebrated the focused mission and core values, gave every employee a wallet-sized card containing the mission statement, and provided other symbolic items—pins, coffee mugs, pencils, hats—that focused on elements within the mission and its values. Primarily held to share information, the meetings were also used to rally employees and build enthusiasm for the "new" organization. The informal mixing that occurs at such kick-offs is also a valuable time for management to energize employees and talk with them further about the focus.

8. FINANCIAL FOCUS

Well-run companies have a strong financial focus that emphasizes both profitability and cost containment. It can play a significant resource allocation role that simultaneously provides increased funds and resources to programs that support the core values while denying (or at least sharply reducing) funds and resources to established programs that are less important to the mission.

How capital is invested and what activities are expended carry important messages to employees. It is necessary to examine investment decisions in terms of a strategic standard that includes the company's core values and focused mission. Having done so, it may be necessary to withhold capital or budgetary expense dollars for those projects that fail to qualify under this standard. When capital investments and highly visible expenses are consistent with the values and mission of the company, they will provide support for and reinforce this focused mission among employees. But when inconsistency abounds, employees will be confused and may withhold their support.

9. TRAINING

Training programs should be examined closely to ensure that a disproportionate amount of the training budget is dedicated to the organization's core values. First, make sure training programs are increased or enhanced in areas where skills are needed to carry out the mission and implement the core values. For example, if customer service is valued, significant training implications for many employees relate to it and extend to almost all facets of the company.

A bank client of ours had a service quality problem that was identified by both employees and customers. As part of its strategy, the bank made a significant investment in training that emphasized service quality and product knowledge. As a result, employees developed the skills that helped reinforce the customer service core value. The main point, however, is that the firm had to make investment choices. By making a maximum commitment to customer service and dramatically increasing the training budget in this area, the bank declined to fund other activities.

Second, provide systematic training in the core values themselves. Incorporate a section on the company's focused mission in new employee orientation. This is a good time, for example, to pass out any wallet-sized cards or other materials that summarize the values and mission. Similarly, incorporate material on the core values in all or most supervisory and management training programs. Managers and supervisors must set the example where values are concerned. If top management does not make an effort to get this essential group to buy into and adopt the core values and mission, one cannot expect subordinates to do so. This is especially the case when change is taking place and supervisors and managers are still operating according to the old set of perceived values.

Finally, training involves much more than classroom or group activities. Executives should take every opportunity to coach employees on a one-to-one basis, sharing the core values with new people and reaffirming them with long-time employees.

10. PERSONAL RECOGNITION PROGRAMS

This may be the most influential contributor to gaining focus that we can discuss. Our research consistently shows that employees who feel appreciated for their efforts—that is, are recognized by management for their contributions—are active and enthusiastic supporters of every aspect of the organization. Similarly, those who don't feel appreciated are negative and critical about the entire organization. Unfortunately, in almost every company, fewer than 50 percent of the employees feel appreciated by management.

It is important for a firm's compensation and pay practices to reflect the core values.

At one level, it is important for a firm's compensation and pay practices to reflect the core values. This includes job grades, performance appraisals, salary increases, and bonuses. Even more important, formal and informal recognition programs can be linked to the core values. One of our clients developed a "Hot Ideas" program to provide rapid (within a day or two) recognition to employees who had a good idea or who made an important contribution. Key managers had the discretionary authority to give spot awards for productivity, quality, or customer service contributions that matched the core values. These were relatively inexpensive—$10 cash, dinner for two, tickets to a popular show. Another client gave out golf caps with the company name on them to employees who made a special effort on behalf of the company.

Formalized recognition programs, including award ceremonies and recognition dinners, should reflect the core values. These are particularly important because they are the occasion when top performance is celebrated within the organization and top performers gain wide visibility. If there is a problem in this area it is simply that such occasions occur too infrequently, often only on an annual basis.

More frequent recognition programs are a real option. One of our clients has a monthly celebration for employees who make a special contribution. During an inexpensive catered luncheon, which typically lasts about an hour, executives give the honored employees a special award that emphasizes the company's core values and mission, then heap praise on everyone to let them know how much the organization appreciates them. Employees usually leave the luncheon feeling about 10 feet tall.

People like it when management recognizes them for a good job. Pats on the back, "Attaboys!" and "Attagirls!" are cheap and can fit into any budget. Linking praise and informal recognition efforts like this with the core values can produce a powerful motivating effect among employees. As Herzberg[8] maintains, consistently and frequently applied formal and informal recognition programs provide management with a powerful tool to influence employees to live the company's values and implement its focused mission.

The starting place for building an organization and paying attention to the workforce is clarifying the firm's core values and developing a focused mission.

The starting place for building an organization and paying attention to the workforce is clarifying the firm's core values and developing a focused mission. When there is focus and the mission is clear, you have a driving force that gives direction to the entire organization.

The practical and often inexpensive implemental steps I have identified provide a mechanism for incorporating change and getting the entire workforce to "buy into" and share the core values and focused mission. These steps provide management with the tools to develop the organization and to build excellence within it. Such companies will have significant competitive advantages in the years that lie ahead.

The common view is that cultural change is very time-consuming, painful, and slow. In my judgment this view is exaggerated. Meaningful transformations can take place relatively quickly and the pain can be reduced when top management consistently follows these 10 rules or commandments for systematic cultural change.

ENDNOTES

1. J. H. Reynierse and P. J. Leyden, "Implementing Organizational Change: An Ordinary Effort for an Extraordinary Situation," in R. J. Niehaus and K. F. Price, eds., *Bottom Line Results from Strategic Human Resource Planning* (New York: Plenum, 1992), pp. 133–48.

2. J. H. Reynierse and J. B. Harker, "Measuring and Managing Organizational Culture," *Human Resource Planning* 9 (1986), pp. 1–8.

3. T. J. Peters and R. H. Waterman, *In Search of Excellence* (New York: Harper & Row, 1982).

4. D. J. McLaughlin, B. C. McLaughlin, and S. Lischick, "Company Values: A Key to Managing in Turbulent Times," in R. J. Niehaus and K. F. Price, eds., *Bottom Line Results from Strategic Human Resource Planning* (New York: Plenum, 1992), pp. 261–74.

5. T. Peters, *Liberation Management* (New York: Alfred A. Knopf, 1992).

6. Peters and Waterman, *In Search of Excellence;* T. Peters and N. Austin, *A Passion for Excellence* (New York: Random House, 1985).

7. M. DePree, *Leadership Is an Art* (New York: Doubleday, 1989).

8. F. Herzberg, *Work and the Nature of Man* (Cleveland, OH: World, 1966).

OTHER REFERENCES

1. R. T. Pascale and A. G. Athos, *The Art of Japanese Management* (New York: Simon & Schuster, 1981).

2. B. Z. Posner, J. M. Kouzes, and W. H. Schmidt, "Shared Values Make a Difference: An Empirical Test of Corporate Culture," *Human Resource Management* 24 (1985), pp. 293–309.

BUSINESS ETHICS: A VIEW FROM THE TRENCHES

Joseph L. Badaracco, Jr.
Allen P. Webb

This article chronicles the moral and ethical dilemmas faced by recent graduates of Harvard's MBA program. Interviews with these graduates indicate the very real, very thin line between ethical and unethical. Most had encountered situations that challenged their integrity, situations not uncommon in the workplace. The article illustrates the need for unremitting effort in the task of establishing ethical norms for an organization.

Research and writing in the field of business ethics typically takes the viewpoint of a senior executive or, on occasion, a middle manager. But aside from several questionnaire-based studies, there are no in-depth examinations of how young managers[1] define ethical issues, think about them, and resolve them. This article aims to remedy this skewed perspective. In essence, it sketches a picture of business ethics as viewed not from the generals' headquarters, but from the trenches.[2]

The conventional wisdom and practice of management business ethics is now familiar. Well-intentioned business executives rely on some mix of corporate credos, statements of their own convictions, ethics hotlines, ombudsmen, and training programs to set the ethical standards for their organizations. Scholars study deviance, corporate crime, and the effectiveness of efforts to shape a company's ethical climate. In business ethics classrooms, students learn the basic principles of utilitarianism and deontology and practice applying them to contemporary management dilemmas such as affirmative action, pollution, layoffs, and takeover battles.

The view from the trenches is very different, and it offers little comfort for senior executives who are trying to implement corporate ethics programs, for academics developing philosophy-based approaches to business ethics, or for those who hope that communitarian values will soon take root in corporate soil.

This article, which is based principally upon in-depth interviews with 30 recent graduates of the Harvard MBA Program, reveals several disturbing patterns. First, in many cases, young managers received explicit instructions from their middle-manager bosses or felt strong organizational pressures to do things that they believed

Source: *California Management Review* 37, no. 2 (1995).

were sleazy, unethical, or sometimes illegal. Second, corporate ethics programs, codes of conduct, mission statements, hot lines, and the like provided little help. Third, many of the young managers believed that their company's executives were out-of-touch on ethical issues, either because they were too busy or because they sought to avoid responsibility. Fourth, the young managers resolved the dilemmas they faced largely on the basis of personal reflection and individual values, not through reliance on corporate credos, company loyalty, the exhortations of senior executives, philosophical principles, or religious reflection.

Ironically, however, while many of the interviewees described their experiences as difficult or even traumatic, many believed they learned important lessons about themselves and the world of work. In particular, they came to see themselves even more clearly as self-reliant, mobile, autonomous moral agents in an intensely competitive, sometimes unethical business world.

The 30 young managers interviewed for this study had all taken an elective course on business ethics and had written papers about ethical dilemmas they had faced in their first jobs. These young men and women—and, most importantly, the disheartening answers they gave to our questions—seemed typical of young management candidates. Two-thirds of the interviewees were men and one-third women; 4 of the 30 were African-Americans. Half of the students, at the time of the incident they described, were working for commercial or investment banks, or consulting, accounting, or advertising firms. The young managers' views of organizations, senior executives, and the pressures of management life confirm what several large-sample, questionnaire studies of young managers have found.[3] What the in-depth interviews add, however, is an understanding of what lies behind the questionnaire results.

"JUST DO IT"

The young managers described a variety of situations. For example, a management trainee at a well-known consumer products company was told by his boss to make up data to support a new product introduction. When he began to object, his boss cut him off and said, "Just do it." A young financial analyst had calculated that the return on a significant investment at a refinery was approximately 12 percent. His boss explained to him that no project could be approved without a 25 percent return and told him to redo his numbers and get them right. In other situations, young employees were asked or expected to overlook kickback schemes, fill out time sheets inaccurately (at consulting and accounting firms), overlook safety defects in products, ship products that clearly did not meet customer specifications, or find ways to fire employees in violation of company policies. In several cases, young women reported that they were victims of sexual harassment, sometimes by their immediate superiors, and that they were later expected or asked to acquiesce in coverups of these incidents.[4]

For most of the young managers, such situations proved to be "wake-up calls"—difficult, sometimes traumatic learning experiences in both personal and professional terms.

For most of the young managers, such situations proved to be "wake-up calls"—difficult, sometimes traumatic learning experiences in both personal and professional terms. One young woman, once she realized what was happening to her, said that "her body felt as if all the life had been drained from it . . . I felt as if I were in a dream and trying very hard to awaken, but to no avail." Other interviewees used these phrases: "I felt as if I had been physically punched in the stomach," "It was shattering," "I was white-knuckled incensed at this slap in my face." Most of the interviewees said that they frequently recalled the episode or thought about it whenever they confronted another difficult ethical situation. In general, the interviewees believed that the situations they faced were crises in their careers and important tests of their character.

Despite these strong feelings, the young managers were not cynics and did not blame the flaws of human nature for their predicaments. Few of them believed that the people who pressured them to act unethically were evil. Some, they believed, had been promoted according to the Peter Principle and had responsibilities they could not handle; others were facing personal difficulties; many were themselves under intense organizational pressure.

Indeed, most of the interviewees had optimistic views of human nature. For example, one of the interview questions asked, "What percent of people do their work honestly? What percent are sleazy? What percent are in between—they want to be honest, and basically are, but may need help?" A strong majority of the interviewees said that only a few people in their companies were fundamentally unethical.[5] A clear majority believed that organizational pressures—not character flaws—had led people in their organizations to act unethically. This was a typical comment:

> I fundamentally believe that all people want to do their jobs. I've met very few complete sleazes—50 percent to 60 percent try real hard, 2 percent to 3 percent are sleazes. And then there's the muddy people. These are people who started in the first group, but have been beaten up, or presented with an opportunity to do something sleazy.

FOUR COMMANDMENTS

The young managers believed, in effect, that the people who pressured them to act in sleazy ways were responding to four powerful organizational commandments. First, performance is what really counts, so make your numbers. Second, be loyal and show us that you're a team player. Third, don't break the law. Fourth, don't over-invest in ethical behavior. Taken by themselves, the first three commandments are hardly immoral. But while they are almost certainly necessary for a successful organization, they are hardly sufficient for creating an ethical or responsible one, especially when a fourth powerful norm encourages sleazy behavior.

The first three commandments were described by the interviewees in the following ways:

> There was always pressure to demonstrate that you weren't out of line with your budget. Management took notice of this and had severe actions plans if you were spending too much, or weren't spending enough.

> I felt that the code was you do what you have to in order to satisfy client needs. Period. If it was illegal, not just unethical, they wouldn't tolerate it.

> There's the big benefit of being viewed as a team player, someone who is concerned with making sure that the company remained profitable.

> [Ethics are]not a high priority of theirs. They're interested in making money. Either you're on the team and producing, or you're not. That's it.

Many of the interviewees shared the same view of how these organizational pressures worked. Intense competition was the starting point. Clients, customers, and competitors demanded ever lower costs, higher quality, and faster action. One interviewee said, "These pressures are translated straight through the organization." Another said, "There was so much revenue pressure . . . There was this aura of pressure around everybody." Another added, "It was a tough place to work . . . The stress level at this office is so high that three of the partners have died in the last five years. These were guys under 35!" One interviewee, speaking from the perspective of the military, said:

> Because of the downsizing in the military, and because everything you do has such an impact on your evaluations, I think one of the dangers we face is that people are going to take the easier wrong, rather than the tougher right because they are very worried about their careers. This is especially true for young officers. In the past, they could make mistakes without having it become a career-stopper. Today, make a mistake and you're gone . . . Because your boss is also worried about his job, there is a lot of pressure on people at the lowest levels to make things happen. So they are doing things they might not otherwise do.

Personal reputation is, in effect, a brand name to be carefully developed and safeguarded. Bosses have power not because they can threaten to fire or demote people, but because they can damage or strengthen these reputations.

Whether and how a young manager responds to the three commandments is crucial. The interviewees believed that a young manager's reputation begins to take shape very early in a career. The "grapevine" lets others know who makes his or her numbers and whether someone is a candidate for the fast track and a team player. Personal reputation is, in effect, a brand name to be carefully developed and safeguarded. Bosses have power not because they can threaten to fire or demote people, but because they can damage or strengthen these reputations. One young manager, who persistently called attention to bogus numbers that her boss insisted on using, reported that:

> He started treating other people better. He wasn't on my side anymore, and you needed him on your side to do things. He wasn't my buddy anymore . . . There were other cases of this. He did it by acting like you weren't that smart anymore. It made it really difficult to get the kind of support you needed to be a really top performer.

The young managers believed that their bosses, who were typically middle managers, confronted the same basic commandments but with ever more acute pressures.[6] Taken together, the following quotations present a composite picture of middle-management life as viewed from the trenches:

> I really feel for people who are middle management, with a wife and four kids, under financial strain . . . You see it happen all the time, that people are indicted for fraud or larceny. You can empathize with their situation. The world is changing fast. And a lot of people have been blindsided by it—so they've done things that they don't like. I can't say that will never happen to me. It's easy for me as a single person . . . but when you're desperate, you're desperate.

> [My boss] was not willfully unethical. It was the pressure of the time . . . I have no idea what pressures were on him to drive the project. It probably wasn't [his] initiative to fudge the numbers. There may have been a good intention at some point in the organization. But as it got filtered through the organization, it changed. Some executive may have said, "This is an interesting project." Unfortunately this got translated as, "The vice president really wants this project." This sort of thing can happen a lot. Things start on high. As they go down they are filtered, modified. What was a positive comment several levels above becomes "do this or die" several levels down.

The first three commandments become troublesome when coupled with the fourth: don't overinvest in ethical behavior. In fact, two of our interview questions revealed strong pressures to act unethically. One asked, "Do sleazy people get ahead faster or slower?" Only a handful of the interviewees responded with unambiguous "no's." In essence, only a few believed that sleazy behavior was a drag on a career in their organization. In other words, only a small minority believed that "ethics pays" in terms of career advancement. A larger number had firm convictions that sleazy people progressed faster. This was a typical comment:

Only a small minority believed that "ethics pays" in terms of career advancement. A larger number had firm convictions that sleazy people progressed faster.

> It depends on how smart they are. If they're smart, they get ahead fast. If they're not smart, they get caught and they get fired, or they get ahead more slowly.

The majority also believed that sleaze advanced careers, but they qualified their comments. Most of them believed that sleazy behavior involved significant risks, particularly in the long run. The remainder simply believed that ethical behavior made no difference.

We also asked about whistleblowers. Less than a third of the interviewees believed that their organizations respected or encouraged whistleblowing. A similar number were unsure how whistleblowers would be treated, and the other interviewees believed that whistleblowing was dangerous:

> If I had been a whistleblower, nothing positive would have happened. The senior VP who was harassing me would have undermined me. I knew someone else who had complained . . . and he gunned for her. I don't remember anything else. This woman was forced out . . . and people were warned off. It was terrible.

> I've had a few experiences. In the Army—fraud, misuse of government property—they always lost, and lost big. People always encouraged them to do it. But in every case they were hung out to dry. Then the people who encouraged them backed off. The whistleblowers are devastated by the experience. Some will never recover. I would never recommend that someone be a whistleblower.

The interviewees' own experiences underscored the more pessimistic views. Only a handful (one in 10) reported that their supervisor or the promoter or perpetrator of the unethical activity they confronted was seriously punished.[7] Several expressed deep concern that no action was taken:

> Nothing ever happened to him. I felt bad, because I heard he went after other people, too.

> It's really awful that there was no resolution. Who won? I didn't. I had to leave something I loved. He didn't. That's the weird part of all of this. He was stripped of his client responsibilities in _____; that's how we kept this client. He couldn't be fired, but he was made a research partner—ironically enough, he was supposed to deal with the most technical issues. He is still with _____, but in a different office. He left before I came to HBS, which contributed to my belief that the firm was a good place. I thought he'd been fired until I got back. That's what I'd been told, because I'd threatened to sue if nothing was done. Now I question whether the whole thing was an attempt to keep me from suing—I even question my own mentor.

We also asked, "For what sorts of offenses do you remember your company punishing people?" We learned that the first "three commandments" typically drove the process of discipline. In essence, the young managers learned they could avoid punishment by doing their jobs, listening to their bosses, and not rocking the boat. Failure to perform, be a team player, or avoid gross transgressions such as stealing, lying, or drinking on the job was hazardous. Poor performance was the surest way of earning discipline. In contrast, unethical behavior was rarely mentioned.

When we asked the young managers, "Did fear of punishment motivate you to do the right thing?" the answers were astounding. Only five interviewees said that they were more inclined to do the right thing because they feared the consequences if they did not. More than half of the 30 stood our question on its head. They feared the repercussions of doing *what they saw as "the right thing."* These were some typical comments:

> There is a great deal of general fear of the partners. We had CLMs—Career Limiting Moves. That was mentioned to me in my first week at the firm. It was never defined. But whistleblowing was definitely on the list.

> I've seen the opposite. In every organization, someone's been screwed for standing up.

> No one was ever punished for sexual harassment. I had always heard that at companies in general your reputation would be lost if you created a stir about being harassed. I was very concerned that my own reputation would be besmirched. People would have seen me as a problem because it happened to me. I had always heard this.

> I would have been punished. If I stood up, I would have lost my job.

> If anything, I figured that by taking a strong stand I might get myself in trouble. People might look at me as a "goody two shoes." Someone might try to force me out.

In short, a clear pattern of implicit norms and values had taken shape in the minds of many of these young managers. This pattern is what we have called the "fourth commandment." In only a minority of cases did ethics seem to pay. Middle managers who pressed subordinates for sleazy or illegal behavior went unpunished. Whistleblowing was often a professional hazard. And sleazy behavior didn't hurt or even seemed to accelerate career advancement, especially in the short run and sometimes in the long run too.

FECKLESS ETHICS PROGRAMS

Roughly half of the young managers we interviewed had worked for companies with a formal ethics program of some sort. In general, these ethics programs seemed to make little difference. Indeed, their impact was often described in terms like those that H. L. Menken suggested as an epitaph for Calvin Coolidge: "He did no harm and was not a nuisance." Only four of the interviewees whose organizations had formal ethics programs actually consulted them while grappling with the episode they described. Remarkably, three of these four were serving in branches of the U.S. military at the time and had been inculcated with the code of ethics from the age of 18, when they entered military academics. In short, only one young manager in a corporate setting actually tried to make use of a code of conduct or any other corporate ethics device.

The programs failed to address the issues commonly faced by young managers, other people in the organization paid no attention to them, and the principles espoused in the codes and programs seemed inconsistent with "what the company was all about."

The young managers were dubious about ethics programs for several reasons. The programs failed to address the issues commonly faced by young managers, other people in the organization paid no attention to them, and the principles espoused in the codes and programs seemed inconsistent with "what the company was all about." To the extent there was implicit ethics codes, it reinforced the first three commandments— don't break the law, rock the boat, or fail to make your numbers.

> There was a code of conduct you read when you came in. They were mostly based on legal issues—what you could and shouldn't do with customers. There wasn't a whole lot above that said. I had to sign a code saying I wouldn't take gifts from customers. But ethics weren't discussed with my group.

There was a formal code responding to statutory pressure [insider trading] at that time. Outside of that, there really wasn't anything.

There was an unwritten code of conduct. Don't steal. It's easy to do in a refinery. Operators who drove company vehicles around might fill up their gas tanks free. This was fine. Others, however, did it with their own cars. Others "borrowed" tools. There was an unwritten code not to do this. No one ever commented to me about what you should and shouldn't do. It was just handed down.

Some companies tried to link ethics with the commandments to be loyal and perform well. One common approach was making a corporate code of conduct one plank of a "total quality" push. Another was to focus efforts entirely on "serving the customer," with a passing reference to the types of behavior that constituted ethical service. The young managers often expressed skepticism at the company's commitments to these hybrid efforts:

It's all part of TQM. We hired a company called _____. Five or six years ago, they started with us. The central part of the program is "THE BIG Q." This means doing the right things right, the first time. Our ethics "module" falls under the auspices of the big Q. When we're in Big Q training sessions, we talk about it. But it's only 1 of 15 things. It doesn't receive the treatment that I would hope it would.

As far as I know, there was nothing [no code of ethics]. Ethics had to do with clients. Protect clients interests. Client confidentiality. Serve the clients. I don't remember any other type of ethics statements. Just protect the client. That's paramount at _____.

Many interviewees indicted their company's ethics effort more harshly:

I saw it as total hypocrisy. The woman writing documents about total quality was now asking me to fabricate data!

I'm cynical. To me, corporate codes of conduct exist to cover the potential problems companies may have. It provides deniability. It gives the employers an excuse . . . The top officers can say, "These employees messed up. They violated our way of doing business."

After the whole Drexel Burnham thing exploded, there was a push to codify ethics. A big-ass policy book came out. No one read it. People said, "If we were doing anything illegal, we would have been caught." Investment banking isn't like Johnson and Johnson with this phony-ass ethics stuff pinned to the wall. There may be a book. But I'll bet 90 percent of the revenue-generating professionals don't even know that it exists.

The handful of young managers who found themselves in cultures they believed to be ethical *did* respect their organization's ethics efforts. In essence, what many young managers were criticizing were ethics programs that existed in vacuums. For them, the main value of these devices was confirming and reinforcing an ethical climate that already existed, not creating one.

OUT-OF-TOUCH SENIOR EXECUTIVES

The desire of young managers to work in companies with healthy ethical climates is hardly surprising. Most CEOs would like to preside over such organizations, and the difficult task, of course, is creating them. In general, the young managers believed that corporate cultures were set, not by the intentions and pronouncements of those at the top, but by their actions. The message for executives was that they were being watched all the time. One young manager said, "Never forget that there is not a moment that goes by when the people who work for you aren't looking at you and listening."

> Most Important: What many managers miss is that there is a very tight, silent, observational relationship between bosses and subordinates. Because subordinates want to be promoted and get higher pay and status. You want to offer people an opportunity to see good conduct in action—and to emphasize that this is part of how you got where you are."

Unfortunately, senior executives often set poor examples for their organizations; in common parlance, they "just don't get it"—or perhaps they don't want to. Not all of the interviewees were critical of the senior executives of their organizations or cynical about them, but a clear majority were.

In the minds of the young managers, there were several reasons why senior executives were out of touch. For several of the interviewees, company size was a crucial factor. Interviewees said:

> It's such a huge organization . . . When you're in a branch, you couldn't be further away from where the real minds of the business are. You're just executing. It shows why it's so hard to communicate ethics in a big company.

> There are so many layers of management. Consultants. Associates. Managers. Senior managers. Partners. Partners who run offices. Partners who run the firm. By the time you reach the top, you have no memory of what it's like at the bottom. You rarely have a case where the staff meets the partner. If the staff does work with a partner, that means it's not an important partner . . . There is this feeling that a partner shouldn't deal with the staff. It's your turn to enjoy it once you're a partner."

Other interviewees believed senior managers had simply forgotten what life was like in the trenches or had become jaded as their careers advanced. They made comments like these:

> One of the sad things that I've observed, and I hope I don't fall prey to this, is that experience jades you. Good people see things . . . and each time they become less sensitive. There are lots of things that go on that to me aren't illegal, immoral, but they make me and the people who do them uncomfortable. Experience really hardens your heart.

> The bank was huge, had a lot of employees and bureaucracy. Senior management was very detached from day-to-day ethical issues. I never really had a direct response from any of the senior people in the organization after my decision. I don't think they realized something like that might even come up.

> Top management in an organization like _____ doesn't walk among the masses. People report to them. But they can't see or understand what's happening. Also, no one wants to report bad news up. What they should be hearing gets filtered. I doubt that any senior management would want any ethical violations to happen.

Other interviewees were more cynical, believing that senior managers were sometimes wanting to be out of touch. In other words, they sought to isolate themselves from certain decisions and used management layers and other organizational devices as protective cover. These are some of the young managers' comments:

> I would have to say that a partner has to be a complete idiot not to know what is going on. But they keep their noses clean . . . Managers often hope you will do the wrong thing. They hope you can get away with it, that it will work out. But they will deny it if it doesn't.

> A lot of upper level managers only want to hear the good news. No one wants to be the bearer of bad news. The messenger gets shot a lot.

Other interviewees believed that a combination of generational and gender issues left senior executives out of touch:

There's always going to be a generational difference. There are people who didn't have to deal with competition. A lot of older managers got out of college and started working at good jobs. It was an easier time. They didn't need a master's degree. They went to work and worked eight hours a day. And they got ahead. They thought they were doing great work. These older managers are now competing in a world we are accustomed to. We're quicker on our feet. They're slower.

Older managers, in their fifties and sixties, have come from a more traditional world. Banking was dominated by men . . . They aren't as comfortable with women. This feels unnatural to them. They look at women as "ladies," not as business peers.

I sometimes feel sorry for men at the tops of companies who are in their fifties because they just don't think they're doing things that are wrong . . . But I think it would be immature not to recognize that it is hard. It's hard to foresee what the world will be like when I'm fifty-five. Attitudes are generational . . . It's a generational gap. Who knows how difficult it will be for me to adjust.

You know, a lot of this comes down to what club you're in. What you end up with is a homogeneous environment where it's all white men in their 50s and 60s from the midwest, who develop a certain culture. That is the company's mind-set.

Not all of the interviewees were critical of senior managers. A few acknowledged that senior executives brought more experience and a broader perspective on difficult issues. However, even these generally positive comments were tempered with ambivalence; for example:

The biggest reason is that they [senior managers] have the benefit of experience. They've seen the repercussions which come from making decisions. They see the bigger picture . . . In the military, as you progress through certain ranks, you realize that you have only enough time and energy to put your heart and soul into so many decisions. You are so busy, you have total responsibility for whole groups of people. So you recognize that things are relatively more important or less important over time. You've been beaten up enough that you realize concessions have to be made . . . not just on ethical lines . . . that whole aspect of gaining experience continues through your career.

Finally, it is important to note what the young managers did not say. Like the dog that did not bark in the Sherlock Holmes story, this omission may be as significant as some of their actual statements. Only two of the interviewees expressed admiration for the senior executives of their organizations. In both cases, the young managers said that they respected certain senior managers for their unambiguous commitments to ethical values and for the persistent, conspicuous adherence to these values that was displayed in their actions and decisions. In all the other cases, there seemed to be a significant "disconnect" between the younger managers and senior executives.[8] Perhaps this is unsurprising in view of the feckless ethics efforts many of these executives had sponsored and the immunity that many companies, even those with elaborate ethics program, seem to have granted to sleazy, but high-performing middle and upper managers.

THE "SLEEP TEST"

How did the young managers resolve the dilemmas they faced? Their basic approach emphasized simple, quasi-intuitive decision making based on what many of them called the "sleep test." In general, they were confident that by listening to their hearts and avoiding activities that made them feel uncomfortable, they could lead ethical lives. They often expressed this

> *They were confident that by listening to their hearts and avoiding activities that made them feel uncomfortable, they could lead ethical lives.*

approach in simple formulas: "If I do this, can I sleep at night?" "Can I look at myself in the mirror in the morning?" "Will I be the kind of person I want to be?" It was questions such as these—not corporate credos, the exhortations and examples of senior executives, or philosophical principles or religious reflection—that guided the young managers' thinking. Here are some typical comments:

> The other guide [for young managers], and this sounds hokey, is how they feel. If someone makes you feel bad, that's untenable. If you feel weird, then that's the guide.

> One of the things I like to think about is, am I comfortable with this decision? Can I live with it? Will it bother me? If it will, then rethink it. Maybe there's something wrong with it.

> Can you sleep easily at night?

> I guess my thought is, "How does it make you feel?" If it's being done to you, "How does it make you feel?" If you're getting sick all the time, that tells you something. It has to be wrong. You've got to get past the rationalization. I got sick every morning on the way to work. That's wrong.

> The bottom line is what you're comfortable with. I want to know that in a year, I want to be able to both meet my house payments, and have some dignity left.

> They [young managers] should use their gut feel. If you feel something is awkward, there's nothing wrong with that. Once you feel that way, take the time for yourself to see why you feel that. Is it what you're being asked to do? Why you're being asked? How you're being asked?

"Gut feel" is a deceptively simple term. Reliance on one's "heart" or "gut" begs questions of how a person has acquired his or her intuitions and whether they are morally sound. For most of the young managers, simple phrases such as the "sleep test" were actually proxies for more complex considerations, largely derived from traditional sources of values—fidelity to family values, long-standing moral maxims, and advice from trusted individuals—as well as reputational concerns. Moreover, as we asked about the sleep test and gut feel, we learned that it was not a substitute for reflection but a way of validating or confirming personal deliberation. Many of the young managers emphasized the importance of thinking carefully about ethical difficulties.

The most important single source of ethical wisdom was the family, particularly the young managers' parents:

> Values from upbringing [should guide ethical decision making].

> Ummm . . . This is going to sound sort of trite. But if you can comfortably tell your parents, I think you are probably doing the right thing.

> You can't go out and build a sense of morality in someone if they weren't brought up with it.

> Can you tell your grandfather about it and be proud? Upbringing is important. What do you perceive as right and wrong?

> I think your own family values are most important. I hate to sound like Dan Quayle. That was the only thing that helped me through this. I knew we might never get caught, but at the end of the day, I felt like I didn't want to do it. Yuck! That's what helps when you start in business. Have a strong knowledge of what those convictions are. We have them, but we don't know it until they are tested. At this time, I was tested, and at first I didn't act on them. I kept the options open too long.

Fundamentally, it has to be personal integrity, meaning the way they were raised, their religion, their level of social consciousness . . . That should be the fallback. That's all you have.

Only two of the young managers explicitly cited their religious beliefs as important sources of ethical guidance. However, four or five of the interviewees mentioned their reliance upon simple moral principles that were variants of the "Golden Rule."

Many interviewees recognized that they could make better decisions with help from others. They strongly recommended that young managers seek advice, though they also stressed the pitfalls of talking openly with others—particularly older managers—in their companies. The young managers often felt more comfortable seeking advice from parents, friends, or peers in the organization than they did talking to their bosses. Nevertheless, even their endorsements of external advice are laced with affirmations of the importance of relying upon one's own values. This was a typical comment:

> It's always been my experience that whenever you find yourself in a situation where there is no obvious choice, you need to talk to people you trust, get advice, and use that as a guidepost. It's ultimately up to you, and you have to live with it. But don't do it in a vacuum. You need to figure out what the questions are that you should be asking, and you may need help answering them.

The "sleep test" was also a proxy for how the world would view their actions. The young managers we spoke to believed that their reputations in the eyes of others were extremely important. Clearly, the principal loyalty of these young managers—as they see themselves, at least—is to their own sense of integrity and, to a lesser degree, to their careers.

Clearly, the principal loyalty of these young managers—as they see themselves, at least—is to their own sense of integrity and, to a lesser degree, to their careers.

> If you wouldn't share it with a "60 Minutes" news camera, don't do it.

> Probably, the best compass is: "Imagine that whatever you did was going to be reported on the front page of the *New York Times*. How would you like that? Would you be comfortable?" People use that rule in a lot of organizations. If anybody that you told would find that to be a horrendous way to conduct yourself, then you probably shouldn't do it.

> It was a lot easier for me to come to a conclusion than you might think. I've seen other circumstances that would have been a lot tougher. Mine wouldn't have had any bad ramifications for my career had I pursued it, but there may have been reputational issues at stake. For me, that was a big deal. For someone else, they might not have been. But I just couldn't violate the trust of the entrepreneur whom I'd been dealing with.

RESILIENCE, CONFIDENCE, AND MOBILITY

How did the young managers look back upon their experiences? What did they hope and fear for the future? In several important and surprising ways, their difficult experiences proved to be valuable:[9]

> You mature. You get a better perspective . . . You learn so much about yourself, as well as about how to handle situations. That's were the growing comes. It helps you with other tough situations down the road.

> It made me step back and ask, "What matters to me in life. What are the things that I want to do?" . . . It made me more willing to ask in advance and to try to prevent situations from evolving. It made me more proactive.

It's made me a lot tougher. Every time I meet someone new in the company—a new manager or a co-worker—I'm careful. I'm a lot tougher. This is unfortunate. I don't trust people as much as I used to . . . Before, I thought everything was done on the up and up. Now I know a lot of things are done on the sly, through blackmail. Deals are cut every which way behind closed doors.

I learned a lot from it. The whole concept of picking your battles . . . People who think they will be true to their ethics have probably never examined their ethics. Very few people have never winked.

I had a very idealistic view of the way things worked. This woke me up to the fact that there are times when projects don't go forward not because of their merits, but rather because of politics, the desire of many managers to see lots of projects done on their watch so they'll get promoted . . . I'm likely to be more wary when people asked me to do things."

It was a wake-up call in a lot of ways. Definitely on how organizations work. You can get stranded alone. It showed me that you alone are responsible for yourself, for your professional and personal development. It gave me a bit of distance on people. But I don't overwhelmingly distrust people.

Perhaps I was a bit naive about how the business world worked. This hardened me, and it also made me realize how inexperienced I was.

It showed me that not all people in the business world are adults. It's a dog-eat-dog world. You really have to watch out.

It made me realize how naive I was. This was literally my first job. I had previously worked at summer camps. After this happened, I said to myself, "This is the real world now."

After living through these difficult, sometimes traumatic, experiences, many of the interviewees defined professional ethics in terms of self-reliance and mobility rather than community and commitment.

After living through these difficult, sometimes traumatic, experiences, many of the interviewees defined professional ethics in terms of self-reliance and mobility rather than community and commitment. Throughout the interviews, the young managers expressed a willingness to walk out the door rather than compromise their values. For them, being ethical involves fidelity to one's own values and willingness to leave an organization that fails to match these values. In short, it means being able to take a stand and walk away. Ethics was a matter of exit, rather than loyalty or voice:

The main thing [is] . . . you've got to be able to live with yourself. How many of these situations are going to be career makers or breakers? If it is a clear-cut career breaker, then in my opinion, you need to rethink whether that's the kind of organization you want to be in.

A professor once gave my class some great advice: Get a "go to hell account." Get three to six months pay in the bank. Be prepared to tell someone to "go to hell," and then walk.

Thank God we're not Japan, and can move in and out of organizations. It's self-selecting. At some point, when people realize they're in a bad environment, they move. That's better than in our parents' day, I think.

The young managers believed that it was necessary to look closely at organizations before joining them and to be willing to walk away from them if the "fit" turned out to be poor. For these young people, changing a large organization's ethical climate from within was a futile challenge.

When we asked them to discuss the future, many of the young managers were confident they could maintain their personal integrity, but mainly because they believed that age brought status, wealth, and the ability to ignore problems that occurred further down in the organization. For example:

> If you're lucky, and you become well off, and have the luxury of being able to make tough choices, then it's easier to do the right thing. When you're stretched all of the time, then it's really tough. It's not age, but how constrained are you? I'm not constrained now. I'm single. If I go bankrupt, it's no big deal. I'd feel differently if I had 2 kids, a wife, a mortgage out the butt . . . and that will happen to me (I hope). That's one thing you see.

> It seems like a lot of people, like that guy at Johnson and Johnson . . . it's easy for him to preach ethics. He's got 50 million bucks in the bank. It's tougher when you're struggling. You can't classify people as young or old. For example, when I was 23, I had no experience, no money . . . I was more willing to compromise than I am now. HBS, some financial comfort, more self-confidence—those things have given me a higher risk profile.

> The choices may be hard, but the challenges become less significant relative to your career . . . As you rise, you have more control over the conduct around you. It is less likely to impact negatively on your job. When you're younger, you have a livelihood issue that is much more pressing. You have a much greater likelihood of damaging your career when you're young.

The interviewees' confidence about their ability to remain self-reliant and ethical had one significant qualification, the perils of middle management.[10] Middle managers, they believed, were often squeezed from above and below. Often, they also had family commitments that restricted their ability to walk away from an employer; in effect, their families were held hostage. The young managers frequently emphasized how easy it was for people in this situation to start cutting corners and progressively do things that were worse and worse.

> Once you're older, it's harder, you've invested more. You're further along. You have more to lose. But you've also been bloodied. So you're more careful.

> It's tougher if you're a middle manager than if you're in an entry-level position. That's because there is less to lose when you're young. If you're 2 or 3 rungs from the top, you have the most to lose.

> I can't say it [career advancement] should have no impact. At the youngest age, this should be a smaller concern. The real struggle comes when you're 45 years old, and don't know where to go next.

> It's something I keep in mind all of the time. The challenges are, as you enter middle management, you have people tugging at you from both ends; top and bottom. You want to become a top executive. It's easy to say "this one thing will help me. I've been good for so long. This can't hurt." There is always pressure to cross the line in order to advance [your] career.

> Yes [it becomes more difficult to behave ethically as one ages]. Family responsibilities take over. You make one slip at one level, then you think you can tell a bigger lie, then a bigger lie. Soon it's one big lie, and you're at the top of the company.

> Yes [it becomes more difficult to behave ethically as one ages]. There is more pressure. So you have to actively check yourself to avoid doing shady things. I am conscious of doing this more often now than when I was younger.

> I don't think I can iterate strongly enough the problem from an economic standpoint . . . the problem of how people may conduct themselves when they feel there is no effective out for them.

Only 4 of our 30 interviewees described the top management of their employers in positive terms. Far more of the interviewees had serious misgivings about top management and the likely reactions of their organizations to employees who might take difficult moral stands.

> *There was very little idealism about corporate visions, the values of top managers, or the role of companies in society.*

Perhaps as significant as the young managers' negative statements about the companies they had worked in and their willingness to leave them was what was missing from their remarks. There was very little idealism about corporate visions, the values of top managers, or the role of companies in society. When such statements appeared, they were in stark contrast to the bulk of the comments we heard.

The bottom line for many interviewees was that very few companies embodied values consistent with those they hoped to live by. Many of the young managers were willing to change jobs in search of one that did. In essence, as the interviewees anticipated the pressures, constraints, and slippery slopes of middle management, they feared becoming like their bosses. This presumably reinforced their reluctance to commit themselves to particular companies. Many of those who were relatively happy with their employer worked for smaller companies and believed that this was a significant advantage in the maintenance of an ethical culture.

Given the importance our interviewees attached to corporate culture, and change jobs, their willingness to move about and the fact that many believed "small is beautiful," we wonder whether prevailing organizational realities in corporate America discourage bright young managers who might shake things up from considering employment with traditional, large firms. If this is the case, then the ethical concerns we have highlighted may be self-perpetuating.

IMPLICATIONS

The implications of this study run in several important directions. For business managers and executives, the following seem especially important:

- The difficulty of establishing sound ethical norms for an organization, especially a large one, can hardly be underestimated. The task requires unremitting effort.

- Many people, perhaps most, in business organizations are intensely concerned about their careers, and about their job performance. This creates strong pressures to choose the easier wrong rather than the tougher right in a difficult situation.

- Ethics codes can be helpful, though not decisive, particularly if they are specific about acceptable and unacceptable behavior and provide advice on handling "gray area" matters.

- The ethical climate of an organization is extremely fragile. The "grapevine" quickly communicates situations in which executives have chosen the expedient action over the right one. This, in turn, significantly undermines the credibility of subsequent pronouncements by senior executives of their commitment to ethics.

- Young managers are much more likely to believe that a code means what it says if the code is enforced. This means punishing individuals who are guilty of violating the code; it also means letting the organization know that these infractions have been punished. Our interviewees came the closest to unanimity when answering the question, "Do you think companies should punish managers who ask people to do sleazy things?" In contrast, when violations go unpunished, codes become simply another wall decoration or file-drawer filler.

- In a culture of suspicion, both inside organizations and in the general culture, the pronouncements of senior executives on business ethics, no matter how heartfelt, count for very little. Actions are what matter. And when senior executives do choose the right thing over the expedient or profitable, they are much more likely to be sending a signal that will be clearly understood. One interviewee said he worked in a company where the CEO had made it clear through a series of decisions that he would say "good-bye in a heartbeat" to a $20 million deal if it were not ethically sound.

- If a company's leaders are not going to make an unremitting effort to high ethical standards, and if they will not investigate and discipline violators of codes of conduct, they should abandon or avoid creating company ethics credos, announcing their personal dedication to high ethical standards, and implementing other parts of the standard, corporate business ethics program. They may simply be setting themselves up to be viewed with suspicion and cynicism.

For those who teach in the field of business ethics, and perhaps for those who teach in other general management areas, this study suggests:

- While the focus on moral dilemmas—situations in which one genuine moral claim conflicts with another—is valuable in conceptual, pedagogical, and practical terms, it may be valuable to spend larger portions of courses on issues of "right versus wrong" rather than issues of "right versus right." The reason is simply that many students have been or will be in situations where they are strongly pressured to do something sleazy or worse.

- Parts of ethics courses could be oriented toward teaching students what to do in these situations: advising them on various ways of exerting organizational pressure to defend themselves, or explaining the various ways of blowing the whistle and the hazards that typically accompany such efforts.

- Inevitably, the task of teaching business ethics will become more difficult, if these first two guidelines are followed, because teachers will have to tread a fine line between being usefully realistic, on the one hand, and further encouraging cynicism, pessimism, and the sleazy sorts of behavior that they hope young managers and organizations will avoid.

- The two favorite philosophers of business ethics—Mill and Kant—should perhaps share the spotlight with Aristotle and Machiavelli. (It is telling that the tables of contents, indexes, and teaching material in most of the major textbooks and casebooks on ethics contain only a handful of references to either of these philosophers.) Aristotle's emphasis on the role of character and the influence of a community on the shaping of one's values and virtues may be a powerful starting point for teaching ethics to young people who instinctively prefer the individualistic, "sleep test" to ethical issues. Machiavelli—whose ideas could, of course, be viewed as corrupting the young—may nevertheless be another plausible starting point since he expresses a world view that is consistent with the experiences that many students have had or anticipate.

- Nevertheless, it remains valuable to teach deontology and utilitarianism, though not simply as analytical principles, but as ways of helping students to understand the broader ramifications of their actions. This could serve as a valuable counterbalance to the highly individualistic and potentially solipsistic views that lie behind the "sleep test" and the preference for doing things that "*I* can live with."

Finally, we believe that there are many important studies yet to be done that would be variants of this one. These would rely upon in-depth interviews rather than questionnaires, and they would examine business ethics from the viewpoint of people at lower levels of an organization. Our belief is that these studies—for understanding the role of business ethics in organizations and for making it more effective—could prove quite significant.

ENDNOTES

1. For simplicity, we refer to the interviewees as "young managers." This is not accurate in every case since some of the interviewees faced dilemmas when they were working as analysts or loan officers or in other positions in which they did not supervise other people. Also, a few had management responsibilities in nonbusiness organizations, such as branches of the U.S. Armed Forces.

2. Except for a handful of articles in scholarly journals, most of which are cited below, the principal focus of research on managerial wrongdoing has focused on senior and middle managers and on issues of illegal behavior, also known as white-collar crime, corporate crime, and corporate deviance. The seminal work in this field was carried out by Edwin H. Sutherland, whose classic, *White Collar Crime*, examined court decisions over a span of four decades and focused upon the incidence, pattern, and causes of illegal activity by large corporations. In contrast to the sleazy behavior which many of our interviewees described, Sutherland focused upon legal violations such as actions in restraint of trade, advertising, misrepresentation, copyright and patent infringement, and unfair labor practices. See Edwin H. Sutherland, *White Collar Crime* (New Haven, CT: Yale University Press, 1983). Other important books in this field are Marshall B. Clinard, *Corporate Corruption* (New York: Praeger, 1990); Marshall B. Clinard and Peter C. Yeager, *Corporate Crime* (New York: Free Press, 1983); N. David Ermann and Richard J. Lundman, *Corporate and Governmental Deviance* (New York: Oxford University Press, 1992). Middle management deviance is examined in Marshall B. Clinard, *Corporate Ethics and Crime* (Beverly Hills, CA: Sage, 1983); Earl Shorris, *The Oppressed Middle* (Garden City, NY: Anchor Press/Doubleday, 1981).

3. These studies are cited at various points in this article. Our findings were also consistent with three other sets of data. First, we analyzed all 57 papers about personal ethical dilemmas written for a second-year MBA elective at Harvard called "Moral Dilemmas of Management." Thirty-nine of these papers described dilemmas the students had faced at work. Of these, 18 involved situations in which a young manager received direct orders from his or her boss to do something that seemed uncomfortable, sleazy, or worse. In 11 other cases, there was no direct order, but the young

manager reported clear, strong organizational pressure to do something that he or she believed to be inappropriate or wrong.

The same pattern appeared in a second and much more extensive body of data. We randomly selected and analyzed 10 percent of the applications submitted by the 820 applicants accepted in a recent year by the Harvard MBA Program. The application form asked candidates to describe an ethical dilemma they had confronted. Approximately 75 percent of the applicants in our sample described episodes at work. A full two-thirds of the work-related dilemmas involved strong organizational pressures to act—in the minds of the applicants—in inappropriate ways. In more than half the cases, they had been given explicit instructions by their bosses. Additional confirmation of this pattern appeared in a third sample, our interviews. A strong majority of the interviewees said they knew of other cases, involving other young people in their organizations, who had to deal with situations like theirs.

4. In principle, it is possible that some young and inexperienced managers may perceive ethical problems where they do not exist, or they may perceive an implicit order when there is none—a phenomenon typically called "anticipatory socialization." Young managers today might have been led to such expectations through the consistent portrayal of business executives on television as crooks of various kinds and through the highly publicized scandals of recent years' business leaders. Nevertheless, in all the incidents they reported to us, the interviewees could cite other evidence—such as indications that the behavior they were asked to engage in was common in their organizations—which at least corroborated their perception of the situations they faced.

5. It is impossible to determine whether corporate crime, or lower-grade nefarious activity—i.e., "corporate sleaze"—has become more common or less common in recent years. The difficulties of making statistical comparisons are discussed in Irwin Ross, *Shady Business* (New York: The Twentieth Century Fund Press, 1992), pp. 6–15. Ross does, however, reach this tentative conclusion:

> Business crime today is rarely as blatant and is hardly as pervasive as in the post–Civil War era or the robber barons or the manic years of the 1920s stock market boom. On the other hand, the corporate delinquencies of the past, however outrageous, were not always perceived as criminal when they occurred. They often enjoyed de facto legality . . . Today, by contrast, both the common and the more exotic forms of corporate misbehavior have long been statutorily illegal, and are almost universally condemned as unethical . . . Judged by the shifting criteria of social acceptability, corporate criminality today is worse than in the past.[p. 15]

Raymond C. Baumhart, S. J., has examined survey data on business ethics since the 1960s, and he concluded in 1977 that "business behavior is more ethical than it was 15 years ago, but that the expectations of a better educated and ethically sensitized public have risen more rapidly than the behavior." See Steven E. Brenner and Early A. Molander, "Is the Ethics of Business Changing?" *Harvard Business Review*, January–February 1977, p. 68.

6. Several studies provide evidence that managers and other employees often feel pressure to compromise their personal principles, and some of these studies indicate that these pressures are even more severe at lower levels of the organization. See, for example, Archie B. Carroll, "Linking Business Ethics to Behavior in Organizations," *S.A.N. Advanced Management Journal*, Summer 1978, pp. 4–11; James R. Harris, "Ethical Values of Individuals at Different Levels in the Organization Hierarchy of a Single Firm," *Journal of Business Ethics* 9 (1990), pp. 741–50; Douglas J. Lincoln et al., "Ethical Beliefs and Personal Values of Top Level Executives," *Journal of Business Research* 10 (1982), pp. 475–87; and Barry Z. Posner and Warren H. Schmidt, "Values and the American Manager: An Update," *California Management Review* 26 no. 3 (Spring 1984), pp. 202–16.

7. The difficulties of relying upon punishment to deter corporate crime have been examined in John C. Coffee, Jr., "Making the Punishment Fit The Corporation: The problems of Finding an Optimal Corporation Criminal Sanction," *Northern Illinois University Law Review*, (Fall 1980), pp. 3–55; John C. Coffee, Jr., "Corporate Crime and Punishment: A Non-Chicago View of the Economics of Criminal Sanctions. *American Criminal Law Review* 17 (1980), pp. 419–71; and John C. Coffee, Jr., " 'No Soul to Damn: No Body to Kick': An Unscandalized Inquiry into the Problem of Corporate Punishment," *Michigan Law Review*, January 1981, pp. 386–459.

   To our knowledge, only one study has examined the frequency with which senior executives have been punished for serious infractions. Robert Nathan found that only half of all the senior executives indicted for or convicted of serious offenses—such as illegal political contributions, fraud, price-fixing, or securities violations—had not been retained or rehired by their firms. See Robert Stuart Nathan, "Corporate Criminals Who Kept Their Jobs," *Business and Society Review*, Spring 1980, pp. 19–21.

8. According to the Ethics Resource Center, in a recent survey of 700 U.S. companies, the most important ethics issues facing these firms were: drug and alcohol abuse, employee theft, conflicts of interest, quality control, discrimination, abuse of proprietary information, abuse of expense accounts, plant closings and layoffs, misuse of company assets, and environmental pollution. Few of these issues figured prominently in the dilemmas described by the interviewees, suggesting again a significant difference between the way ethics is viewed at the top of an organization and a view from the trenches. See *Ethics Policies and Programs*, a report by the Ethics Resource Center and the Behavior Research Center, Washington, DC, 1990, pp. 4–5.

9. The young managers' less trusting, more skeptical attitudes may indeed be sound preparation for at least some of the individuals they will meet in their professional lives. John Woody's study of 2,500 students and managers and their approach to ethical reasoning concluded that 8–10 percent of both groups were "strongly unprincipled and egoistic." See John Wood, "Ethical Attitudes of Students and Business Professionals: A Study of Moral Reasoning," *Journal of Business* 1988, pp. 249–57. These skeptical or cynical views are hardly a recent phenomenon even though there are many reasons to think that these viewpoints have become more widespread. Evidence of "growing cynicism" among business managers appears, for

example, in studies conducted during the 1950s. See Brenner and Molander, "Is the Ethics of Business Changing?"

10. The young managers' views of themselves, as well as their views of their middle-manager bosses, is consistent with Phillip Lewis's longitudinal study of the ethical principles used by executives, middle managers, and students as guidelines for making decisions. He characterized the students as "self-reliant ethical seekers," while describing the middle managers he studied as "organizational realists." See Phillip V. Lewis, "Ethical Principles for Decision Makers: A Longitudinal Survey," *Journal of Business Ethics,* 1989, pp. 271–78. John Wood's survey of more than 2,000 business professionals and business students concluded that the students were more individualistic and egoistic in their ethical reasoning than the managers. See Wood, "Ethical Attitudes of Students and Business Professionals."

A GUIDE TO CASE ANALYSIS

I keep six honest serving men
(They taught me all I knew);
Their names are What and Why and
When;
And How and Where and Who.

Rudyard Kipling

In most courses in strategic management, students use cases about actual companies to practice strategic analysis and to gain some experience in the tasks of crafting and implementing strategy. A case sets forth, in a factual manner, the events and organizational circumstances surrounding a particular managerial situation. It puts readers at the scene of the action and familiarizes them with all the relevant circumstances. A case on strategic management can concern a whole industry, a single organization, or some part of an organization; the organization involved can be either profit seeking or not-for-profit. The essence of the student's role in case analysis is to *diagnose* and *size up* the situation described in the case and then to *recommend* appropriate action steps.

WHY USE CASES TO PRACTICE STRATEGIC MANAGEMENT?

A student of business with tact
Absorbed many answers he lacked.
But acquiring a job,
He said with a sob,
"How does one fit answer to fact?"

The foregoing limerick was used some years ago by Professor Charles Gragg to characterize the plight of business students who had no exposure to cases.[1] The facts are that the mere act of listening to lectures and sound advice about managing does little for anyone's management skills and that the accumulated managerial wisdom cannot effectively be passed on by lectures and assigned readings alone. If anything had been learned about the practice of management, it is that a storehouse of ready-made textbook answers does not exist. Each managerial situation has unique aspects, requiring its own diagnosis, judgment, and tailor-made actions. Cases provide would-be managers with a valuable way to practice wrestling with the actual problems of actual managers in actual companies.

The case approach to strategic analysis is, first and foremost, an exercise in learning by doing. Because cases provide you with detailed information about conditions and problems of different industries and companies, your task of analyz-

---

[1]Charles I. Gragg, "Because Wisdom Can't Be Told," in *The Case Method at the Harvard Business School*, ed. M. P. McNair (New York: McGraw-Hill, 1954), p. 11.

ing company after company and situation after situation has the twin benefit of boosting your analytical skills and exposing you to the ways companies and managers actually do things. Most college students have limited managerial backgrounds and only fragmented knowledge about companies and real-life strategic situations. Cases help substitute for on-the-job experience by (1) giving you broader exposure to a variety of industries, organizations, and strategic problems; (2) forcing you to assume a managerial role (as opposed to that of just an onlooker); (3) providing a test of how to apply the tools and techniques of strategic management; and (4) asking you to come up with pragmatic managerial action plans to deal with the issues at hand.

OBJECTIVES OF CASE ANALYSIS

Using cases to learn about the practice of strategic management is a powerful way for you to accomplish five things:[2]

1. Increase your understanding of what managers should and should not do in guiding a business to success.
2. Build your skills in sizing up company resource strengths and weaknesses and in conducting strategic analysis in a variety of industries and competitive situations.
3. Get valuable practice in identifying strategic issues that need to be addressed, evaluating strategic alternatives, and formulating workable plans of action.
4. Enhance your sense of business judgment, as opposed to uncritically accepting the authoritative crutch of the professor or "back-of-the-book" answers.
5. Gaining in-depth exposure to different industries and companies, thereby acquiring something close to actual business experience.

If you understand that these are the objectives of case analysis, you are less likely to be consumed with curiosity about "the answer to the case." Students who have grown comfortable with and accustomed to textbook statements of fact and definitive lecture notes are often frustrated when discussions about a case do not produce concrete answers. Usually, case discussions produce good arguments for more than one course of action. Differences of opinion nearly always exist. Thus, should a class discussion conclude without a strong, unambiguous consensus on what do to, don't grumble too much when you are *not* told what the answer is or what the company actually did. Just remember that in the business world answers don't come in conclusive black-and-white terms. There are nearly always several feasible courses of action and approaches, each of which may work out satisfactorily. Moreover, in the business world, when one elects a particular course of action, there is no peeking at the back of a book to see if you have chosen the best thing to do and no one to turn to for a provably correct answer. The only valid test of management action is *results*. If the results of an action turn out to be "good," the decision to take it may be presumed "right." If not, then the action chosen was "wrong" in the sense that it didn't work out.

Hence, the important thing for a student to understand in case analysis is that the managerial exercise of identifying, diagnosing, and recommending builds your skills;

---

[2]Ibid., pp. 12–14; and D. R. Schoen and Philip A. Sprague, "What Is the Case Method?" in *The Case Method at the Harvard Business School*, ed. M. P. McNair, pp. 78–79.

discovering the right answer or finding out what actually happened is no more than frosting on the cake. Even if you learn what the company did, you can't conclude that it was necessarily right or best. All that can be said is "here is what they did . . ."

The point is this: *The purpose of giving you a case assignment is not to cause you to run to the library or surf the Internet to discover what the company actually did but, rather, to enhance your skills in sizing up situations and developing your managerial judgment about what needs to be done and how to do it.* The aim of case analysis is for *you* to bear the strains of thinking actively, of offering your analysis, of proposing action plans, and of explaining and defending your assessments—this is how cases provide you with meaningful practice at being a manager.

PREPARING A CASE FOR CLASS DISCUSSION

If this is your first experience with the case method, you may have to reorient your study habits. Unlike lecture courses where you can get by without preparing intensively for each class and where you have latitude to work assigned readings and reviews of lecture notes into your schedule, a case assignment requires conscientious preparation before class. You will not get much out of hearing the class discuss a case you haven't read, and you certainly won't be able to contribute anything yourself to the discussion. What you have got to do to get ready for class discussion of a case is to study the case, reflect carefully on the situation presented, and develop some reasoned thoughts. Your goal in preparing the case should be to end up with what you think is a sound, well-supported analysis of the situation and a sound, defensible set of recommendations about which managerial actions need to be taken. The Strat-Tutor software package that accompanies this edition will assist you in preparing the cases—it contains a set of study questions for each case and step-by-step tutorials to walk you through the process of analyzing and developing reasonable recommendations.

To prepare a case for class discussion, we suggest the following approach:

1. *Read the case through rather quickly for familiarity.* The initial reading should give you the general flavor of the situation and indicate which issue or issues are involved. If your instructor has provided you with study questions for the case, now is the time to read them carefully.

2. *Read the case a second time.* On this reading, try to gain full command of the facts. Begin to develop some tentative answers to the study questions your instructor has provided or that are provided on the Strat-Tutor software package. If your instructor has elected not to give you assignment questions or has elected not to use Strat-Tutor, then start forming your own picture of the overall situation being described.

3. *Study all the exhibits carefully.* Often, there is an important story in the numbers contained in the exhibits. Expect the information in the case exhibits to be crucial enough to materially affect your diagnosis of the situation.

4. *Decide what the strategic issues are.* Until you have identified the strategic issues and problems in the case, you don't know what to analyze, which tools and analytical techniques are called for, or otherwise how to proceed. At times the strategic issues are clear—either being stated in the case or else obvious from reading the case. At other times you will have to dig them out from all the information given; if so, the study questions and the case preparation exercises on Strat-Tutor will guide you.

5. *Start your analysis of the issues with some number crunching.* A big majority of strategy cases call for some kind of number crunching—calculating assorted financial ratios to check out the company's financial condition and recent performance, calculating growth rates of sales or profits or unit volume, checking out profit margins and the makeup of the cost structure, and understanding whatever revenue-cost-profit relationships are present. See Table 1 for a summary of key financial ratios, how they are calculated, and what they show. If you are using Strat-TUTOR, much of the number-crunching has been computerized and you'll spend most of your time interpreting the growth rates, financial ratios, and other calculations provided.

6. *Use whichever tools and techniques of strategic analysis are called for.* Strategic analysis is not just a collection of opinions; rather, it entails application of a growing number of powerful tools and techniques that cut beneath the surface and produce important insight and understanding of strategic situations. Every case assigned is strategy related and contains an opportunity to usefully apply the weapons of strategic analysis. Your instructor is looking for you to demonstrate that you know *how* and *when* to use the strategic management concepts presented in the text chapters. The case preparation guides on Strat-TUTOR will point you toward the proper analytical tools needed to analyze the case situation.

7. *Check out conflicting opinions and make some judgments about the validity of all the data and information provided.* Many times cases report views and contradictory opinions (after all, people don't always agree on things, and different people see the same things in different ways). Forcing you to evaluate the data and information presented in the case helps you develop your powers of inference and judgment. Asking you to resolve conflicting information "comes with the territory" because a great many managerial situations entail opposing points of view, conflicting trends, and sketchy information.

8. *Support your diagnosis and opinions with reasons and evidence.* The most important things to prepare for are your answers to the question "Why?" For instance, if after studying the case you are of the opinion that the company's managers are doing a poor job, then it is your answer to "Why?" that establishes just how good your analysis of the situation is. If your instructor has provided you with specific study questions for the case or if you are using the case preparation guides on Strat-TUTOR, by all means prepare answers that include all the reasons and number-crunching evidence you can muster to support your diagnosis. Work through the case preparation exercises on Strat-TUTOR *conscientiously* or, if you are using study questions provided by the instructor, *generate at least two pages of notes!*

9. *Develop an appropriate action plan and set of recommendations.* Diagnosis divorced from corrective action is sterile. The test of a manager is always to convert sound analysis into sound actions—actions that will produce the desired results. Hence, the final and most telling step in preparing a case is to develop an action agenda for management that lays out a set of specific recommendations on what to do. Bear in mind that proposing realistic, workable solutions is far preferable to casually tossing out off-the-top-of-your-head suggestions. Be prepared to argue why your recommendations are more attractive than other courses of action that are open. You'll find Strat-TUTOR's case preparation guides helpful in performing this step, too.

TABLE 1   A Summary of Key Financial Ratios, How They Are Calculated, and What They Show

Ratio	How Calculated	What It Shows
Profitability Ratios		
1. Gross profit margin	$\dfrac{\text{Sales} - \text{Cost of goods sold}}{\text{Sales}}$	An indication of the total margin available to cover operating expenses and yield a profit.
2. Operating profit margin (or return on sales)	$\dfrac{\text{Profits before taxes and before interest}}{\text{Sales}}$	An indication of the firm's profitability from current operations without regard to the interest charges accruing from the capital structure.
3. Net profit margin (or net return on sales)	$\dfrac{\text{Profits after taxes}}{\text{Sales}}$	Shows after tax profits per dollar of sales. Subpar profit margins indicate that the firm's sales prices are relatively low or that costs are relatively high, or both.
4. Return on total assets	$\dfrac{\text{Profits after taxes}}{\text{Total assets}}$ or $\dfrac{\text{Profits after taxes} + \text{interest}}{\text{Total assets}}$	A measure of the return on total investment in the enterprise. It is sometimes desirable to add interest to aftertax profits to form the numerator of the ratio since total assets are financed by creditors as well as by stockholders; hence, it is accurate to measure the productivity of assets by the returns provided to both classes of investors.
5. Return on stockholder's equity (or return on net worth)	$\dfrac{\text{Profits after taxes}}{\text{Total stockholders' equity}}$	A measure of the rate of return on stockholders' investment in the enterprise.
6. Return on common equity	$\dfrac{\text{Profits after taxes} - \text{Preferred stock dividends}}{\text{Total stockholders' equity} - \text{Par value of preferred stock}}$	A measure of the rate of return on the investment the owners of the common stock have made in the enterprise.
7. Earnings per share	$\dfrac{\text{Profits after taxes} - \text{Preferred stock dividends}}{\text{Number of shares of common stock outstanding}}$	Shows the earnings available to the owners of each share of common stock.
Liquidity Ratios		
1. Current ratio	$\dfrac{\text{Current assets}}{\text{Current liabilities}}$	Indicates the extent to which the claims of short-term creditors are covered by assets that are expected to be converted to cash in a period roughly corresponding to the maturity of the liabilities.
2. Quick ratio (or acid-test ratio)	$\dfrac{\text{Current assets} - \text{Inventory}}{\text{Current liabilities}}$	A measure of the firm's ability to pay off short-term obligations without relying on the sale of its inventories.
3. Inventory to net working capital	$\dfrac{\text{Inventory}}{\text{Current assets} - \text{Current liabilities}}$	A measure of the extent to which the firm's working capital is tied up in inventory.
Leverage Ratios		
1. Debt-to-assets ratio	$\dfrac{\text{Total debt}}{\text{Total assets}}$	Measures the extent to which borrowed funds have been used to finance the firm's operations.
2. Debt-to-equity ratio	$\dfrac{\text{Total debt}}{\text{Total stockholders' equity}}$	Provides another measure of the funds provided by creditors versus the funds provided by owners.

TABLE 1 Ratios, How They Are Calculated, and What They Show (*cont.*)

Ratio	How Calculated	What It Shows
Leverage Ratios (*cont.*)		
3. Long-term debt-to-equity ratio	$\dfrac{\text{Long-term debt}}{\text{Total stockholders' equity}}$	A widely used measure of the balance between debt and equity in the firm's long-term capital structure.
4. Times-interest-earned (or coverage) ratio	$\dfrac{\text{Profits before interest and taxes}}{\text{Total interest charges}}$	Measures the extent to which earnings can decline without the firm becoming unable to meet its annual interest costs.
5. Fixed-charge coverage	$\dfrac{\text{Profits before taxes and interest} + \text{Lease obligations}}{\text{Total interest charges} + \text{Lease obligations}}$	A more inclusive indication of the firm's ability to meet all of its fixed-charge obligations.
Activity Ratios		
1. Inventory turnover	$\dfrac{\text{Sales}}{\text{Inventory of finished goods}}$	When compared to industry averages, it provides an indication of whether a company has excessive or perhaps inadequate finished goods inventory.
2. Fixed assets turnover	$\dfrac{\text{Sales}}{\text{Fixed assets}}$	A measure of the sales productivity and utilization of plant and equipment.
3. Total assets turnover	$\dfrac{\text{Sales}}{\text{Total assets}}$	A measure of the utilization of all the firm's assets; a ratio below the industry average indicates the company is not generating a sufficient volume of business, given the size of its asset investment.
4. Accounts receivable turnover	$\dfrac{\text{Annual credit sales}}{\text{Accounts receivable}}$	A measure of the average length of time it takes the firm to collect the sales made on credit.
5. Average collection period	$\dfrac{\text{Accounts receivable}}{\text{Total sales} \div 365}$ or $\dfrac{\text{Accounts receivable}}{\text{Average daily sales}}$	Indicates the average length of time the firm must wait after making a sale before it receives payment.
Other Ratios		
1. Dividend yield on common stock	$\dfrac{\text{Annual dividends per share}}{\text{Current market price per share}}$	A measure of the return to owners received in the form of dividends.
2. Price-earnings ratio	$\dfrac{\text{Current market price per share}}{\text{After tax earnings per share}}$	Faster-growing or less-risky firms tend to have higher price-earnings ratios than slower-growing or more-risky firms.
3. Dividend payout ratio	$\dfrac{\text{Annual dividends per share}}{\text{After tax earnings per share}}$	Indicates the percentage of profits paid out as dividends.
4. Cash flow per share	$\dfrac{\text{After tax profits} + \text{Depreciation}}{\text{Number of common shares outstanding}}$	A measure of the discretionary funds over and above expenses that are available for use by the firm.

Note: Industry-average ratios against which a particular company's ratios may be judged are available in *Modern Industry* and *Dun's Reviews* published by Dun & Bradstreet (14 ratios for 125 lines of business activities), Robert Morris Associates' Annual Statement Studies (11 ratios for 156 lines of business), and the FTC-SEC's *Quarterly Financial Report* for manufacturing corporations.

As long as you are conscientious in preparing your analysis and recommendations, and have ample reasons, evidence, and arguments to support your views, you shouldn't fret unduly about whether what you've prepared is the right answer to the case. In case analysis there is rarely just one right approach or set of recommendations. Managing companies and devising and implementing strategies are not such exact sciences that there exists a single provably correct analysis and action plan for each strategic situation. Of course, some analyses and action plans are better than others; but, in truth, there's nearly always more than one good way to analyze a situation and more than one good plan of action. So, if you have carefully prepared the case using either the Strat-TUTOR case preparation guides or your instructor's assignment questions, don't lose confidence in the correctness of your work and judgment.

PARTICIPATING IN CLASS DISCUSSION OF A CASE

Classroom discussions of cases are sharply different from attending a lecture class. In a case class students do most of the talking. The instructor's role is to solicit student participation, keep the discussion on track, ask "Why?" often, offer alternative views, play the devil's advocate (if no students jump in to offer opposing views), and otherwise lead the discussion. The students in the class carry the burden for analyzing the situation and for being prepared to present and defend their diagnoses and recommendations. Expect a classroom environment, therefore, that calls for *your* size-up of the situation, *your* analysis, what actions *you* would take, and why *you* would take them. Do not be dismayed if, as the class discussion unfolds, some insightful things are said by your fellow classmates that you did not think of. It is normal for views and analyses to differ and for the comments of others in the class to expand your own thinking about the case. As the old adage goes, "Two heads are better than one." So it is to be expected that the class as a whole will do a more penetrating and searching job of case analysis than will any one person working alone. This is the power of group effort, and its virtues are that it will help you see more analytical applications, let you test your analyses and judgments against those of your peers, and force you to wrestle with differences of opinion and approaches.

To orient you to the classroom environment on the days a case discussion is scheduled, we compiled the following list of things to expect:

1. Expect students to dominate the discussion and do most of the talking. The case method enlists a maximum of individual participation in class discussion. It is not enough to be present as a silent observer; if every student took this approach, there would be no discussion. (Thus, expect a portion of your grade to be based on your participation in case discussions.)

2. Expect the instructor to assume the role of extensive questioner and listener.

3. Be prepared for the instructor to probe for reasons and supporting analysis.

4. Expect and tolerate challenges to the views expressed. All students have to be willing to submit their conclusions for scrutiny and rebuttal. Each student needs to learn to state his or her views without fear of disapproval and to overcome the hesitation of speaking out. Learning respect for the views and approaches of others is an integral part of case analysis exercises. But there are times when it is OK to swim against the tide of majority opinion. In the practice of management, there is always room for originality and unorthodox

approaches. So while discussion of a case is a group process, there is no compulsion for you or anyone else to cave in and conform to group opinions and group consensus.

5. Don't be surprised if you change your mind about some things as the discussion unfolds. Be alert to how these changes affect your analysis and recommendations (in the event you get called on).

6. Expect to learn a lot from each case discussion; use what you learned to be better prepared for the next case discussion.

There are several things you can do on your own to be good and look good as a participant in class discussions:

- Although you should do your own independent work and independent thinking, don't hesitate before (and after) class to discuss the case with other students. In real life, managers often discuss the company's problems and situation with other people to refine their own thinking.

- In participating in the discussion, make a conscious effort to contribute, rather than just talk. There is a big difference between saying something that builds the discussion and offering a long-winded, off-the-cuff remark that leaves the class wondering what the point was.

- Avoid the use of "I think," "I believe," and "I feel"; instead, say, "My analysis shows —" and "The company should do . . . because —" Always give supporting reasons and evidence for your views; then your instructor won't have to ask you "Why?" every time you make a comment.

- In making your points, assume that everyone has read the case and knows what it says; avoid reciting and rehashing information in the case—instead, use the data and information to explain your assessment of the situation and to support your position.

- Bring the printouts of the work you've done on Strat-Tutor or the notes you've prepared (usually two or three pages' worth) to class and rely on them extensively when you speak. There's no way you can remember everything off the top of your head—especially the results of your number crunching. To reel off the numbers or to present all five reasons why, instead of one, you will need good notes. When you have prepared thoughtful answers to the study questions and use them as the basis for your comments, *everybody* in the room will know you are well prepared, and your contribution to the case discussion will stand out.

PREPARING A WRITTEN CASE ANALYSIS

Preparing a written case analysis is much like preparing a case for class discussion, except that your analysis must be more complete and put in report form. Unfortunately, though, there is no ironclad procedure for doing a written case analysis. All we can offer are some general guidelines and words of wisdom—this is because company situations and management problems are so diverse that no one mechanical way to approach a written case assignment always works.

Your instructor may assign you a specific topic around which to prepare your written report. Or, alternatively, you may be asked to do a comprehensive written case analysis, where the expectation is that you will (1) *identify* all the pertinent issues that management needs to address, (2) perform whatever *analysis* and *evaluation* is appropriate, and (3) propose an *action plan* and *set of recommendations* addressing the issues you have identified. In going through the exercise of identify, evaluate, and recommend, keep the following pointers in mind.[3]

Identification   It is essential early on in your paper that you provide a sharply focused diagnosis of strategic issues and key problems and that you demonstrate a good grasp of the company's present situation. Make sure you can identify the firm's strategy (use the concepts and tools in Chapters 1–8 as diagnostic aids) and that you can pinpoint whatever strategy implementation issues may exist (again, consult the material in Chapters 9–11 for diagnostic help). Consult the key points we have provided at the end of each chapter for further diagnostic suggestions. Review the study questions for the case on Strat-TUTOR. Consider beginning your paper with an overview of the company's situation, its strategy, and the significant problems and issues that confront management. State problems/issues as clearly and precisely as you can. Unless it is necessary to do so for emphasis, avoid recounting facts and history about the company (assume your professor has read the case and is familiar with the organization).

Analysis and Evaluation   This is usually the hardest part of the report. Analysis is hard work! Check out the firm's financial ratios, its profit margins and rates of return, and its capital structure, and decide how strong the firm is financially. Table 1 contains a summary of various financial ratios and how they are calculated. Use it to assist in your financial diagnosis. Similarly, look at marketing, production, managerial competence, and other factors underlying the organization's strategic successes and failures. Decide whether the firm has valuable resource strengths and competencies and, if so, whether it is capitalizing on them.

Check to see if the firm's strategy is producing satisfactory results and determine the reasons why or why not. Probe the nature and strength of the competitive forces confronting the company. Decide whether and why the firm's competitive position is getting stronger or weaker. Use the tools and concepts you have learned about to perform whatever analysis and evaluation is appropriate. Work through the case preparation exercise on Strat-TUTOR if one is available for the case you've been assigned.

In writing your analysis and evaluation, bear in mind four things:

1. You are obliged to offer analysis and evidence to back up your conclusions. Do not rely on unsupported opinions, over-generalizations, and platitudes as a substitute for tight, logical argument backed up with facts and figures.

2. If your analysis involves some important quantitative calculations, use tables and charts to present the calculations clearly and efficiently. Don't just tack the exhibits on at the end of your report and let the reader figure out what they mean and why they were included. Instead, in the body of your report cite some of the key numbers, highlight the conclusions to be

---

[3]For some additional ideas and viewpoints, you may wish to consult Thomas J. Raymond, "Written Analysis of Cases," in *The Case Method at the Harvard Business School*, ed. M. P. McNair, pp. 139–63. Raymond's article includes an actual case, a sample analysis of the case, and a sample of a student's written report on the case.

drawn from the exhibits, and refer the reader to your charts and exhibits for more details.

3. Demonstrate that you have command of the strategic concepts and analytical tools to which you have been exposed. Use them in your report.

4. Your interpretation of the evidence should be reasonable and objective. Be wary of preparing a one-sided argument that omits all aspects not favorable to your conclusions. Likewise, try not to exaggerate or overdramatize. Endeavor to inject balance into your analysis and to avoid emotional rhetoric. Strike phrases such as "I think," "I feel," and "I believe" when you edit your first draft and write in "My analysis shows," instead.

Recommendations The final section of the written case analysis should consist of a set of definite recommendations and a plan of action. Your set of recommendations should address all of the problems/issues you identified and analyzed. If the recommendations come as a surprise or do not follow logically from the analysis, the effect is to weaken greatly your suggestions of what to do. Obviously, your recommendations for actions should offer a reasonable prospect of success. High-risk, bet-the-company recommendations should be made with caution. State how your recommendations will solve the problems you identified. Be sure the company is financially able to carry out what you recommend; also check to see if your recommendations are workable in terms of acceptance by the persons involved, the organization's competence to implement them, and prevailing market and environmental constraints. Try not to hedge or weasel on the actions you believe should be taken.

By all means state your recommendations in sufficient detail to be meaningful—get down to some definite nitty-gritty specifics. Avoid such unhelpful statements as "the organization should do more planning" or "the company should be more aggressive in marketing its product." For instance, do not simply say "the firm should improve its market position" but state exactly how you think this should be done. Offer a definite agenda for action, stipulating a timetable and sequence for initiating actions, indicating priorities, and suggesting who should be responsible for doing what.

In proposing an action plan, remember there is a great deal of difference between, on the one hand, being responsible for a decision that may be costly if it proves in error and, on the other hand, casually suggesting courses of action that might be taken when you do not have to bear the responsibility for any of the consequences. A good rule to follow in making your recommendations is: *Avoid recommending anything you would not yourself be willing to do if you were in management's shoes.* The importance of learning to develop good judgment in a managerial situation is indicated by the fact that, even though the same information and operating data may be available to every manager or executive in an organization, the quality of the judgments about what the information means and which actions need to be taken does vary from person to person.[4]

It goes without saying that your report should be well organized and well written. Great ideas amount to little unless others can be convinced of their merit—this takes tight logic, the presentation of convincing evidence, and persuasively written arguments.

---

[4]Gragg, "Because Wisdom Can't Be Told," p. 10.

RESEARCHING COMPANIES AND INDUSTRIES VIA THE INTERNET AND ON-LINE DATA SERVICES

Very likely, there will be occasions when you need to get additional information about some of the assigned cases, perhaps because your instructor has asked you to do further research on the industry or because you are simply curious about what has happened to the company since the case was written. These days it is relatively easy to run down recent industry developments and to find out whether a company's strategic and financial situation has improved, deteriorated, or changed little since the conclusion of the case. The amount of information about companies and industries available on the Internet and through on-line data services is formidable and expanding rapidly.

On-Line Data Services   Lexis/Nexis, Bloomberg Financial News Services, and other on-line subscription services available in many university libraries provide access to a wide array of business reference material. For example, the Lexis/Nexis COMPANY library contains full-text 10-Ks, 10-Qs, annual reports, company profiles for more than 11,000 U.S. and international companies, and a variety of other valuable data files. The Lexis/Nexis files listed below are particularly useful in researching companies and industries:

Publication/subject	Lexis/Nexis file name
Market Share Reporter (an excellent source of market share statistics)	MKTSHR
Hoover company profiles	HOOVER
Hoover profiles of international companies	HVRWLD
Standard & Poor's Register	SPCORP
Securities and Exchange Commission	SEC
Company annual reports	ARS
Company annual 10-K filings	10-K
Company quarterly 10-Q filings	10-Q
Company newswire stories	CONEWS
Business wire	BWIRE
Public relations newswire	PRNEWS
S&P Daily News	SPNEWS

Company Web Pages and Other Websites Containing Business Information   Many companies (and the number increases daily) have Websites with information about products, financial performance, recent accomplishments, late-breaking company developments, and rundowns on company objectives, strategy, and future plans. Some company Web pages include links to the home pages of industry trade associations where you can find information about industry size, growth, recent industry news, statistical trends, and future outlook. A number of business periodicals like *Business Week, The Wall Street Journal,* and *Fortune* have Internet editions that contain the full text of many of the articles that appear in their paper editions. You can access these sites by typing in the proper Internet address for the company, trade association, or publication. The following Websites are particularly good locations for company and industry information:

- Securities and Exchange Commission EDGAR database (contains company 10-Ks, 10-Qs, etc.) *http://www.sec.gov/cgi-bin/srch-edgar/*
- NASDAQ *http://www.nasdaq.com/*
- CNNfn: The Financial Network *http://cnnfn.com/*
- Hoover's Online *http://hoovers.com/*
- *American Demographics/*Marketing Tools *http://www.marketingtools.com/*
- Industry Net *http://www.industry.net/*
- *Wall Street Journal*—Interactive edition *http://update.wsj.com/*
- *Business Week http://www.businessweek.com/*
- *Fortune http://www.pathfinder/com/@@cUyeVQQAtmYhdMyb/fortune/*
- MSNBC Commerce News *http://www.msnbc.com/news/COM__front.asp/*
- *Los Angeles Times http://www.latimes.com/*
- *New York Times http://www.nytimes.com/*
- News Page *http://www.newspage.com/*
- Electric Library *http://www.elibrary/com/*
- International Business Resources on the WWW *http://ciber.bus.msu.edu/ busref.html/*

Some of these Internet sources require subscriptions in order to access their entire databases.

Using a Search Engine   Alternatively, or in addition, you can quickly locate and retrieve information on companies, industries, products, individuals, or other subjects of interest using such Internet search engines as Lycos, Alta Vista, Infoseek, Excite, Yahoo!, and Magellan. Search engines find articles and other information sources that relate to a particular industry, company name, topic, phrase, or "keyword" of interest. Some search engines contain bigger indexes of submitted Uniform Resource Locator addresses than others, so it is essential to be alert to the coverage of each search engine—*the information sources covered by each search engine are specified on the search engine's Website.* Each of the search engines also provide guidelines for how to formulate your query for information sources. You may find the following brief descriptions of frequently-used search engines helpful in selecting which one to try:

- Alta Vista (*http://www.altavista.digital.com/*)—Digital Equipment claims that Alta Vista searches the largest index and database on the Web of any engine: over 30 million Web pages on over 475,000 servers plus 14,000 articles posted in various news groups as of early 1997. For the latest information on what you can find using the Alta Vista search engine, visit the Website. Alta Vista searches the full text of all documents in its database. The search results give a higher score to documents where the keywords are in the first few words of the document or title; higher scores are also given to documents containing multiple use of the keywords.
- Infoseek Net Search (*http://www.infoseek.com/*)—Infoseek lets you use natural language phrases like "find information on discounted Caribbean cruises" as well as traditional keyword searches. It is good for searching popular Web

pages but is considered less efficient than Alta Vista in finding obscure names and keywords. Infoseek looks for keywords in the title of a document or at the beginning of a document page. It is more likely to return Internet addresses to a query where the keyword(s) appear frequently in the document.

- Yahoo (*http://www.yahoo.com*)—Yahoo is not actually a search engine, but a catalog of Websites that have been submitted to Yahoo by Webpage authors. Yahoo identifies the Internet addresses for a query that contain the specified keywords in the title of the document or in the description of the document.
- Lycos (*http://www.lycos.com*)—An up-to-date list of the sources that Lycos searches can be found on its Webpage. Lycos searches abstracts based on titles and the first few words of key paragraphs for the keywords listed in a query. It does not search the full text of a document.
- Excite (*http://www.excite.com*)—Excite is a full-text search engine that scans Websites, Usenet news, and other sources as described on its opening Web pages. Like Alta Vista, it gives a higher score to documents that contain the keyword in the title or is repeated frequently in the full text of the document. Excite is unusual in that it understands synonyms. Not only does it return documents that match keywords in a query, but it also returns documents that contain synonyms of keywords listed in a query.

Our tips for making the quickest and most effective use of search engines are listed below:

- Make your search as specific as possible. Search engines are very efficient and may retrieve thousands of matches to a very general request.
- Use Boolean operators like AND, AND NOT, OR, and parentheses to narrow the scope of your search. These operators help zero in on those items of greatest relevance to what you are looking for.
- Each search engine will have specific commands that will further limit the search results. Make sure that you inspect the search engine's advanced search tips to determine how to use those capabilities.
- Some search engines are upper- and lower-case sensitive. As a rule, your query should be entered with the correct upper-case and lower-case letters because of the capitalization-sensitive nature of certain search engines.

Keep in mind that the information retrieved by a search engine is "unfiltered" and may include sources that are not reliable or that contain inaccurate or misleading information. Be wary of information provided by authors who are unaffiliated with reputable organizations or publications or which doesn't come from the company or a credible trade association—be especially careful in relying on the accuracy of information you find posted on various bulletin boards. Articles covering a company or issue should be copyrighted or published by a reputable source. If you are turning in a paper containing information gathered from the Internet, you should cite your sources (providing the Internet address and date visited); it is also wise to print Web pages for your research file (some Web pages are updated frequently).

The Learning Curve Is Steep   With a modest investment of time, you will learn how to use Internet sources and search engines to run down information on companies and industries quickly and efficiently. And it is a skill that will serve you well into the future. Once you become familiar with the data available at the different Websites

TABLE 2 The Ten Commandments of Case Analysis

To be observed in written reports and oral presentations, and while participating in class discussions.

1. Read the case twice, once for an overview and once to gain full command of the facts; then take care to explore every one of the exhibits.

2. Make a list of the problems and issues that have to be confronted.

3. Do enough number crunching to discover the story told by the data presented in the case. (To help you comply with this commandment, consult Table 1 to guide your probing of a company's financial condition and financial performance.)

4. Look for opportunities to apply the concepts and analytical tools in the text chapters.

5. Be thorough in your diagnosis of the situation (either make a one- or two-page outline of your assessment or work through the exercises on Strat-Tutor).

6. Support any and all opinions with well-reasoned arguments and numerical evidence; don't stop until you can purge "I think" and "I feel" from your assessment and, instead, are able to rely completely on "My analysis shows."

7. Develop charts, tables, and graphs to expose more clearly the main points of your analysis.

8. Prioritize your recommendations and make sure they can be carried out in an acceptable time frame with the available skills and financial resources.

9. Review your recommended action plan to see if it addresses all of the problems and issues you identified.

10. Avoid recommending any course of action that could have disastrous consequences if it doesn't work out as planned; therefore, be as alert to the downside risks of your recommendations as you are to their upside potential and appeal.

mentioned above and with using a search engine, you will know where to go to look for the particular information that you want. Search engines nearly always turn up too many information sources that match your request rather than two few; the trick is to learn to zero in on those most relevant to what you are looking for. Like most things, once you get a little experience under your belt on how to do company and industry research on the Internet, you will find that you can readily find the information you need.

THE TEN COMMANDMENTS OF CASE ANALYSIS

As a way of summarizing our suggestions about how to approach the task of case analysis, we have compiled what we like to call "The Ten Commandments of Case Analysis." They are shown in Table 2. If you observe all or even most of these commandments faithfully as you prepare a case either for class discussion or for a written report, your chances of doing a good job on the assigned cases will be much improved. Hang in there, give it your best shot, and have some fun exploring what the real world of strategic management is all about.

INDEXES

NAME INDEX

SUBJECT INDEX